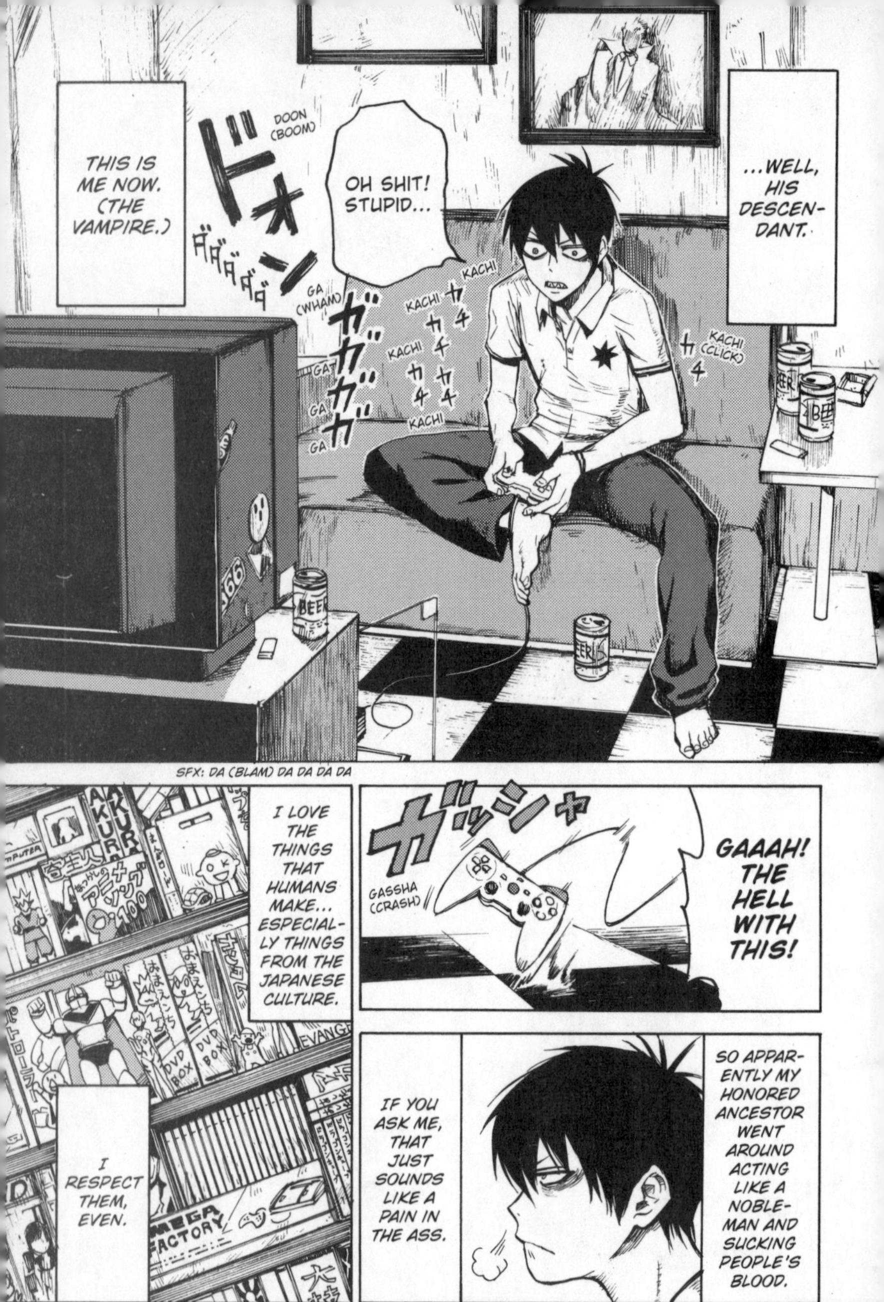
...WELL, HIS DESCENDANT.
DOON (BOOM)
THIS IS ME NOW. (THE VAMPIRE.)
OH SHIT! STUPID...
KACHI KACHI (CLICK)
KACHI KACHI KACHI KACHI
GA (WHAM) GA GA GA
SFX: DA (BLAM) DA DA DA DA
GAAAH! THE HELL WITH THIS!
GASSHA (CRASH)
SO APPARENTLY MY HONORED ANCESTOR WENT AROUND ACTING LIKE A NOBLEMAN AND SUCKING PEOPLE'S BLOOD.
IF YOU ASK ME, THAT JUST SOUNDS LIKE A PAIN IN THE ASS.
I LOVE THE THINGS THAT HUMANS MAKE... ESPECIALLY THINGS FROM THE JAPANESE CULTURE.
I RESPECT THEM, EVEN.
MEGA FACTORY
DVD BOX
EVANGE

MEDIA (TOP TO BOTTOM): SWEET REVENGE, 100 CLASSIC ANIME SONGS, MANGA ROAD / PATROLLER, OMAENCHI DVD BOX, GUNDAM / DRAGONCUBE

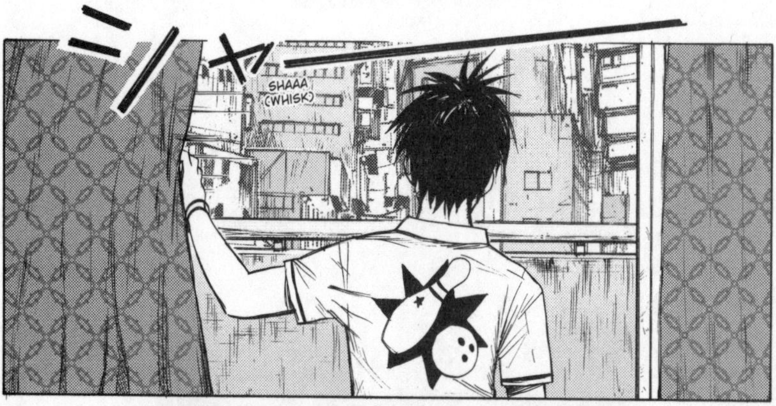
SHAAA (WHISK)

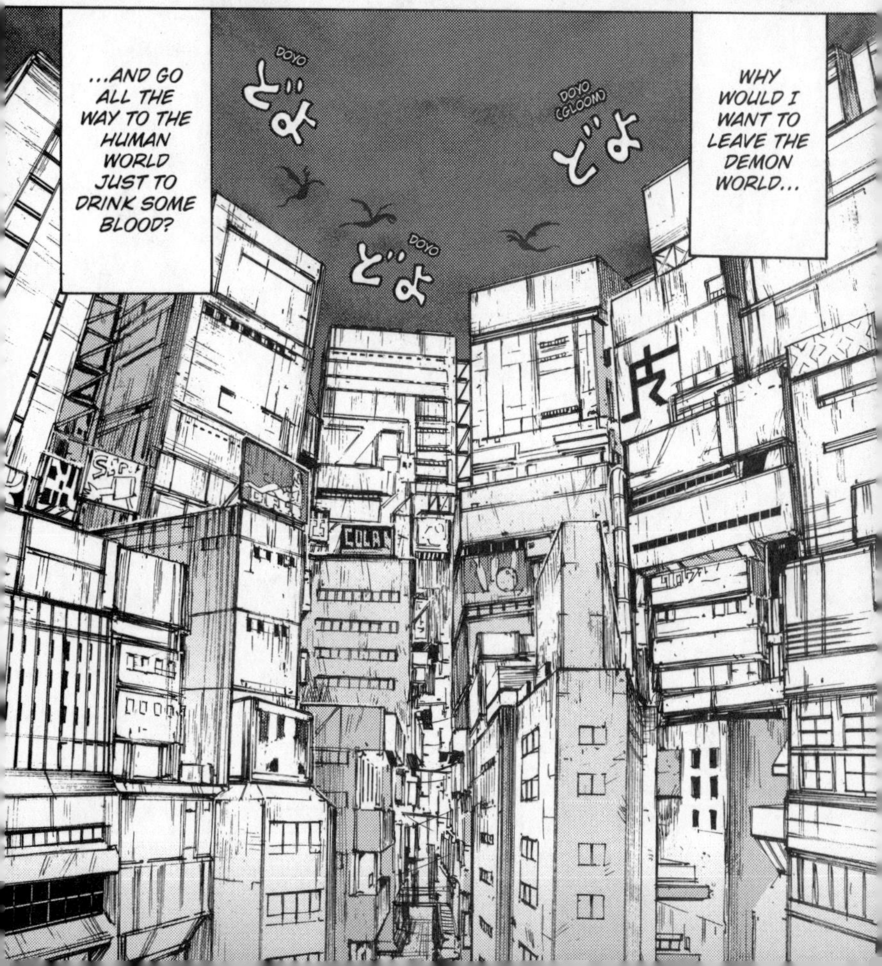
WHY WOULD I WANT TO LEAVE THE DEMON WORLD...
DOYO (GLOOM)
どよ
DOYO
どよ
DOYO
どよ
...AND GO ALL THE WAY TO THE HUMAN WORLD JUST TO DRINK SOME BLOOD?

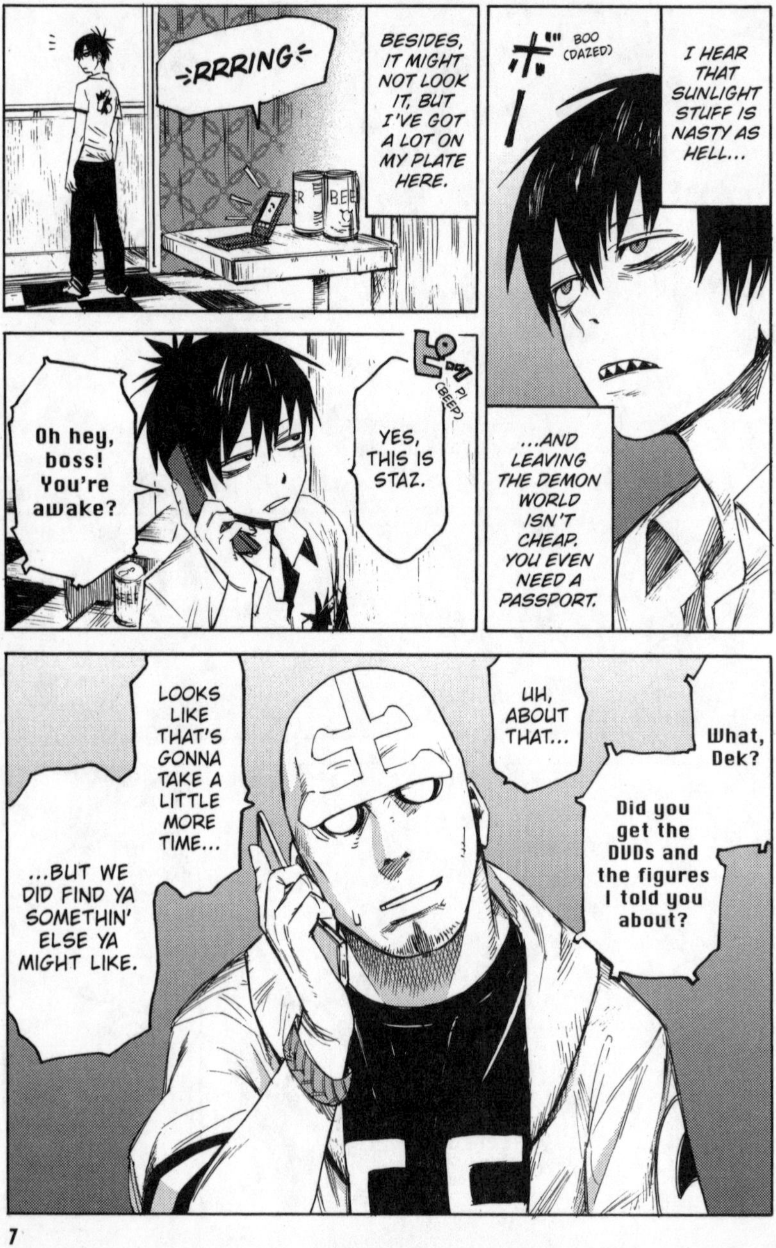
BOO (DAZED)
I HEAR THAT SUNLIGHT STUFF IS NASTY AS HELL...
...AND LEAVING THE DEMON WORLD ISN'T CHEAP. YOU EVEN NEED A PASSPORT.
BESIDES, IT MIGHT NOT LOOK IT, BUT I'VE GOT A LOT ON MY PLATE HERE.
RRRING
PI (BEEP)
YES, THIS IS STAZ.
Oh hey, boss! You're awake?
What, Dek?
Did you get the DVDs and the figures I told you about?
UH, ABOUT THAT...
LOOKS LIKE THAT'S GONNA TAKE A LITTLE MORE TIME...
...BUT WE DID FIND YA SOMETHIN' ELSE YA MIGHT LIKE.

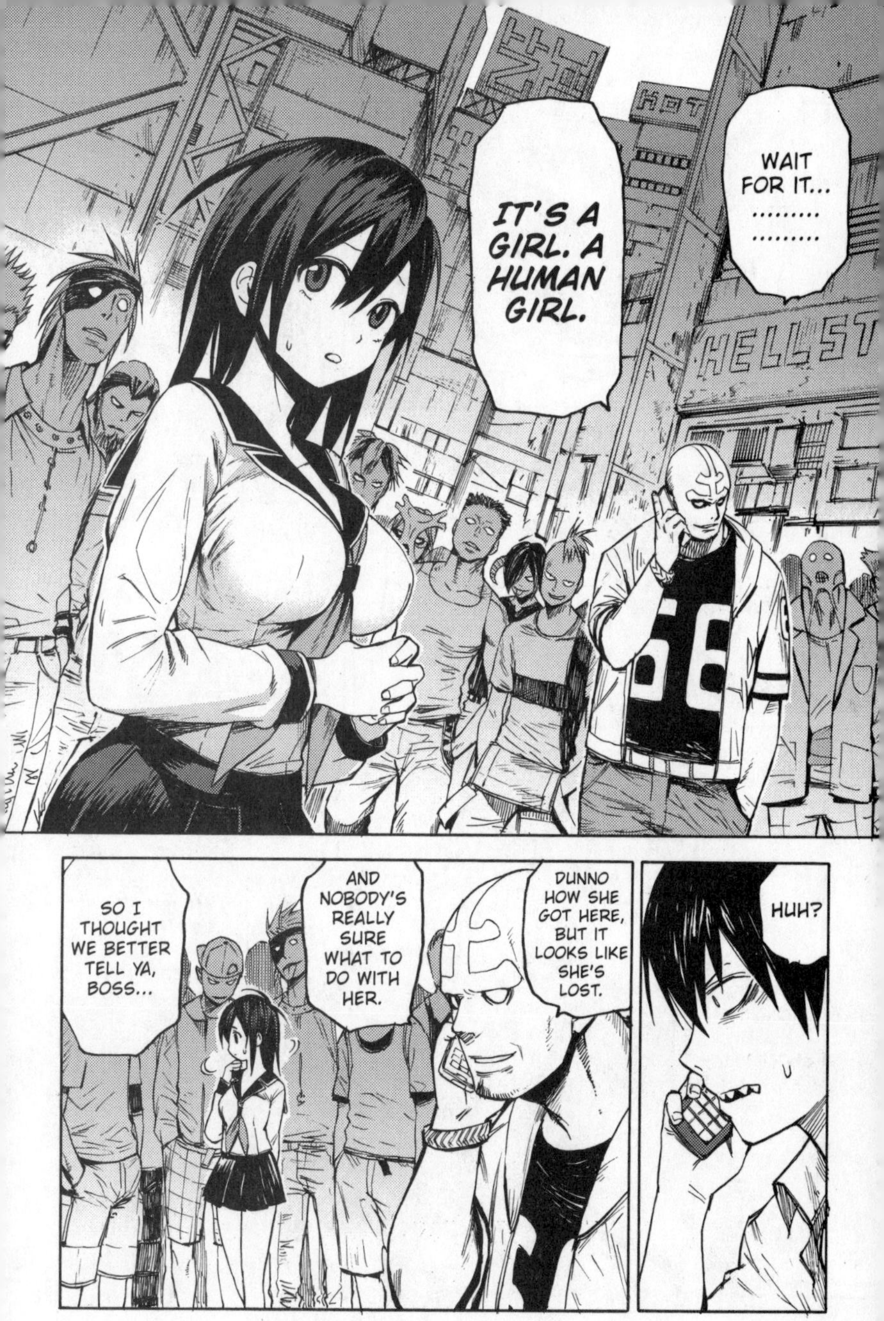
WAIT FOR IT... ......... .........
IT'S A GIRL. A HUMAN GIRL.
HELLST
HUH?
DUNNO HOW SHE GOT HERE, BUT IT LOOKS LIKE SHE'S LOST.
AND NOBODY'S REALLY SURE WHAT TO DO WITH HER.
SO I THOUGHT WE BETTER TELL YA, BOSS...

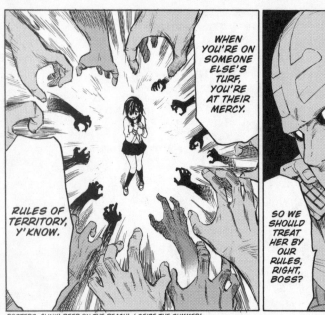

'COS FACT IS, THIS AIN'T THE HUMAN WORLD.
SO WE SHOULD TREAT HER BY OUR RULES, RIGHT, BOSS?
WHEN YOU'RE ON SOMEONE ELSE'S TURF, YOU'RE AT THEIR MERCY.
RULES OF TERRITORY, Y'KNOW.
POSTERS: CLINK! BEER ON THE BEACH! / SEIZE THE SUMMER!
Huh? You there, boss?
A HUMAN ... GIRL...
A GIRL... IN THE DEMON WORLD ...
A HUMAN ...!!
BRING HER HERE. NOW...

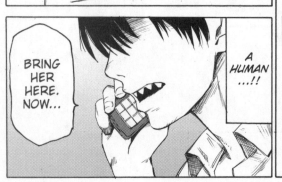

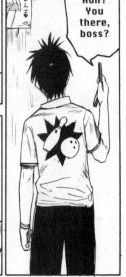

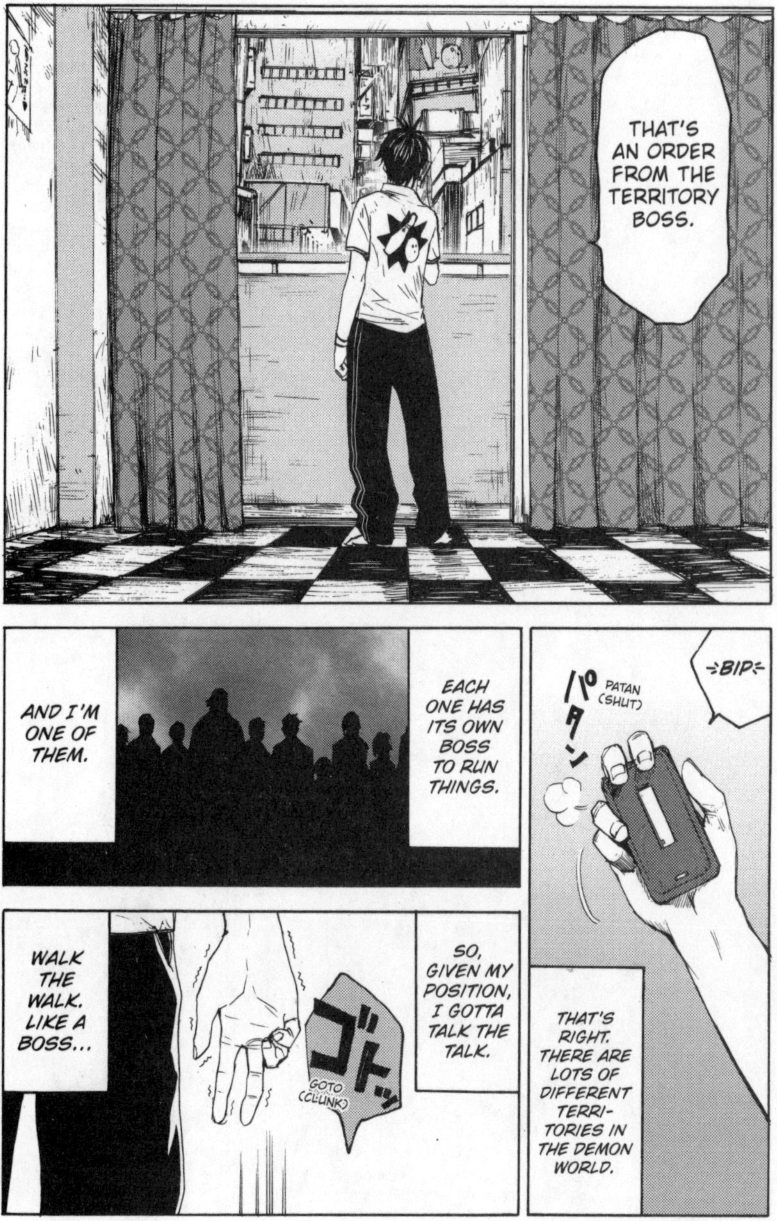
THAT'S AN ORDER FROM THE TERRITORY BOSS.
-BIP-
パタン
PATAN (SHUT)
THAT'S RIGHT. THERE ARE LOTS OF DIFFERENT TERRI-TORIES IN THE DEMON WORLD.
EACH ONE HAS ITS OWN BOSS TO RUN THINGS.
AND I'M ONE OF THEM.
SO, GIVEN MY POSITION, I GOTTA TALK THE TALK.
ゴトッ
GOTO (CL-UNK)
WALK THE WALK. LIKE A BOSS...

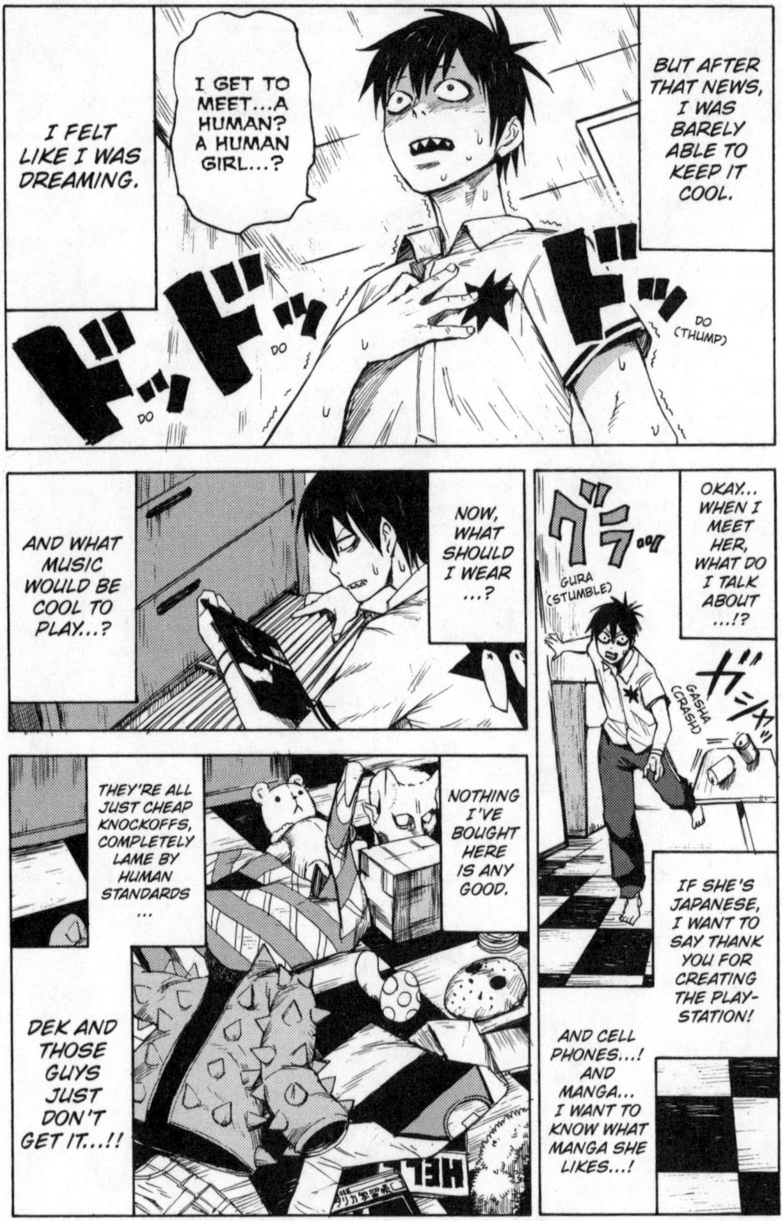
BUT AFTER THAT NEWS, I WAS BARELY ABLE TO KEEP IT COOL.
I GET TO MEET...A HUMAN? A HUMAN GIRL...?
I FELT LIKE I WAS DREAMING.
ドッ
DO (THUMP)
ドッ
DO
ドッ
DO
OKAY... WHEN I MEET HER, WHAT DO I TALK ABOUT...!?
グラッ
GURA (STUMBLE)
ガシャッ
GASHA (CRASH)
IF SHE'S JAPANESE, I WANT TO SAY THANK YOU FOR CREATING THE PLAY-STATION!
AND CELL PHONES...! AND MANGA... I WANT TO KNOW WHAT MANGA SHE LIKES...!
NOW, WHAT SHOULD I WEAR...?
AND WHAT MUSIC WOULD BE COOL TO PLAY...?
NOTHING I'VE BOUGHT HERE IS ANY GOOD.
THEY'RE ALL JUST CHEAP KNOCKOFFS, COMPLETELY LAME BY HUMAN STANDARDS...
DEK AND THOSE GUYS JUST DON'T GET IT...!!

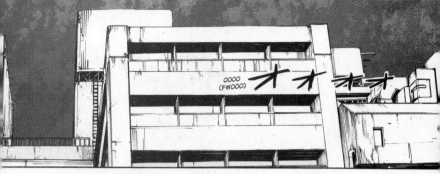

OOOO
(FWOOO)
オオオオオオ

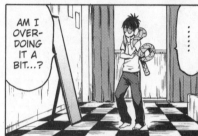

AM I OVER-DOING IT A BIT...?

· · · · ·

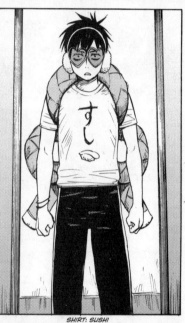

SHIRT: SUSHI

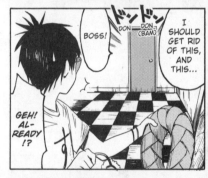

ドン ドン
DON DON (BAM)

BOSS!

I SHOULD GET RID OF THIS, AND THIS...

GEH! AL-READY !?

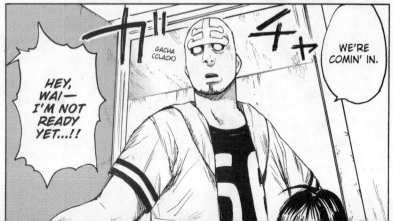

ガ
GACHA (CLACK)

チャ

WE'RE COMIN' IN.

HEY, WAI— I'M NOT READY YET...!!

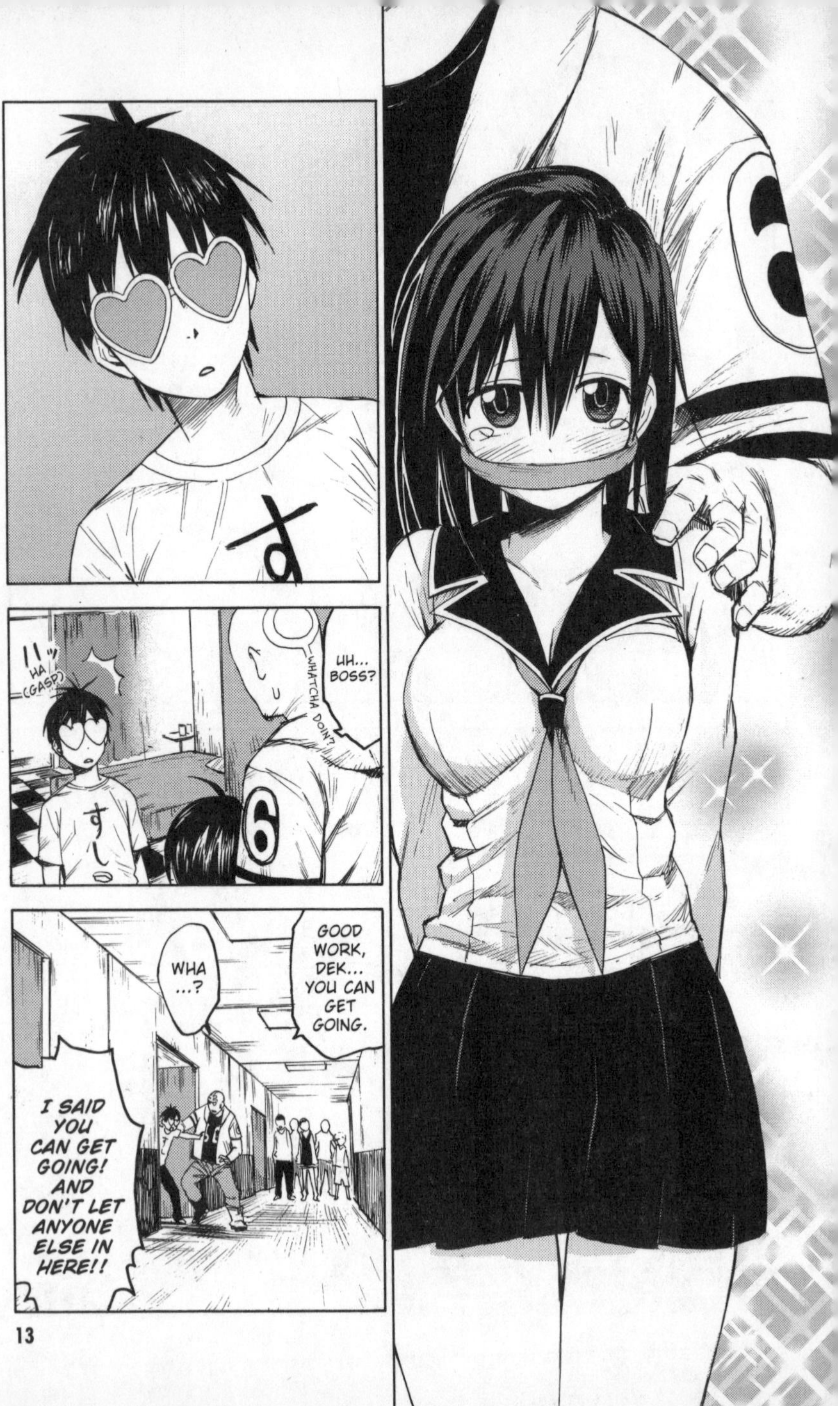
UH... BOSS?
WHATCHA DOIN'?
ハッ HA (GASP)
GOOD WORK, DEK... YOU CAN GET GOING.
WHA ...?
I SAID YOU CAN GET GOING! AND DON'T LET ANYONE ELSE IN HERE!!

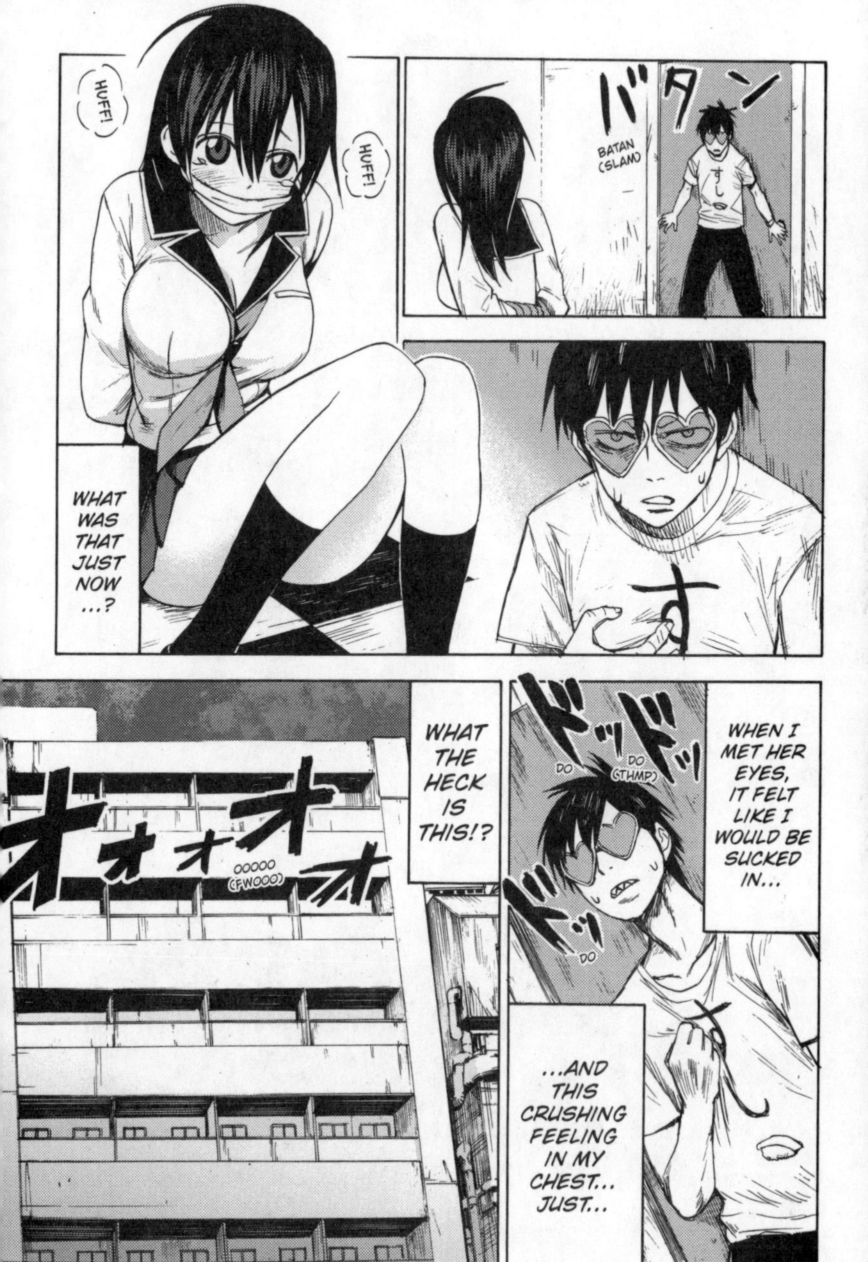
バタン
BATAN (SLAM)
すし
す
HUFF!
HUFF!
WHAT WAS THAT JUST NOW ...?
WHEN I MET HER EYES, IT FELT LIKE I WOULD BE SUCKED IN...
ドッドッ
DO
DO (THMP)
ドッ
DO
...AND THIS CRUSHING FEELING IN MY CHEST... JUST...
WHAT THE HECK IS THIS!?
オォォオオ
OOOOO (FWOOO)

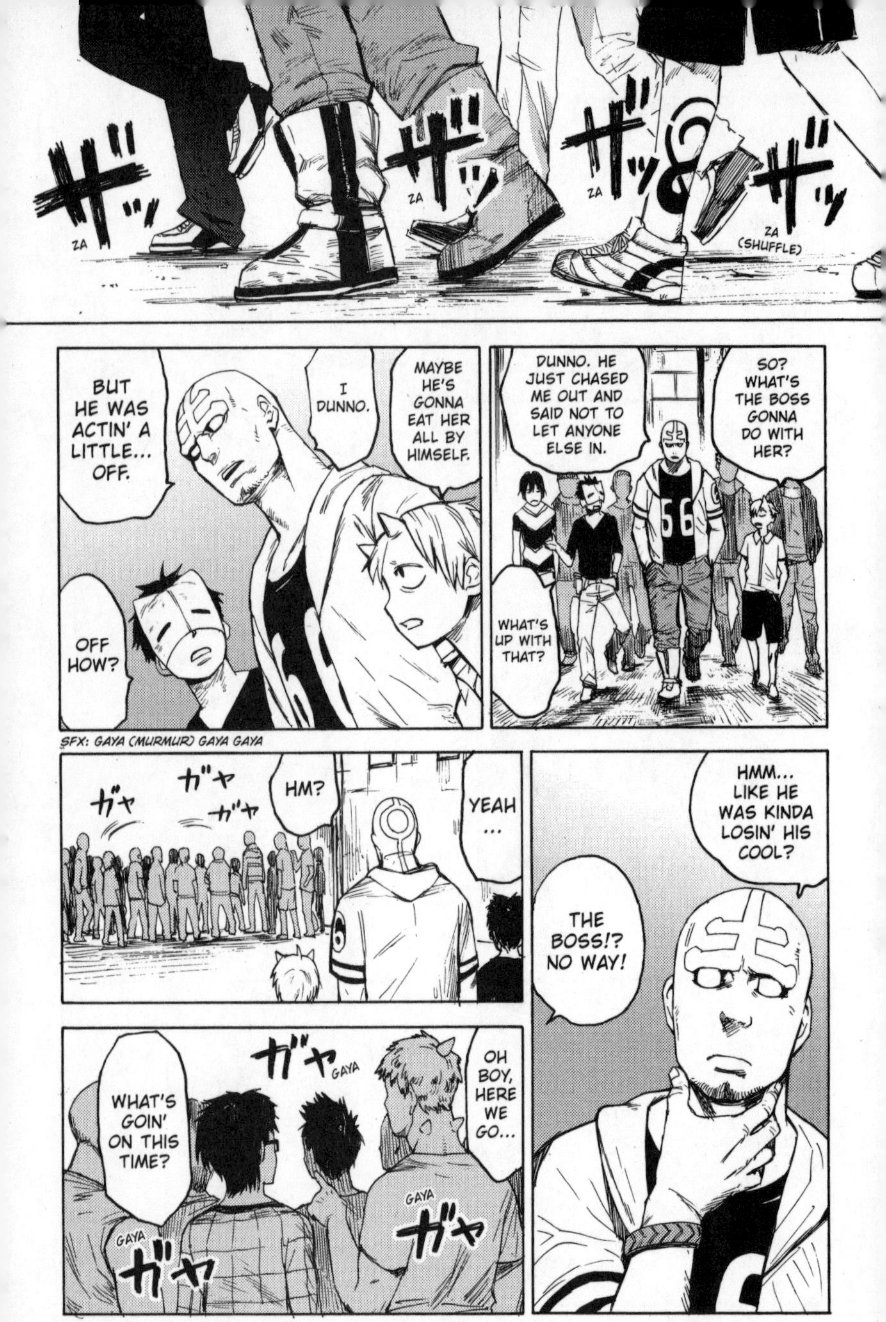
ザッ
ZA (SHUFFLE)
ザッ
ZA
ザッ
ZA
ザッ
ZA
SO? WHAT'S THE BOSS GONNA DO WITH HER?
DUNNO. HE JUST CHASED ME OUT AND SAID NOT TO LET ANYONE ELSE IN.
WHAT'S UP WITH THAT?
MAYBE HE'S GONNA EAT HER ALL BY HIMSELF.
I DUNNO.
BUT HE WAS ACTIN' A LITTLE... OFF.
OFF HOW?
SFX: GAYA (MURMUR) GAYA GAYA
HMM... LIKE HE WAS KINDA LOSIN' HIS COOL?
THE BOSS!? NO WAY!
YEAH...
HM?
ガヤ
ガヤ
ガヤ
OH BOY, HERE WE GO...
ガヤ GAYA
WHAT'S GOIN' ON THIS TIME?
ガヤ GAYA
ガヤ GAYA

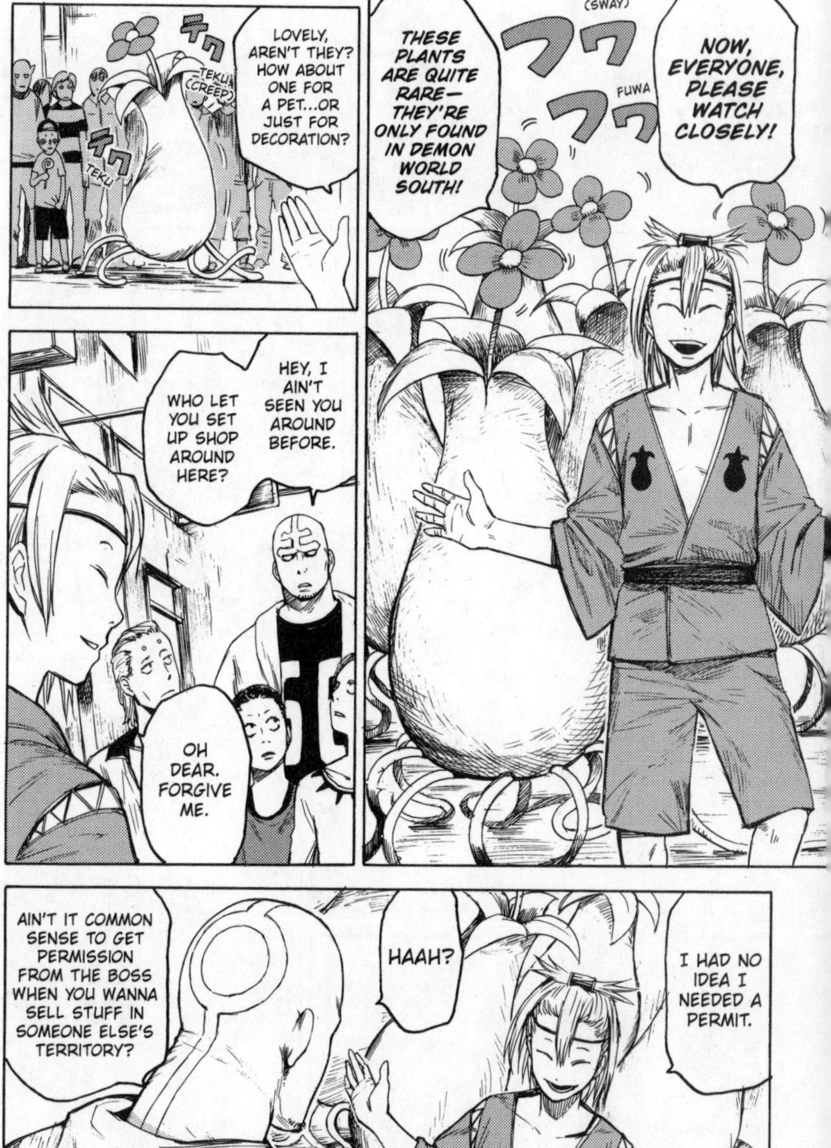
FUWA (SWAY)
FUWA
NOW, EVERYONE, PLEASE WATCH CLOSELY!
THESE PLANTS ARE QUITE RARE—THEY'RE ONLY FOUND IN DEMON WORLD SOUTH!
LOVELY, AREN'T THEY? HOW ABOUT ONE FOR A PET...OR JUST FOR DECORATION?
TEKU (CREEP)
TEKU
HEY, I AIN'T SEEN YOU AROUND BEFORE.
WHO LET YOU SET UP SHOP AROUND HERE?
OH DEAR. FORGIVE ME.
I HAD NO IDEA I NEEDED A PERMIT.
HAAH?
AIN'T IT COMMON SENSE TO GET PERMISSION FROM THE BOSS WHEN YOU WANNA SELL STUFF IN SOMEONE ELSE'S TERRITORY?

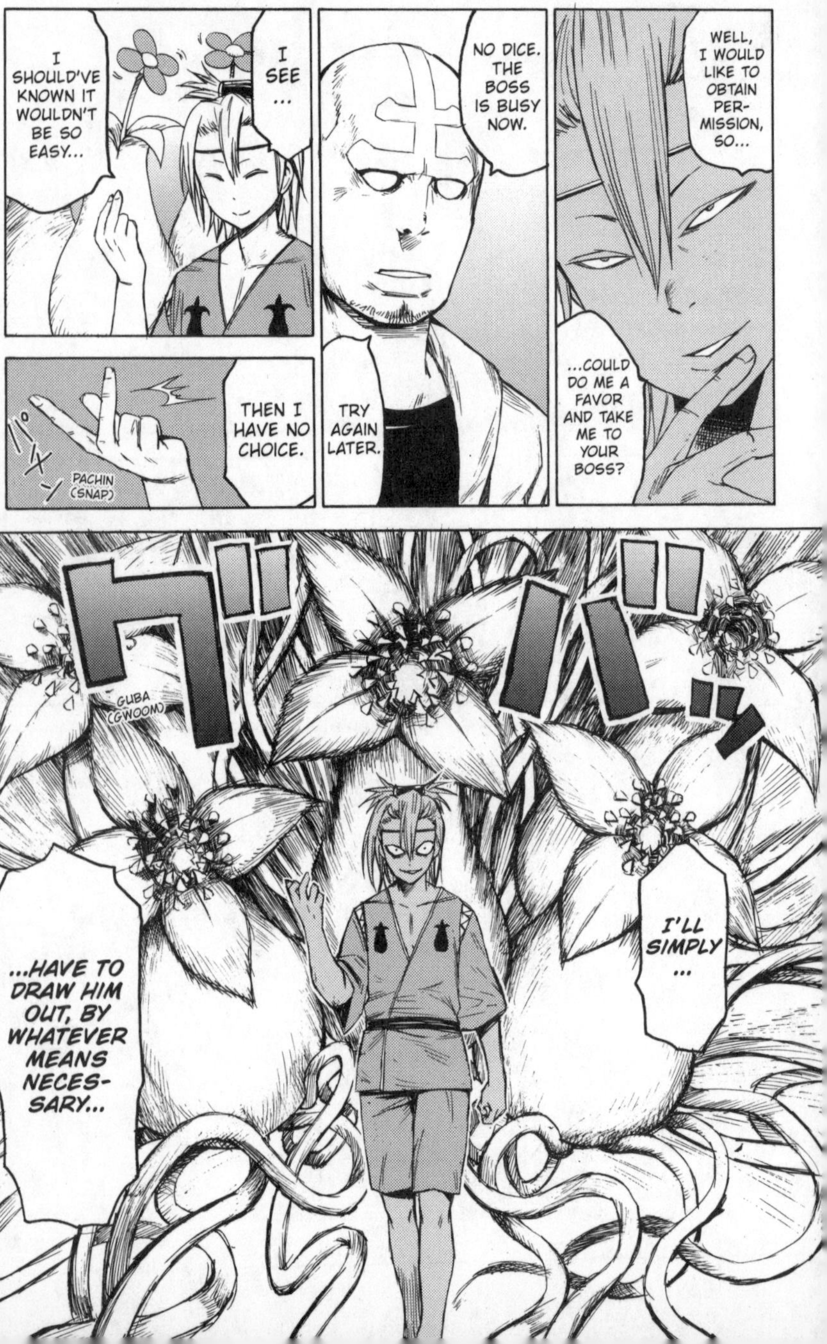
WELL, I WOULD LIKE TO OBTAIN PER-MISSION, SO...
...COULD DO ME A FAVOR AND TAKE ME TO YOUR BOSS?
NO DICE. THE BOSS IS BUSY NOW.
TRY AGAIN LATER.
I SEE ...
I SHOULD'VE KNOWN IT WOULDN'T BE SO EASY...
THEN I HAVE NO CHOICE.
PACHIN (SNAP)
GUBA (GWOOM)
I'LL SIMPLY ...
...HAVE TO DRAW HIM OUT, BY WHATEVER MEANS NECES-SARY...

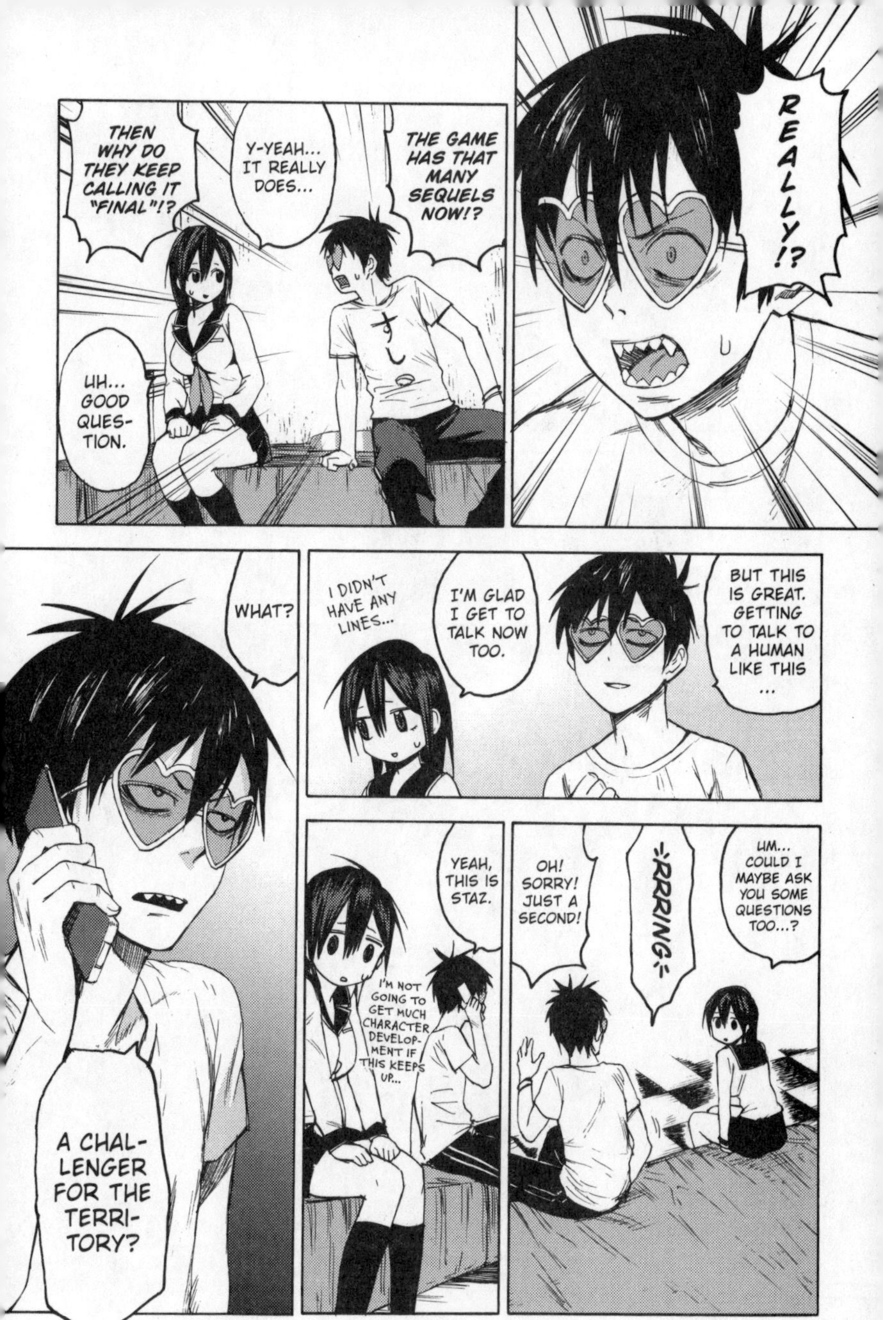
REALLY!?
THE GAME HAS THAT MANY SEQUELS NOW!?
Y-YEAH... IT REALLY DOES...
THEN WHY DO THEY KEEP CALLING IT "FINAL"!?
UH... GOOD QUES-TION.
BUT THIS IS GREAT. GETTING TO TALK TO A HUMAN LIKE THIS ...
I'M GLAD I GET TO TALK NOW TOO.
I DIDN'T HAVE ANY LINES...
UM... COULD I MAYBE ASK YOU SOME QUESTIONS TOO...?
RRRING
OH! SORRY! JUST A SECOND!
YEAH, THIS IS STAZ.
I'M NOT GOING TO GET MUCH CHARACTER DEVELOP-MENT IF THIS KEEPS UP...
WHAT?
A CHAL-LENGER FOR THE TERRI-TORY?

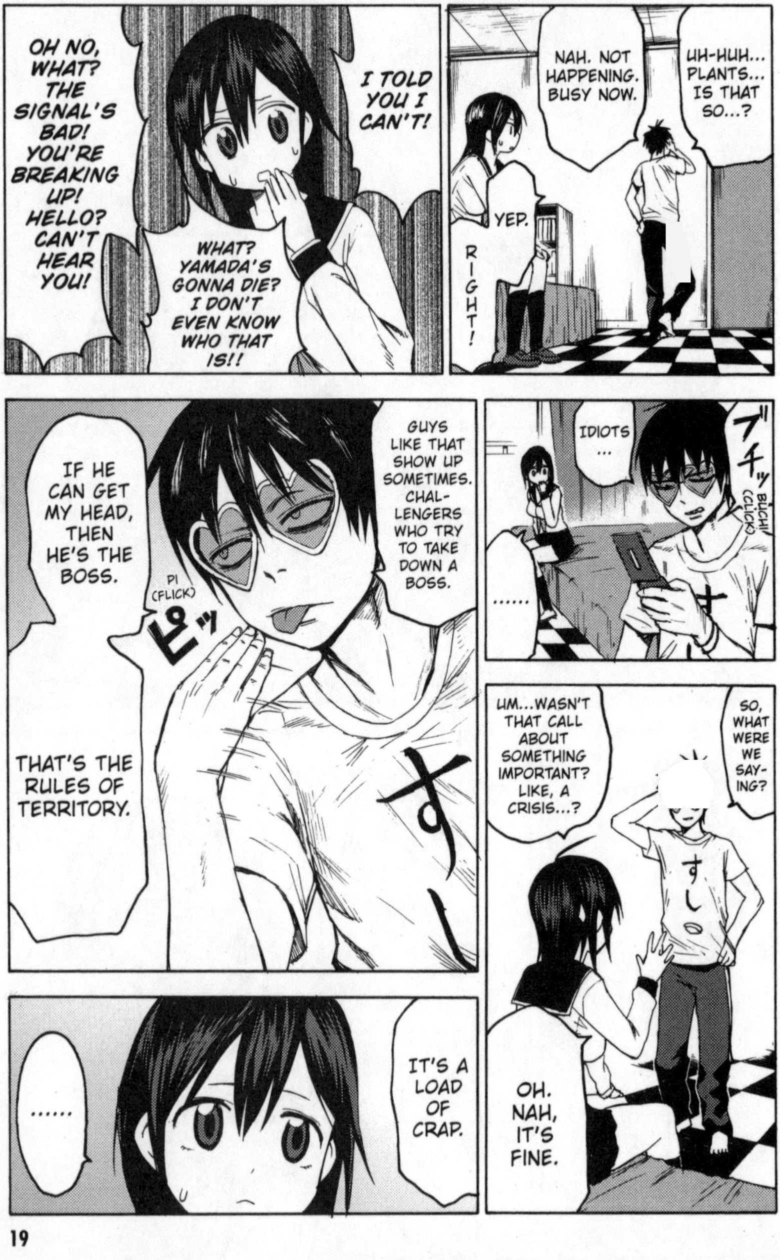
UH-HUH... PLANTS... IS THAT SO...?
NAH. NOT HAPPENING. BUSY NOW.
YEP.
RIGHT!
I TOLD YOU I CAN'T!
OH NO, WHAT? THE SIGNAL'S BAD! YOU'RE BREAKING UP! HELLO? CAN'T HEAR YOU!
WHAT? YAMADA'S GONNA DIE? I DON'T EVEN KNOW WHO THAT IS!!
ブチッ
BUCHI! (CLICK)
IDIOTS...
......
SO, WHAT WERE WE SAYING?
UM...WASN'T THAT CALL ABOUT SOMETHING IMPORTANT? LIKE, A CRISIS...?
OH. NAH, IT'S FINE.
GUYS LIKE THAT SHOW UP SOMETIMES. CHALLENGERS WHO TRY TO TAKE DOWN A BOSS.
IF HE CAN GET MY HEAD, THEN HE'S THE BOSS.
ピッ
PI (FLICK)
THAT'S THE RULES OF TERRITORY.
IT'S A LOAD OF CRAP.
......

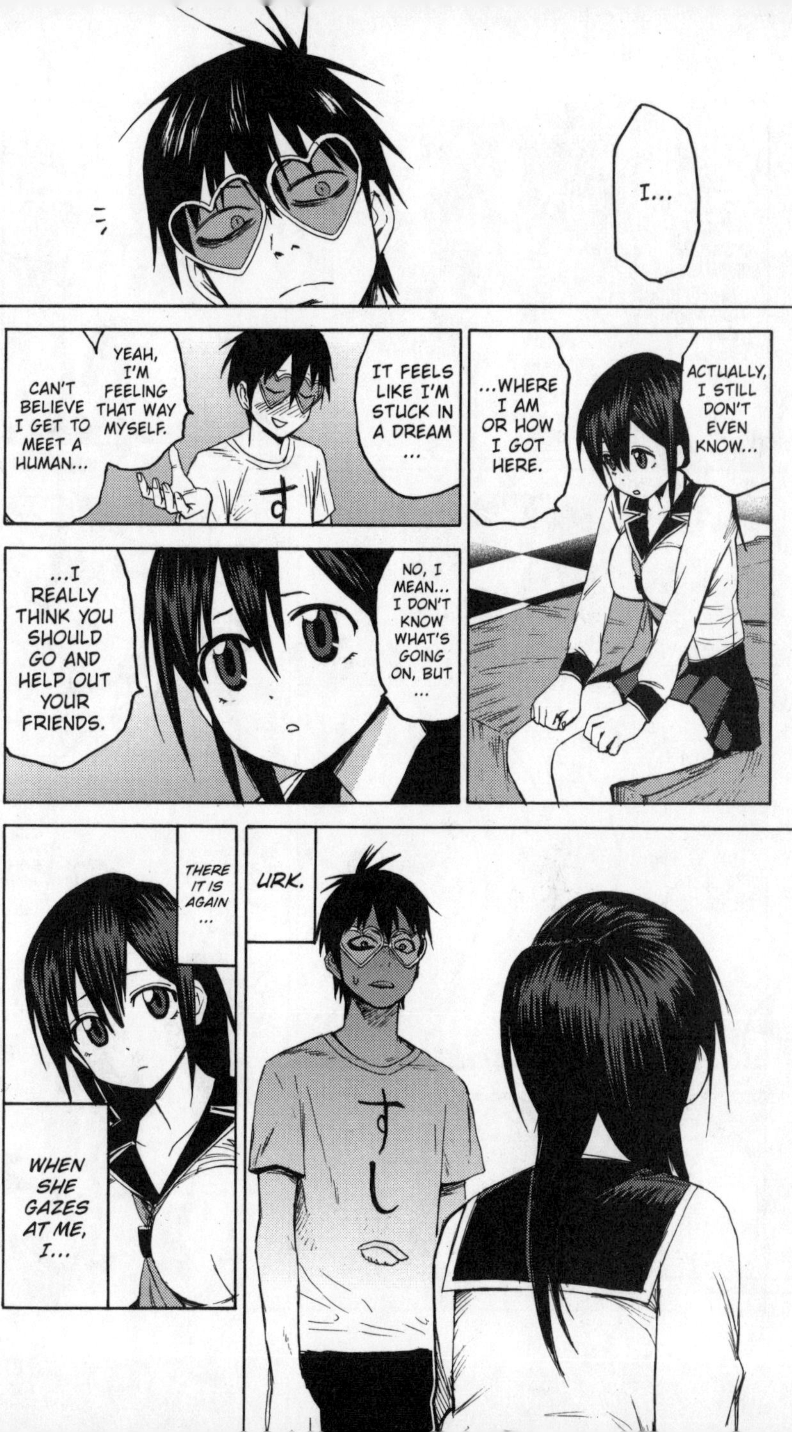
I...
ACTUALLY, I STILL DON'T EVEN KNOW...
...WHERE I AM OR HOW I GOT HERE.
IT FEELS LIKE I'M STUCK IN A DREAM...
YEAH, I'M FEELING THAT WAY MYSELF.
CAN'T BELIEVE I GET TO MEET A HUMAN...
NO, I MEAN... I DON'T KNOW WHAT'S GOING ON, BUT...
...I REALLY THINK YOU SHOULD GO AND HELP OUT YOUR FRIENDS.
URK.
THERE IT IS AGAIN...
WHEN SHE GAZES AT ME, I...

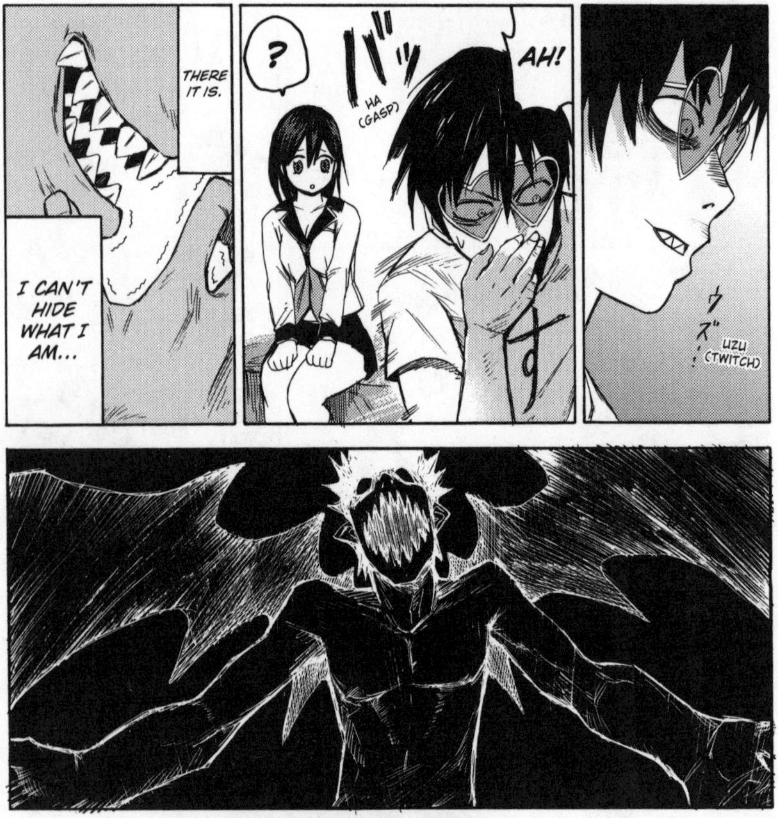
ウズ…
UZU (TWITCH)
AH!
バッ
HA (GASP)
?
THERE IT IS.
I CAN'T HIDE WHAT I AM…

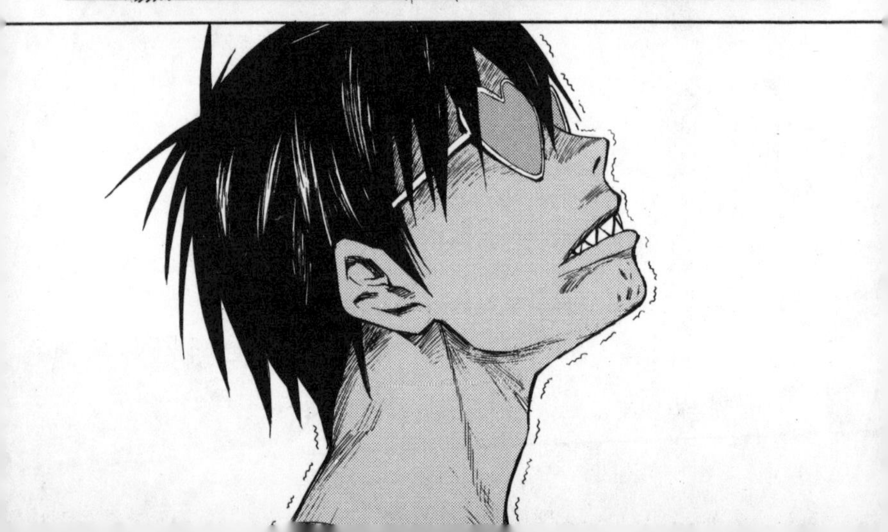

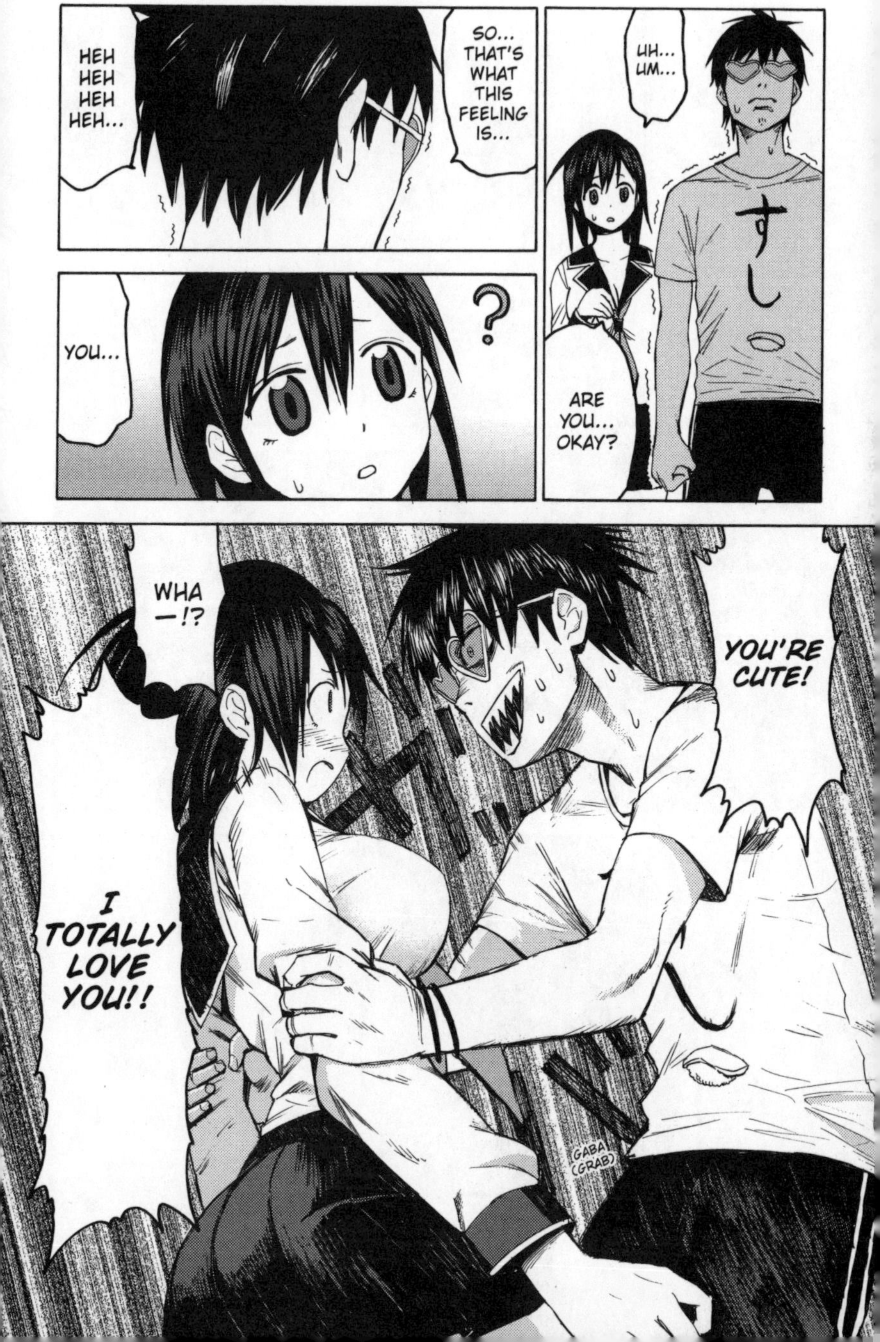
UH... UM...
すし
ARE YOU... OKAY?
SO... THAT'S WHAT THIS FEELING IS...
HEH HEH HEH HEH...
?
YOU...
YOU'RE CUTE!
WHA—!?
I TOTALLY LOVE YOU!!
GABA (GRAB)

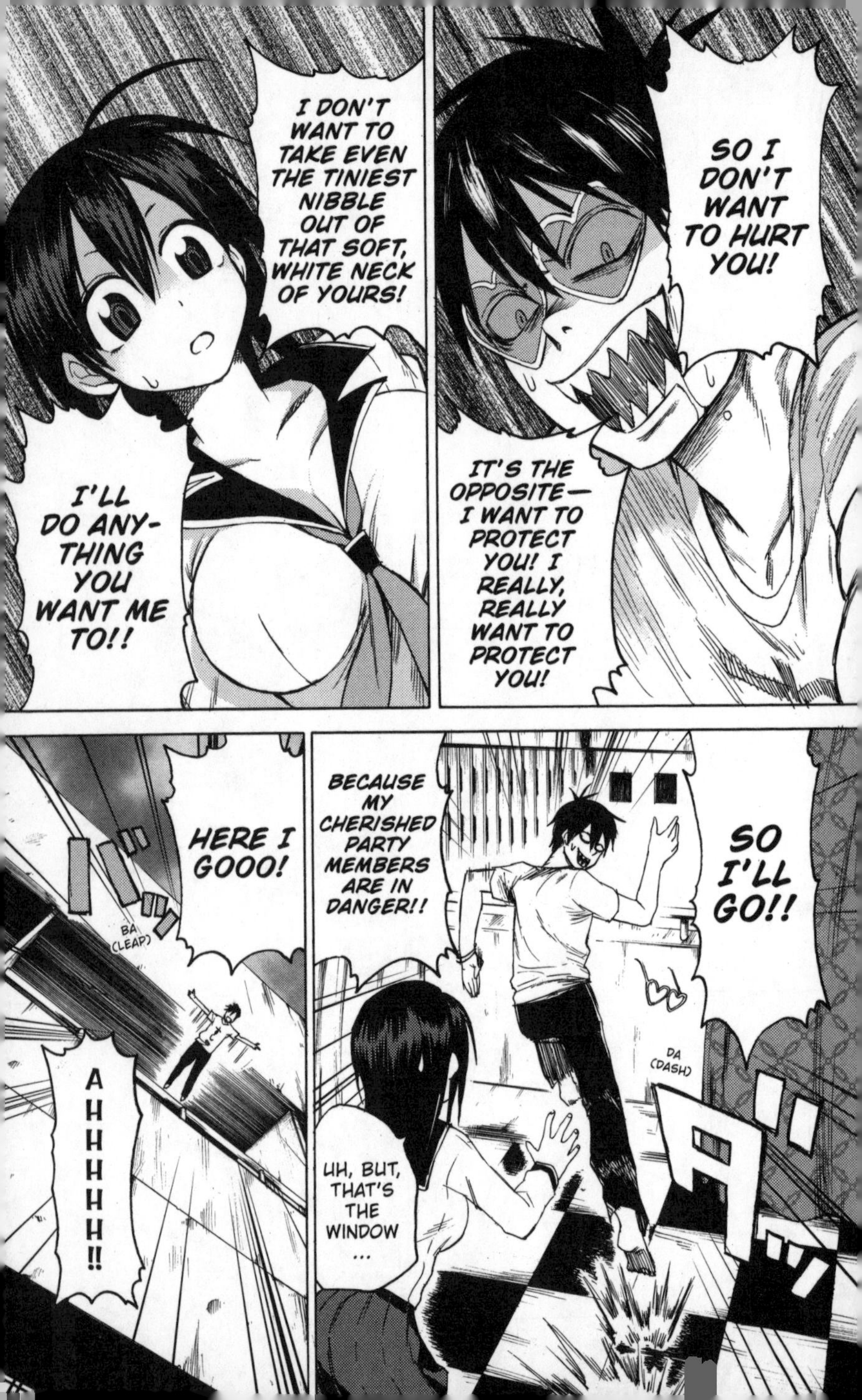
SO I DON'T WANT TO HURT YOU!
IT'S THE OPPOSITE— I WANT TO PROTECT YOU! I REALLY, REALLY WANT TO PROTECT YOU!
I DON'T WANT TO TAKE EVEN THE TINIEST NIBBLE OUT OF THAT SOFT, WHITE NECK OF YOURS!
I'LL DO ANY-THING YOU WANT ME TO!!
SO I'LL GO!!
BECAUSE MY CHERISHED PARTY MEMBERS ARE IN DANGER!!
DA (DASH)
UH, BUT, THAT'S THE WINDOW ...
HERE I GOOO!
BA (LEAP)
AHHHHHH!!

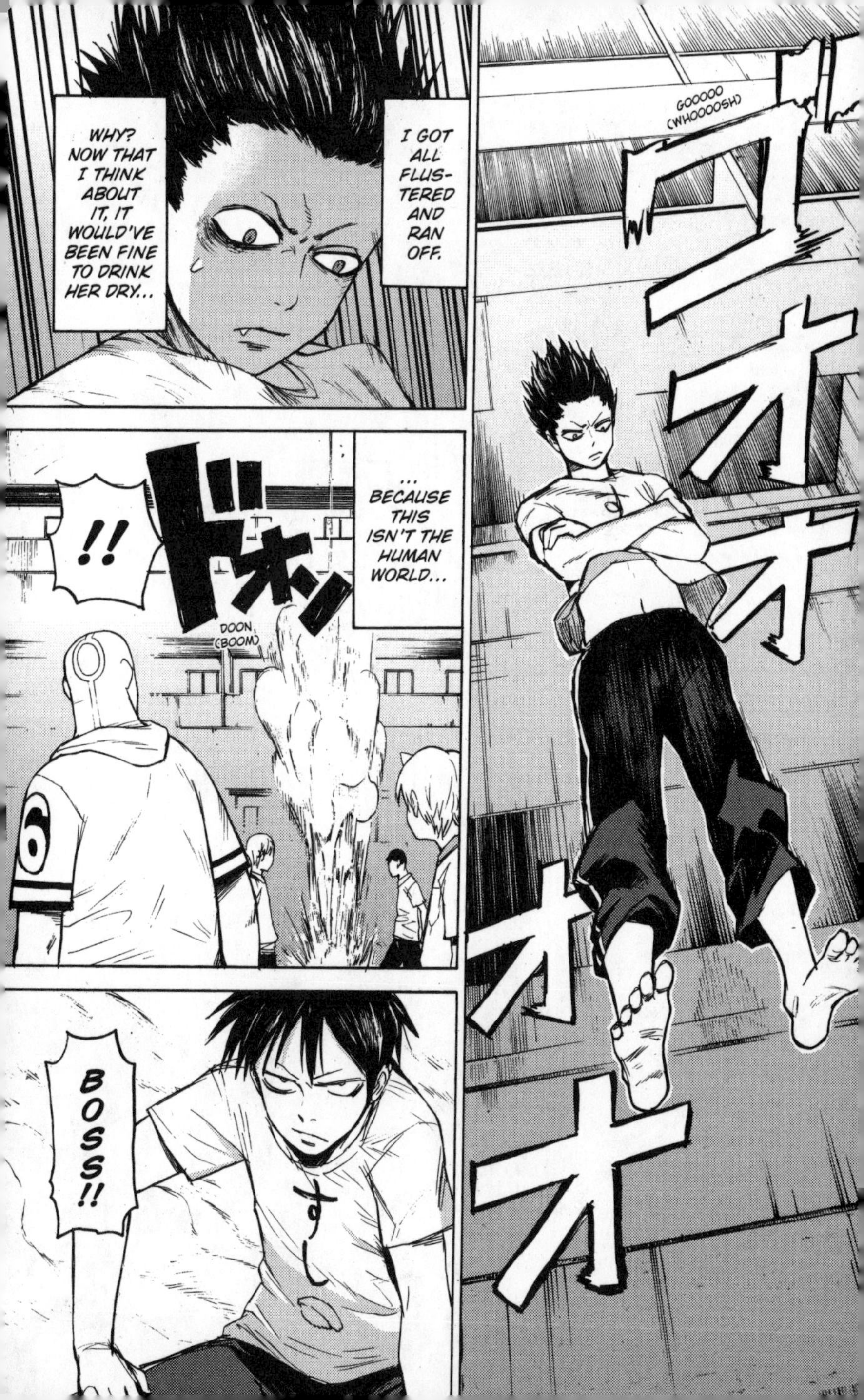
GOOOOO (WHOOOOSH)
I GOT ALL FLUS-TERED AND RAN OFF.
WHY? NOW THAT I THINK ABOUT IT, IT WOULD'VE BEEN FINE TO DRINK HER DRY...
... BECAUSE THIS ISN'T THE HUMAN WORLD...
DOON (BOOM)
!!
BOSS!!

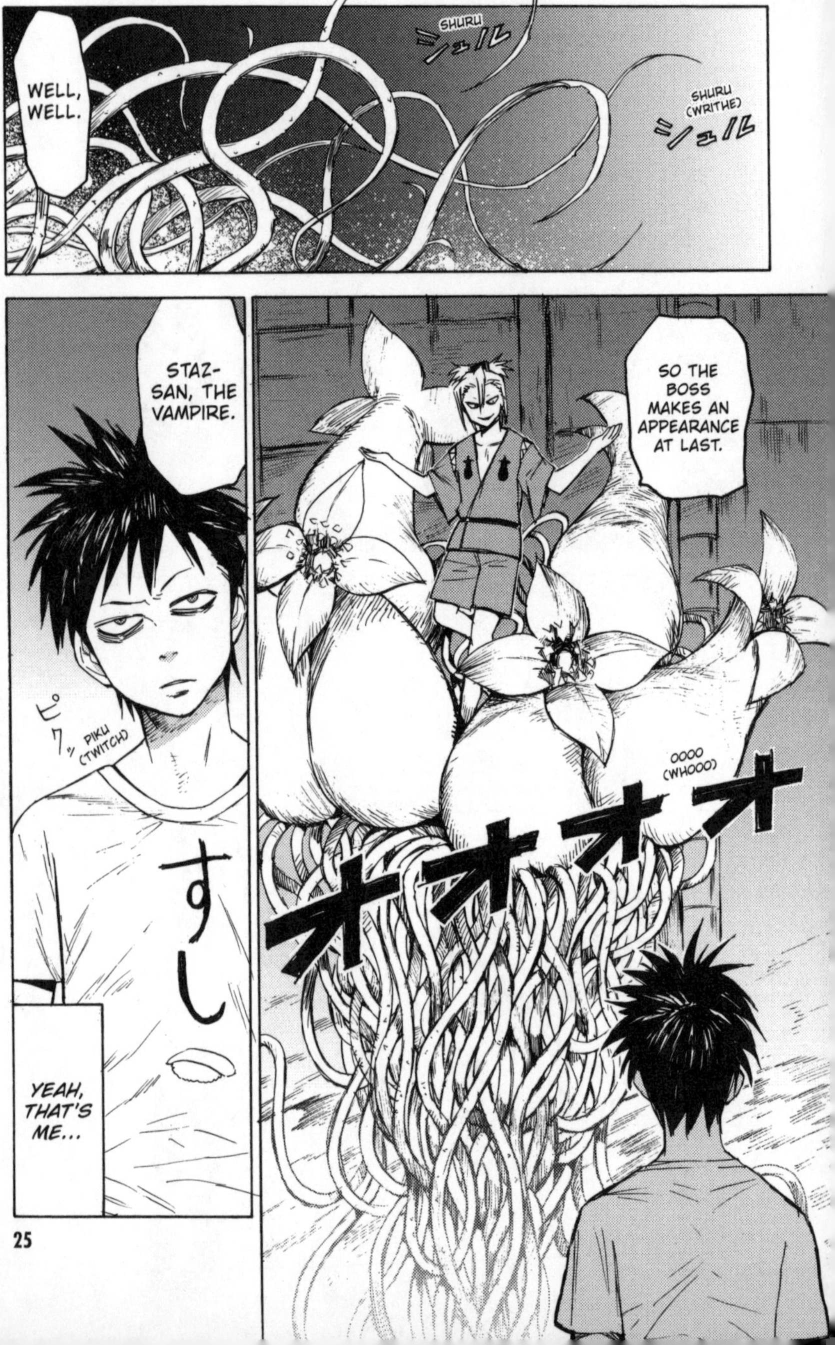
SHURU
シュル
SHURU (WRITHE)
シュル
WELL, WELL.
SO THE BOSS MAKES AN APPEARANCE AT LAST.
OOOO (WHOOO)
オオオオ
STAZ-SAN, THE VAMPIRE.
ピクッ
PIKU (TWITCH)
すし
YEAH, THAT'S ME...

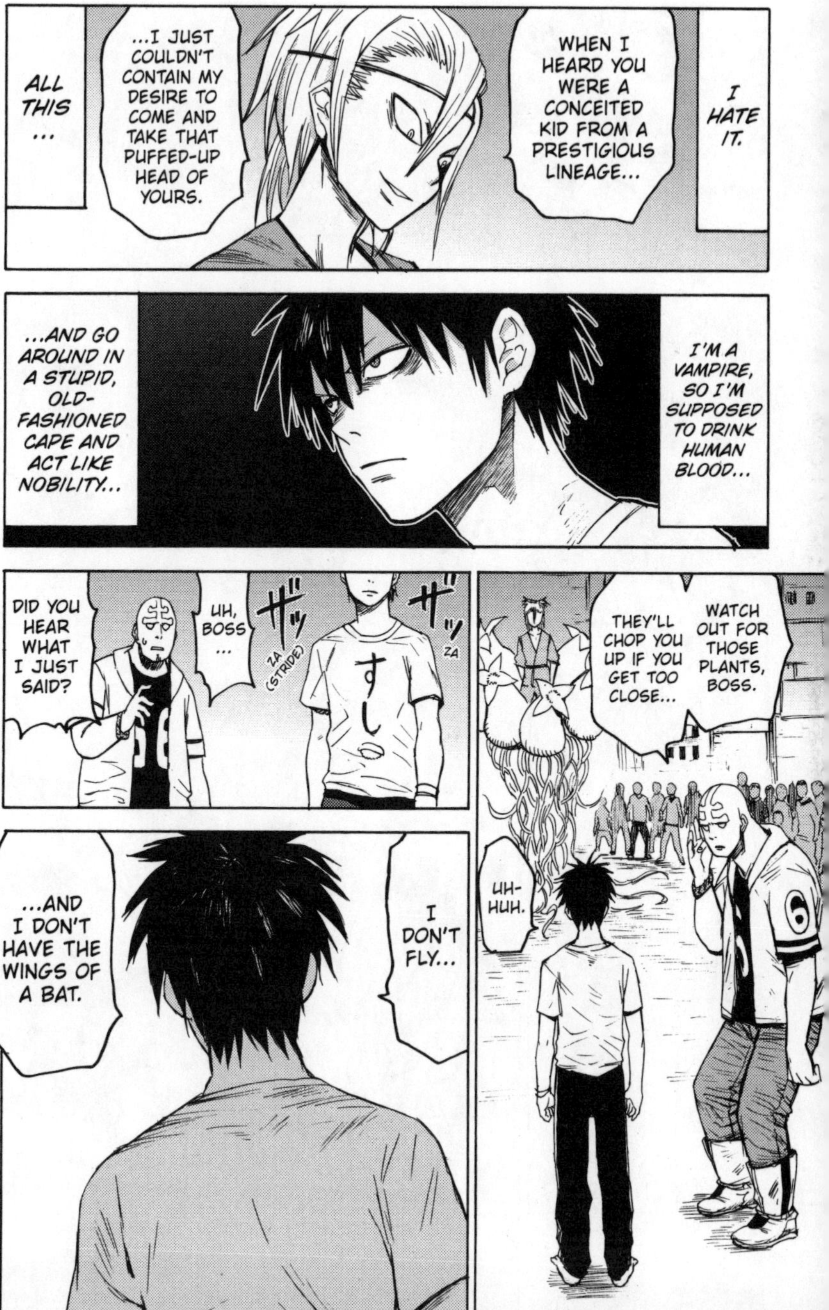
I HATE IT.
WHEN I HEARD YOU WERE A CONCEITED KID FROM A PRESTIGIOUS LINEAGE...
...I JUST COULDN'T CONTAIN MY DESIRE TO COME AND TAKE THAT PUFFED-UP HEAD OF YOURS.
ALL THIS...
I'M A VAMPIRE, SO I'M SUPPOSED TO DRINK HUMAN BLOOD...
...AND GO AROUND IN A STUPID, OLD-FASHIONED CAPE AND ACT LIKE NOBILITY...
WATCH OUT FOR THOSE PLANTS, BOSS.
THEY'LL CHOP YOU UP IF YOU GET TOO CLOSE...
UH-HUH.
ザッ ZA
すし
UH, BOSS...
ザッ ZA (STRIDE)
DID YOU HEAR WHAT I JUST SAID?
I DON'T FLY...
...AND I DON'T HAVE THE WINGS OF A BAT.

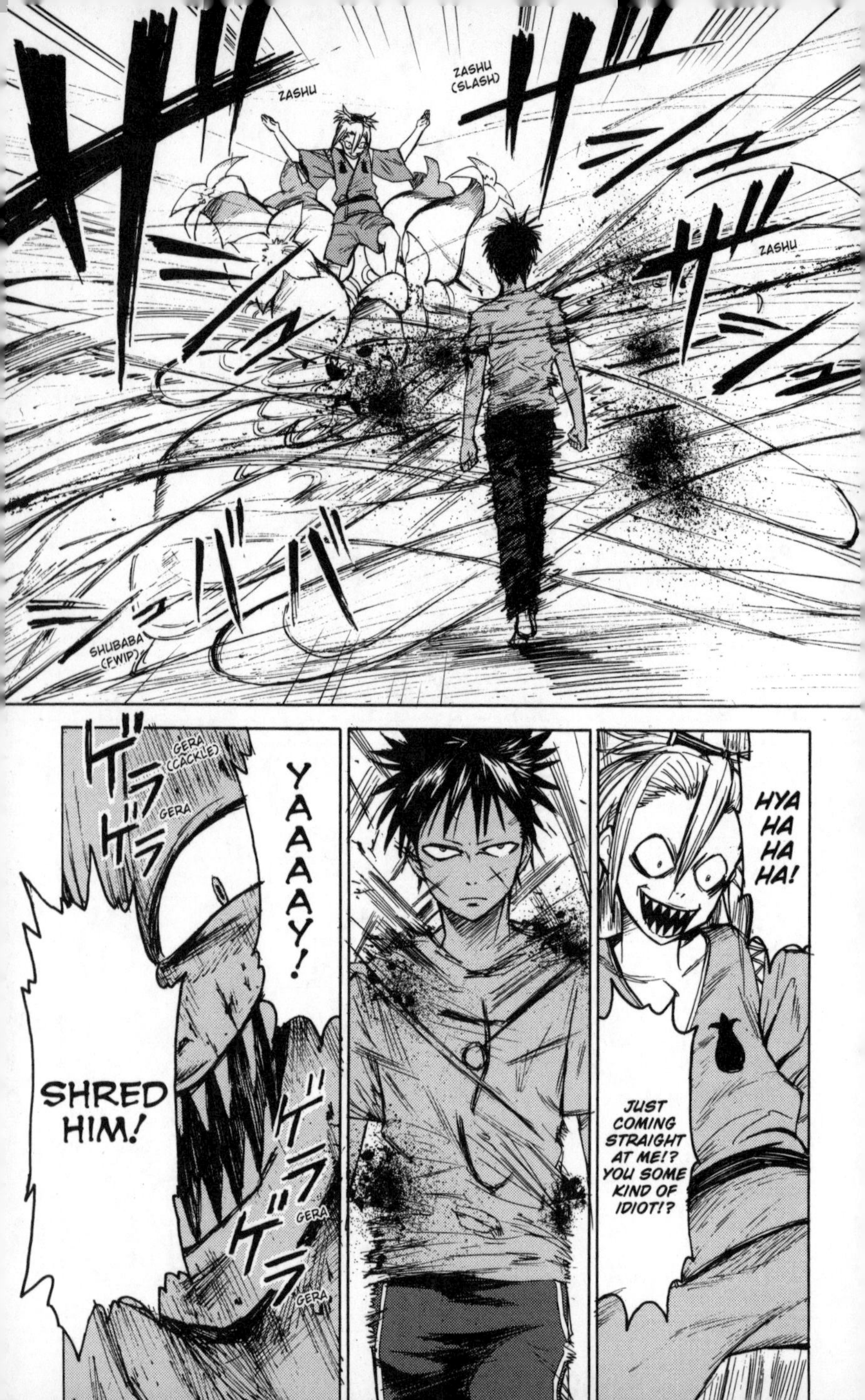
ZASHU (SLASH)
ZASHU
ZASHU
SHUBABA (FWIP)
HYA HA HA HA HA!
JUST COMING STRAIGHT AT ME!? YOU SOME KIND OF IDIOT!?
YAAAAAY!
GERA (CACKLE)
GERA
SHRED HIM!
GERA
GERA

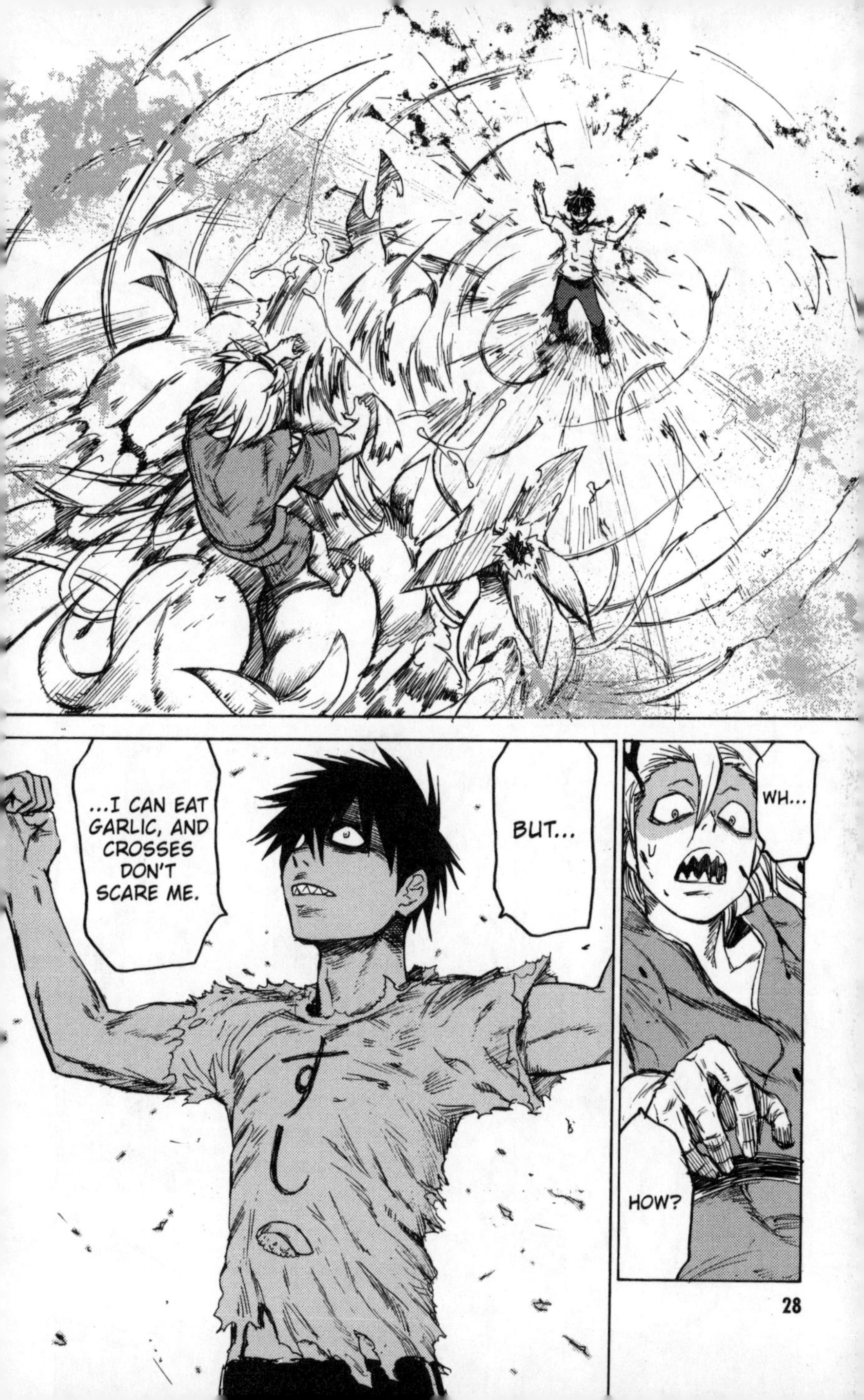
WH...
HOW?
BUT...
...I CAN EAT GARLIC, AND CROSSES DON'T SCARE ME.

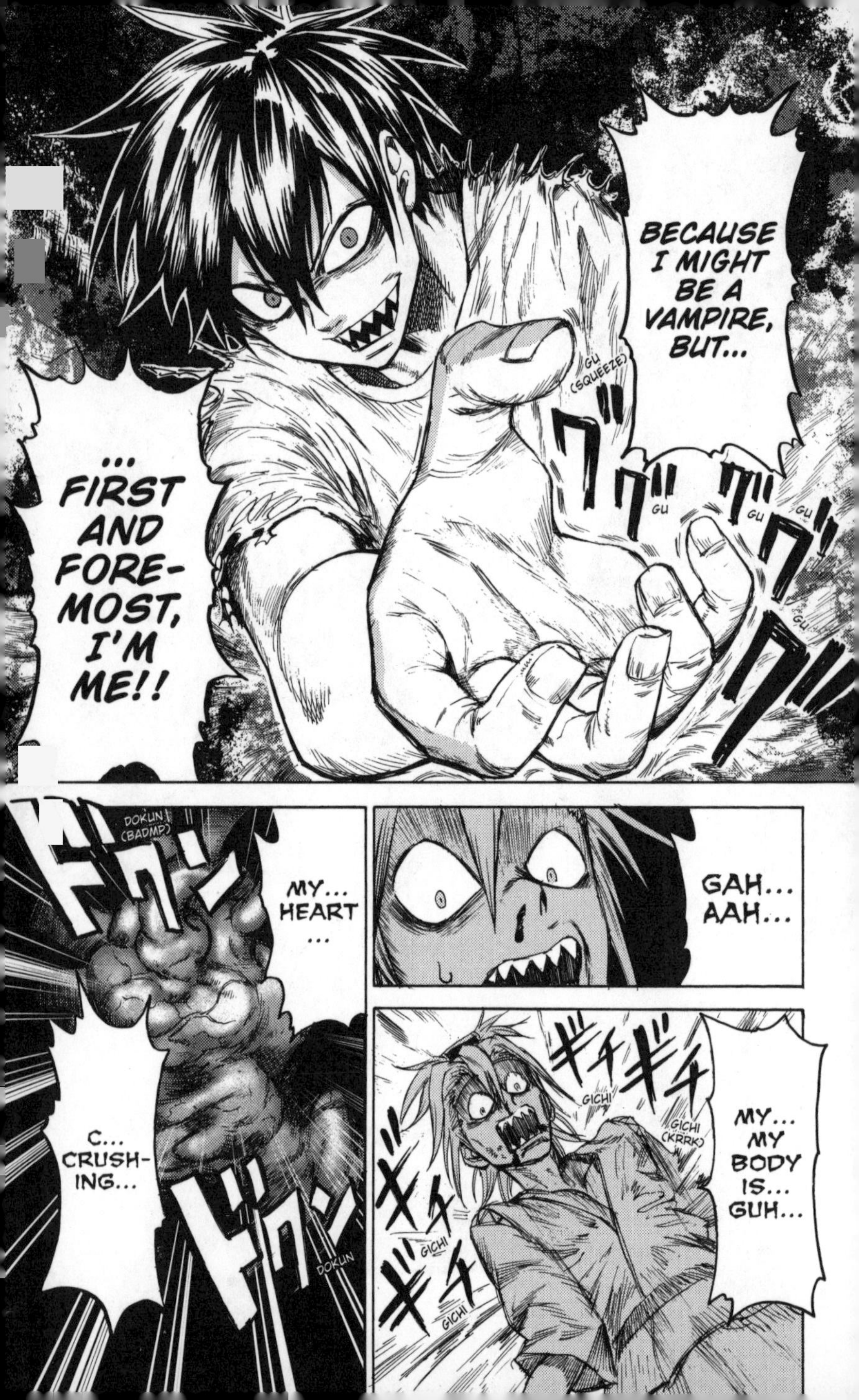
BECAUSE I MIGHT BE A VAMPIRE, BUT...
GU (SQUEEZE)
GU
GU
GU
GU
... FIRST AND FORE-MOST, I'M ME!!
GAH... AAH...
MY... MY BODY IS... GUH...
GICHI
GICHI (KRRK)
GICHI
GICHI
DOKUN (BADMP)
MY... HEART ...
C... CRUSH-ING...
DOKUN

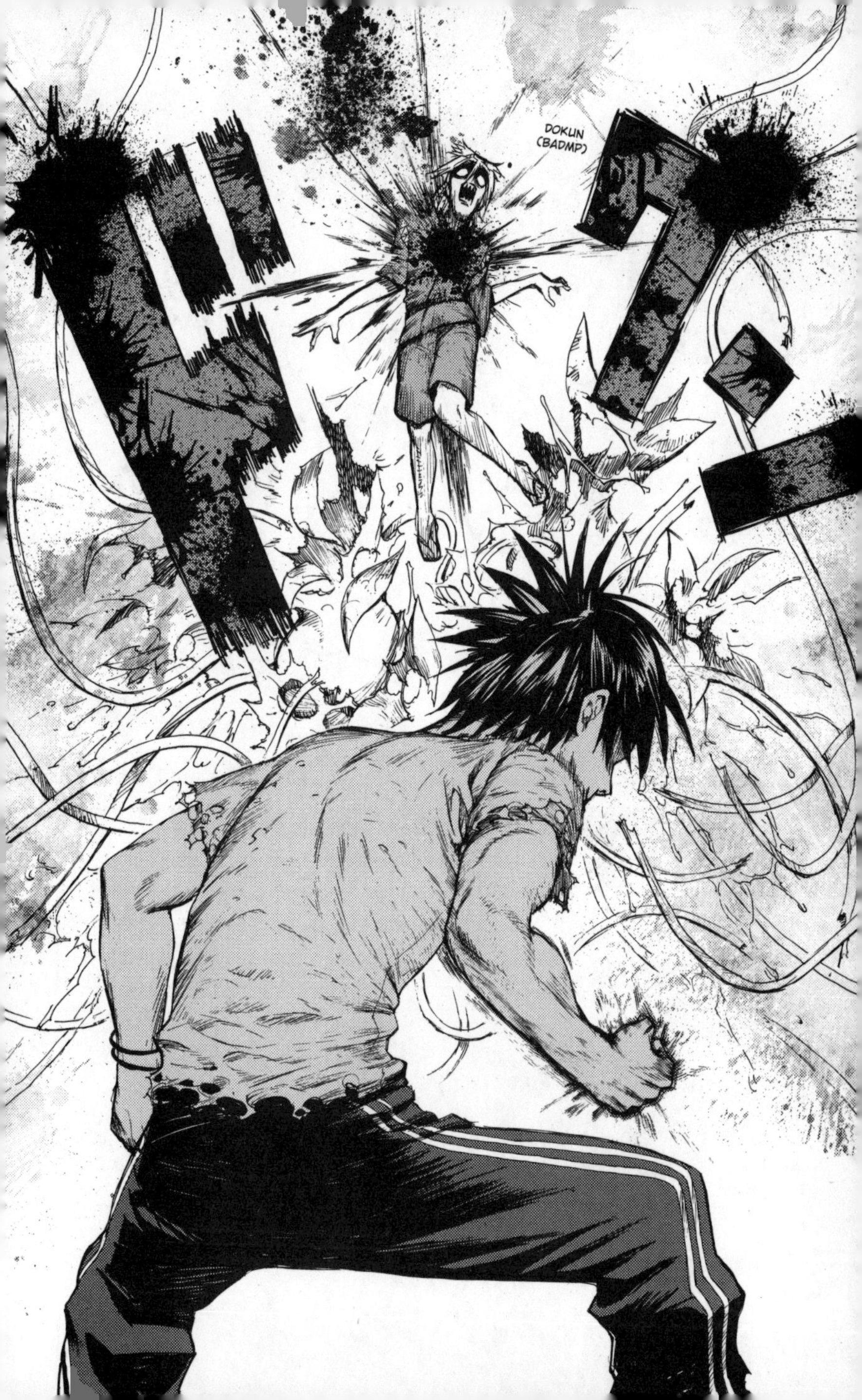
DOKUN
(BADMP)

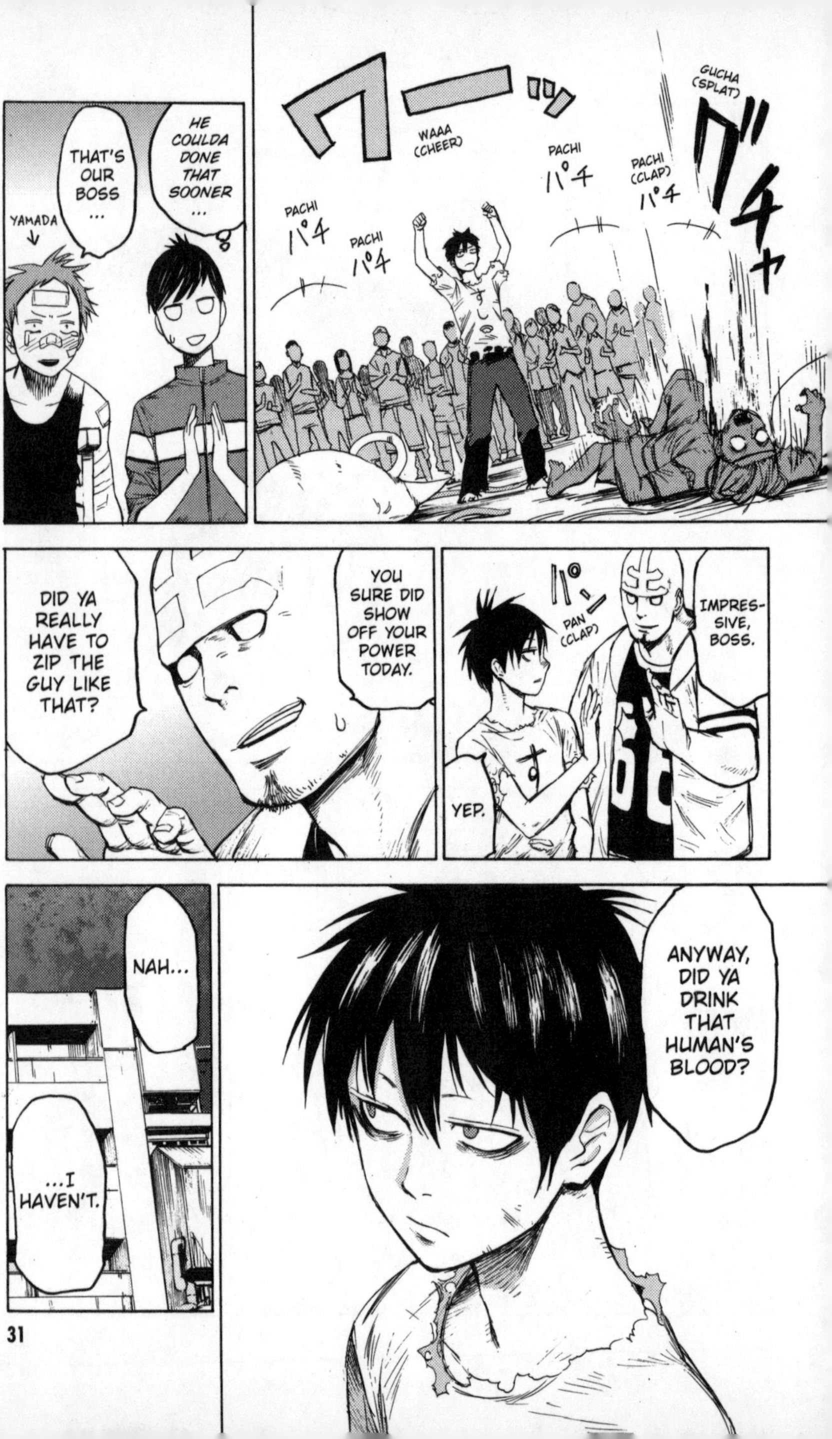
GUCHA (SPLAT)
グチャ
ワーッ
WAAA (CHEER)
PACHI
パチ
PACHI (CLAP)
パチ
PACHI
パチ
PACHI
パチ
HE COULDA DONE THAT SOONER...
THAT'S OUR BOSS...
YAMADA
IMPRES-SIVE, BOSS.
パン
PAN (CLAP)
YEP.
YOU SURE DID SHOW OFF YOUR POWER TODAY.
DID YA REALLY HAVE TO ZIP THE GUY LIKE THAT?
ANYWAY, DID YA DRINK THAT HUMAN'S BLOOD?
NAH...
...I HAVEN'T.

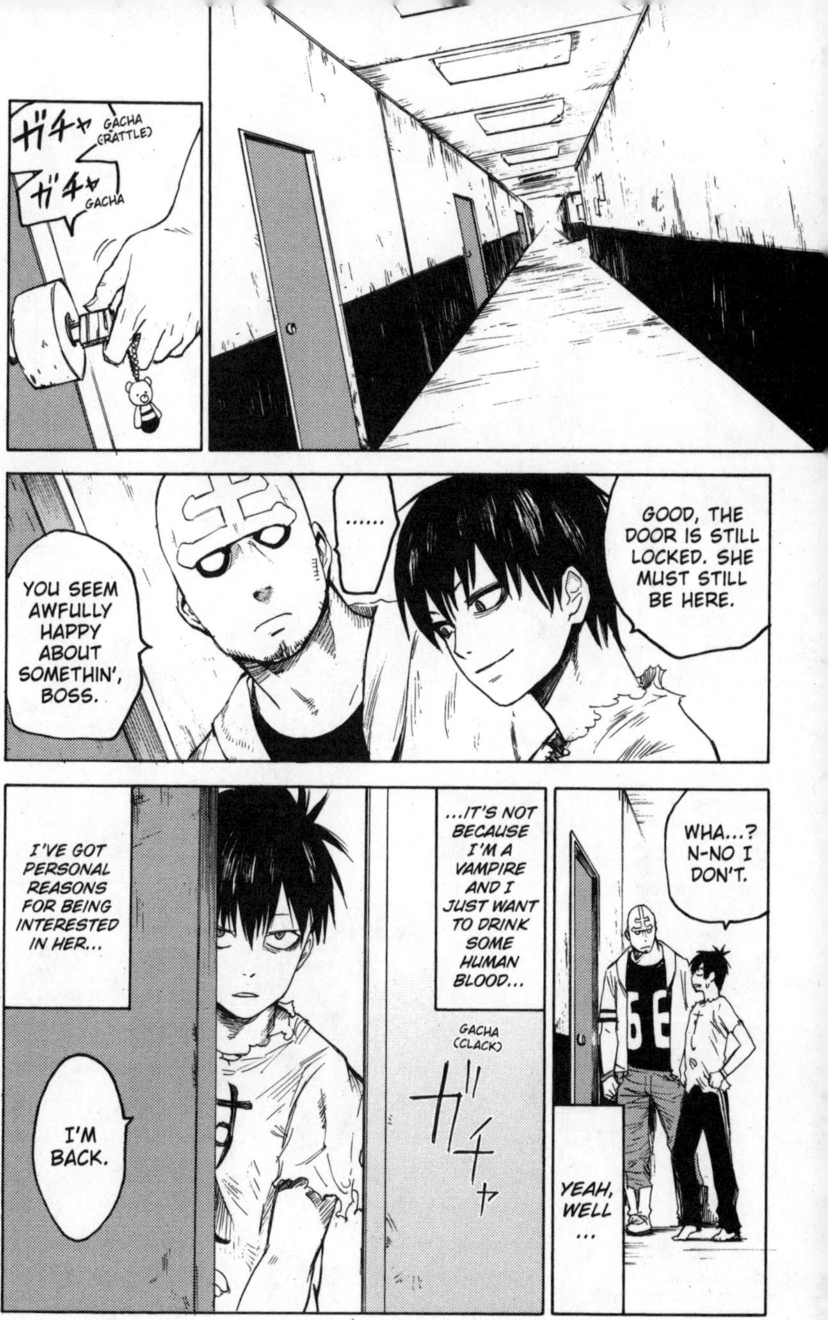
ガチャ
GACHA (RATTLE)
ガチャ
GACHA
GOOD, THE DOOR IS STILL LOCKED. SHE MUST STILL BE HERE.
......
YOU SEEM AWFULLY HAPPY ABOUT SOMETHIN', BOSS.
WHA...? N-NO I DON'T.
YEAH, WELL ...
...IT'S NOT BECAUSE I'M A VAMPIRE AND I JUST WANT TO DRINK SOME HUMAN BLOOD...
GACHA (CLACK)
ガチャ
I'VE GOT PERSONAL REASONS FOR BEING INTERESTED IN HER...
I'M BACK.

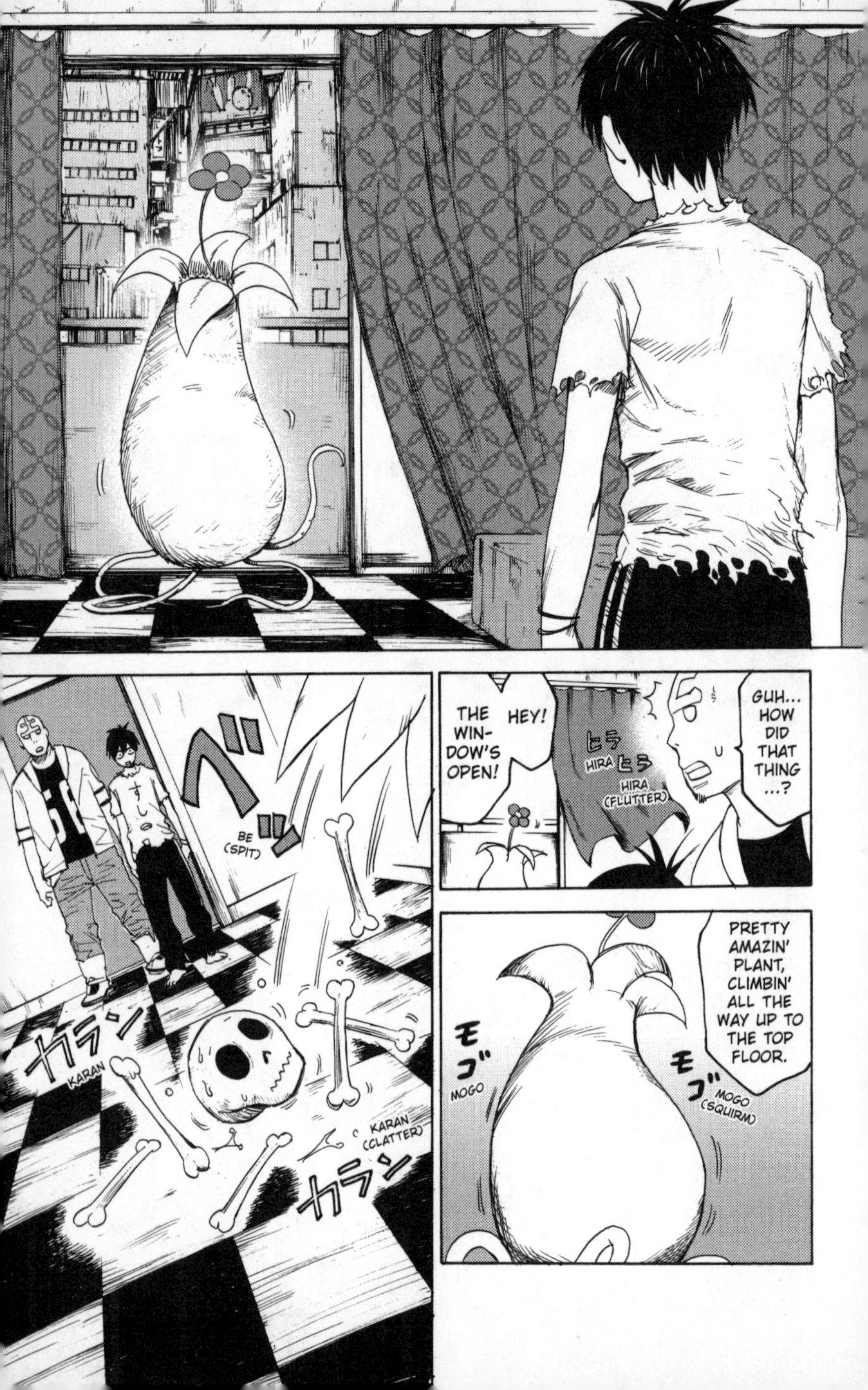
GUH... HOW DID THAT THING...?
HEY!
THE WIN-DOW'S OPEN!
HIRA HIRA (FLUTTER)
PRETTY AMAZIN' PLANT, CLIMBIN' ALL THE WAY UP TO THE TOP FLOOR.
MOGO MOGO (SQUIRM)
BE (SPIT)
KARAN
KARAN (CLATTER)

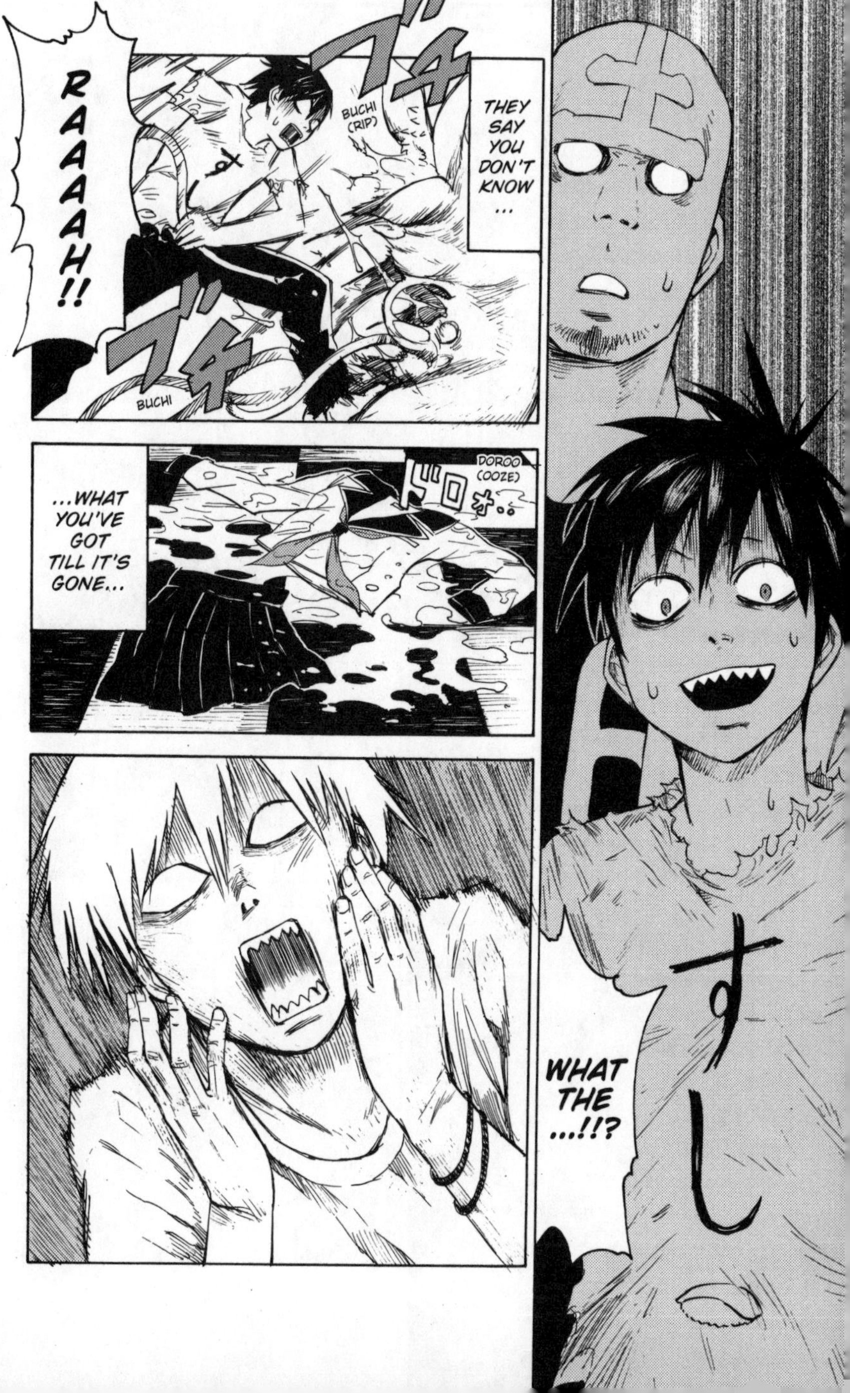
WHAT THE ...!!?
THEY SAY YOU DON'T KNOW ...
BUCHI (RIP)
RAAAAAH!!
BUCHI
DOROO (OOZE)
...WHAT YOU'VE GOT TILL IT'S GONE...

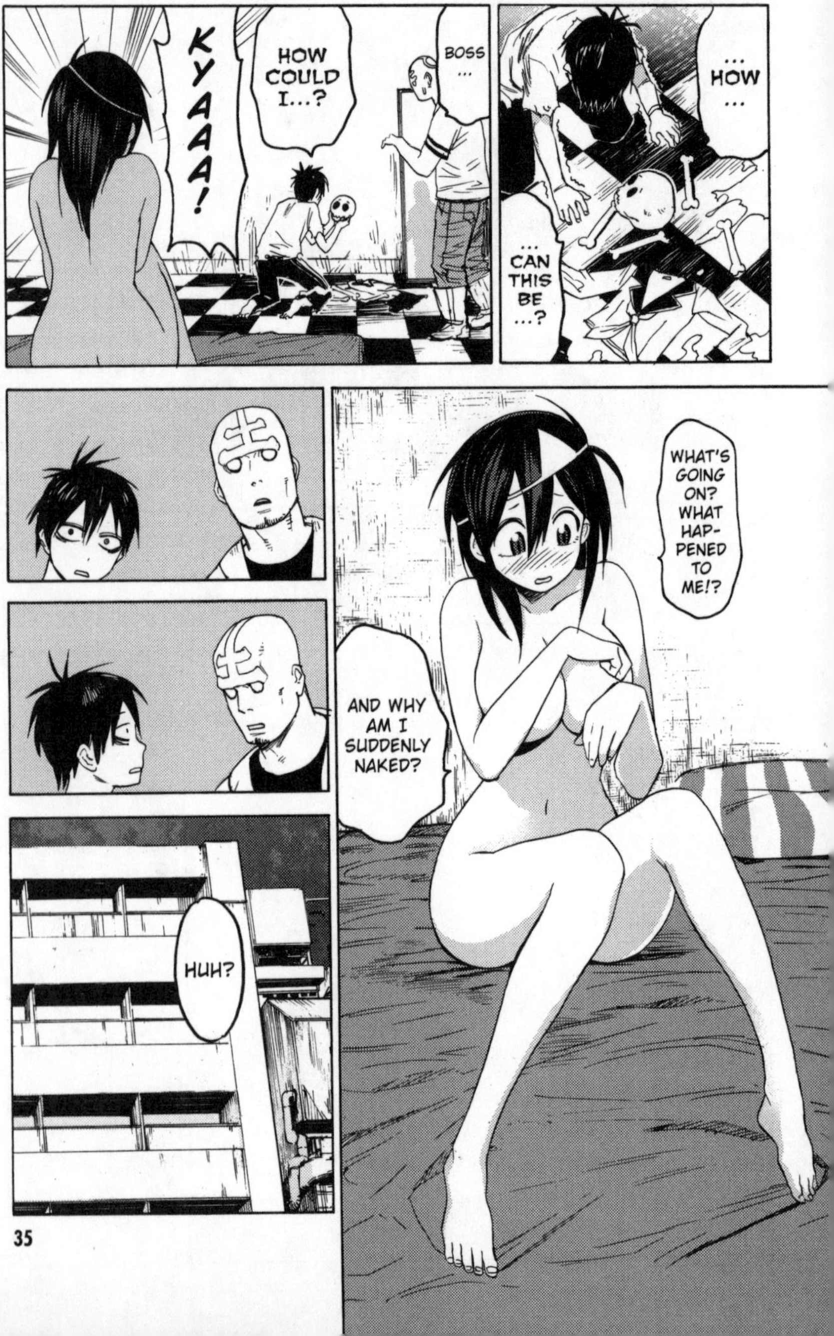
... HOW ...
... CAN THIS BE ...?
BOSS ...
HOW COULD I...?
KYAAAA!
WHAT'S GOING ON? WHAT HAP-PENED TO ME!?
AND WHY AM I SUDDENLY NAKED?
HUH?

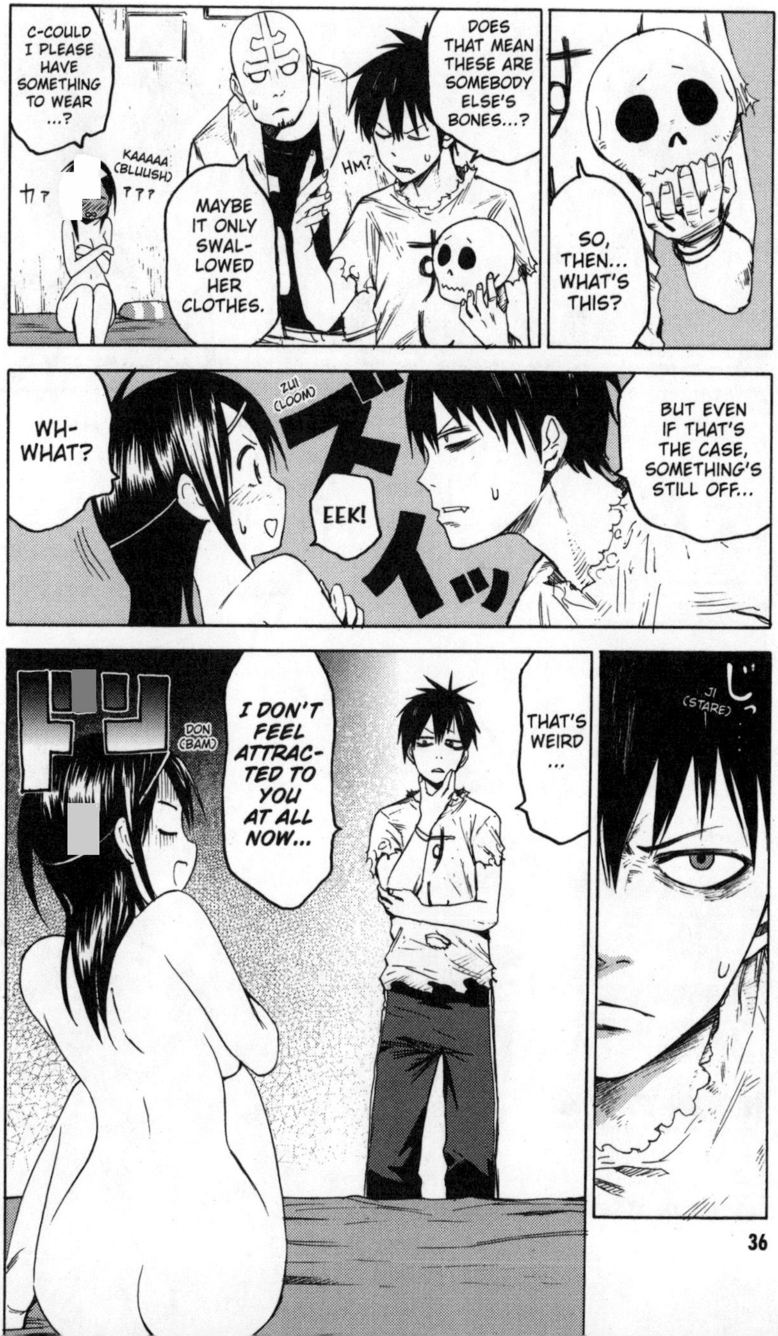
SO, THEN... WHAT'S THIS?
DOES THAT MEAN THESE ARE SOMEBODY ELSE'S BONES...?
HM?
MAYBE IT ONLY SWALLOWED HER CLOTHES.
KAAAAA (BLUUSH)
???
C-COULD I PLEASE HAVE SOMETHING TO WEAR ...?
BUT EVEN IF THAT'S THE CASE, SOMETHING'S STILL OFF...
ZUI (LOOM)
EEK!
WH-WHAT?
JI (STARE)
THAT'S WEIRD ...
I DON'T FEEL ATTRACTED TO YOU AT ALL NOW...
DON (BAM)

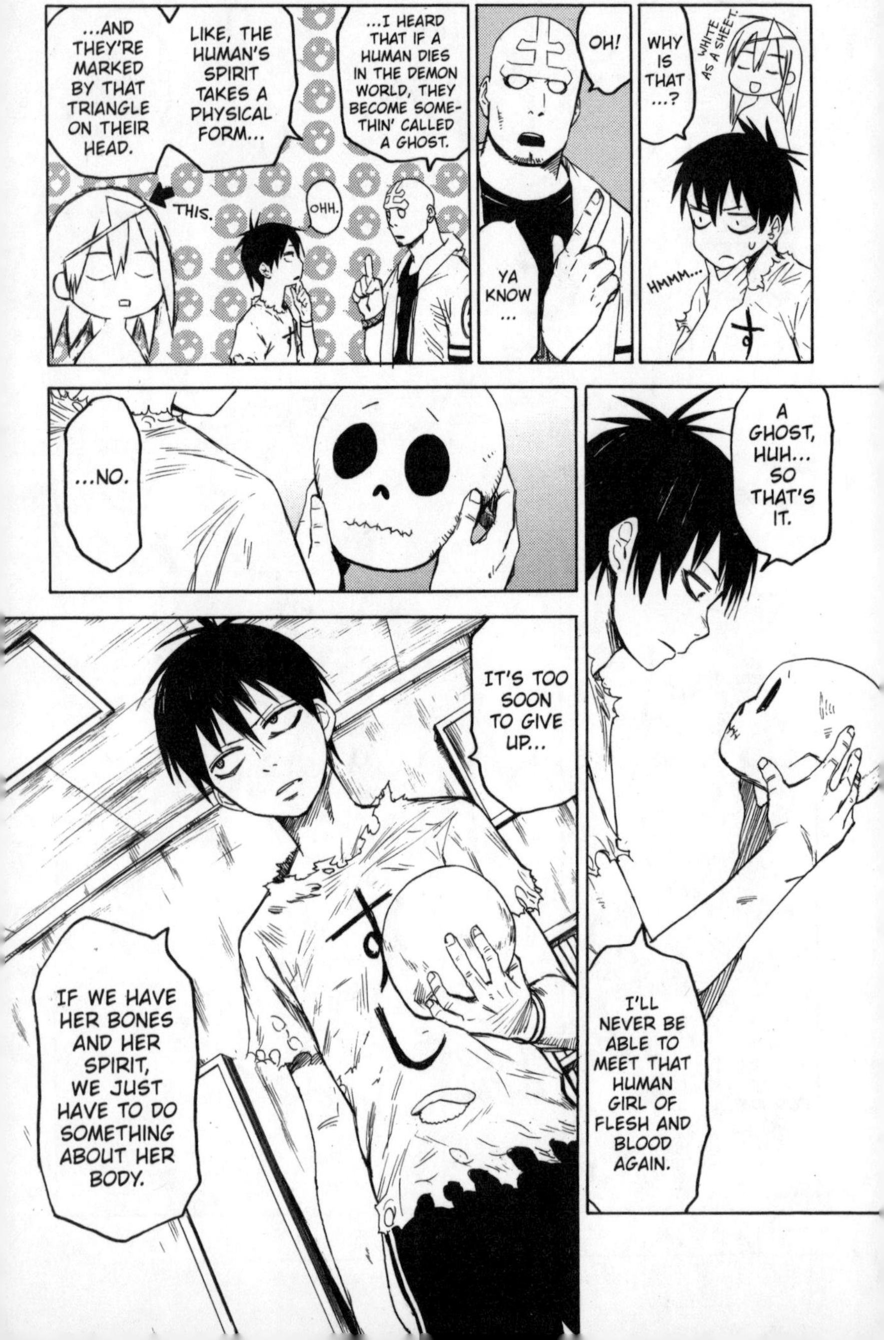
WHY IS THAT ...?
WHITE AS A SHEET.
HMMM...
OH!
YA KNOW ...
...I HEARD THAT IF A HUMAN DIES IN THE DEMON WORLD, THEY BECOME SOMETHIN' CALLED A GHOST.
LIKE, THE HUMAN'S SPIRIT TAKES A PHYSICAL FORM...
...AND THEY'RE MARKED BY THAT TRIANGLE ON THEIR HEAD.
OHH.
THIS.
A GHOST, HUH... SO THAT'S IT.
I'LL NEVER BE ABLE TO MEET THAT HUMAN GIRL OF FLESH AND BLOOD AGAIN.
...NO.
IT'S TOO SOON TO GIVE UP...
IF WE HAVE HER BONES AND HER SPIRIT, WE JUST HAVE TO DO SOMETHING ABOUT HER BODY.

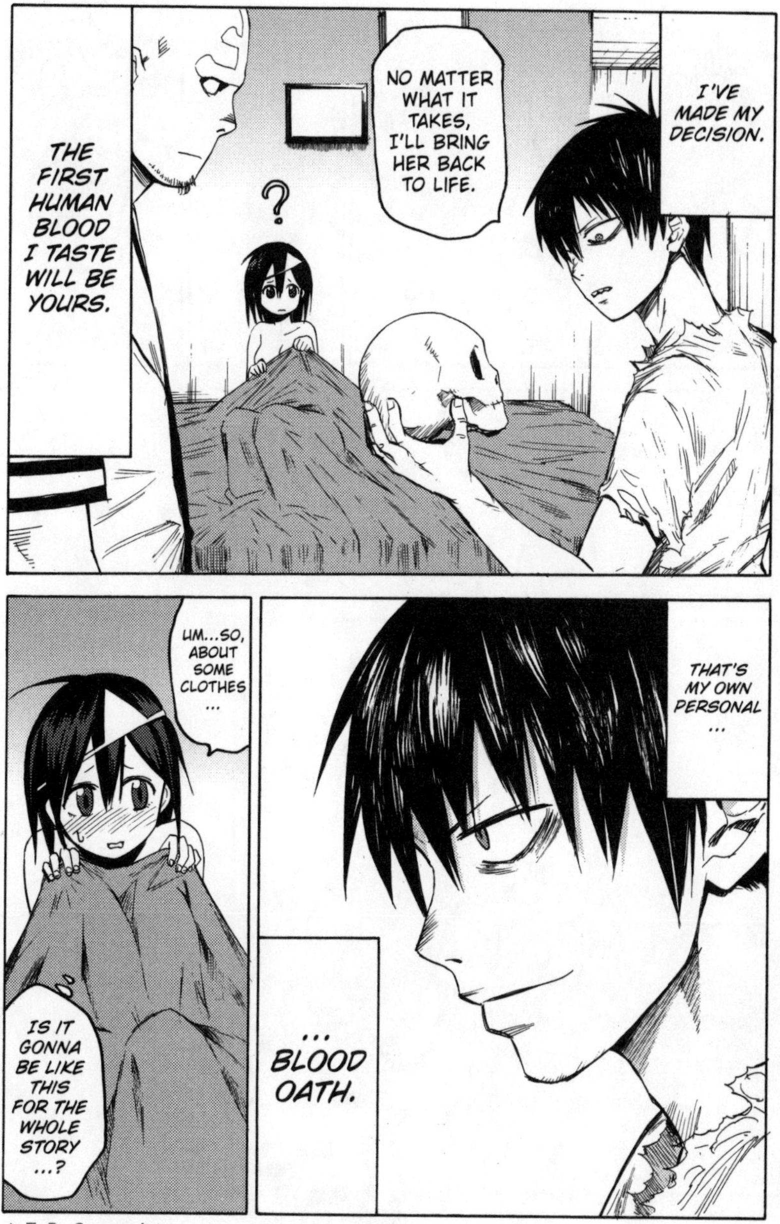
I'VE MADE MY DECISION.
NO MATTER WHAT IT TAKES, I'LL BRING HER BACK TO LIFE.
?
THE FIRST HUMAN BLOOD I TASTE WILL BE YOURS.
THAT'S MY OWN PERSONAL ...
... BLOOD OATH.
UM...SO, ABOUT SOME CLOTHES ...
IS IT GONNA BE LIKE THIS FOR THE WHOLE STORY ...?

♠ To Be Continued ♠

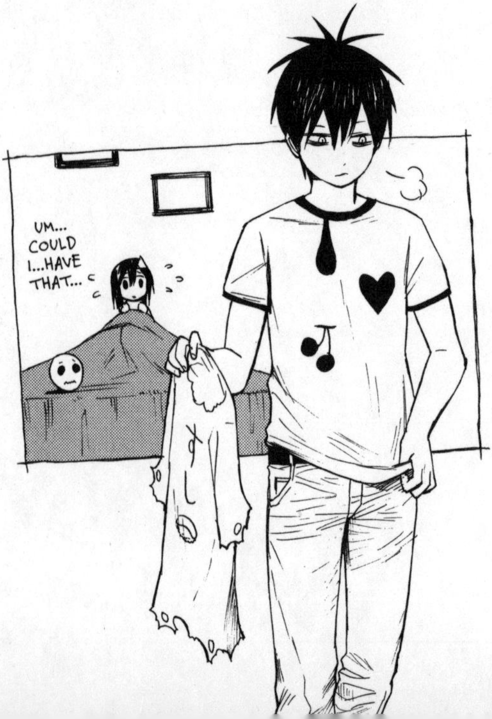
UM... COULD I...HAVE THAT...

BLOOD LAD

# CHAPTER 2 ♠ NOKO BUFFET

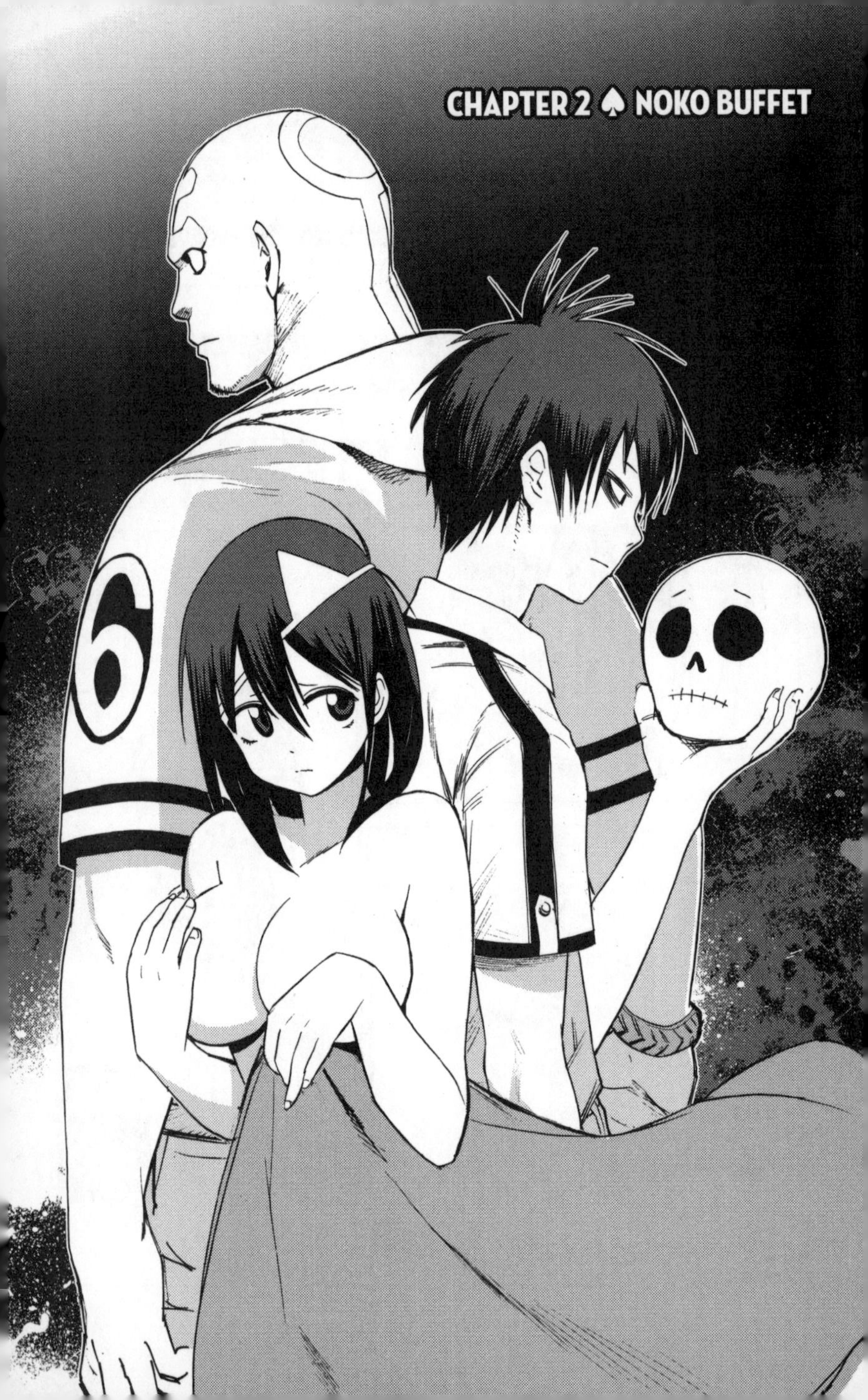

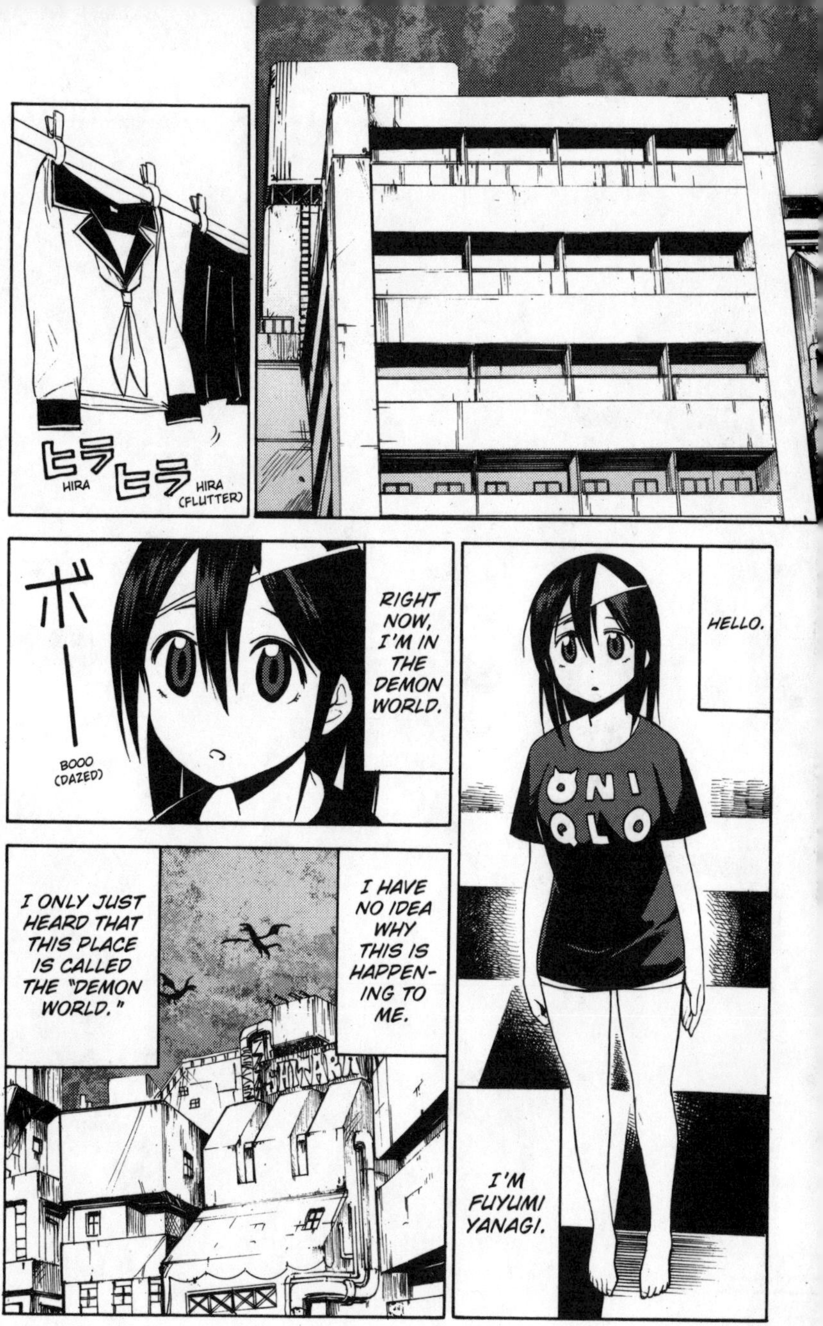

ヒラ
HIRA
ヒラ
HIRA (FLUTTER)
HELLO.
I'M FUYUMI YANAGI.
RIGHT NOW, I'M IN THE DEMON WORLD.
ボー
BOOO (DAZED)
I HAVE NO IDEA WHY THIS IS HAPPENING TO ME.
I ONLY JUST HEARD THAT THIS PLACE IS CALLED THE "DEMON WORLD."

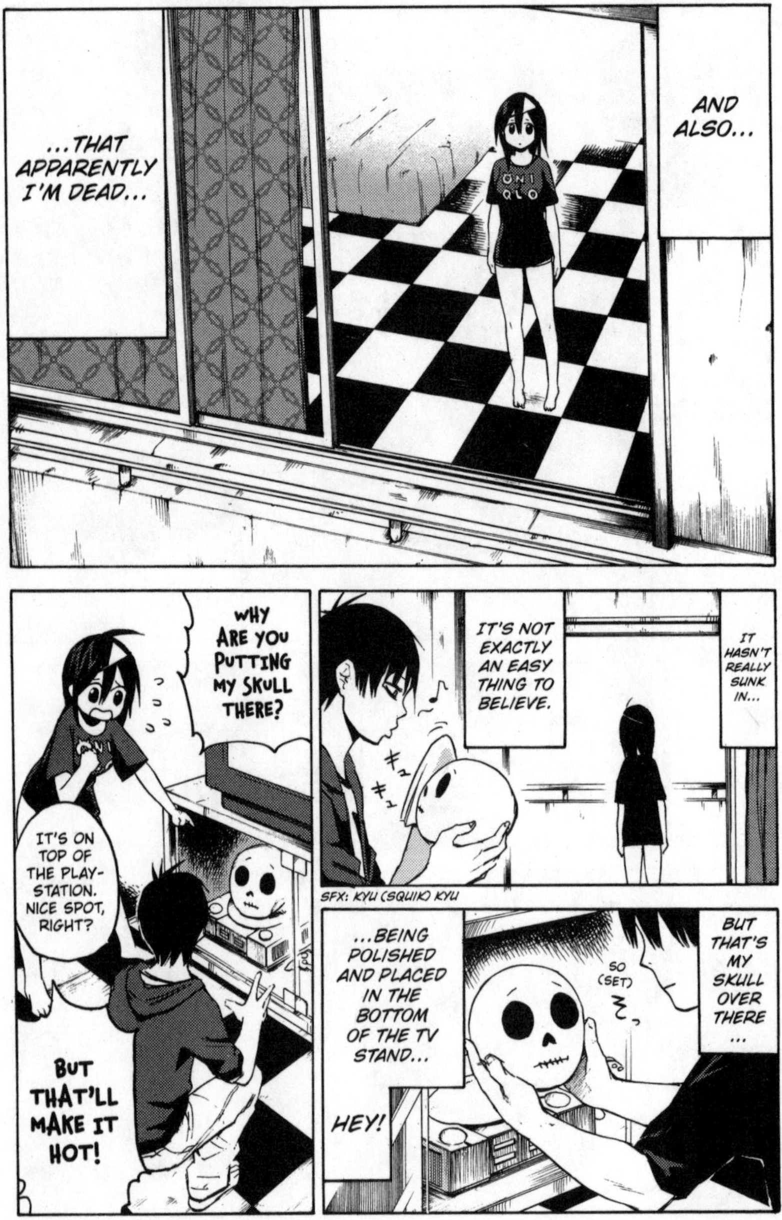
AND ALSO...
...THAT APPARENTLY I'M DEAD...
IT HASN'T REALLY SUNK IN...
IT'S NOT EXACTLY AN EASY THING TO BELIEVE.
SFX: KYU (SQUIK) KYU
BUT THAT'S MY SKULL OVER THERE...
SO (SET)
...BEING POLISHED AND PLACED IN THE BOTTOM OF THE TV STAND...
HEY!
WHY ARE YOU PUTTING MY SKULL THERE?
IT'S ON TOP OF THE PLAY-STATION. NICE SPOT, RIGHT?
BUT THAT'LL MAKE IT HOT!

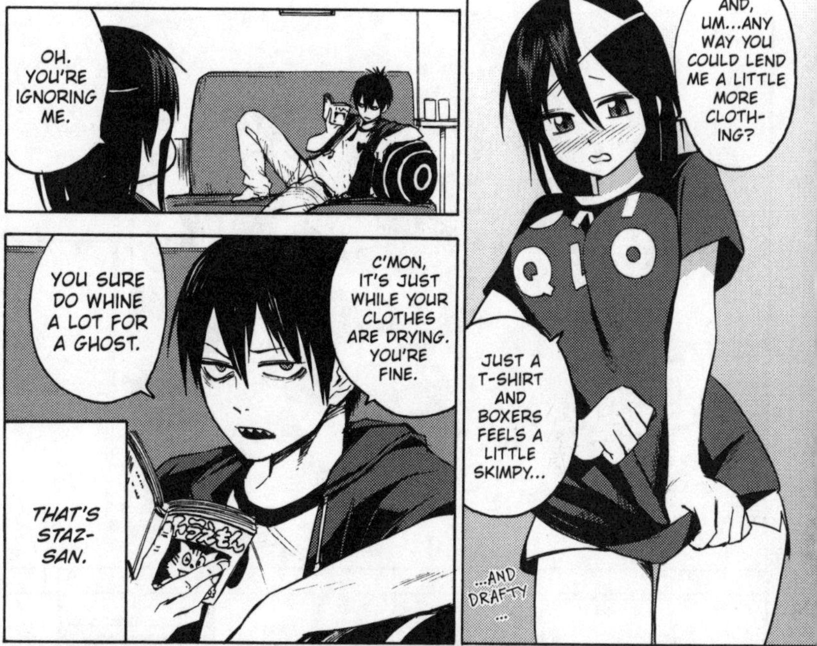
AND, UM...ANY WAY YOU COULD LEND ME A LITTLE MORE CLOTH-ING?
JUST A T-SHIRT AND BOXERS FEELS A LITTLE SKIMPY...
...AND DRAFTY...
OH. YOU'RE IGNORING ME.
C'MON, IT'S JUST WHILE YOUR CLOTHES ARE DRYING. YOU'RE FINE.
YOU SURE DO WHINE A LOT FOR A GHOST.
THAT'S STAZ-SAN.

BOOK: TORAEMON (NOTE: A SPOOF ON THE CLASSIC MANGA DORAEMON; TORA MEANS "TIGER.")

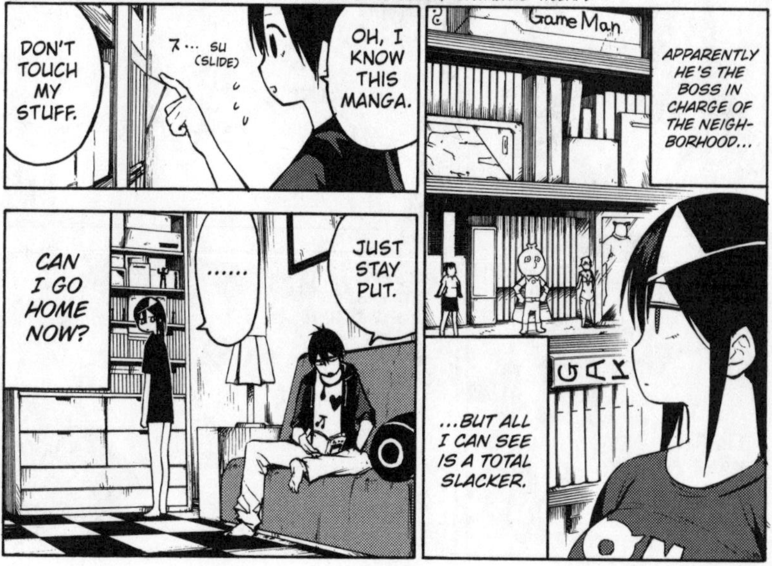
Game Man
APPARENTLY HE'S THE BOSS IN CHARGE OF THE NEIGH-BORHOOD...
OH, I KNOW THIS MANGA.
ス… SU (SLIDE)
DON'T TOUCH MY STUFF.
...BUT ALL I CAN SEE IS A TOTAL SLACKER.
JUST STAY PUT.
......
CAN I GO HOME NOW?

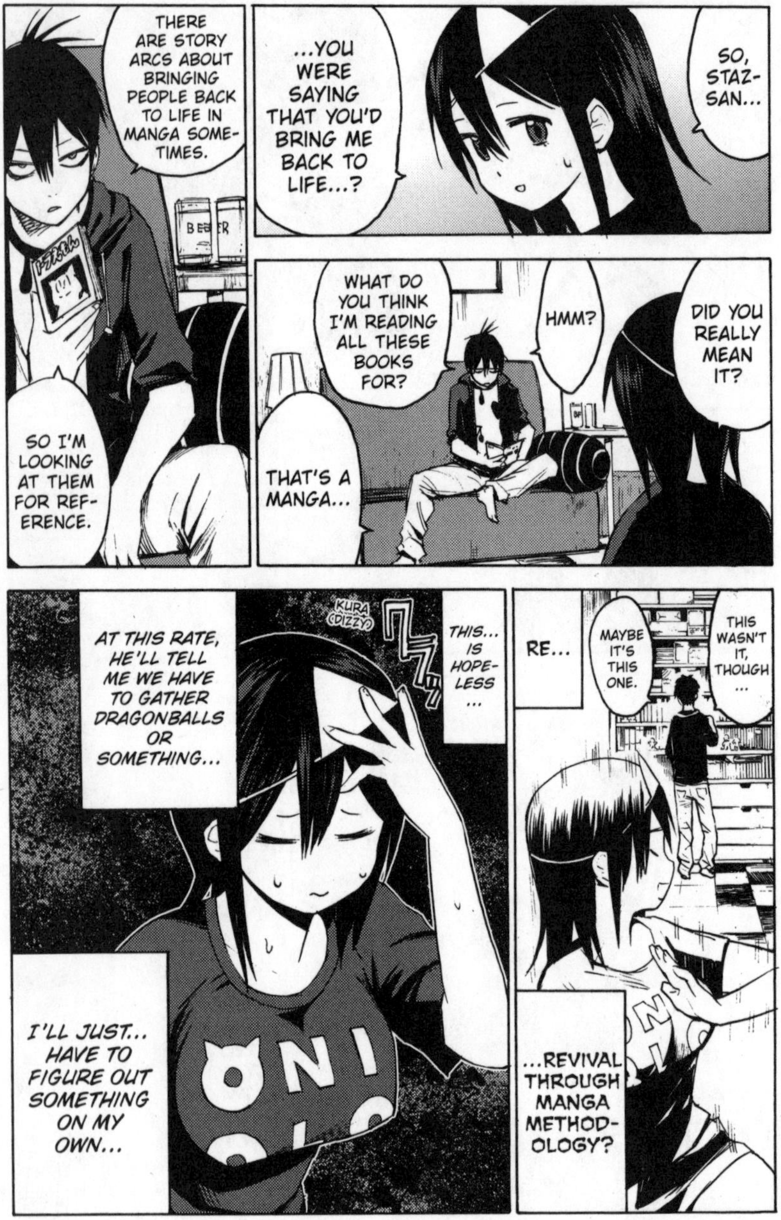
SO, STAZ-SAN...
...YOU WERE SAYING THAT YOU'D BRING ME BACK TO LIFE...?
DID YOU REALLY MEAN IT?
HMM?
WHAT DO YOU THINK I'M READING ALL THESE BOOKS FOR?
THAT'S A MANGA...
THERE ARE STORY ARCS ABOUT BRINGING PEOPLE BACK TO LIFE IN MANGA SOMETIMES.
SO I'M LOOKING AT THEM FOR REFERENCE.
THIS WASN'T IT, THOUGH...
MAYBE IT'S THIS ONE.
RE...
...REVIVAL THROUGH MANGA METHODOLOGY?
THIS... IS HOPELESS...
KURA (DIZZY)
AT THIS RATE, HE'LL TELL ME WE HAVE TO GATHER DRAGONBALLS OR SOMETHING...
I'LL JUST... HAVE TO FIGURE OUT SOMETHING ON MY OWN...

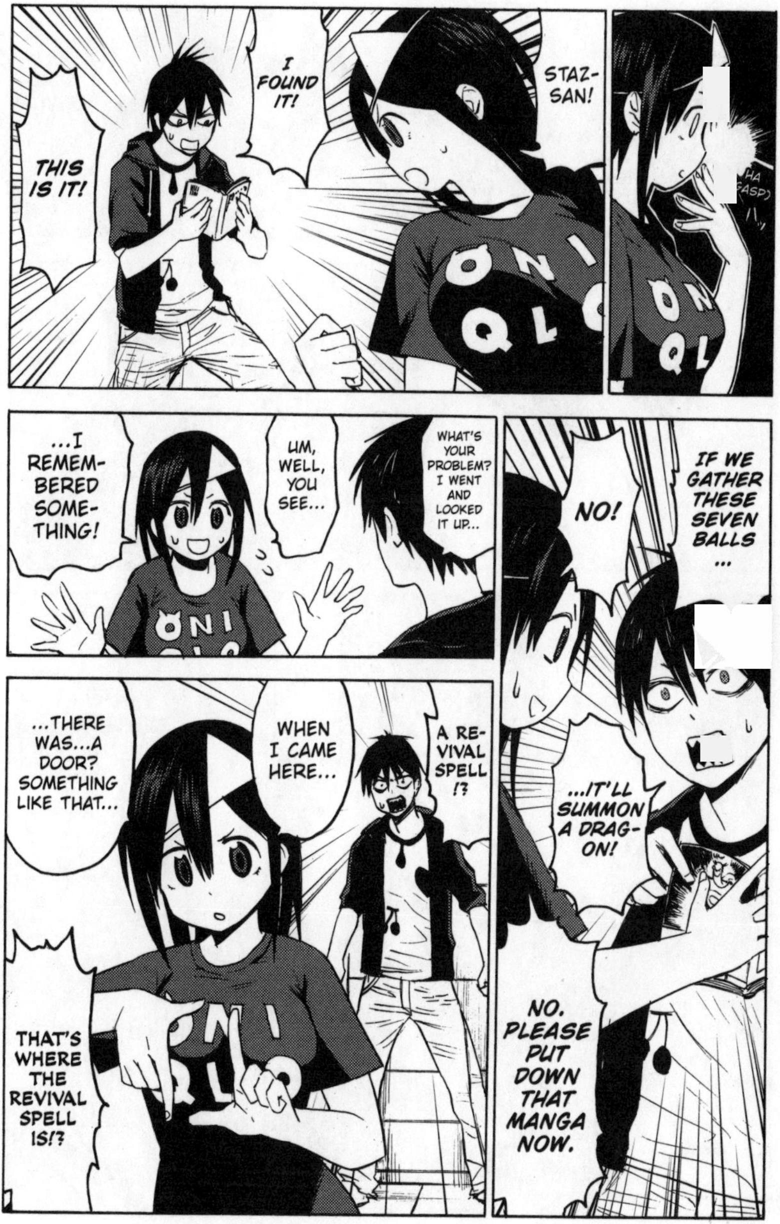
HA
STAZ-SAN!
I FOUND IT!
THIS IS IT!
IF WE GATHER THESE SEVEN BALLS ...
NO!
...IT'LL SUMMON A DRAG-ON!
NO. PLEASE PUT DOWN THAT MANGA NOW.
WHAT'S YOUR PROBLEM? I WENT AND LOOKED IT UP...
UM, WELL, YOU SEE...
...I REMEM-BERED SOME-THING!
A RE-VIVAL SPELL !?
WHEN I CAME HERE...
...THERE WAS...A DOOR? SOMETHING LIKE THAT...
THAT'S WHERE THE REVIVAL SPELL IS!?

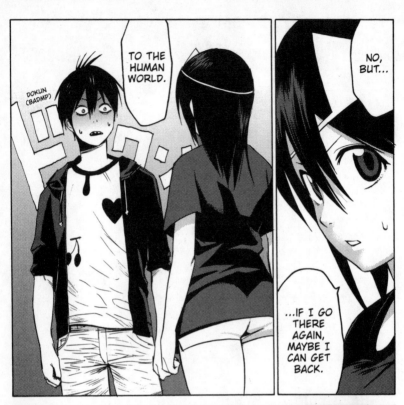

NO, BUT...
...IF I GO THERE AGAIN, MAYBE I CAN GET BACK.
TO THE HUMAN WORLD.
DOKUN (BADMP)
NO...
ヒク... HIKU (TWITCH)
NO WAY CAN THAT EXIST.
Y-YOU CAN'T FOOL ME...WHAT IDIOT WOULD BELIEVE THAT...?
OH... THEN I'LL GO BY MYSELF.
HUH ...?
...OH. WELL... ACTUALLY, I'M, UH, OUT OF SHAMPOO. I HAVE TO GO OUT ANYWAY.
......

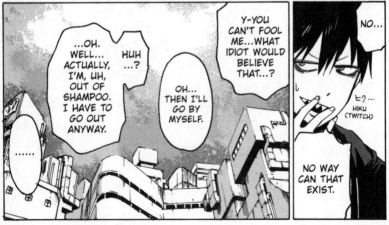

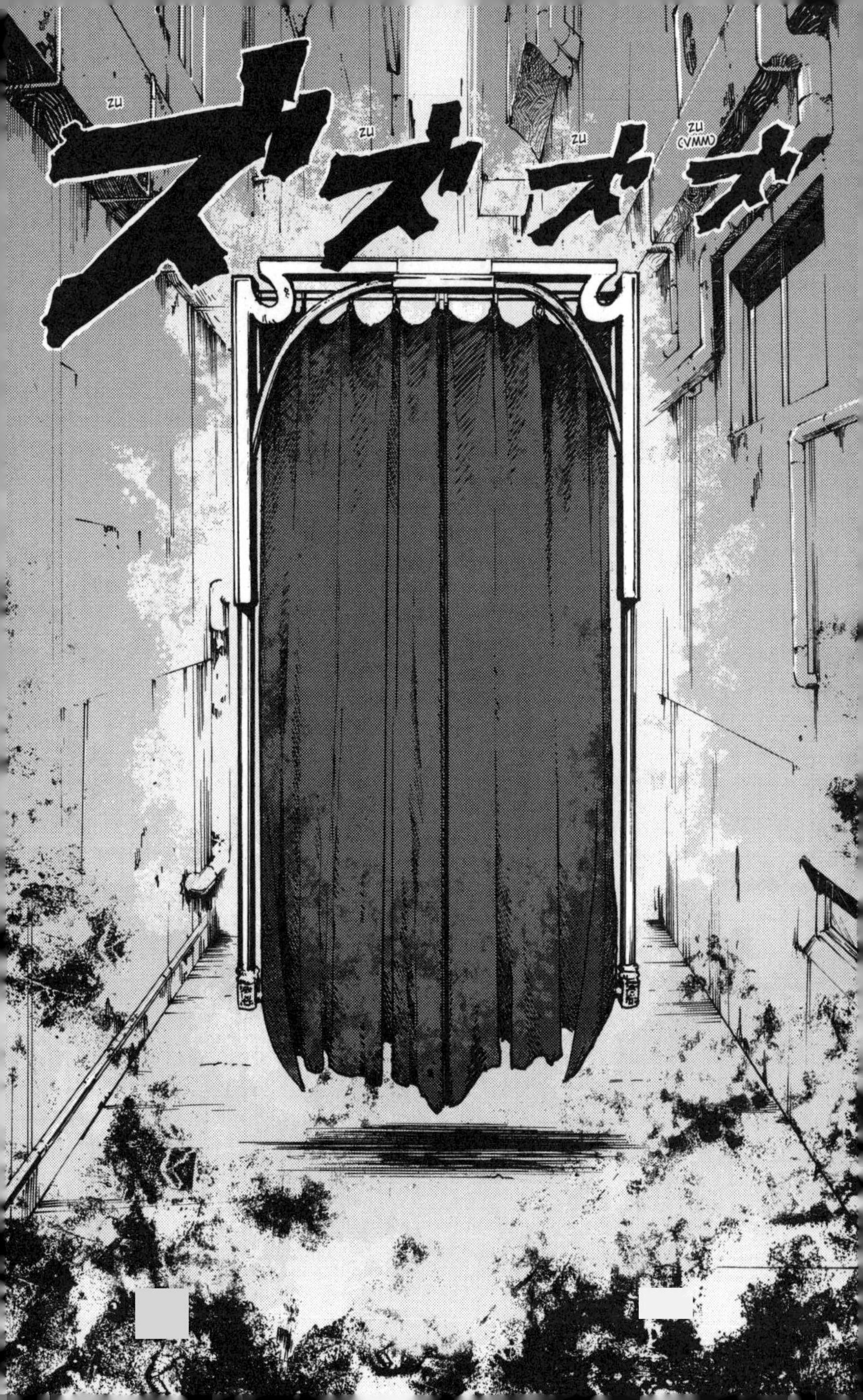
ズズズズ
ZU ZU ZU ZU (VMM)

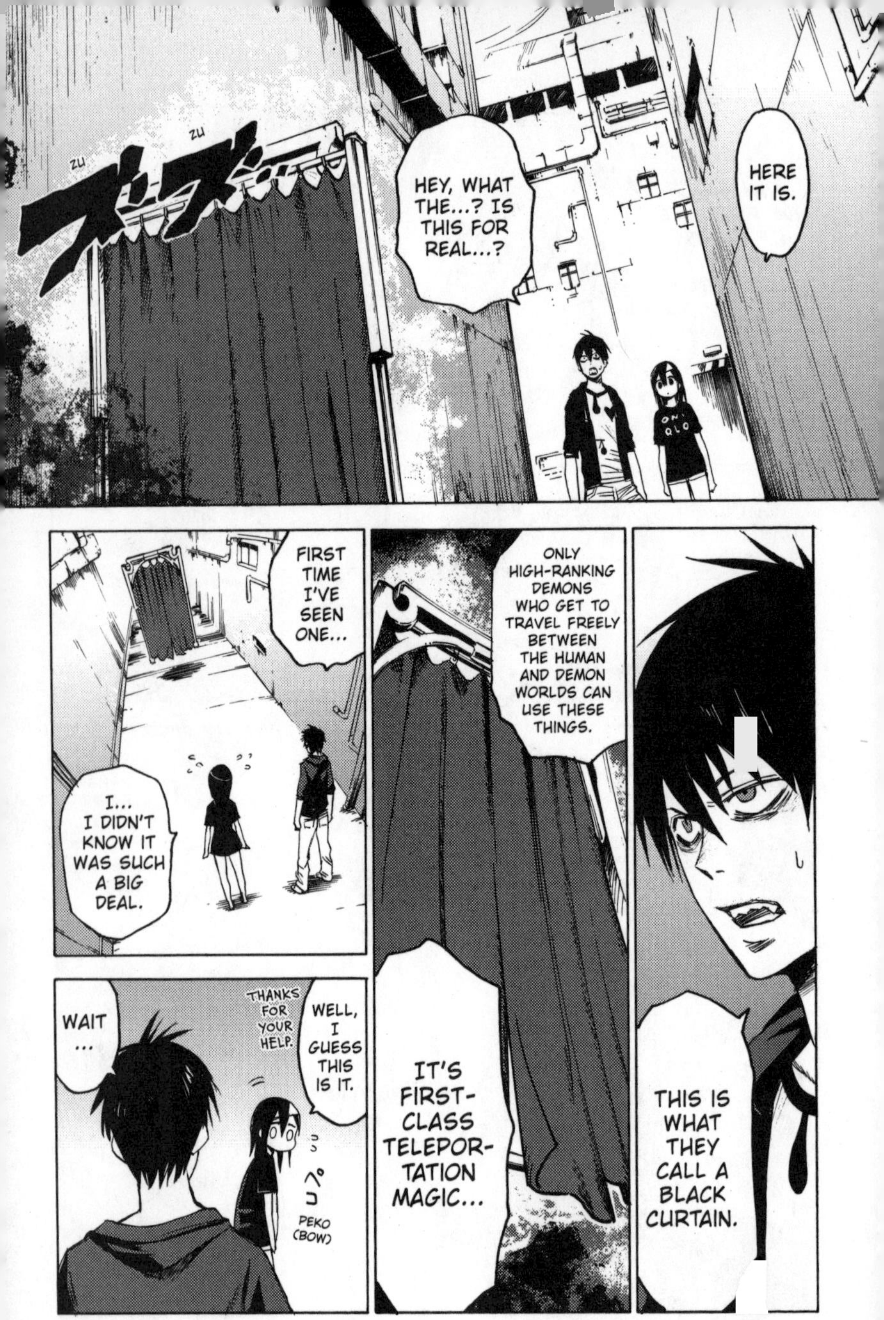
HERE IT IS.
HEY, WHAT THE...? IS THIS FOR REAL...?
ZU
ZU
THIS IS WHAT THEY CALL A BLACK CURTAIN.
ONLY HIGH-RANKING DEMONS WHO GET TO TRAVEL FREELY BETWEEN THE HUMAN AND DEMON WORLDS CAN USE THESE THINGS.
IT'S FIRST-CLASS TELEPORTATION MAGIC...
FIRST TIME I'VE SEEN ONE...
I... I DIDN'T KNOW IT WAS SUCH A BIG DEAL.
WELL, I GUESS THIS IS IT.
THANKS FOR YOUR HELP.
PEKO (BOW)
WAIT...

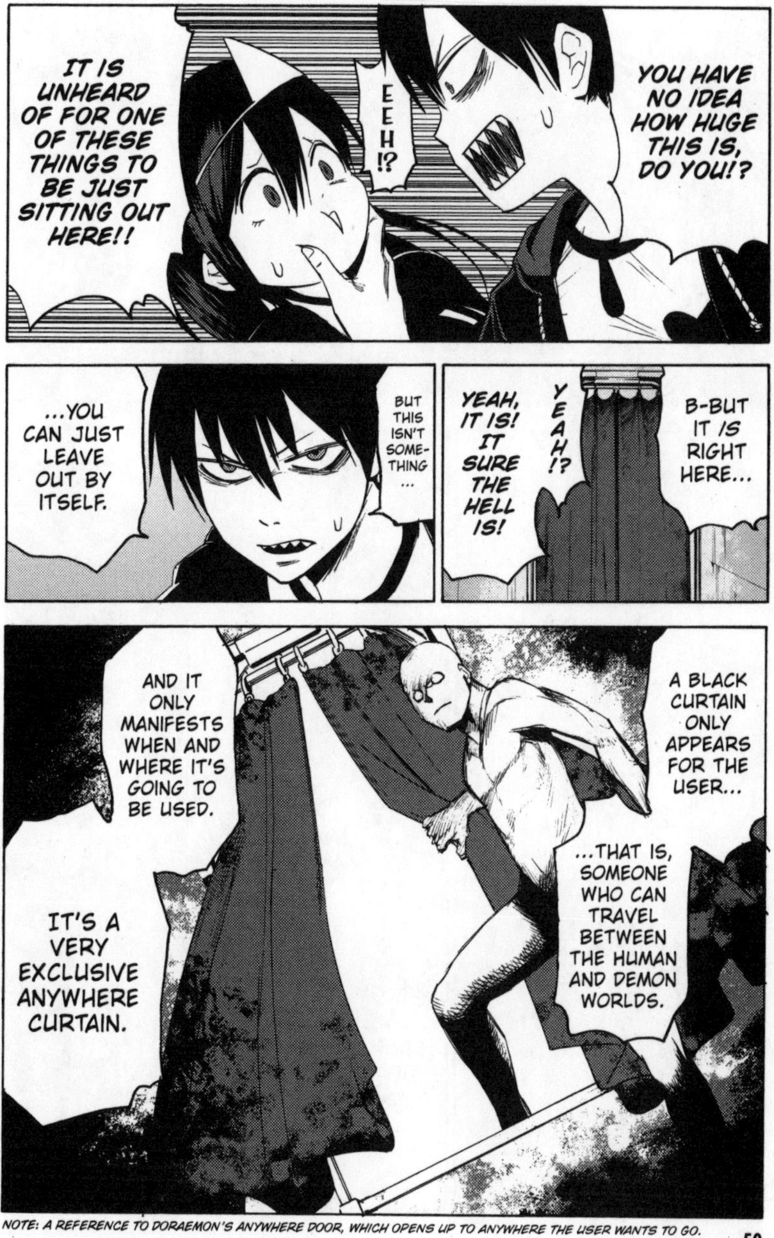
YOU HAVE NO IDEA HOW HUGE THIS IS, DO YOU!?
EEH!?
IT IS UNHEARD OF FOR ONE OF THESE THINGS TO BE JUST SITTING OUT HERE!!
B-BUT IT *IS* RIGHT HERE...
YEAH!?
YEAH, IT IS! IT SURE THE HELL IS!
BUT THIS ISN'T SOME-THING ...
...YOU CAN JUST LEAVE OUT BY ITSELF.
A BLACK CURTAIN ONLY APPEARS FOR THE USER...
AND IT ONLY MANIFESTS WHEN AND WHERE IT'S GOING TO BE USED.
...THAT IS, SOMEONE WHO CAN TRAVEL BETWEEN THE HUMAN AND DEMON WORLDS.
IT'S A VERY EXCLUSIVE ANYWHERE CURTAIN.

NOTE: A REFERENCE TO DORAEMON'S ANYWHERE DOOR, WHICH OPENS UP TO ANYWHERE THE USER WANTS TO GO.

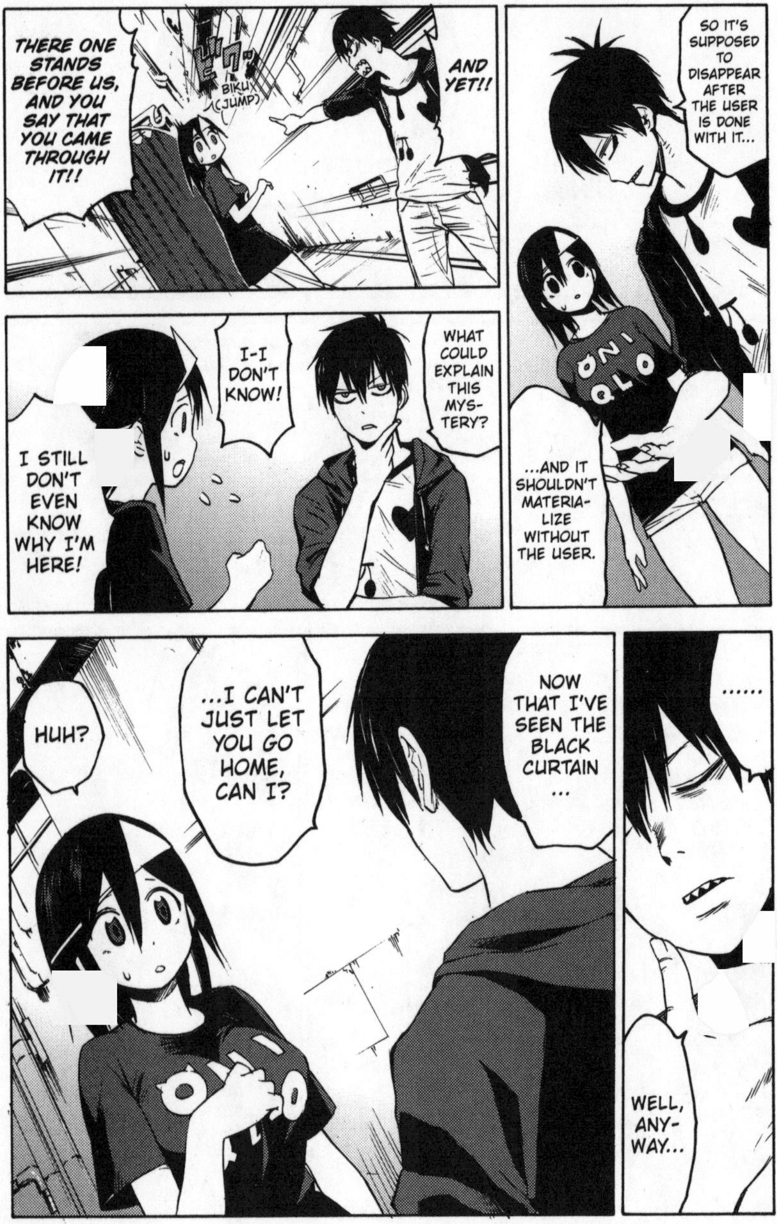
SO IT'S SUPPOSED TO DISAPPEAR AFTER THE USER IS DONE WITH IT...
...AND IT SHOULDN'T MATERIALIZE WITHOUT THE USER.
AND YET!!
BIKU (JUMP)
THERE ONE STANDS BEFORE US, AND YOU SAY THAT YOU CAME THROUGH IT!!
WHAT COULD EXPLAIN THIS MYSTERY?
I-I DON'T KNOW!
I STILL DON'T EVEN KNOW WHY I'M HERE!
......
WELL, ANYWAY...
NOW THAT I'VE SEEN THE BLACK CURTAIN...
...I CAN'T JUST LET YOU GO HOME, CAN I?
HUH?

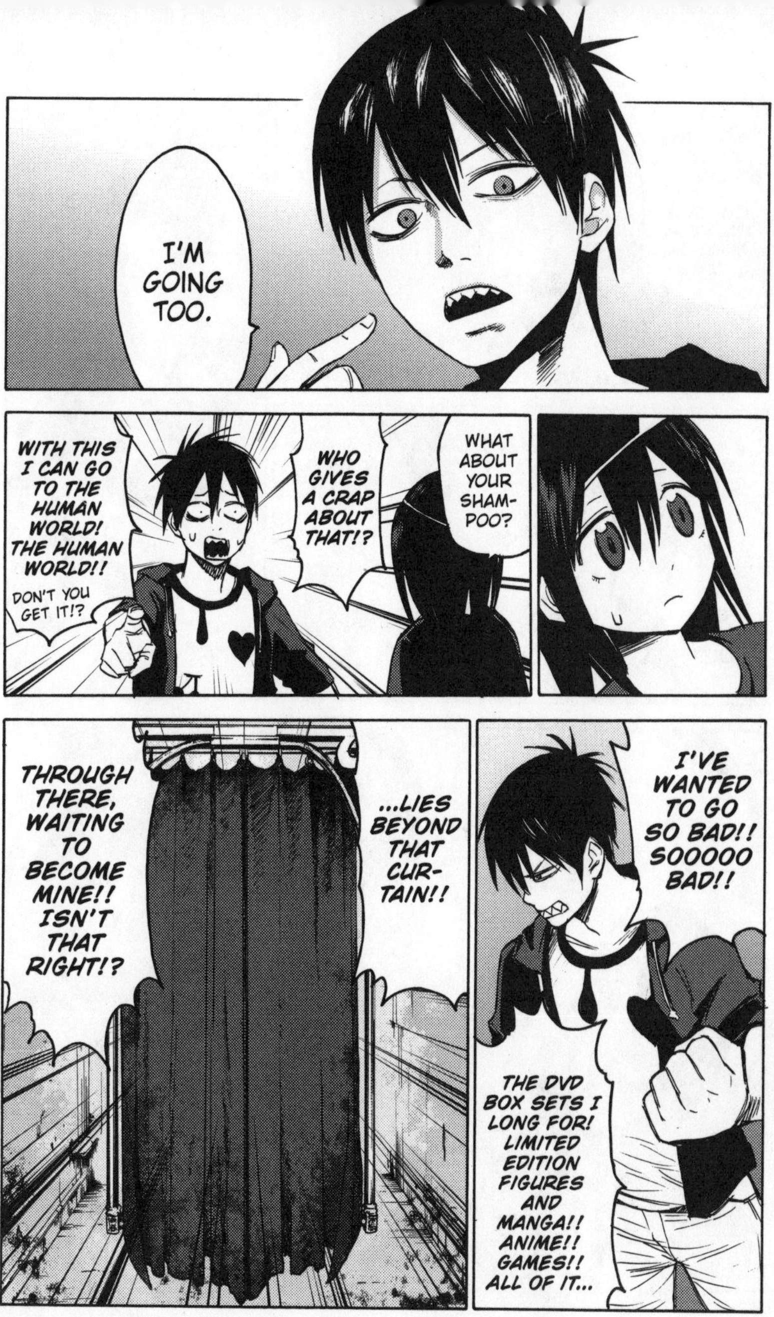
I'M GOING TOO.
WHAT ABOUT YOUR SHAMPOO?
WHO GIVES A CRAP ABOUT THAT!?
WITH THIS I CAN GO TO THE HUMAN WORLD! THE HUMAN WORLD!!
DON'T YOU GET IT!?
I'VE WANTED TO GO SO BAD!! SOOOOO BAD!!
THE DVD BOX SETS I LONG FOR! LIMITED EDITION FIGURES AND MANGA!! ANIME!! GAMES!! ALL OF IT...
...LIES BEYOND THAT CUR-TAIN!!
THROUGH THERE, WAITING TO BECOME MINE!! ISN'T THAT RIGHT!?

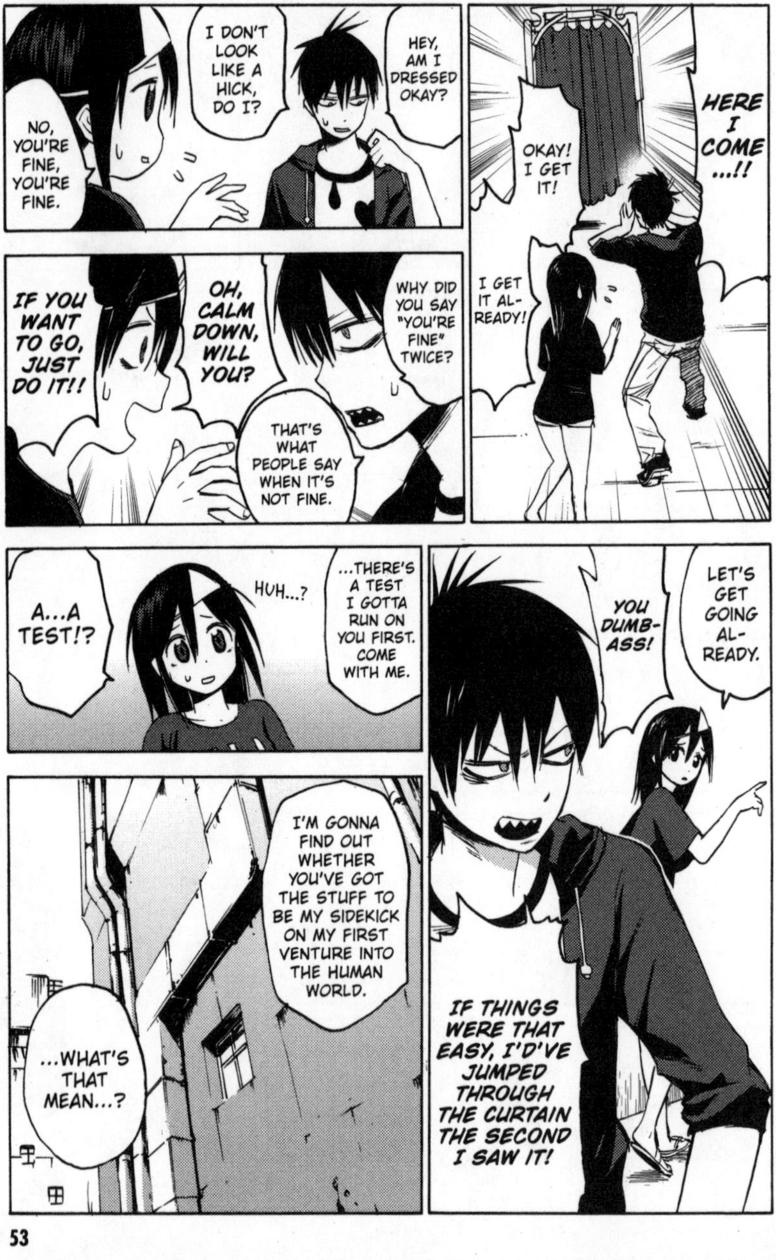
HERE I COME...!!
OKAY! I GET IT!
I GET IT ALREADY!
HEY, AM I DRESSED OKAY?
I DON'T LOOK LIKE A HICK, DO I?
NO, YOU'RE FINE, YOU'RE FINE.
WHY DID YOU SAY "YOU'RE FINE" TWICE?
THAT'S WHAT PEOPLE SAY WHEN IT'S NOT FINE.
OH, CALM DOWN, WILL YOU?
IF YOU WANT TO GO, JUST DO IT!!
LET'S GET GOING ALREADY.
YOU DUMBASS!
IF THINGS WERE THAT EASY, I'D'VE JUMPED THROUGH THE CURTAIN THE SECOND I SAW IT!
...THERE'S A TEST I GOTTA RUN ON YOU FIRST. COME WITH ME.
HUH...?
A...A TEST!?
I'M GONNA FIND OUT WHETHER YOU'VE GOT THE STUFF TO BE MY SIDEKICK ON MY FIRST VENTURE INTO THE HUMAN WORLD.
...WHAT'S THAT MEAN...?

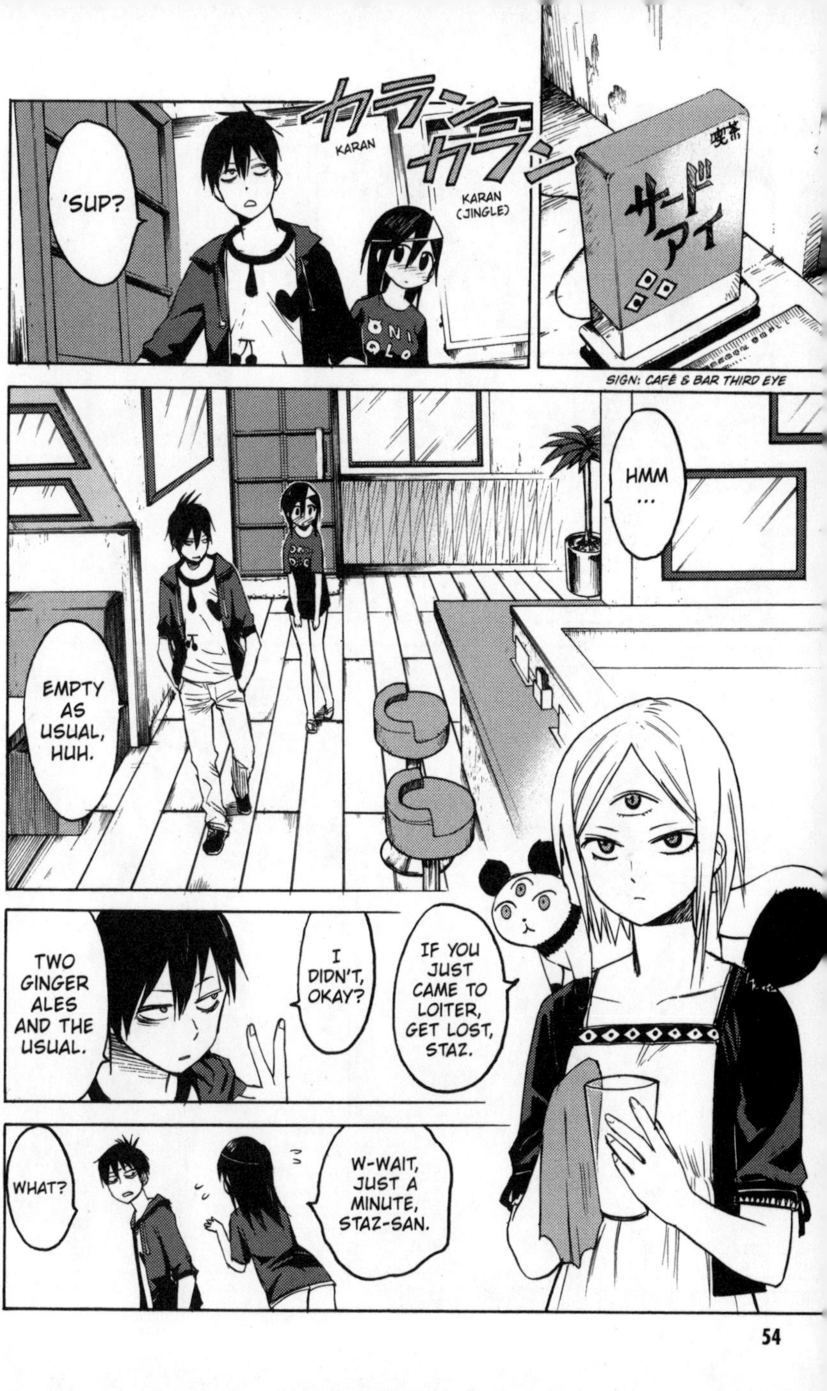
サードアイ
SIGN: CAFÉ & BAR THIRD EYE
カラン
カラン
KARAN
KARAN (JINGLE)
'SUP?
HMM ...
EMPTY AS USUAL, HUH.
IF YOU JUST CAME TO LOITER, GET LOST, STAZ.
I DIDN'T, OKAY?
TWO GINGER ALES AND THE USUAL.
W-WAIT, JUST A MINUTE, STAZ-SAN.
WHAT?

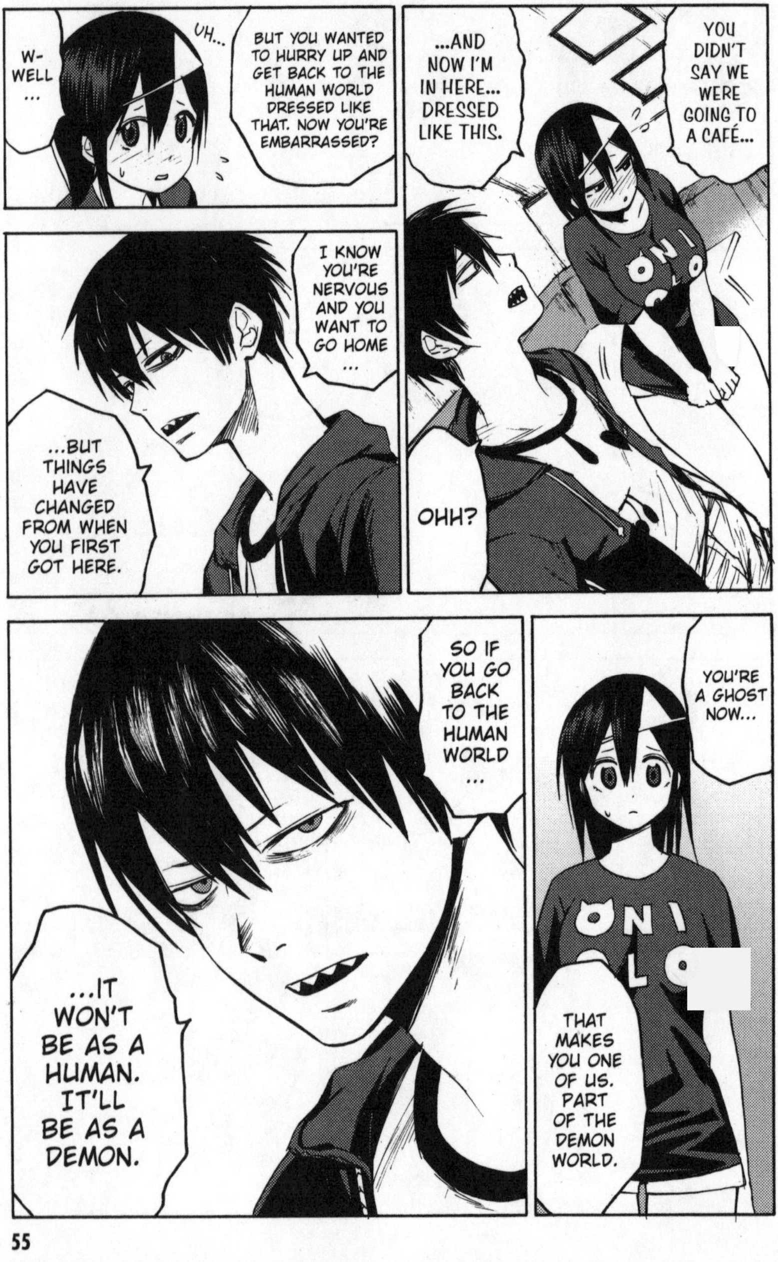
YOU DIDN'T SAY WE WERE GOING TO A CAFÉ...
...AND NOW I'M IN HERE... DRESSED LIKE THIS.
OHH?
BUT YOU WANTED TO HURRY UP AND GET BACK TO THE HUMAN WORLD DRESSED LIKE THAT. NOW YOU'RE EMBARRASSED?
UH...
W-WELL...
I KNOW YOU'RE NERVOUS AND YOU WANT TO GO HOME...
...BUT THINGS HAVE CHANGED FROM WHEN YOU FIRST GOT HERE.
YOU'RE A GHOST NOW...
THAT MAKES YOU ONE OF US. PART OF THE DEMON WORLD.
SO IF YOU GO BACK TO THE HUMAN WORLD...
...IT WON'T BE AS A HUMAN. IT'LL BE AS A DEMON.

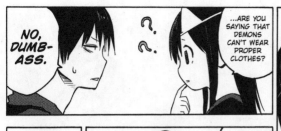

......
SO, THEN ...
...ARE YOU SAYING THAT DEMONS CAN'T WEAR PROPER CLOTHES?
NO, DUMB-ASS.
HEY, YOU JUST GOT HERE, AND YOU'RE FIGHTING ALREADY?
トク
TOKU (GLUG)
トク
TOKU
GIVE IT A REST, WOULD YA!?
コト
KOTO (TNK)
SFX: KYAAA (SQUEAL)
D-DID THAT ANIMAL JUST TALK!?
AND IT POURED THE SODA!!
ギャーッ
IT... IT'S SOOO CUUUU-UTE!!
......
AWW, SO SOFT.
H-HEY ...
STAZ, WHO IS THIS ...?
WHOOOA!
GOOD LUCK WITH THAT...
ガタ
GATA (CLATTER)
NOW...

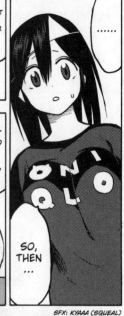

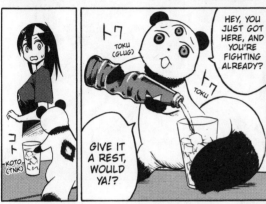

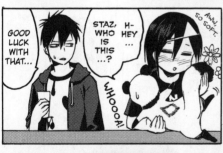

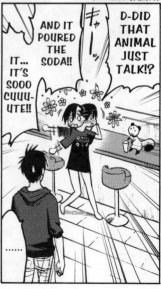

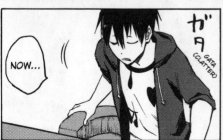

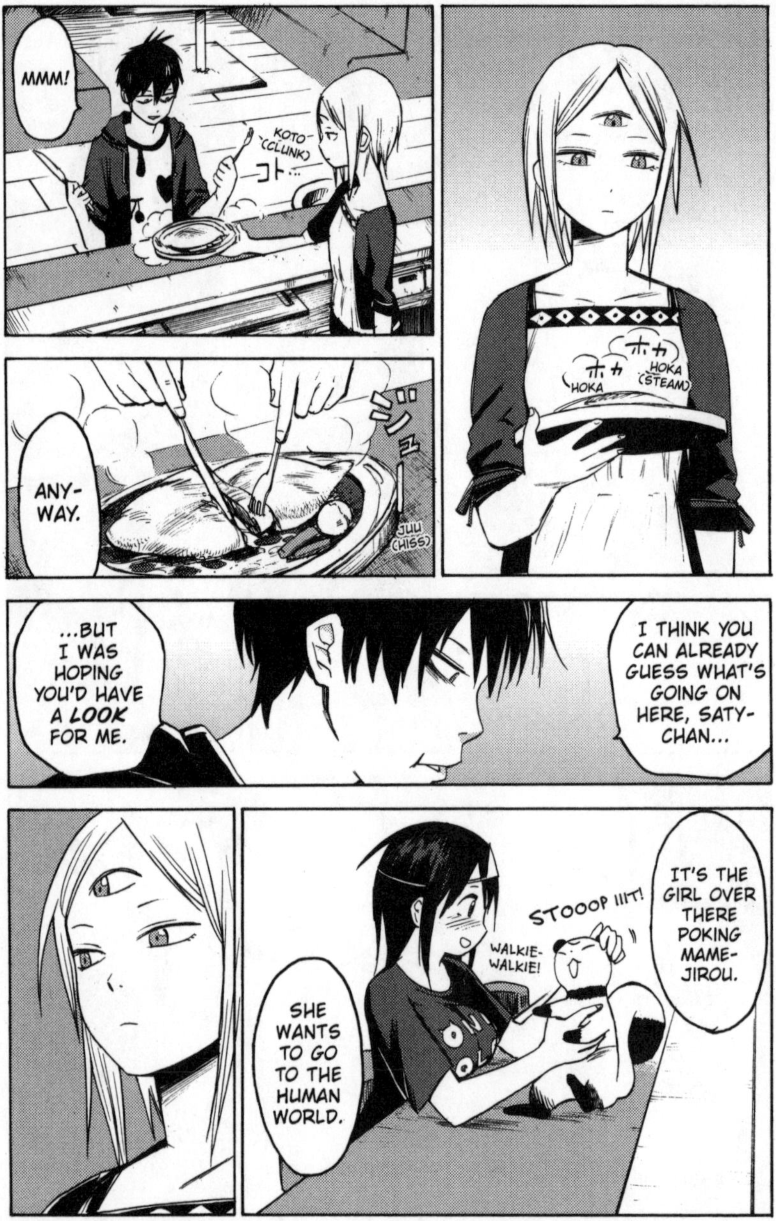
HOKA HOKA (STEAM)
MMM!
KOTO (CLUNK)
ANY-WAY.
JUU (HISS)
I THINK YOU CAN ALREADY GUESS WHAT'S GOING ON HERE, SATY-CHAN...
...BUT I WAS HOPING YOU'D HAVE A ***LOOK*** FOR ME.
IT'S THE GIRL OVER THERE POKING MAME-JIROU.
STOOOP IIIT!
WALKIE-WALKIE!
SHE WANTS TO GO TO THE HUMAN WORLD.

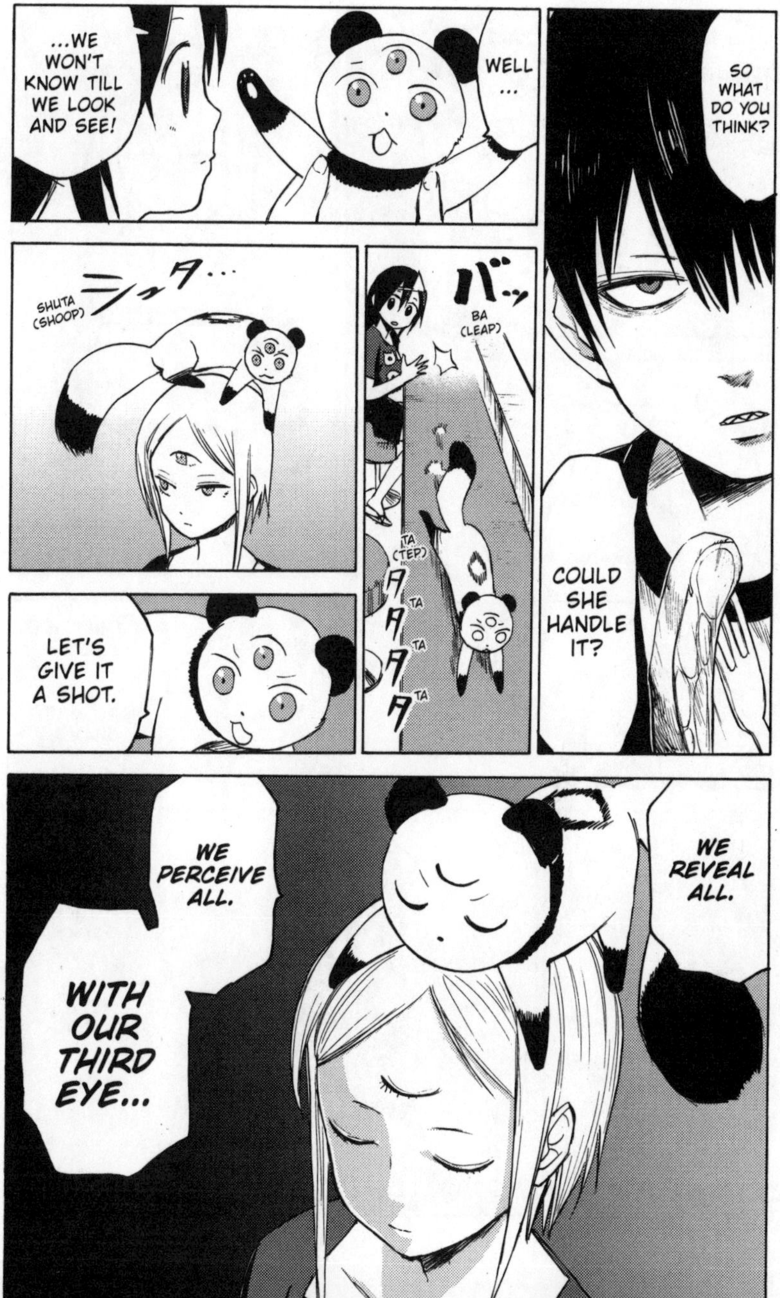
SO WHAT DO YOU THINK?
COULD SHE HANDLE IT?
WELL...
...WE WON'T KNOW TILL WE LOOK AND SEE!
バッ
BA (LEAP)
タタタタ
TA (TEP) TA TA TA
シュタ…
SHUTA (SHOOP)
LET'S GIVE IT A SHOT.
WE REVEAL ALL.
WE PERCEIVE ALL.
WITH OUR THIRD EYE...

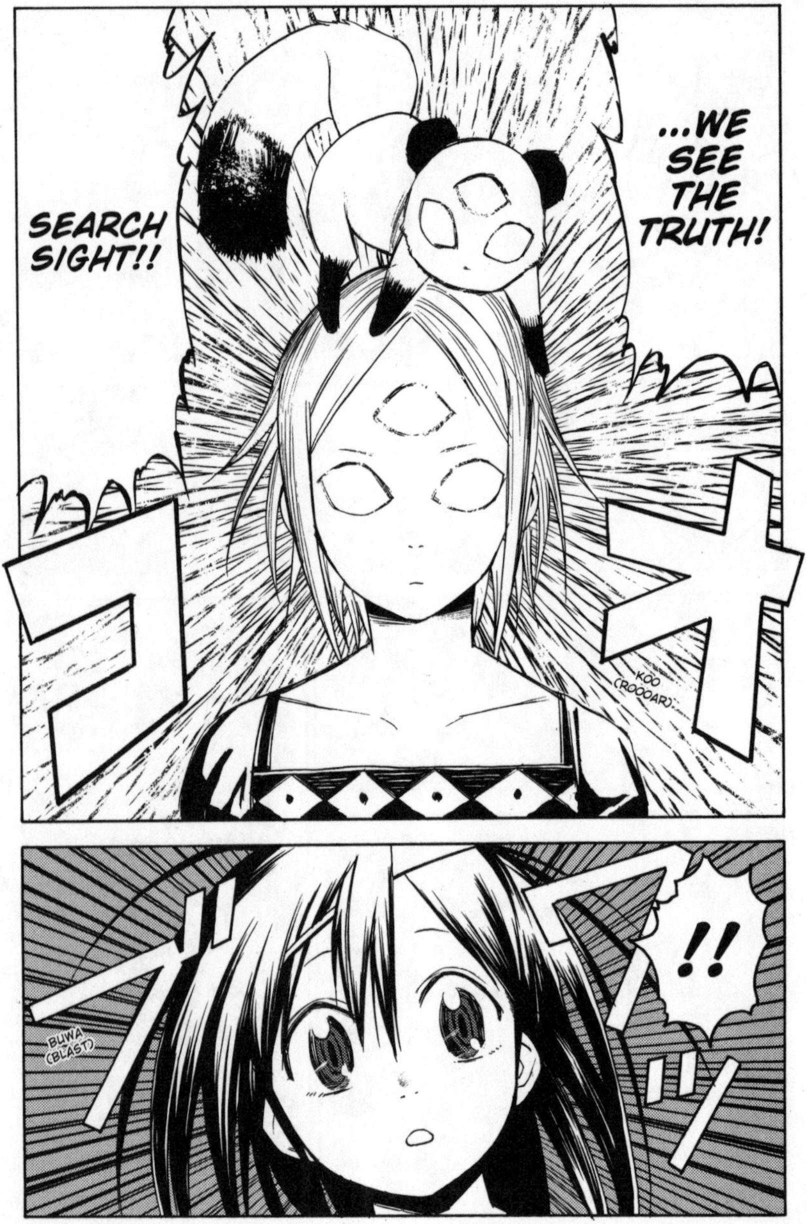
...WE SEE THE TRUTH!
SEARCH SIGHT!!
KOO (ROOOAR)
!!
BUWA (BLAST)

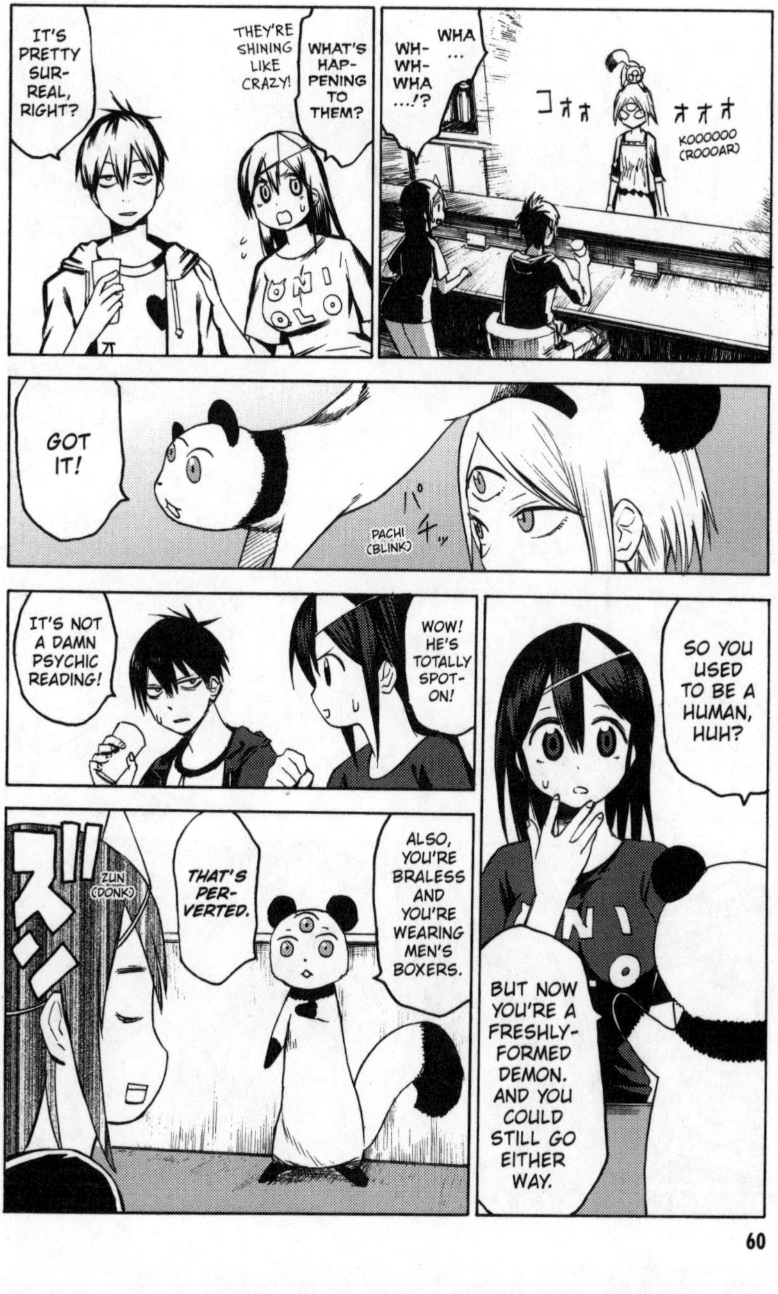
WHA ...
WH-WH-WHA ...!?
コォォ
オオオ
KOOOOOO (ROOOAR)
WHAT'S HAP-PENING TO THEM?
THEY'RE SHINING LIKE CRAZY!
IT'S PRETTY SUR-REAL, RIGHT?
パチッ
PACHI (BLINK)
GOT IT!
SO YOU USED TO BE A HUMAN, HUH?
BUT NOW YOU'RE A FRESHLY-FORMED DEMON. AND YOU COULD STILL GO EITHER WAY.
WOW! HE'S TOTALLY SPOT-ON!
IT'S NOT A DAMN PSYCHIC READING!
ALSO, YOU'RE BRALESS AND YOU'RE WEARING MEN'S BOXERS.
THAT'S PER-VERTED.
ズン
ZUN (DONK)

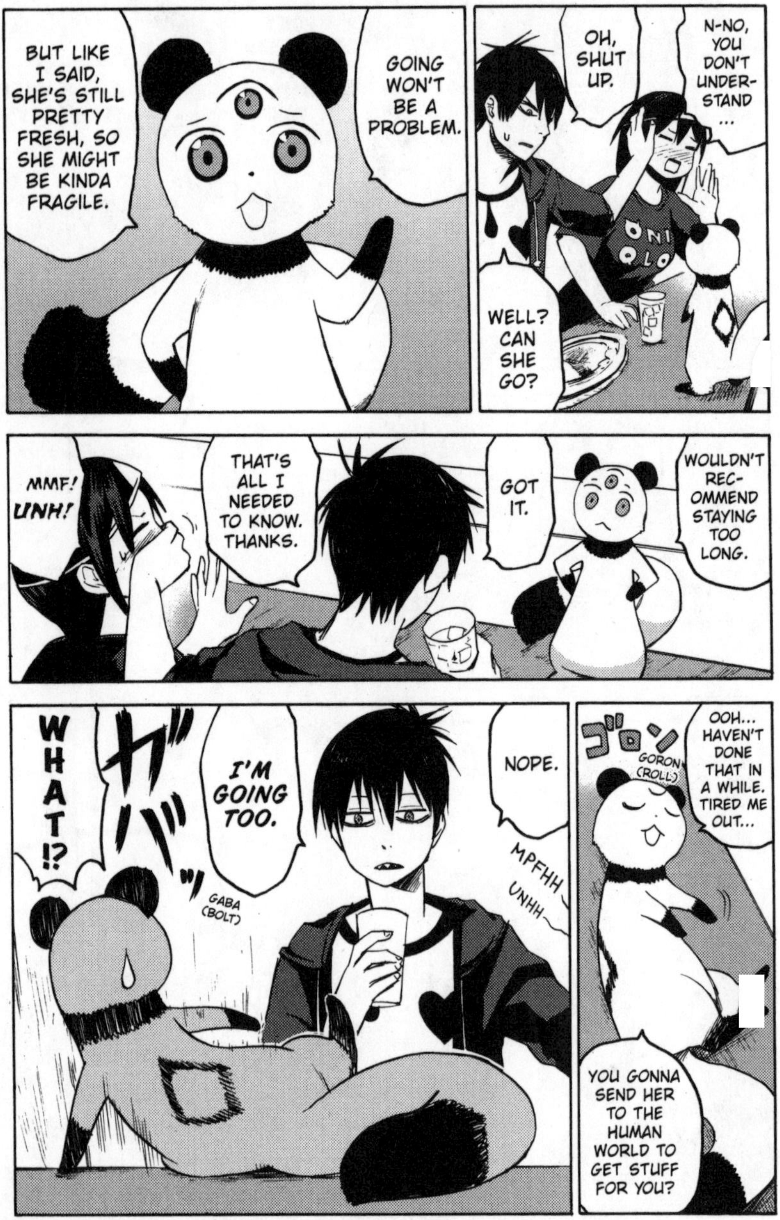
N-NO, YOU DON'T UNDER-STAND ...
OH, SHUT UP.
WELL? CAN SHE GO?
GOING WON'T BE A PROBLEM.
BUT LIKE I SAID, SHE'S STILL PRETTY FRESH, SO SHE MIGHT BE KINDA FRAGILE.
WOULDN'T REC-OMMEND STAYING TOO LONG.
GOT IT.
THAT'S ALL I NEEDED TO KNOW. THANKS.
MMF! UNH!
OOH... HAVEN'T DONE THAT IN A WHILE. TIRED ME OUT...
ゴロン
GORON (ROLL)
YOU GONNA SEND HER TO THE HUMAN WORLD TO GET STUFF FOR YOU?
NOPE.
MPFHH UNHH
I'M GOING TOO.
ガバッ
GABA (BOLT)
WHAT!?

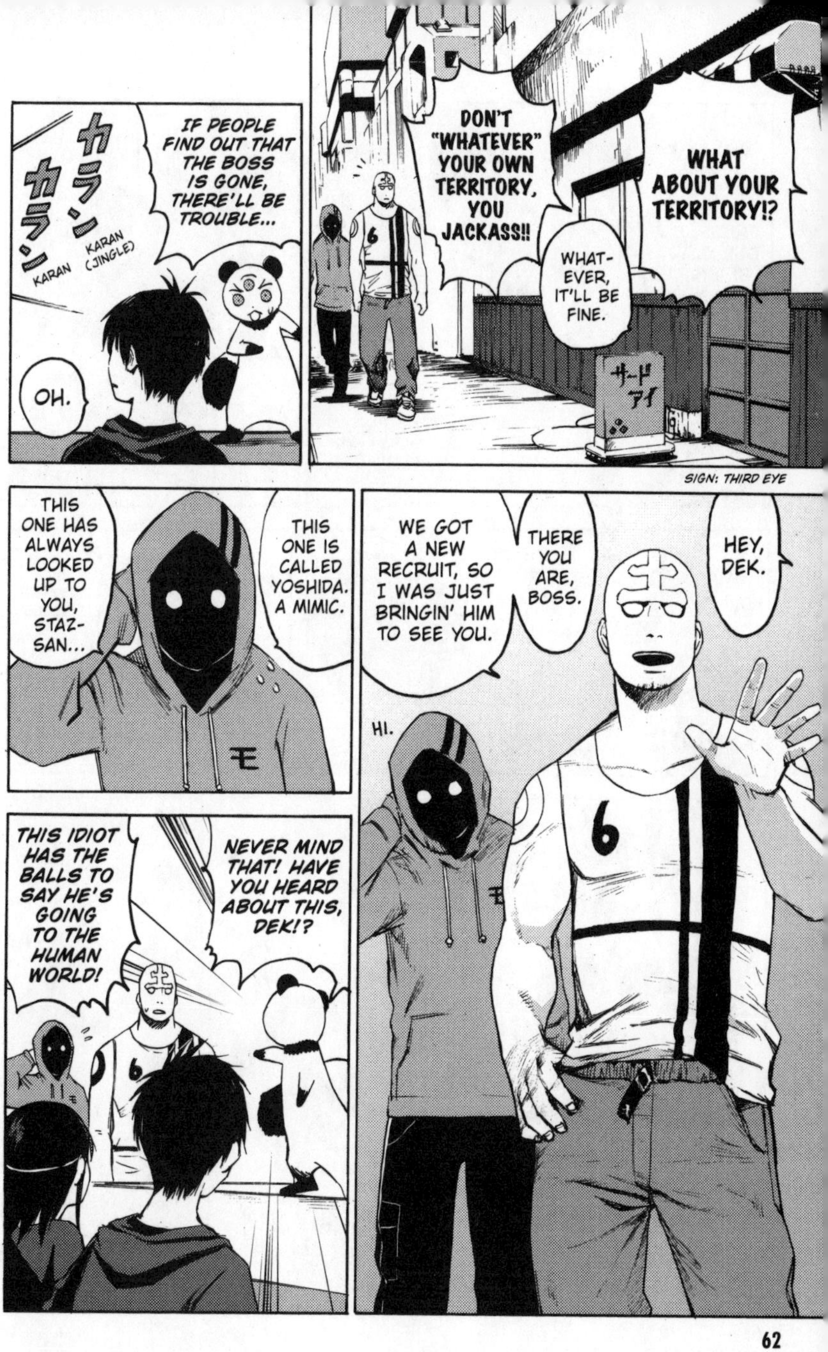
WHAT ABOUT YOUR TERRITORY!?
DON'T "WHATEVER" YOUR OWN TERRITORY, YOU JACKASS!!
WHAT-EVER, IT'LL BE FINE.
サード アイ
SIGN: THIRD EYE
IF PEOPLE FIND OUT THAT THE BOSS IS GONE, THERE'LL BE TROUBLE...
カラン カラン
KARAN KARAN (JINGLE)
OH.
HEY, DEK.
THERE YOU ARE, BOSS.
WE GOT A NEW RECRUIT, SO I WAS JUST BRINGIN' HIM TO SEE YOU.
HI.
THIS ONE IS CALLED YOSHIDA. A MIMIC.
THIS ONE HAS ALWAYS LOOKED UP TO YOU, STAZ-SAN...
NEVER MIND THAT! HAVE YOU HEARD ABOUT THIS, DEK!?
THIS IDIOT HAS THE BALLS TO SAY HE'S GOING TO THE HUMAN WORLD!

SFX: BURU (TREMBLE) BURU BURU

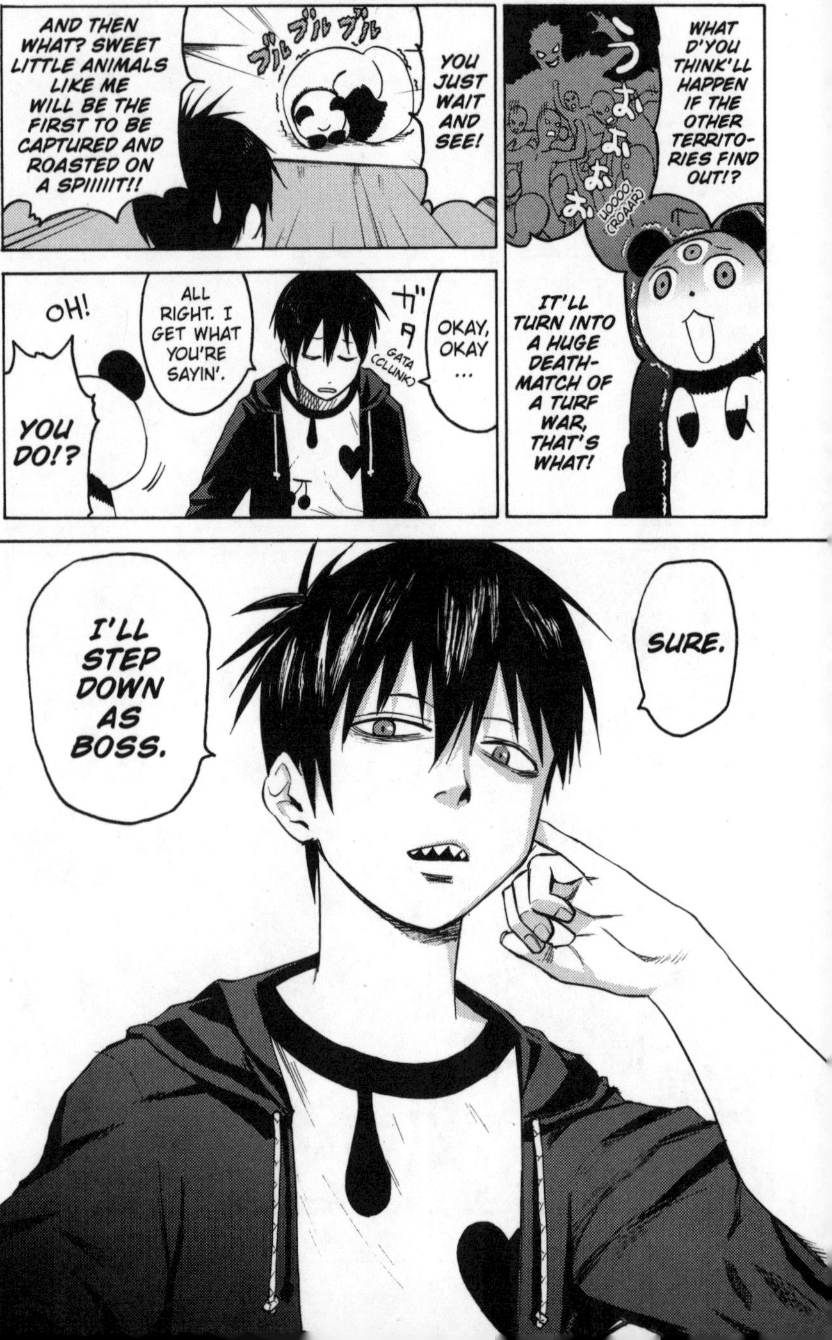
WHAT D'YOU THINK'LL HAPPEN IF THE OTHER TERRITORIES FIND OUT!?
UOOOO (ROAAR)
IT'LL TURN INTO A HUGE DEATH-MATCH OF A TURF WAR, THAT'S WHAT!
YOU JUST WAIT AND SEE!
AND THEN WHAT? SWEET LITTLE ANIMALS LIKE ME WILL BE THE FIRST TO BE CAPTURED AND ROASTED ON A SPIIIIIT!!
OKAY, OKAY ...
GATA (CLUNK)
ALL RIGHT. I GET WHAT YOU'RE SAYIN'.
OH!
YOU DO!?
SURE.
I'LL STEP DOWN AS BOSS.

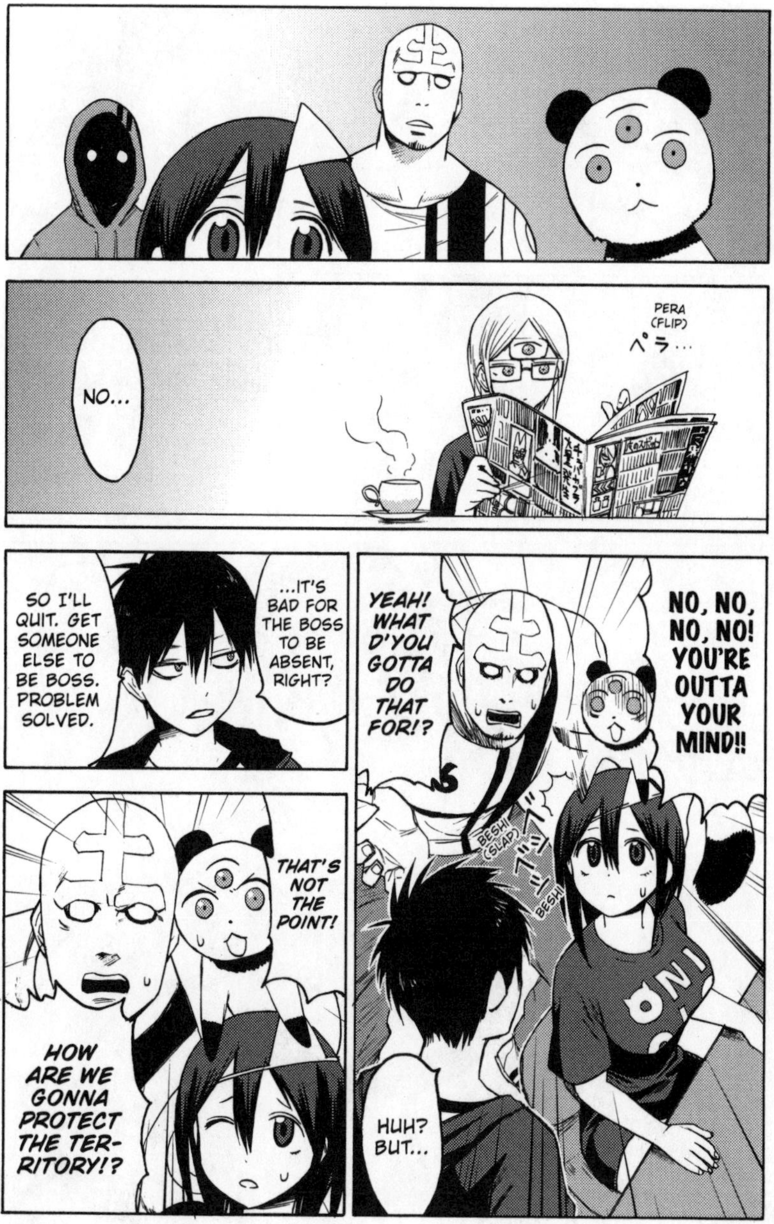
PERA (FLIP)
ペラ…
NO…
NO, NO, NO, NO! YOU'RE OUTTA YOUR MIND!!
YEAH! WHAT D'YOU GOTTA DO THAT FOR!?
BESHI (SLAP)
BESHI
HUH? BUT…
…IT'S BAD FOR THE BOSS TO BE ABSENT, RIGHT?
SO I'LL QUIT. GET SOMEONE ELSE TO BE BOSS. PROBLEM SOLVED.
THAT'S NOT THE POINT!
HOW ARE WE GONNA PROTECT THE TER-RITORY!?

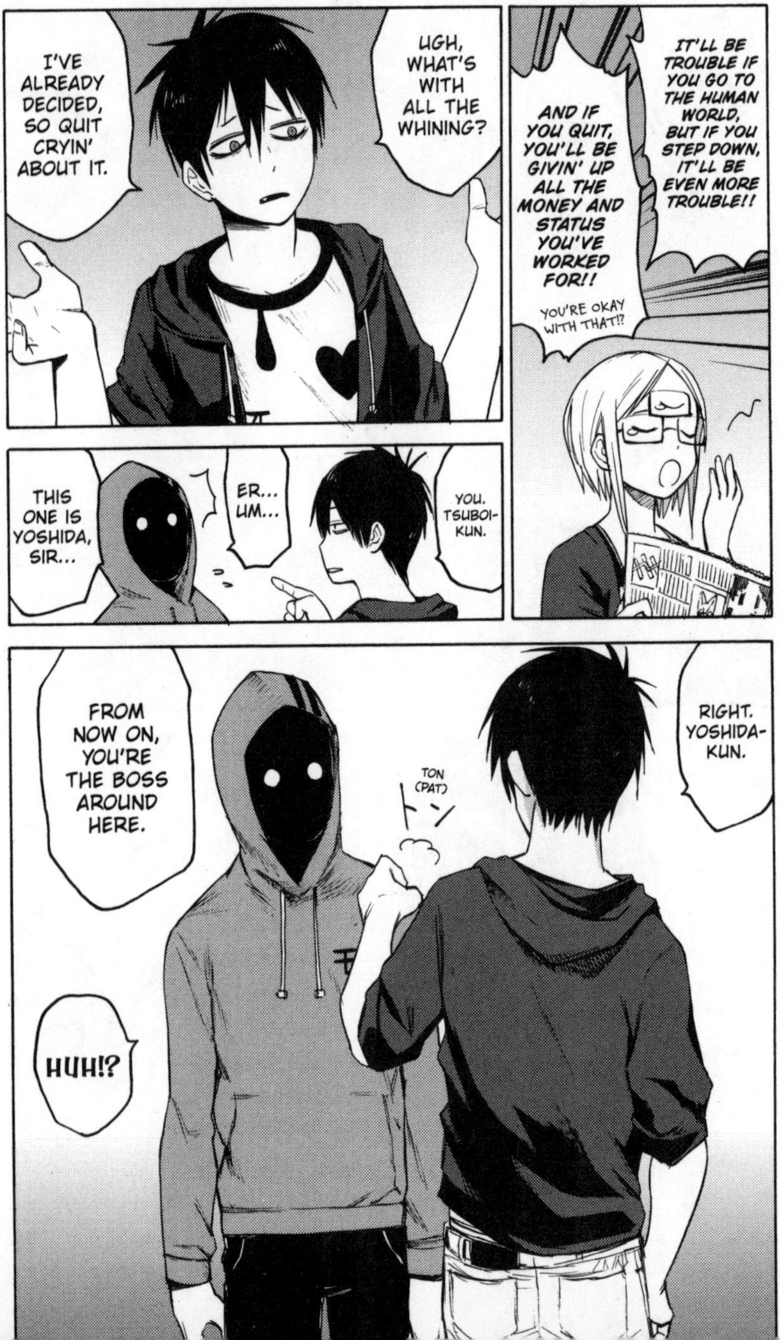
IT'LL BE TROUBLE IF YOU GO TO THE HUMAN WORLD, BUT IF YOU STEP DOWN, IT'LL BE EVEN MORE TROUBLE!!
AND IF YOU QUIT, YOU'LL BE GIVIN' UP ALL THE MONEY AND STATUS YOU'VE WORKED FOR!!
YOU'RE OKAY WITH THAT!?
UGH, WHAT'S WITH ALL THE WHINING?
I'VE ALREADY DECIDED, SO QUIT CRYIN' ABOUT IT.
YOU. TSUBOI-KUN.
ER... UM...
THIS ONE IS YOSHIDA, SIR...
RIGHT. YOSHIDA-KUN.
TON (PAT)
FROM NOW ON, YOU'RE THE BOSS AROUND HERE.
HUH!?

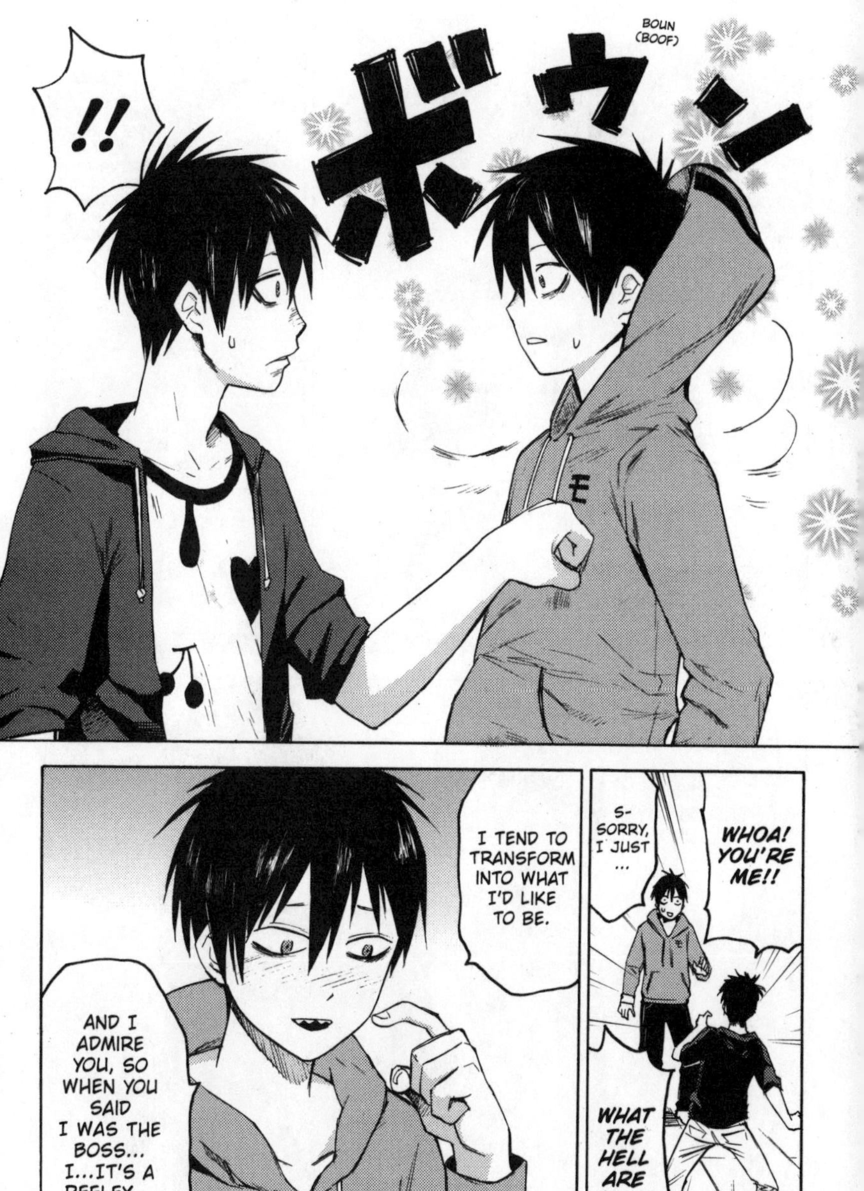
BOUN
(BOOF)
ボウン
!!
WHOA! YOU'RE ME!!
S-SORRY, I JUST ...
WHAT THE HELL ARE YOU!?
I TEND TO TRANSFORM INTO WHAT I'D LIKE TO BE.
AND I ADMIRE YOU, SO WHEN YOU SAID I WAS THE BOSS... I...IT'S A REFLEX...

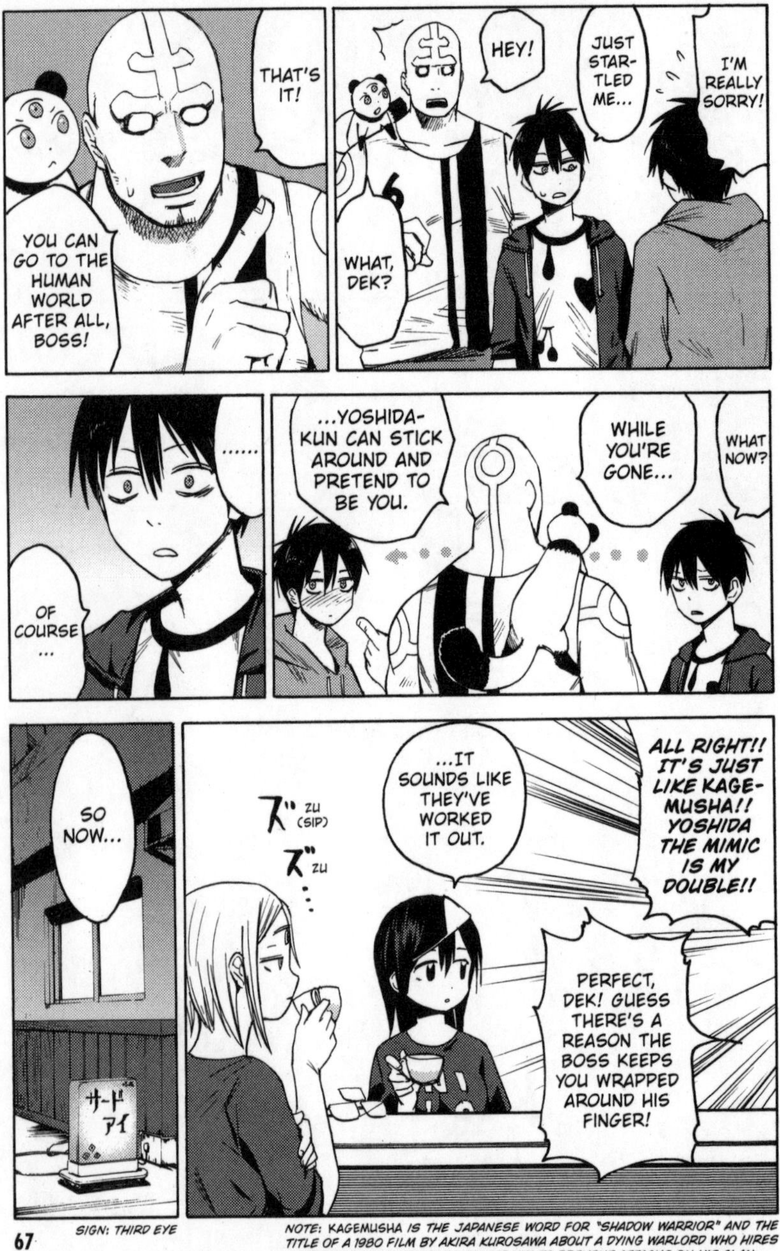
I'M REALLY SORRY!
JUST STARTLED ME...
HEY!
WHAT, DEK?
THAT'S IT!
YOU CAN GO TO THE HUMAN WORLD AFTER ALL, BOSS!
WHAT NOW?
WHILE YOU'RE GONE...
...YOSHIDA-KUN CAN STICK AROUND AND PRETEND TO BE YOU.
......
OF COURSE ...
ALL RIGHT!! IT'S JUST LIKE KAGE-MUSHA!! YOSHIDA THE MIMIC IS MY DOUBLE!!
PERFECT, DEK! GUESS THERE'S A REASON THE BOSS KEEPS YOU WRAPPED AROUND HIS FINGER!
...IT SOUNDS LIKE THEY'VE WORKED IT OUT.
ズ ZU (SIP)
ズ ZU
...
SO NOW...
サード アイ

SIGN: THIRD EYE

NOTE: KAGEMUSHA IS THE JAPANESE WORD FOR "SHADOW WARRIOR" AND THE TITLE OF A 1980 FILM BY AKIRA KUROSAWA ABOUT A DYING WARLORD WHO HIRES A PETTY CRIMINAL THAT LOOKS LIKE HIM TO PREVENT ATTACKS ON HIS CLAN.

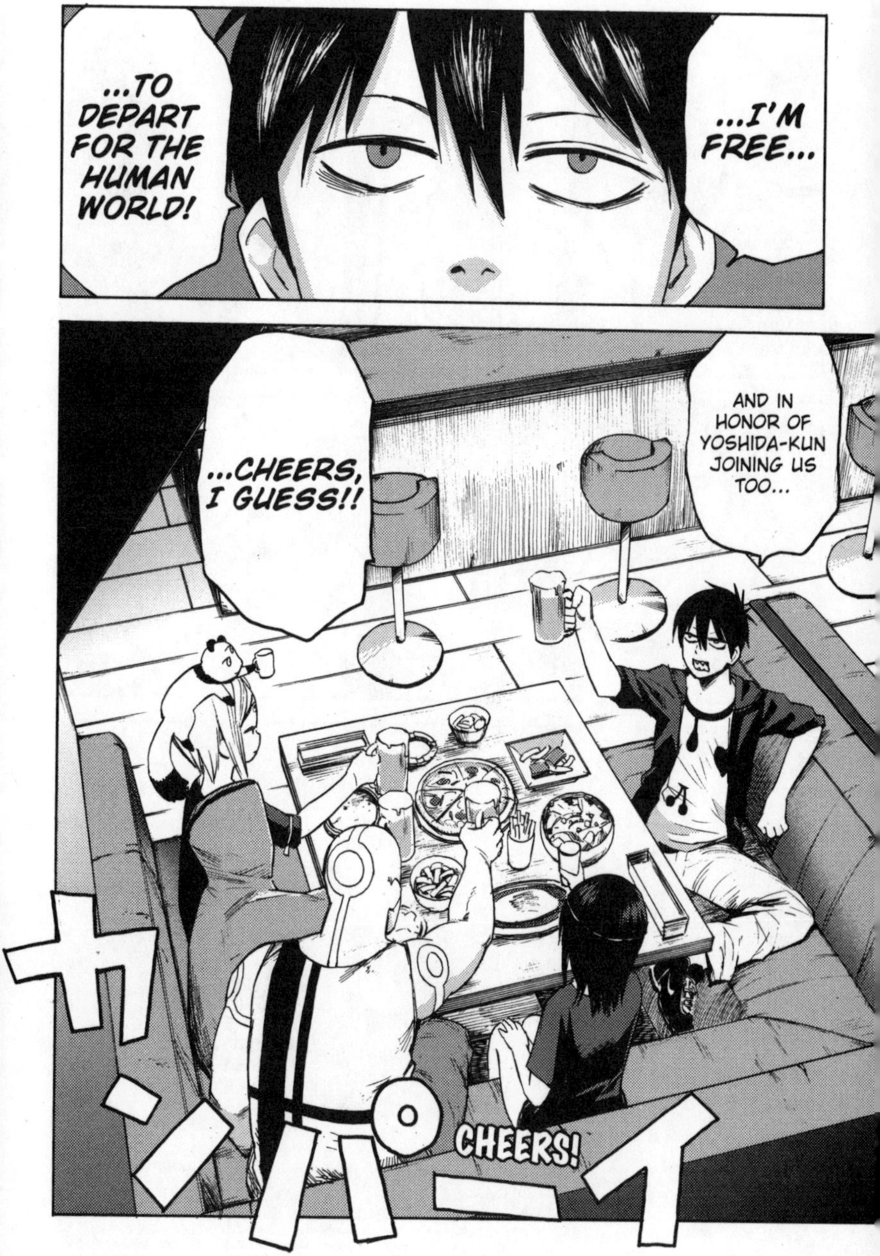
...I'M FREE...
...TO DEPART FOR THE HUMAN WORLD!
AND IN HONOR OF YOSHIDA-KUN JOINING US TOO...
...CHEERS, I GUESS!!
カンパーイ
CHEERS!

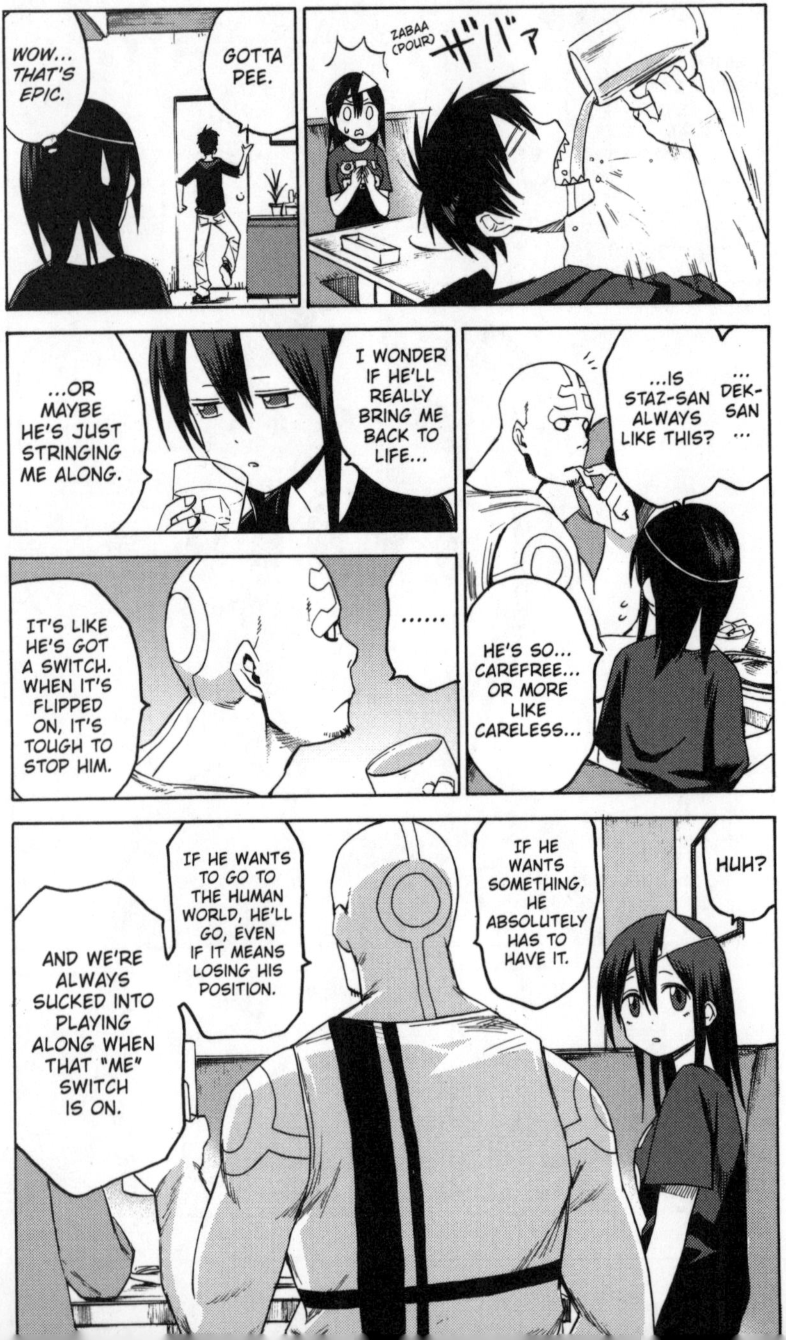
ZABAA (POUR)
ザバァ
GOTTA PEE.
WOW... THAT'S EPIC.
... DEK-SAN ...
...IS STAZ-SAN ALWAYS LIKE THIS?
HE'S SO... CAREFREE... OR MORE LIKE CARELESS...
I WONDER IF HE'LL REALLY BRING ME BACK TO LIFE...
...OR MAYBE HE'S JUST STRINGING ME ALONG.
......
IT'S LIKE HE'S GOT A SWITCH. WHEN IT'S FLIPPED ON, IT'S TOUGH TO STOP HIM.
HUH?
IF HE WANTS SOMETHING, HE ABSOLUTELY HAS TO HAVE IT.
IF HE WANTS TO GO TO THE HUMAN WORLD, HE'LL GO, EVEN IF IT MEANS LOSING HIS POSITION.
AND WE'RE ALWAYS SUCKED INTO PLAYING ALONG WHEN THAT "ME" SWITCH IS ON.

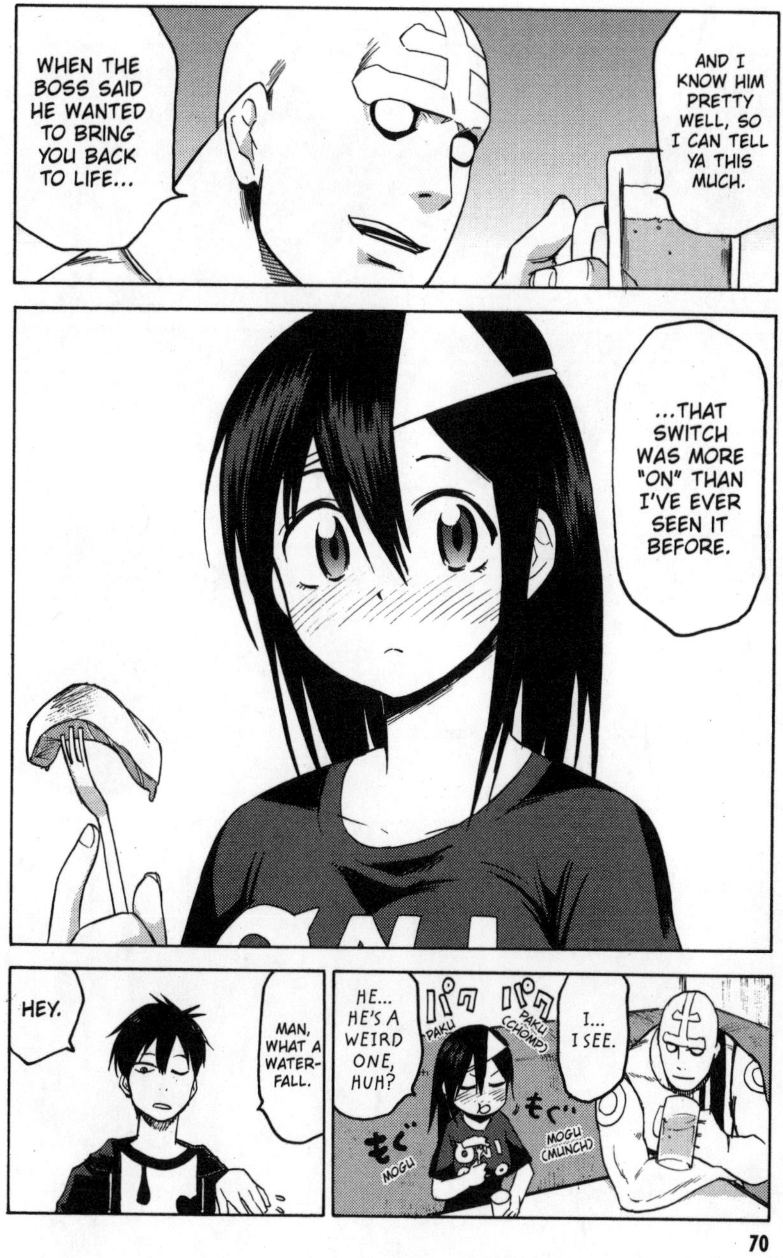
AND I KNOW HIM PRETTY WELL, SO I CAN TELL YA THIS MUCH.
WHEN THE BOSS SAID HE WANTED TO BRING YOU BACK TO LIFE...
...THAT SWITCH WAS MORE "ON" THAN I'VE EVER SEEN IT BEFORE.
I... I SEE.
パク PAKU (CHOMP)
パク PAKU
HE... HE'S A WEIRD ONE, HUH?
もぐ MOGU (MUNCH)
もぐ MOGU
MAN, WHAT A WATER-FALL.
HEY.

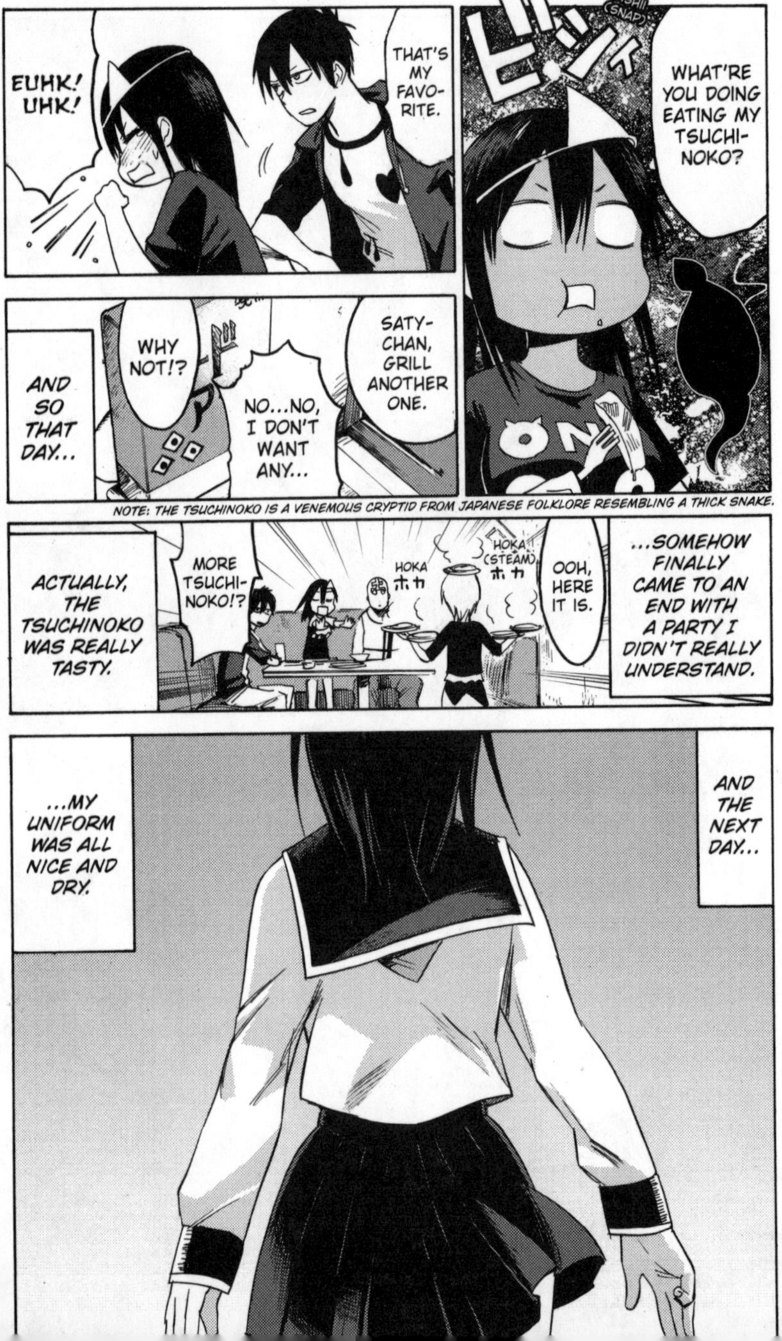
BISHI! (SNAP)
WHAT'RE YOU DOING EATING MY TSUCHI-NOKO?
THAT'S MY FAVO-RITE.
EUHK! UHK!
SATY-CHAN, GRILL ANOTHER ONE.
NO...NO, I DON'T WANT ANY...
WHY NOT!?
AND SO THAT DAY...
NOTE: THE TSUCHINOKO IS A VENEMOUS CRYPTID FROM JAPANESE FOLKLORE RESEMBLING A THICK SNAKE.
...SOMEHOW FINALLY CAME TO AN END WITH A PARTY I DIDN'T REALLY UNDERSTAND.
OOH, HERE IT IS.
HOKA (STEAM)
HOKA
MORE TSUCHI-NOKO!?
ACTUALLY, THE TSUCHINOKO WAS REALLY TASTY.
AND THE NEXT DAY...
...MY UNIFORM WAS ALL NICE AND DRY.

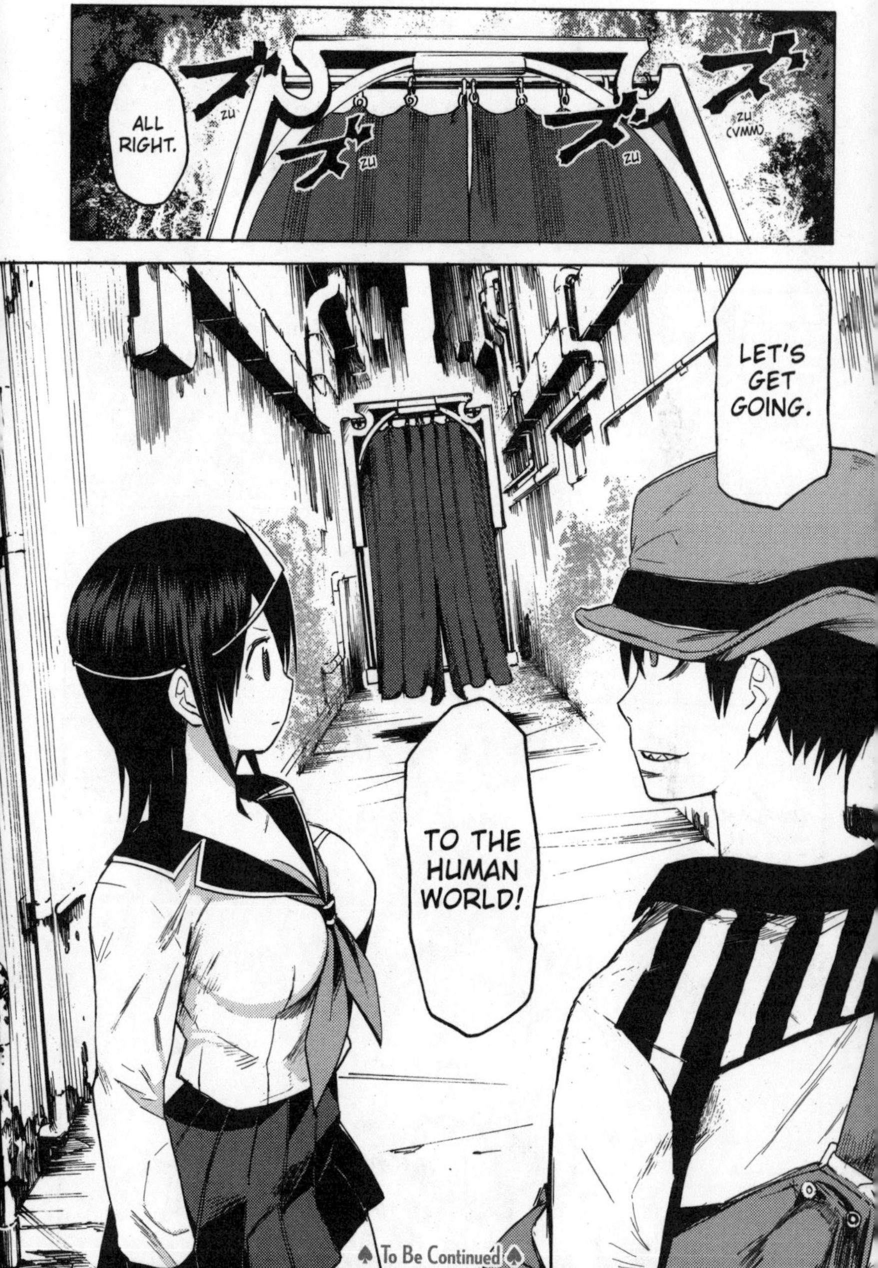
ZU (VMM)
ZU
ZU
ZU
ALL RIGHT.
LET'S GET GOING.
TO THE HUMAN WORLD!
To Be Continued

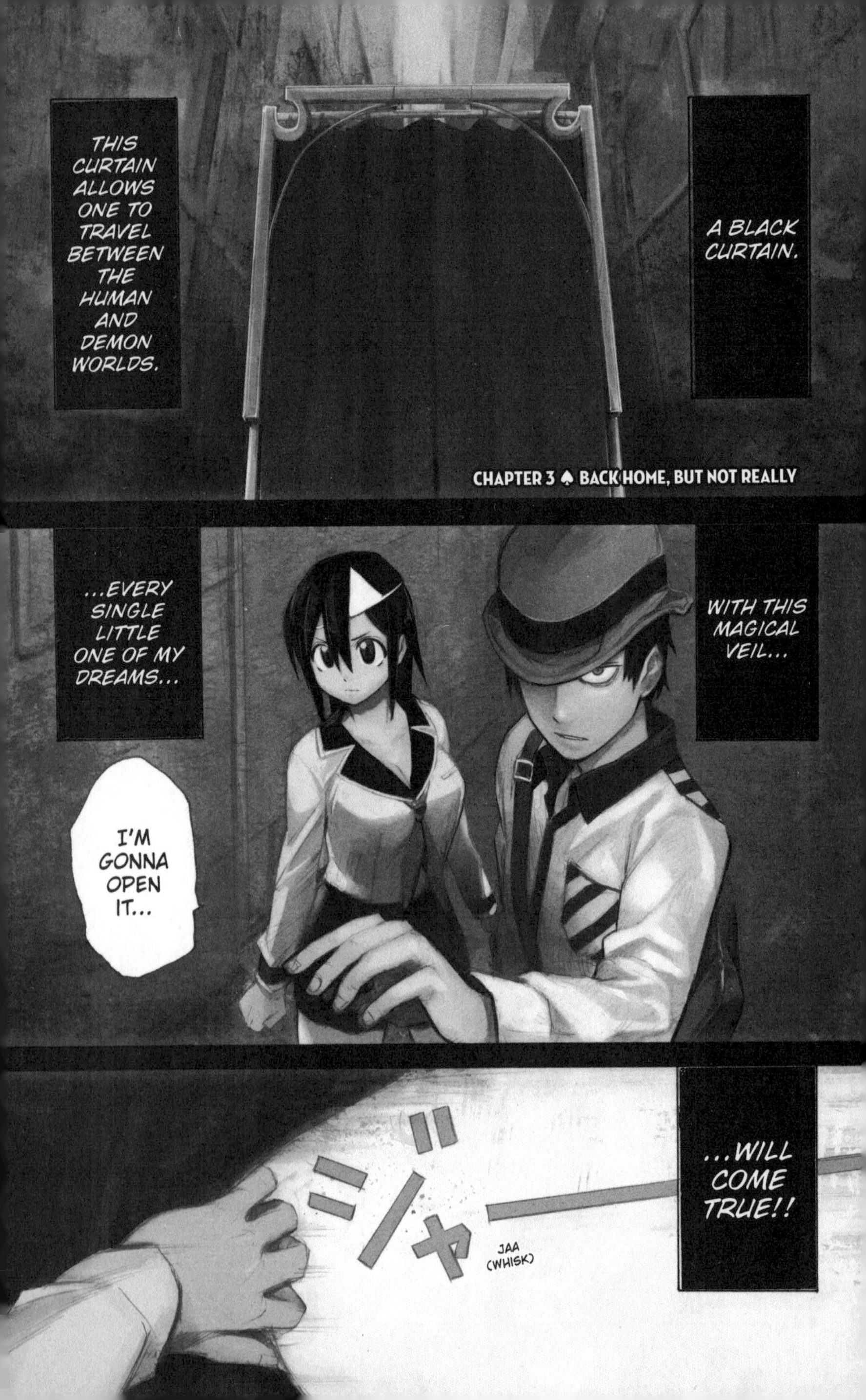
A BLACK CURTAIN.
THIS CURTAIN ALLOWS ONE TO TRAVEL BETWEEN THE HUMAN AND DEMON WORLDS.
CHAPTER 3 ♠ BACK HOME, BUT NOT REALLY
WITH THIS MAGICAL VEIL...
...EVERY SINGLE LITTLE ONE OF MY DREAMS...
I'M GONNA OPEN IT...
...WILL COME TRUE!!
ジャー
JAA (WHISK)

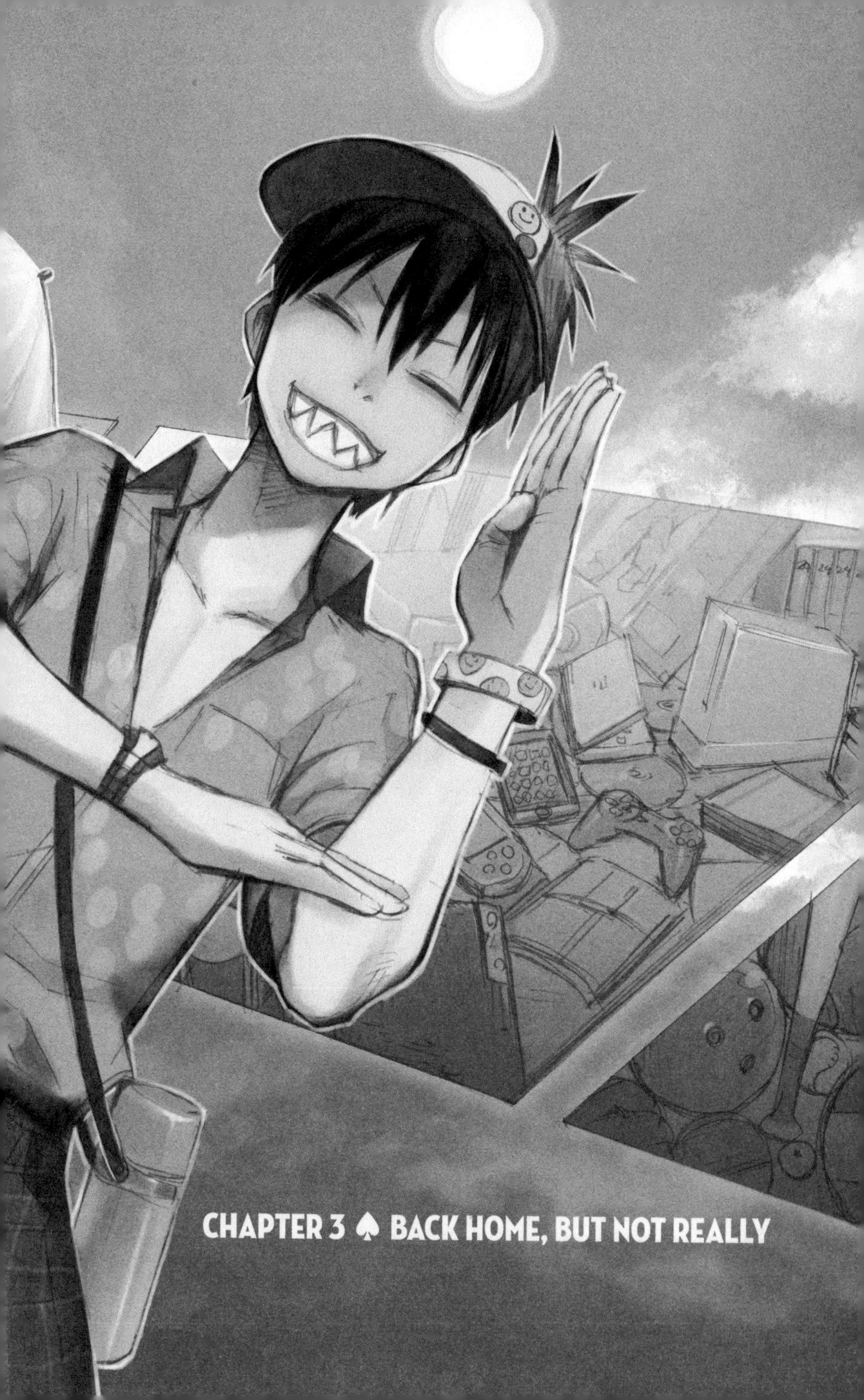

# CHAPTER 3 ♠ BACK HOME, BUT NOT REALLY

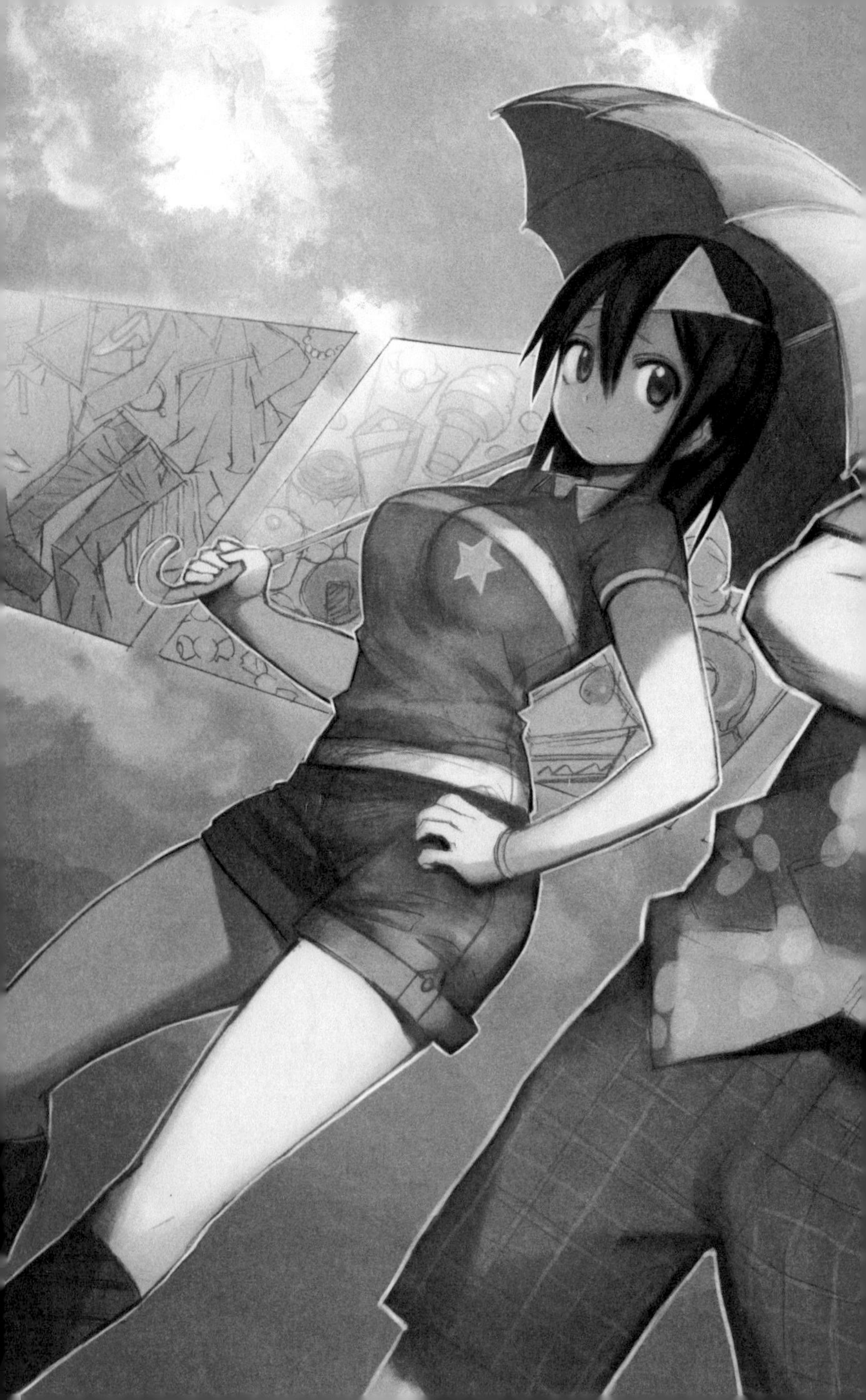

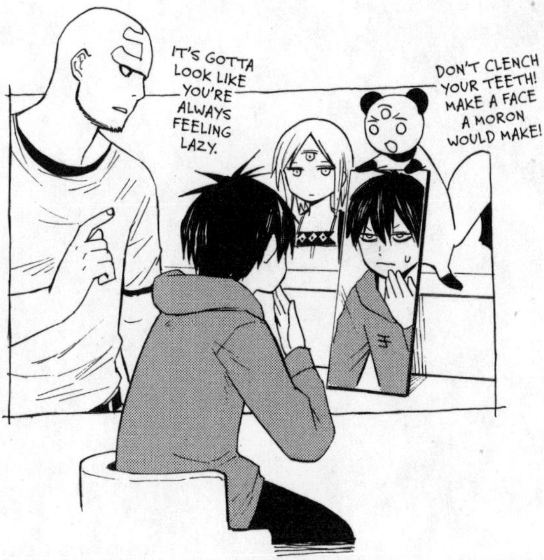
DON'T CLENCH YOUR TEETH! MAKE A FACE A MORON WOULD MAKE!
IT'S GOTTA LOOK LIKE YOU'RE ALWAYS FEELING LAZY.

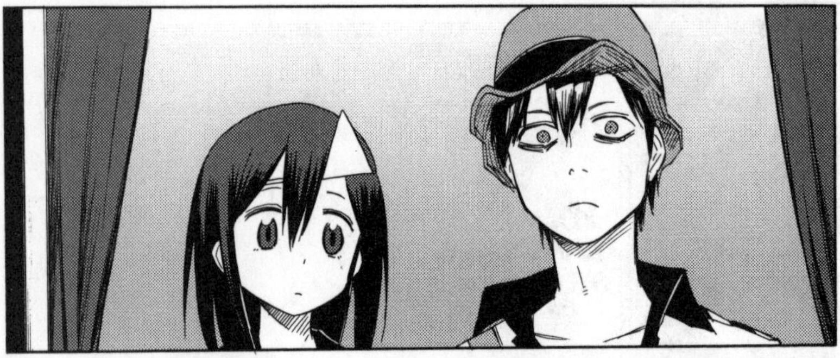

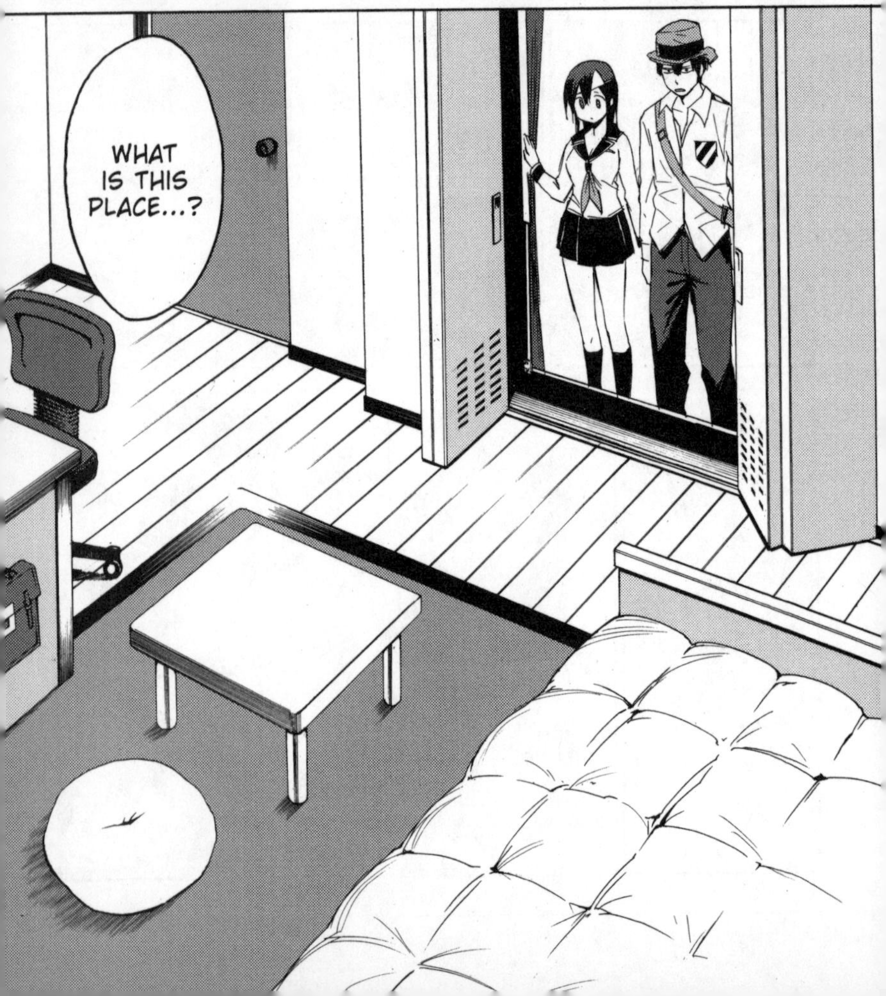
WHAT IS THIS PLACE...?

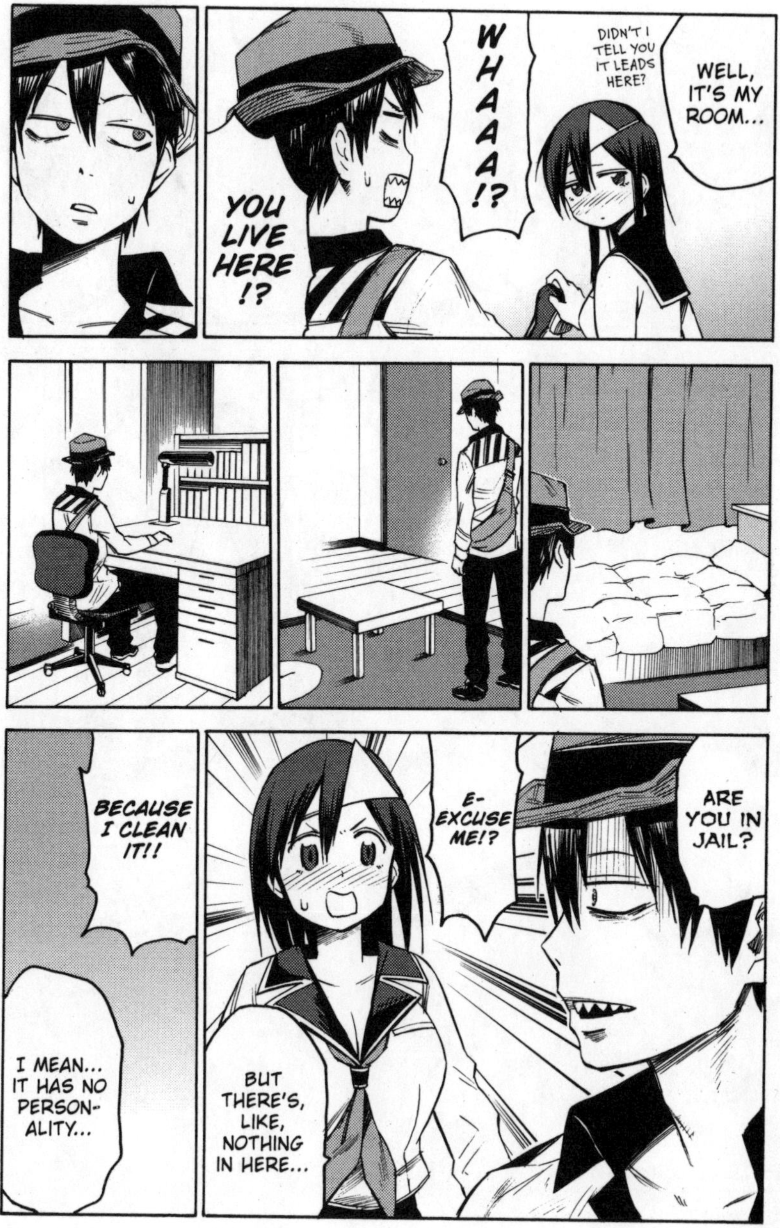
WELL, IT'S MY ROOM...
DIDN'T I TELL YOU IT LEADS HERE?
WHAAAA!?
YOU LIVE HERE!?
ARE YOU IN JAIL?
E-EXCUSE ME!?
BUT THERE'S, LIKE, NOTHING IN HERE...
BECAUSE I CLEAN IT!!
I MEAN... IT HAS NO PERSON-ALITY...

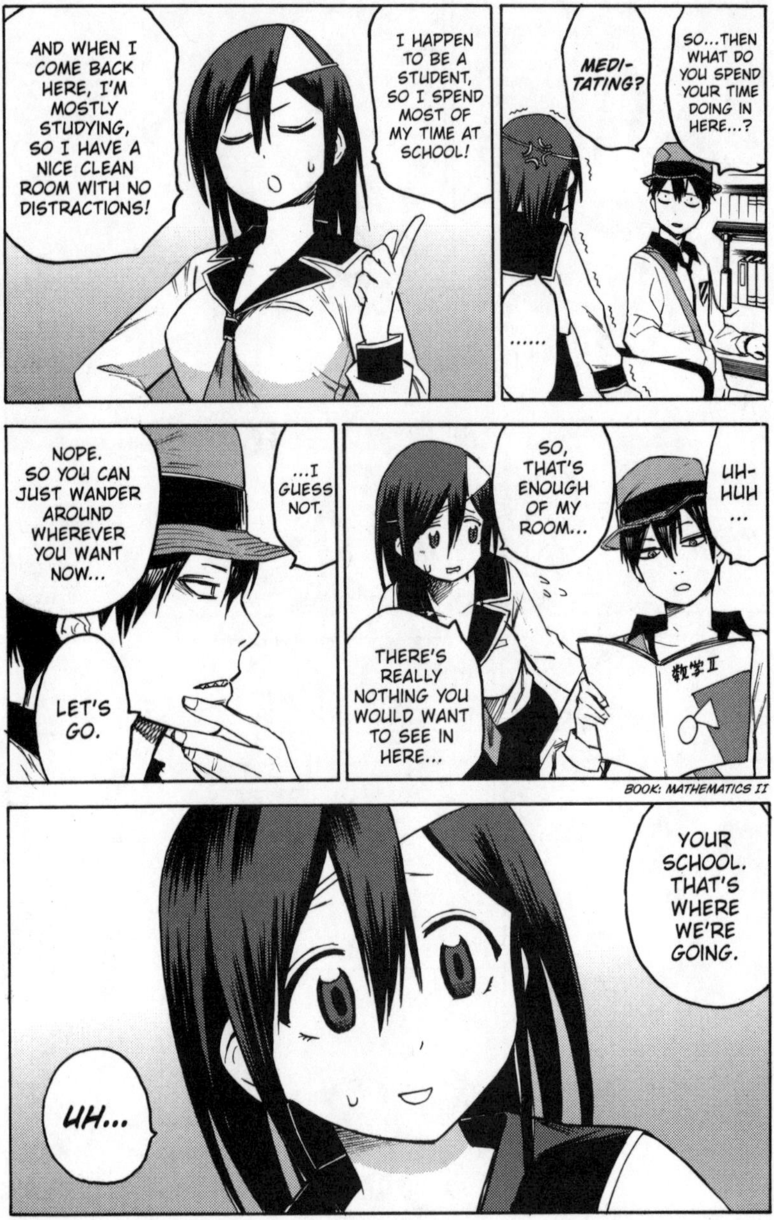
SO...THEN WHAT DO YOU SPEND YOUR TIME DOING IN HERE...?
MEDI-TATING?
......
I HAPPEN TO BE A STUDENT, SO I SPEND MOST OF MY TIME AT SCHOOL!
AND WHEN I COME BACK HERE, I'M MOSTLY STUDYING, SO I HAVE A NICE CLEAN ROOM WITH NO DISTRACTIONS!
UH-HUH ...
SO, THAT'S ENOUGH OF MY ROOM...
THERE'S REALLY NOTHING YOU WOULD WANT TO SEE IN HERE...
数学II
BOOK: MATHEMATICS II
...I GUESS NOT.
NOPE. SO YOU CAN JUST WANDER AROUND WHEREVER YOU WANT NOW...
LET'S GO.
YOUR SCHOOL. THAT'S WHERE WE'RE GOING.
UH...

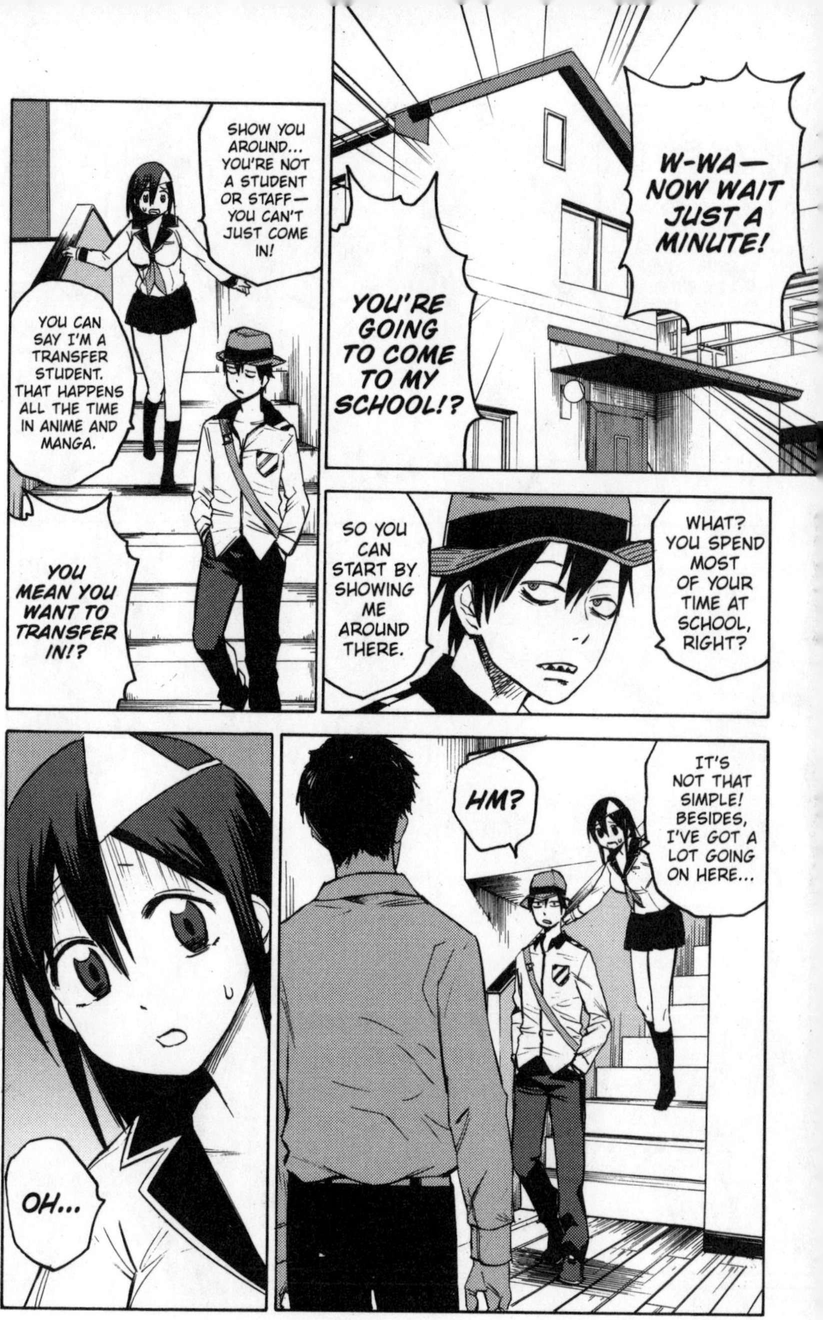

W-WA— NOW WAIT JUST A MINUTE!
YOU'RE GOING TO COME TO MY SCHOOL!?
WHAT? YOU SPEND MOST OF YOUR TIME AT SCHOOL, RIGHT?
SO YOU CAN START BY SHOWING ME AROUND THERE.
SHOW YOU AROUND... YOU'RE NOT A STUDENT OR STAFF— YOU CAN'T JUST COME IN!
YOU CAN SAY I'M A TRANSFER STUDENT. THAT HAPPENS ALL THE TIME IN ANIME AND MANGA.
YOU MEAN YOU WANT TO TRANSFER IN!?
IT'S NOT THAT SIMPLE! BESIDES, I'VE GOT A LOT GOING ON HERE...
HM?
OH...

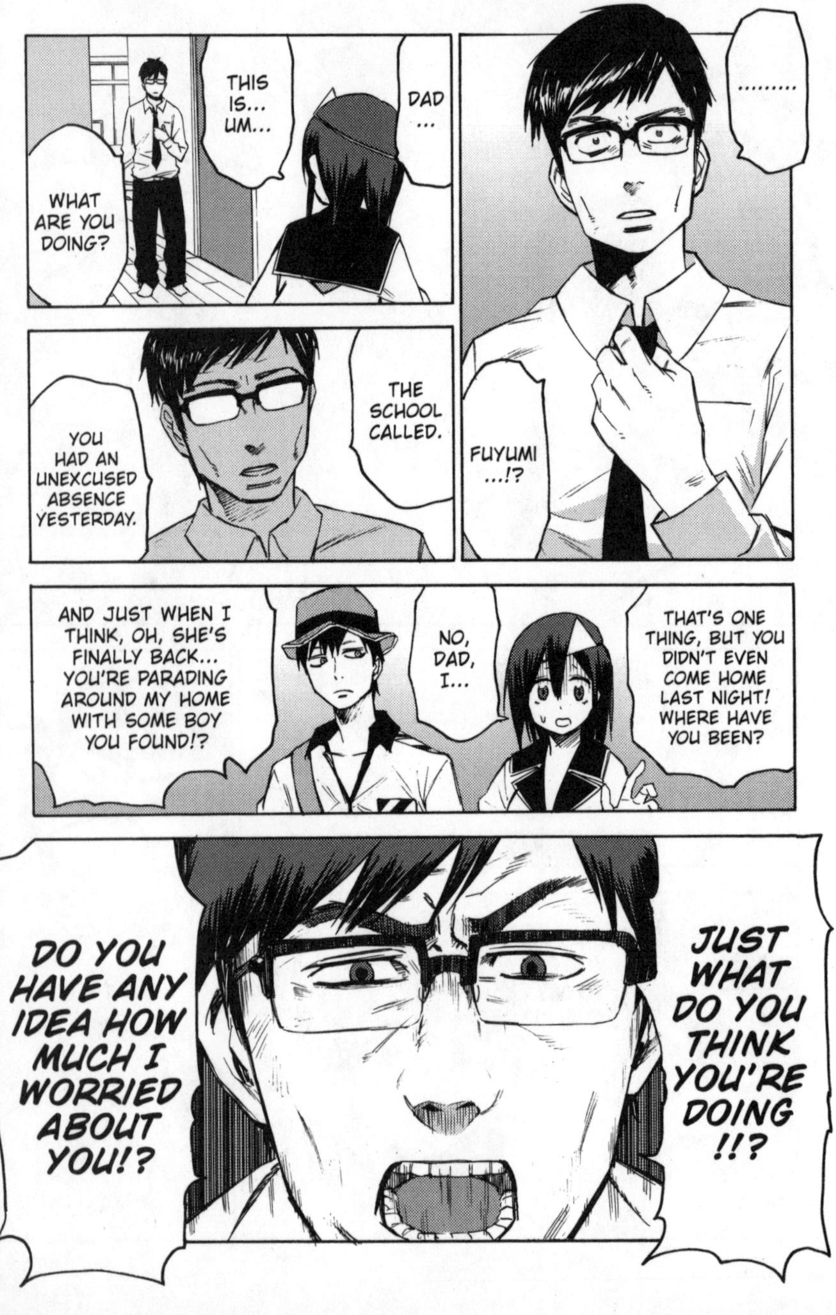
.........
FUYUMI ...!?
DAD ...
THIS IS... UM...
WHAT ARE YOU DOING?
THE SCHOOL CALLED.
YOU HAD AN UNEXCUSED ABSENCE YESTERDAY.
THAT'S ONE THING, BUT YOU DIDN'T EVEN COME HOME LAST NIGHT! WHERE HAVE YOU BEEN?
NO, DAD, I...
AND JUST WHEN I THINK, OH, SHE'S FINALLY BACK... YOU'RE PARADING AROUND MY HOME WITH SOME BOY YOU FOUND!?
JUST WHAT DO YOU THINK YOU'RE DOING!!?
DO YOU HAVE ANY IDEA HOW MUCH I WORRIED ABOUT YOU!?

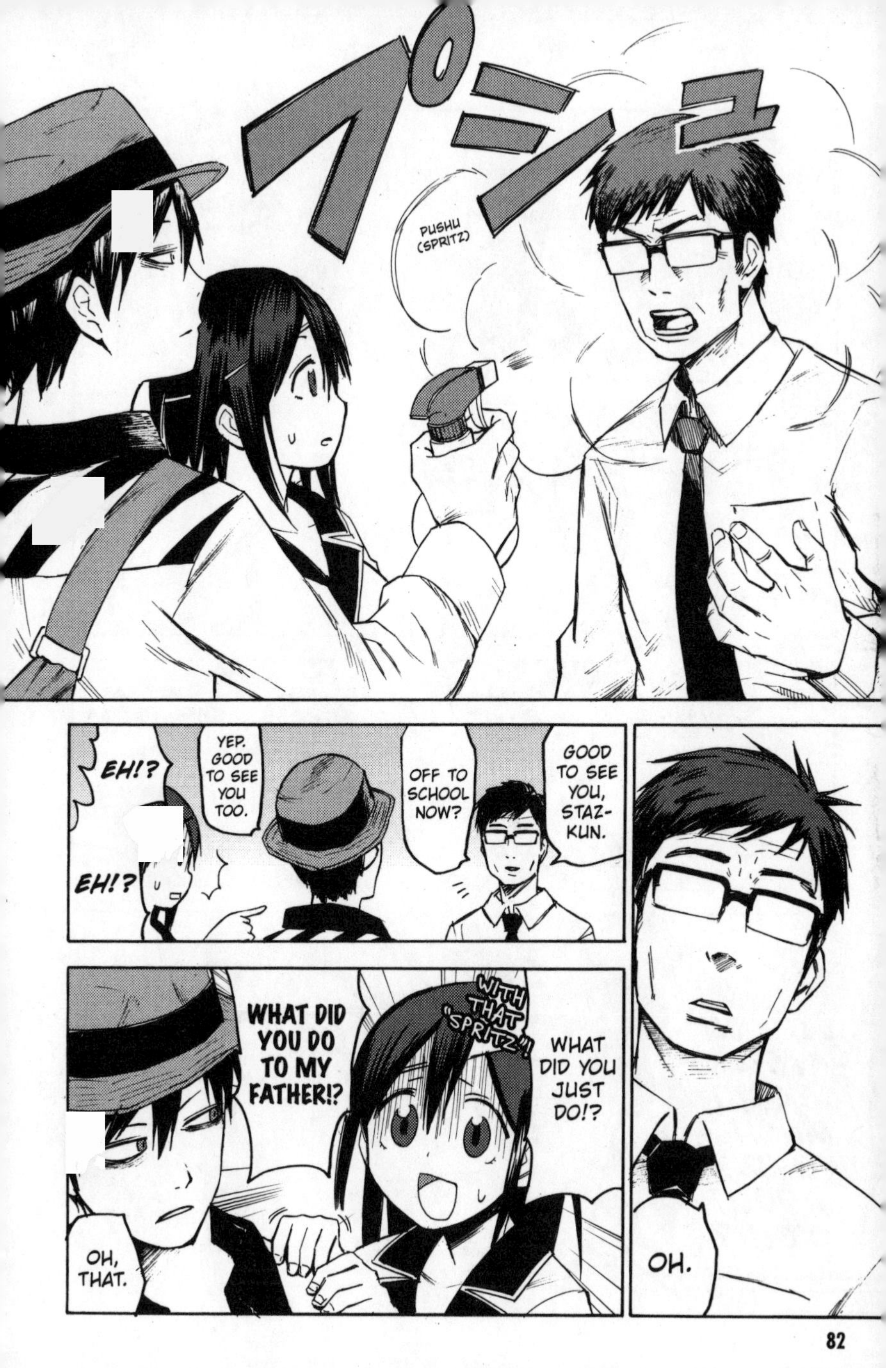
プシュ
PUSHU (SPRITZ)
OH.
GOOD TO SEE YOU, STAZ-KUN.
OFF TO SCHOOL NOW?
YEP. GOOD TO SEE YOU TOO.
EH!?
EH!?
WHAT DID YOU JUST DO!?
WITH THAT "SPRITZ"!
WHAT DID YOU DO TO MY FATHER!?
OH, THAT.

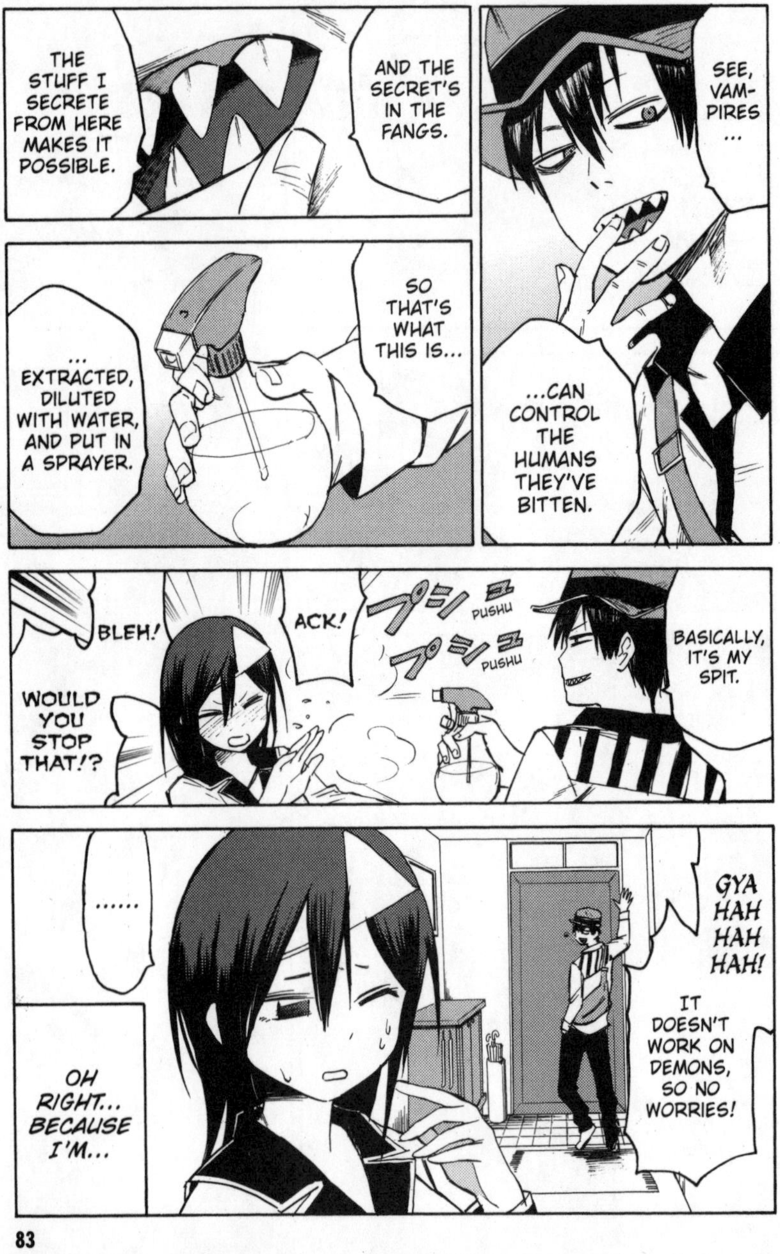
SEE, VAMPIRES ...
...CAN CONTROL THE HUMANS THEY'VE BITTEN.
AND THE SECRET'S IN THE FANGS.
THE STUFF I SECRETE FROM HERE MAKES IT POSSIBLE.
SO THAT'S WHAT THIS IS...
... EXTRACTED, DILUTED WITH WATER, AND PUT IN A SPRAYER.
BASICALLY, IT'S MY SPIT.
プシュ PUSHU
プシュ PUSHU
ACK!
BLEH!
WOULD YOU STOP THAT!?
GYA HAH HAH HAH!
IT DOESN'T WORK ON DEMONS, SO NO WORRIES!
......
OH RIGHT... BECAUSE I'M...

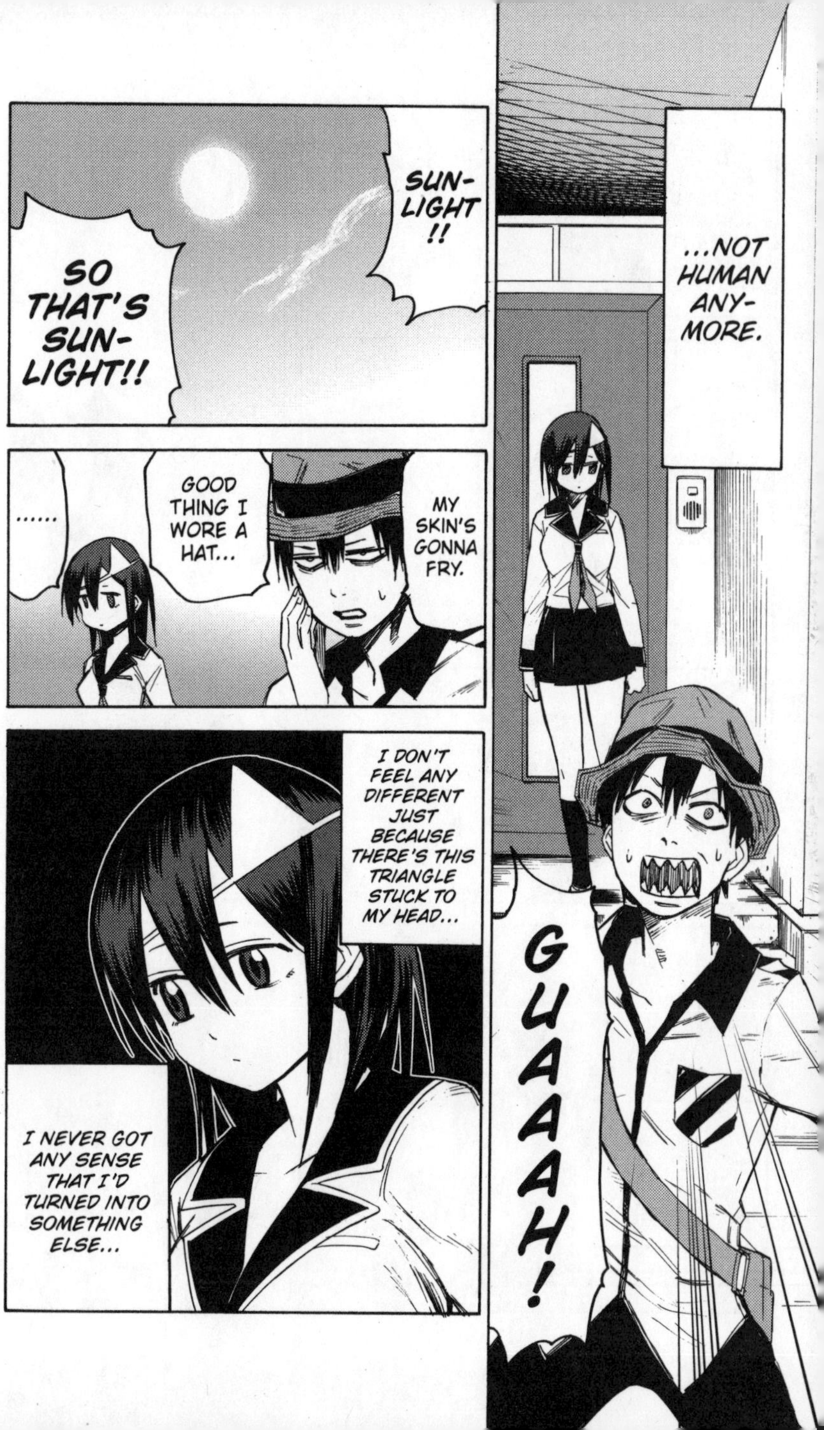
...NOT HUMAN ANY-MORE.
GUAAAAH!
SUN-LIGHT!!
SO THAT'S SUN-LIGHT!!
MY SKIN'S GONNA FRY.
GOOD THING I WORE A HAT...
......
I DON'T FEEL ANY DIFFERENT JUST BECAUSE THERE'S THIS TRIANGLE STUCK TO MY HEAD...
I NEVER GOT ANY SENSE THAT I'D TURNED INTO SOMETHING ELSE...

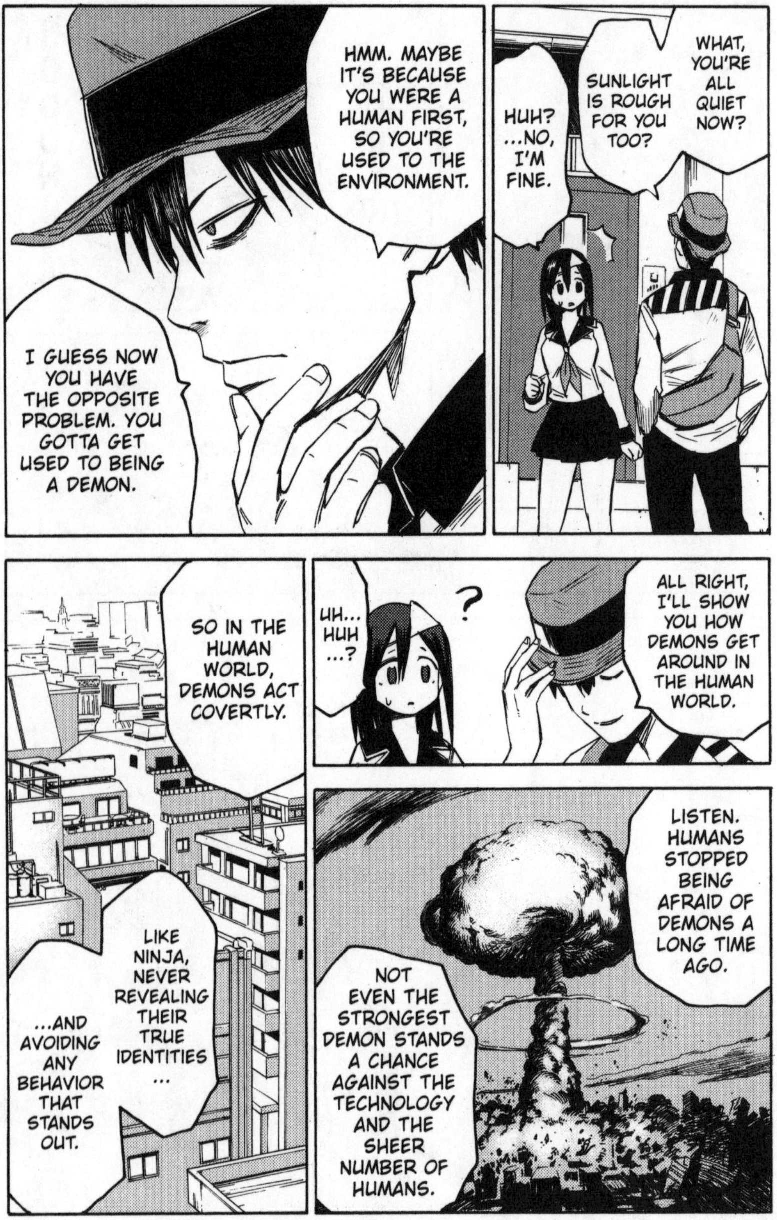
WHAT, YOU'RE ALL QUIET NOW?
SUNLIGHT IS ROUGH FOR YOU TOO?
HUH? ...NO, I'M FINE.
HMM. MAYBE IT'S BECAUSE YOU WERE A HUMAN FIRST, SO YOU'RE USED TO THE ENVIRONMENT.
I GUESS NOW YOU HAVE THE OPPOSITE PROBLEM. YOU GOTTA GET USED TO BEING A DEMON.
ALL RIGHT, I'LL SHOW YOU HOW DEMONS GET AROUND IN THE HUMAN WORLD.
?
UH... HUH ...?
LISTEN. HUMANS STOPPED BEING AFRAID OF DEMONS A LONG TIME AGO.
NOT EVEN THE STRONGEST DEMON STANDS A CHANCE AGAINST THE TECHNOLOGY AND THE SHEER NUMBER OF HUMANS.
SO IN THE HUMAN WORLD, DEMONS ACT COVERTLY.
LIKE NINJA, NEVER REVEALING THEIR TRUE IDENTITIES ...
...AND AVOIDING ANY BEHAVIOR THAT STANDS OUT.

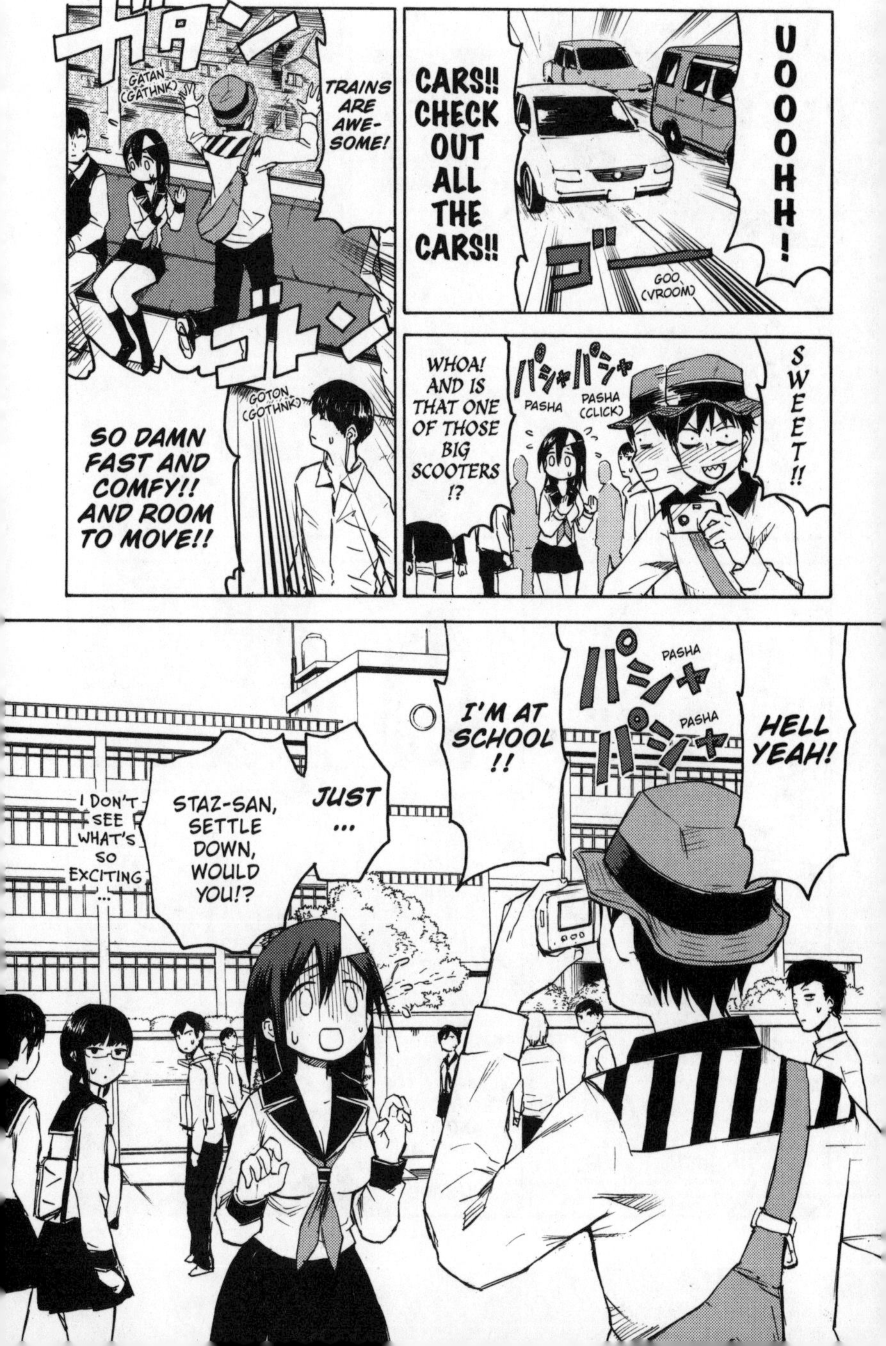
UOOOOHH!
CARS!! CHECK OUT ALL THE CARS!!
ゴー
GOO (VROOM)
SWEET!!
パシャパシャ
PASHA (CLICK)
PASHA
WHOA! AND IS THAT ONE OF THOSE BIG SCOOTERS!?
ガタン
GATAN (GATHNK)
TRAINS ARE AWE-SOME!
ゴトン
GOTON (GOTHNK)
SO DAMN FAST AND COMFY!! AND ROOM TO MOVE!!
HELL YEAH!
パシャ
PASHA
パシャ
PASHA
I'M AT SCHOOL!!
JUST...
STAZ-SAN, SETTLE DOWN, WOULD YOU!?
I DON'T SEE WHAT'S SO EXCITING...

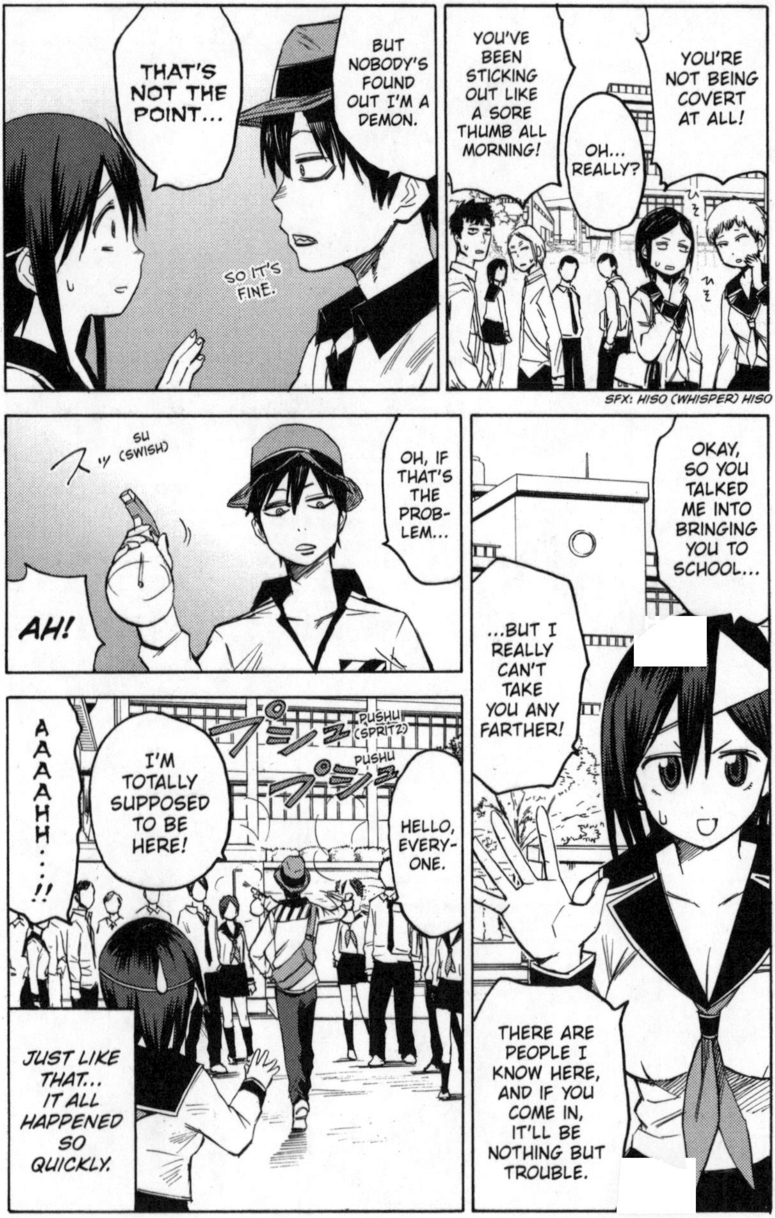
YOU'RE NOT BEING COVERT AT ALL!
YOU'VE BEEN STICKING OUT LIKE A SORE THUMB ALL MORNING!
OH... REALLY?
SFX: HISO (WHISPER) HISO
BUT NOBODY'S FOUND OUT I'M A DEMON.
SO IT'S FINE.
THAT'S NOT THE POINT...
OKAY, SO YOU TALKED ME INTO BRINGING YOU TO SCHOOL...
...BUT I REALLY CAN'T TAKE YOU ANY FARTHER!
THERE ARE PEOPLE I KNOW HERE, AND IF YOU COME IN, IT'LL BE NOTHING BUT TROUBLE.
OH, IF THAT'S THE PROB-LEM...
SU (SWISH)
AH!
PUSHU (SPRITZ)
PUSHU
HELLO, EVERY-ONE.
I'M TOTALLY SUPPOSED TO BE HERE!
AAAAHH...!!
JUST LIKE THAT... IT ALL HAPPENED SO QUICKLY.

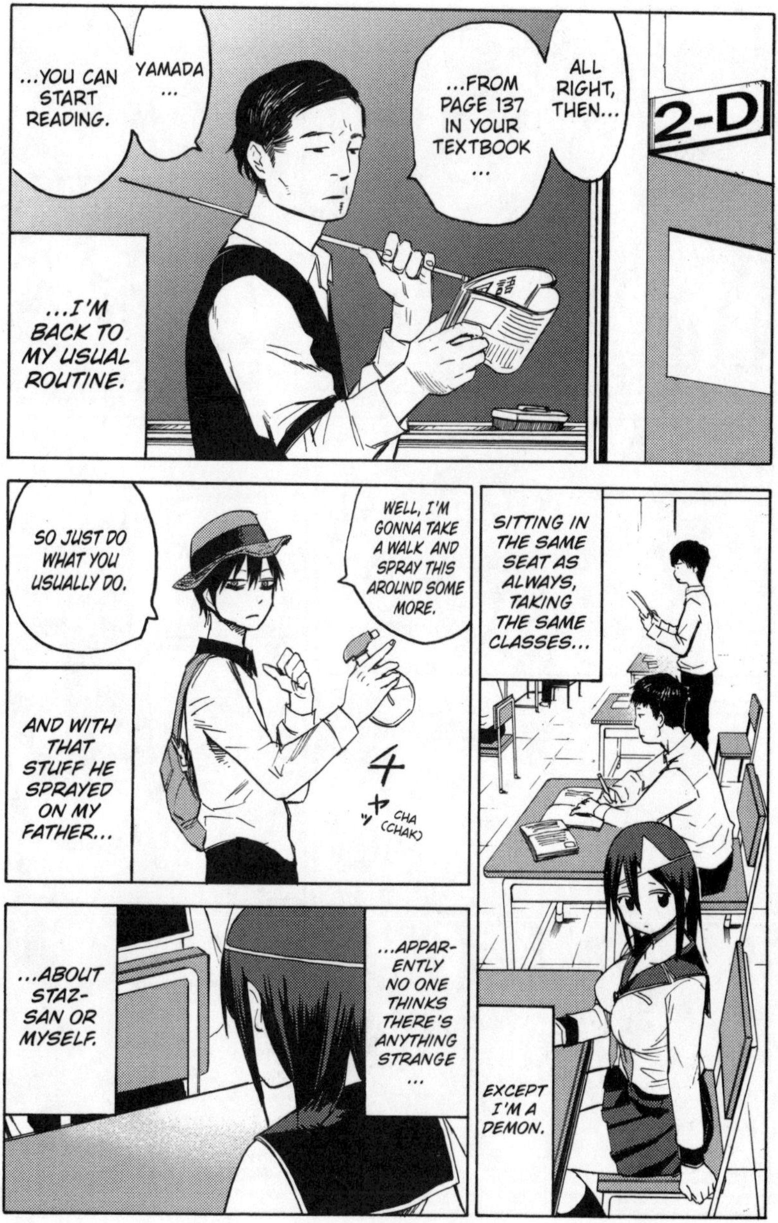
2-D
ALL RIGHT, THEN...
...FROM PAGE 137 IN YOUR TEXTBOOK ...
YAMADA ...
...YOU CAN START READING.
...I'M BACK TO MY USUAL ROUTINE.
SITTING IN THE SAME SEAT AS ALWAYS, TAKING THE SAME CLASSES...
EXCEPT I'M A DEMON.
WELL, I'M GONNA TAKE A WALK AND SPRAY THIS AROUND SOME MORE.
SO JUST DO WHAT YOU USUALLY DO.
CHA (CHAK)
AND WITH THAT STUFF HE SPRAYED ON MY FATHER...
...APPAR-ENTLY NO ONE THINKS THERE'S ANYTHING STRANGE ...
...ABOUT STAZ-SAN OR MYSELF.

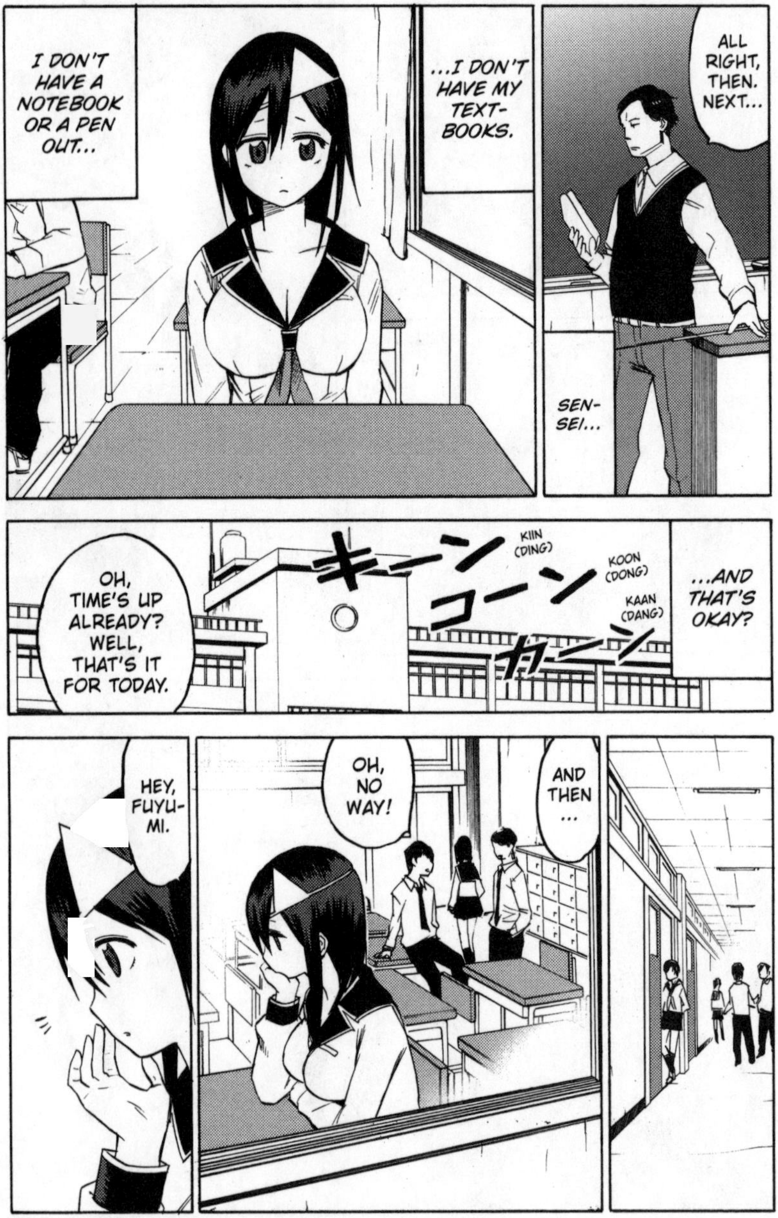
ALL RIGHT, THEN. NEXT...
SEN-SEI...
...I DON'T HAVE MY TEXT-BOOKS.
I DON'T HAVE A NOTEBOOK OR A PEN OUT...
...AND THAT'S OKAY?
KIIN (DING)
KOON (DONG)
KAAN (DANG)
OH, TIME'S UP ALREADY? WELL, THAT'S IT FOR TODAY.
AND THEN...
OH, NO WAY!
HEY, FUYU-MI.

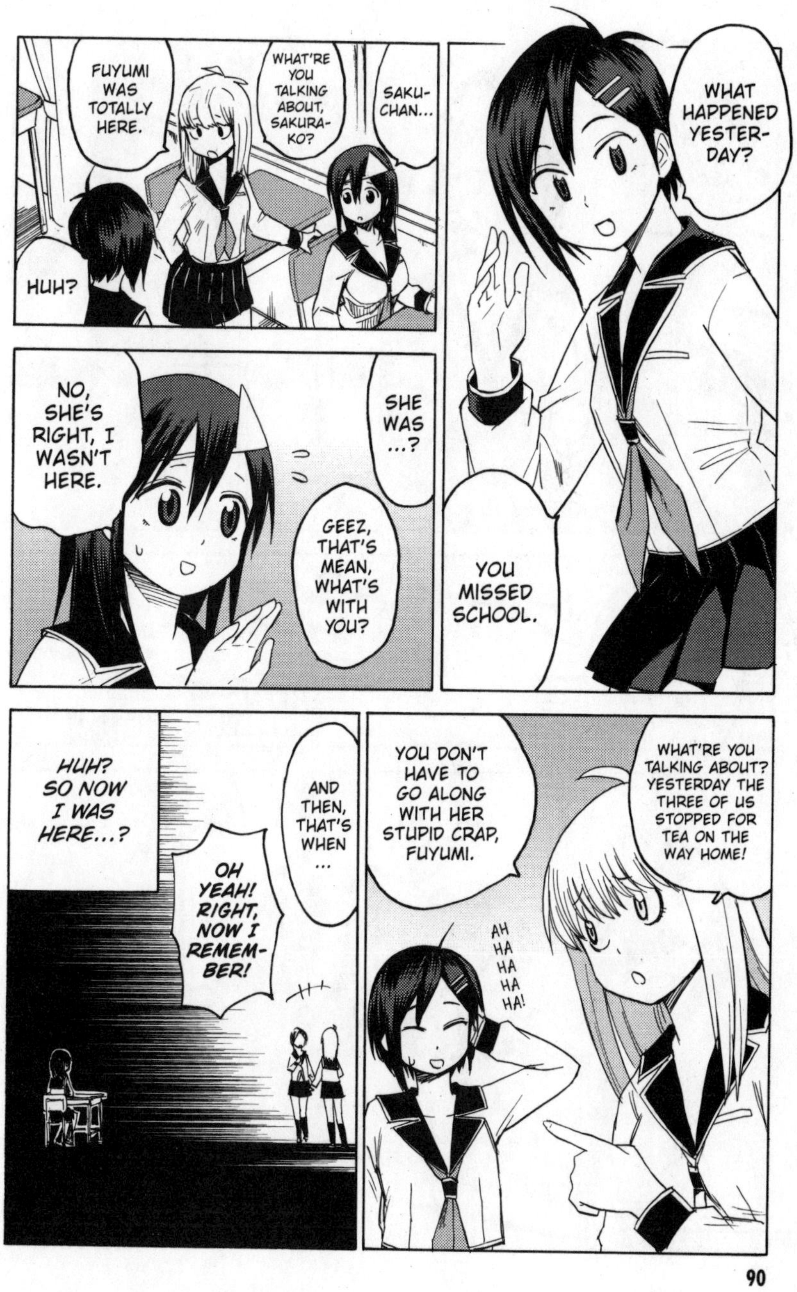
WHAT HAPPENED YESTER-DAY?
YOU MISSED SCHOOL.
SAKU-CHAN...
WHAT'RE YOU TALKING ABOUT, SAKURAKO?
FUYUMI WAS TOTALLY HERE.
HUH?
SHE WAS ...?
NO, SHE'S RIGHT, I WASN'T HERE.
GEEZ, THAT'S MEAN, WHAT'S WITH YOU?
WHAT'RE YOU TALKING ABOUT? YESTERDAY THE THREE OF US STOPPED FOR TEA ON THE WAY HOME!
YOU DON'T HAVE TO GO ALONG WITH HER STUPID CRAP, FUYUMI.
AH HA HA HA HA!
AND THEN, THAT'S WHEN ...
OH YEAH! RIGHT, NOW I REMEMBER!
HUH? SO NOW I WAS HERE...?

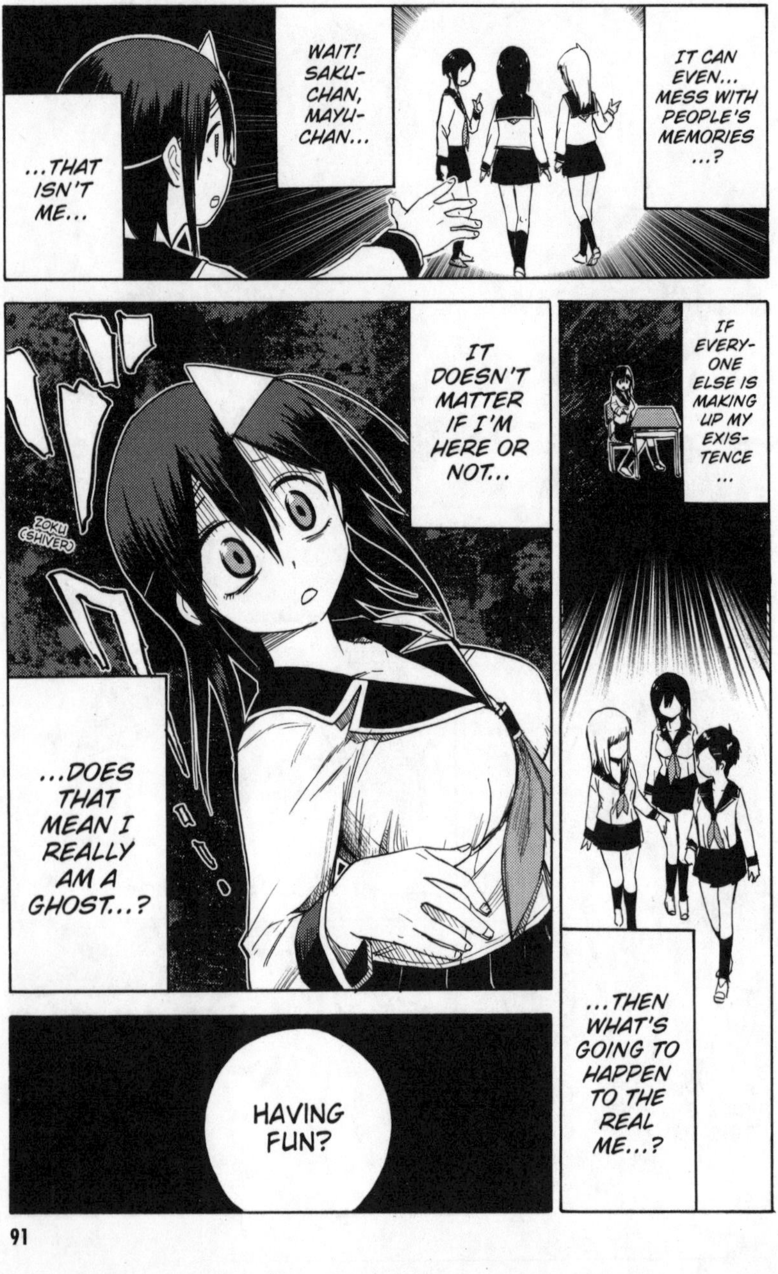
IT CAN EVEN... MESS WITH PEOPLE'S MEMORIES...?
WAIT! SAKU-CHAN, MAYU-CHAN...
...THAT ISN'T ME...
IF EVERY-ONE ELSE IS MAKING UP MY EXIS-TENCE...
...THEN WHAT'S GOING TO HAPPEN TO THE REAL ME...?
IT DOESN'T MATTER IF I'M HERE OR NOT...
ZOKU (SHIVER)
...DOES THAT MEAN I REALLY AM A GHOST...?
HAVING FUN?

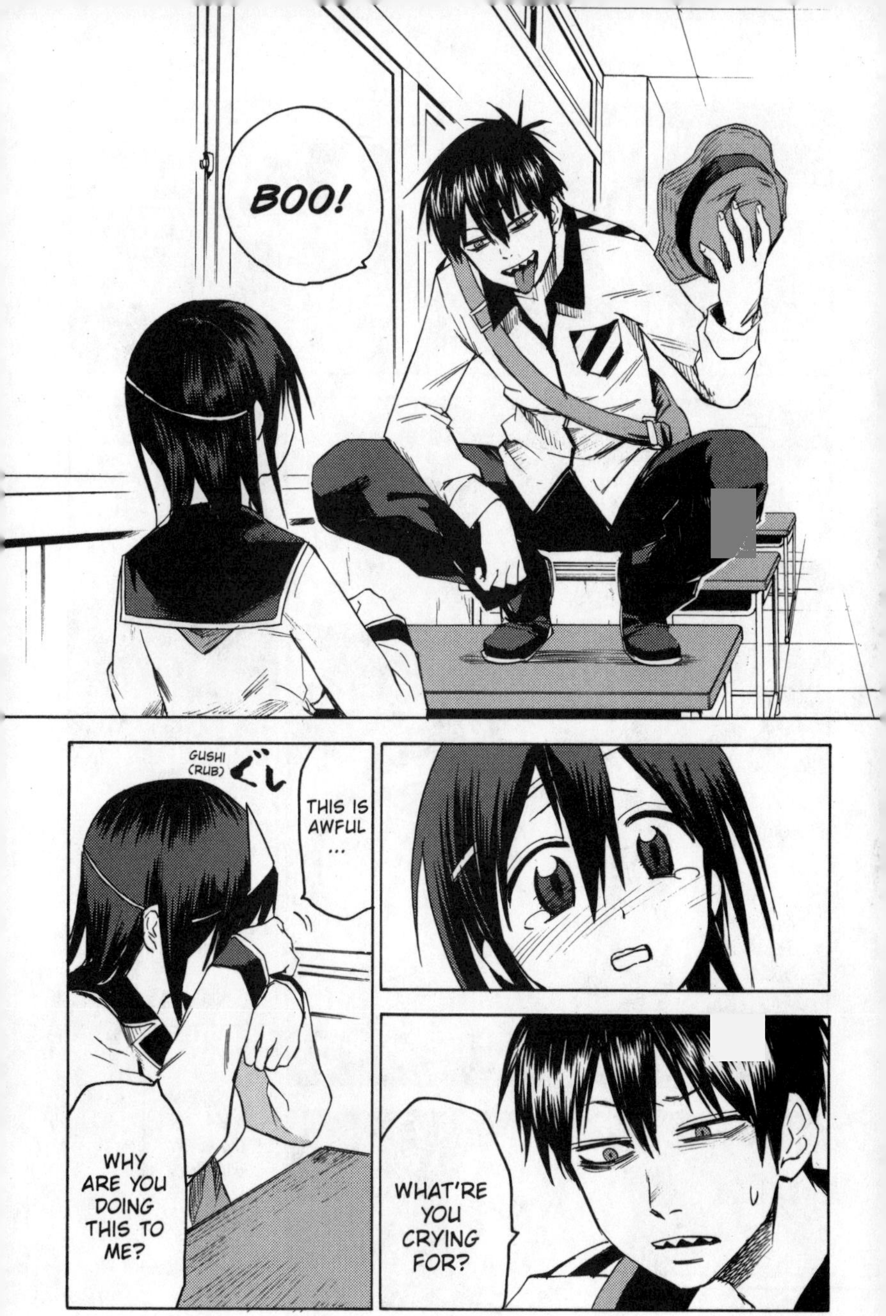
BOO!
WHAT'RE YOU CRYING FOR?
GUSHI (RUB) ぐし
THIS IS AWFUL ...
WHY ARE YOU DOING THIS TO ME?

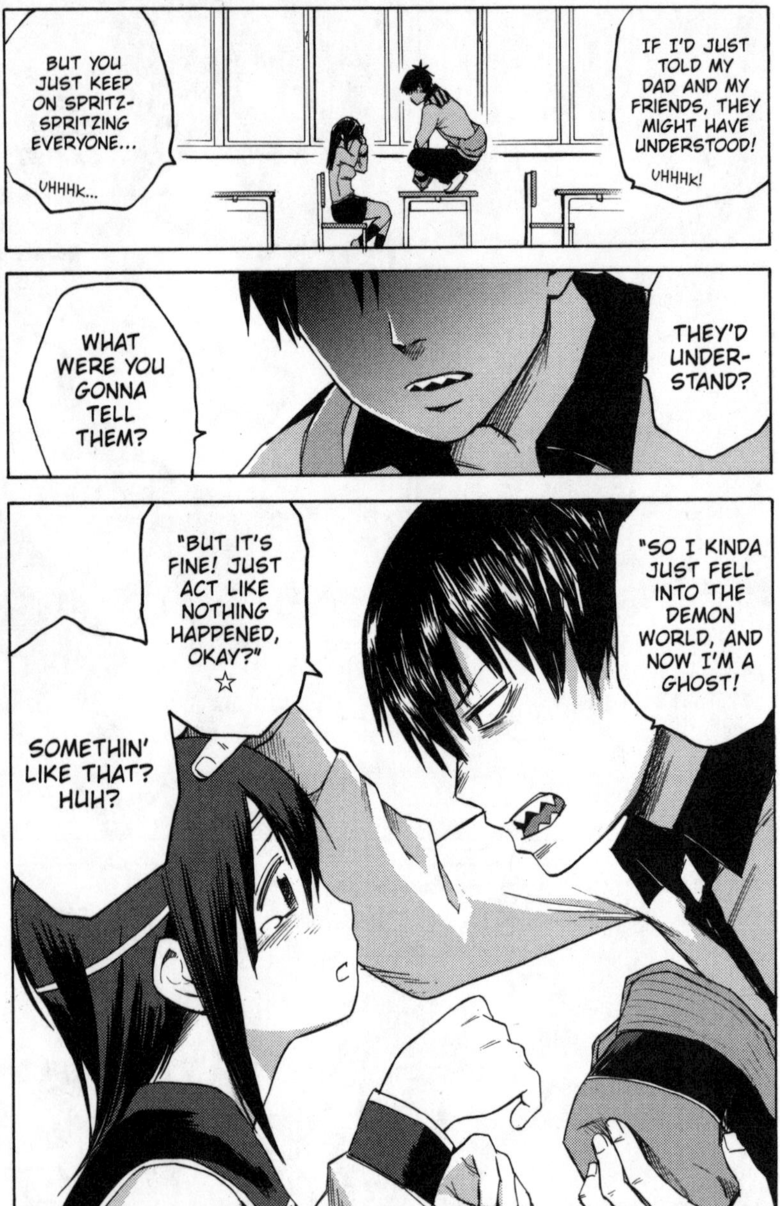
IF I'D JUST TOLD MY DAD AND MY FRIENDS, THEY MIGHT HAVE UNDERSTOOD!
UHHHK!
BUT YOU JUST KEEP ON SPRITZ-SPRITZING EVERYONE...
UHHHK...
THEY'D UNDER-STAND?
WHAT WERE YOU GONNA TELL THEM?
"SO I KINDA JUST FELL INTO THE DEMON WORLD, AND NOW I'M A GHOST!
"BUT IT'S FINE! JUST ACT LIKE NOTHING HAPPENED, OKAY?" ☆
SOMETHIN' LIKE THAT? HUH?

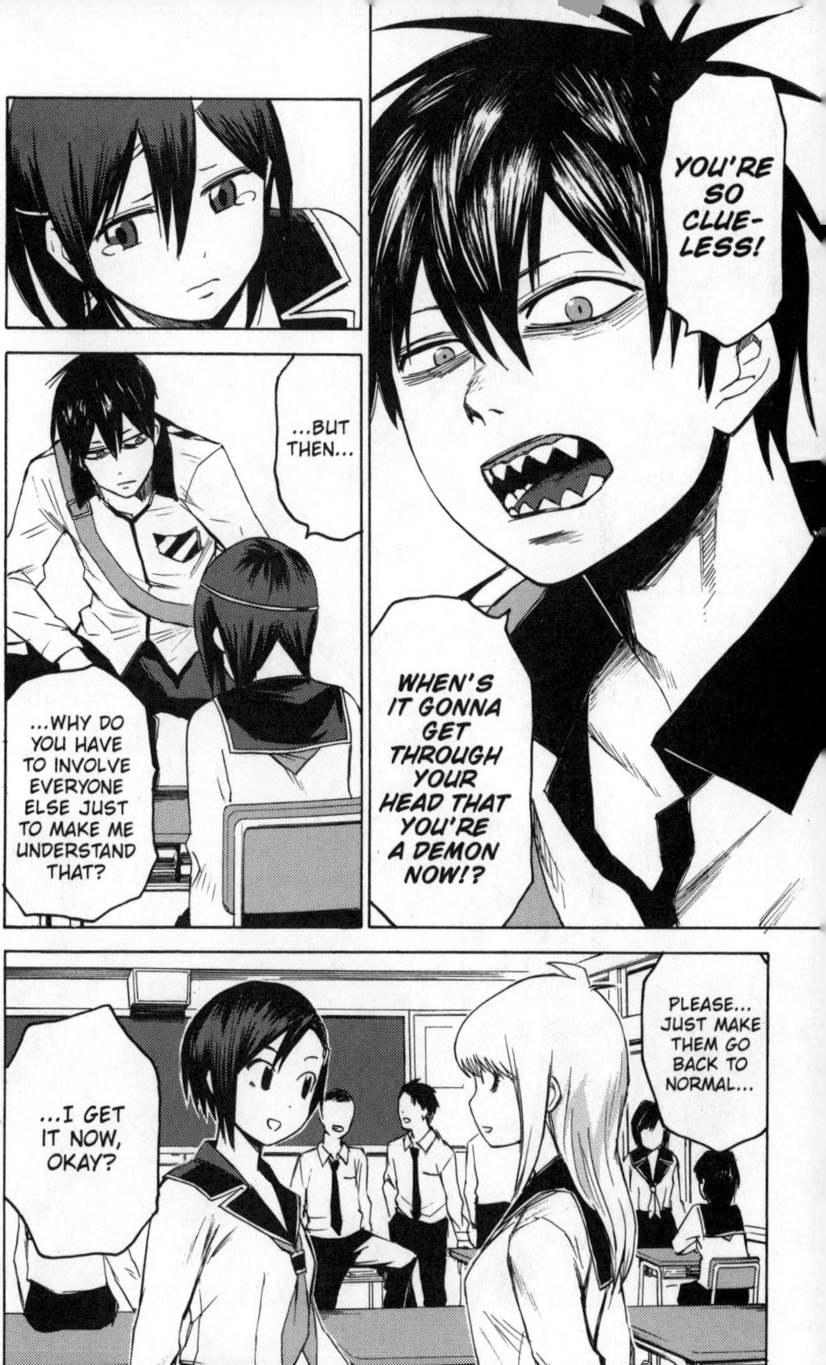
YOU'RE SO CLUE-LESS!
WHEN'S IT GONNA GET THROUGH YOUR HEAD THAT YOU'RE A DEMON NOW!?
...BUT THEN...
...WHY DO YOU HAVE TO INVOLVE EVERYONE ELSE JUST TO MAKE ME UNDERSTAND THAT?
PLEASE... JUST MAKE THEM GO BACK TO NORMAL...
...I GET IT NOW, OKAY?

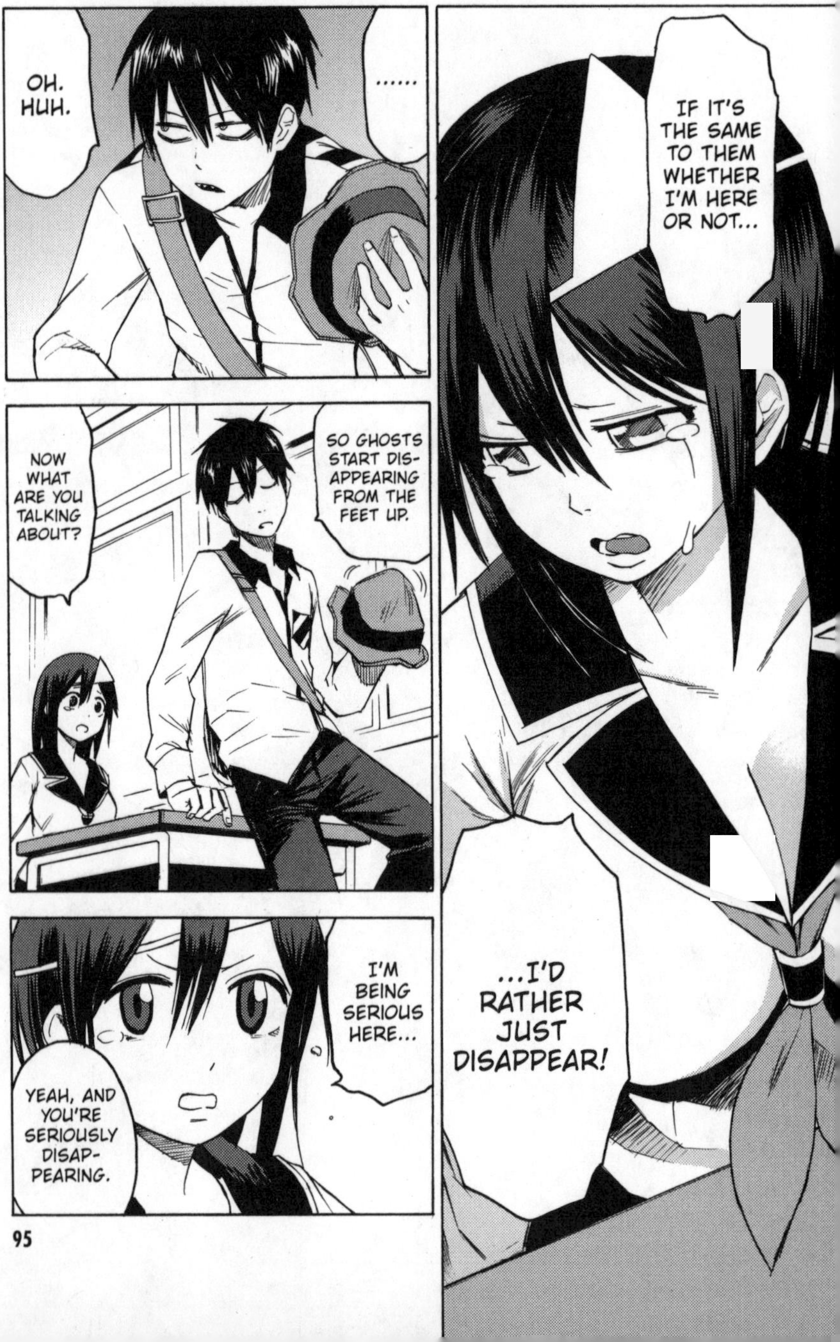
IF IT'S THE SAME TO THEM WHETHER I'M HERE OR NOT...
...I'D RATHER JUST DISAPPEAR!
......
OH. HUH.
SO GHOSTS START DIS-APPEARING FROM THE FEET UP.
NOW WHAT ARE YOU TALKING ABOUT?
I'M BEING SERIOUS HERE...
YEAH, AND YOU'RE SERIOUSLY DISAP-PEARING.

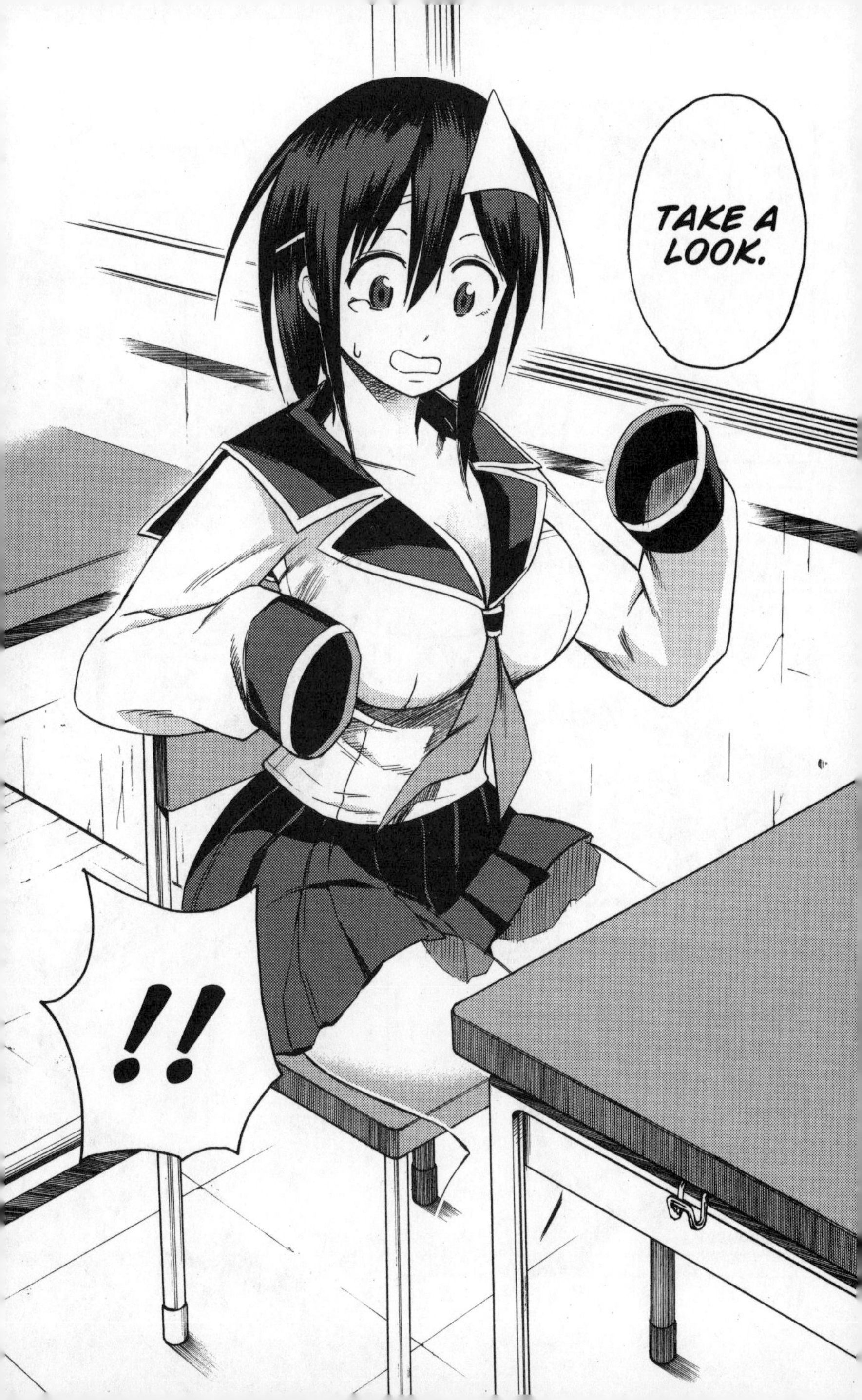
TAKE A LOOK.
!!

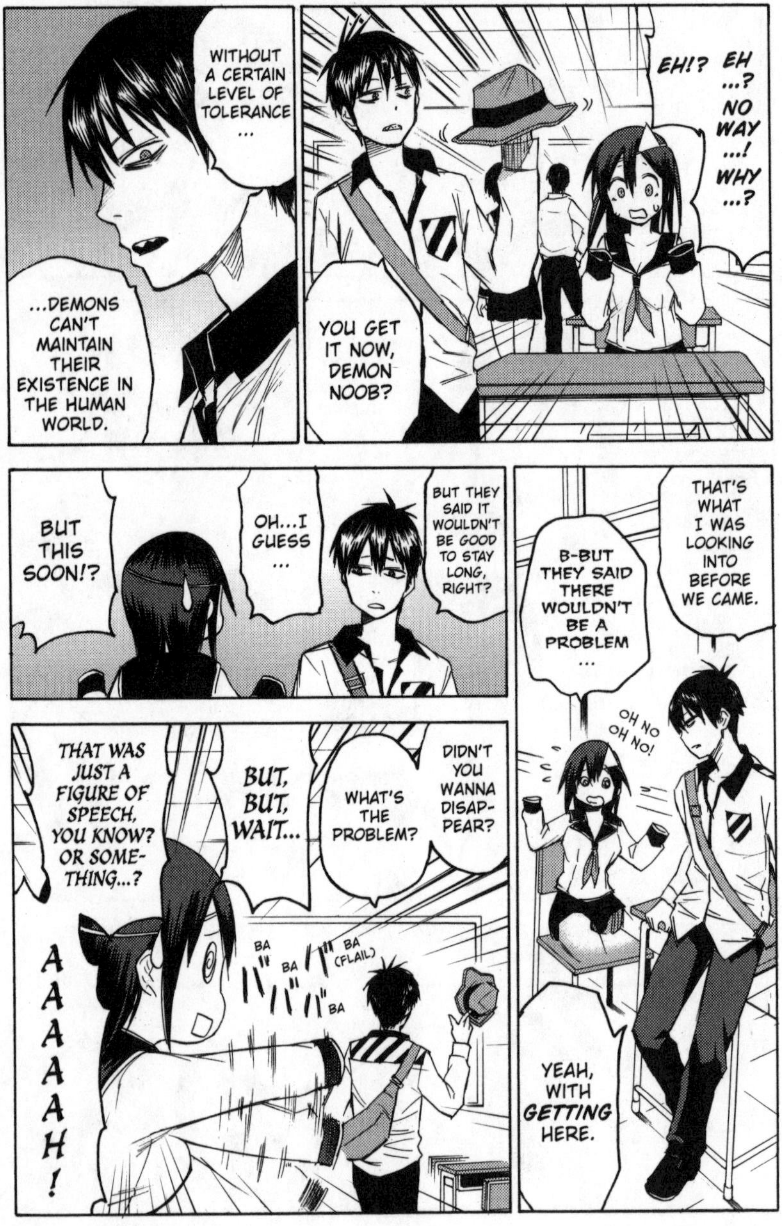
EH!? EH...? NO WAY...! WHY...?
YOU GET IT NOW, DEMON NOOB?
WITHOUT A CERTAIN LEVEL OF TOLERANCE...
...DEMONS CAN'T MAINTAIN THEIR EXISTENCE IN THE HUMAN WORLD.
THAT'S WHAT I WAS LOOKING INTO BEFORE WE CAME.
B-BUT THEY SAID THERE WOULDN'T BE A PROBLEM...
OH NO OH NO!
YEAH, WITH GETTING HERE.
BUT THEY SAID IT WOULDN'T BE GOOD TO STAY LONG, RIGHT?
OH...I GUESS...
BUT THIS SOON!?
DIDN'T YOU WANNA DISAPPEAR?
WHAT'S THE PROBLEM?
BUT, BUT, WAIT...
THAT WAS JUST A FIGURE OF SPEECH, YOU KNOW? OR SOME-THING...?
BA BA BA (FLAIL) BA
AAAAAAH!

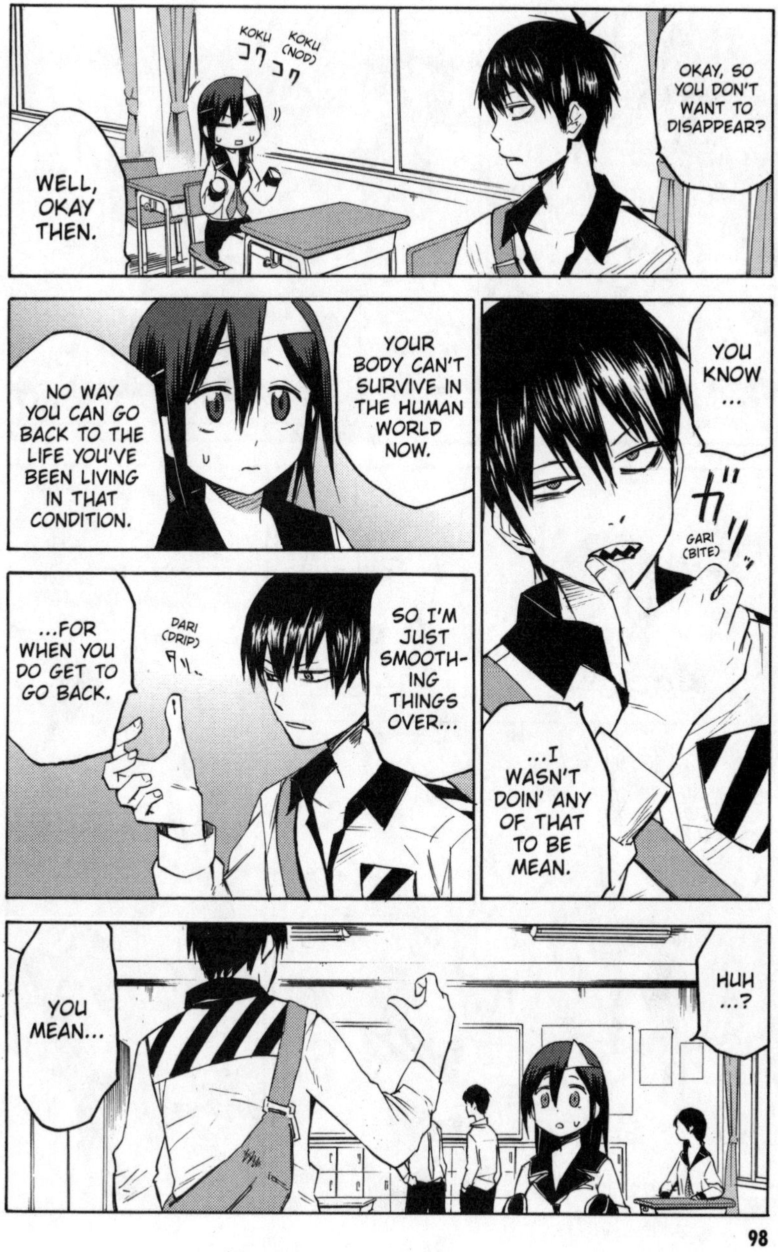
OKAY, SO YOU DON'T WANT TO DISAPPEAR?
KOKU KOKU (NOD) コクコク
WELL, OKAY THEN.
YOU KNOW ...
ガリッ GARI (BITE)
...I WASN'T DOIN' ANY OF THAT TO BE MEAN.
YOUR BODY CAN'T SURVIVE IN THE HUMAN WORLD NOW.
NO WAY YOU CAN GO BACK TO THE LIFE YOU'VE BEEN LIVING IN THAT CONDITION.
SO I'M JUST SMOOTHING THINGS OVER...
DARI (DRIP) タリ…
...FOR WHEN YOU DO GET TO GO BACK.
HUH ...?
YOU MEAN...

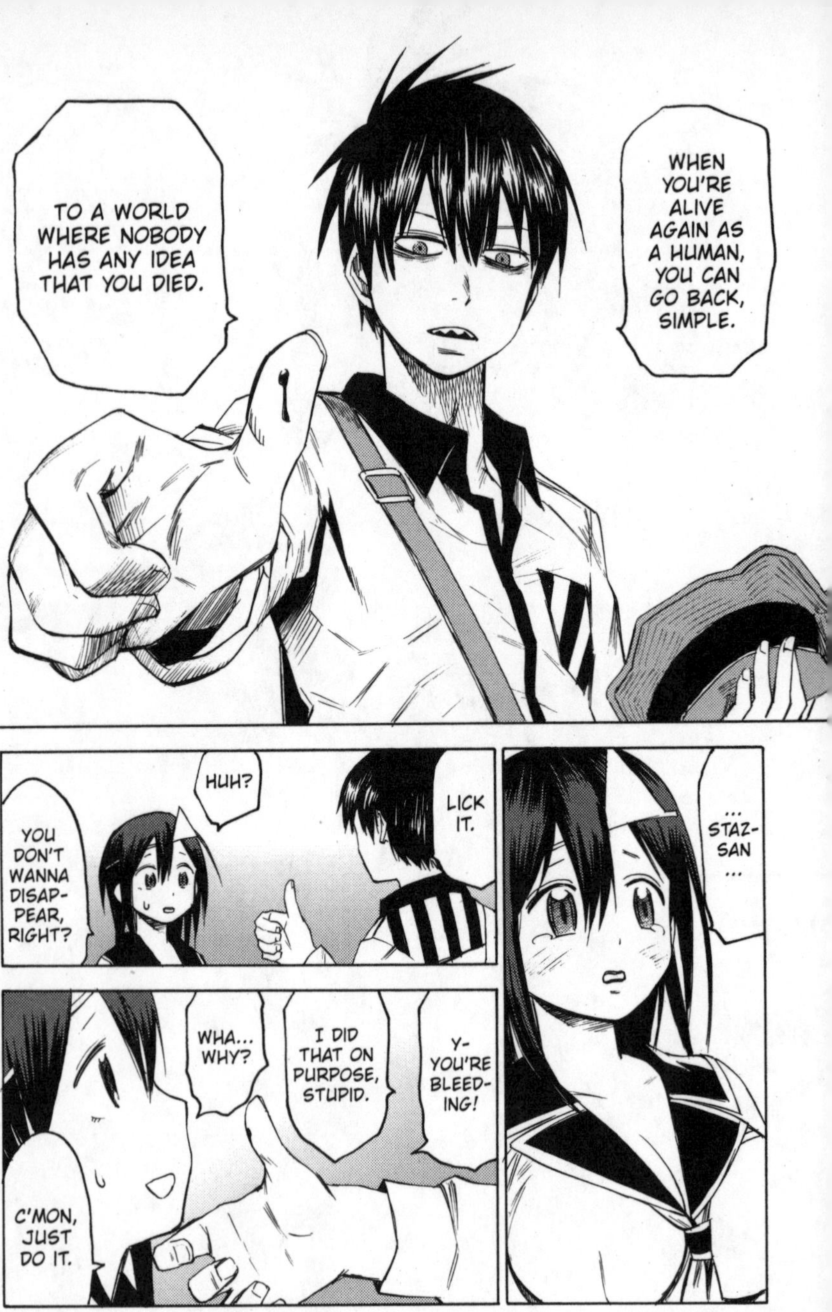
WHEN YOU'RE ALIVE AGAIN AS A HUMAN, YOU CAN GO BACK, SIMPLE.
TO A WORLD WHERE NOBODY HAS ANY IDEA THAT YOU DIED.
... STAZ-SAN ...
LICK IT.
HUH?
YOU DON'T WANNA DISAP-PEAR, RIGHT?
Y-YOU'RE BLEED-ING!
I DID THAT ON PURPOSE, STUPID.
WHA... WHY?
C'MON, JUST DO IT.

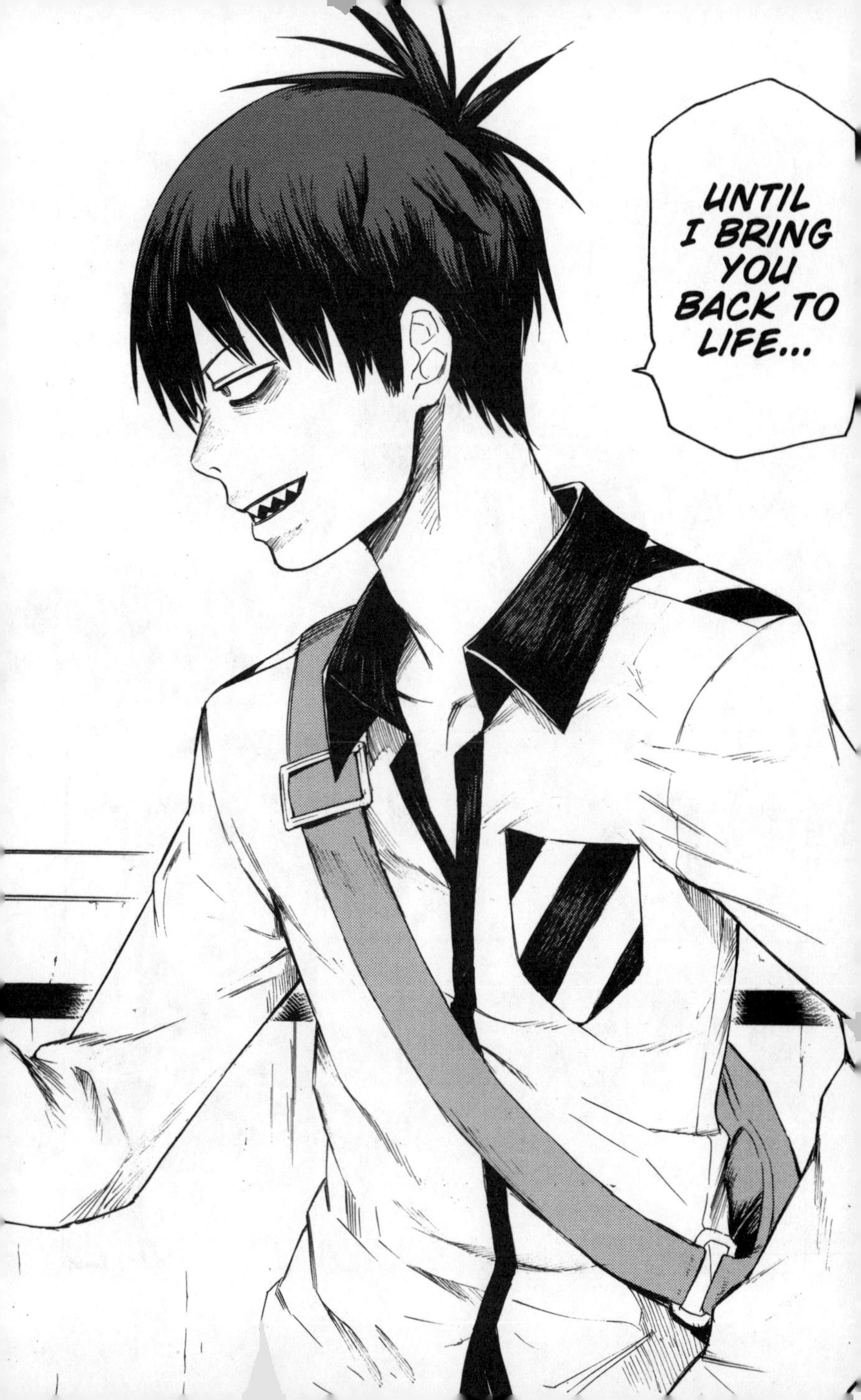
UNTIL I BRING YOU BACK TO LIFE...

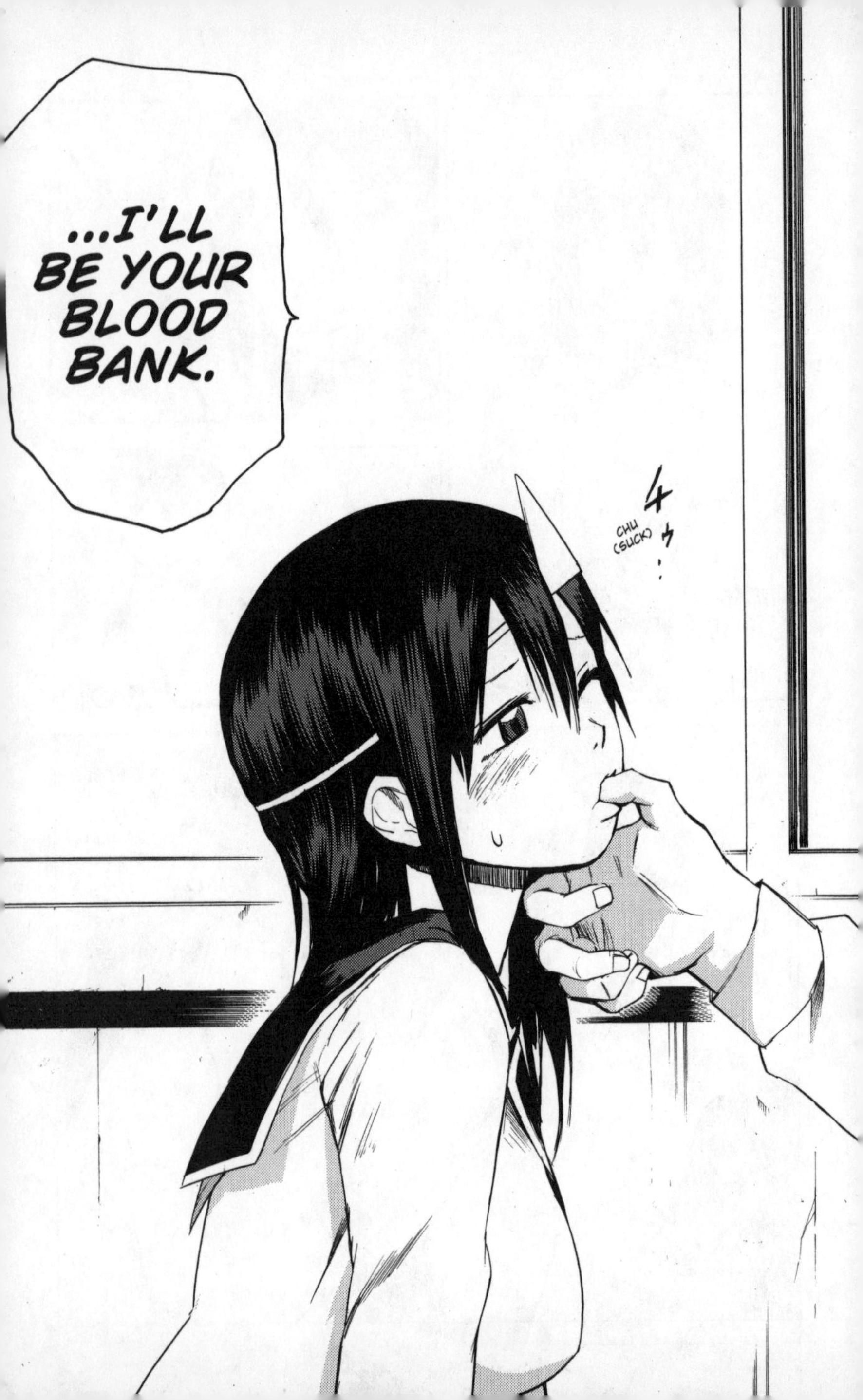
...I'LL BE YOUR BLOOD BANK.
CHU (SUCK)

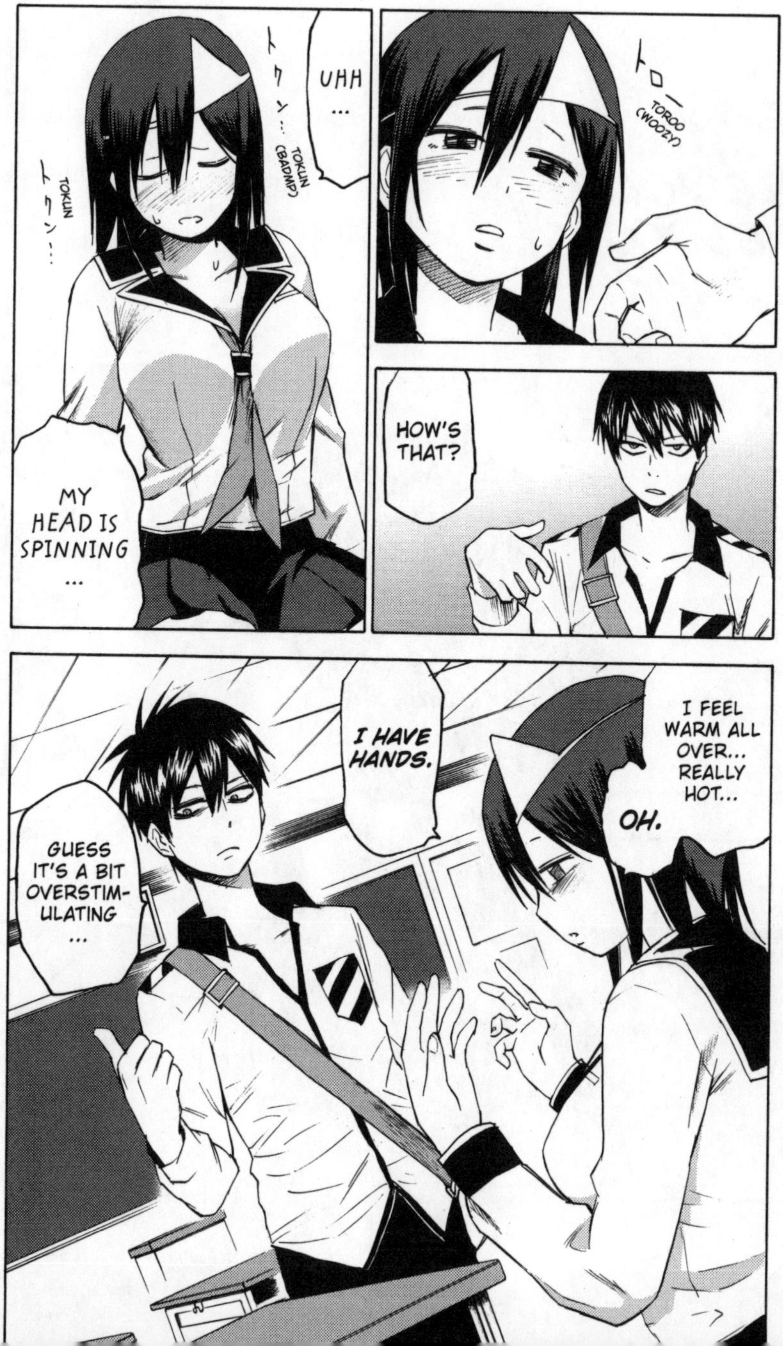

トロー
TOROO (WOOZY)
HOW'S THAT?
UHH ...
トクン…
TOKUN (BADMP)
トクン…
TOKUN
MY HEAD IS SPINNING ...
I FEEL WARM ALL OVER... REALLY HOT...
I HAVE HANDS.
OH.
GUESS IT'S A BIT OVERSTIMULATING ...

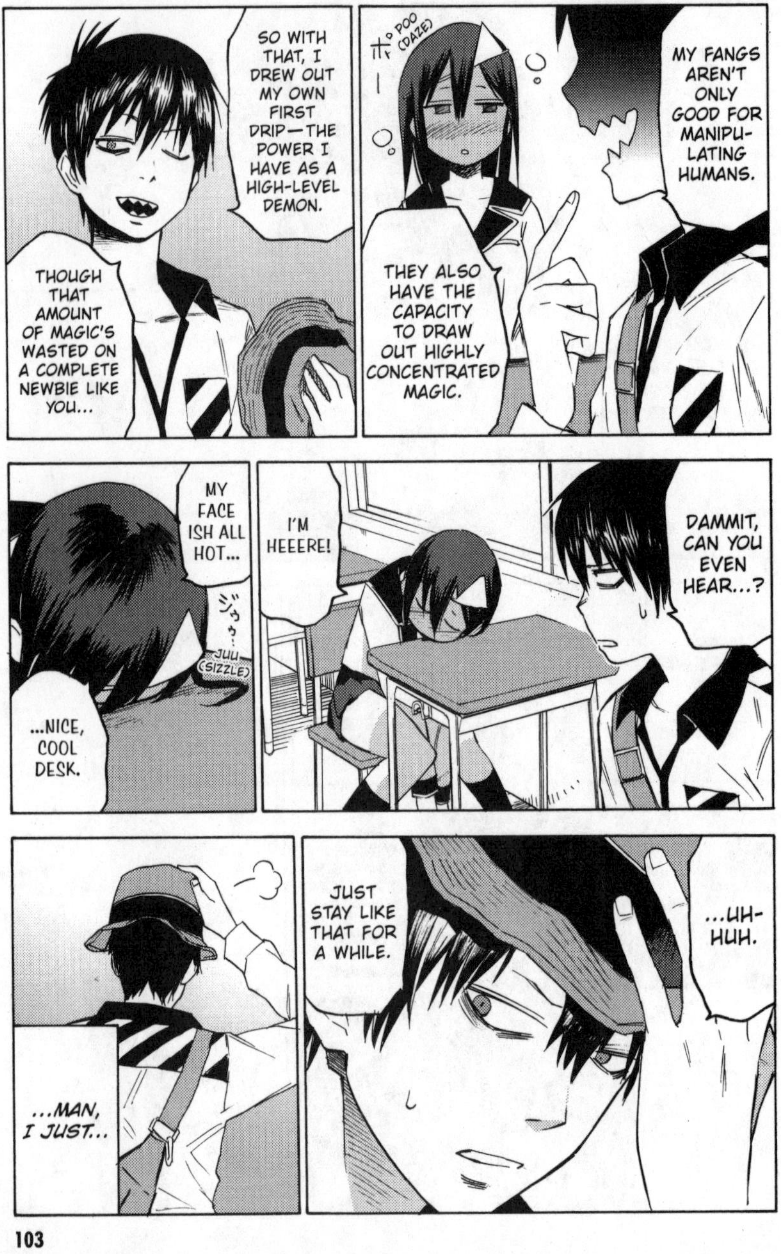
MY FANGS AREN'T ONLY GOOD FOR MANIPU-LATING HUMANS.
POO (DAZE)
THEY ALSO HAVE THE CAPACITY TO DRAW OUT HIGHLY CONCENTRATED MAGIC.
SO WITH THAT, I DREW OUT MY OWN FIRST DRIP—THE POWER I HAVE AS A HIGH-LEVEL DEMON.
THOUGH THAT AMOUNT OF MAGIC'S WASTED ON A COMPLETE NEWBIE LIKE YOU...
DAMMIT, CAN YOU EVEN HEAR...?
I'M HEEERE!
MY FACE ISH ALL HOT...
JUU (SIZZLE)
...NICE, COOL DESK.
...UH-HUH.
JUST STAY LIKE THAT FOR A WHILE.
...MAN, I JUST...

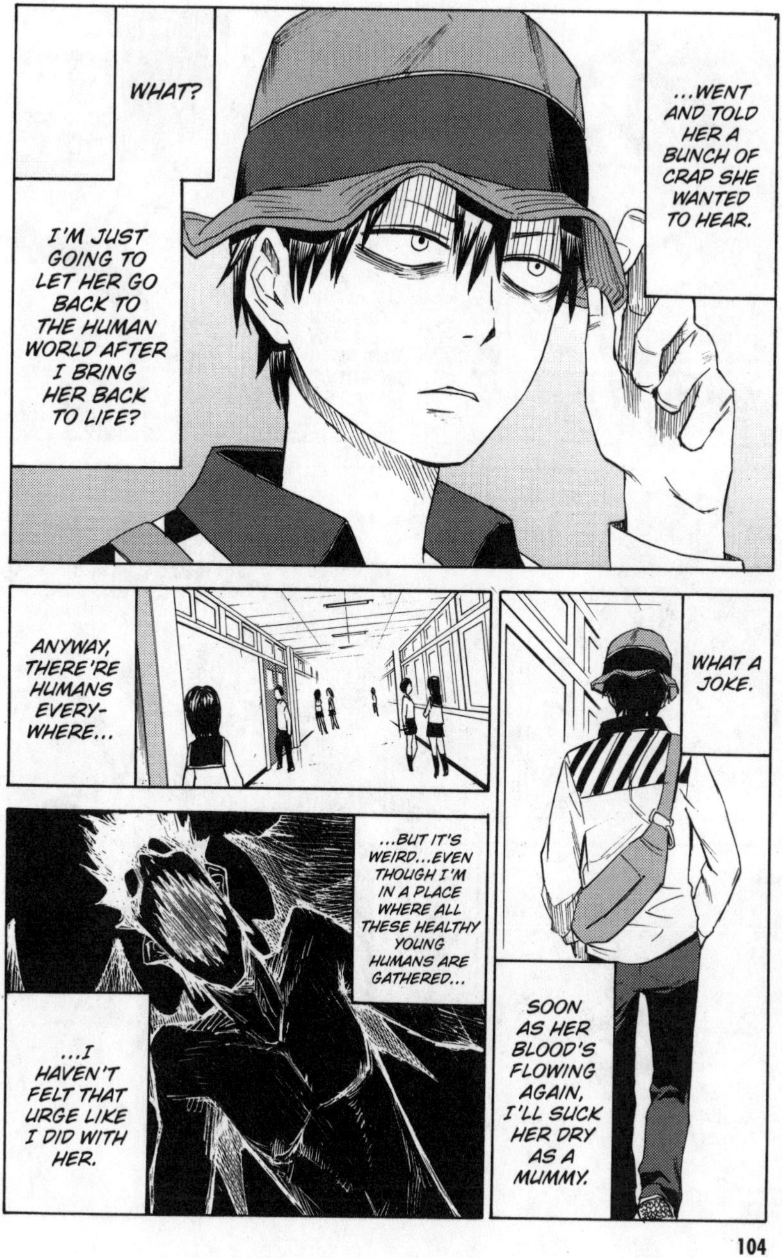
...WENT AND TOLD HER A BUNCH OF CRAP SHE WANTED TO HEAR.
WHAT?
I'M JUST GOING TO LET HER GO BACK TO THE HUMAN WORLD AFTER I BRING HER BACK TO LIFE?
WHAT A JOKE.
SOON AS HER BLOOD'S FLOWING AGAIN, I'LL SUCK HER DRY AS A MUMMY.
ANYWAY, THERE'RE HUMANS EVERY-WHERE...
...BUT IT'S WEIRD...EVEN THOUGH I'M IN A PLACE WHERE ALL THESE HEALTHY YOUNG HUMANS ARE GATHERED...
...I HAVEN'T FELT THAT URGE LIKE I DID WITH HER.

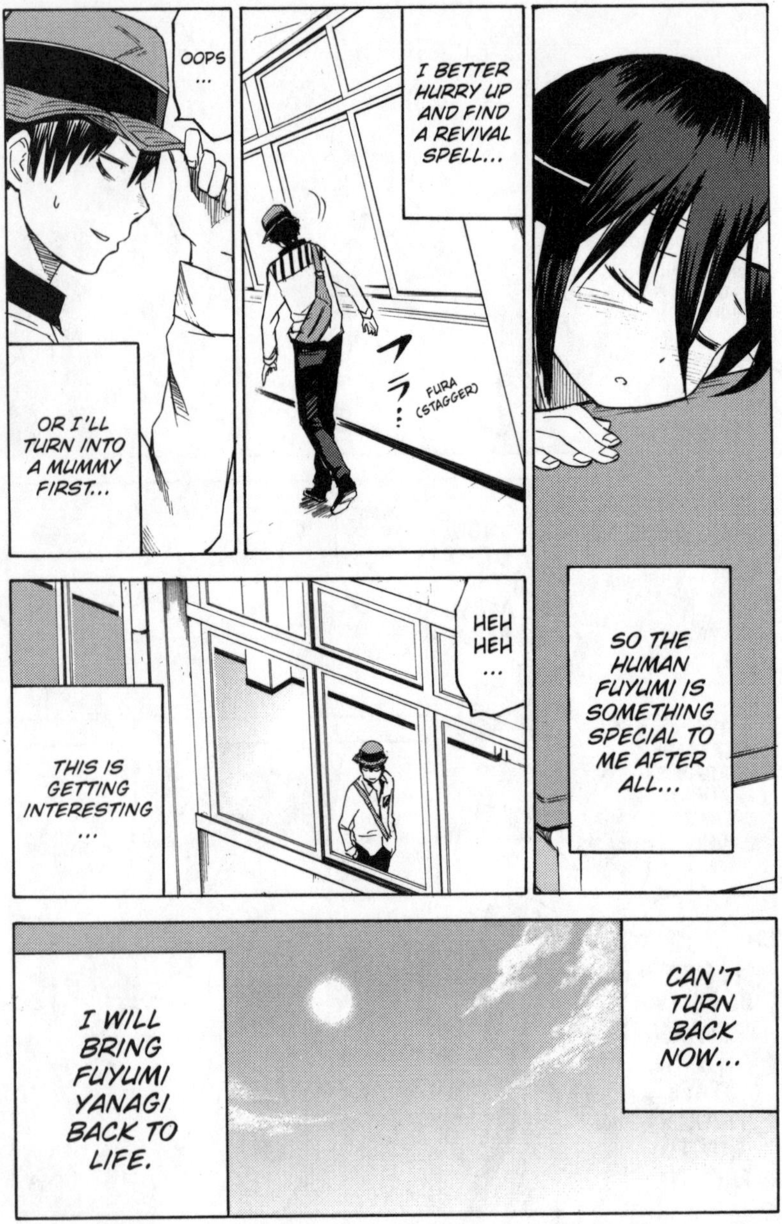
SO THE HUMAN FUYUMI IS SOMETHING SPECIAL TO ME AFTER ALL...
I BETTER HURRY UP AND FIND A REVIVAL SPELL...
FURA (STAGGER)
OOPS ...
OR I'LL TURN INTO A MUMMY FIRST...
HEH HEH ...
THIS IS GETTING INTERESTING ...
CAN'T TURN BACK NOW...
I WILL BRING FUYUMI YANAGI BACK TO LIFE.

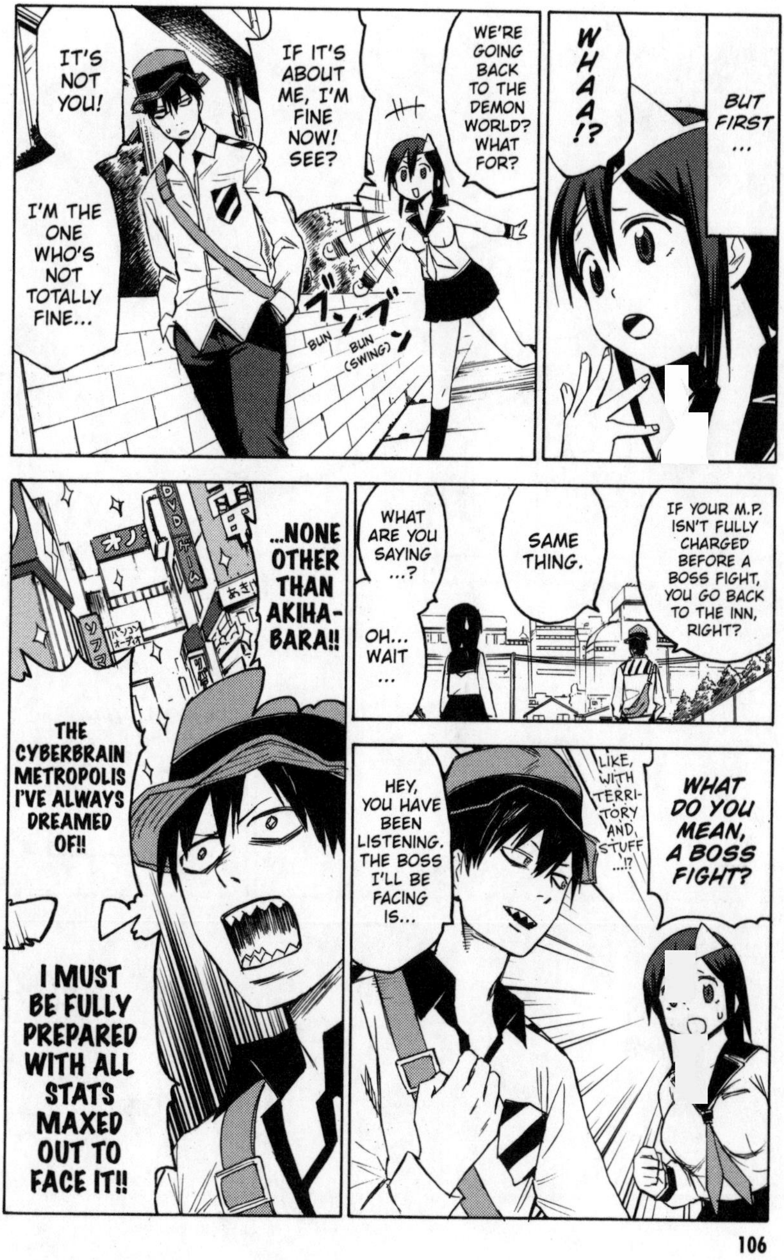
BUT FIRST...
WHAA!?
WE'RE GOING BACK TO THE DEMON WORLD? WHAT FOR?
IF IT'S ABOUT ME, I'M FINE NOW! SEE?
ブン ブン
BUN BUN (SWING)
IT'S NOT YOU!
I'M THE ONE WHO'S NOT TOTALLY FINE...
IF YOUR M.P. ISN'T FULLY CHARGED BEFORE A BOSS FIGHT, YOU GO BACK TO THE INN, RIGHT?
SAME THING.
WHAT ARE YOU SAYING...?
OH... WAIT...
WHAT DO YOU MEAN, A BOSS FIGHT?
LIKE, WITH TERRITORY AND STUFF...!?
HEY, YOU HAVE BEEN LISTENING. THE BOSS I'LL BE FACING IS...
...NONE OTHER THAN AKIHABARA!!
THE CYBERBRAIN METROPOLIS I'VE ALWAYS DREAMED OF!!
I MUST BE FULLY PREPARED WITH ALL STATS MAXED OUT TO FACE IT!!

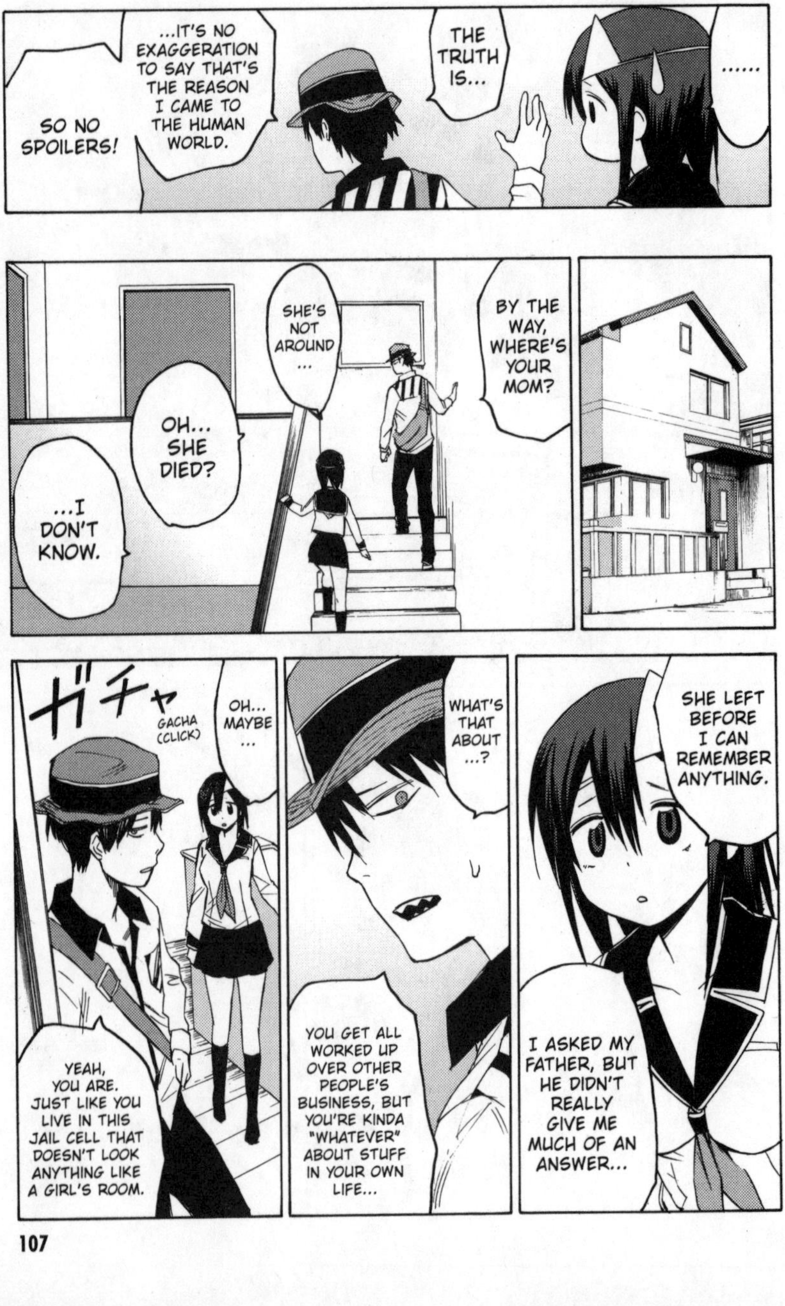
......
THE TRUTH IS...
...IT'S NO EXAGGERATION TO SAY THAT'S THE REASON I CAME TO THE HUMAN WORLD.
SO NO SPOILERS!
BY THE WAY, WHERE'S YOUR MOM?
SHE'S NOT AROUND...
OH... SHE DIED?
...I DON'T KNOW.
SHE LEFT BEFORE I CAN REMEMBER ANYTHING.
I ASKED MY FATHER, BUT HE DIDN'T REALLY GIVE ME MUCH OF AN ANSWER...
WHAT'S THAT ABOUT...?
YOU GET ALL WORKED UP OVER OTHER PEOPLE'S BUSINESS, BUT YOU'RE KINDA "WHATEVER" ABOUT STUFF IN YOUR OWN LIFE...
ガチャ
GACHA (CLICK)
OH... MAYBE...
YEAH, YOU ARE. JUST LIKE YOU LIVE IN THIS JAIL CELL THAT DOESN'T LOOK ANYTHING LIKE A GIRL'S ROOM.

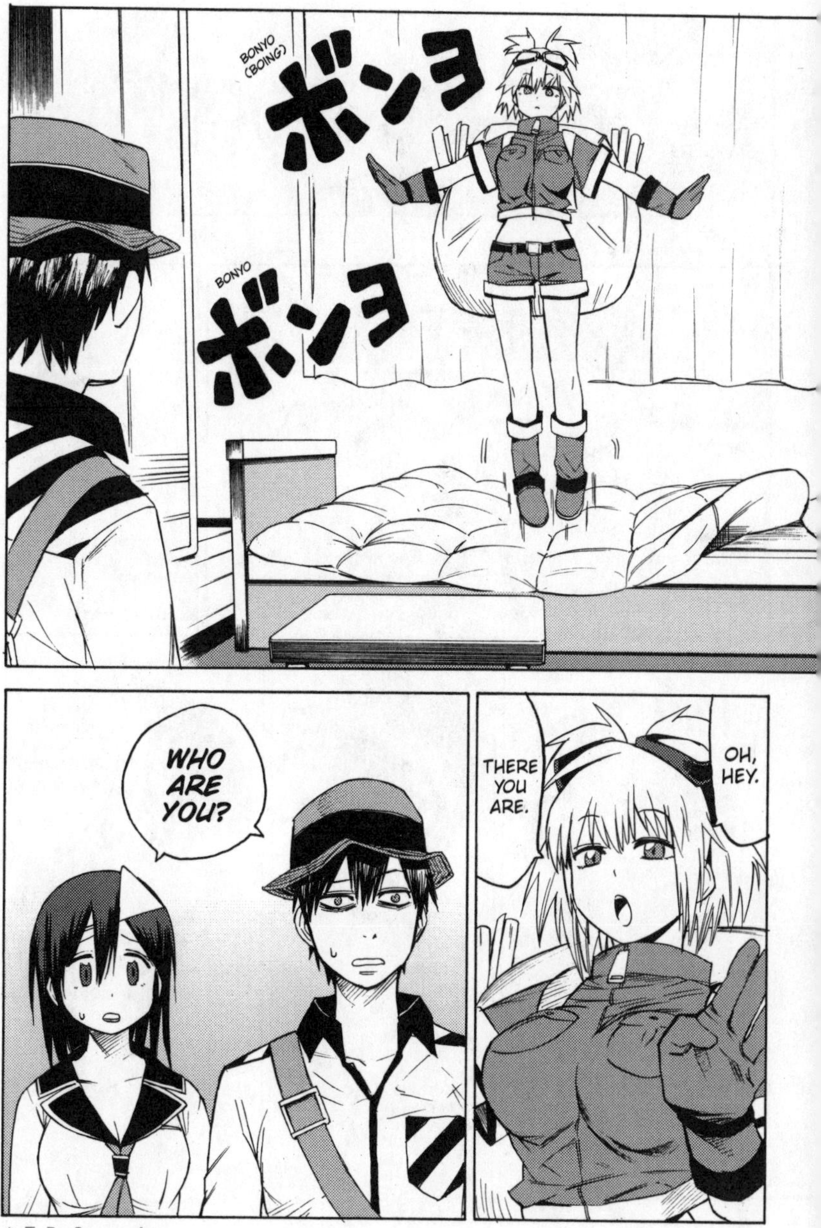
BONYO (BOING)
ボンヨ
BONYO
ボンヨ
OH, HEY.
THERE YOU ARE.
WHO ARE YOU?

♠ To Be Continued ♠

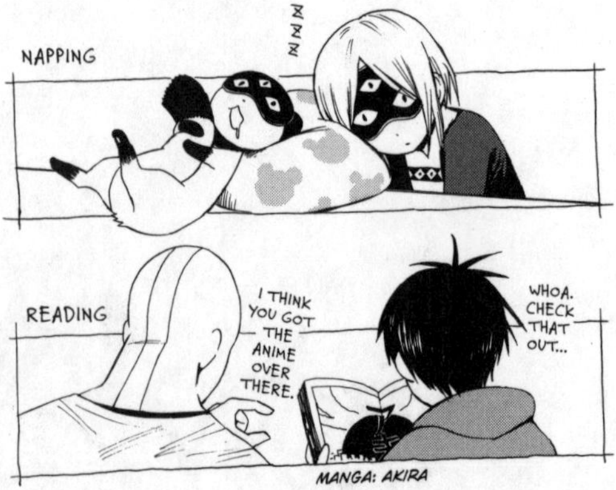
NAPPING
ZZZ
READING
WHOA. CHECK THAT OUT...
I THINK YOU GOT THE ANIME OVER THERE.

MANGA: AKIRA

BLOOD LAD

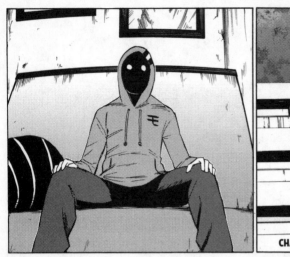

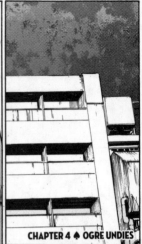

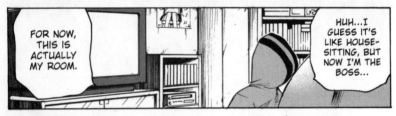

CHAPTER 4 ♠ OGRE UNDIES
HUH...I GUESS IT'S LIKE HOUSE-SITTING, BUT NOW I'M THE BOSS...
FOR NOW, THIS IS ACTUALLY MY ROOM.
MAN, THE BOSS WENT ALL-OUT ON HIS LIBRARY!!
ALL THESE GAMES AND DVDs HE ORDERED FROM THE HUMAN WORLD!!
AND THE ELECTRONICS ARE ALL JAPANESE!!
DISCERNING AND ALL-OUT!!

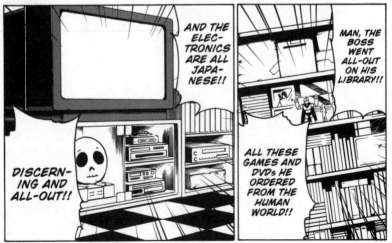

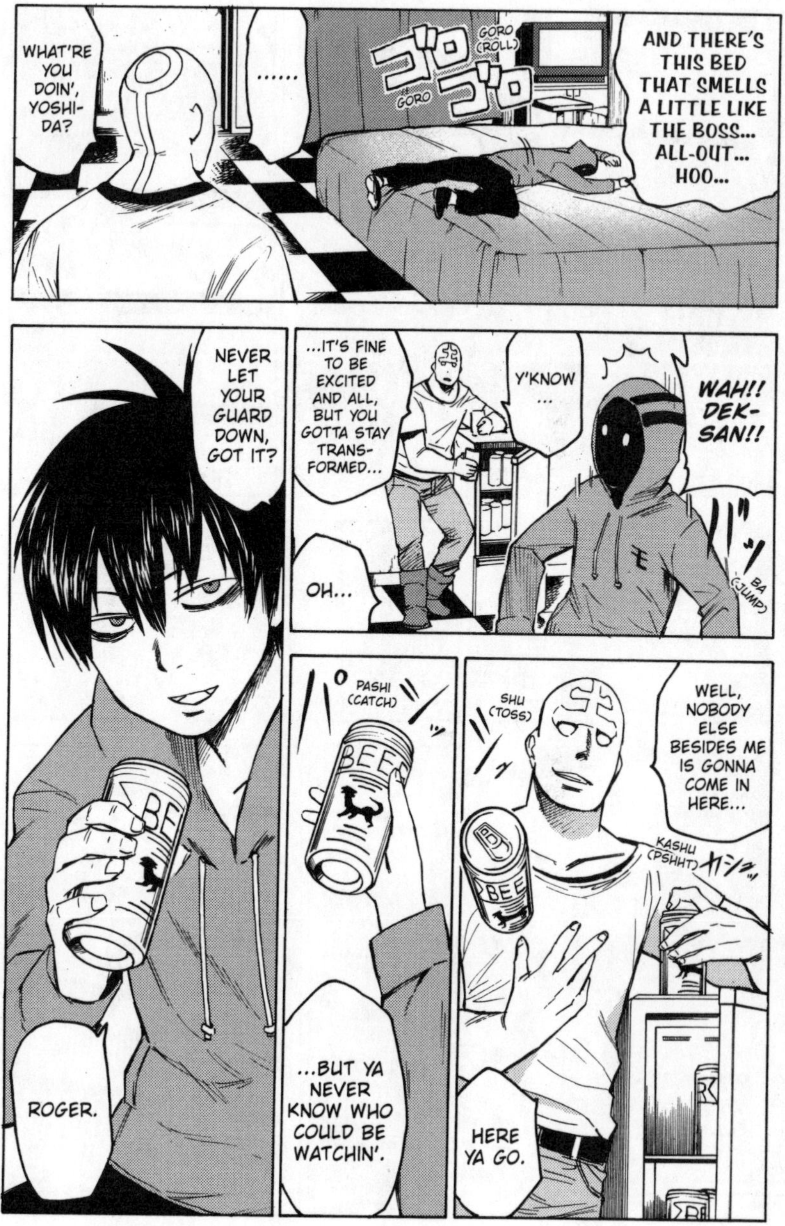
AND THERE'S THIS BED THAT SMELLS A LITTLE LIKE THE BOSS... ALL-OUT... HOO...
GORO (ROLL)
GORO
......
WHAT'RE YOU DOIN', YOSHIDA?
WAH!! DEK-SAN!!
Y'KNOW ...
BA (JUMP)
...IT'S FINE TO BE EXCITED AND ALL, BUT YOU GOTTA STAY TRANSFORMED...
OH...
WELL, NOBODY ELSE BESIDES ME IS GONNA COME IN HERE...
SHU (TOSS)
KASHU (PSHHT)
HERE YA GO.
PASHI (CATCH)
...BUT YA NEVER KNOW WHO COULD BE WATCHIN'.
NEVER LET YOUR GUARD DOWN, GOT IT?
ROGER.

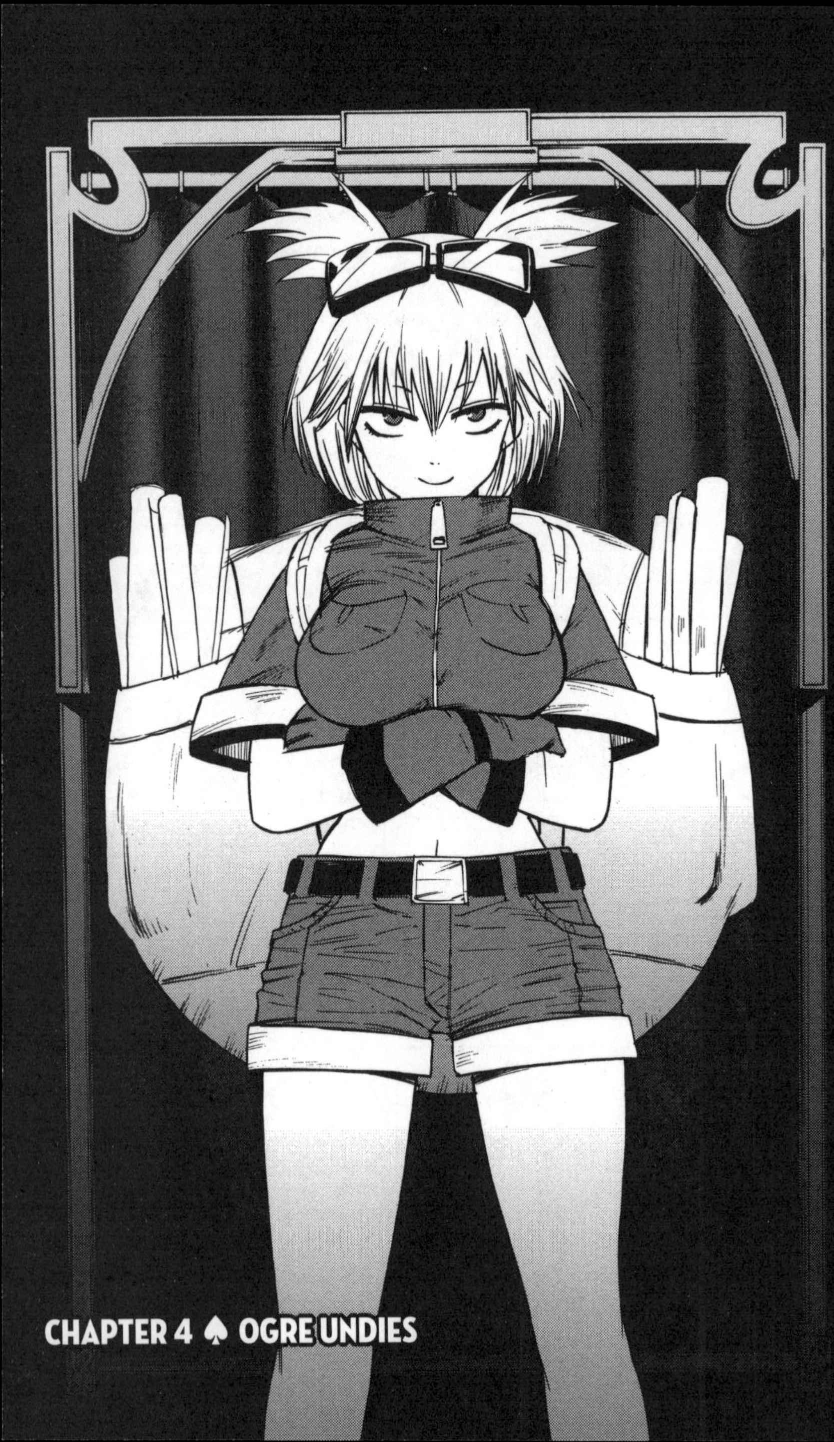

# CHAPTER 4 ♠ OGRE UNDIES

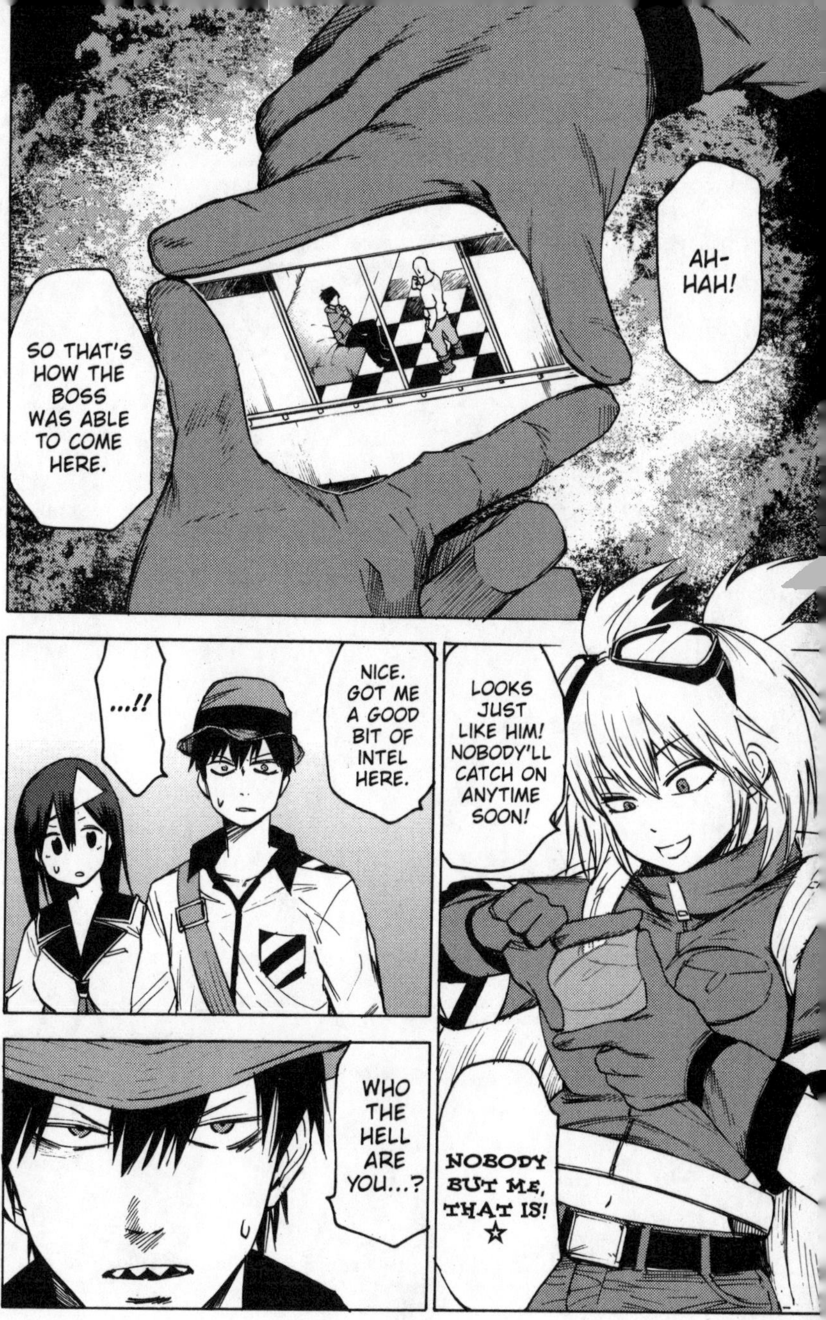
AH-HAH!
SO THAT'S HOW THE BOSS WAS ABLE TO COME HERE.
LOOKS JUST LIKE HIM! NOBODY'LL CATCH ON ANYTIME SOON!
NOBODY BUT ME, THAT IS! ☆
NICE. GOT ME A GOOD BIT OF INTEL HERE.
...!!
WHO THE HELL ARE YOU...?

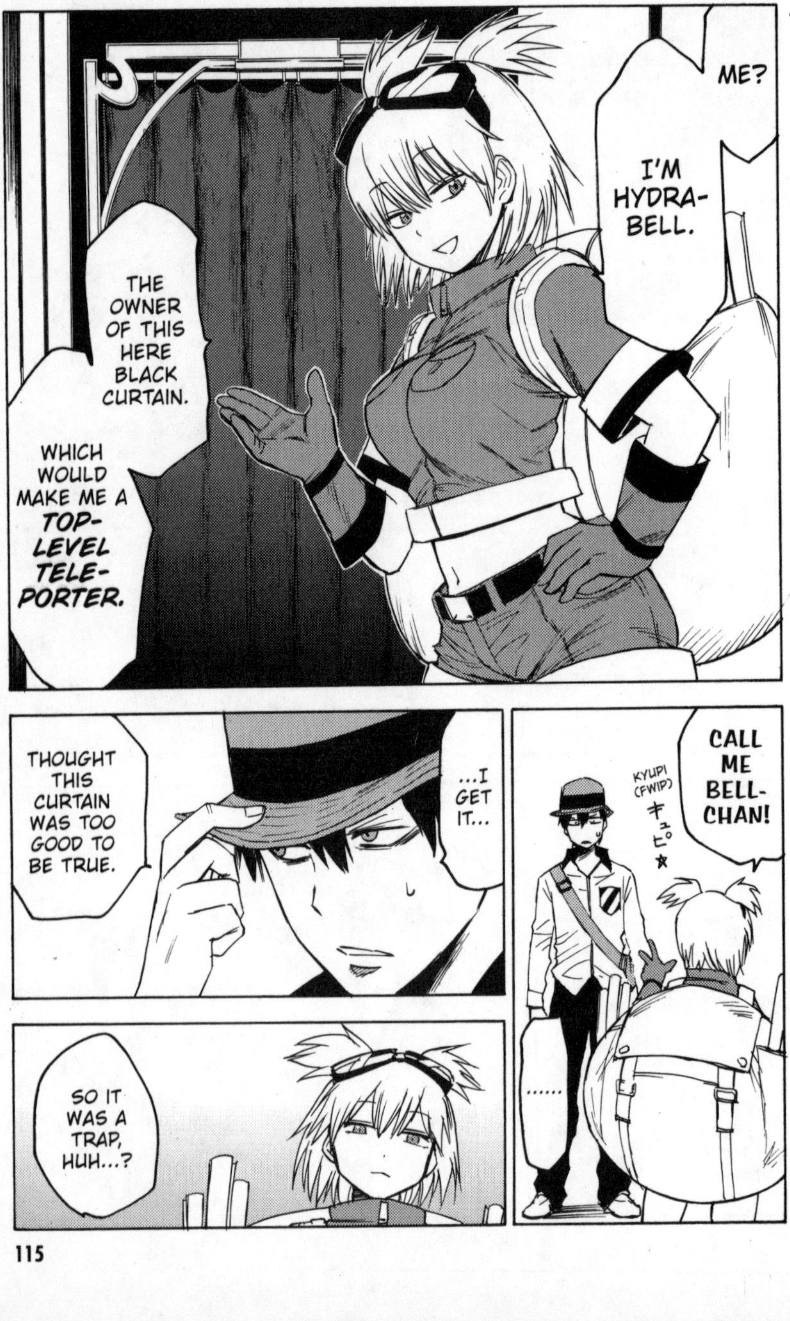
ME?
I'M HYDRA-BELL.
THE OWNER OF THIS HERE BLACK CURTAIN.
WHICH WOULD MAKE ME A *TOP-LEVEL TELE-PORTER.*
CALL ME BELL-CHAN!
KYUPI (FWIP) キュピ☆
......
...I GET IT...
THOUGHT THIS CURTAIN WAS TOO GOOD TO BE TRUE.
SO IT WAS A TRAP, HUH...?

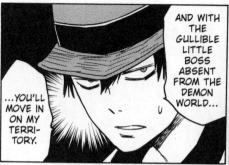

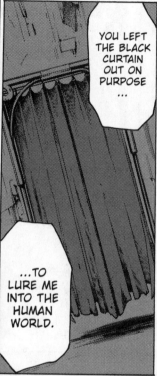

YOU LEFT THE BLACK CURTAIN OUT ON PURPOSE ...
...TO LURE ME INTO THE HUMAN WORLD.
AND WITH THE GULLIBLE LITTLE BOSS ABSENT FROM THE DEMON WORLD...
...YOU'LL MOVE IN ON MY TERRI-TORY.
WAS THAT YOUR CUN-NING PLAN !?
TIME TO EAT!
.........
SORRY, WASN'T LISTEN-ING.
WHAT'S UP?
もぐ もぐ
MOGU (MUNCH)
MOGU
YOU'RE WAY TOO FREE AND EASY ABOUT THIS...
IS THAT... SUPPOSED TO BE...A RICE BALL?
FREE ...
むぐ むぐ
MUGU
MUGU (CHEW)
NOW THERE'S A NICE WORD.

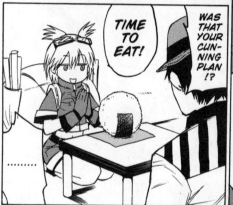

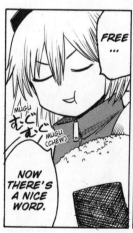

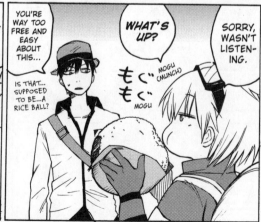

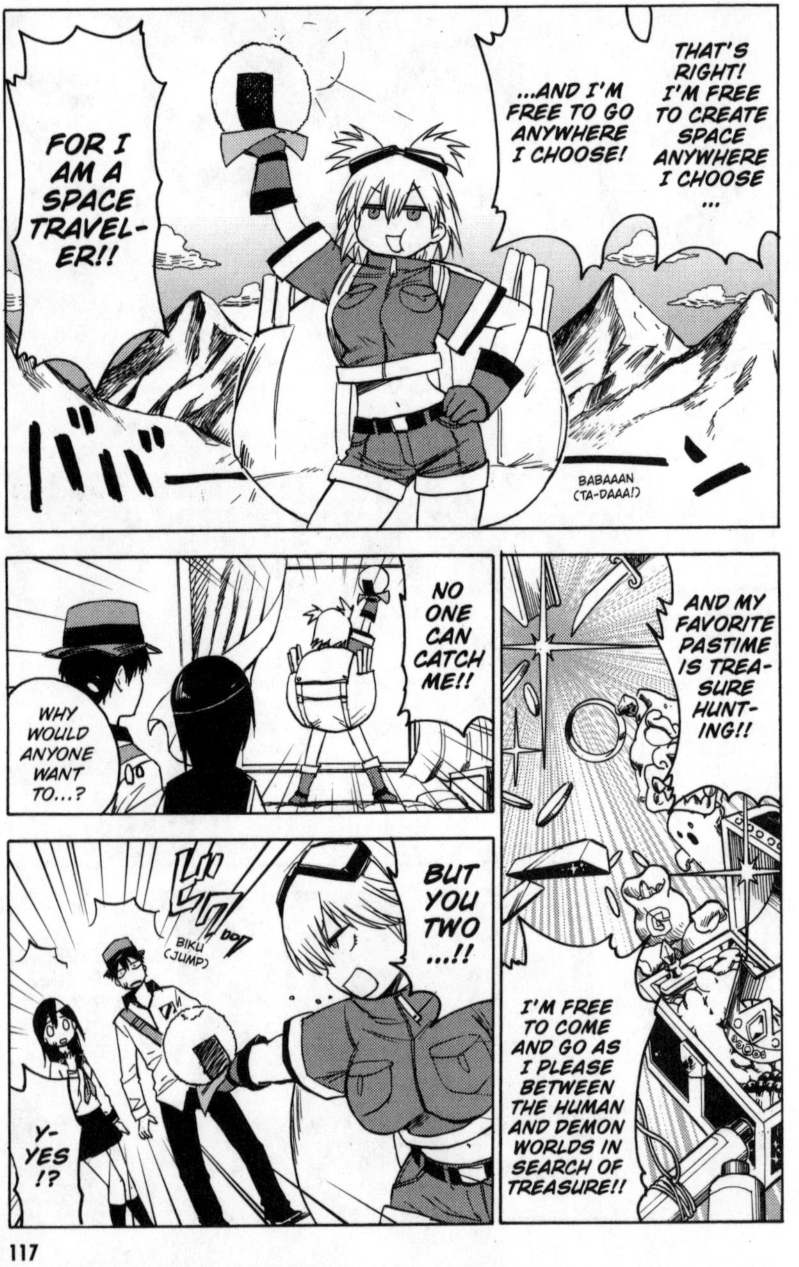
THAT'S RIGHT! I'M FREE TO CREATE SPACE ANYWHERE I CHOOSE ...
...AND I'M FREE TO GO ANYWHERE I CHOOSE!
FOR I AM A SPACE TRAVEL-ER!!
BABAAAN (TA-DAAA!)
AND MY FAVORITE PASTIME IS TREA-SURE HUNT-ING!!
I'M FREE TO COME AND GO AS I PLEASE BETWEEN THE HUMAN AND DEMON WORLDS IN SEARCH OF TREASURE!!
NO ONE CAN CATCH ME!!
WHY WOULD ANYONE WANT TO...?
BUT YOU TWO ...!!
BIKU (JUMP)
Y-YES !?

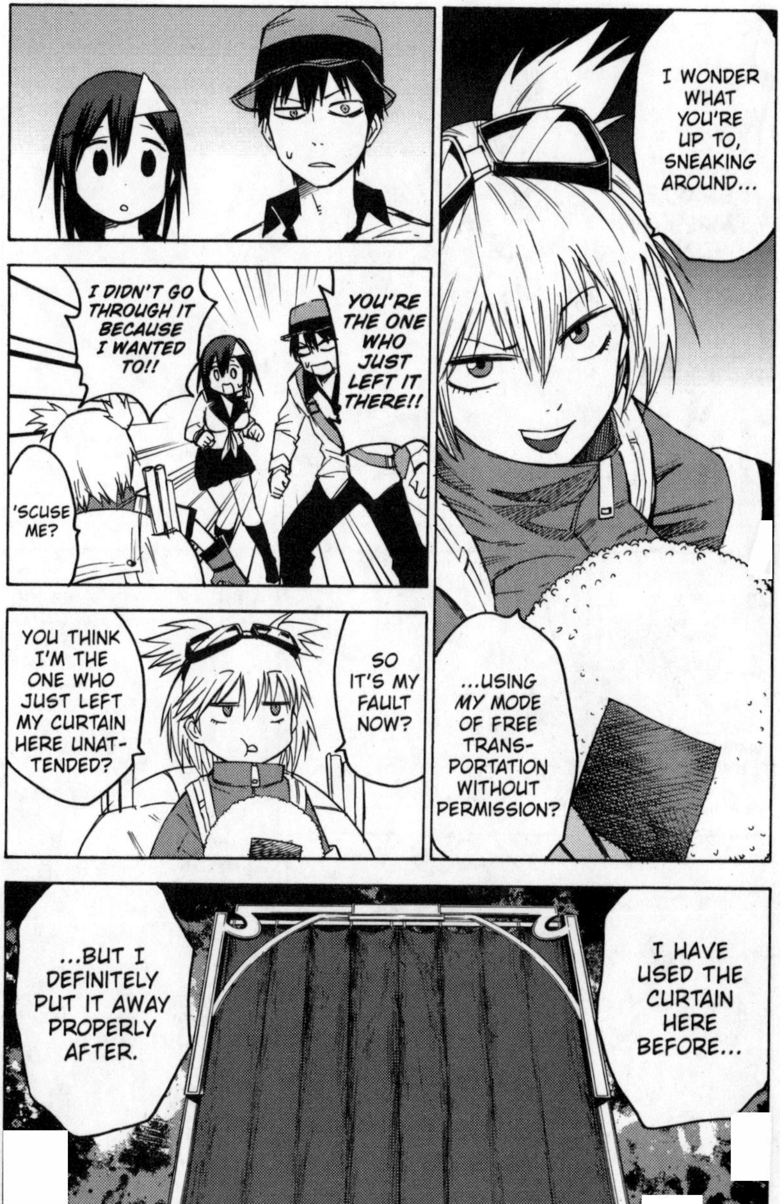
I WONDER WHAT YOU'RE UP TO, SNEAKING AROUND...
...USING MY MODE OF FREE TRANS-PORTATION WITHOUT PERMISSION?
YOU'RE THE ONE WHO JUST LEFT IT THERE!!
I DIDN'T GO THROUGH IT BECAUSE I WANTED TO!!
'SCUSE ME?
SO IT'S MY FAULT NOW?
YOU THINK I'M THE ONE WHO JUST LEFT MY CURTAIN HERE UNAT-TENDED?
I HAVE USED THE CURTAIN HERE BEFORE...
...BUT I DEFINITELY PUT IT AWAY PROPERLY AFTER.

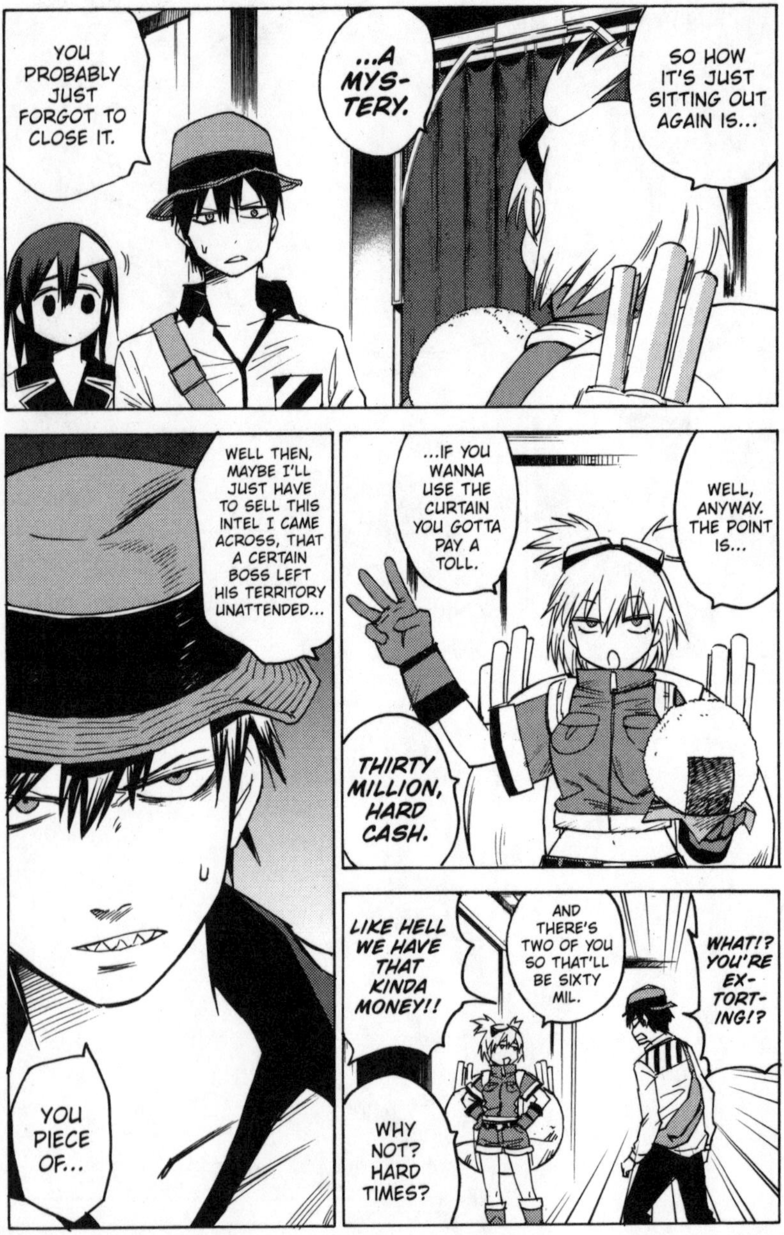
SO HOW IT'S JUST SITTING OUT AGAIN IS...
...A MYS-TERY.
YOU PROBABLY JUST FORGOT TO CLOSE IT.
WELL, ANYWAY. THE POINT IS...
...IF YOU WANNA USE THE CURTAIN YOU GOTTA PAY A TOLL.
THIRTY MILLION, HARD CASH.
WHAT!? YOU'RE EX-TORT-ING!?
AND THERE'S TWO OF YOU SO THAT'LL BE SIXTY MIL.
LIKE HELL WE HAVE THAT KINDA MONEY!!
WHY NOT? HARD TIMES?
WELL THEN, MAYBE I'LL JUST HAVE TO SELL THIS INTEL I CAME ACROSS, THAT A CERTAIN BOSS LEFT HIS TERRITORY UNATTENDED...
YOU PIECE OF...

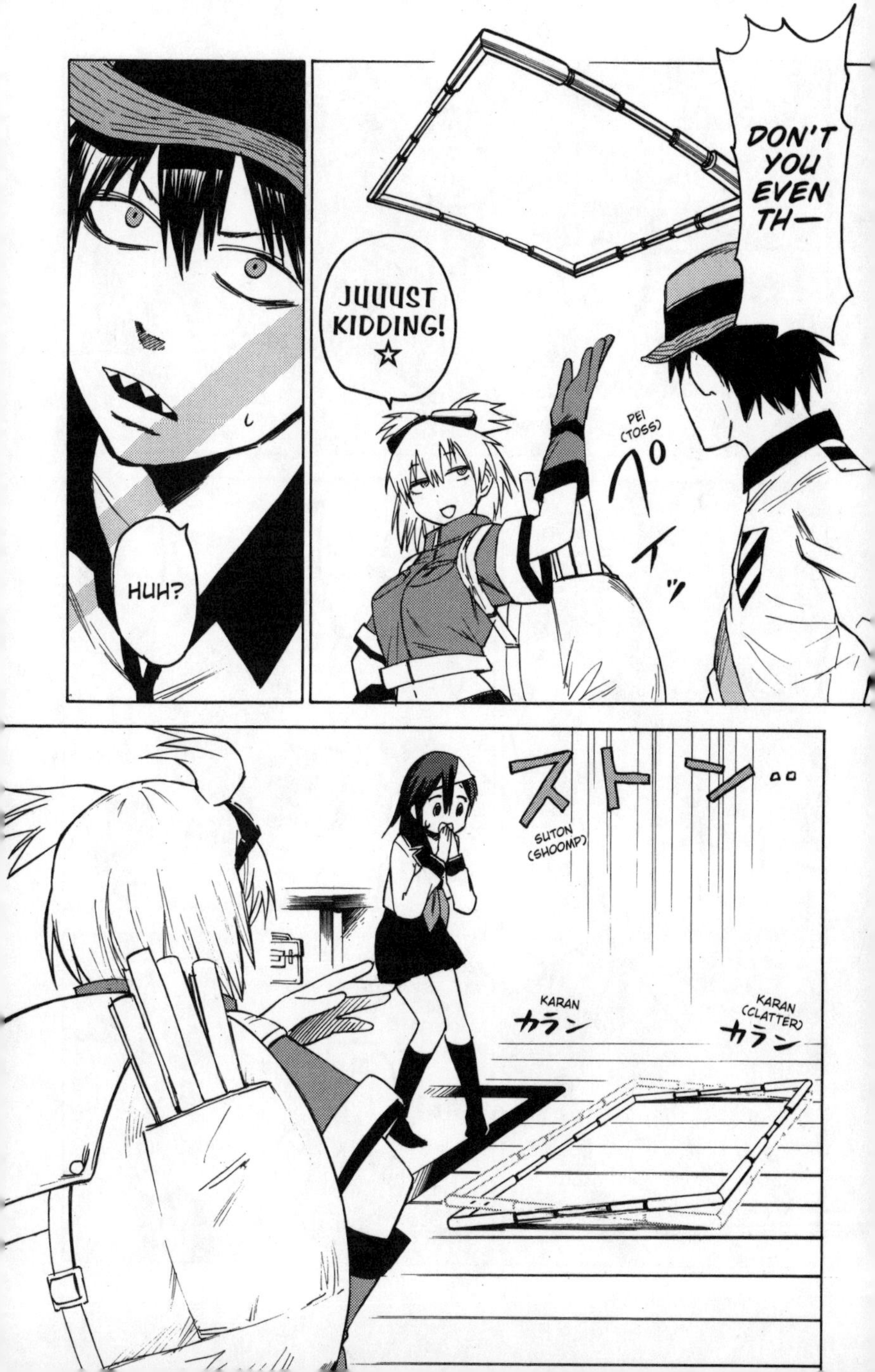

DON'T YOU EVEN TH—
JUUUST KIDDING! ☆
PEI (TOSS)
ペイッ
HUH?
ストーン..
SUTON (SHOOMP)
KARAN (CLATTER)
カラン
KARAN
カラン

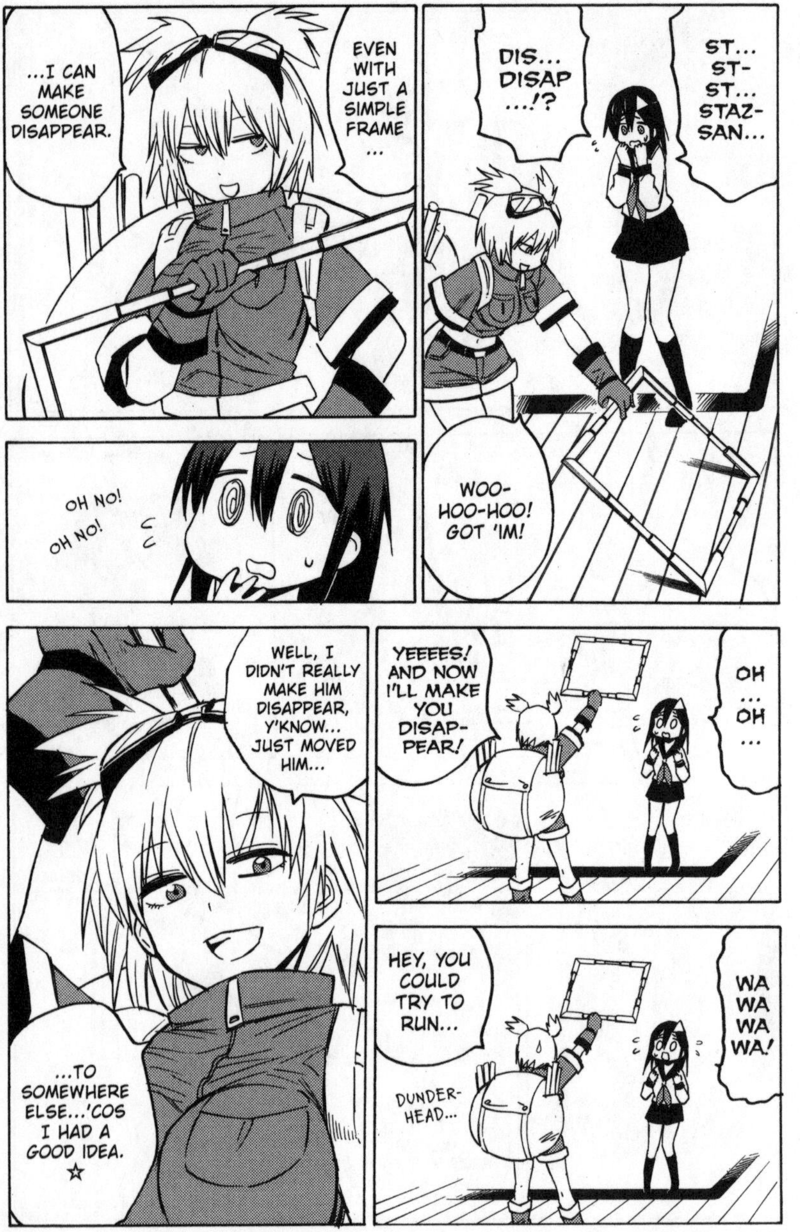
ST... ST- ST... STAZ-SAN...
DIS... DISAP ...!?
WOO-HOO-HOO! GOT 'IM!
EVEN WITH JUST A SIMPLE FRAME ...
...I CAN MAKE SOMEONE DISAPPEAR.
OH NO! OH NO!
OH ... OH ...
YEEEES! AND NOW I'LL MAKE YOU DISAP-PEAR!
WA WA WA WA!
HEY, YOU COULD TRY TO RUN...
DUNDER-HEAD...
WELL, I DIDN'T REALLY MAKE HIM DISAPPEAR, Y'KNOW... JUST MOVED HIM...
...TO SOMEWHERE ELSE...'COS I HAD A GOOD IDEA. ☆

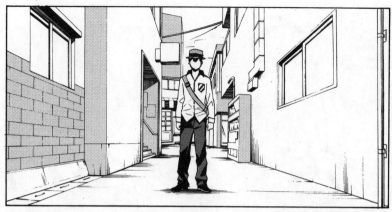

WHERE AM I...?
LOOKS LIKE I'M STILL IN THE HUMAN WORLD, BUT...
THAT BROAD... IS SHE GONNA KEEP ME ...
...FROM GOING BACK TO THE DEMON WORLD SO SHE CAN SELL HER INTEL?
AU CONTRAIRE!☆ THAT LITTLE TIDBIT'D BARELY GET ME SOME POCKET CHANGE.
BA (WHIP)

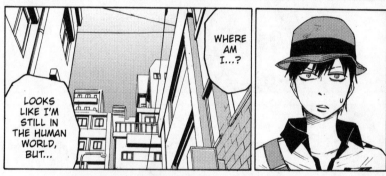

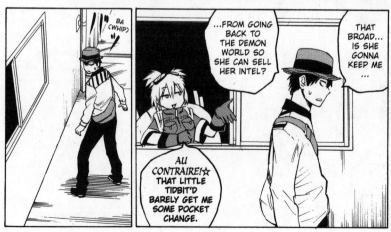

SFX: GASSHA (SMASH)

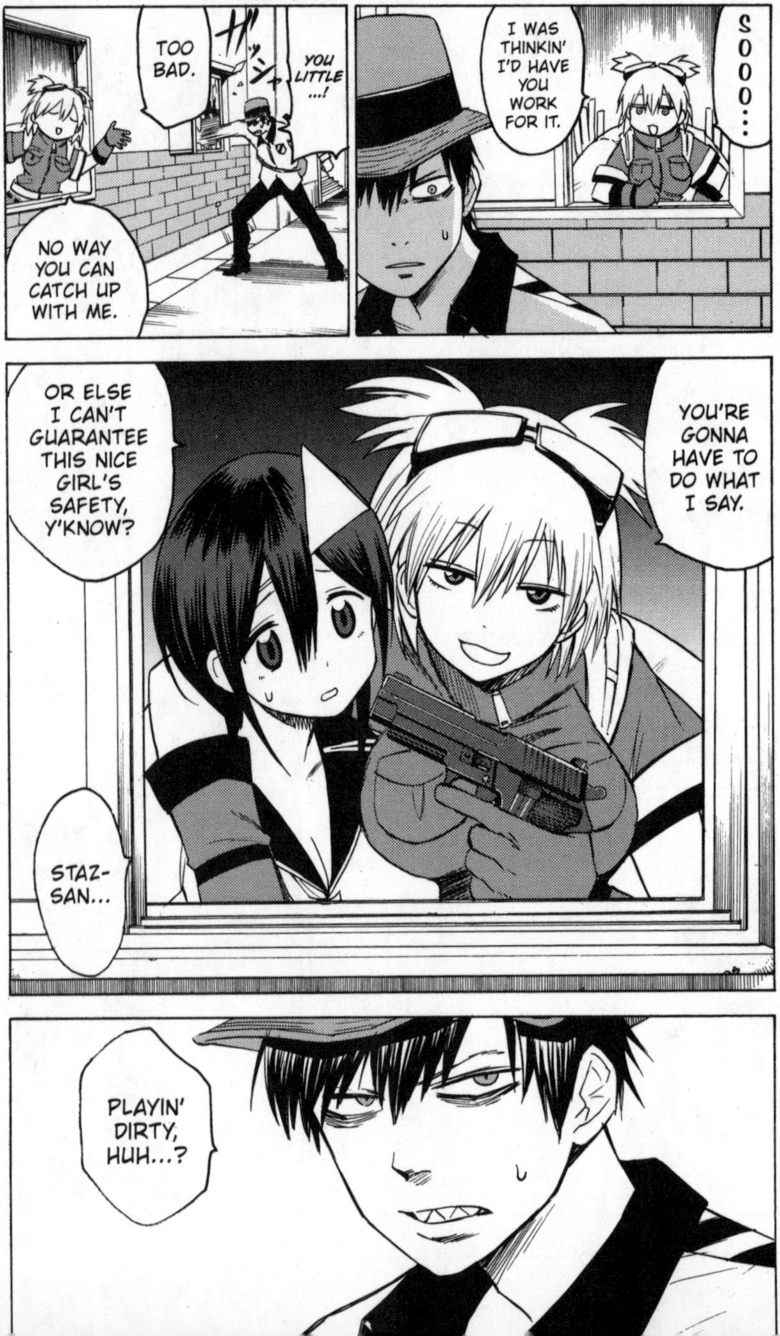
SOOO...
I WAS THINKIN' I'D HAVE YOU WORK FOR IT.
TOO BAD.
YOU LITTLE ...!
NO WAY YOU CAN CATCH UP WITH ME.
YOU'RE GONNA HAVE TO DO WHAT I SAY.
OR ELSE I CAN'T GUARANTEE THIS NICE GIRL'S SAFETY, Y'KNOW?
STAZ-SAN...
PLAYIN' DIRTY, HUH...?

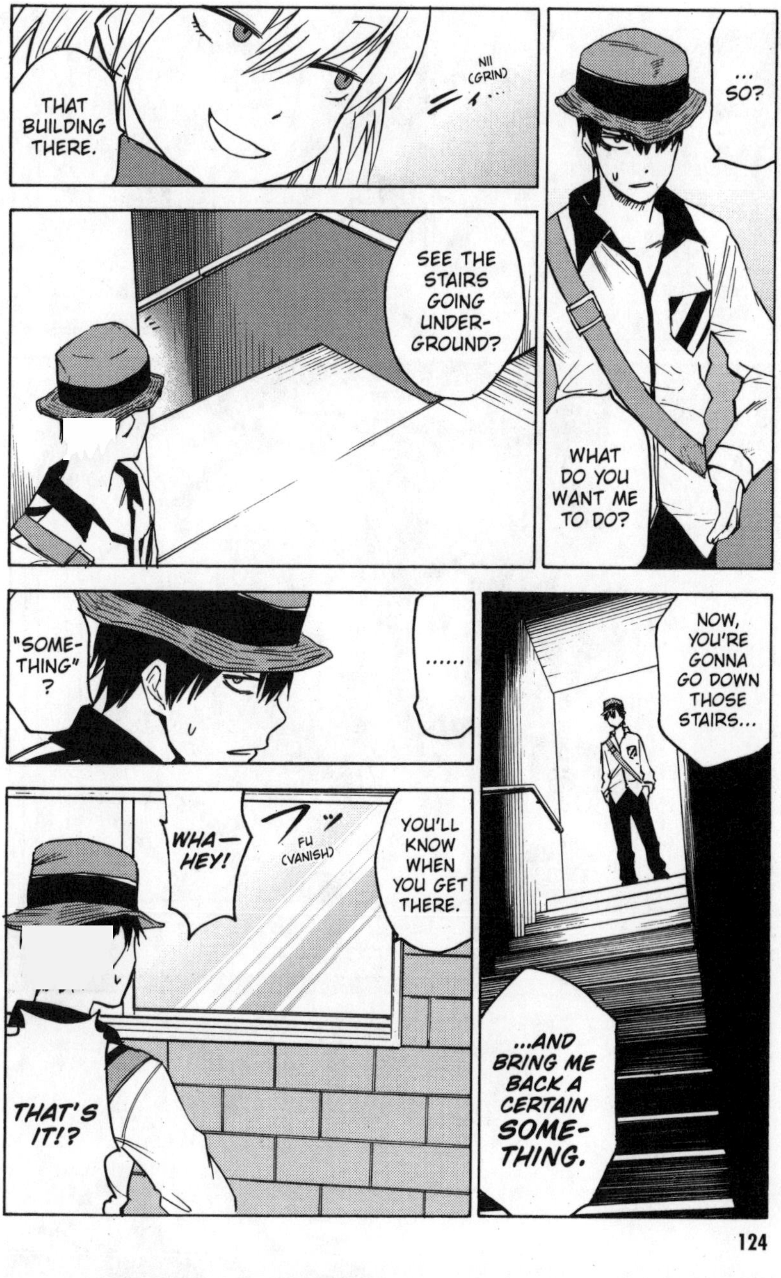
...
SO?
WHAT DO YOU WANT ME TO DO?
NII (GRIN)
THAT BUILDING THERE.
SEE THE STAIRS GOING UNDER-GROUND?
NOW, YOU'RE GONNA GO DOWN THOSE STAIRS...
...AND BRING ME BACK A CERTAIN SOME-THING.
......
"SOME-THING"?
YOU'LL KNOW WHEN YOU GET THERE.
FU (VANISH)
WHA—HEY!
THAT'S IT!?

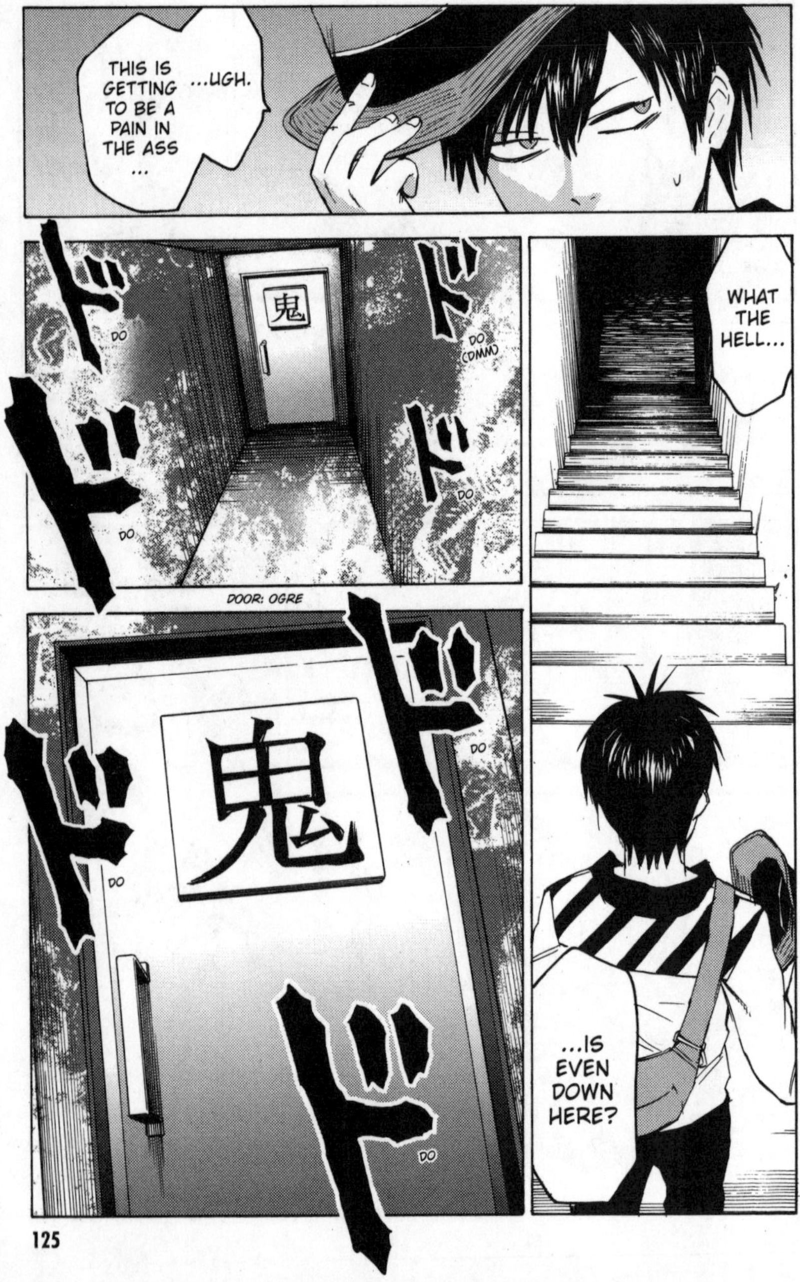
...UGH.
THIS IS GETTING TO BE A PAIN IN THE ASS ...
WHAT THE HELL...
...IS EVEN DOWN HERE?
ド DO (DMM)
ド DO
ド DO
ド DO
鬼
DOOR: OGRE
ド DO
ド DO
ド DO
鬼

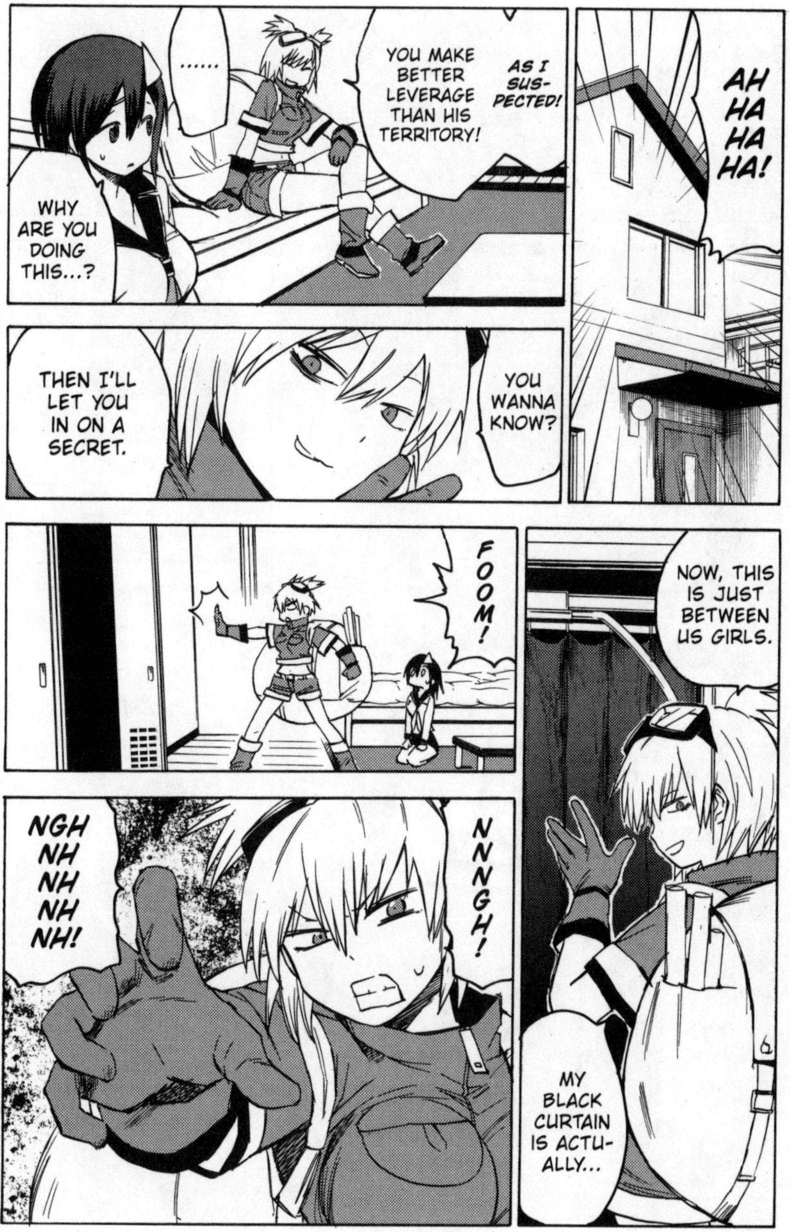
AH HA HA HA!
AS I SUS-PECTED!
YOU MAKE BETTER LEVERAGE THAN HIS TERRITORY!
......
WHY ARE YOU DOING THIS...?
YOU WANNA KNOW?
THEN I'LL LET YOU IN ON A SECRET.
NOW, THIS IS JUST BETWEEN US GIRLS.
MY BLACK CURTAIN IS ACTU-ALLY...
FOOOM!
NNNGH!
NGH NH NH NH NH!

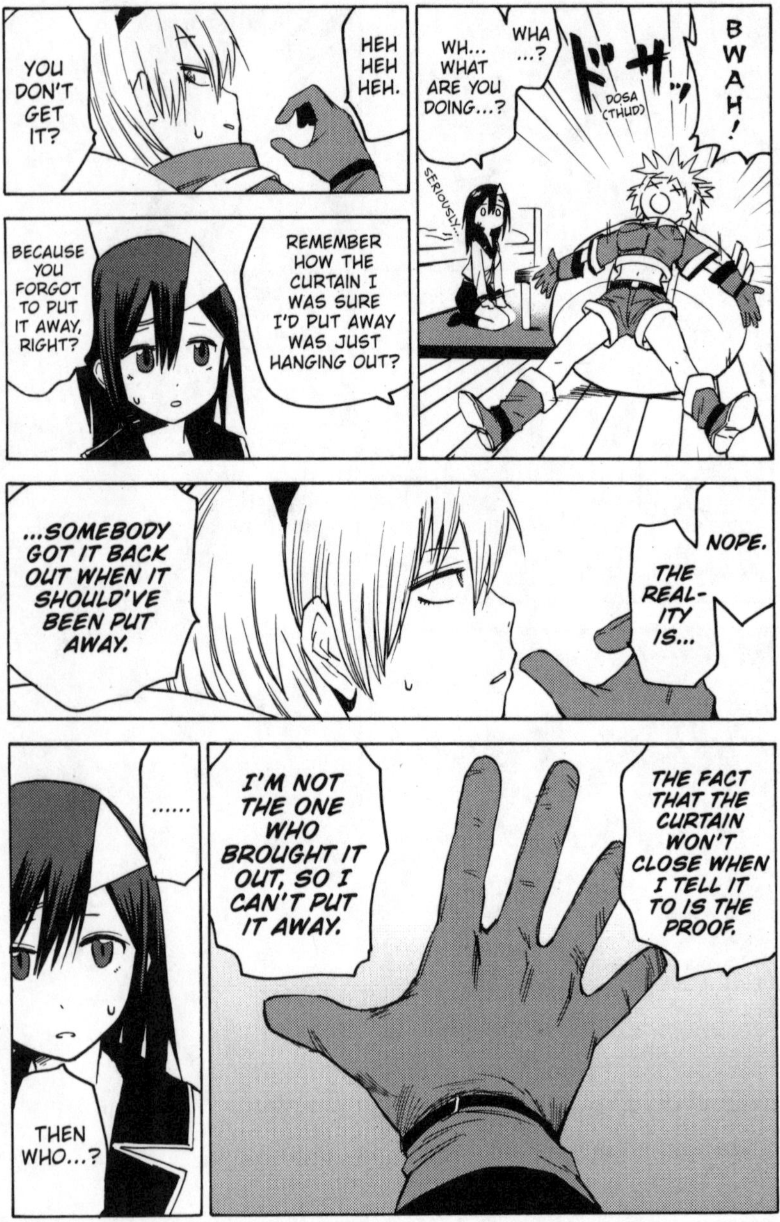
BWAH!
ドサッ
DOSA (THUD)
WHA ...?
WH... WHAT ARE YOU DOING...?
SERIOUSLY...
HEH HEH HEH.
YOU DON'T GET IT?
REMEMBER HOW THE CURTAIN I WAS SURE I'D PUT AWAY WAS JUST HANGING OUT?
BECAUSE YOU FORGOT TO PUT IT AWAY, RIGHT?
NOPE.
THE REALITY IS...
...SOMEBODY GOT IT BACK OUT WHEN IT SHOULD'VE BEEN PUT AWAY.
THE FACT THAT THE CURTAIN WON'T CLOSE WHEN I TELL IT TO IS THE PROOF.
I'M NOT THE ONE WHO BROUGHT IT OUT, SO I CAN'T PUT IT AWAY.
......
THEN WHO...?

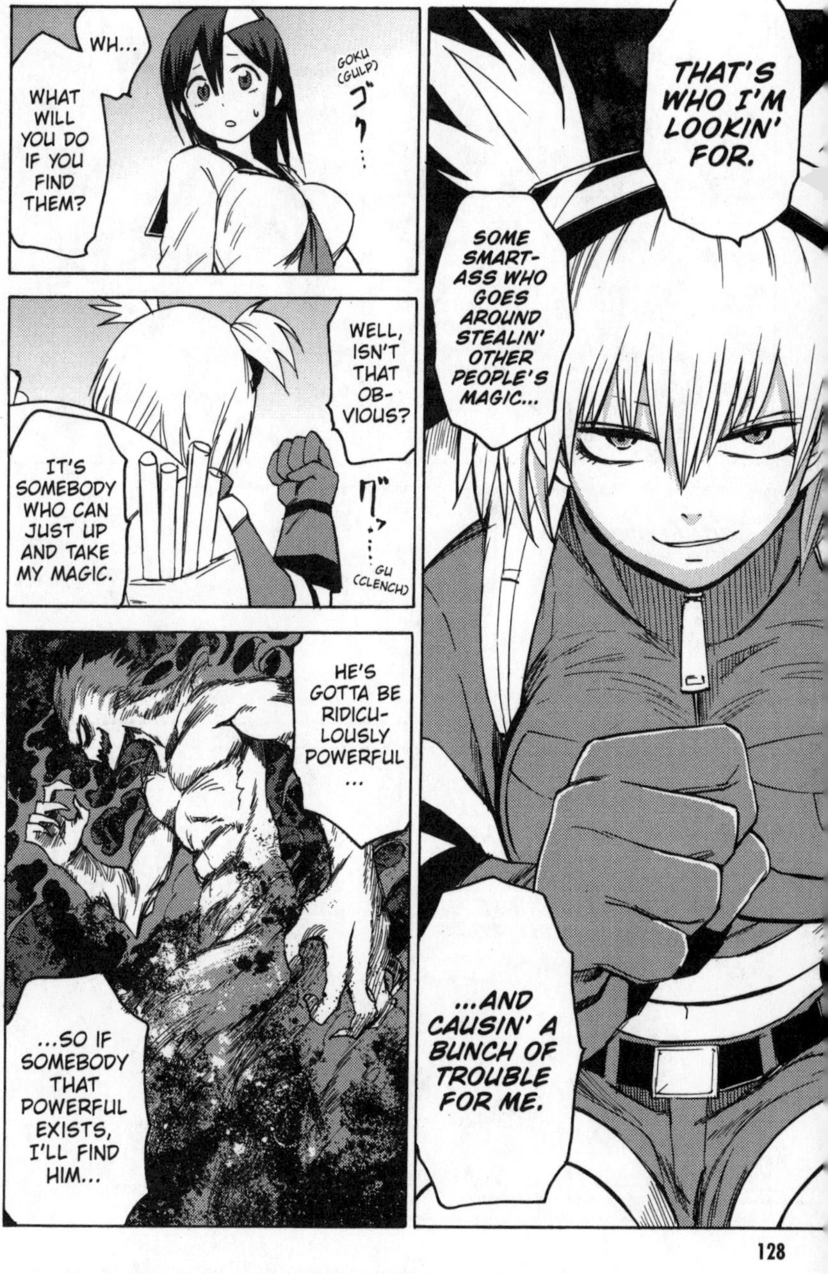
THAT'S WHO I'M LOOKIN' FOR.
SOME SMART-ASS WHO GOES AROUND STEALIN' OTHER PEOPLE'S MAGIC...
...AND CAUSIN' A BUNCH OF TROUBLE FOR ME.
GOKU (GULP)
ゴク…
WH...
WHAT WILL YOU DO IF YOU FIND THEM?
WELL, ISN'T THAT OBVIOUS?
グッ…
GU (CLENCH)
IT'S SOMEBODY WHO CAN JUST UP AND TAKE MY MAGIC.
HE'S GOTTA BE RIDICULOUSLY POWERFUL...
...SO IF SOMEBODY THAT POWERFUL EXISTS, I'LL FIND HIM...

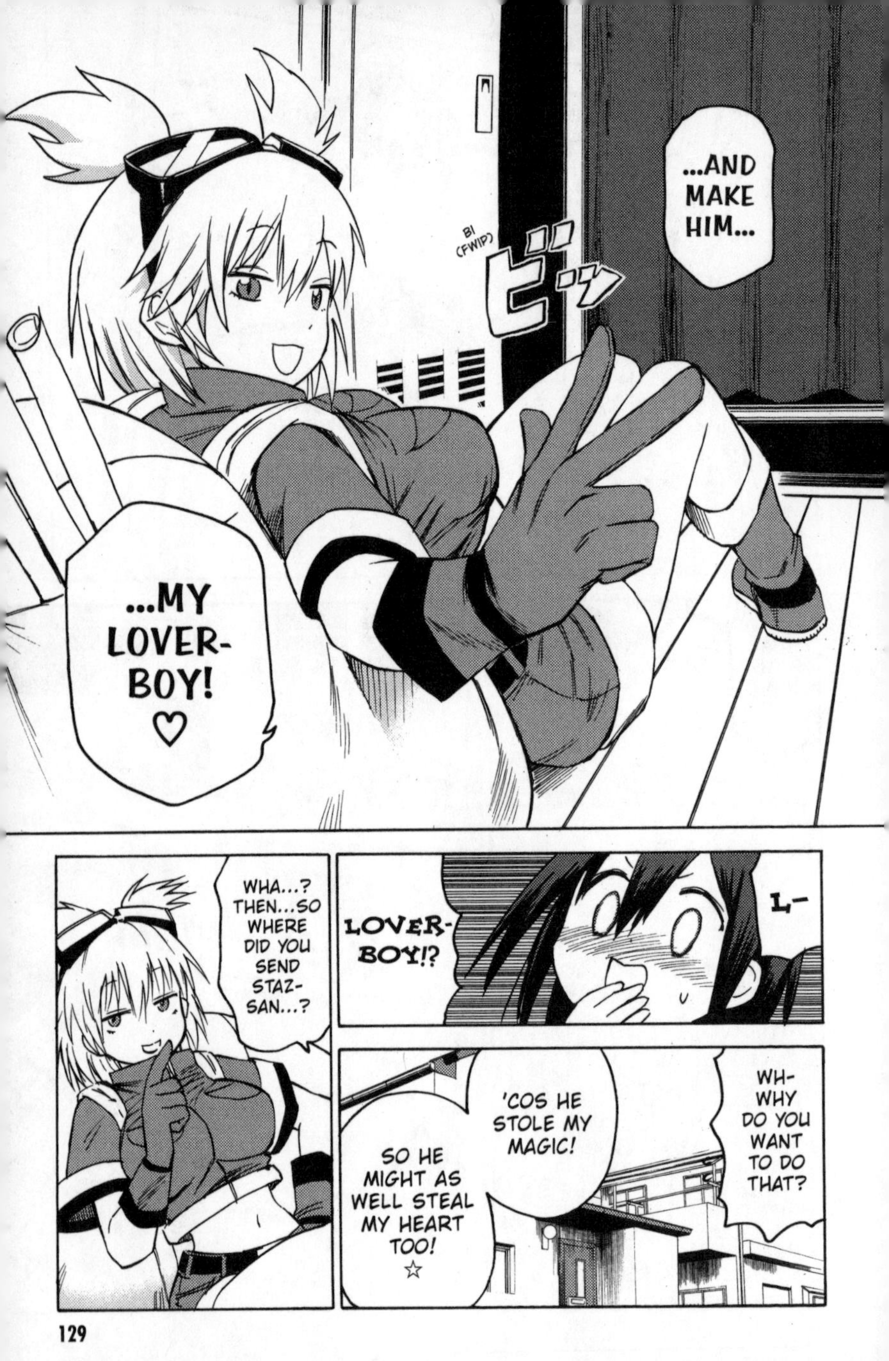
...AND MAKE HIM...
BI (FWIP)
...MY LOVER-BOY! ♡
L,-
LOVER-BOY!?
WH-WHY DO YOU WANT TO DO THAT?
'COS HE STOLE MY MAGIC!
SO HE MIGHT AS WELL STEAL MY HEART TOO! ☆
WHA...? THEN...SO WHERE DID YOU SEND STAZ-SAN...?

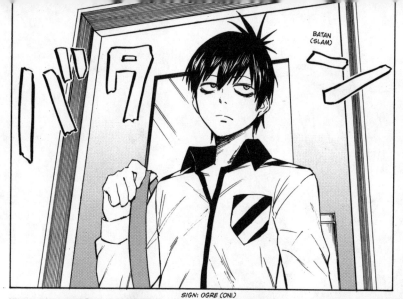

BATAN (SLAM)
SIGN: OGRE (ONI)
WHY, HELLO THERE.
......
WHAT IS THIS JOINT ...?
鬼
OH, IS THIS YOUR FIRST TIME?
BUT YOU DID OPEN THAT DOOR. SO YOU MUST BE A DEMON?

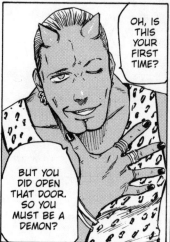

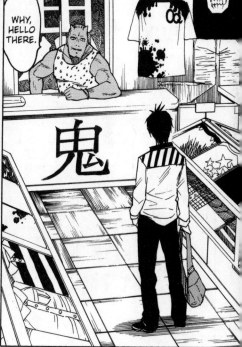

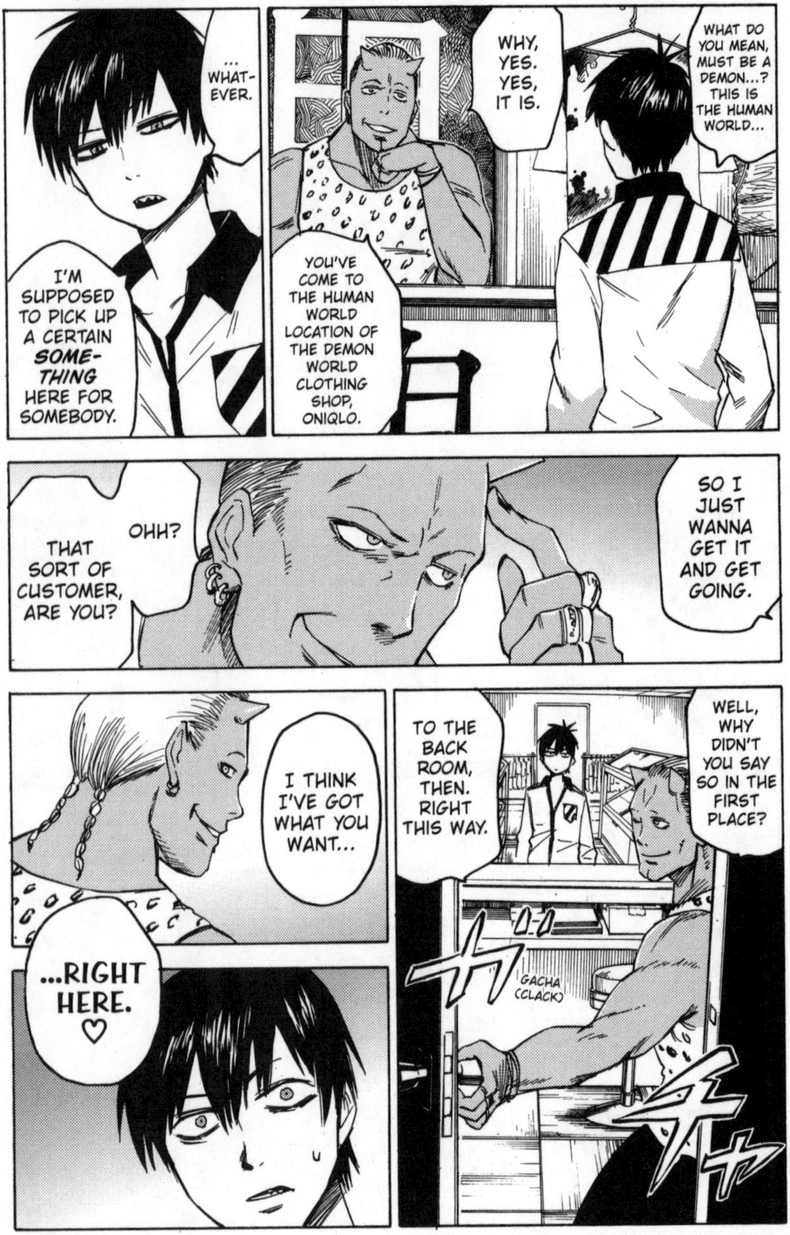
WHAT DO YOU MEAN, MUST BE A DEMON...? THIS IS THE HUMAN WORLD...
WHY, YES. YES, IT IS.
YOU'VE COME TO THE HUMAN WORLD LOCATION OF THE DEMON WORLD CLOTHING SHOP, ONIQLO.
... WHAT-EVER.
I'M SUPPOSED TO PICK UP A CERTAIN *SOME-THING* HERE FOR SOMEBODY.
SO I JUST WANNA GET IT AND GET GOING.
OHH?
THAT SORT OF CUSTOMER, ARE YOU?
WELL, WHY DIDN'T YOU SAY SO IN THE FIRST PLACE?
TO THE BACK ROOM, THEN. RIGHT THIS WAY.
GACHA (CLACK)
I THINK I'VE GOT WHAT YOU WANT...
...RIGHT HERE. ♡

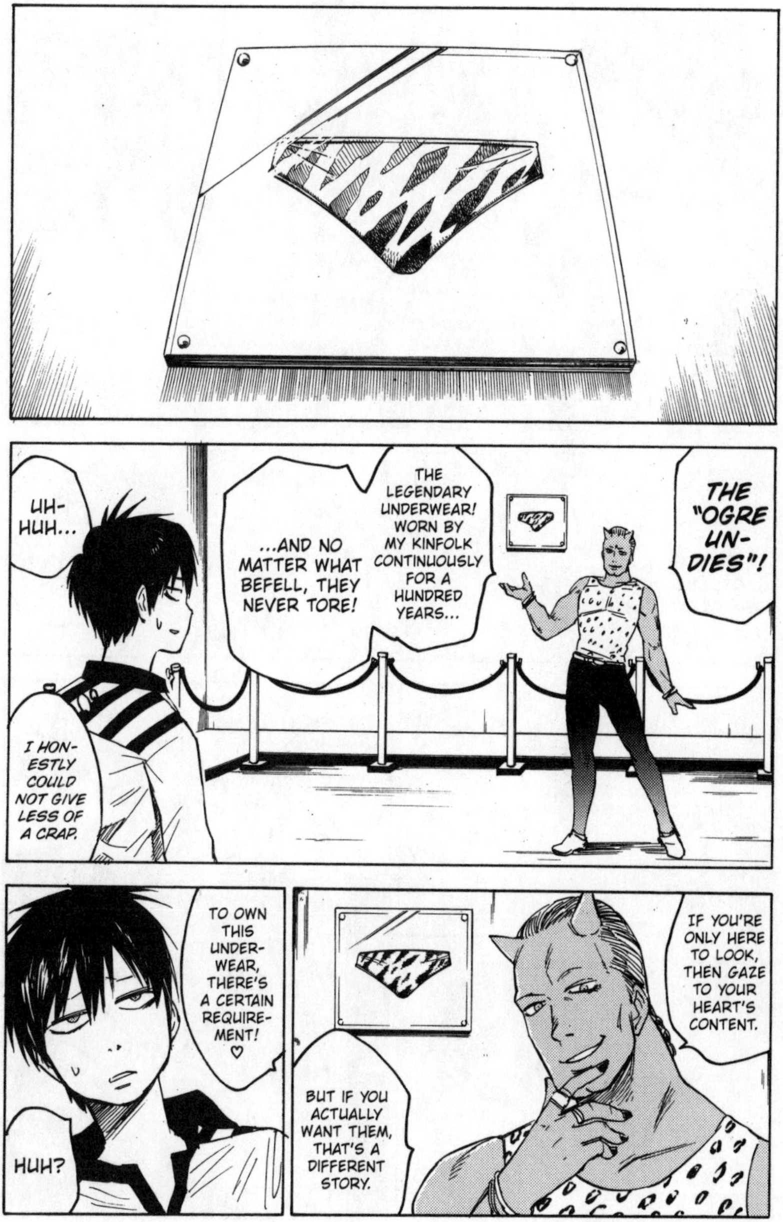
THE "OGRE UNDIES"!
THE LEGENDARY UNDERWEAR! WORN BY MY KINFOLK CONTINUOUSLY FOR A HUNDRED YEARS...
...AND NO MATTER WHAT BEFELL, THEY NEVER TORE!
UH-HUH...
I HONESTLY COULD NOT GIVE LESS OF A CRAP.
IF YOU'RE ONLY HERE TO LOOK, THEN GAZE TO YOUR HEART'S CONTENT.
BUT IF YOU ACTUALLY WANT THEM, THAT'S A DIFFERENT STORY.
TO OWN THIS UNDERWEAR, THERE'S A CERTAIN REQUIREMENT! ♡
HUH?

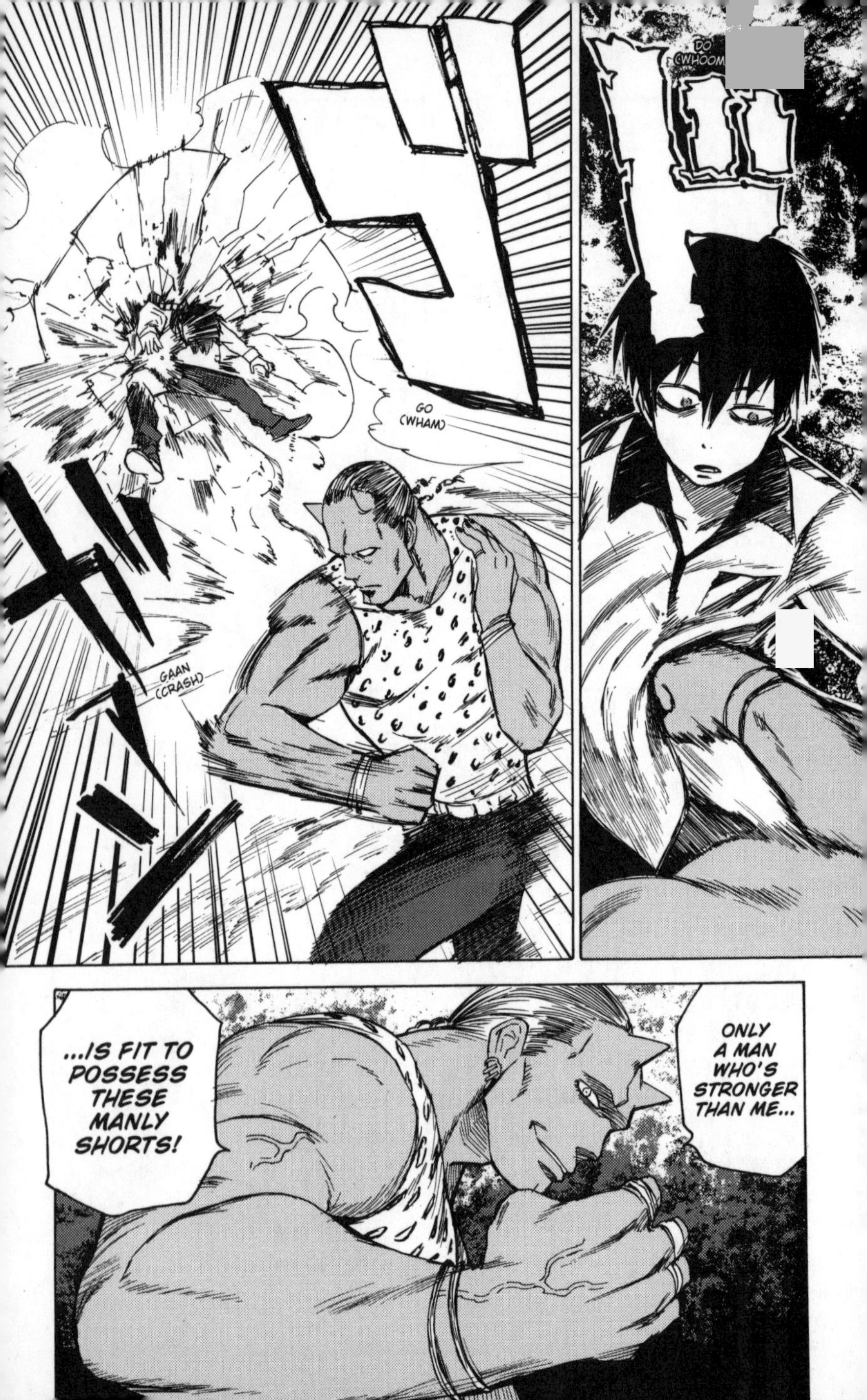
DO (WHOOM)
GO (WHAM)
GAAN (CRASH)
ONLY A MAN WHO'S STRONGER THAN ME...
...IS FIT TO POSSESS THESE MANLY SHORTS!

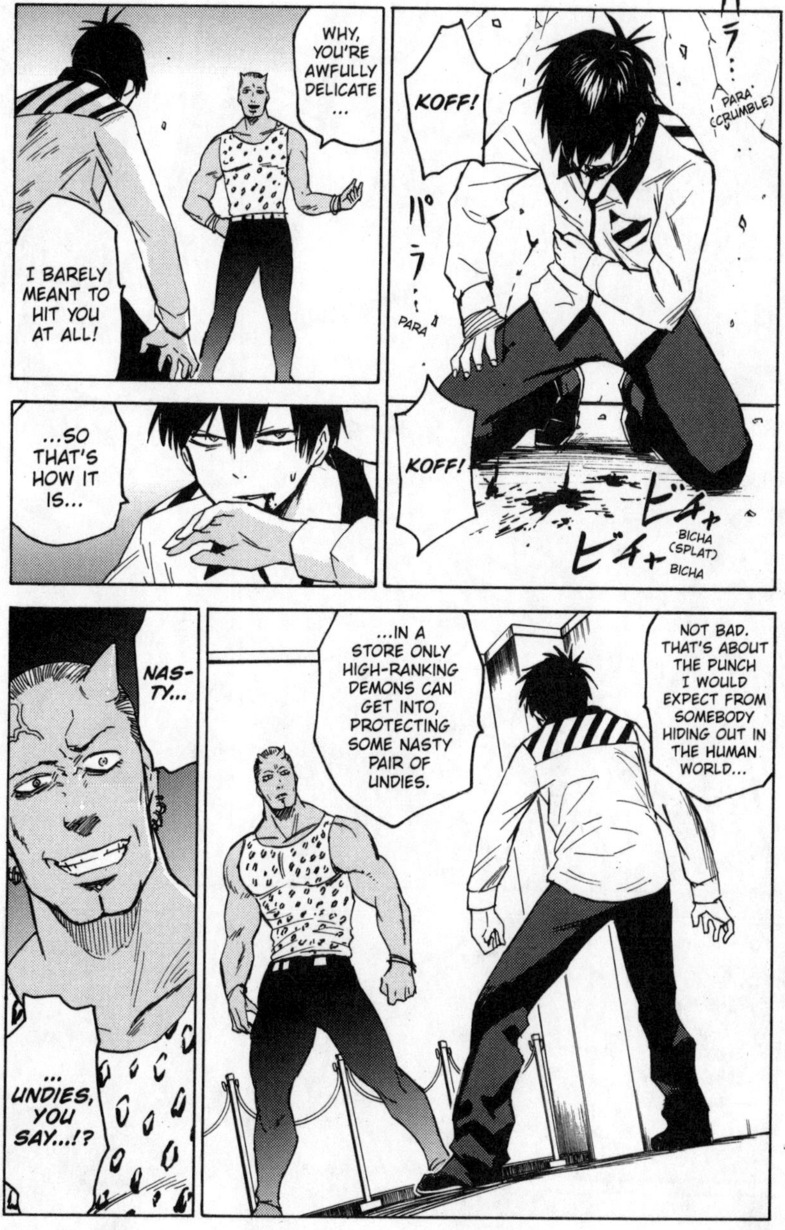
KOFF!
パラ…
PARA PARA (CRUMBLE)
パラ…
PARA
WHY, YOU'RE AWFULLY DELICATE...
I BARELY MEANT TO HIT YOU AT ALL!
KOFF!
ビチャ ビチャ
BICHA (SPLAT) BICHA
...SO THAT'S HOW IT IS...
NOT BAD. THAT'S ABOUT THE PUNCH I WOULD EXPECT FROM SOMEBODY HIDING OUT IN THE HUMAN WORLD...
...IN A STORE ONLY HIGH-RANKING DEMONS CAN GET INTO, PROTECTING SOME NASTY PAIR OF UNDIES.
NAS-TY...
...UNDIES, YOU SAY...!?

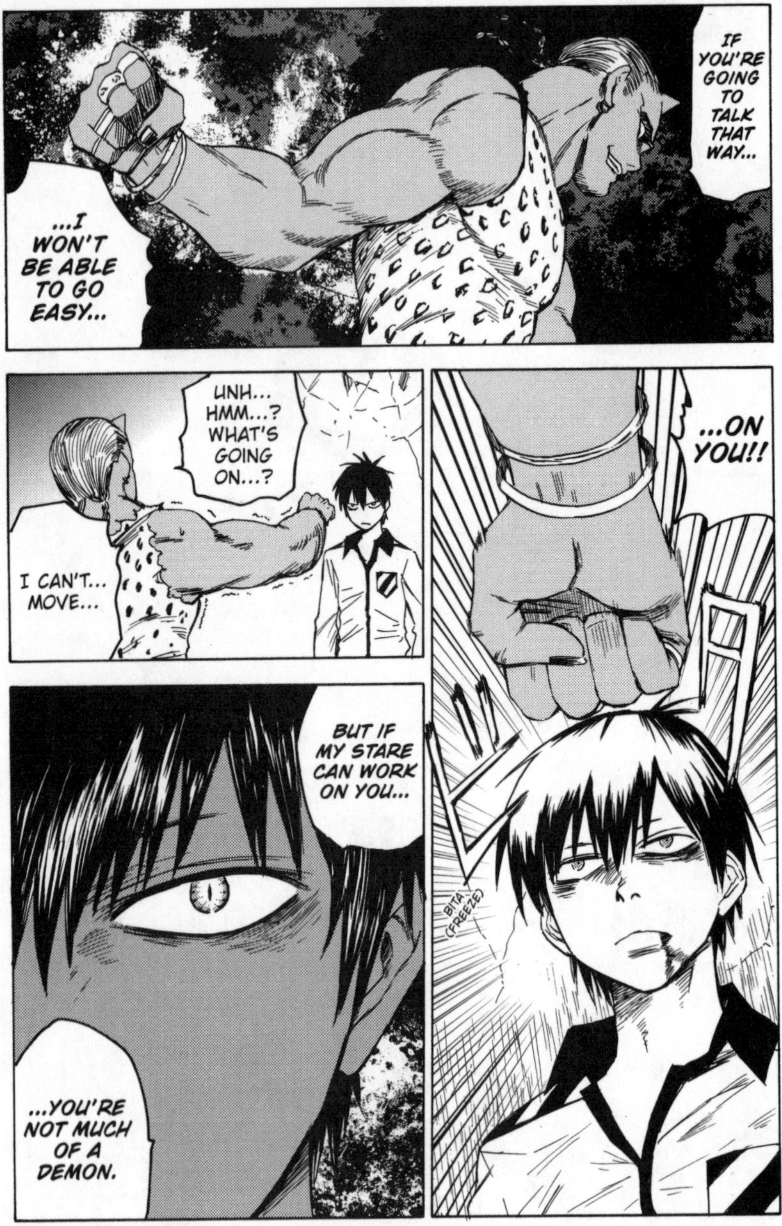
IF YOU'RE GOING TO TALK THAT WAY...
...I WON'T BE ABLE TO GO EASY...
...ON YOU!!
BITA (FREEZE)
UNH... HMM...? WHAT'S GOING ON...?
I CAN'T... MOVE...
BUT IF MY STARE CAN WORK ON YOU...
...YOU'RE NOT MUCH OF A DEMON.

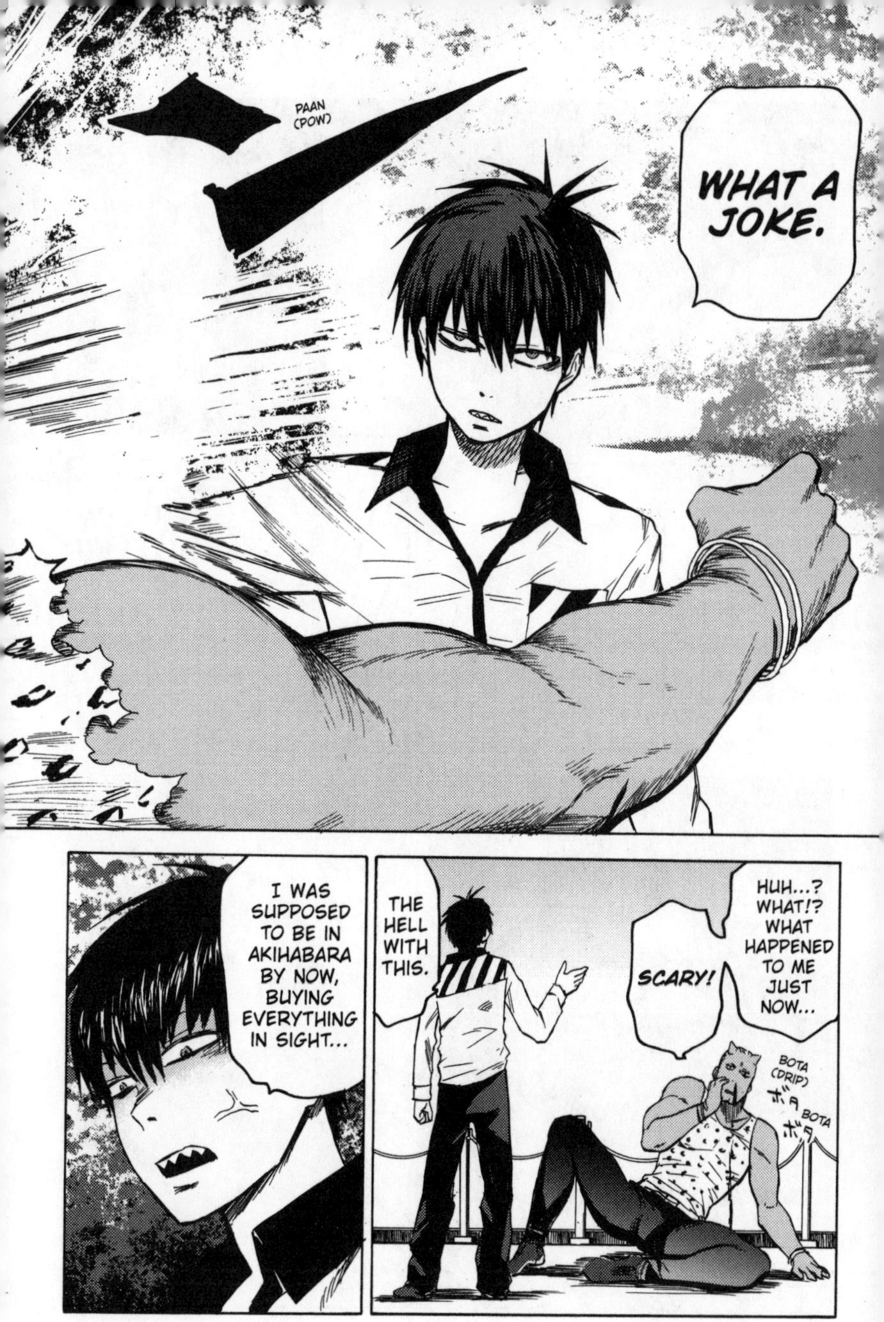
WHAT A JOKE.
PAAN (POW)
HUH...? WHAT!? WHAT HAPPENED TO ME JUST NOW...
SCARY!
BOTA (DRIP)
ボタ
BOTA
ボタ
THE HELL WITH THIS.
I WAS SUPPOSED TO BE IN AKIHABARA BY NOW, BUYING EVERYTHING IN SIGHT...

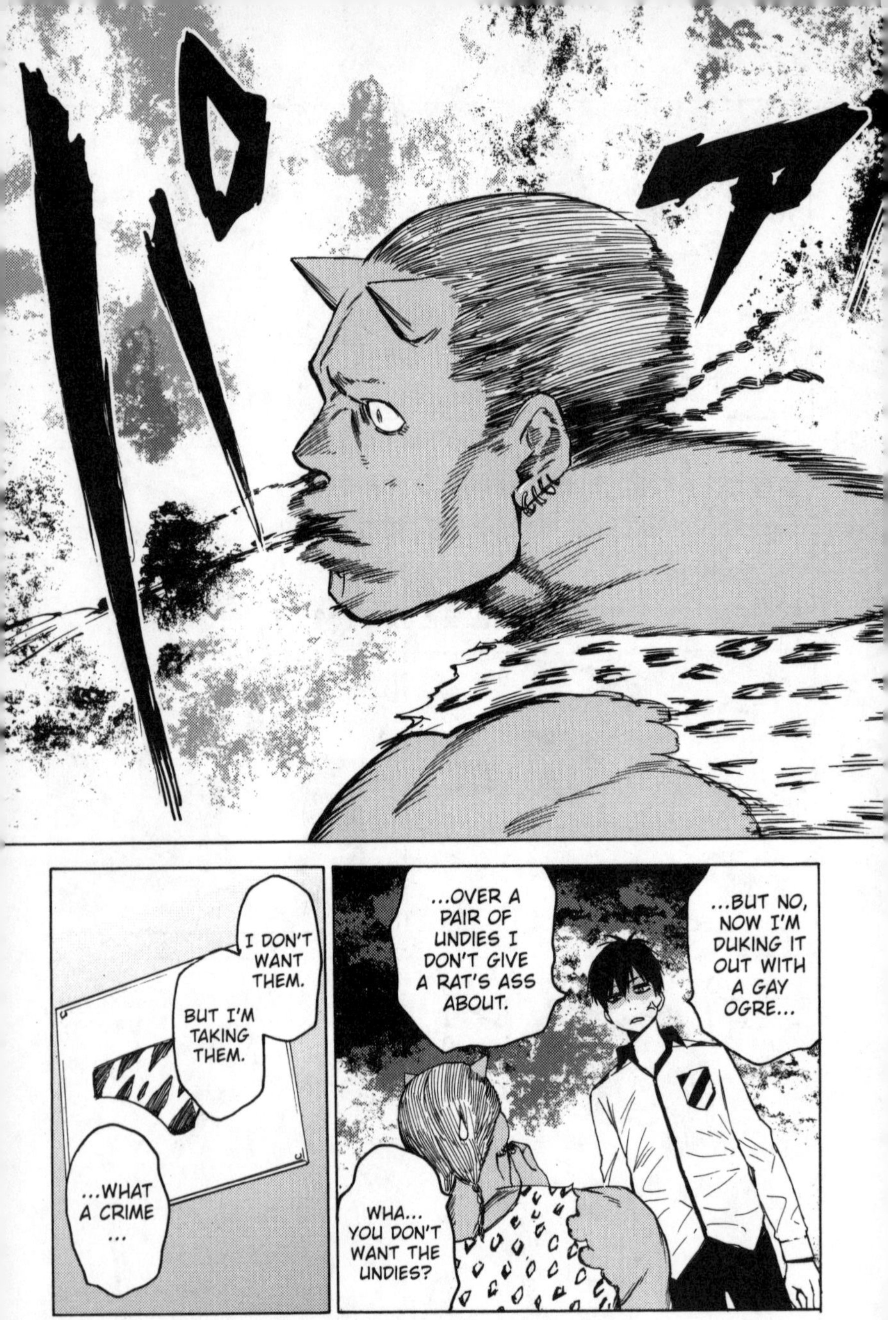
...BUT NO, NOW I'M DUKING IT OUT WITH A GAY OGRE...
...OVER A PAIR OF UNDIES I DON'T GIVE A RAT'S ASS ABOUT.
WHA... YOU DON'T WANT THE UNDIES?
I DON'T WANT THEM.
BUT I'M TAKING THEM.
...WHAT A CRIME ...

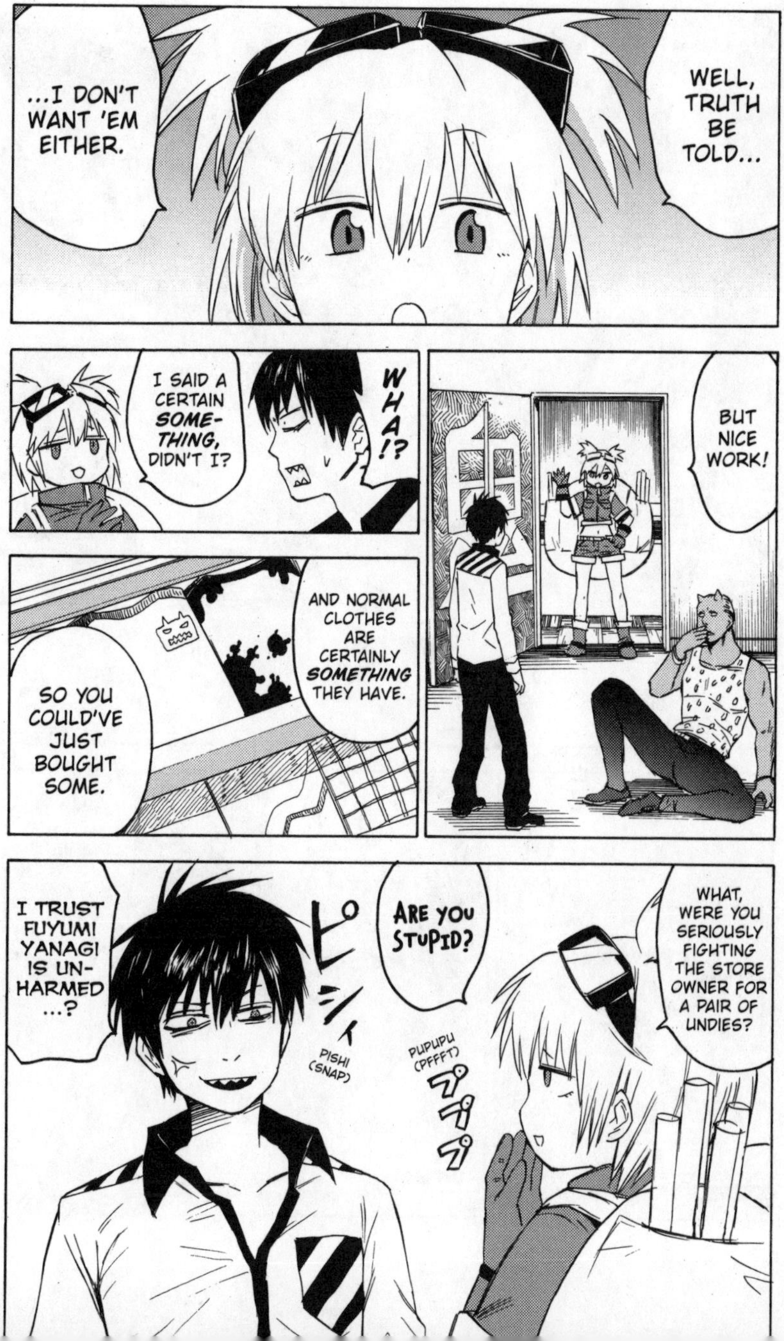
WELL, TRUTH BE TOLD...
...I DON'T WANT 'EM EITHER.
BUT NICE WORK!
WHA!?
I SAID A CERTAIN SOME-THING, DIDN'T I?
AND NORMAL CLOTHES ARE CERTAINLY SOMETHING THEY HAVE.
SO YOU COULD'VE JUST BOUGHT SOME.
WHAT, WERE YOU SERIOUSLY FIGHTING THE STORE OWNER FOR A PAIR OF UNDIES?
ARE YOU STUPID?
PUPUPU (PFFFT)
PISHI (SNAP)
I TRUST FUYUMI YANAGI IS UN-HARMED ...?

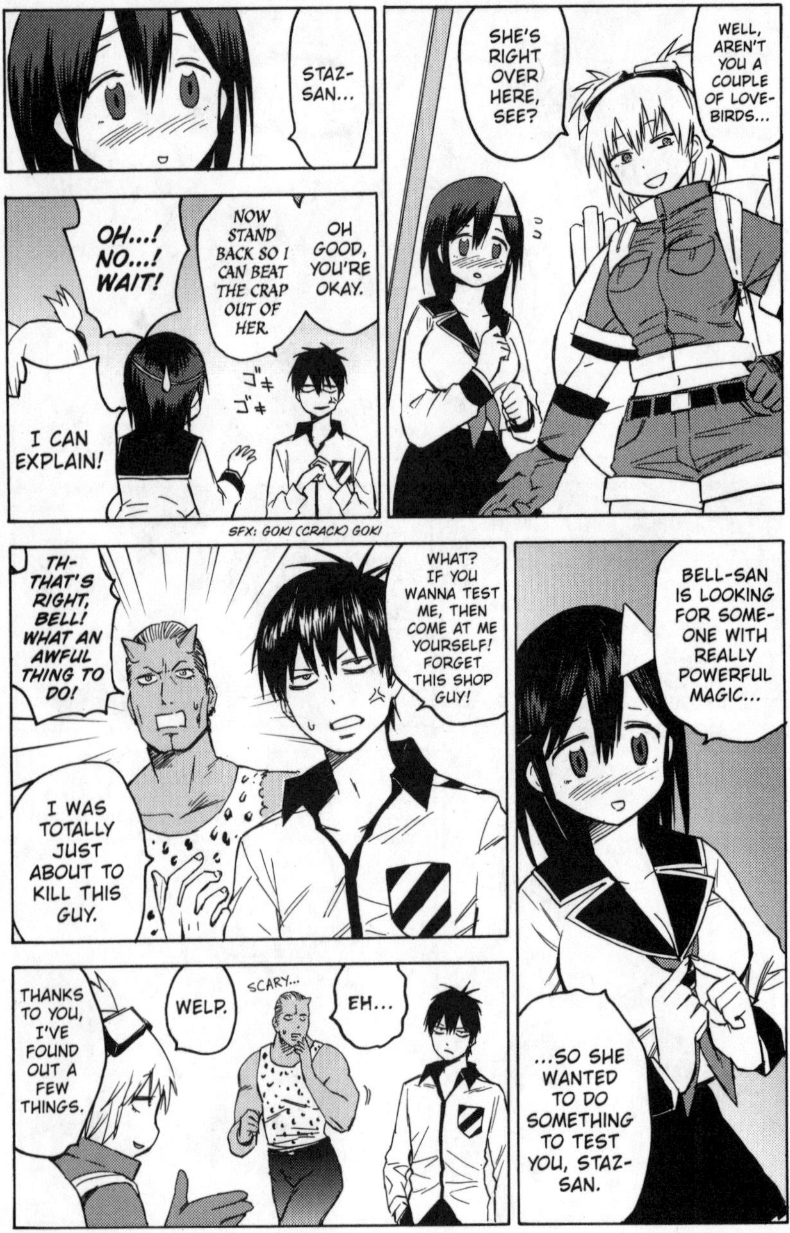
WELL, AREN'T YOU A COUPLE OF LOVE-BIRDS...
SHE'S RIGHT OVER HERE, SEE?
STAZ-SAN...
OH GOOD, YOU'RE OKAY.
NOW STAND BACK SO I CAN BEAT THE CRAP OUT OF HER.
OH...! NO...! WAIT!
I CAN EXPLAIN!
ゴキ ゴキ
SFX: GOKI (CRACK) GOKI
BELL-SAN IS LOOKING FOR SOME-ONE WITH REALLY POWERFUL MAGIC...
...SO SHE WANTED TO DO SOMETHING TO TEST YOU, STAZ-SAN.
WHAT? IF YOU WANNA TEST ME, THEN COME AT ME YOURSELF! FORGET THIS SHOP GUY!
TH-THAT'S RIGHT, BELL! WHAT AN AWFUL THING TO DO!
I WAS TOTALLY JUST ABOUT TO KILL THIS GUY.
EH...
SCARY...
WELP.
THANKS TO YOU, I'VE FOUND OUT A FEW THINGS.

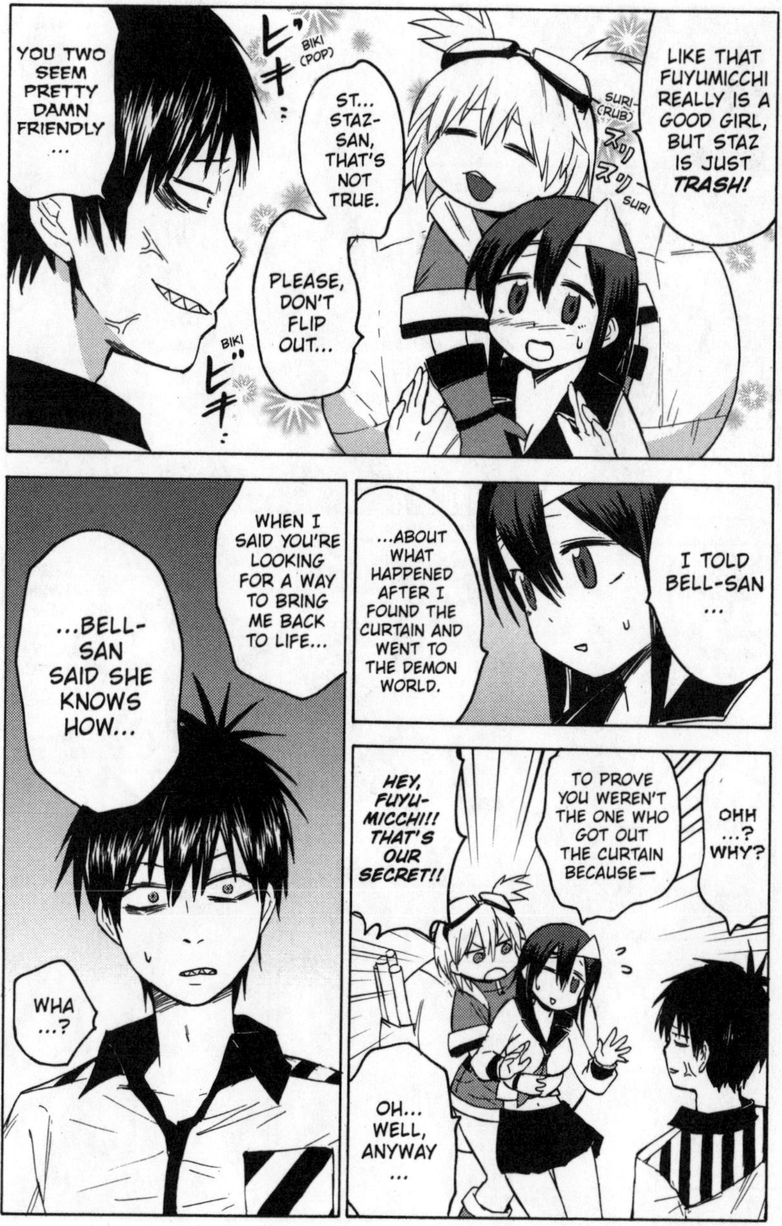
LIKE THAT FUYUMICCHI REALLY IS A GOOD GIRL, BUT STAZ IS JUST TRASH!
SURI (RUB)
SURI
ST... STAZ-SAN, THAT'S NOT TRUE.
BIKI (POP)
PLEASE, DON'T FLIP OUT...
BIKI
YOU TWO SEEM PRETTY DAMN FRIENDLY...
I TOLD BELL-SAN...
...ABOUT WHAT HAPPENED AFTER I FOUND THE CURTAIN AND WENT TO THE DEMON WORLD.
OHH...? WHY?
TO PROVE YOU WEREN'T THE ONE WHO GOT OUT THE CURTAIN BECAUSE—
HEY, FUYUMICCHI!! THAT'S OUR SECRET!!
OH... WELL, ANYWAY...
WHEN I SAID YOU'RE LOOKING FOR A WAY TO BRING ME BACK TO LIFE...
...BELL-SAN SAID SHE KNOWS HOW...
WHA...?

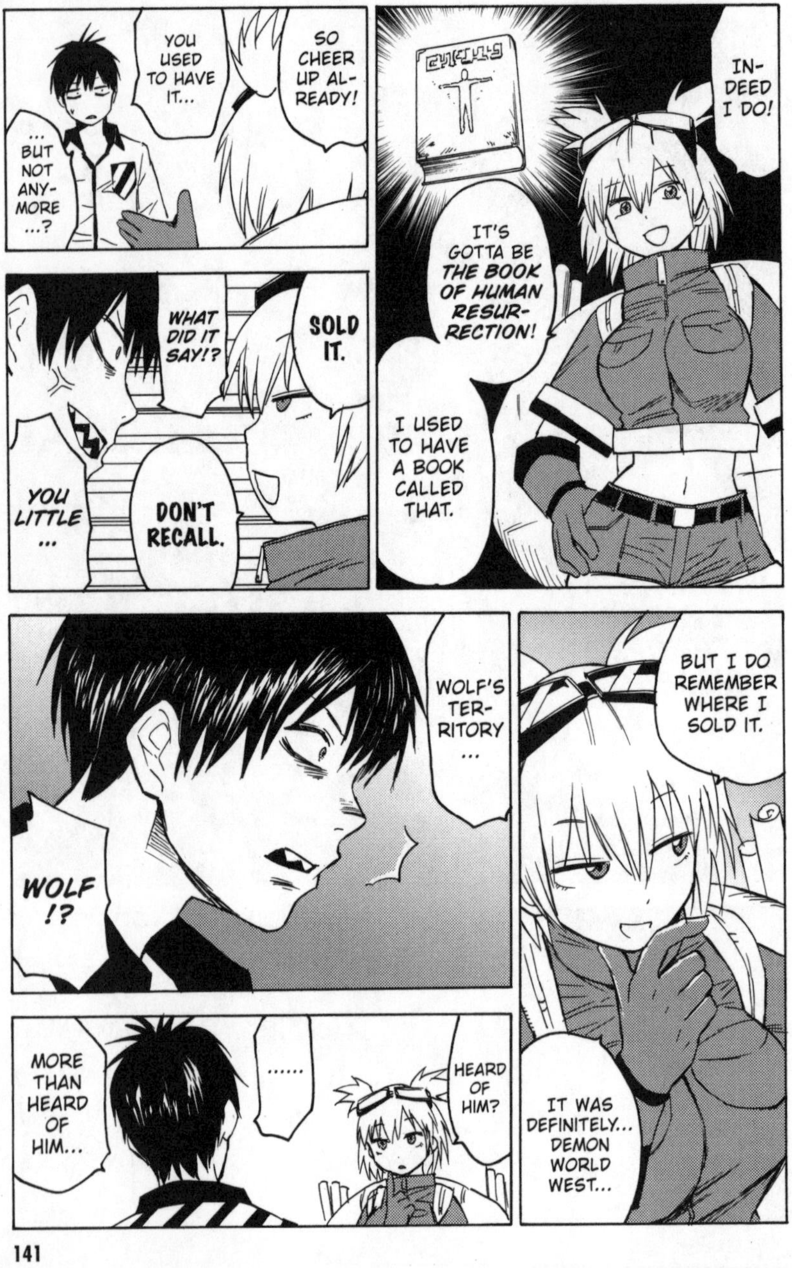
IN-DEED I DO!
IT'S GOTTA BE *THE BOOK OF HUMAN RESURRECTION!*
I USED TO HAVE A BOOK CALLED THAT.
SO CHEER UP AL-READY!
YOU USED TO HAVE IT...
...BUT NOT ANY-MORE ...?
SOLD IT.
WHAT DID IT SAY!?
DON'T RECALL.
YOU LITTLE ...
BUT I DO REMEMBER WHERE I SOLD IT.
IT WAS DEFINITELY... DEMON WORLD WEST...
WOLF'S TER-RITORY ...
WOLF !?
HEARD OF HIM?
......
MORE THAN HEARD OF HIM...

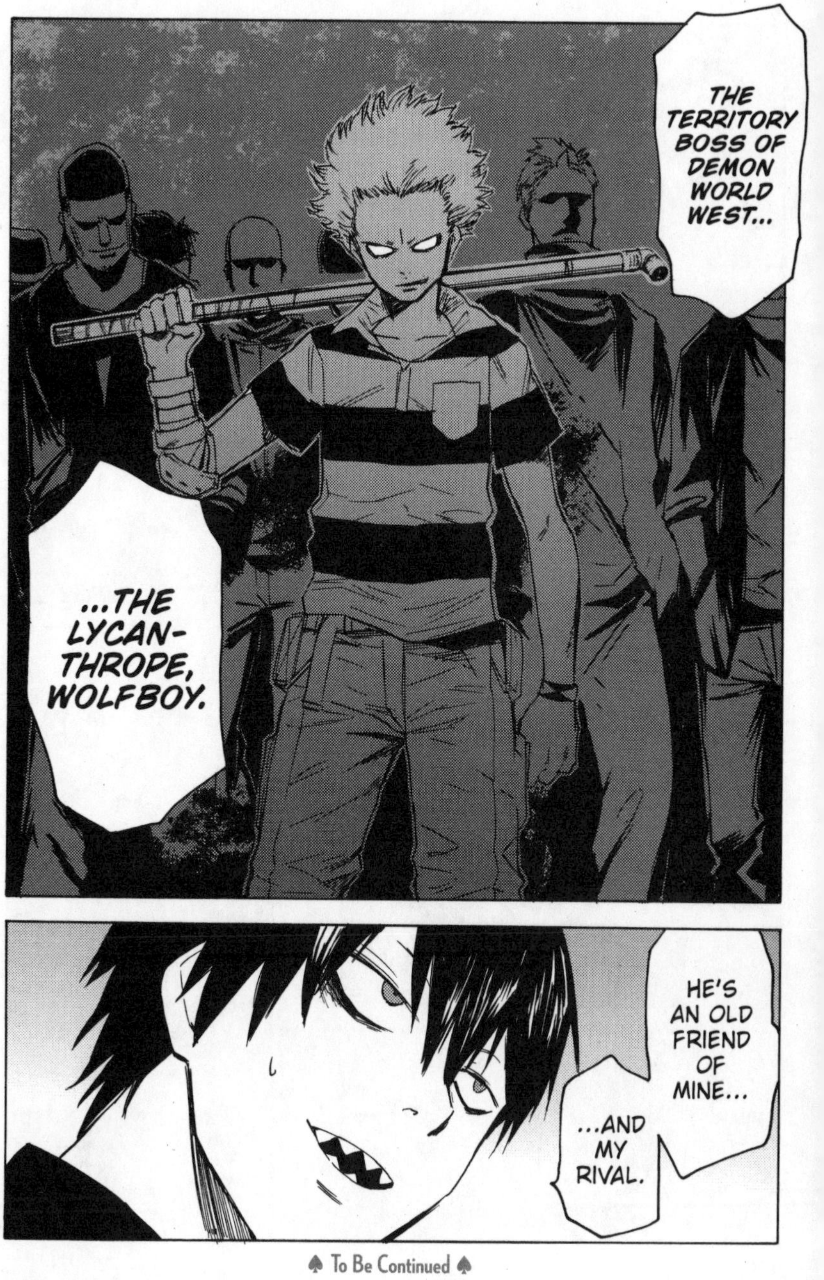
THE TERRITORY BOSS OF DEMON WORLD WEST...
...THE LYCANTHROPE, WOLFBOY.
HE'S AN OLD FRIEND OF MINE...
...AND MY RIVAL.

♠ To Be Continued ♠

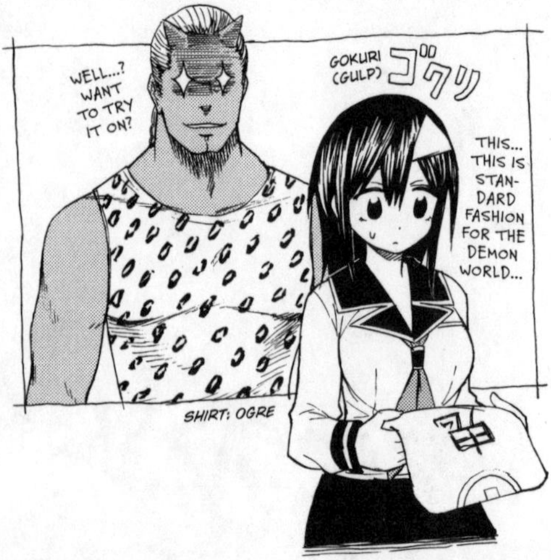
GOKURI (GULP) ゴクリ
WELL...? WANT TO TRY IT ON?
THIS... THIS IS STANDARD FASHION FOR THE DEMON WORLD...
SHIRT: OGRE

BLOOD LAD

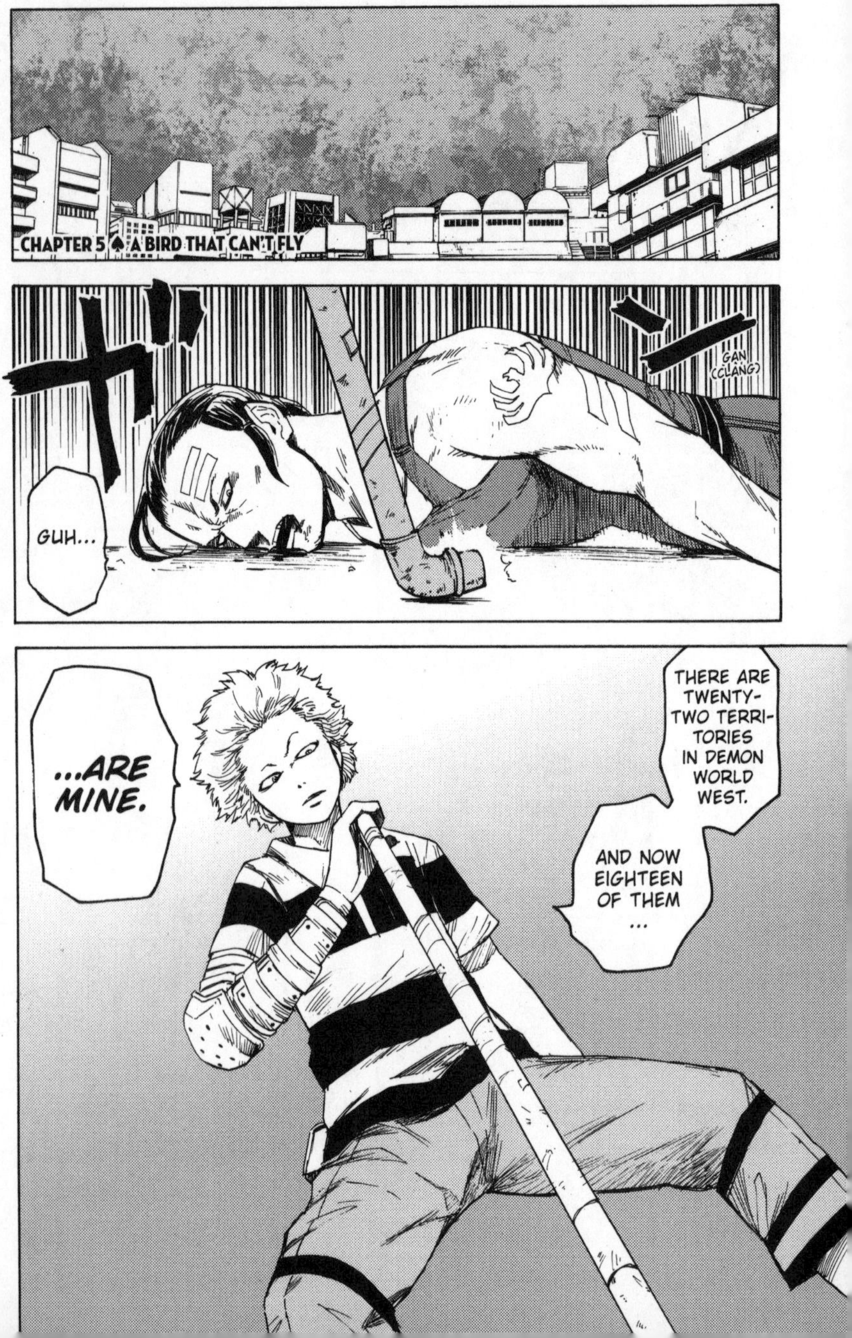
CHAPTER 5 ♠ A BIRD THAT CAN'T FLY
GAN (CLANG)
GUH...
THERE ARE TWENTY-TWO TERRITORIES IN DEMON WORLD WEST.
AND NOW EIGHTEEN OF THEM ...
...ARE MINE.

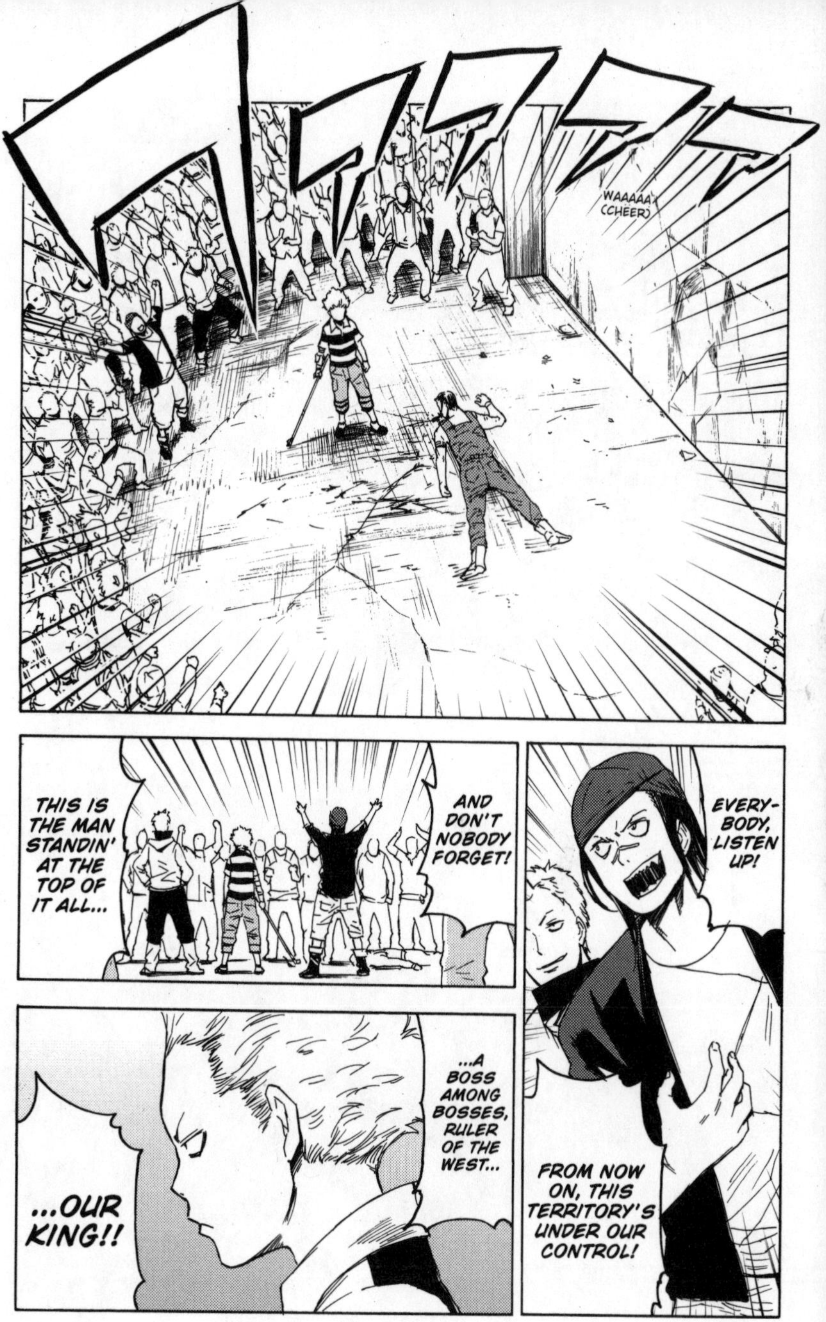
WAAAAA (CHEER)
EVERYBODY, LISTEN UP!
FROM NOW ON, THIS TERRITORY'S UNDER OUR CONTROL!
AND DON'T NOBODY FORGET!
THIS IS THE MAN STANDIN' AT THE TOP OF IT ALL...
...A BOSS AMONG BOSSES, RULER OF THE WEST...
...OUR KING!!

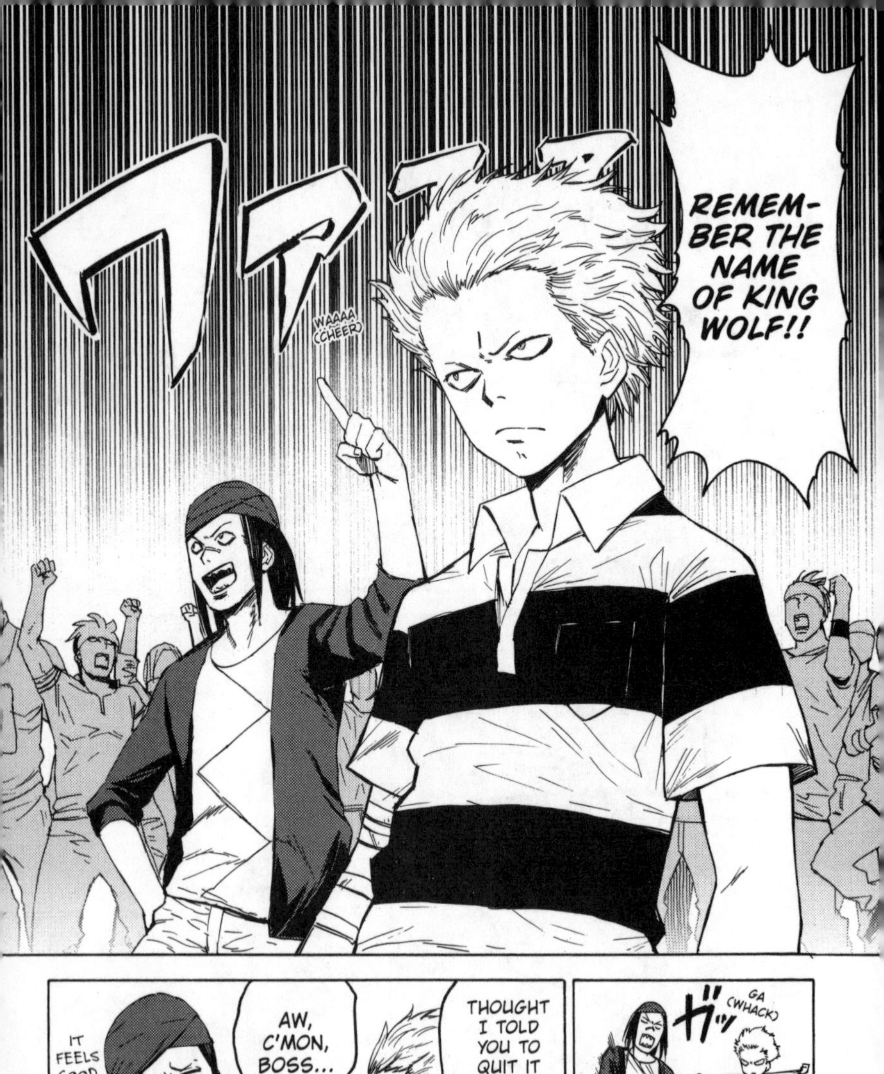
REMEM-
BER THE
NAME
OF KING
WOLF!!
WAAAA
(CHEER)
THOUGHT I TOLD YOU TO QUIT IT WITH THAT YELLIN'.
AW, C'MON, BOSS...
IT FEELS GOOD, YA KNOW ...?
FIRST OF ALL, I AIN'T TAKEN OVER EVERYTHING YET!
GA (WHACK)
OW!!

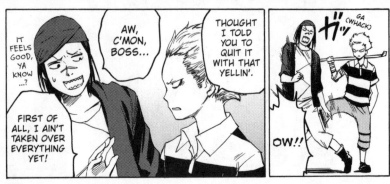

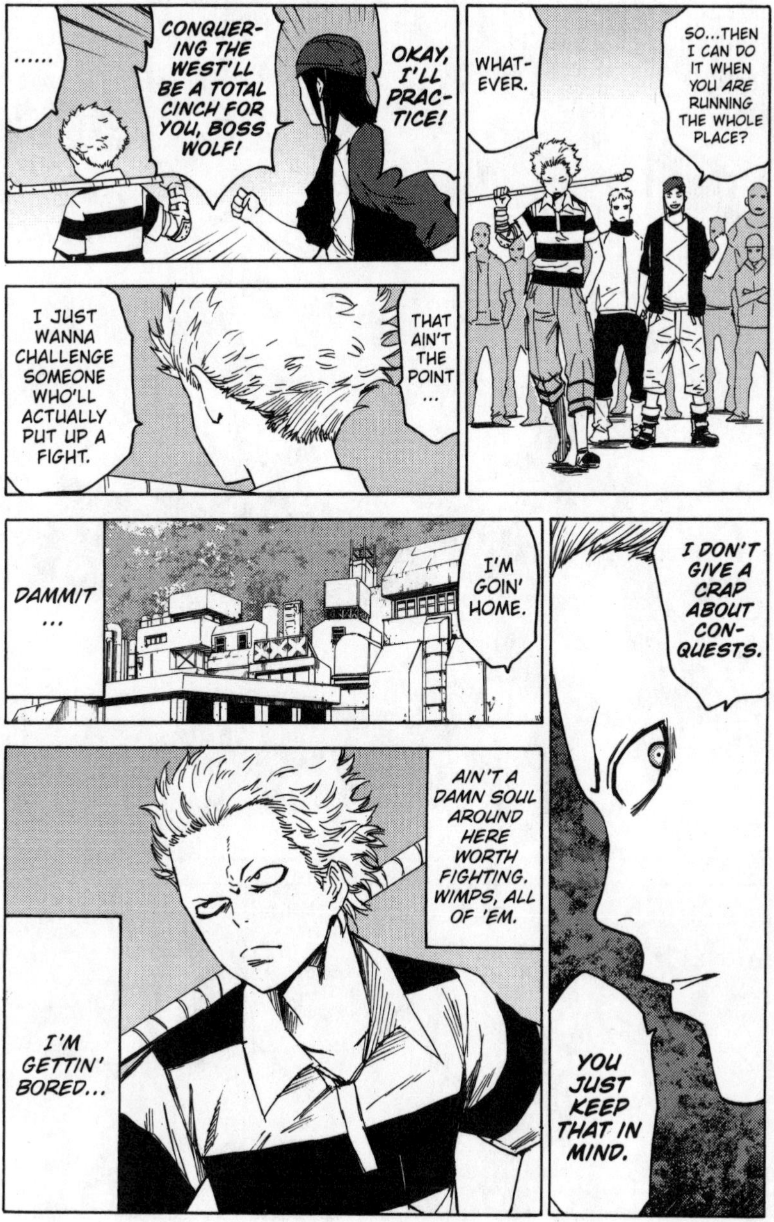
SO...THEN I CAN DO IT WHEN YOU *ARE* RUNNING THE WHOLE PLACE?
WHAT-EVER.
OKAY, I'LL PRAC-TICE!
CONQUER-ING THE WEST'LL BE A TOTAL CINCH FOR YOU, BOSS WOLF!
......
THAT AIN'T THE POINT...
I JUST WANNA CHALLENGE SOMEONE WHO'LL ACTUALLY PUT UP A FIGHT.
I DON'T GIVE A CRAP ABOUT CON-QUESTS.
YOU JUST KEEP THAT IN MIND.
I'M GOIN' HOME.
DAMMIT...
AIN'T A DAMN SOUL AROUND HERE WORTH FIGHTING. WIMPS, ALL OF 'EM.
I'M GETTIN' BORED...

# CHAPTER 5 ♠ A BIRD THAT CAN'T FLY

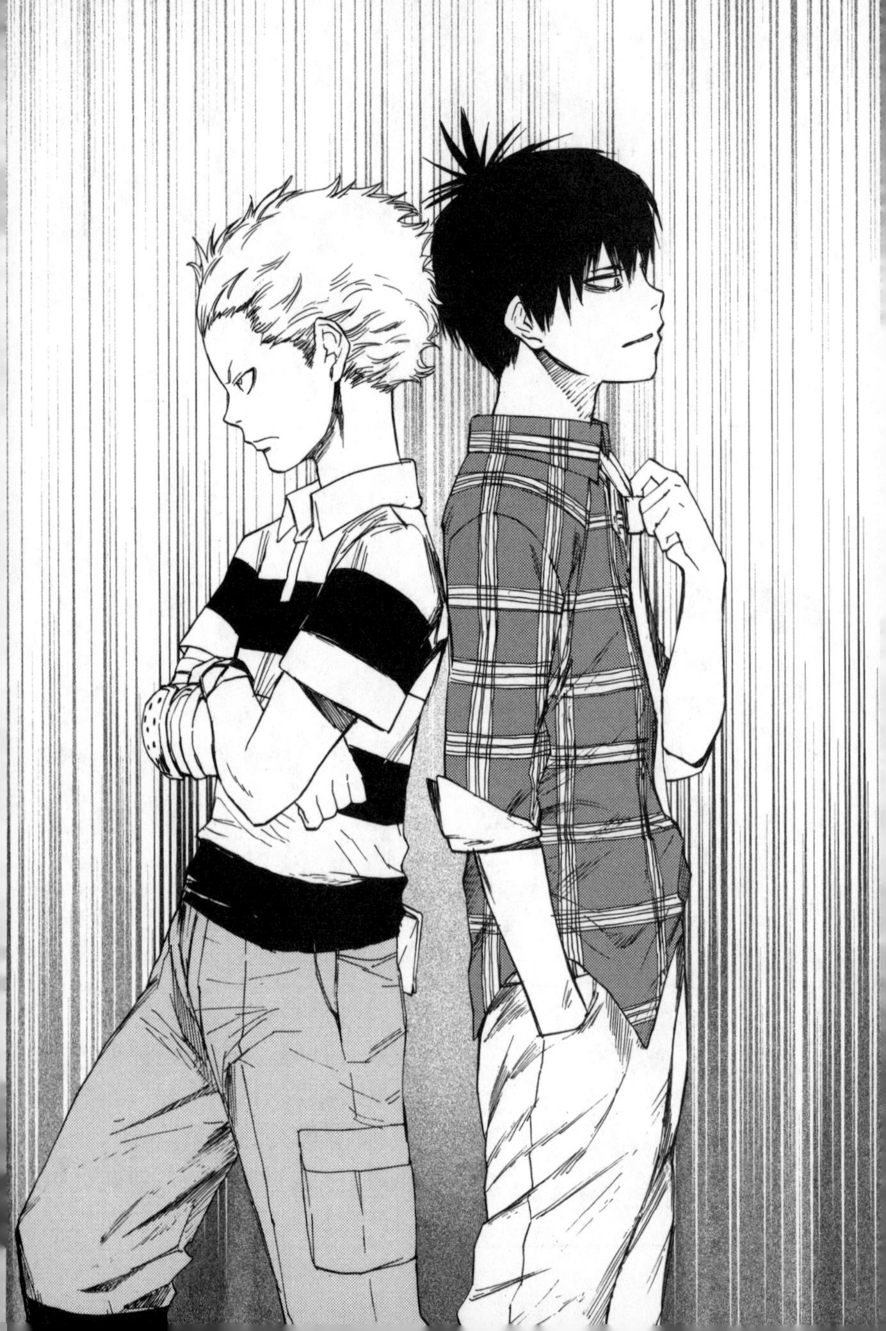

DOOR: OGRE

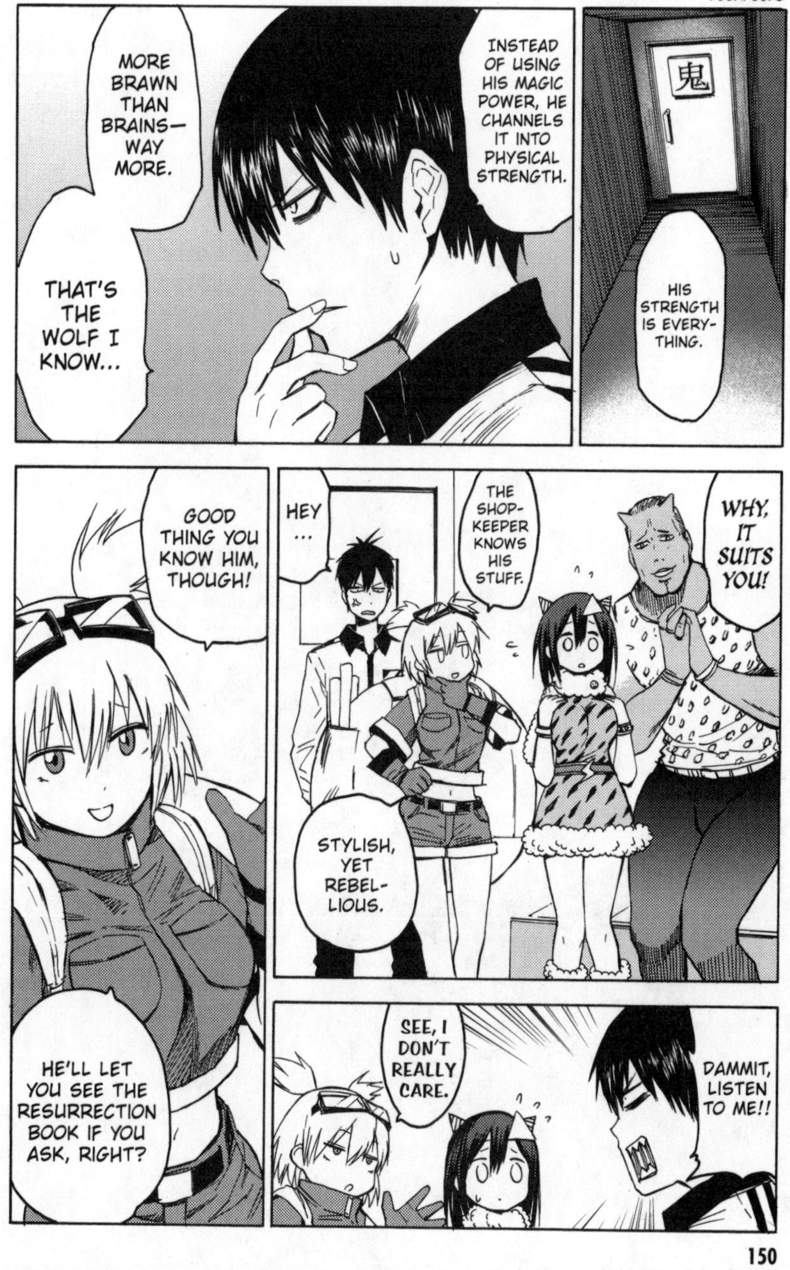
鬼
HIS STRENGTH IS EVERY-THING.
INSTEAD OF USING HIS MAGIC POWER, HE CHANNELS IT INTO PHYSICAL STRENGTH.
MORE BRAWN THAN BRAINS— WAY MORE.
THAT'S THE WOLF I KNOW...
WHY, IT SUITS YOU!
THE SHOP-KEEPER KNOWS HIS STUFF.
HEY ...
STYLISH, YET REBEL-LIOUS.
DAMMIT, LISTEN TO ME!!
SEE, I DON'T REALLY CARE.
GOOD THING YOU KNOW HIM, THOUGH!
HE'LL LET YOU SEE THE RESURRECTION BOOK IF YOU ASK, RIGHT?

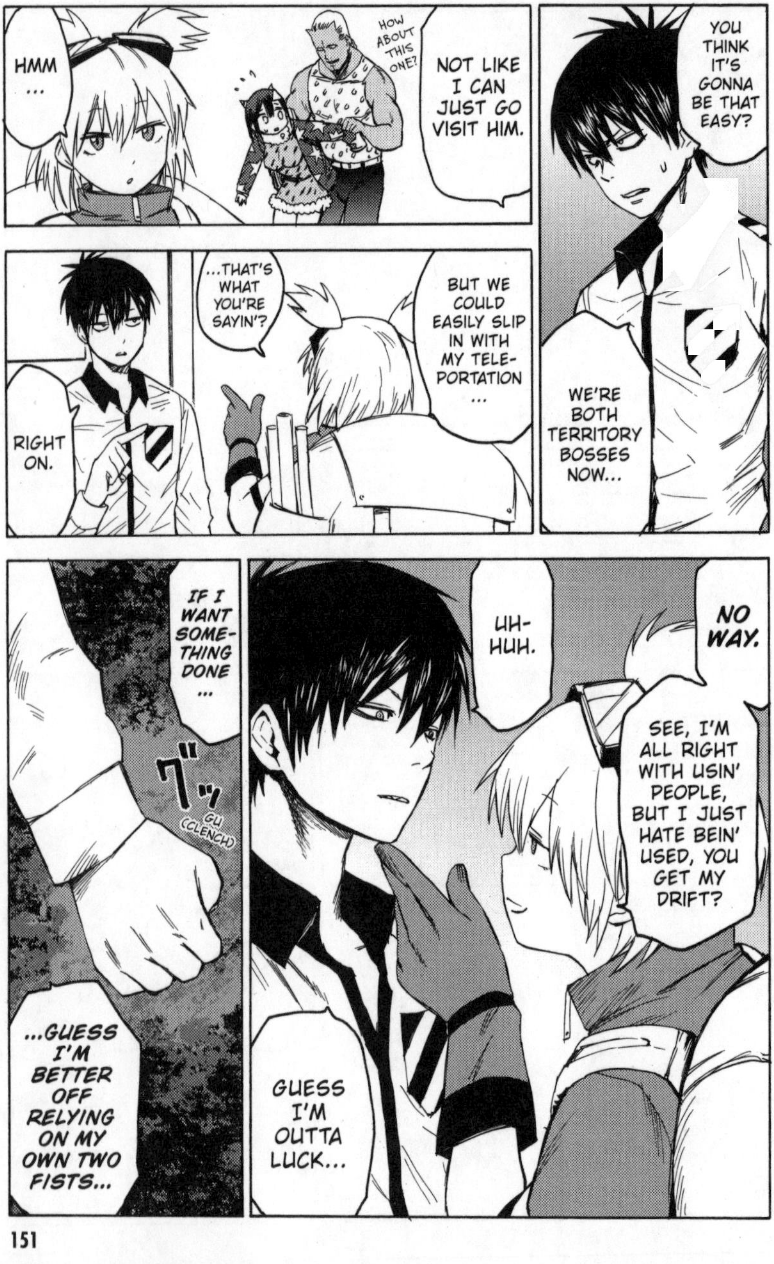
YOU THINK IT'S GONNA BE THAT EASY?
WE'RE BOTH TERRITORY BOSSES NOW...
NOT LIKE I CAN JUST GO VISIT HIM.
HOW ABOUT THIS ONE?
HMM...
BUT WE COULD EASILY SLIP IN WITH MY TELE-PORTATION...
...THAT'S WHAT YOU'RE SAYIN'?
RIGHT ON.
NO WAY.
UH-HUH.
SEE, I'M ALL RIGHT WITH USIN' PEOPLE, BUT I JUST HATE BEIN' USED, YOU GET MY DRIFT?
GUESS I'M OUTTA LUCK...
IF I WANT SOME-THING DONE...
グッ
GU (CLENCH)
...GUESS I'M BETTER OFF RELYING ON MY OWN TWO FISTS...

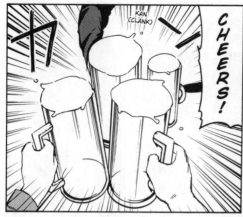

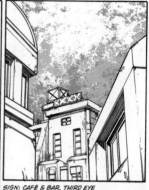

SIGN: CAFÉ & BAR, THIRD EYE
喫茶
サードアイ
KAN (CLANK)
CHEERS!
ゴッ GO ゴッ GO ゴッ GO ゴッ GO ゴッ GO ゴッ
(GLUG)
AHHHH!
MAN, THIS IS AWESOME!
WITH THAT GUY OUT OF TOWN, WE CAN FINALLY HAVE A DAY TO RELAX!!
BOOZE NEVER TASTED BETTER!!
YOU'RE REALLY PULLIN' IT OFF TOO, YOSHIDA!
HOW ABOUT WE JUST KEEP IT LIKE THIS!?
カラン KARAN (JINGLE)
カラン KARAN
WE DON'T NEED THAT GUY AT ALL!
WAH HA HA HA!

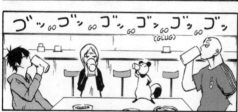

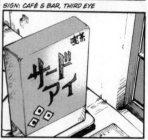

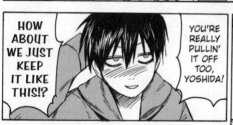

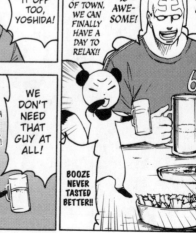

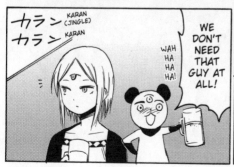

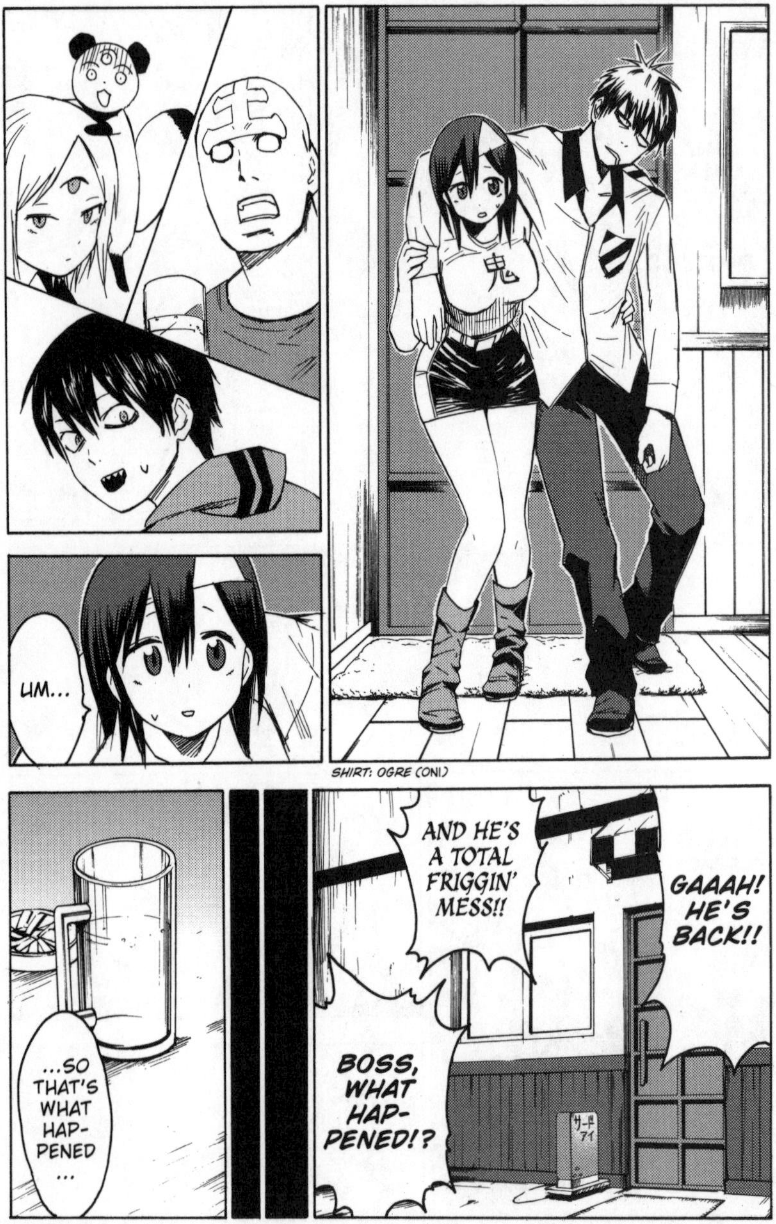
SHIRT: OGRE (ONI)
UM...
GAAAH! HE'S BACK!!
AND HE'S A TOTAL FRIGGIN' MESS!!
BOSS, WHAT HAP-PENED!?
...SO THAT'S WHAT HAP-PENED ...

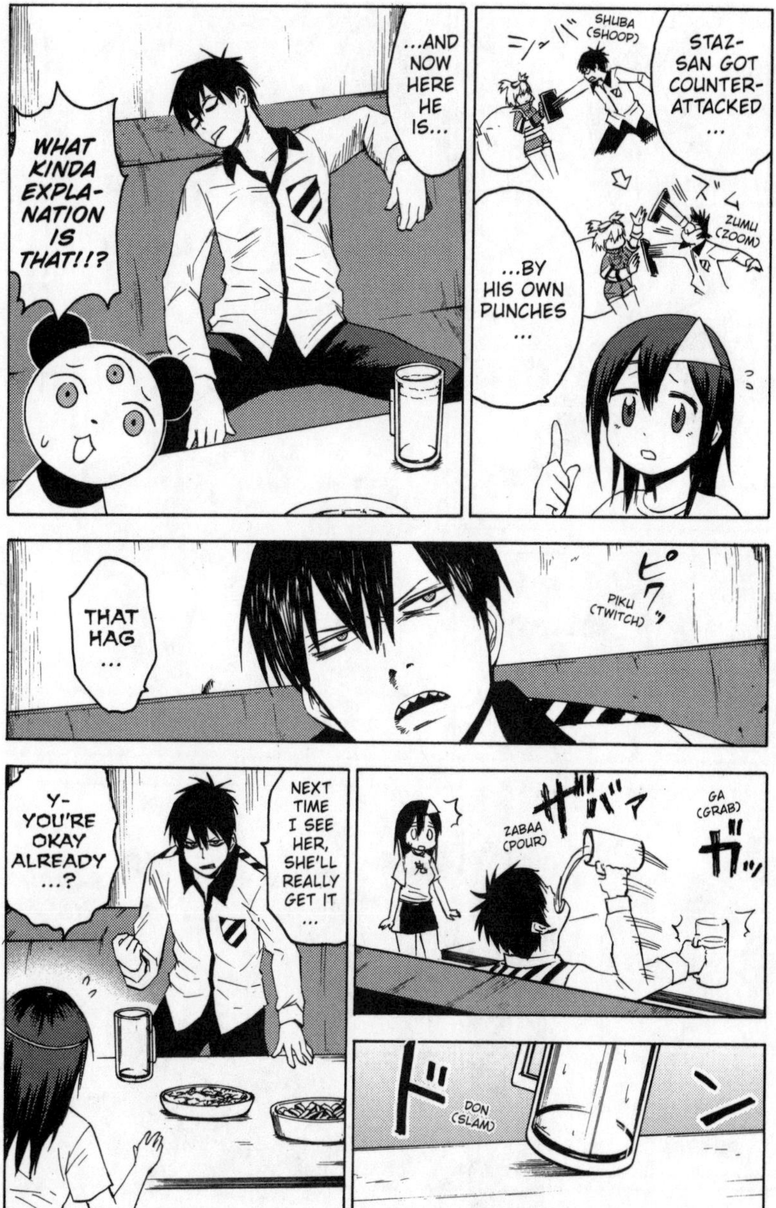
SHUBA (SHOOP)
STAZ-SAN GOT COUNTER-ATTACKED ...
ZUMU (ZOOM)
...BY HIS OWN PUNCHES ...
...AND NOW HERE HE IS...
WHAT KINDA EXPLANATION IS THAT!!?
PIKU (TWITCH)
THAT HAG ...
GA (GRAB)
ZABAA (POUR)
DON (SLAM)
NEXT TIME I SEE HER, SHE'LL REALLY GET IT ...
Y-YOU'RE OKAY ALREADY ...?

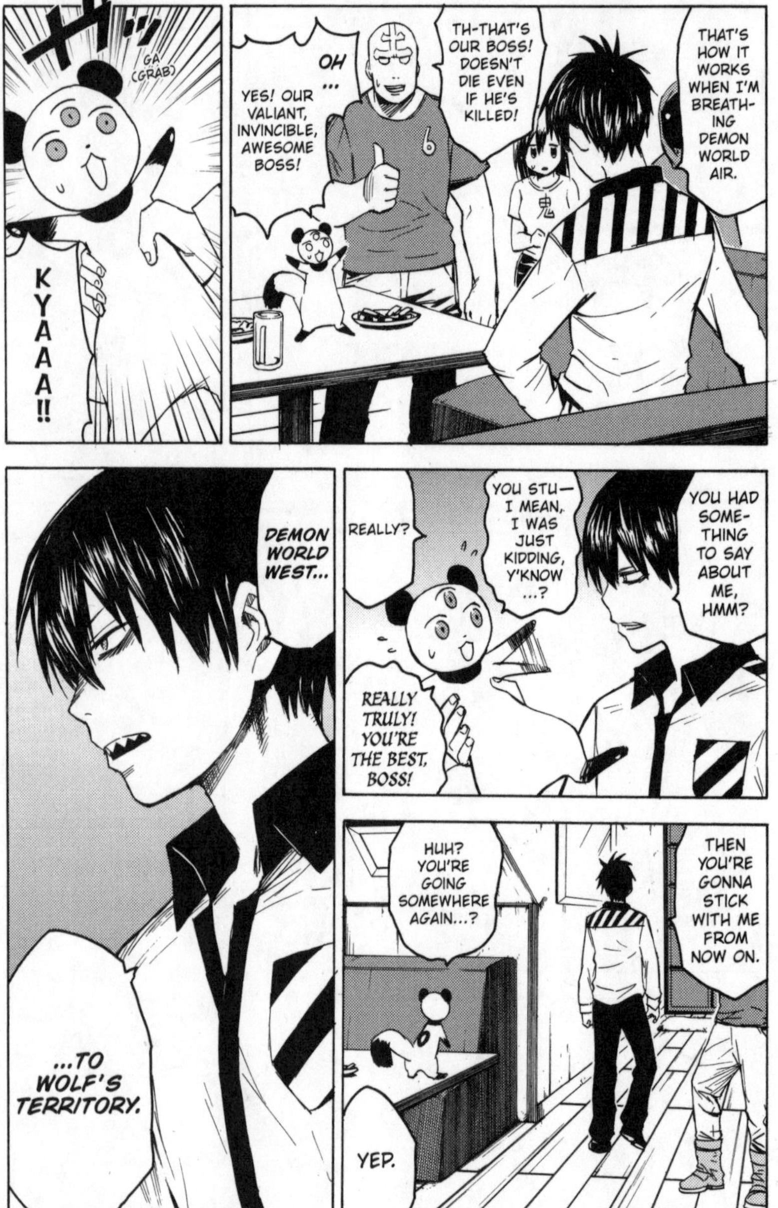
THAT'S HOW IT WORKS WHEN I'M BREATHING DEMON WORLD AIR.
TH-THAT'S OUR BOSS! DOESN'T DIE EVEN IF HE'S KILLED!
OH ...
YES! OUR VALIANT, INVINCIBLE, AWESOME BOSS!
GA (GRAB)
KYAAAA!!
YOU HAD SOMETHING TO SAY ABOUT ME, HMM?
YOU STU— I MEAN, I WAS JUST KIDDING, Y'KNOW ...?
REALLY?
REALLY TRULY! YOU'RE THE BEST, BOSS!
THEN YOU'RE GONNA STICK WITH ME FROM NOW ON.
HUH? YOU'RE GOING SOMEWHERE AGAIN...?
YEP.
DEMON WORLD WEST...
...TO WOLF'S TERRITORY.

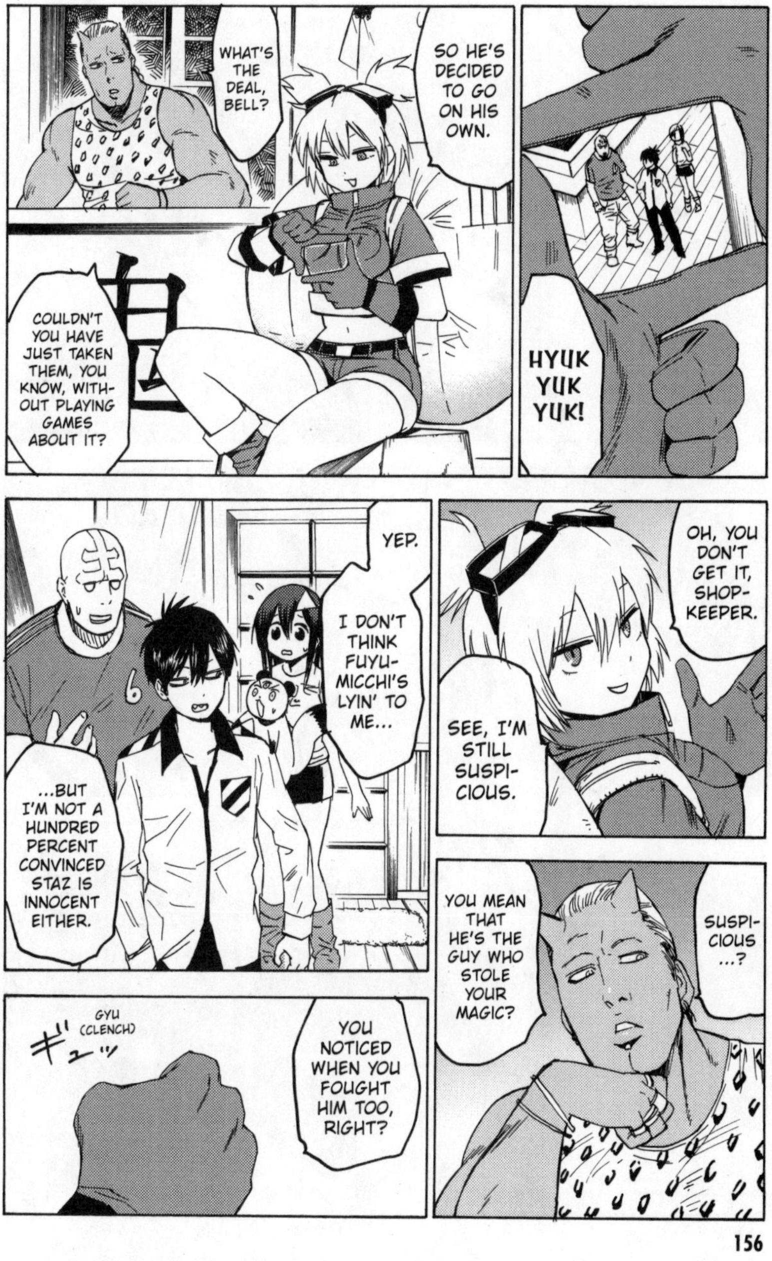
HYUK YUK YUK!
SO HE'S DECIDED TO GO ON HIS OWN.
WHAT'S THE DEAL, BELL?
COULDN'T YOU HAVE JUST TAKEN THEM, YOU KNOW, WITHOUT PLAYING GAMES ABOUT IT?
OH, YOU DON'T GET IT, SHOPKEEPER.
SEE, I'M STILL SUSPICIOUS.
YEP.
I DON'T THINK FUYUMICCHI'S LYIN' TO ME...
...BUT I'M NOT A HUNDRED PERCENT CONVINCED STAZ IS INNOCENT EITHER.
SUSPICIOUS...?
YOU MEAN THAT HE'S THE GUY WHO STOLE YOUR MAGIC?
YOU NOTICED WHEN YOU FOUGHT HIM TOO, RIGHT?
GYU (CLENCH)
ギュッ

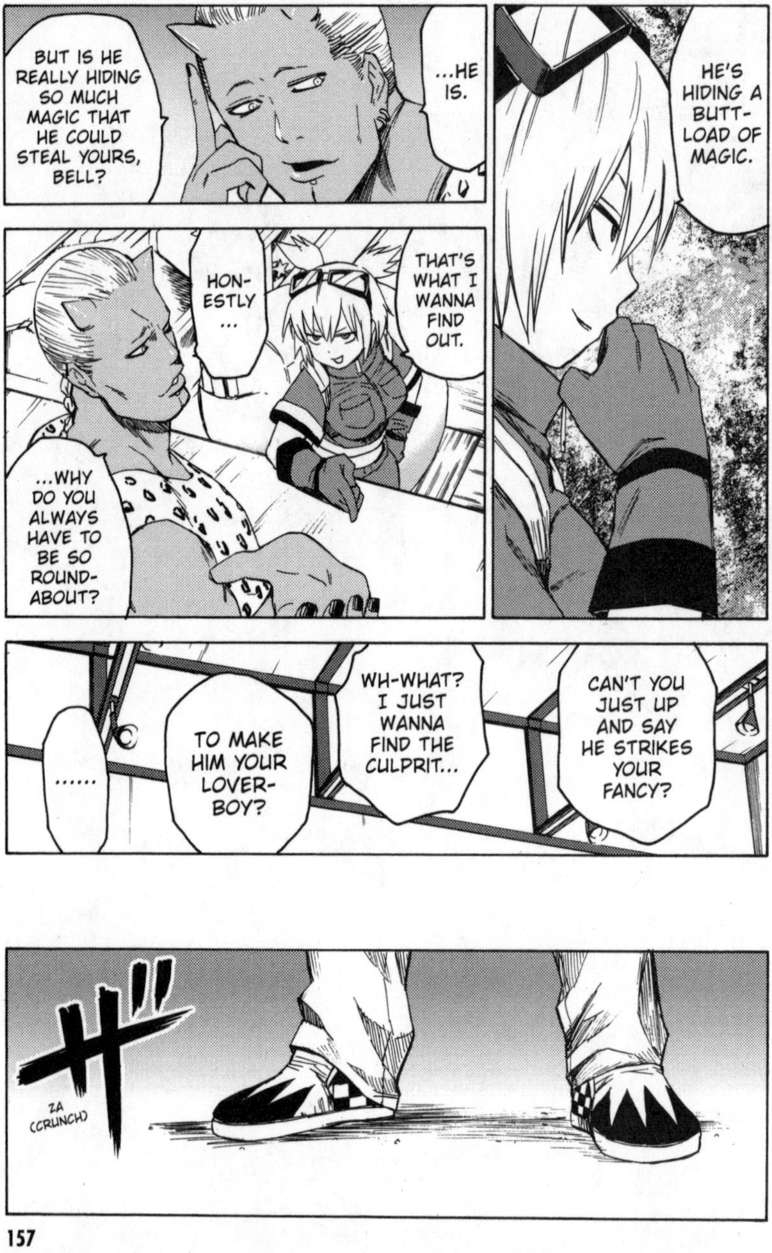
HE'S HIDING A BUTT-LOAD OF MAGIC.
BUT IS HE REALLY HIDING SO MUCH MAGIC THAT HE COULD STEAL YOURS, BELL?
...HE IS.
THAT'S WHAT I WANNA FIND OUT.
HON-ESTLY ...
...WHY DO YOU ALWAYS HAVE TO BE SO ROUND-ABOUT?
CAN'T YOU JUST UP AND SAY HE STRIKES YOUR FANCY?
WH-WHAT? I JUST WANNA FIND THE CULPRIT...
TO MAKE HIM YOUR LOVER-BOY?
......
ザ
ZA (CRUNCH)

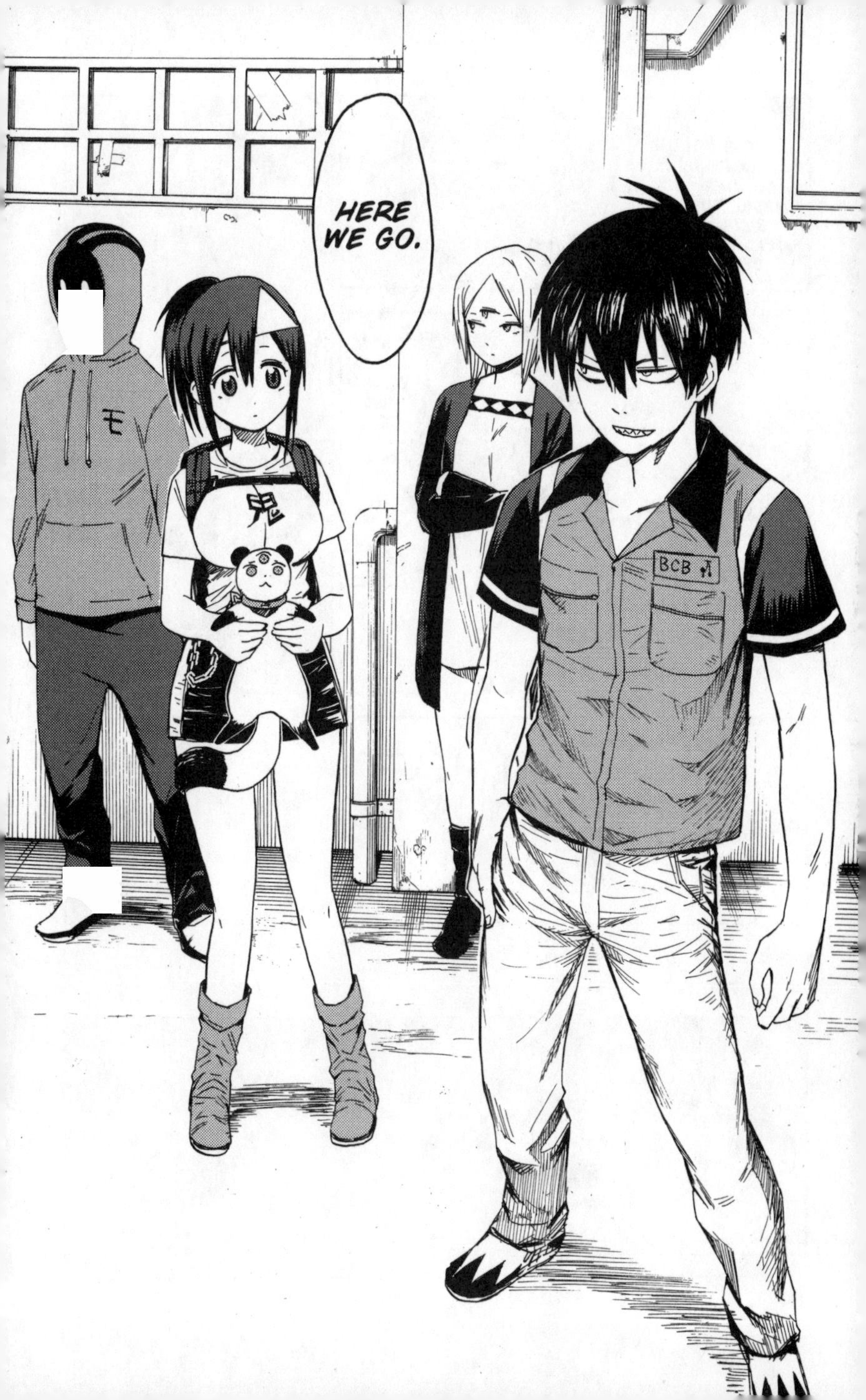
HERE WE GO.

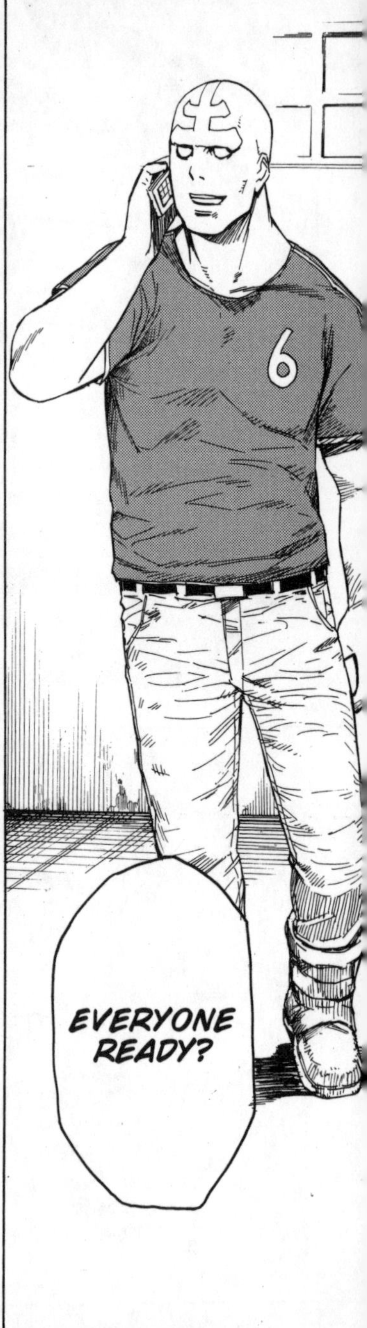
EVERYONE READY?

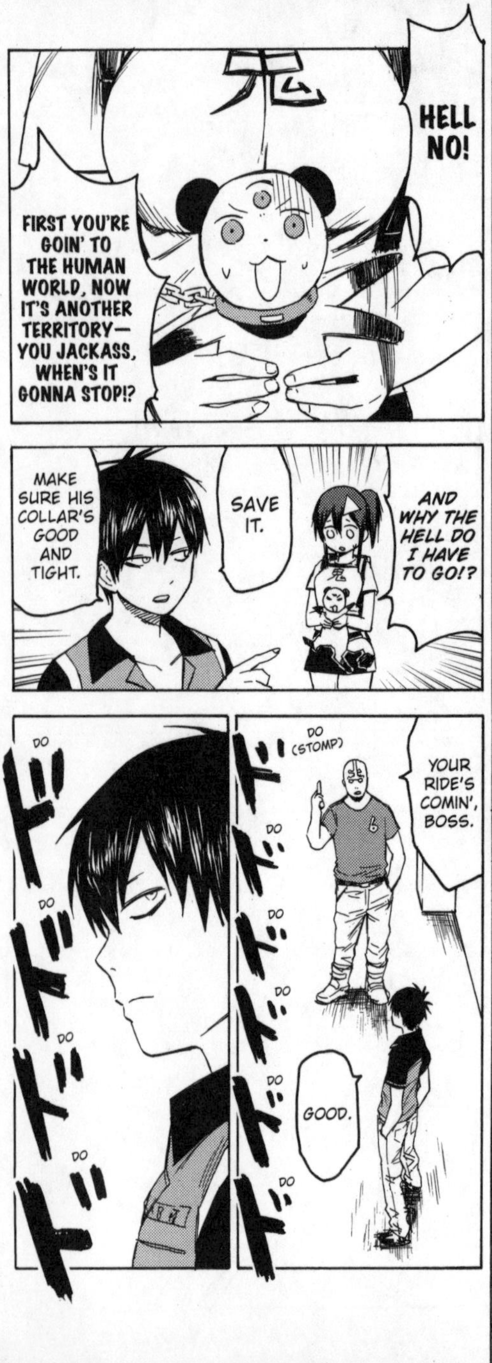
HELL NO!
FIRST YOU'RE GOIN' TO THE HUMAN WORLD, NOW IT'S ANOTHER TERRITORY—YOU JACKASS, WHEN'S IT GONNA STOP!?
AND WHY THE HELL DO I HAVE TO GO!?
SAVE IT.
MAKE SURE HIS COLLAR'S GOOD AND TIGHT.
DO (STOMP)
YOUR RIDE'S COMIN', BOSS.
DO
DO
DO
DO
GOOD.
DO
DO
DO
DO
DO
DO

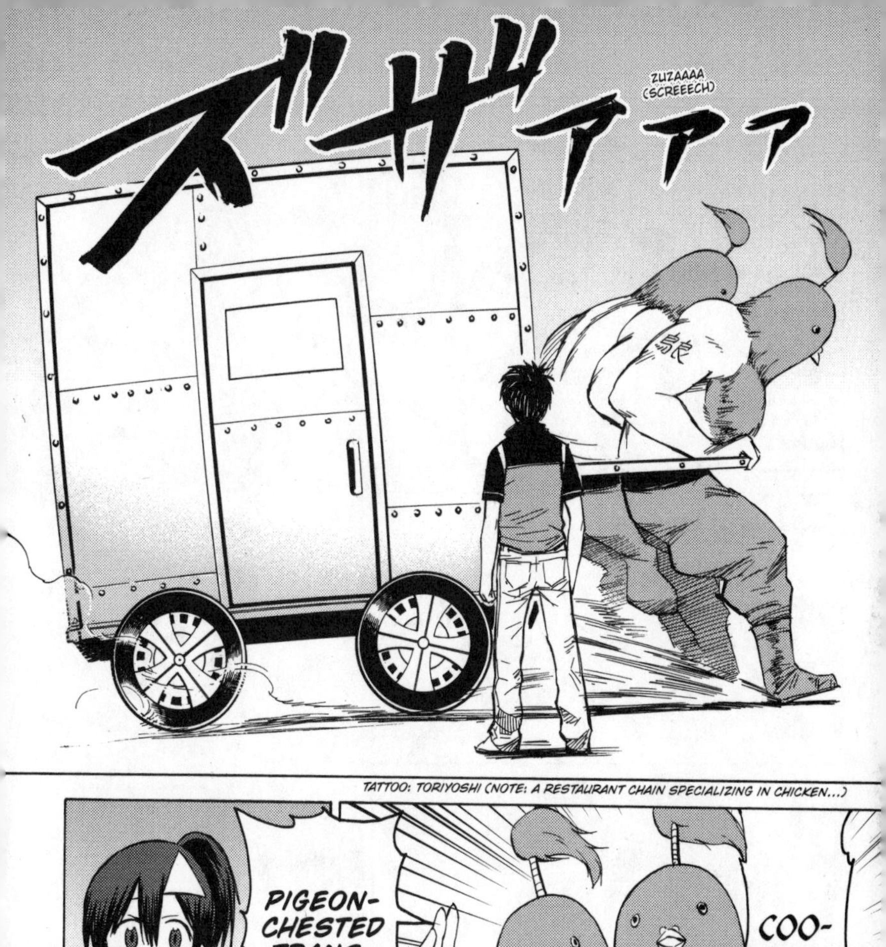
ZUZAAAA
(SCREEECH)

TATTOO: TORIYOSHI (NOTE: A RESTAURANT CHAIN SPECIALIZING IN CHICKEN...)

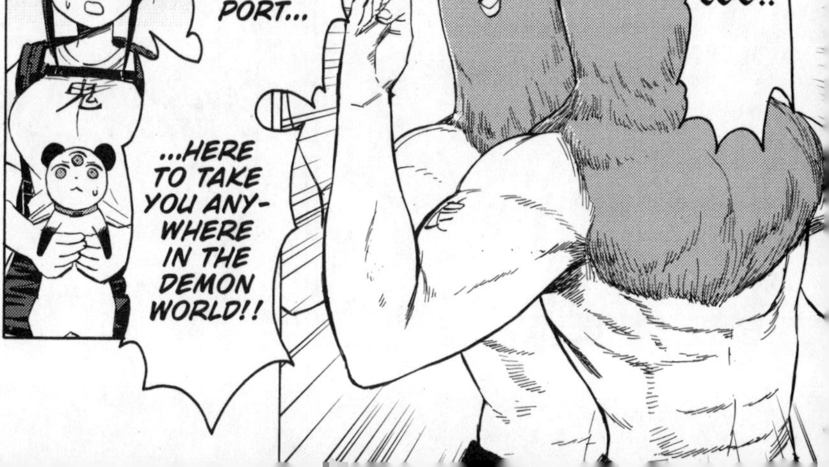
COO-COO!!
PIGEON-CHESTED TRANSPORT...
...HERE TO TAKE YOU ANYWHERE IN THE DEMON WORLD!!

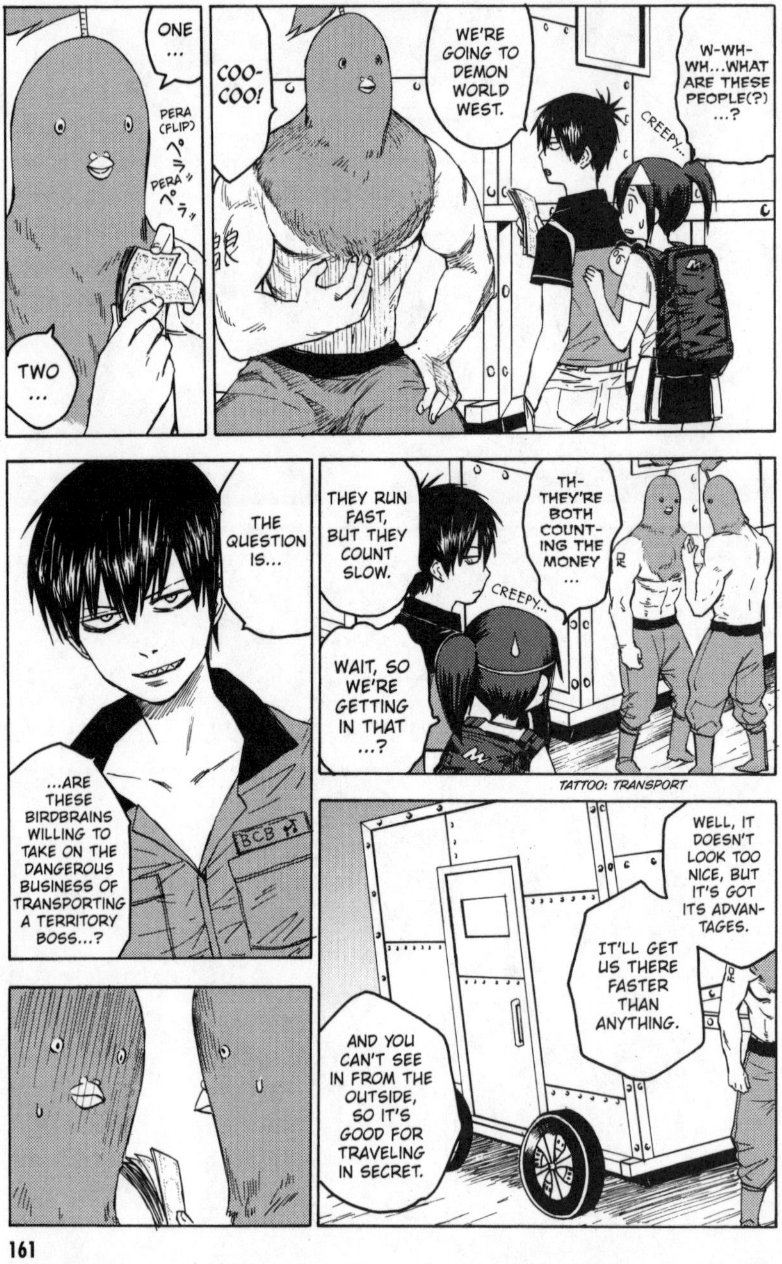
W-WH- WH...WHAT ARE THESE PEOPLE(?) ...?
CREEPY...
WE'RE GOING TO DEMON WORLD WEST.
COO-COO!
ONE ...
PERA (FLIP)
PERA
TWO ...
TH- THEY'RE BOTH COUNTING THE MONEY ...
CREEPY...
THEY RUN FAST, BUT THEY COUNT SLOW.
WAIT, SO WE'RE GETTING IN THAT ...?
TATTOO: TRANSPORT
THE QUESTION IS...
...ARE THESE BIRDBRAINS WILLING TO TAKE ON THE DANGEROUS BUSINESS OF TRANSPORTING A TERRITORY BOSS...?
BCB
WELL, IT DOESN'T LOOK TOO NICE, BUT IT'S GOT ITS ADVANTAGES.
IT'LL GET US THERE FASTER THAN ANYTHING.
AND YOU CAN'T SEE IN FROM THE OUTSIDE, SO IT'S GOOD FOR TRAVELING IN SECRET.

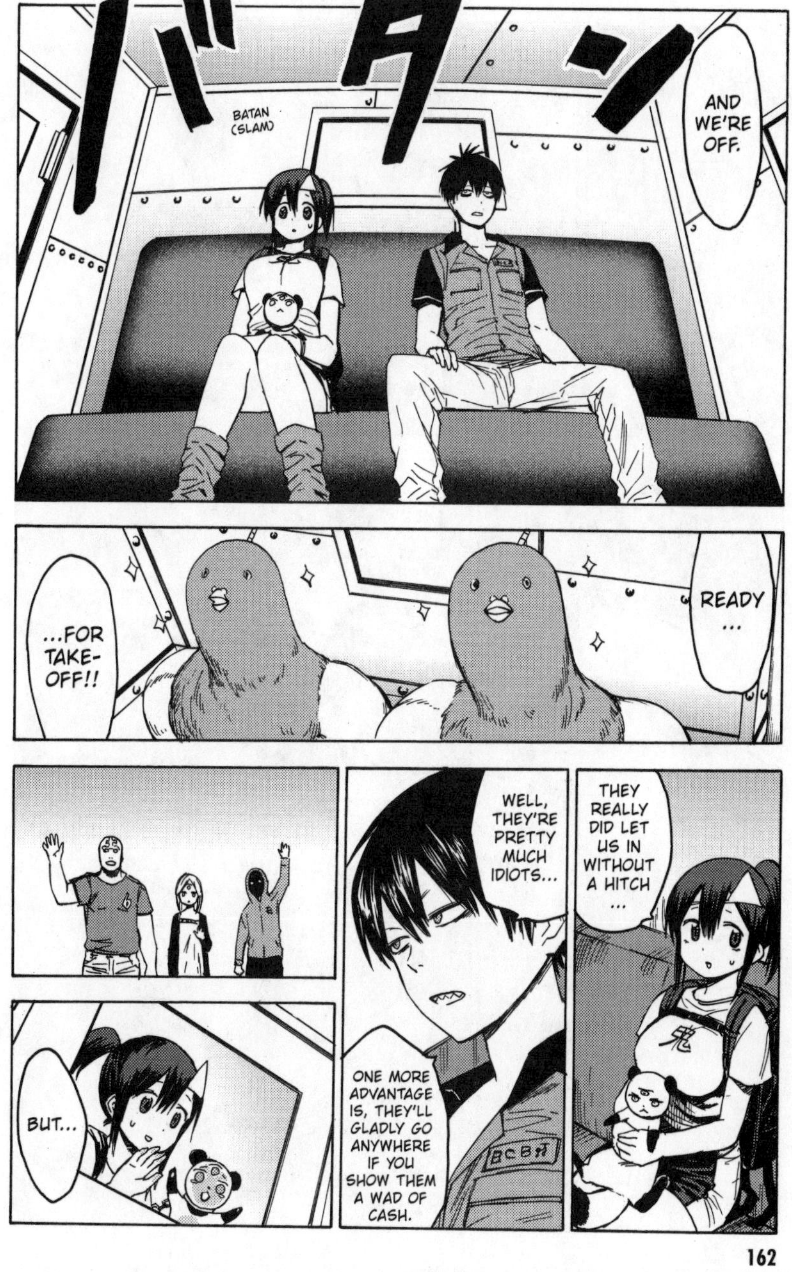
AND WE'RE OFF.
バタッ
BATAN (SLAM)
READY...
...FOR TAKE-OFF!!
THEY REALLY DID LET US IN WITHOUT A HITCH...
鬼
WELL, THEY'RE PRETTY MUCH IDIOTS...
ONE MORE ADVANTAGE IS, THEY'LL GLADLY GO ANYWHERE IF YOU SHOW THEM A WAD OF CASH.
BUT...

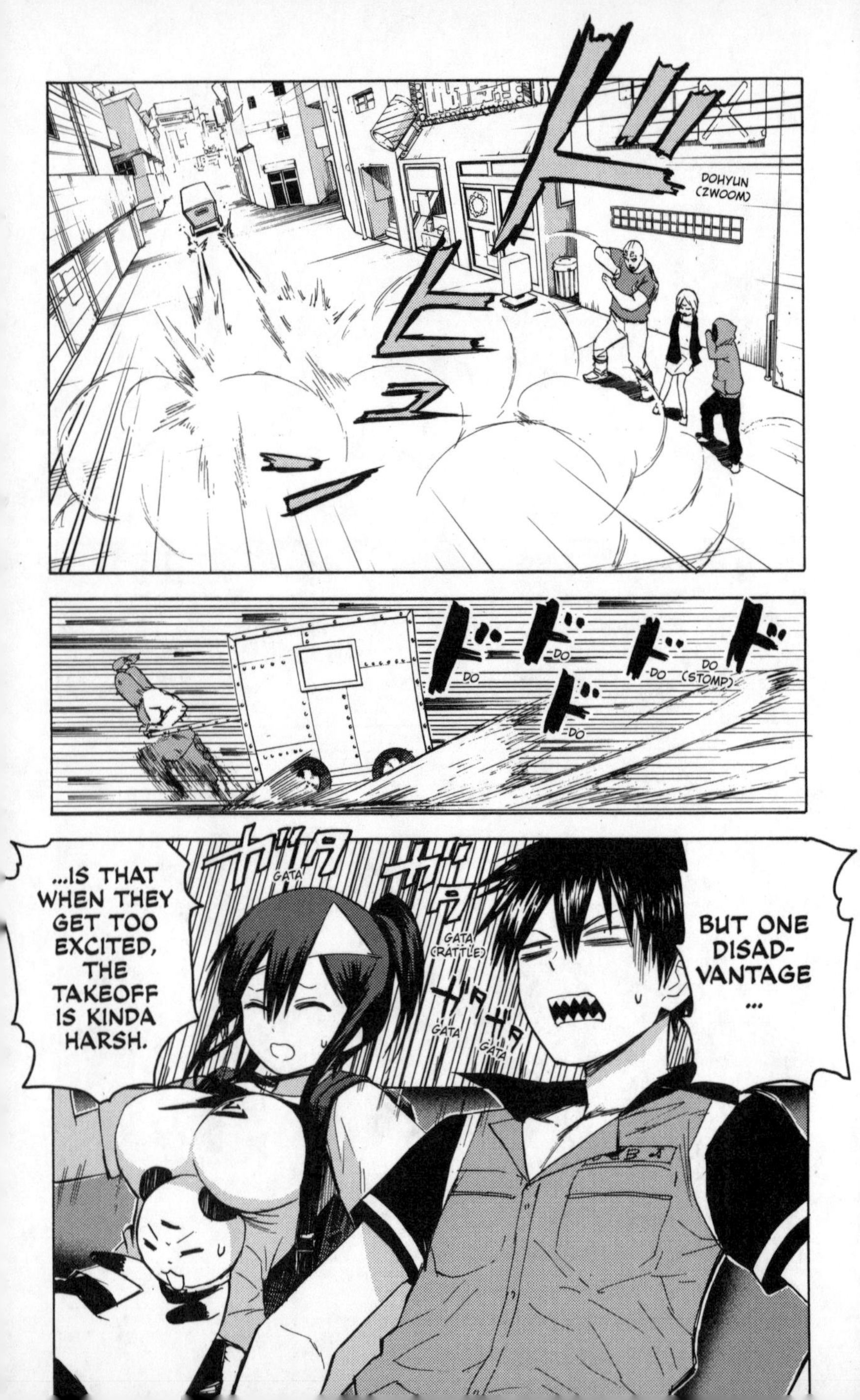
DOHYUN (ZWOOM)
DO (STOMP)
-DO
-DO
-DO
DO
BUT ONE DISAD-VANTAGE ...
GATA (RATTLE)
GATA
GATA
GATA
...IS THAT WHEN THEY GET TOO EXCITED, THE TAKEOFF IS KINDA HARSH.

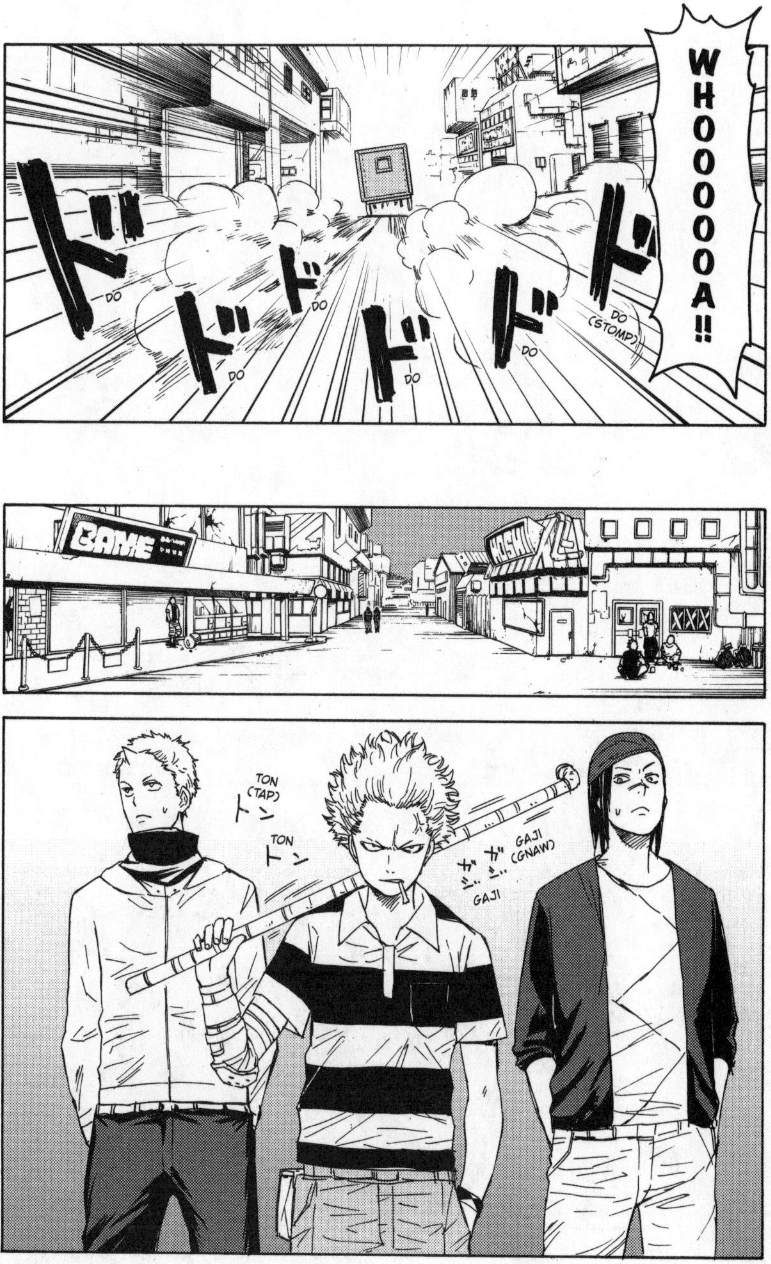
WHOOOOOA!!
DO (STOMP)
DO
DO
DO
DO
DO
GAJI (GNAW)
GAJI
TON (TAP)
TON

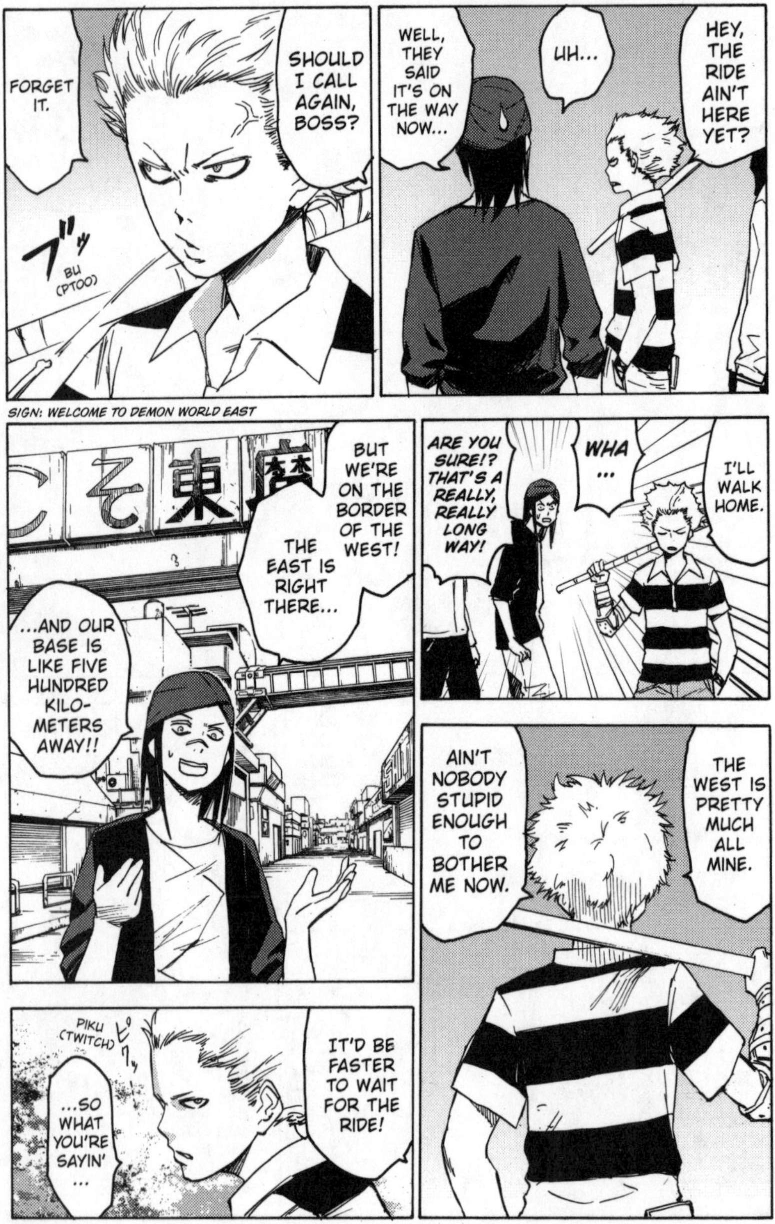
HEY, THE RIDE AIN'T HERE YET?
UH...
WELL, THEY SAID IT'S ON THE WAY NOW...
SHOULD I CALL AGAIN, BOSS?
FORGET IT.
BU (PTOO)
SIGN: WELCOME TO DEMON WORLD EAST
I'LL WALK HOME.
WHA ...
ARE YOU SURE!? THAT'S A REALLY, REALLY LONG WAY!
THE WEST IS PRETTY MUCH ALL MINE.
AIN'T NOBODY STUPID ENOUGH TO BOTHER ME NOW.
BUT WE'RE ON THE BORDER OF THE WEST!
THE EAST IS RIGHT THERE...
...AND OUR BASE IS LIKE FIVE HUNDRED KILO-METERS AWAY!!
IT'D BE FASTER TO WAIT FOR THE RIDE!
PIKU (TWITCH)
...SO WHAT YOU'RE SAYIN' ...

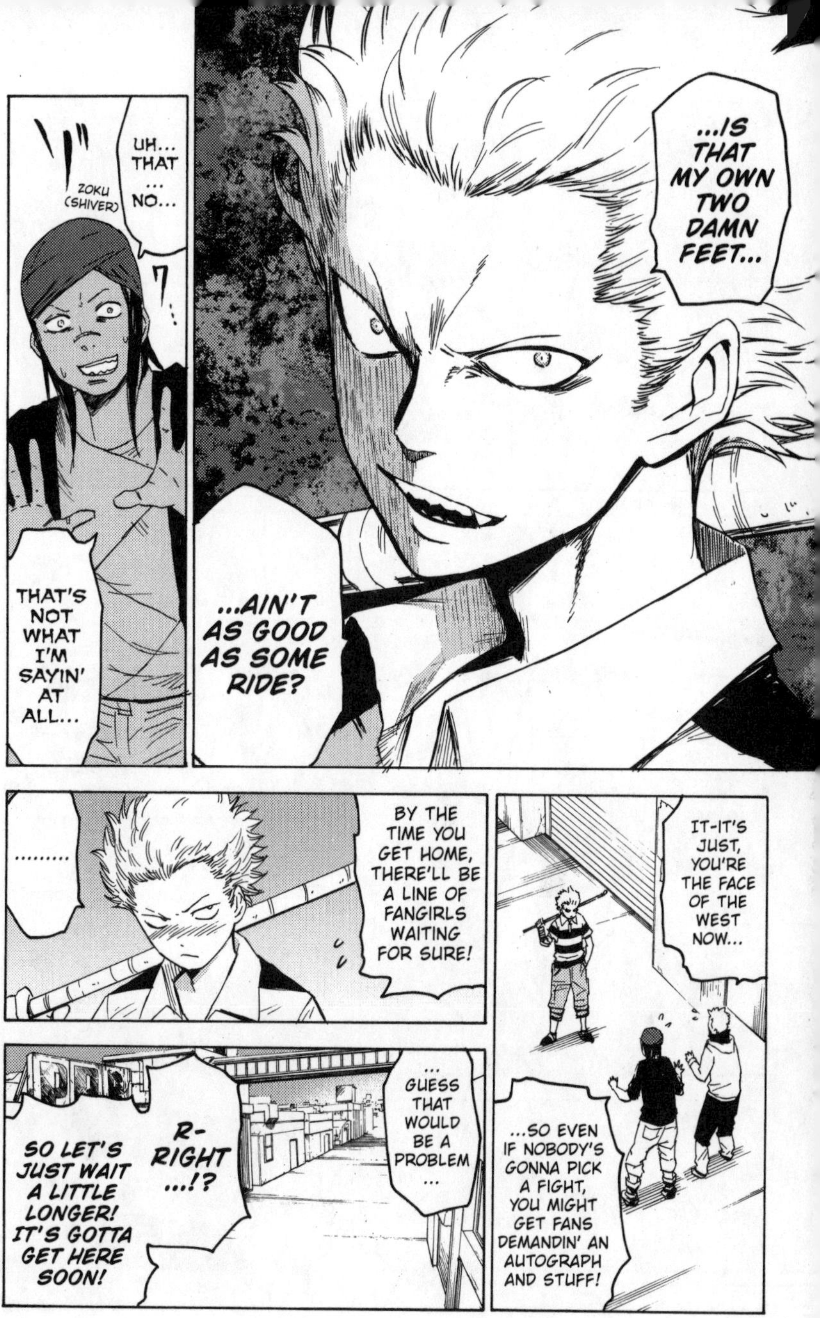

...IS THAT MY OWN TWO DAMN FEET...
...AIN'T AS GOOD AS SOME RIDE?
UH... THAT ... NO...
ZOKU (SHIVER)
THAT'S NOT WHAT I'M SAYIN' AT ALL...
IT-IT'S JUST, YOU'RE THE FACE OF THE WEST NOW...
...SO EVEN IF NOBODY'S GONNA PICK A FIGHT, YOU MIGHT GET FANS DEMANDIN' AN AUTOGRAPH AND STUFF!
BY THE TIME YOU GET HOME, THERE'LL BE A LINE OF FANGIRLS WAITING FOR SURE!
.........
... GUESS THAT WOULD BE A PROBLEM ...
R-RIGHT ...!?
SO LET'S JUST WAIT A LITTLE LONGER! IT'S GOTTA GET HERE SOON!

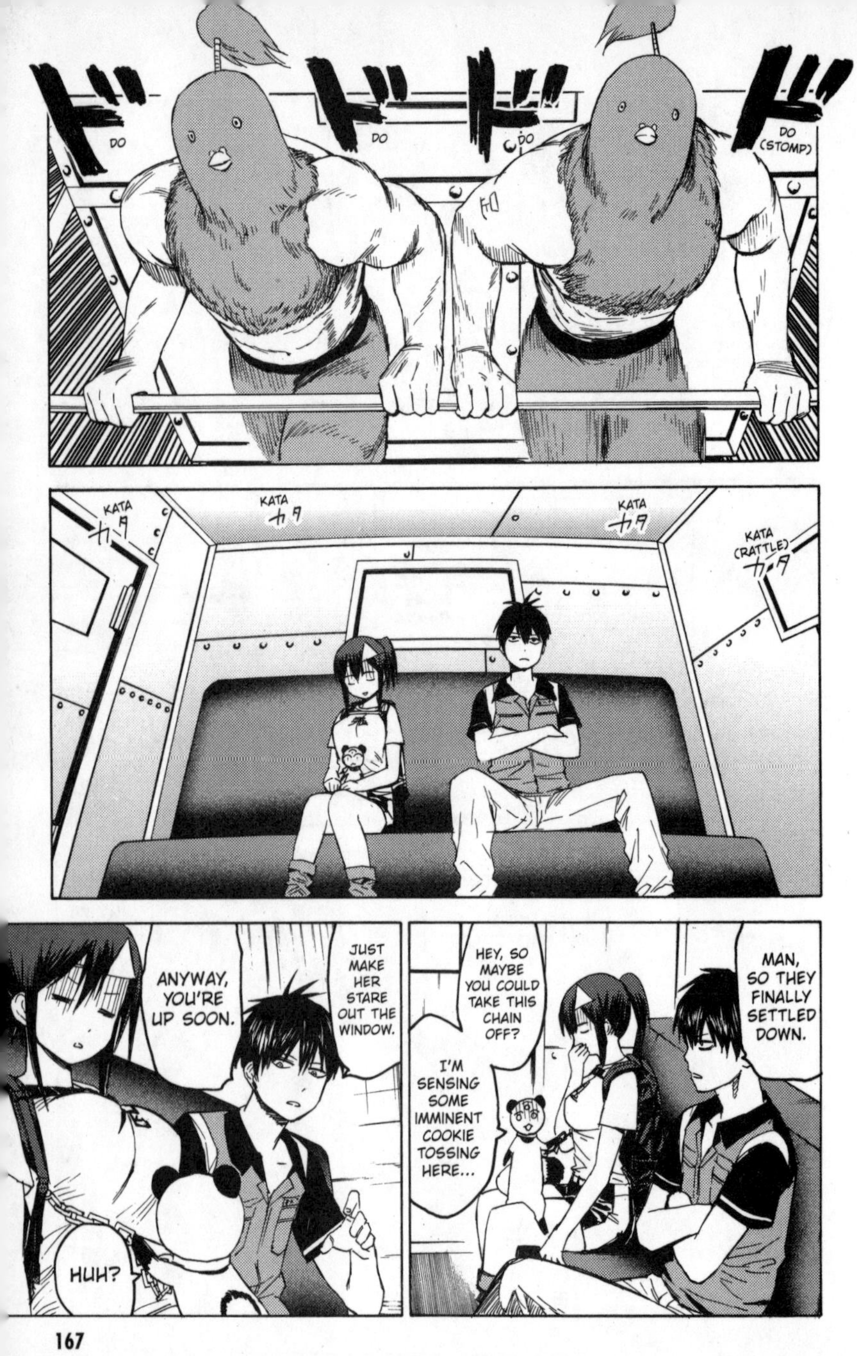
ド
DO (STOMP)
ド
DO
ド
DO
ド
DO
KATA (RATTLE) カタ
KATA カタ
KATA カタ
KATA カタ
MAN, SO THEY FINALLY SETTLED DOWN.
HEY, SO MAYBE YOU COULD TAKE THIS CHAIN OFF?
I'M SENSING SOME IMMINENT COOKIE TOSSING HERE...
JUST MAKE HER STARE OUT THE WINDOW.
ANYWAY, YOU'RE UP SOON.
HUH?

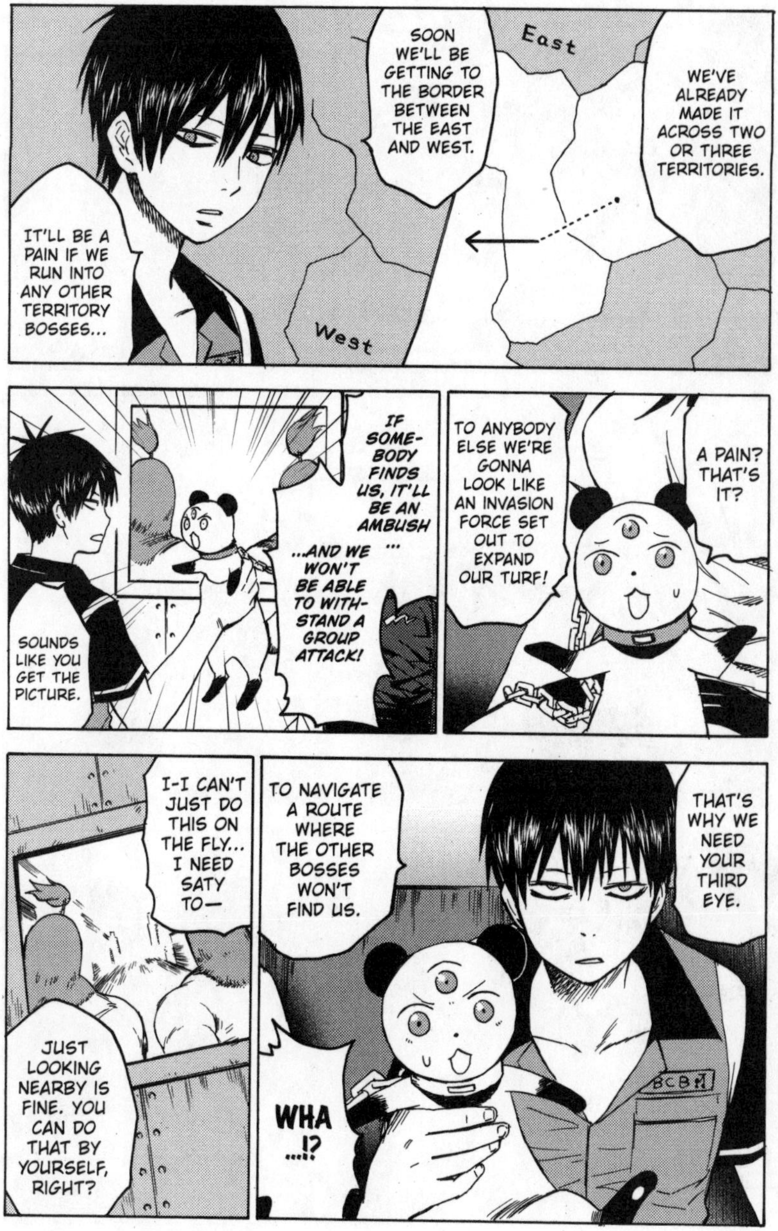
WE'VE ALREADY MADE IT ACROSS TWO OR THREE TERRITORIES.
East
SOON WE'LL BE GETTING TO THE BORDER BETWEEN THE EAST AND WEST.
West
IT'LL BE A PAIN IF WE RUN INTO ANY OTHER TERRITORY BOSSES...
A PAIN? THAT'S IT?
TO ANYBODY ELSE WE'RE GONNA LOOK LIKE AN INVASION FORCE SET OUT TO EXPAND OUR TURF!
IF SOMEBODY FINDS US, IT'LL BE AN AMBUSH ...
...AND WE WON'T BE ABLE TO WITHSTAND A GROUP ATTACK!
SOUNDS LIKE YOU GET THE PICTURE.
THAT'S WHY WE NEED YOUR THIRD EYE.
TO NAVIGATE A ROUTE WHERE THE OTHER BOSSES WON'T FIND US.
WHA ...!?
I-I CAN'T JUST DO THIS ON THE FLY... I NEED SATY TO—
JUST LOOKING NEARBY IS FINE. YOU CAN DO THAT BY YOURSELF, RIGHT?

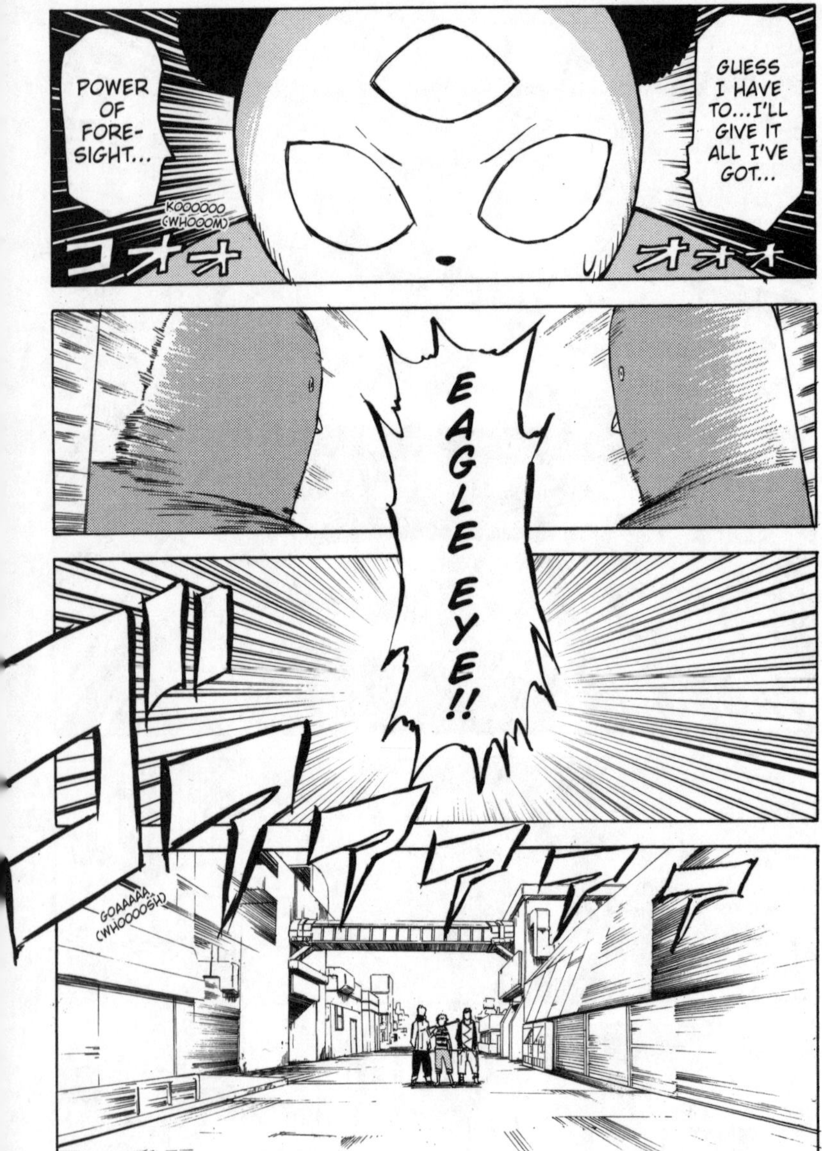
GUESS I HAVE TO...I'LL GIVE IT ALL I'VE GOT...
POWER OF FORE-SIGHT...
KOOOOOO (WHOOOM)
EAGLE EYE!!
GOAAAAA (WHOOOOSH)

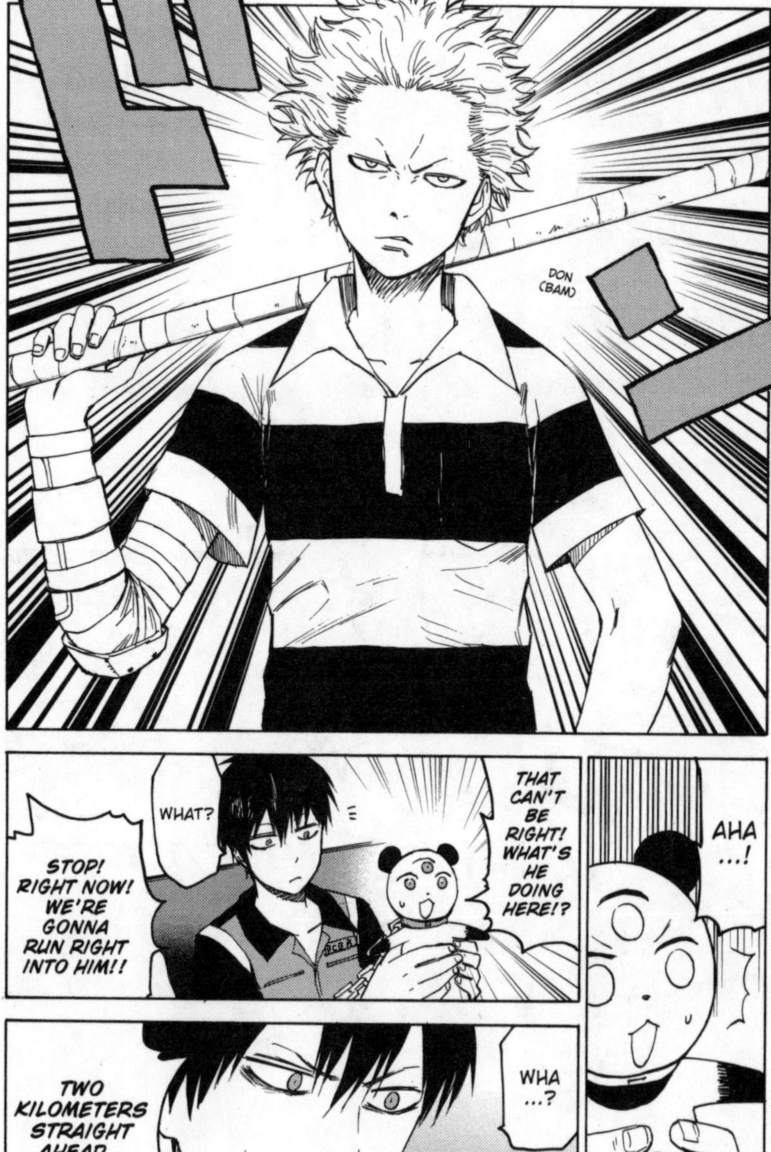
DON (BAM)
AHA ...!
THAT CAN'T BE RIGHT! WHAT'S HE DOING HERE!?
WHAT?
STOP! RIGHT NOW! WE'RE GONNA RUN RIGHT INTO HIM!!
WHA ...?
TWO KILOMETERS STRAIGHT AHEAD...

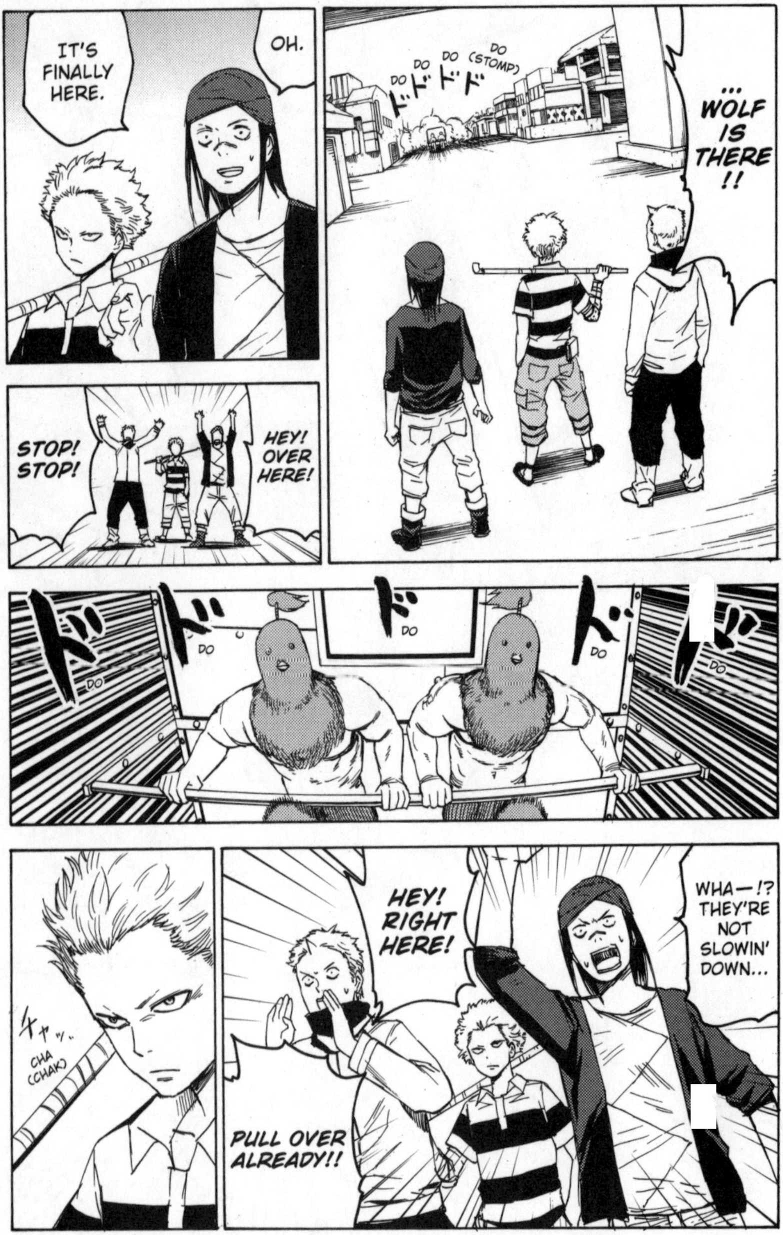
DO DO DO DO (STOMP)
...WOLF IS THERE!!
OH.
IT'S FINALLY HERE.
HEY! OVER HERE!
STOP! STOP!
DO
DO
DO
DO
DO
WHA—!? THEY'RE NOT SLOWIN' DOWN...
HEY! RIGHT HERE!
PULL OVER ALREADY!!
CHA (CHAK)

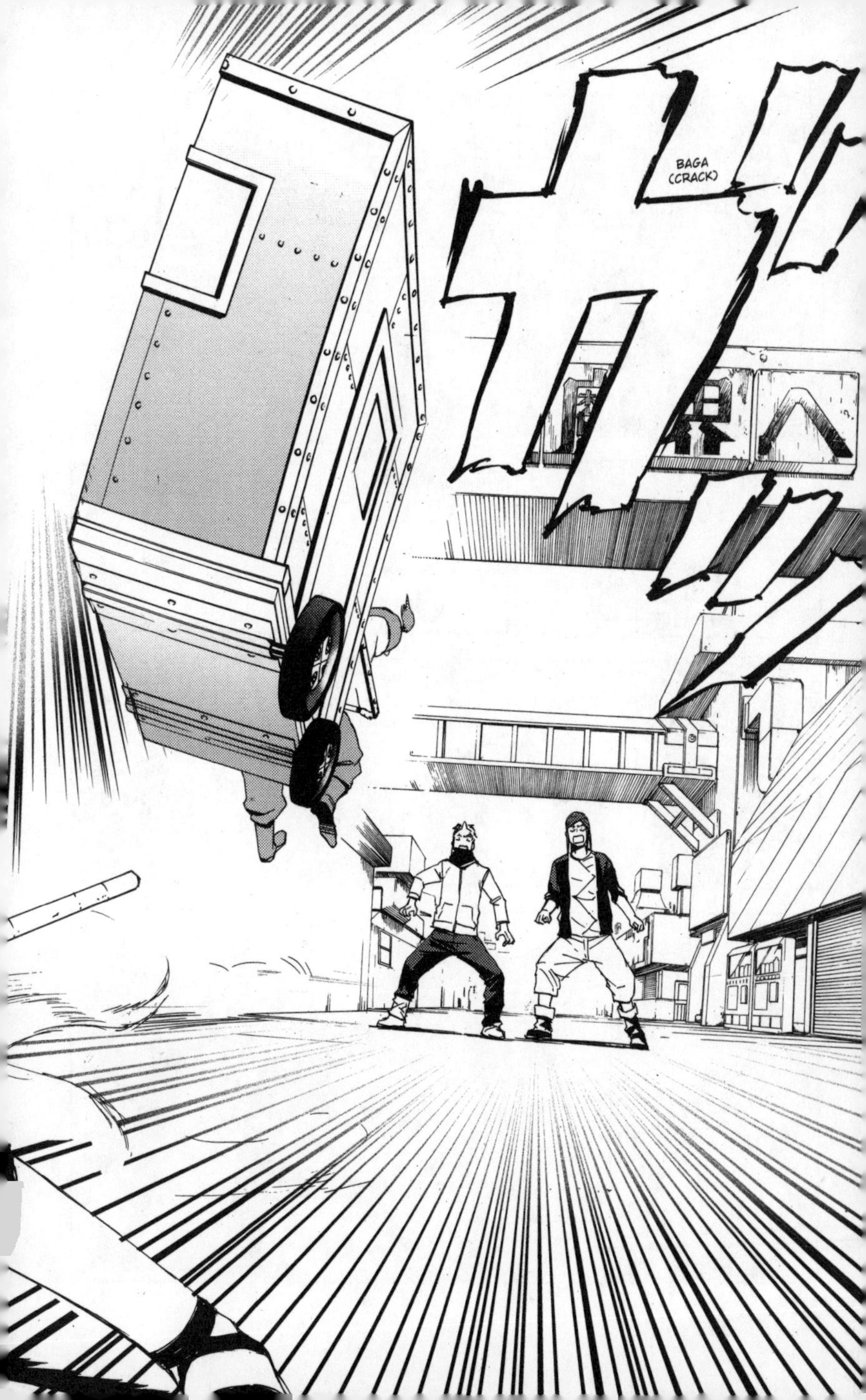
BAGA
(CRACK)

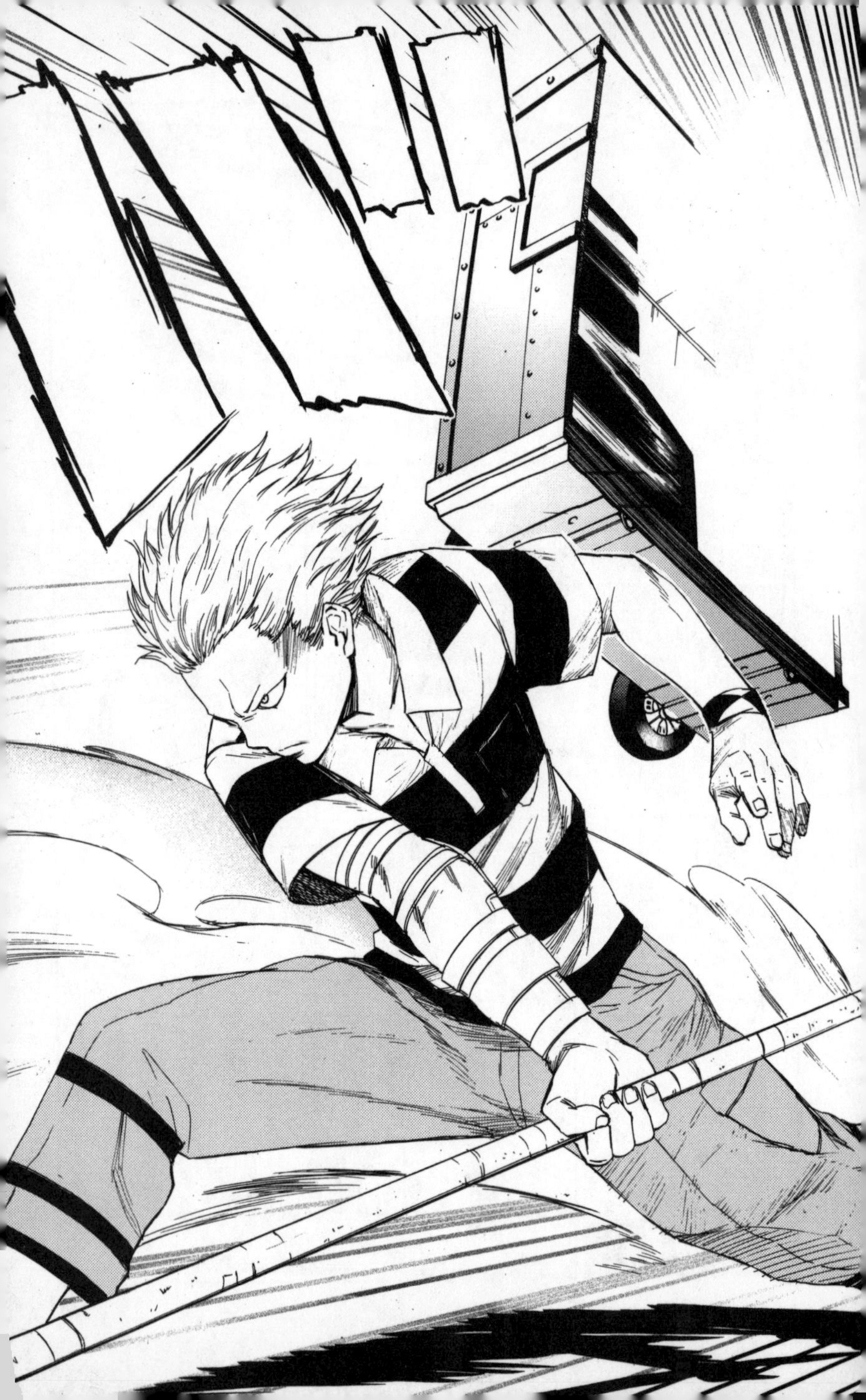

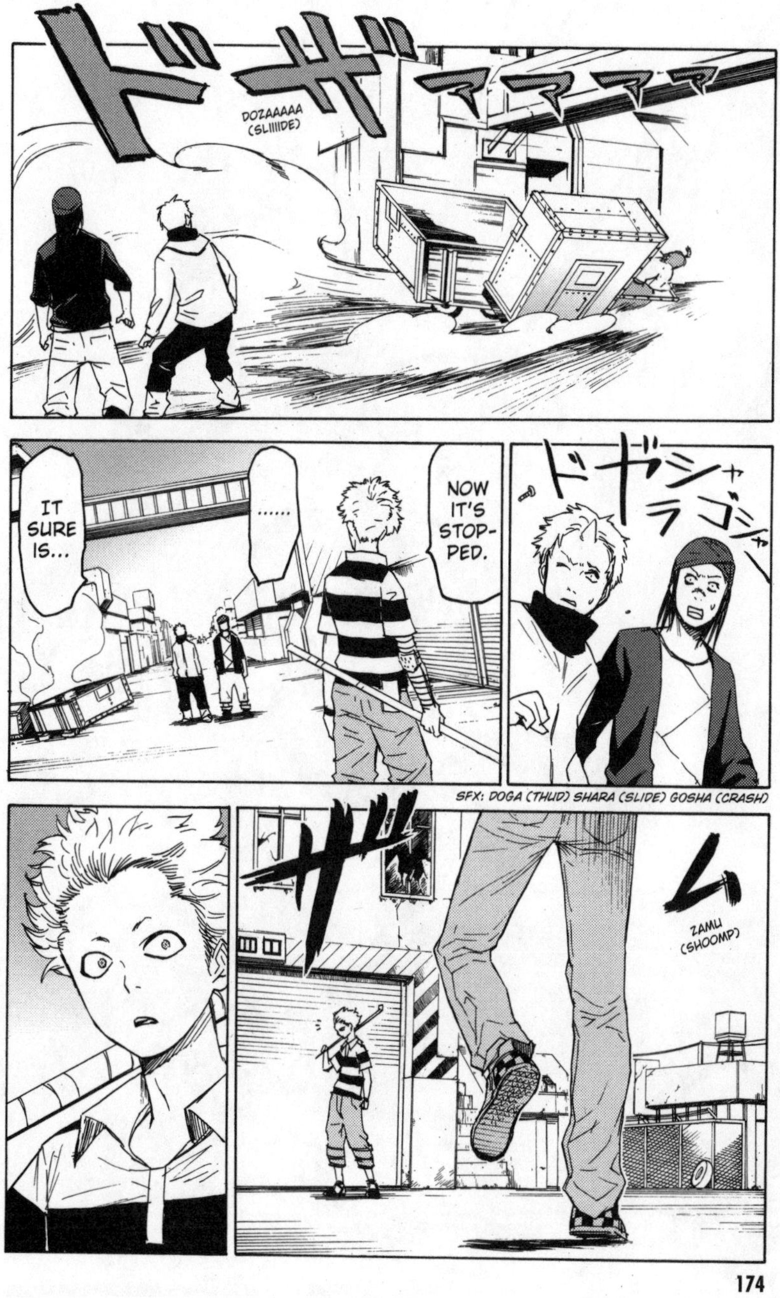
ドザァァァァ
DOZAAAAA (SLIIIIDE)
ドガシャラゴシャ
NOW IT'S STOP-PED.
......
IT SURE IS...
SFX: DOGA (THUD) SHARA (SLIDE) GOSHA (CRASH)
ザム
ZAMU (SHOOMP)

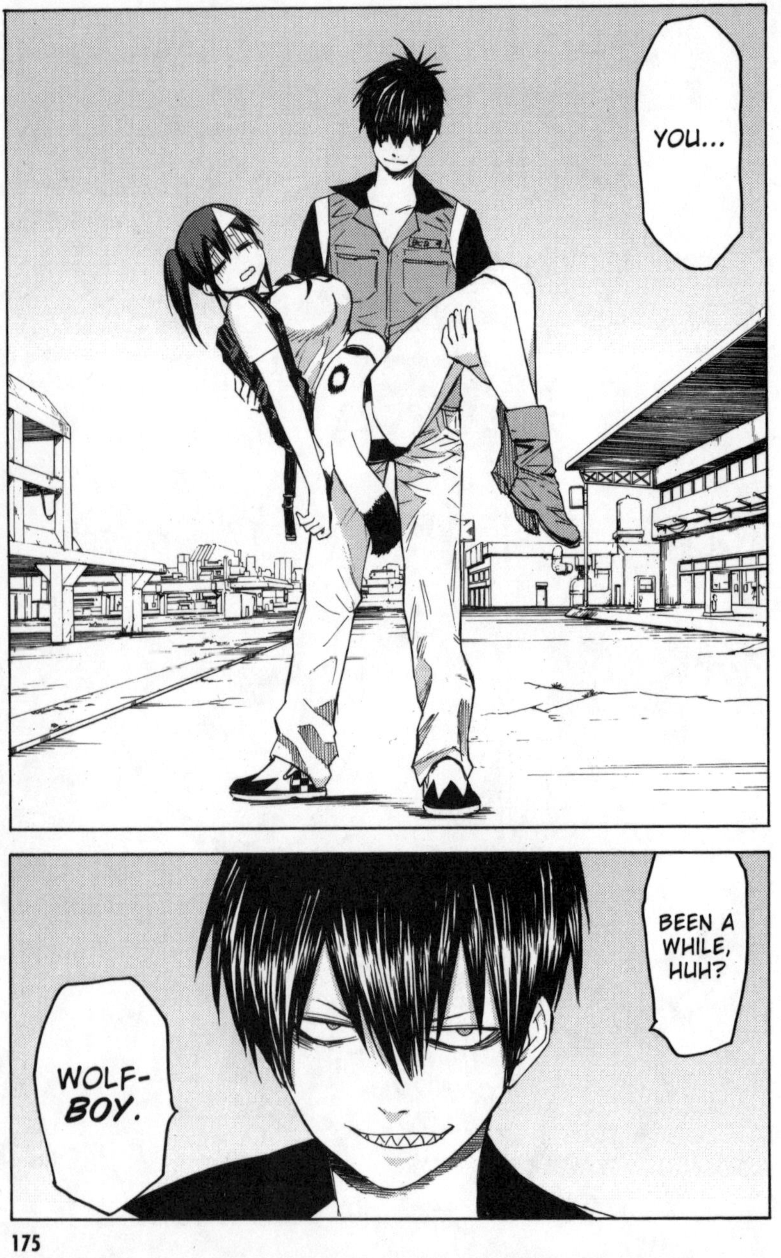
YOU...
BEEN A WHILE, HUH?
WOLF-BOY.

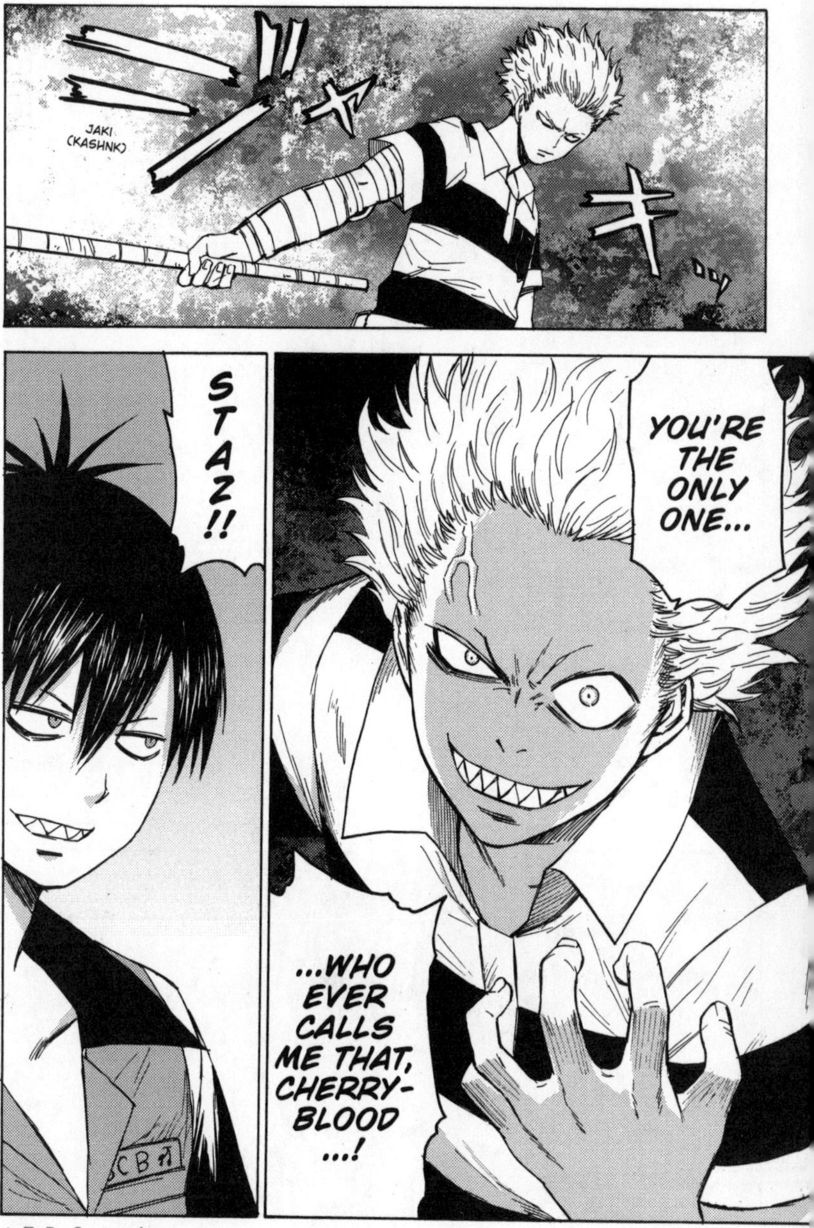
JAKI (KASHNK)
YOU'RE THE ONLY ONE...
...WHO EVER CALLS ME THAT, CHERRY-BLOOD ...!
STAZ!!

♠ To Be Continued ♠

# LIVING IN THE DEMON WORLD

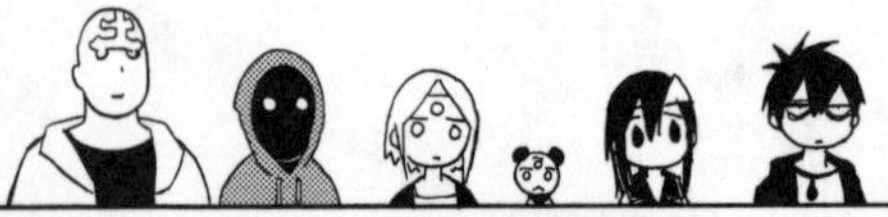

## STAZ'S EVERYDAY LIFE

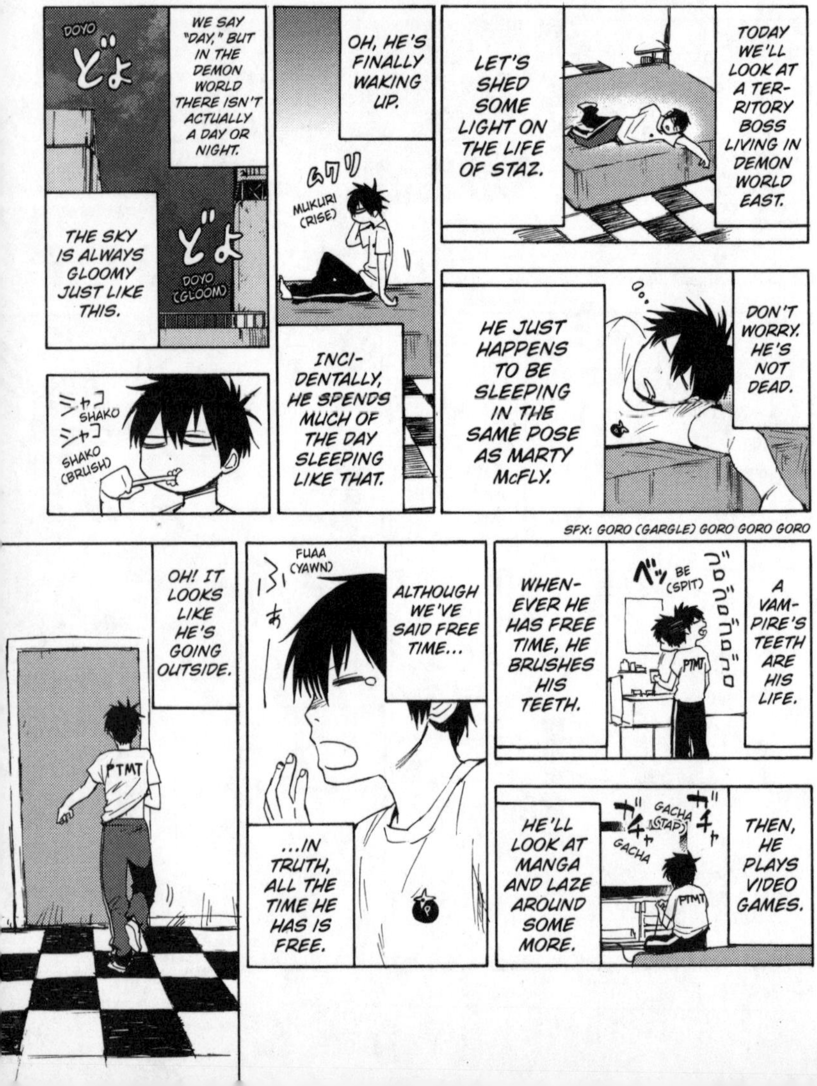
TODAY WE'LL LOOK AT A TERRITORY BOSS LIVING IN DEMON WORLD EAST.
LET'S SHED SOME LIGHT ON THE LIFE OF STAZ.
DON'T WORRY. HE'S NOT DEAD.
HE JUST HAPPENS TO BE SLEEPING IN THE SAME POSE AS MARTY McFLY.
OH, HE'S FINALLY WAKING UP.
ムクリ
MUKURI (RISE)
INCIDENTALLY, HE SPENDS MUCH OF THE DAY SLEEPING LIKE THAT.
WE SAY "DAY," BUT IN THE DEMON WORLD THERE ISN'T ACTUALLY A DAY OR NIGHT.
どよ
DOYO
THE SKY IS ALWAYS GLOOMY JUST LIKE THIS.
どよ
DOYO (GLOOM)
シャコ
SHAKO
シャコ
SHAKO (BRUSH)
SFX: GORO (GARGLE) GORO GORO GORO
A VAMPIRE'S TEETH ARE HIS LIFE.
ゴロゴロゴロ
ベッ
BE (SPIT)
WHENEVER HE HAS FREE TIME, HE BRUSHES HIS TEETH.
THEN, HE PLAYS VIDEO GAMES.
ガチャ
GACHA (TAP)
ガチャ
GACHA
HE'LL LOOK AT MANGA AND LAZE AROUND SOME MORE.
ALTHOUGH WE'VE SAID FREE TIME...
ふぁ
FUAA (YAWN)
...IN TRUTH, ALL THE TIME HE HAS IS FREE.
OH! IT LOOKS LIKE HE'S GOING OUTSIDE.

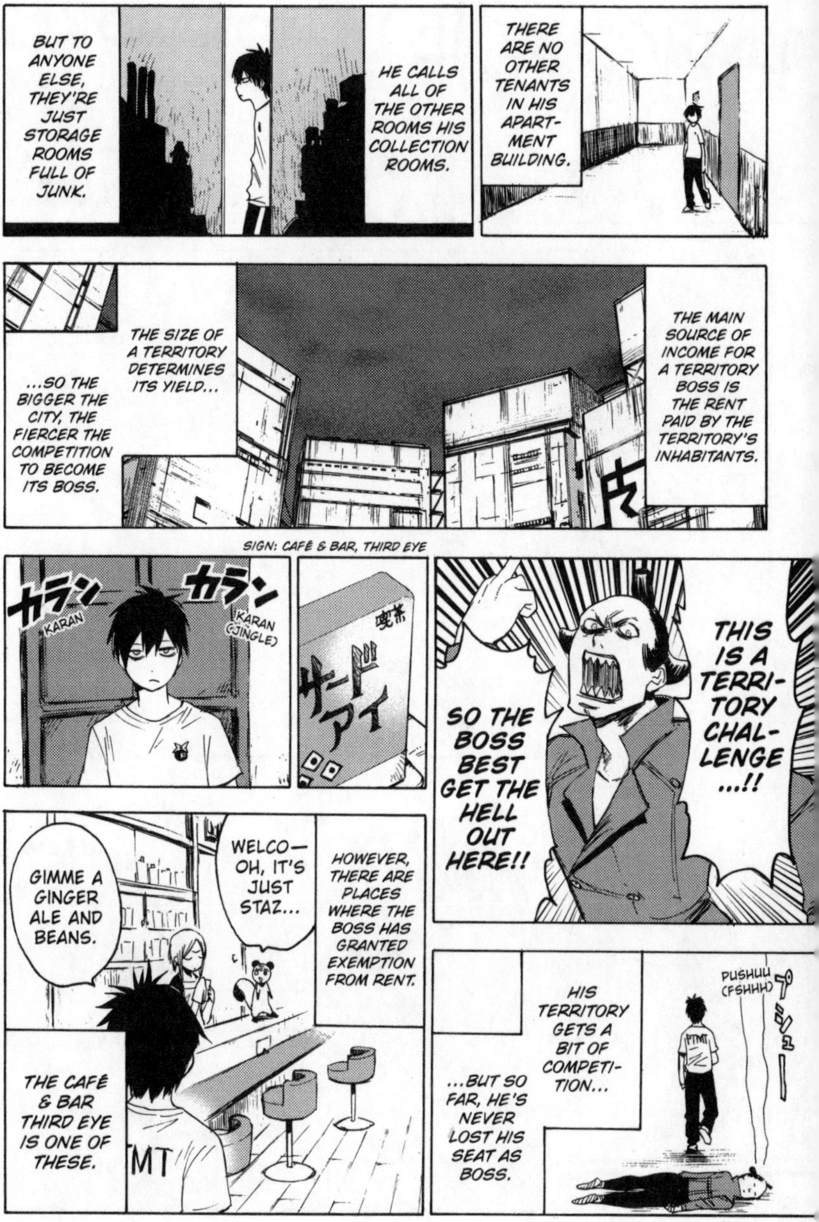
THERE ARE NO OTHER TENANTS IN HIS APARTMENT BUILDING.
HE CALLS ALL OF THE OTHER ROOMS HIS COLLECTION ROOMS.
BUT TO ANYONE ELSE, THEY'RE JUST STORAGE ROOMS FULL OF JUNK.
THE MAIN SOURCE OF INCOME FOR A TERRITORY BOSS IS THE RENT PAID BY THE TERRITORY'S INHABITANTS.
THE SIZE OF A TERRITORY DETERMINES ITS YIELD...
...SO THE BIGGER THE CITY, THE FIERCER THE COMPETITION TO BECOME ITS BOSS.
THIS IS A TERRITORY CHALLENGE...!!
SO THE BOSS BEST GET THE HELL OUT HERE!!
HIS TERRITORY GETS A BIT OF COMPETITION...
...BUT SO FAR, HE'S NEVER LOST HIS SEAT AS BOSS.
プシュー
PUSHUU (FSHHH)
SIGN: CAFÉ & BAR, THIRD EYE
喫茶
サードアイ
カラン
KARAN (JINGLE)
カラン
KARAN
HOWEVER, THERE ARE PLACES WHERE THE BOSS HAS GRANTED EXEMPTION FROM RENT.
WELCO— OH, IT'S JUST STAZ...
GIMME A GINGER ALE AND BEANS.
THE CAFÉ & BAR THIRD EYE IS ONE OF THESE.

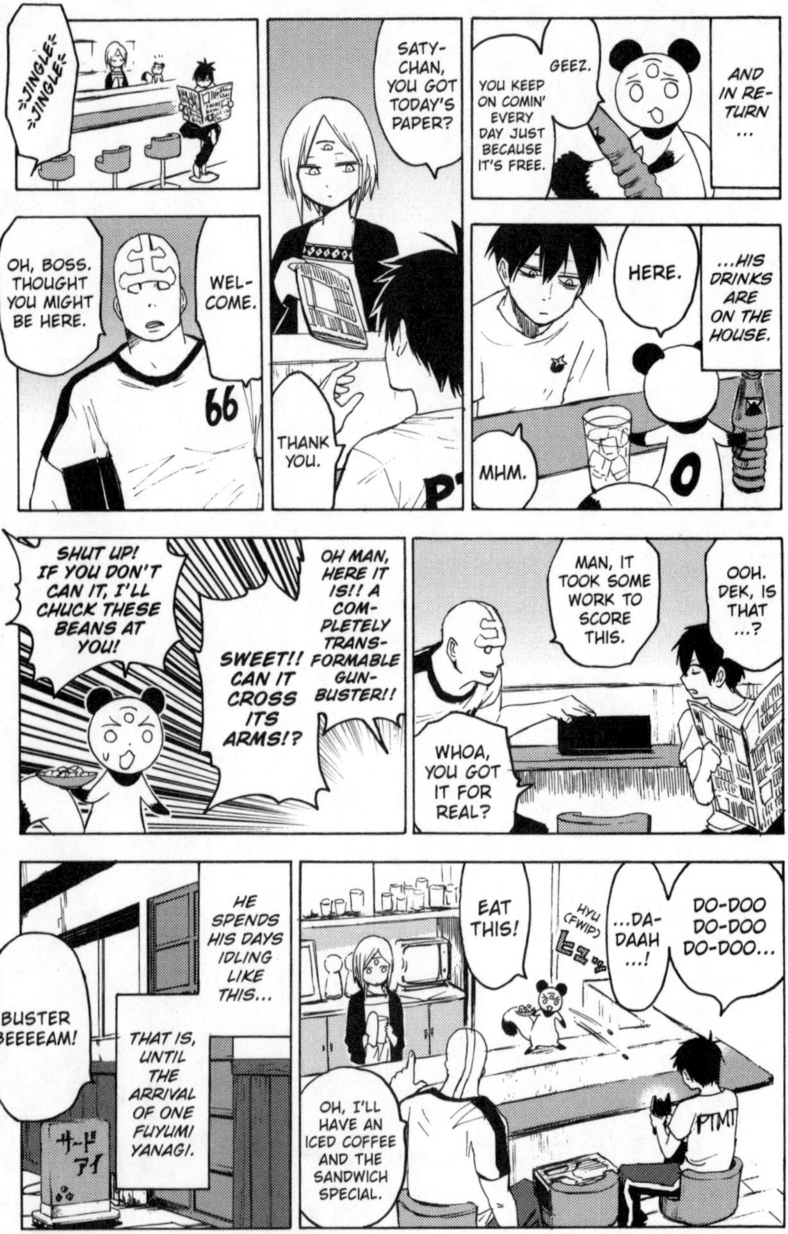
AND IN RE-TURN...
GEEZ.
YOU KEEP ON COMIN' EVERY DAY JUST BECAUSE IT'S FREE.
...HIS DRINKS ARE ON THE HOUSE.
HERE.
MHM.
SATY-CHAN, YOU GOT TODAY'S PAPER?
THANK YOU.
JINGLE JINGLE
WEL-COME.
OH, BOSS. THOUGHT YOU MIGHT BE HERE.
66
OOH. DEK, IS THAT...?
MAN, IT TOOK SOME WORK TO SCORE THIS.
WHOA, YOU GOT IT FOR REAL?
OH MAN, HERE IT IS!! A COM-PLETELY TRANS-FORMABLE GUN-BUSTER!!
SWEET!! CAN IT CROSS ITS ARMS!?
SHUT UP! IF YOU DON'T CAN IT, I'LL CHUCK THESE BEANS AT YOU!
DO-DOO DO-DOO DO-DOO...
...DA-DAAH...!
HYU (FWIP)
EAT THIS!
PTMT
OH, I'LL HAVE AN ICED COFFEE AND THE SANDWICH SPECIAL.
HE SPENDS HIS DAYS IDLING LIKE THIS...
BUSTER BEEEEAM!
THAT IS, UNTIL THE ARRIVAL OF ONE FUYUMI YANAGI.
サード アイ

END

BLOOD LAD

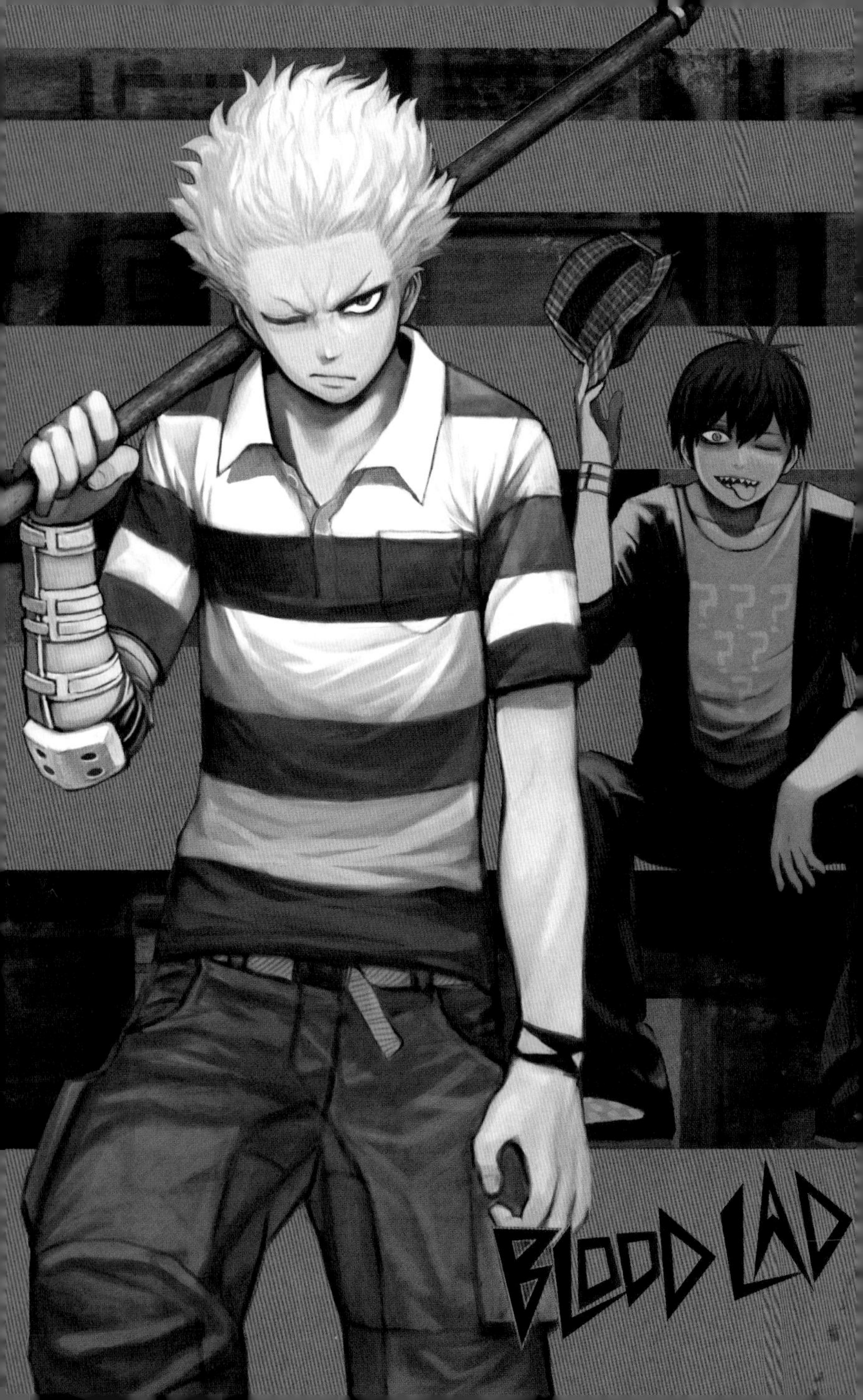
BLOOD LAD

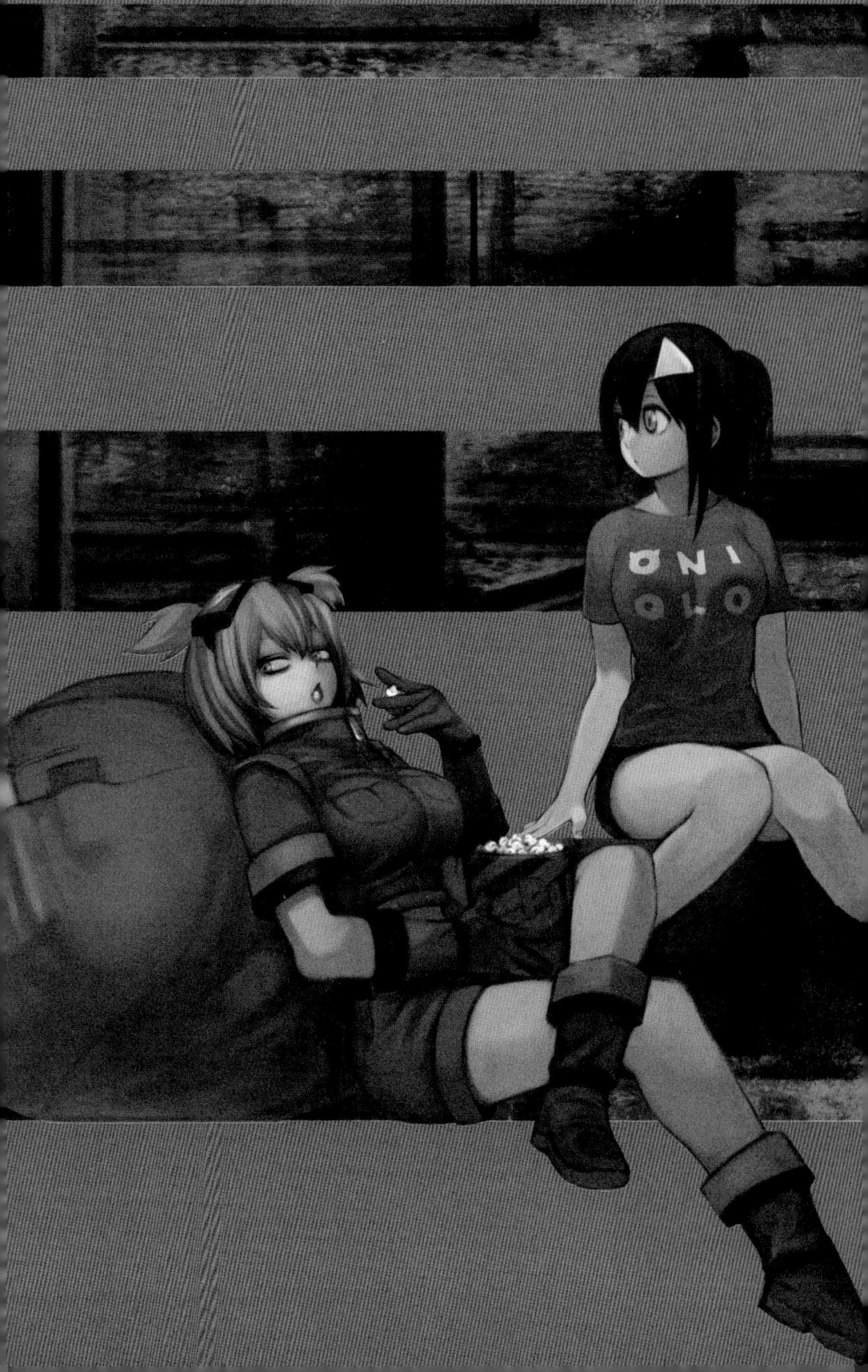

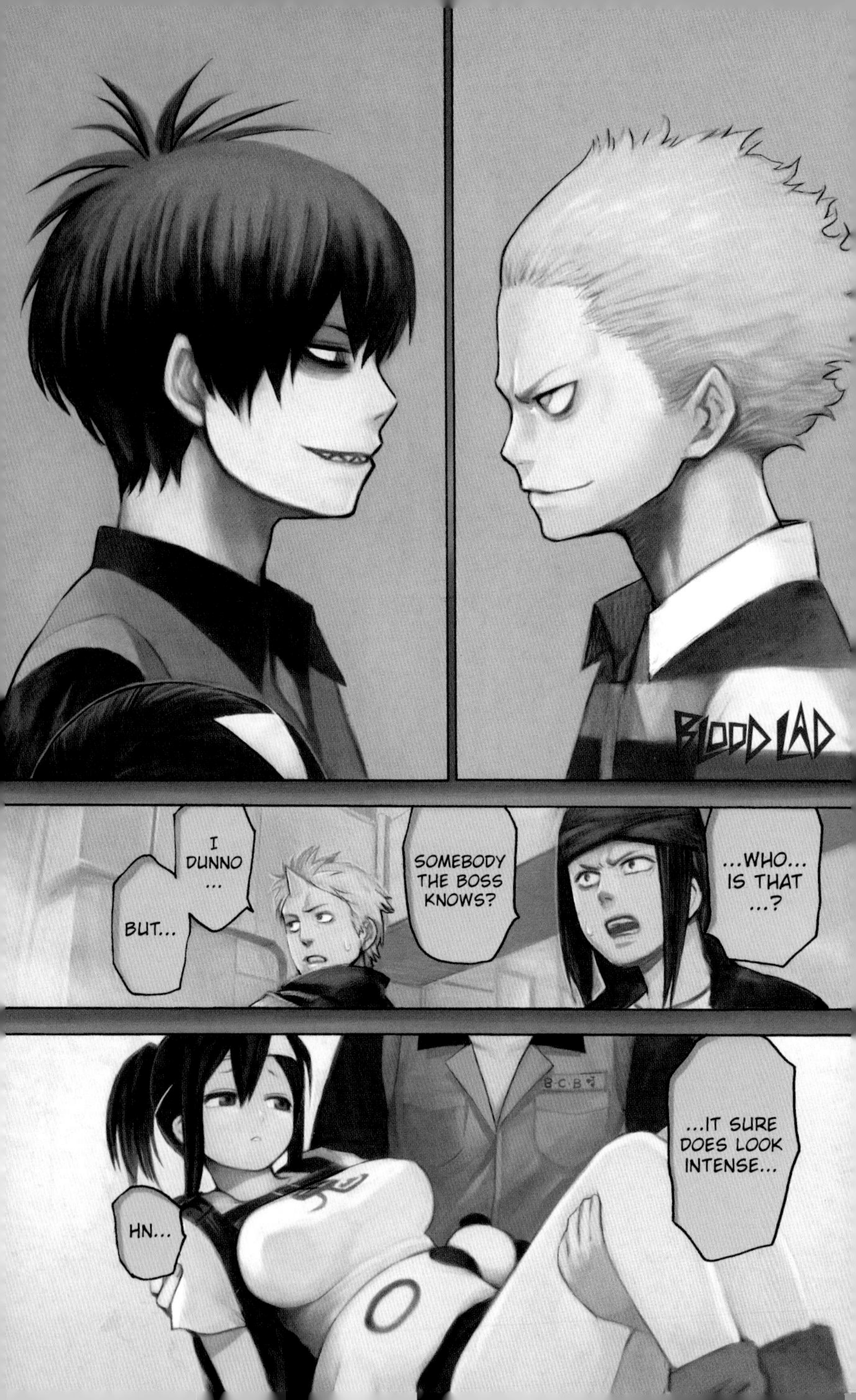
BLOOD LAD
...WHO... IS THAT ...?
SOMEBODY THE BOSS KNOWS?
I DUNNO ... BUT...
...IT SURE DOES LOOK INTENSE...
HN...

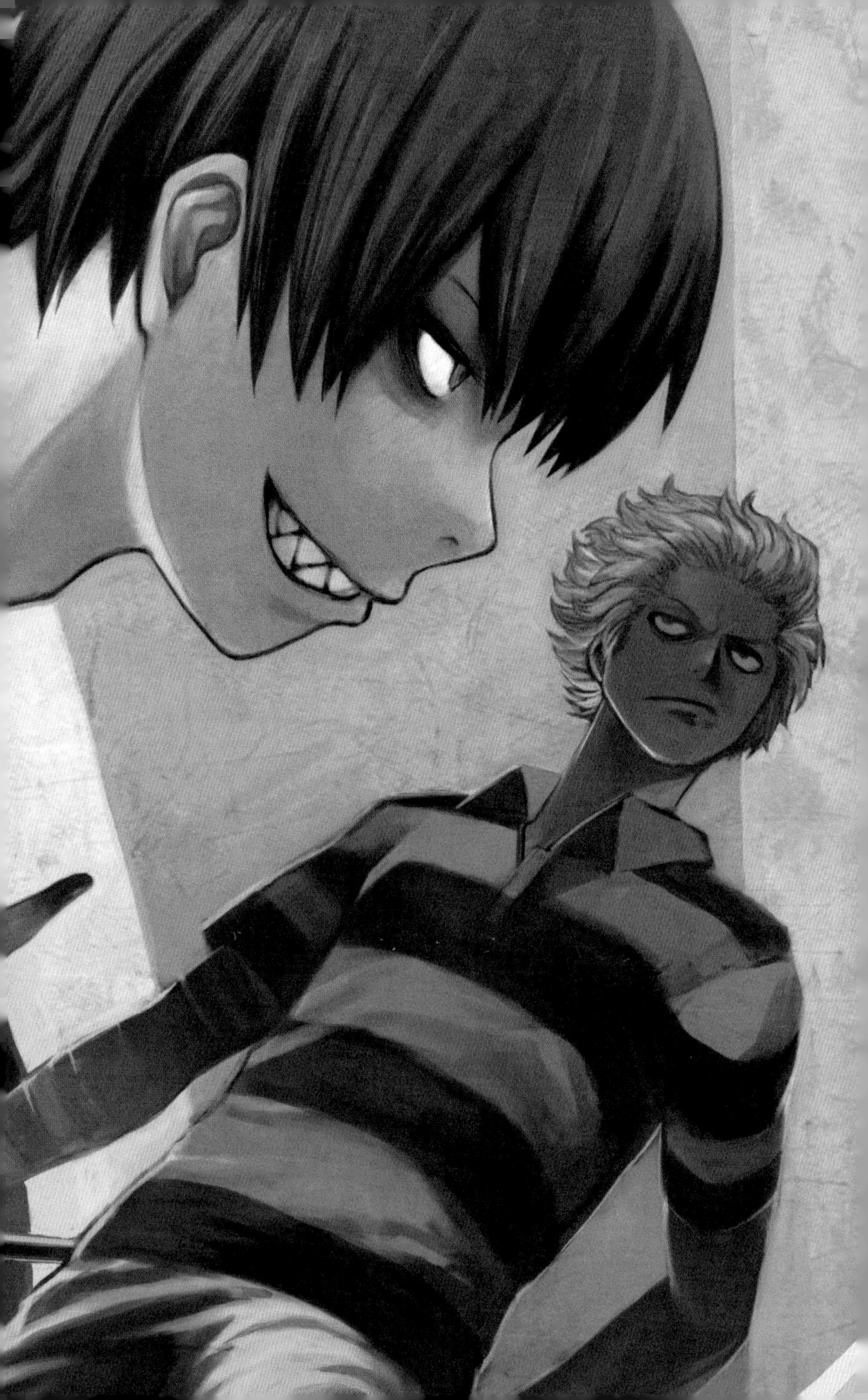

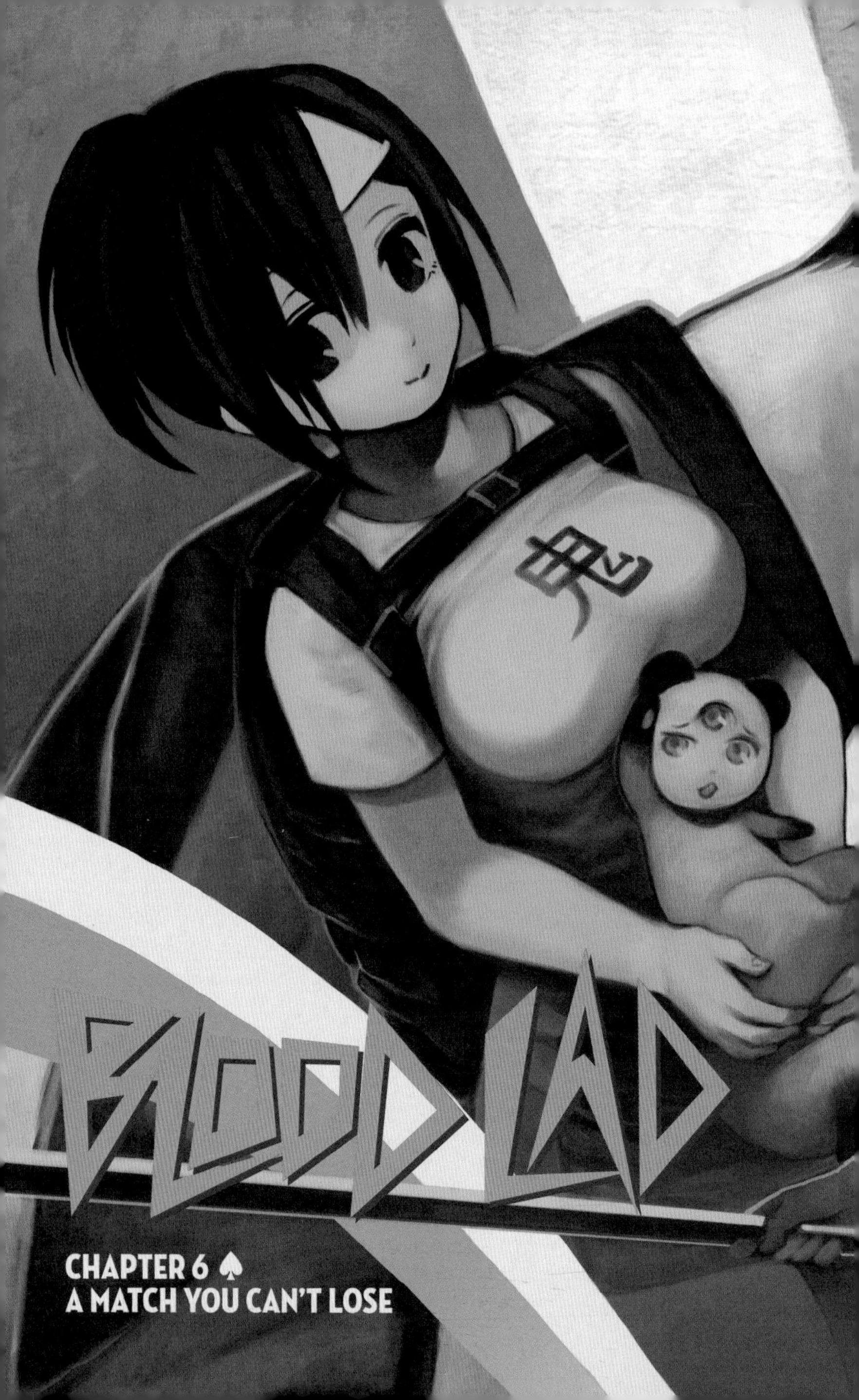
BLOOD LAD
CHAPTER 6 ♠
A MATCH YOU CAN'T LOSE

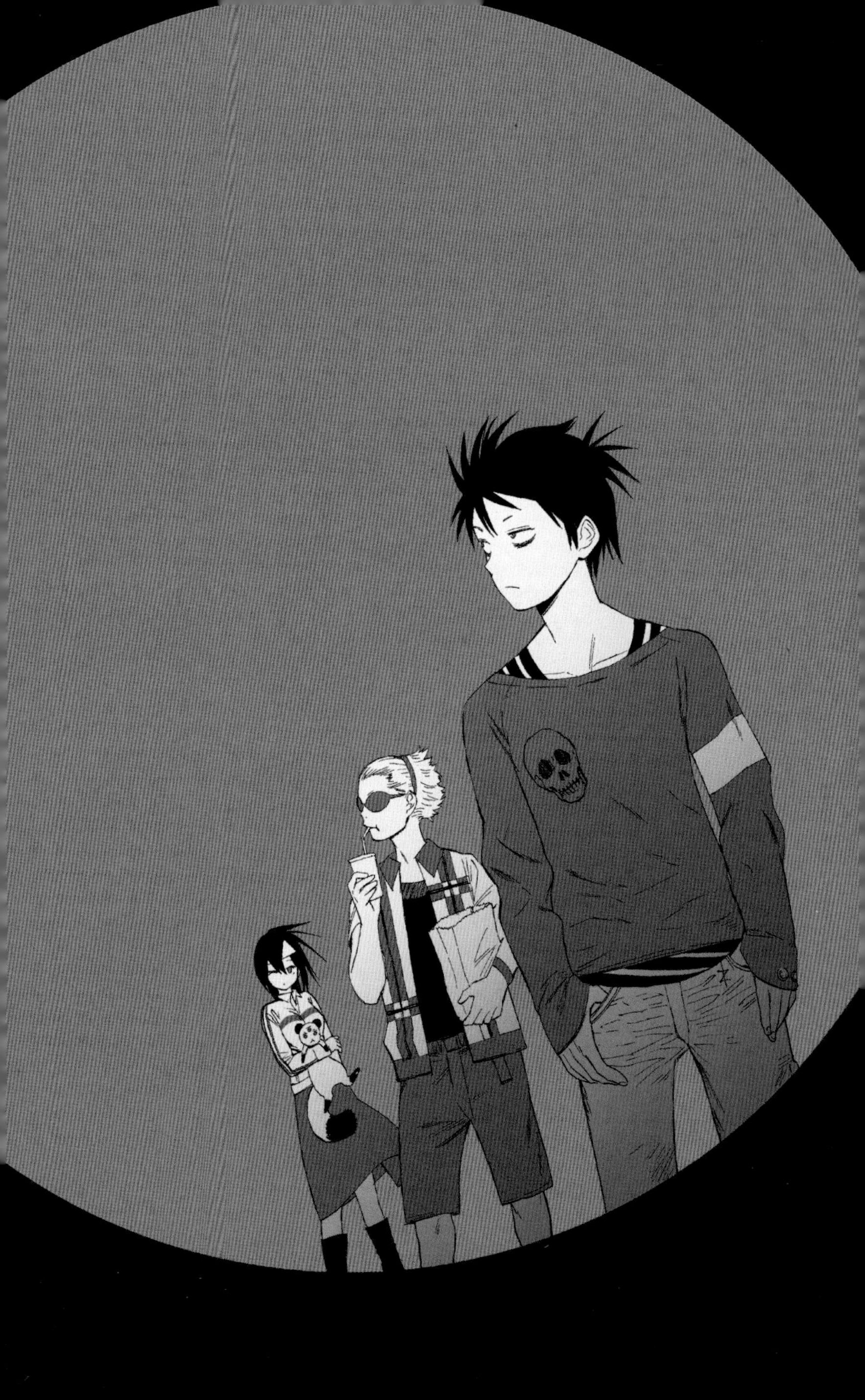

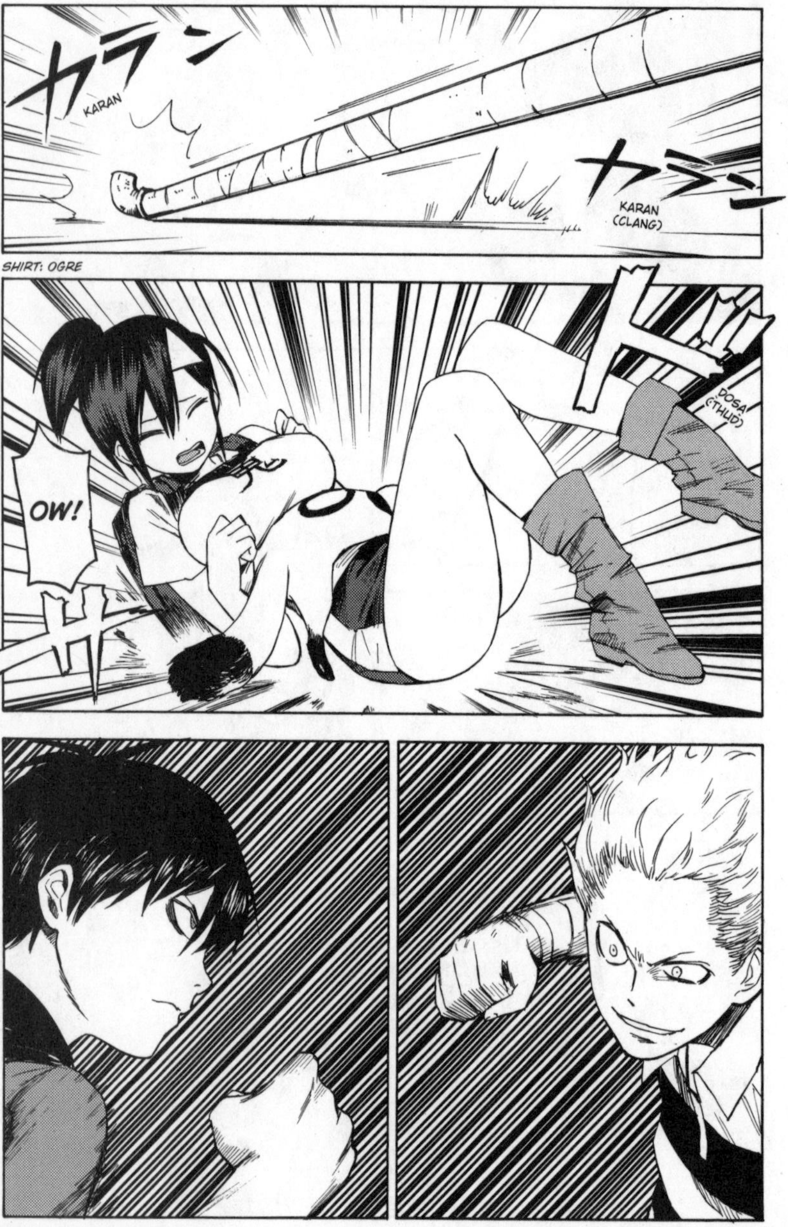

カラン
KARAN (CLANG)
カラン
KARAN
SHIRT: OGRE
DOSA (THUD)
OW!

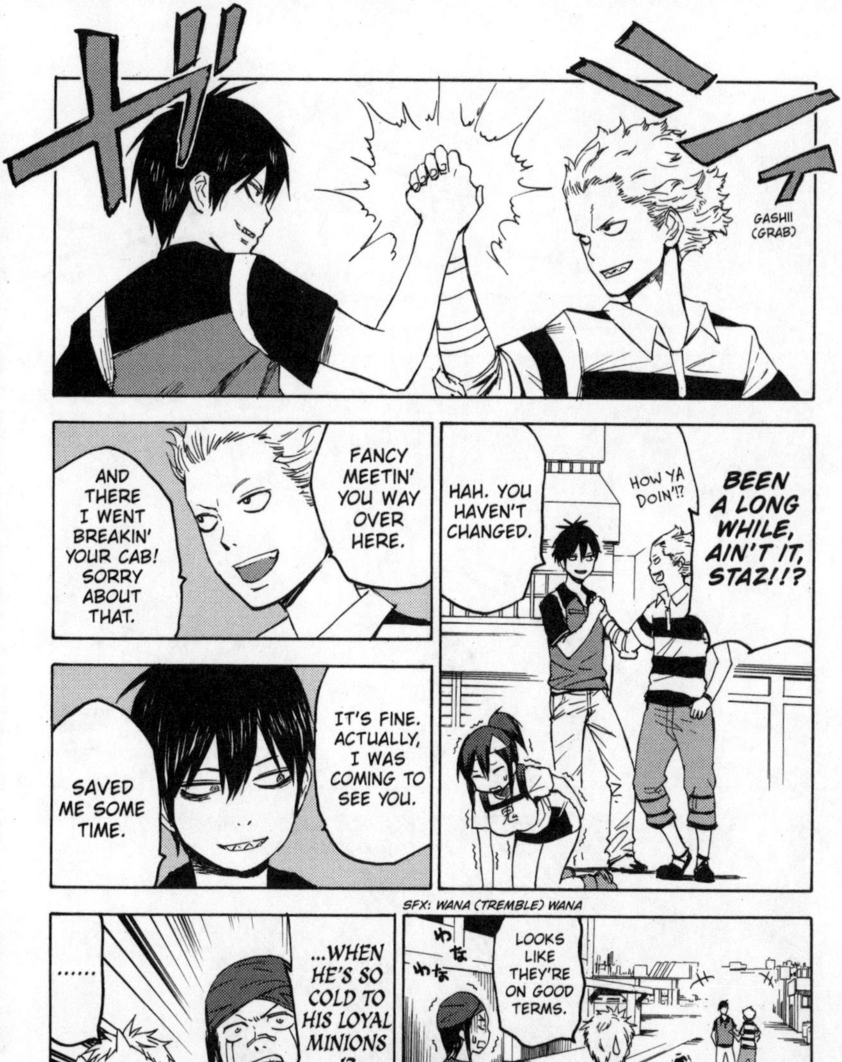
GASHII (GRAB)
BEEN A LONG WHILE, AIN'T IT, STAZ!!?
HOW YA DOIN'!?
HAH. YOU HAVEN'T CHANGED.
FANCY MEETIN' YOU WAY OVER HERE.
AND THERE I WENT BREAKIN' YOUR CAB! SORRY ABOUT THAT.
IT'S FINE. ACTUALLY, I WAS COMING TO SEE YOU.
SAVED ME SOME TIME.
SFX: WANA (TREMBLE) WANA
LOOKS LIKE THEY'RE ON GOOD TERMS.
I CAN'T BELIEVE IT...WHY IS BOSS WOLF ALL HAPPY TO SEE THIS GUY...?
...WHEN HE'S SO COLD TO HIS LOYAL MINIONS!?
......

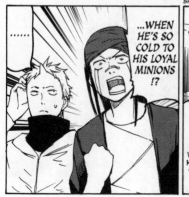

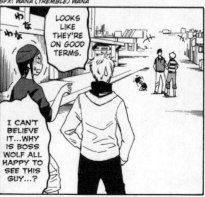

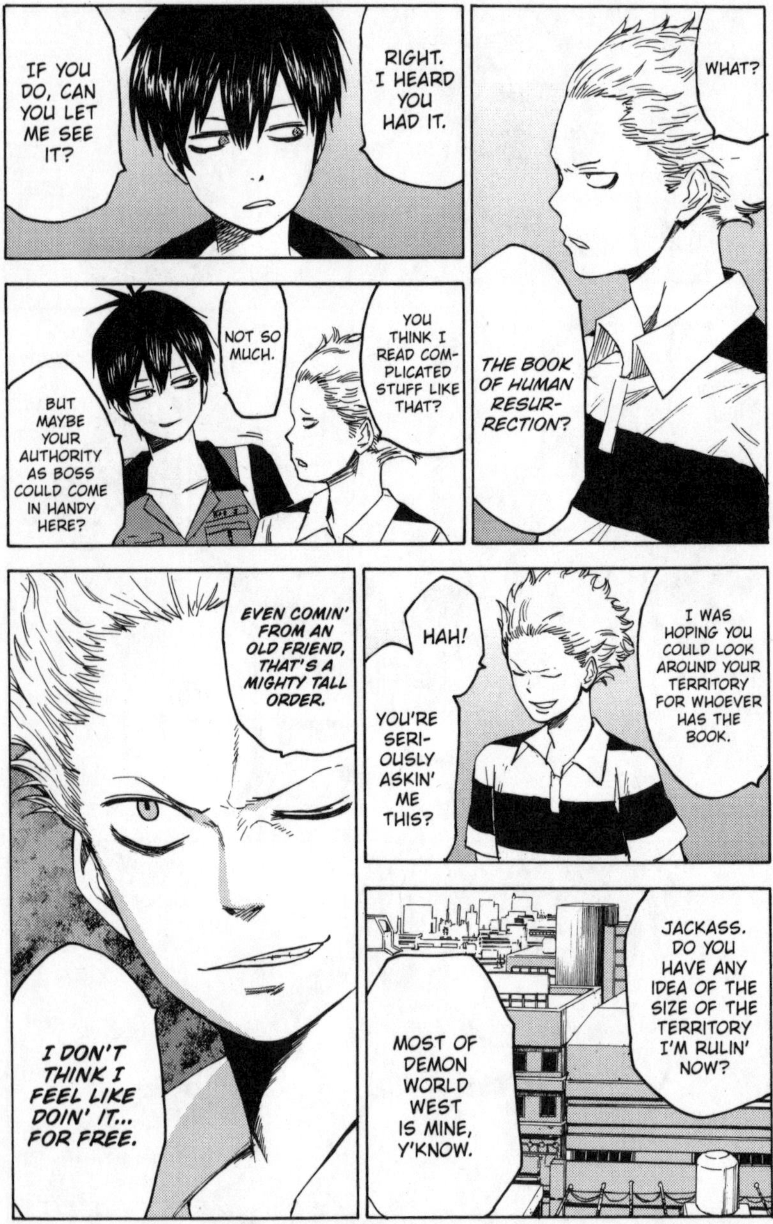
WHAT?
THE BOOK OF HUMAN RESUR-RECTION?
RIGHT. I HEARD YOU HAD IT.
IF YOU DO, CAN YOU LET ME SEE IT?
YOU THINK I READ COM-PLICATED STUFF LIKE THAT?
NOT SO MUCH.
BUT MAYBE YOUR AUTHORITY AS BOSS COULD COME IN HANDY HERE?
I WAS HOPING YOU COULD LOOK AROUND YOUR TERRITORY FOR WHOEVER HAS THE BOOK.
HAH!
YOU'RE SERI-OUSLY ASKIN' ME THIS?
JACKASS. DO YOU HAVE ANY IDEA OF THE SIZE OF THE TERRITORY I'M RULIN' NOW?
MOST OF DEMON WORLD WEST IS MINE, Y'KNOW.
EVEN COMIN' FROM AN OLD FRIEND, THAT'S A MIGHTY TALL ORDER.
I DON'T THINK I FEEL LIKE DOIN' IT... FOR FREE.

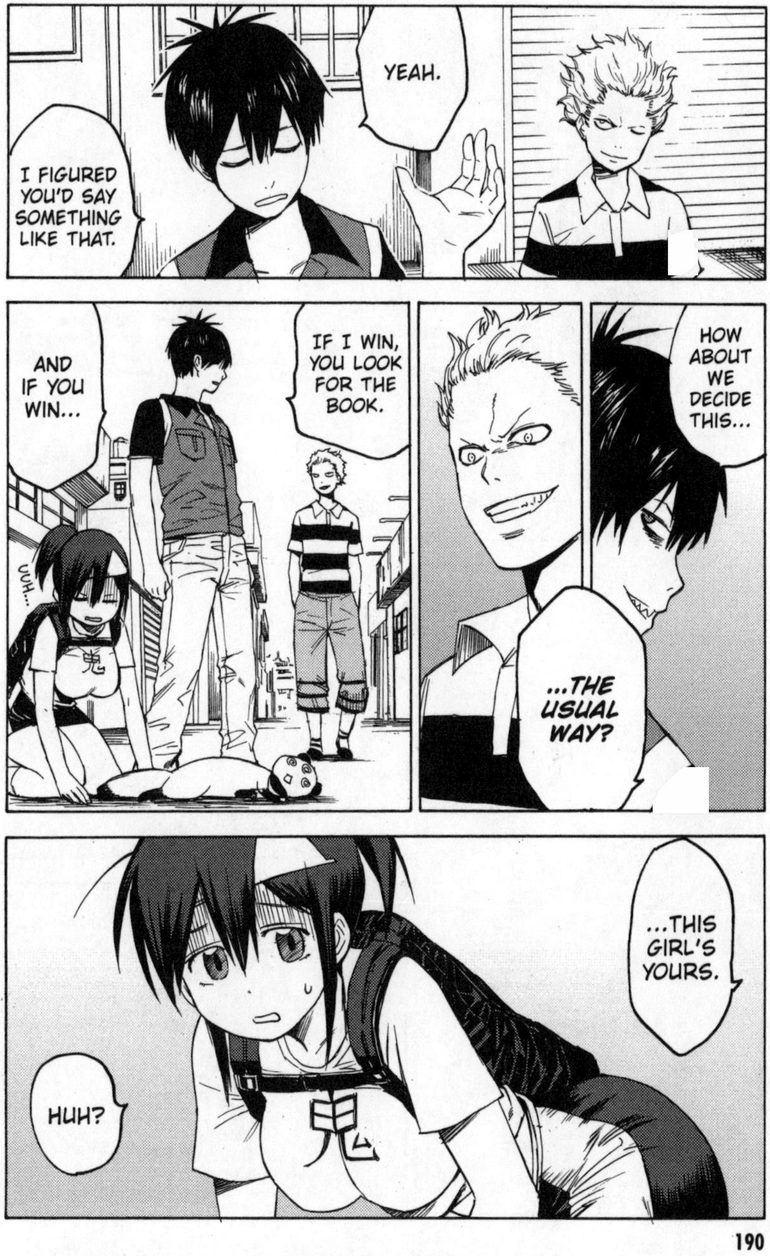
YEAH.
I FIGURED YOU'D SAY SOMETHING LIKE THAT.
HOW ABOUT WE DECIDE THIS...
...THE USUAL WAY?
IF I WIN, YOU LOOK FOR THE BOOK.
AND IF YOU WIN...
UUH...
...THIS GIRL'S YOURS.
HUH?

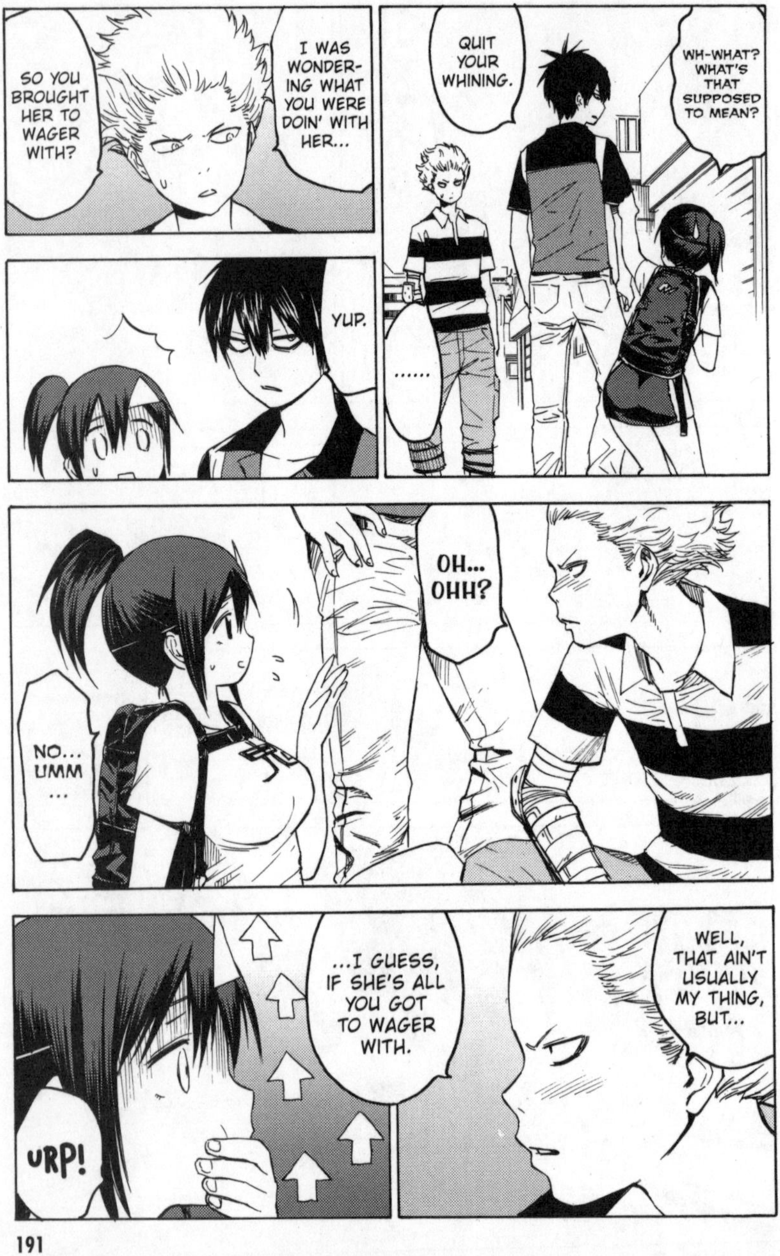
WH-WHAT? WHAT'S THAT SUPPOSED TO MEAN?
QUIT YOUR WHINING.
......
I WAS WONDER-ING WHAT YOU WERE DOIN' WITH HER...
SO YOU BROUGHT HER TO WAGER WITH?
YUP.
OH... OHH?
NO... UMM ...
WELL, THAT AIN'T USUALLY MY THING, BUT...
...I GUESS, IF SHE'S ALL YOU GOT TO WAGER WITH.
URP!

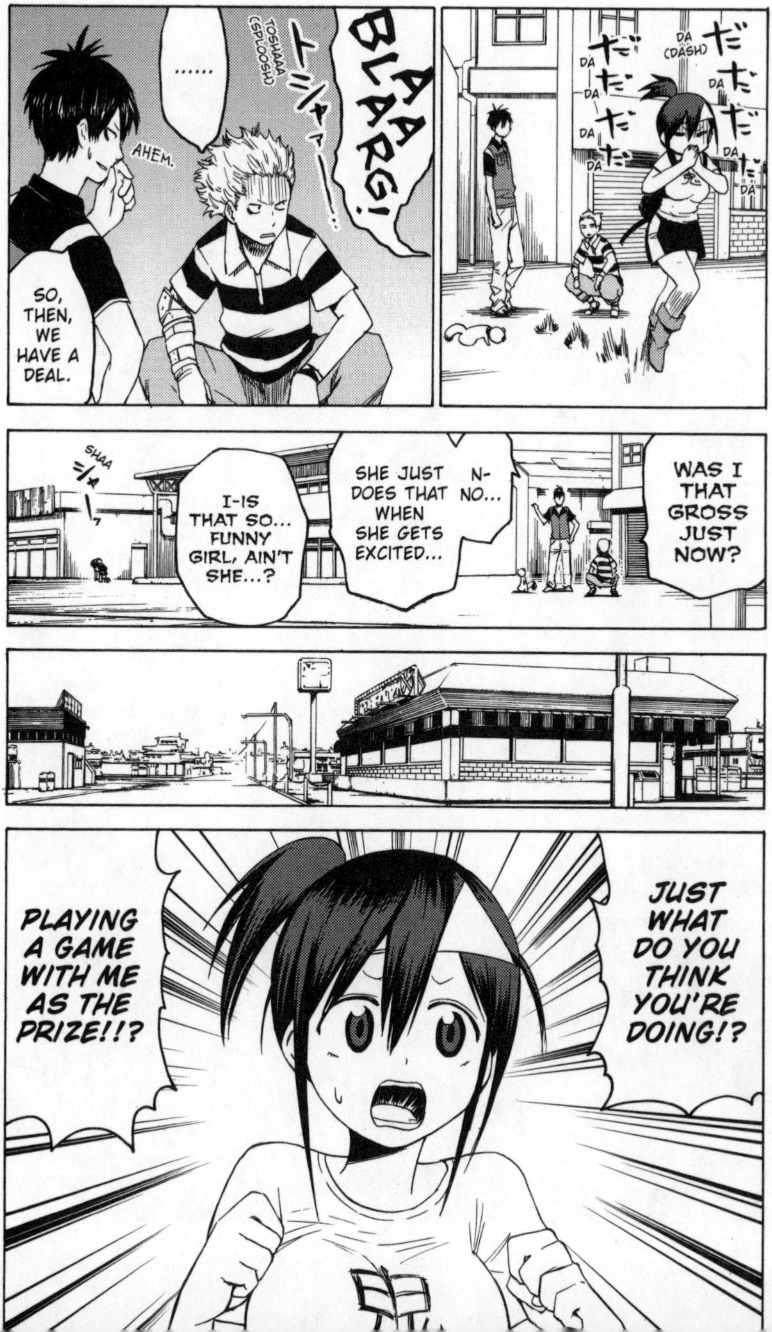

DA (DASH)
DA DA DA DA DA DA DA DA
BLAARG!
TOSHAAA (SPLOOSH)
......
AHEM.
SO, THEN, WE HAVE A DEAL.
WAS I THAT GROSS JUST NOW?
N-NO...
SHE JUST DOES THAT WHEN SHE GETS EXCITED...
I-IS THAT SO... FUNNY GIRL, AIN'T SHE...?
SHAA
JUST WHAT DO YOU THINK YOU'RE DOING!?
PLAYING A GAME WITH ME AS THE PRIZE!!?

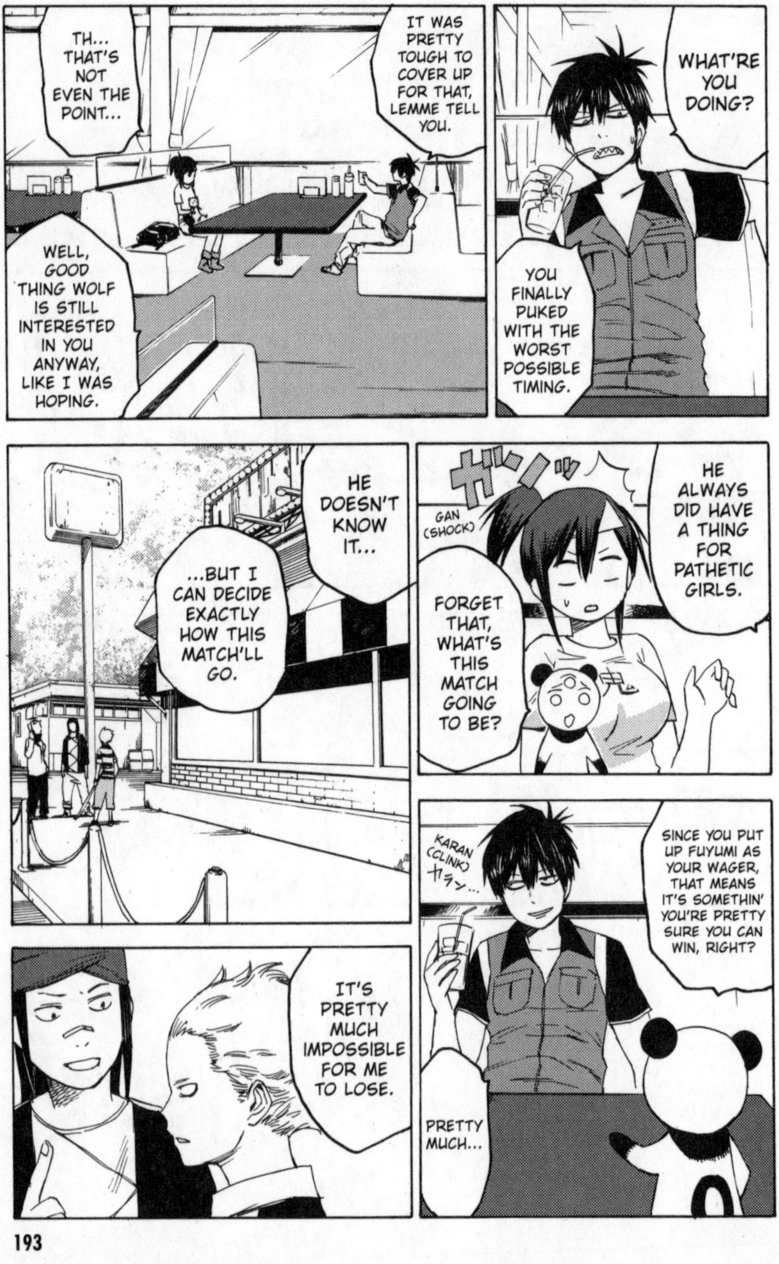
WHAT'RE YOU DOING?
YOU FINALLY PUKED WITH THE WORST POSSIBLE TIMING.
IT WAS PRETTY TOUGH TO COVER UP FOR THAT, LEMME TELL YOU.
TH... THAT'S NOT EVEN THE POINT...
WELL, GOOD THING WOLF IS STILL INTERESTED IN YOU ANYWAY, LIKE I WAS HOPING.
HE ALWAYS DID HAVE A THING FOR PATHETIC GIRLS.
GAN (SHOCK)
FORGET THAT, WHAT'S THIS MATCH GOING TO BE?
SINCE YOU PUT UP FUYUMI AS YOUR WAGER, THAT MEANS IT'S SOMETHIN' YOU'RE PRETTY SURE YOU CAN WIN, RIGHT?
KARAN (CLINK)
PRETTY MUCH...
HE DOESN'T KNOW IT...
...BUT I CAN DECIDE EXACTLY HOW THIS MATCH'LL GO.
IT'S PRETTY MUCH IMPOSSIBLE FOR ME TO LOSE.

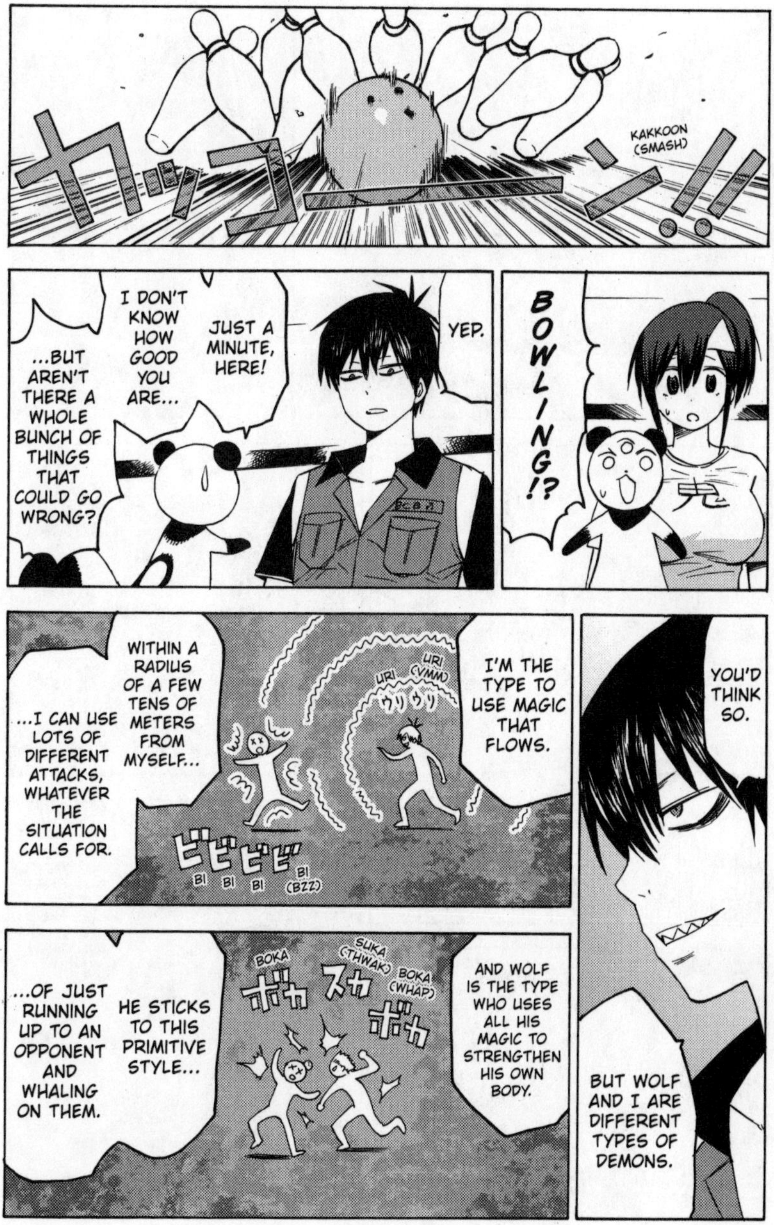
KAKKOON (SMASH)
BOWLING!?
YEP.
JUST A MINUTE, HERE!
I DON'T KNOW HOW GOOD YOU ARE...
...BUT AREN'T THERE A WHOLE BUNCH OF THINGS THAT COULD GO WRONG?
YOU'D THINK SO.
BUT WOLF AND I ARE DIFFERENT TYPES OF DEMONS.
I'M THE TYPE TO USE MAGIC THAT FLOWS.
ウリウリ
URI URI (VMM)
WITHIN A RADIUS OF A FEW TENS OF METERS FROM MYSELF...
...I CAN USE LOTS OF DIFFERENT ATTACKS, WHATEVER THE SITUATION CALLS FOR.
BI BI BI BI (BZZ)
AND WOLF IS THE TYPE WHO USES ALL HIS MAGIC TO STRENGTHEN HIS OWN BODY.
BOKA SUKA (THWAK) BOKA (WHAP)
HE STICKS TO THIS PRIMITIVE STYLE...
...OF JUST RUNNING UP TO AN OPPONENT AND WHALING ON THEM.

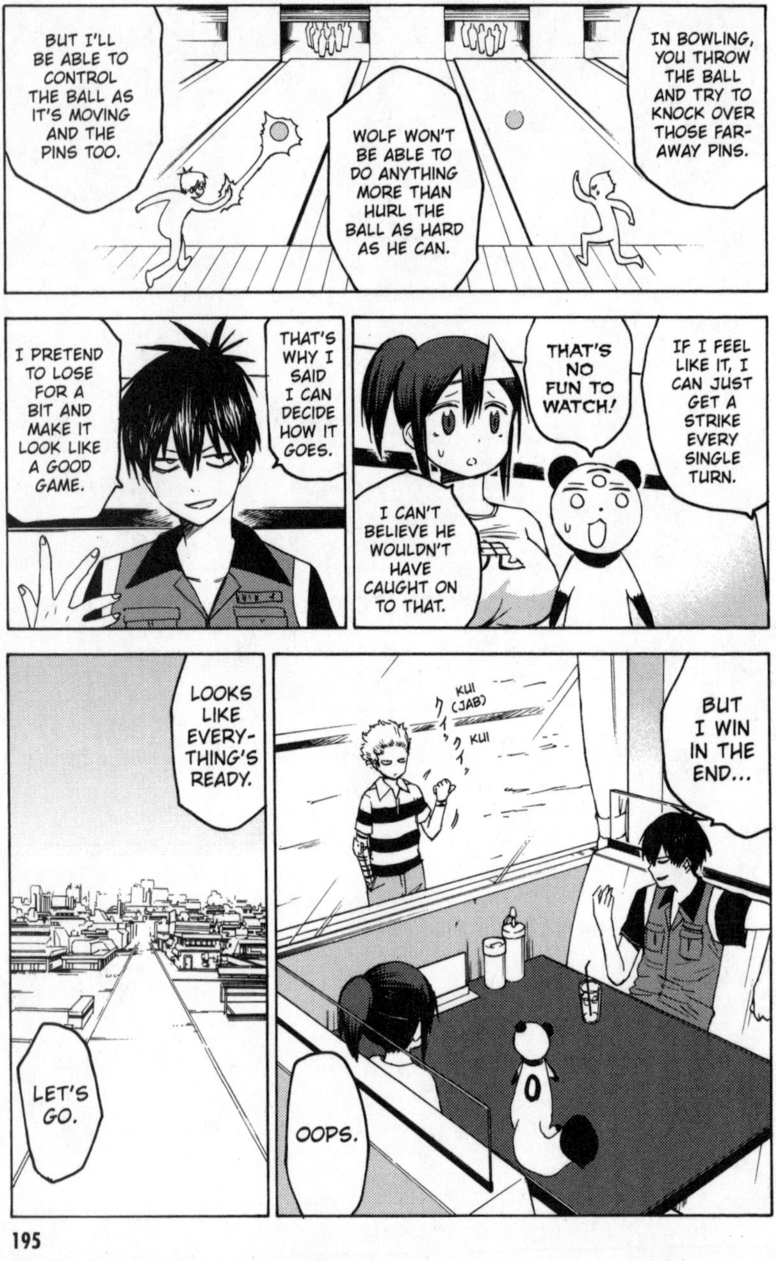
IN BOWLING, YOU THROW THE BALL AND TRY TO KNOCK OVER THOSE FAR-AWAY PINS.
WOLF WON'T BE ABLE TO DO ANYTHING MORE THAN HURL THE BALL AS HARD AS HE CAN.
BUT I'LL BE ABLE TO CONTROL THE BALL AS IT'S MOVING AND THE PINS TOO.
IF I FEEL LIKE IT, I CAN JUST GET A STRIKE EVERY SINGLE TURN.
THAT'S NO FUN TO WATCH!
I CAN'T BELIEVE HE WOULDN'T HAVE CAUGHT ON TO THAT.
THAT'S WHY I SAID I CAN DECIDE HOW IT GOES.
I PRETEND TO LOSE FOR A BIT AND MAKE IT LOOK LIKE A GOOD GAME.
BUT I WIN IN THE END...
KUI (JAB)
KUI
OOPS.
LOOKS LIKE EVERY-THING'S READY.
LET'S GO.

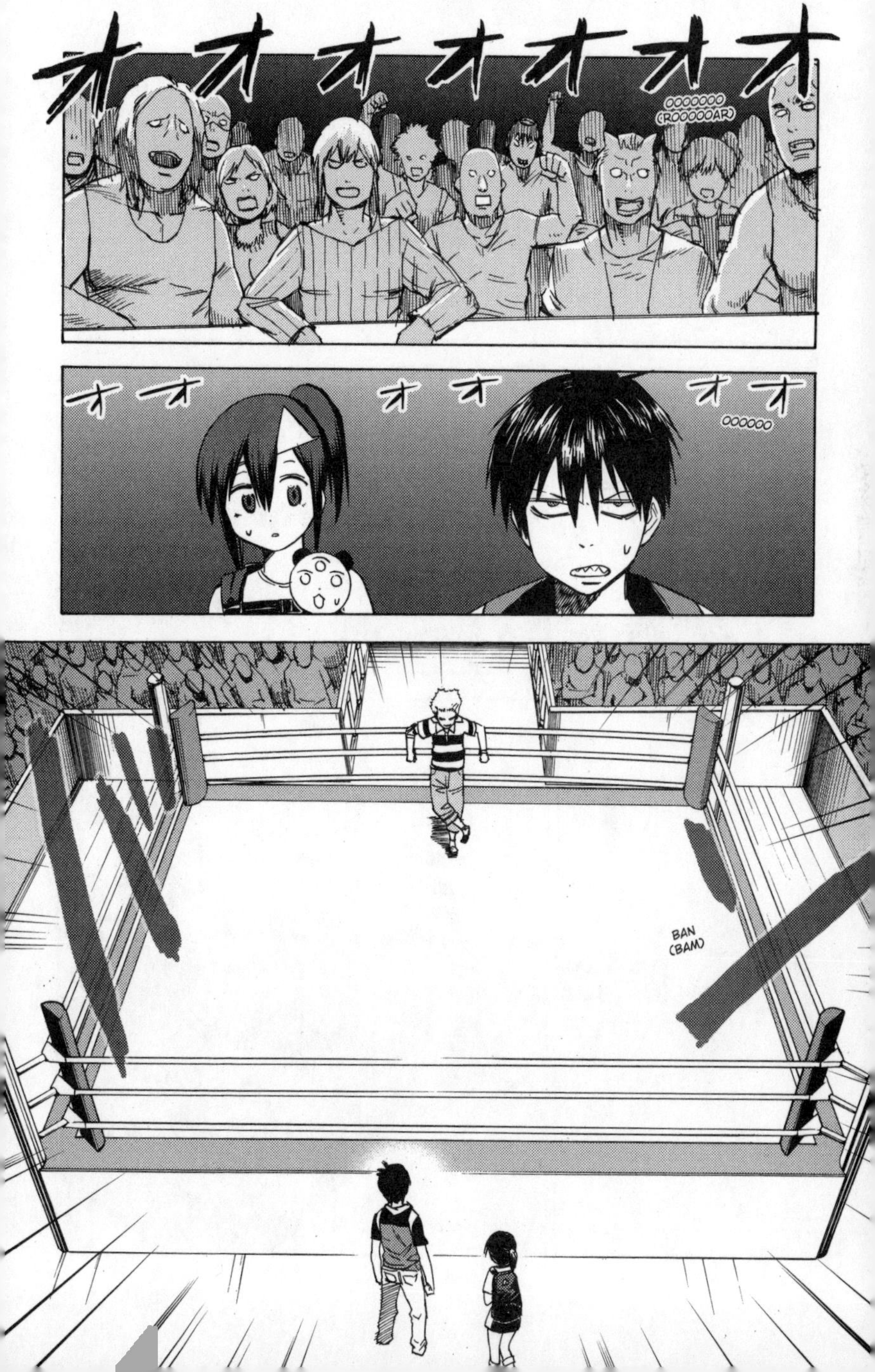
オオオオオオオ
OOOOOOO (ROOOOOAR)
オオ オオ オオ
OOOOOO
BAN (BAM)

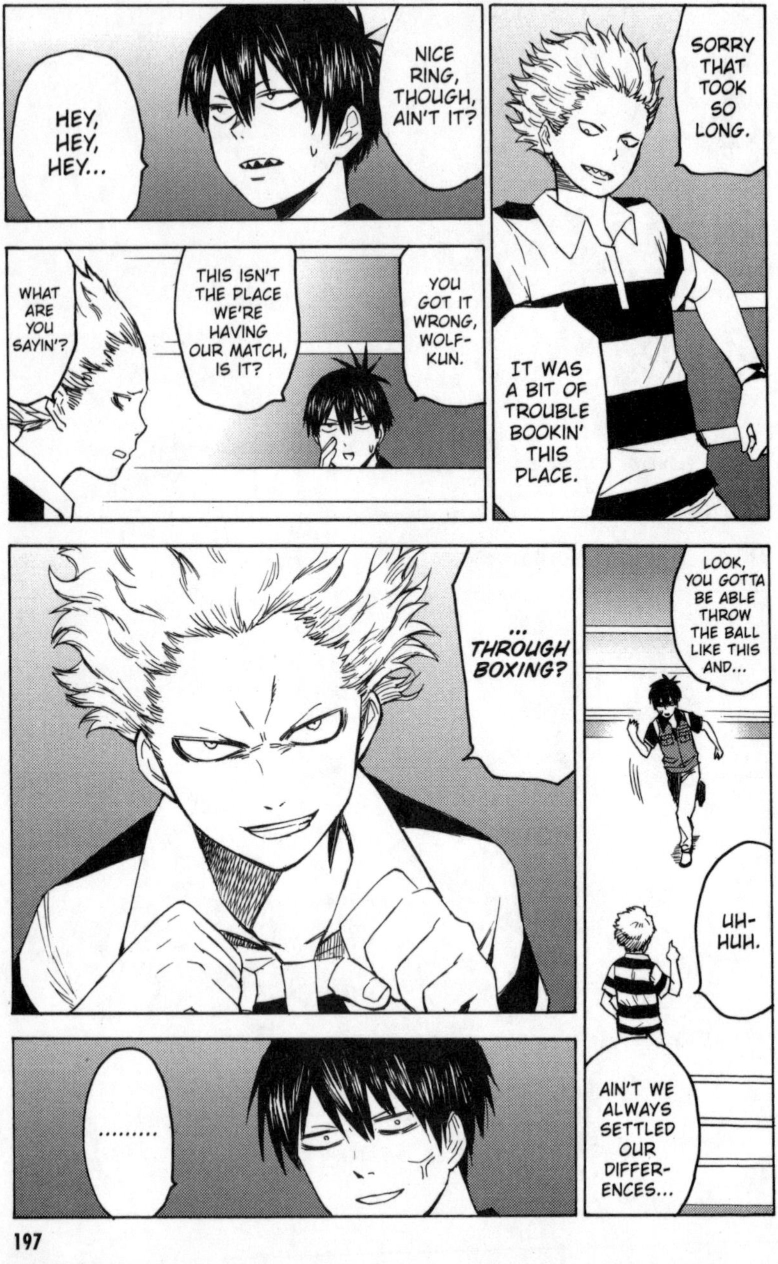
SORRY THAT TOOK SO LONG.
IT WAS A BIT OF TROUBLE BOOKIN' THIS PLACE.
NICE RING, THOUGH, AIN'T IT?
HEY, HEY, HEY...
YOU GOT IT WRONG, WOLF-KUN.
THIS ISN'T THE PLACE WE'RE HAVING OUR MATCH, IS IT?
WHAT ARE YOU SAYIN'?
LOOK, YOU GOTTA BE ABLE THROW THE BALL LIKE THIS AND...
UH-HUH.
AIN'T WE ALWAYS SETTLED OUR DIFFER-ENCES...
... *THROUGH BOXING?*
.........

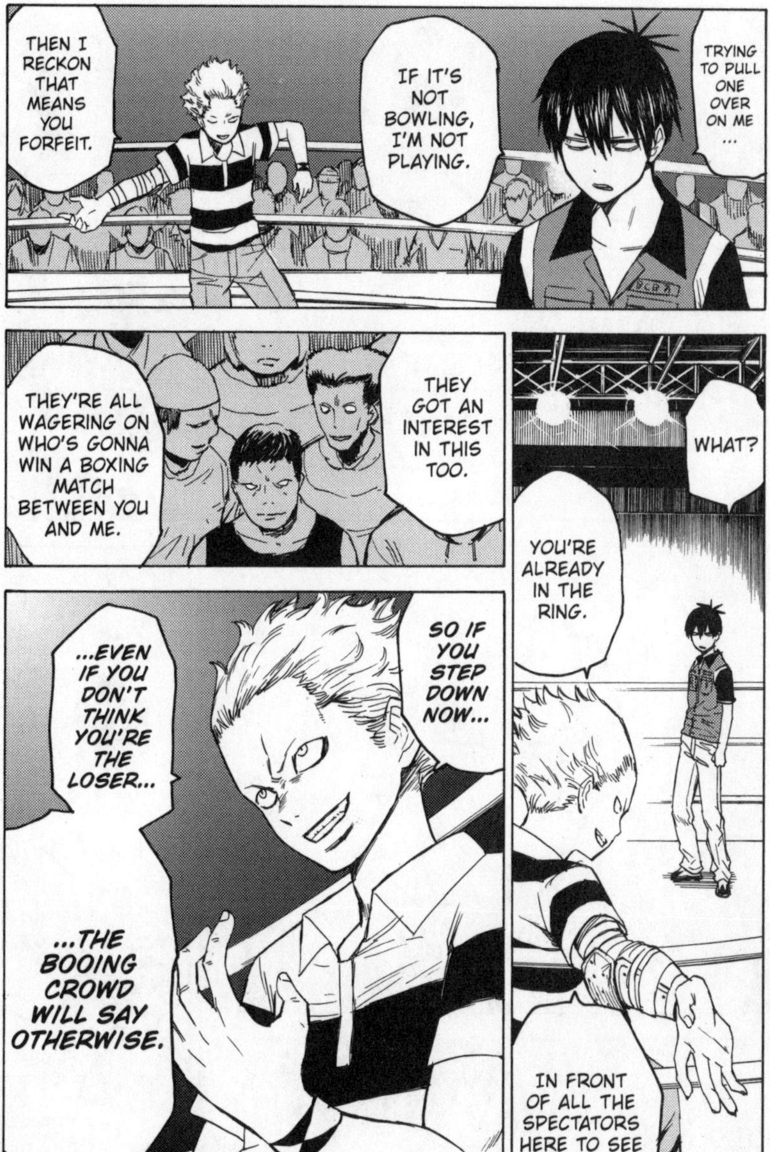
TRYING TO PULL ONE OVER ON ME ...
IF IT'S NOT BOWLING, I'M NOT PLAYING.
THEN I RECKON THAT MEANS YOU FORFEIT.
WHAT?
YOU'RE ALREADY IN THE RING.
IN FRONT OF ALL THE SPECTATORS HERE TO SEE US FIGHT.
THEY GOT AN INTEREST IN THIS TOO.
THEY'RE ALL WAGERING ON WHO'S GONNA WIN A BOXING MATCH BETWEEN YOU AND ME.
SO IF YOU STEP DOWN NOW...
...EVEN IF YOU DON'T THINK YOU'RE THE LOSER...
...THE BOOING CROWD WILL SAY OTHERWISE.

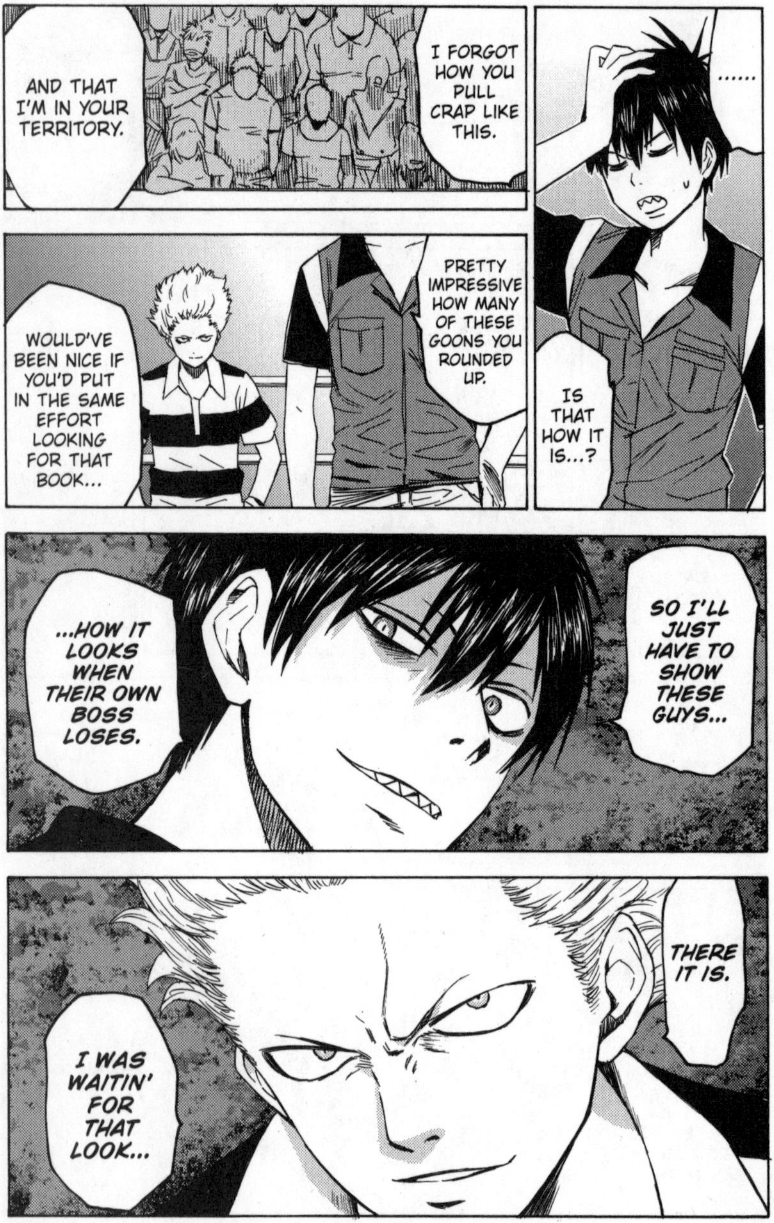
......
IS THAT HOW IT IS...?
I FORGOT HOW YOU PULL CRAP LIKE THIS.
AND THAT I'M IN YOUR TERRITORY.
PRETTY IMPRESSIVE HOW MANY OF THESE GOONS YOU ROUNDED UP.
WOULD'VE BEEN NICE IF YOU'D PUT IN THE SAME EFFORT LOOKING FOR THAT BOOK...
SO I'LL JUST HAVE TO SHOW THESE GUYS...
...HOW IT LOOKS WHEN THEIR OWN BOSS LOSES.
THERE IT IS.
I WAS WAITIN' FOR THAT LOOK...

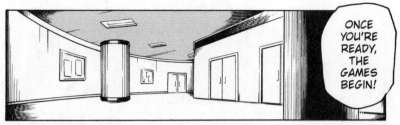

ONCE YOU'RE READY, THE GAMES BEGIN!
THE HELL'S GOING ON NOW!?
THE ONLY THING BOWLING AND BOXING GOT IN COMMON IS THAT THEY BOTH START WITH "BO" AND END WITH "ING"!!
THEN THEY GOT MORE IN COMMON THAN I THOUGHT...
YOU DUMBASS!! DIDN'T YOU STAKE FUYUMI YANAGI ON THIS!?
YOU WERE SUPPOSED TO PULL ONE OVER BUT INSTEAD YOU GOT ONE PULLED OVER ON YOU, AND NOW OUR FUTURE HAS A "PUL" IN IT, ALL RIGHT— PULVERIZED!!
ENOUGH ALREADY. YOU'RE PULLING ENOUGH STUPID PUNS.
HUH? WHERE'D FUYUMI GET TO?
DON'T CHANGE THE SUBJECT!!
SOME GUYS CARTED HER OFF WHILE YOU WERE TALKIN' TO WOLF...
...PROBABLY BECAUSE IT'D BE A PROBLEM IF THE "PRIZE" RAN AWAY.

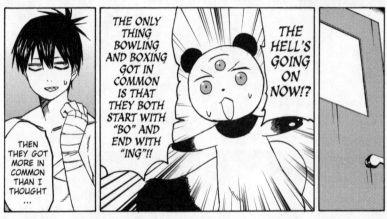

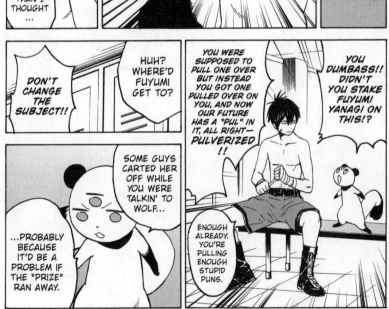

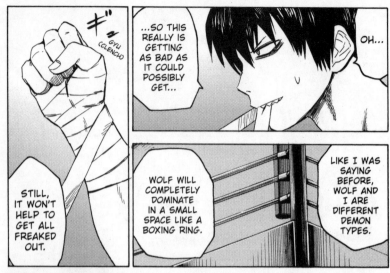

OH...
...SO THIS REALLY IS GETTING AS BAD AS IT COULD POSSIBLY GET...
LIKE I WAS SAYING BEFORE, WOLF AND I ARE DIFFERENT DEMON TYPES.
WOLF WILL COMPLETELY DOMINATE IN A SMALL SPACE LIKE A BOXING RING.
ギュ
GYU (CLENCH)
STILL, IT WON'T HELP TO GET ALL FREAKED OUT.
THIS WHOLE MESS IS MY FAULT...
...
...SO I BETTER CLEAN UP AFTER IT.
AND THEN I'LL BE THE ONE TO BRING FUYUMI BACK TO LIFE.
I GAVE HER A BLOOD OATH.

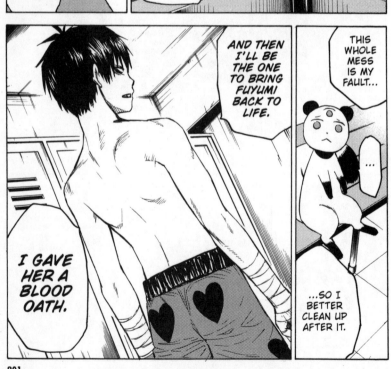

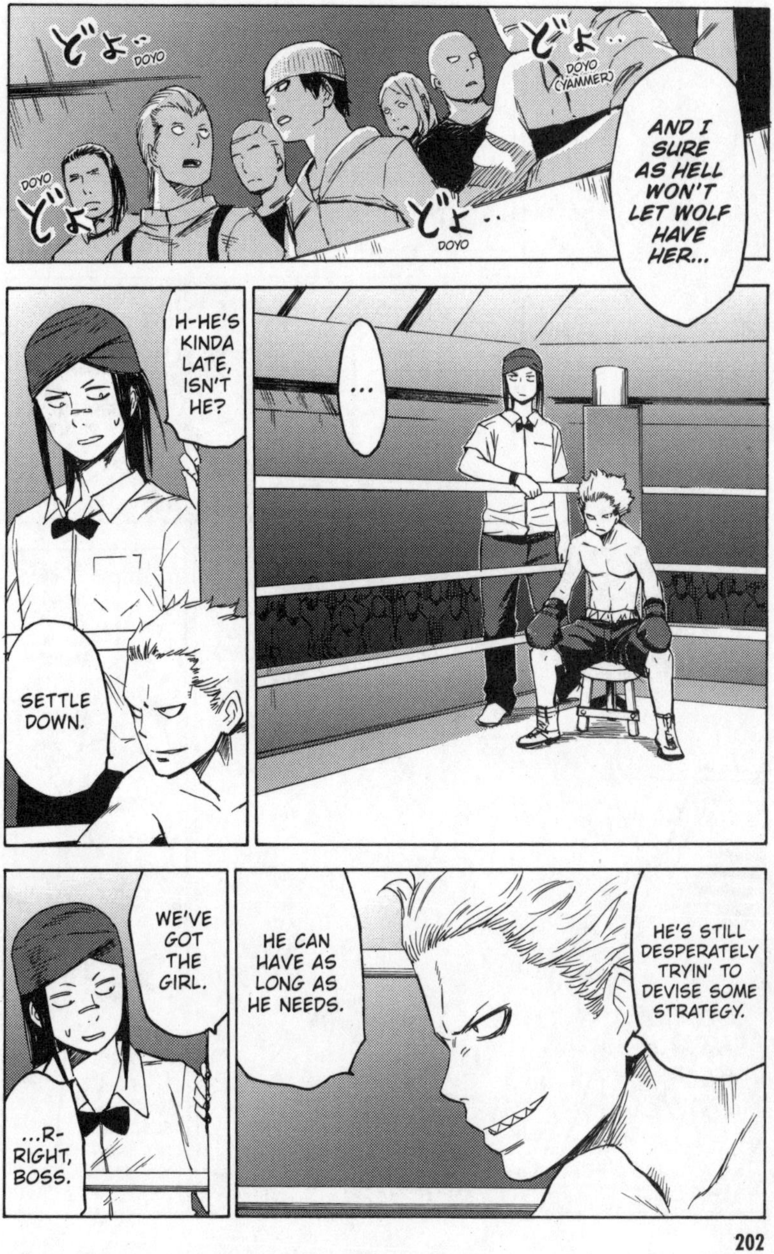
どよ‥
DOYO (YAMMER)
AND I SURE AS HELL WON'T LET WOLF HAVE HER...
どよ‥
DOYO
DOYO
どよ
どよ‥
DOYO
...
H-HE'S KINDA LATE, ISN'T HE?
SETTLE DOWN.
HE'S STILL DESPERATELY TRYIN' TO DEVISE SOME STRATEGY.
HE CAN HAVE AS LONG AS HE NEEDS.
WE'VE GOT THE GIRL.
...R-RIGHT, BOSS.

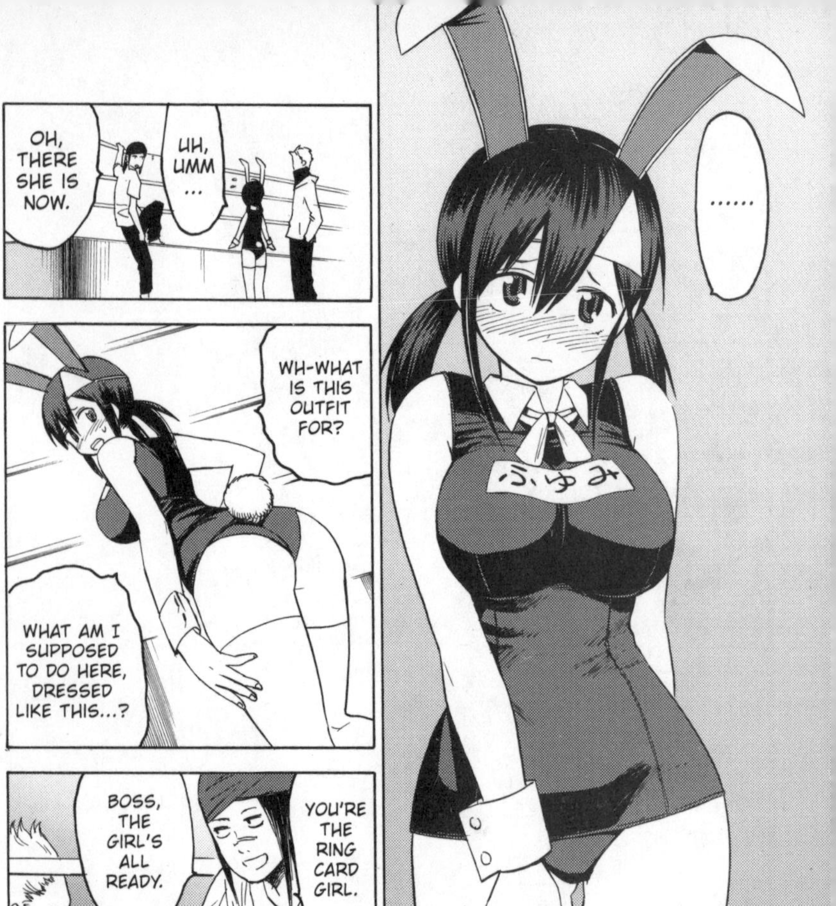
......
ふゆみ
UH, UMM ...
OH, THERE SHE IS NOW.
WH-WHAT IS THIS OUTFIT FOR?
WHAT AM I SUPPOSED TO DO HERE, DRESSED LIKE THIS...?
YOU'RE THE RING CARD GIRL.
BOSS, THE GIRL'S ALL READY.

NAME TAG: FUYUMI

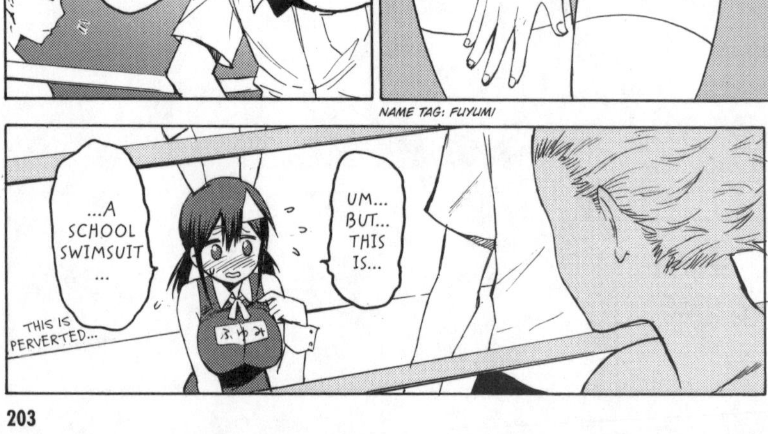
UM... BUT... THIS IS...
...A SCHOOL SWIMSUIT ...
THIS IS PERVERTED...
ふゆみ

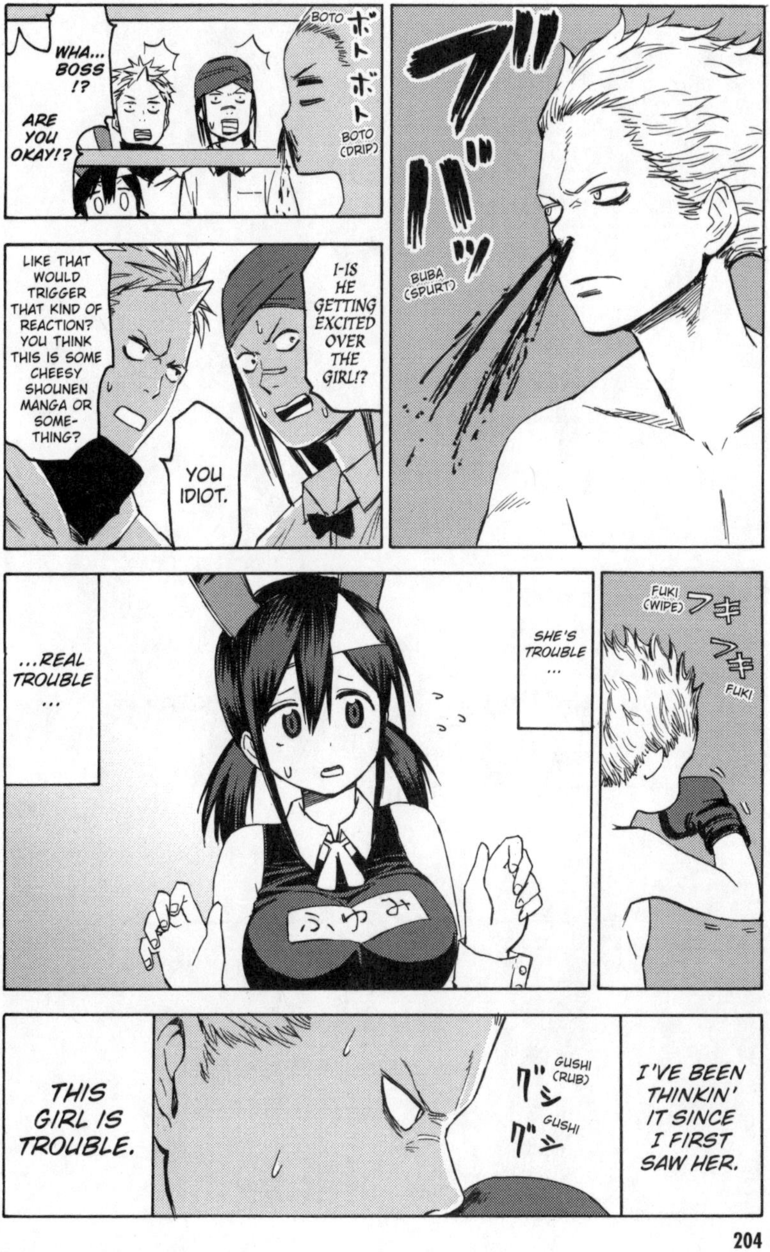
ブバッ
BUBA (SPURT)
ボトボト
BOTO
BOTO (DRIP)
WHA... BOSS !?
ARE YOU OKAY!?
I-IS HE GETTING EXCITED OVER THE GIRL!?
LIKE THAT WOULD TRIGGER THAT KIND OF REACTION? YOU THINK THIS IS SOME CHEESY SHOUNEN MANGA OR SOME-THING?
YOU IDIOT.
フキフキ
FUKI (WIPE)
FUKI
SHE'S TROUBLE ...
ふゆみ
...REAL TROUBLE ...
I'VE BEEN THINKIN' IT SINCE I FIRST SAW HER.
グシグシ
GUSHI (RUB)
GUSHI
THIS GIRL IS TROUBLE.

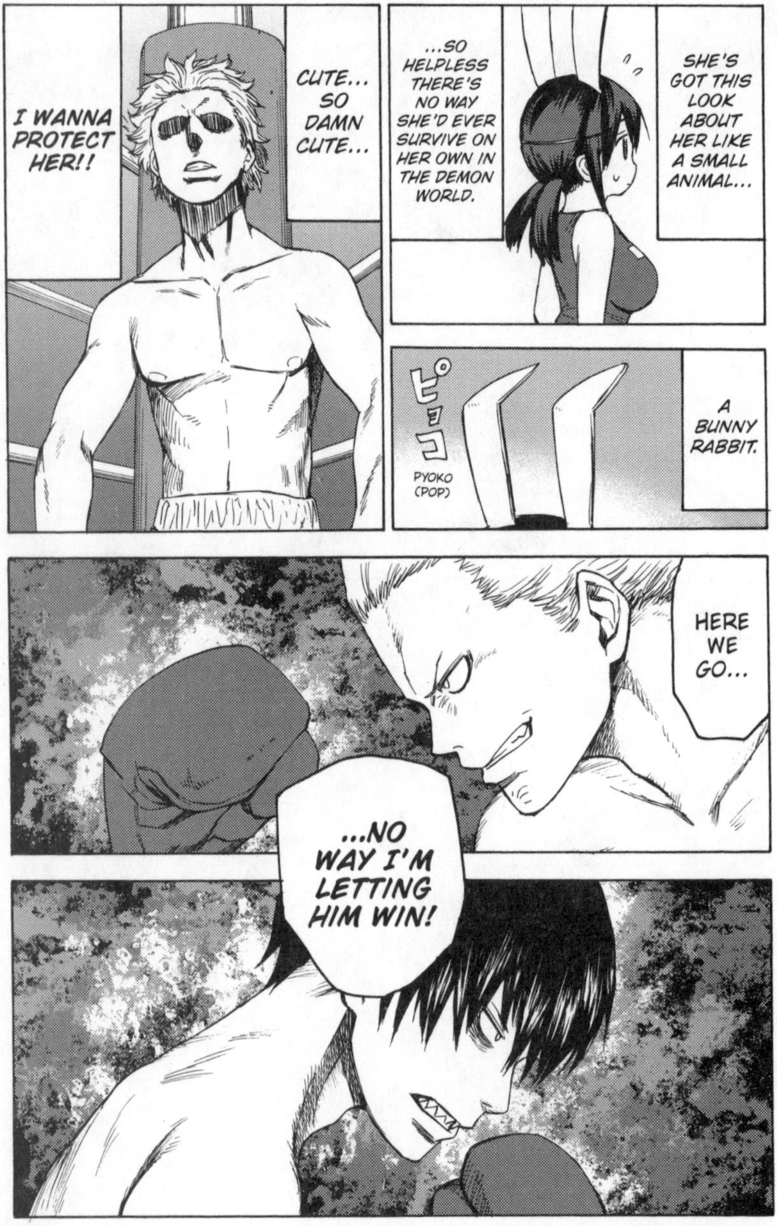
SHE'S GOT THIS LOOK ABOUT HER LIKE A SMALL ANIMAL...
...SO HELPLESS THERE'S NO WAY SHE'D EVER SURVIVE ON HER OWN IN THE DEMON WORLD.
A BUNNY RABBIT.
ピョコ
PYOKO (POP)
CUTE... SO DAMN CUTE...
I WANNA PROTECT HER!!
HERE WE GO...
...NO WAY I'M LETTING HIM WIN!

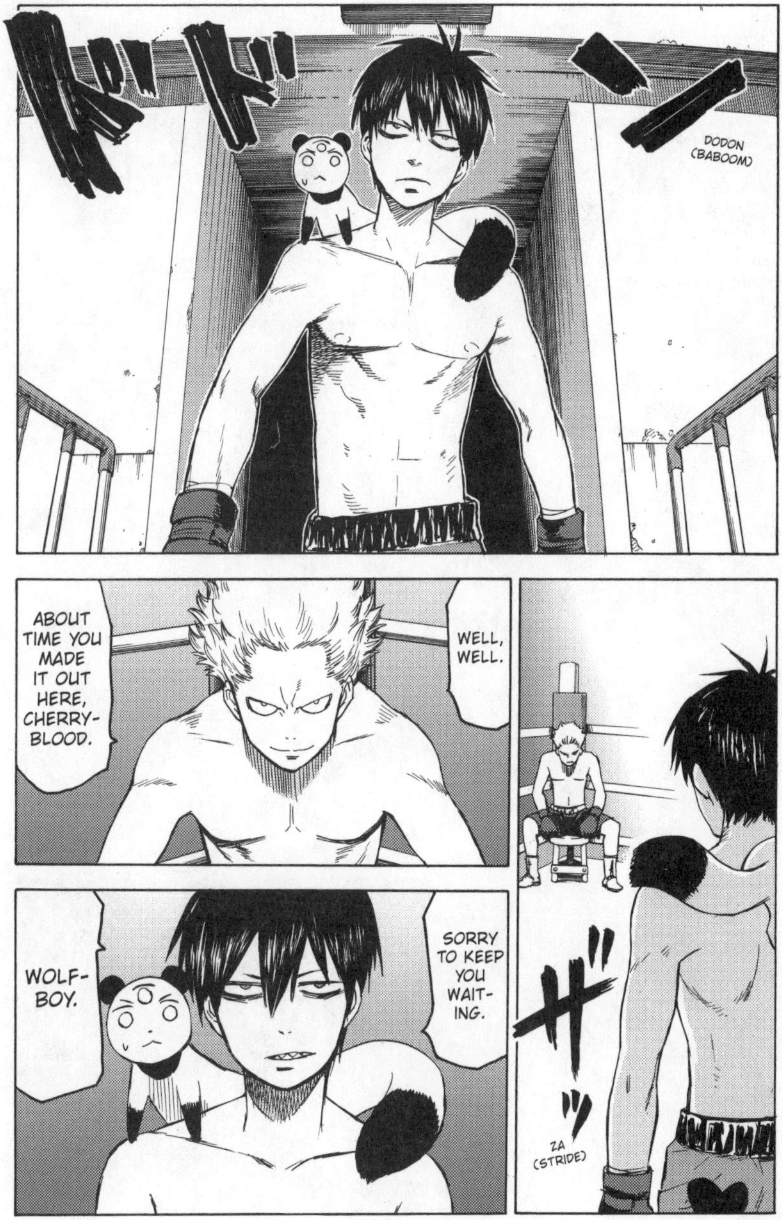
DODON (BABOOM)
ZA (STRIDE)
WELL, WELL.
ABOUT TIME YOU MADE IT OUT HERE, CHERRY-BLOOD.
SORRY TO KEEP YOU WAIT-ING.
WOLF-BOY.

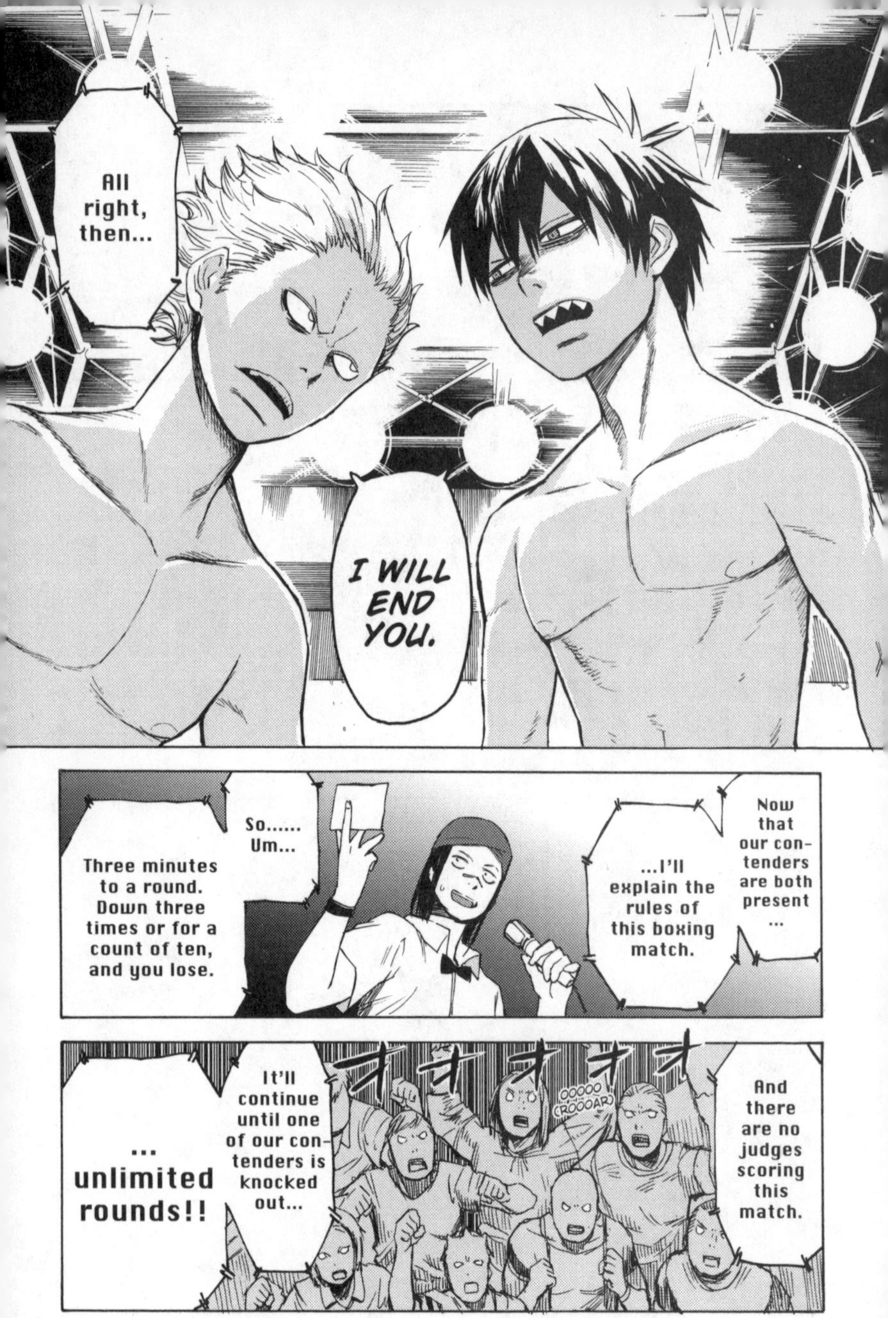
All right, then...
I WILL END YOU.
Now that our contenders are both present...
...I'll explain the rules of this boxing match.
So...... Um...
Three minutes to a round. Down three times or for a count of ten, and you lose.
And there are no judges scoring this match.
OOOOO (ROOOAR)
It'll continue until one of our contenders is knocked out...
...unlimited rounds!!

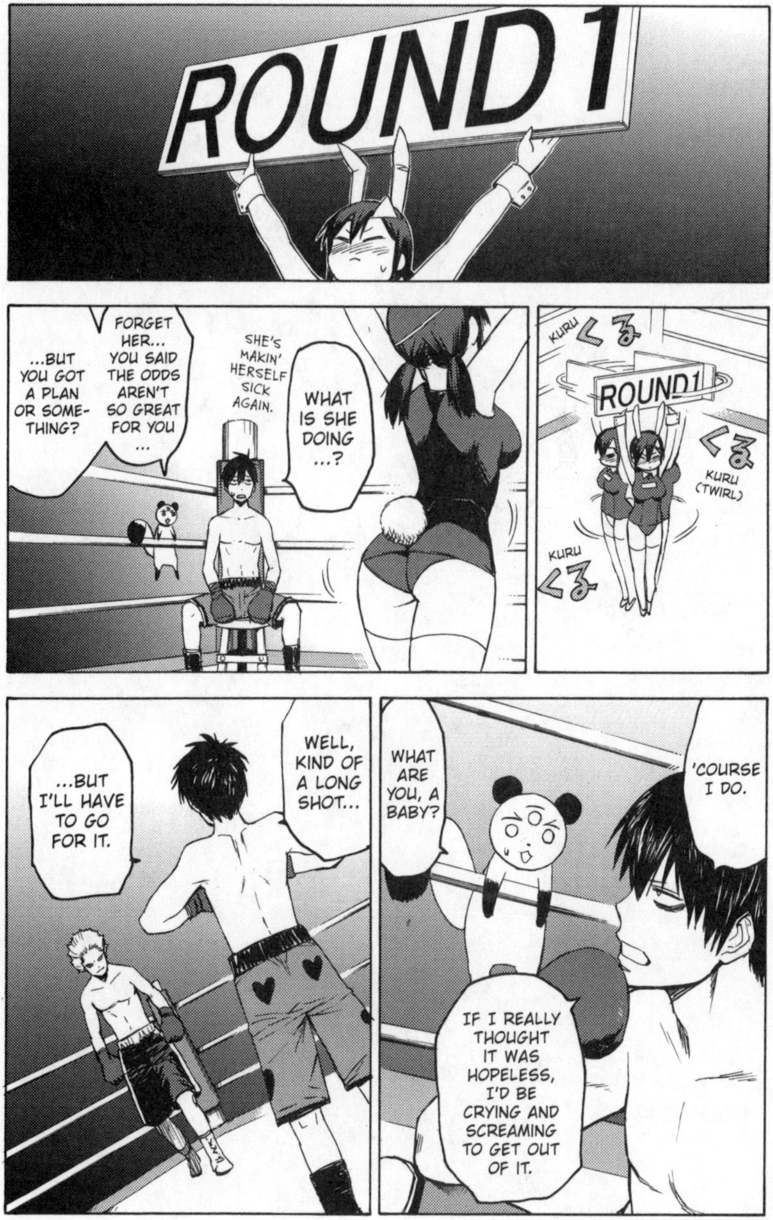
ROUND 1
KURU くる
ROUND 1
くる KURU (TWIRL)
KURU くる
WHAT IS SHE DOING ...?
SHE'S MAKIN' HERSELF SICK AGAIN.
FORGET HER... YOU SAID THE ODDS AREN'T SO GREAT FOR YOU ...
...BUT YOU GOT A PLAN OR SOME-THING?
'COURSE I DO.
WHAT ARE YOU, A BABY?
IF I REALLY THOUGHT IT WAS HOPELESS, I'D BE CRYING AND SCREAMING TO GET OUT OF IT.
WELL, KIND OF A LONG SHOT...
...BUT I'LL HAVE TO GO FOR IT.

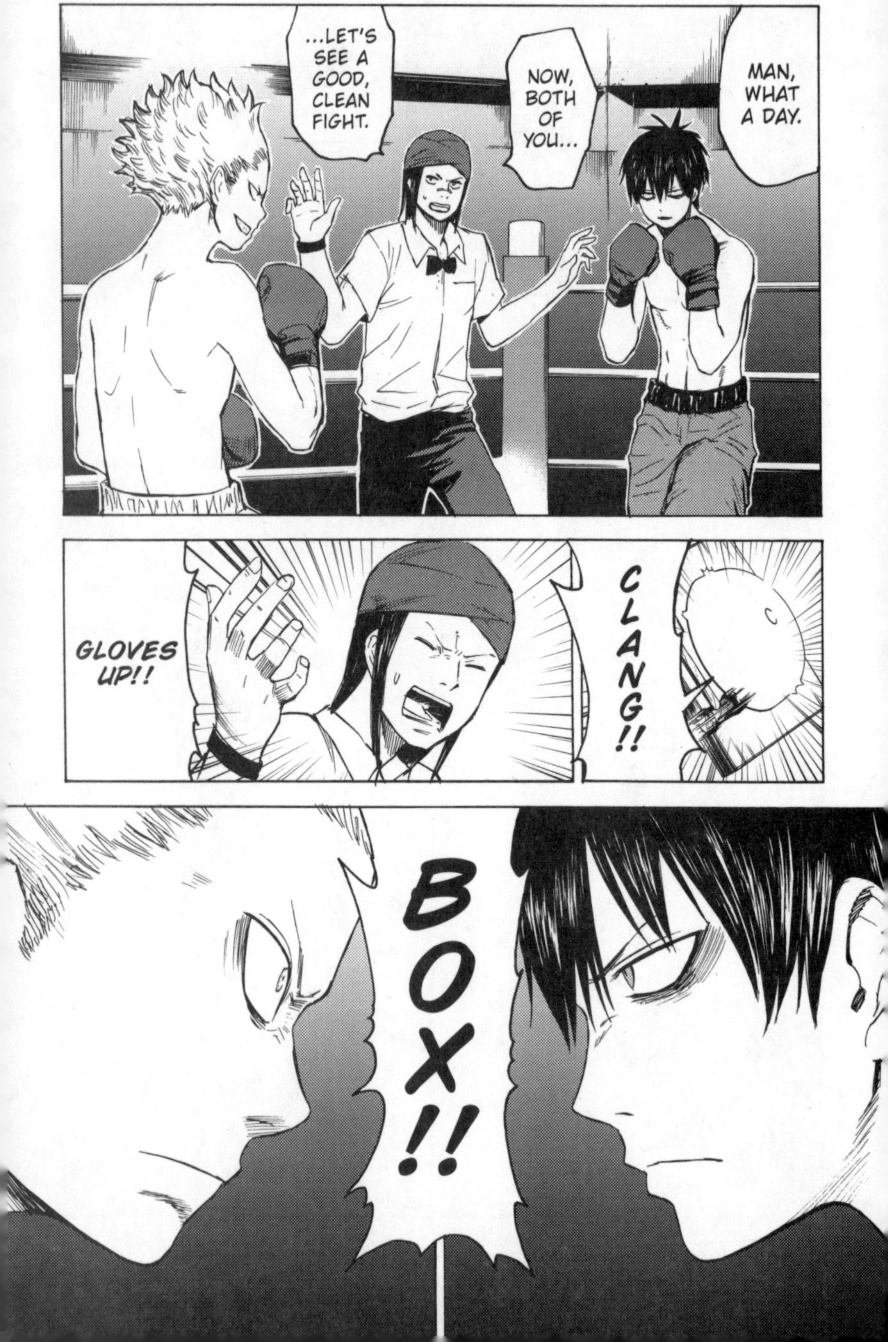
MAN, WHAT A DAY.
NOW, BOTH OF YOU...
...LET'S SEE A GOOD, CLEAN FIGHT.
CLANG!!
GLOVES UP!!
BOX!!

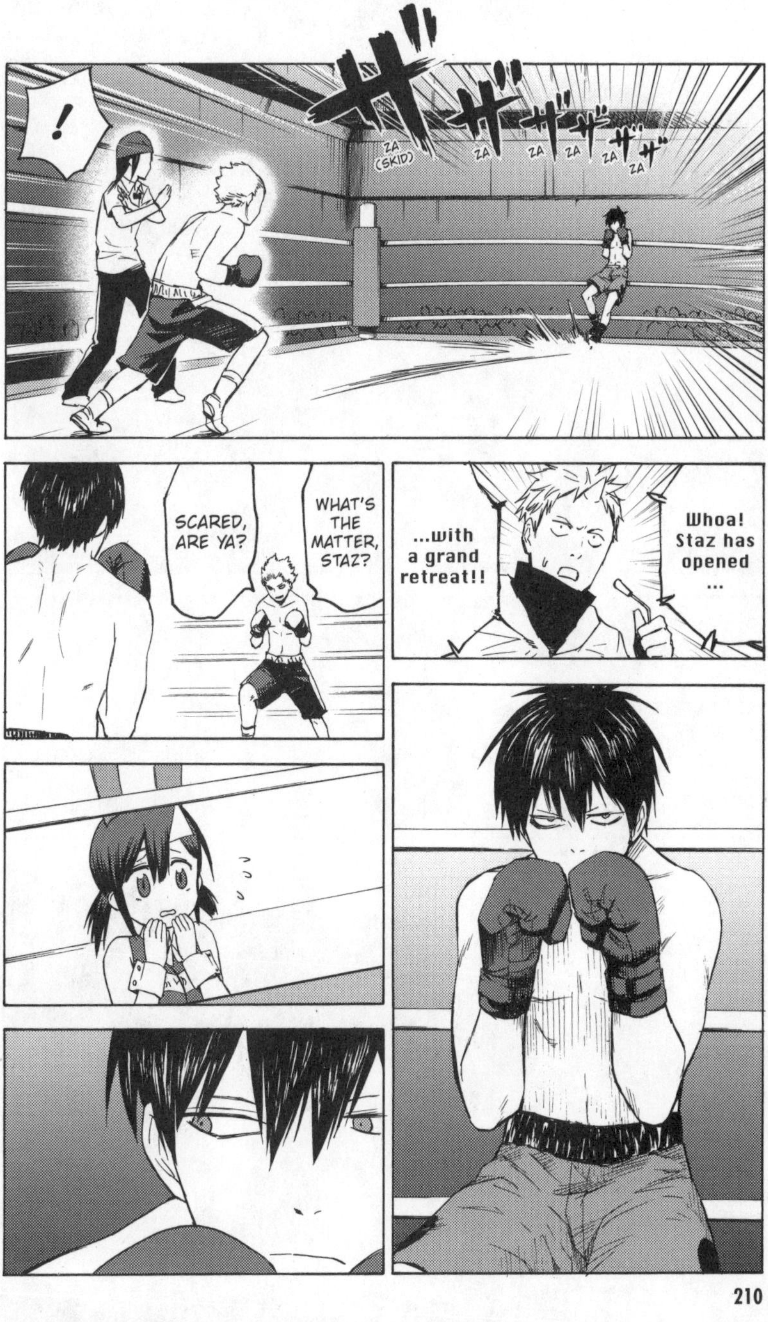

ZA (SKID)
ZA
ZA
ZA
ZA
ZA
!
Whoa! Staz has opened ...
...with a grand retreat!!
WHAT'S THE MATTER, STAZ?
SCARED, ARE YA?

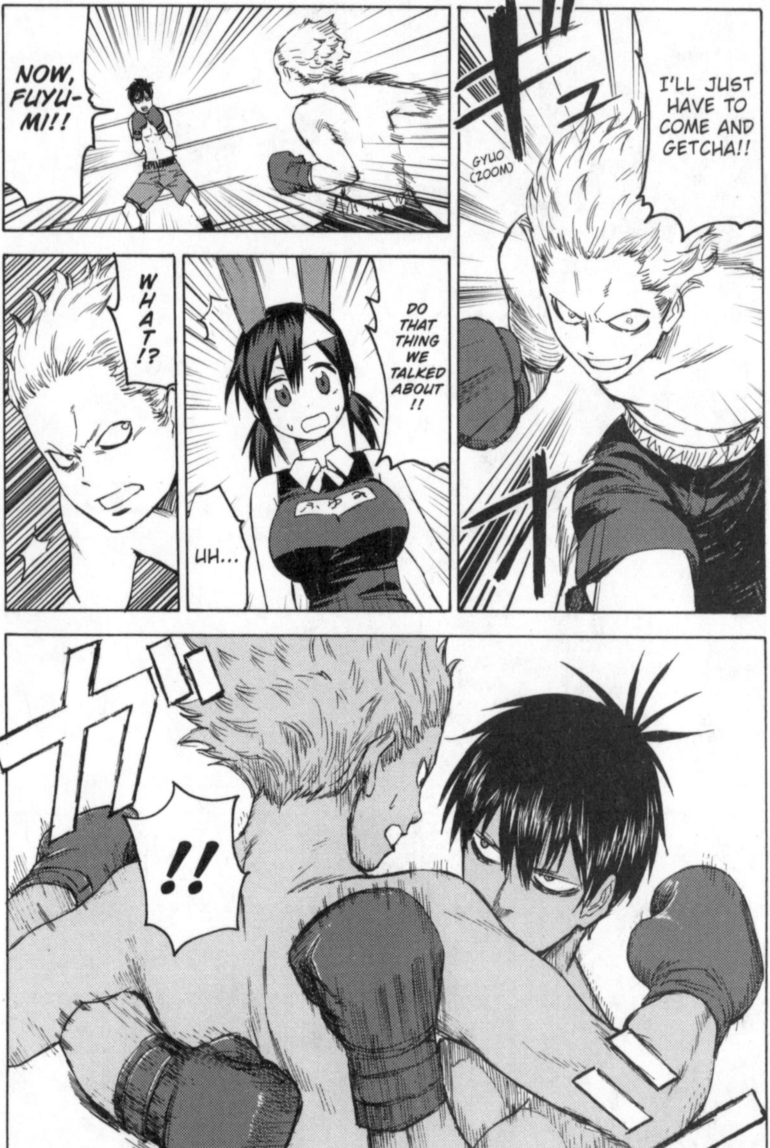
ギュ
GYUO (ZOOM)
I'LL JUST HAVE TO COME AND GETCHA!!
NOW, FUYU-MI!!
DO THAT THING WE TALKED ABOUT!!
UH...
WHAT!?
ガッ
!!
GASHI (GRAB)

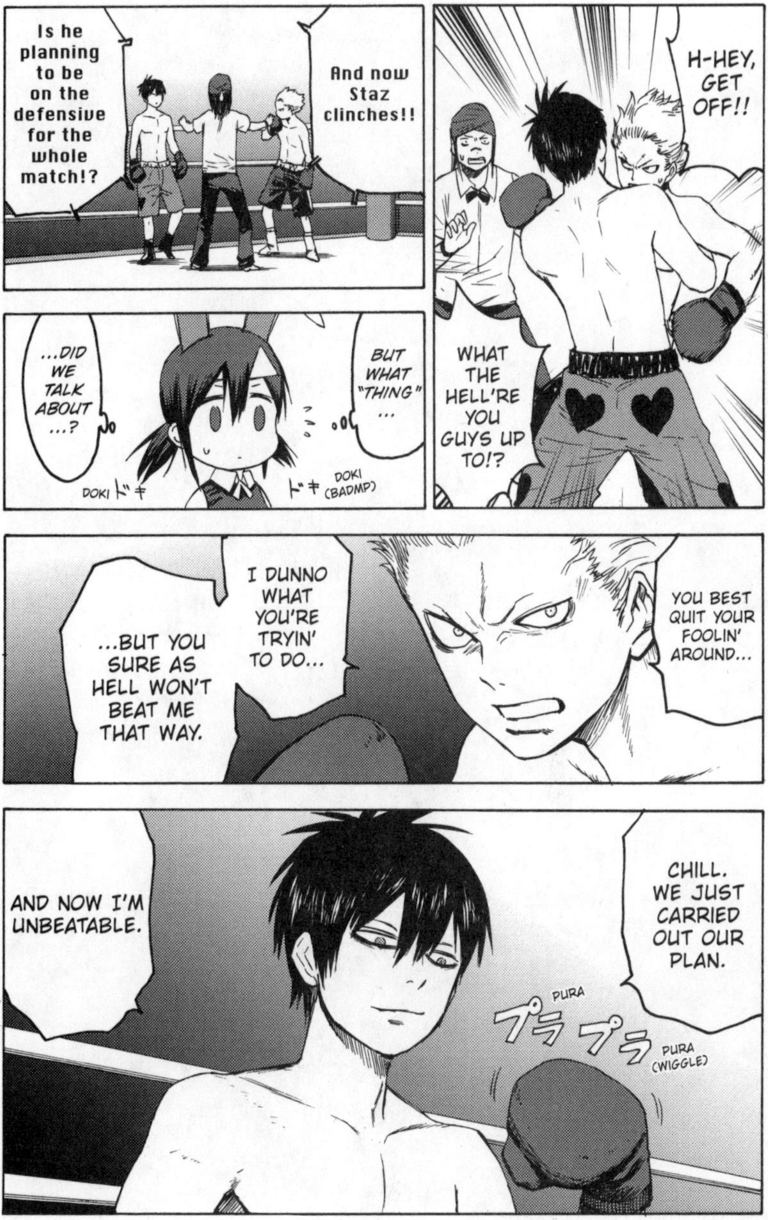
H-HEY, GET OFF!!
WHAT THE HELL'RE YOU GUYS UP TO!?
And now Staz clinches!!
Is he planning to be on the defensive for the whole match!?
BUT WHAT "THING"...
...DID WE TALK ABOUT...?
ドキ DOKI (BADMP)
ドキ DOKI
YOU BEST QUIT YOUR FOOLIN' AROUND...
I DUNNO WHAT YOU'RE TRYIN' TO DO...
...BUT YOU SURE AS HELL WON'T BEAT ME THAT WAY.
CHILL. WE JUST CARRIED OUT OUR PLAN.
プラプラ PURA PURA (WIGGLE)
AND NOW I'M UNBEATABLE.

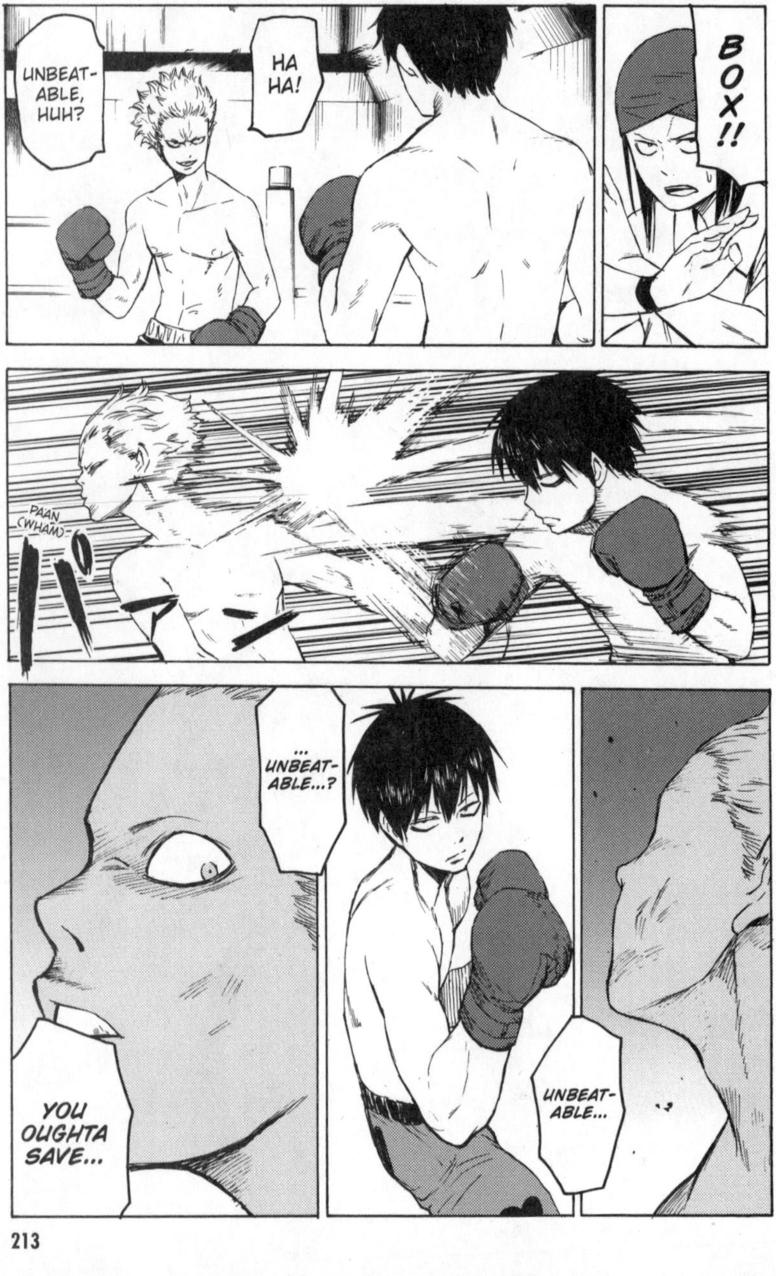
BOX!!
HA HA!
UNBEAT-ABLE, HUH?
PA'AN (WHAM)
... UNBEAT-ABLE...?
UNBEAT-ABLE...
YOU OUGHTA SAVE...

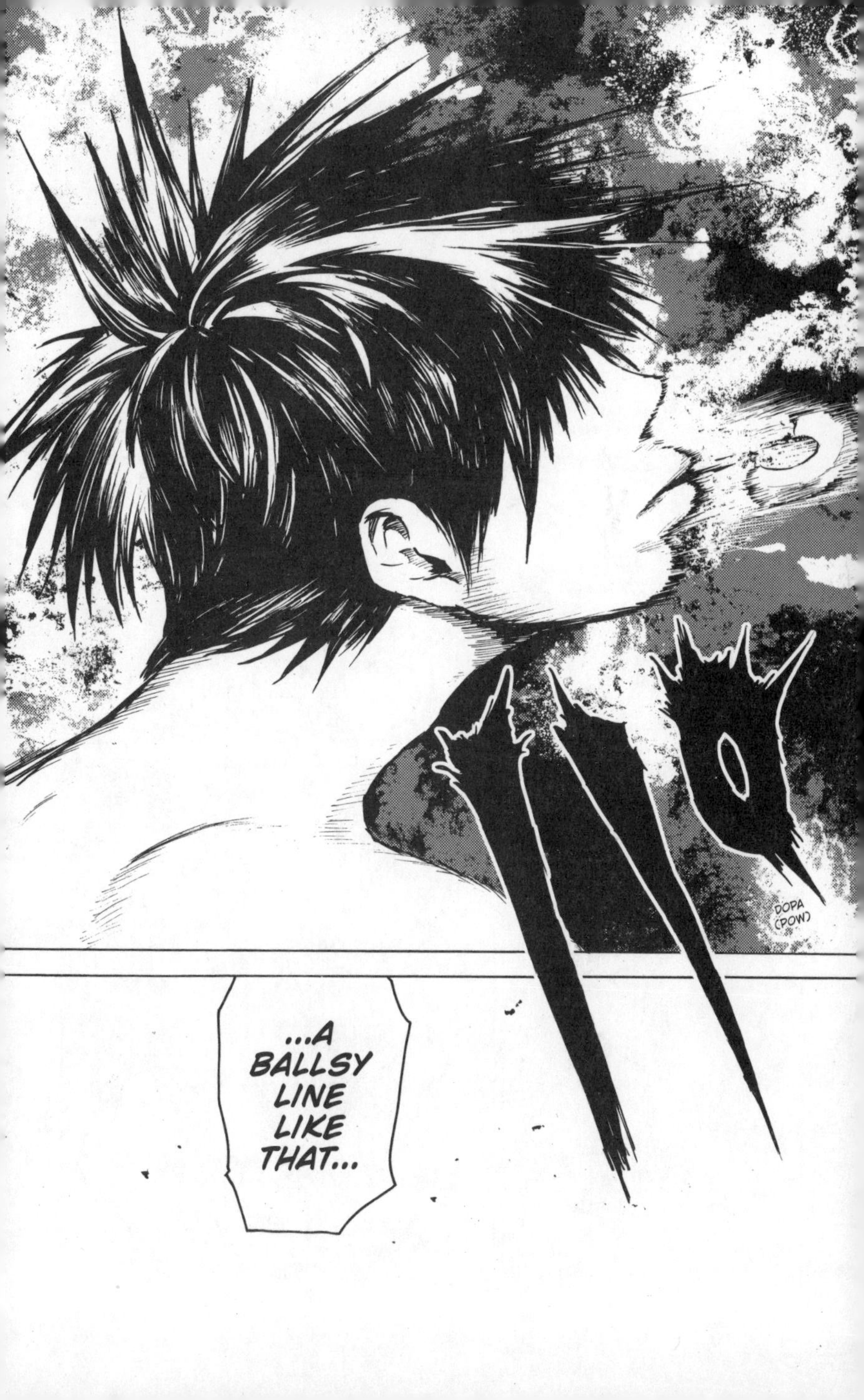
DOPA (POW)
...A BALLSY LINE LIKE THAT...

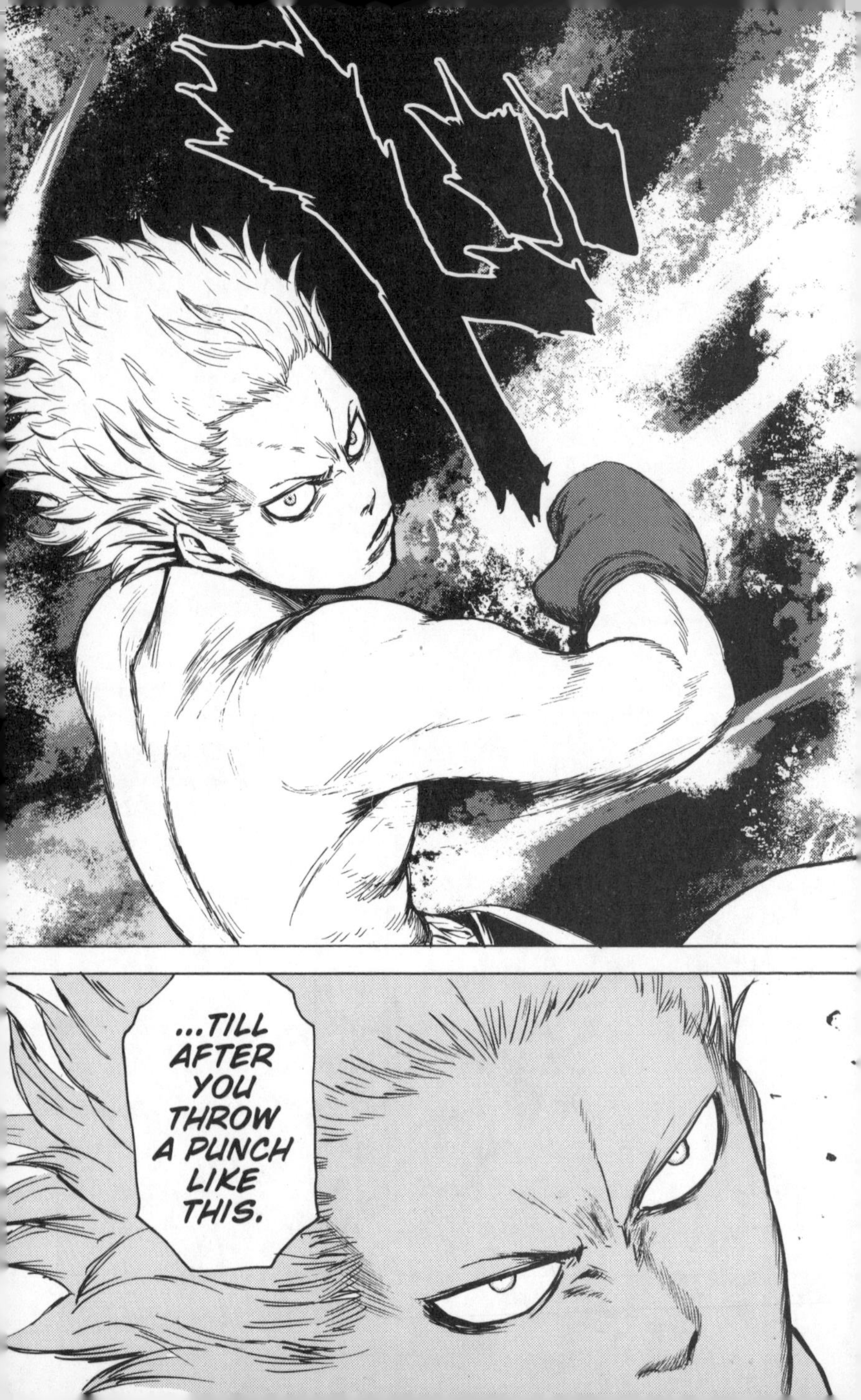
...TILL AFTER YOU THROW A PUNCH LIKE THIS.

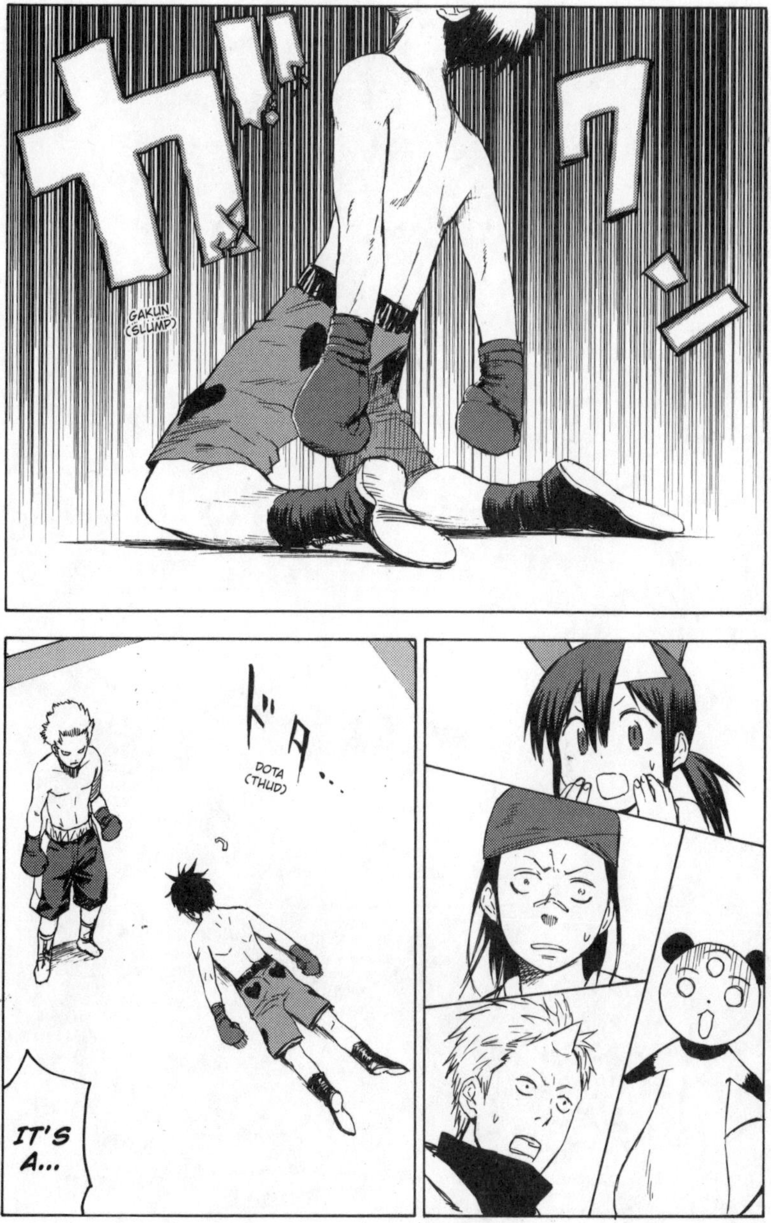
GAKUN (SLUMP)
ドタ…
DOTA (THUD)
IT'S A...

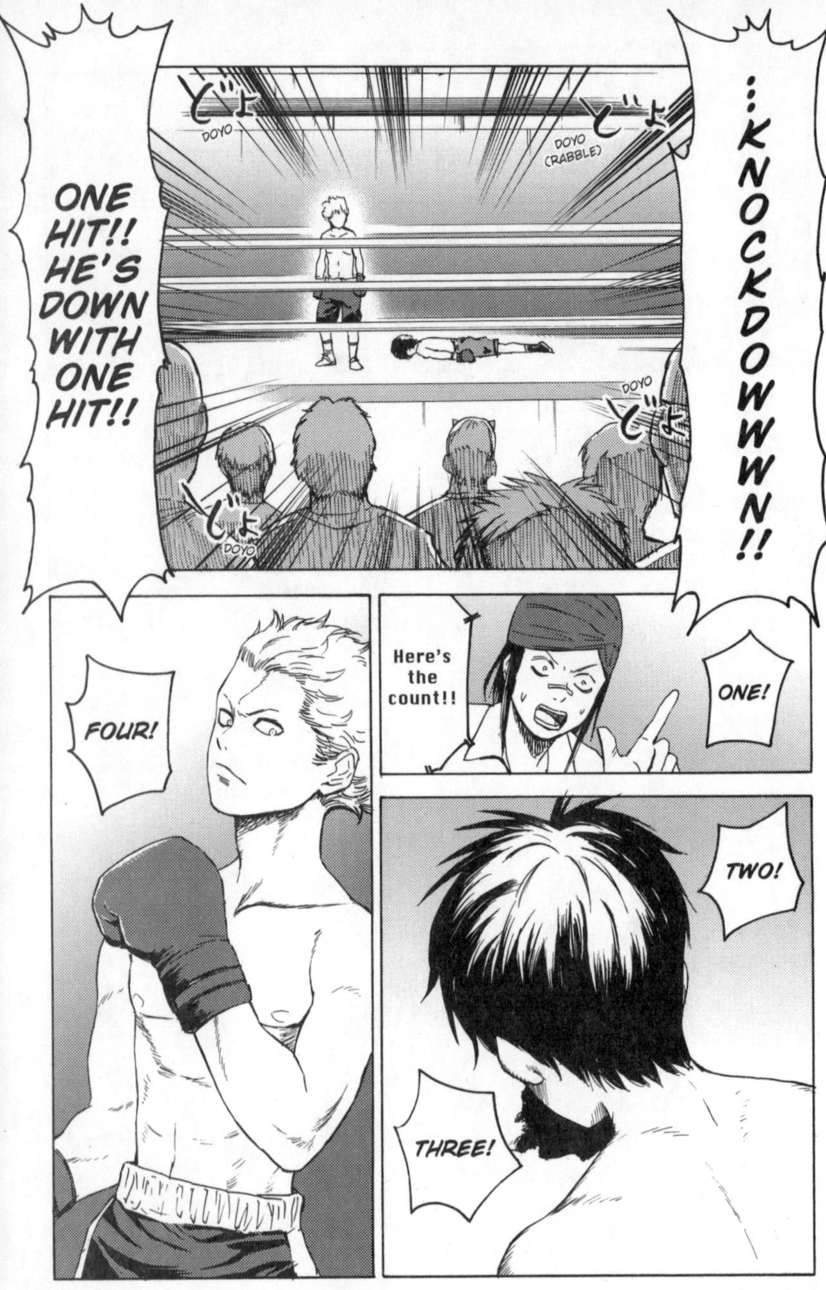

...KNOCKDOWWWWN!!
どよ
DOYO (RABBLE)
どよ
DOYO
ONE HIT!! HE'S DOWN WITH ONE HIT!!
どよ
DOYO
どよ
DOYO
Here's the count!!
ONE!
TWO!
THREE!
FOUR!

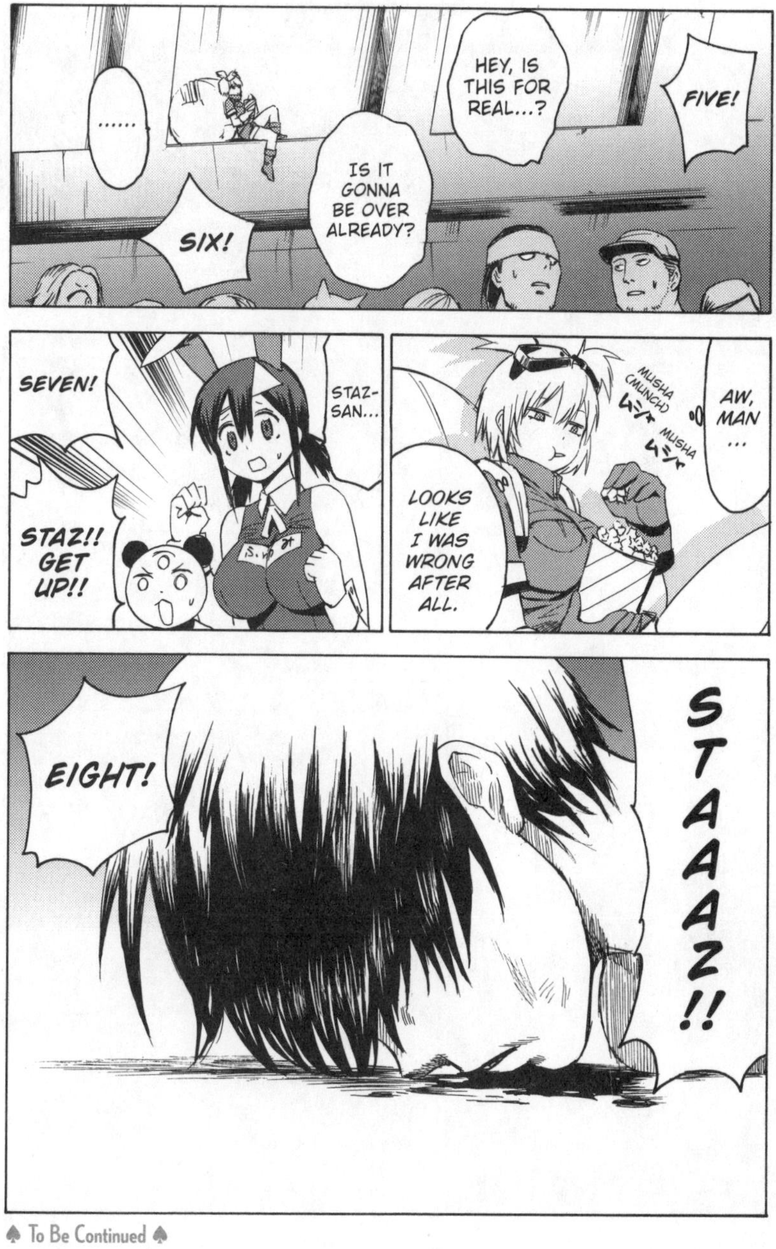
FIVE!
HEY, IS THIS FOR REAL...?
IS IT GONNA BE OVER ALREADY?
......
SIX!
AW, MAN...
MUSHA (MUNCH) ムシャ
MUSHA ムシャ
LOOKS LIKE I WAS WRONG AFTER ALL.
STAZ-SAN...
SEVEN!
STAZ!! GET UP!!
STAAAAZ!!
EIGHT!

♠ To Be Continued ♠

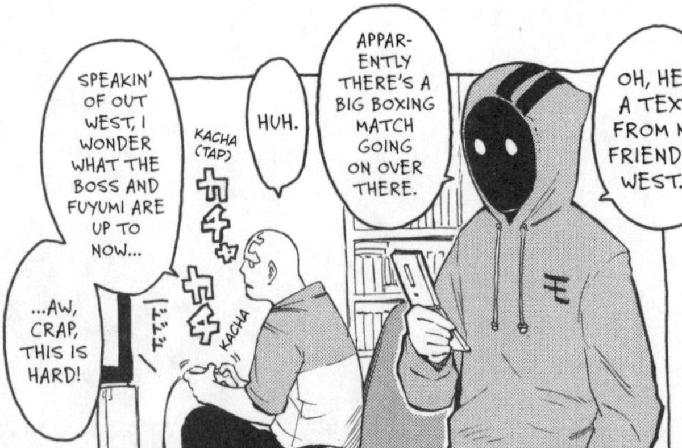
OH, HEY, A TEXT FROM MY FRIEND IN WEST...
APPAR-ENTLY THERE'S A BIG BOXING MATCH GOING ON OVER THERE.
HUH.
SPEAKIN' OF OUT WEST, I WONDER WHAT THE BOSS AND FUYUMI ARE UP TO NOW...
KACHA (TAP)
KACHA
...AW, CRAP, THIS IS HARD!
SFX: DO (BOOP) DO DO

BLOOD LAD

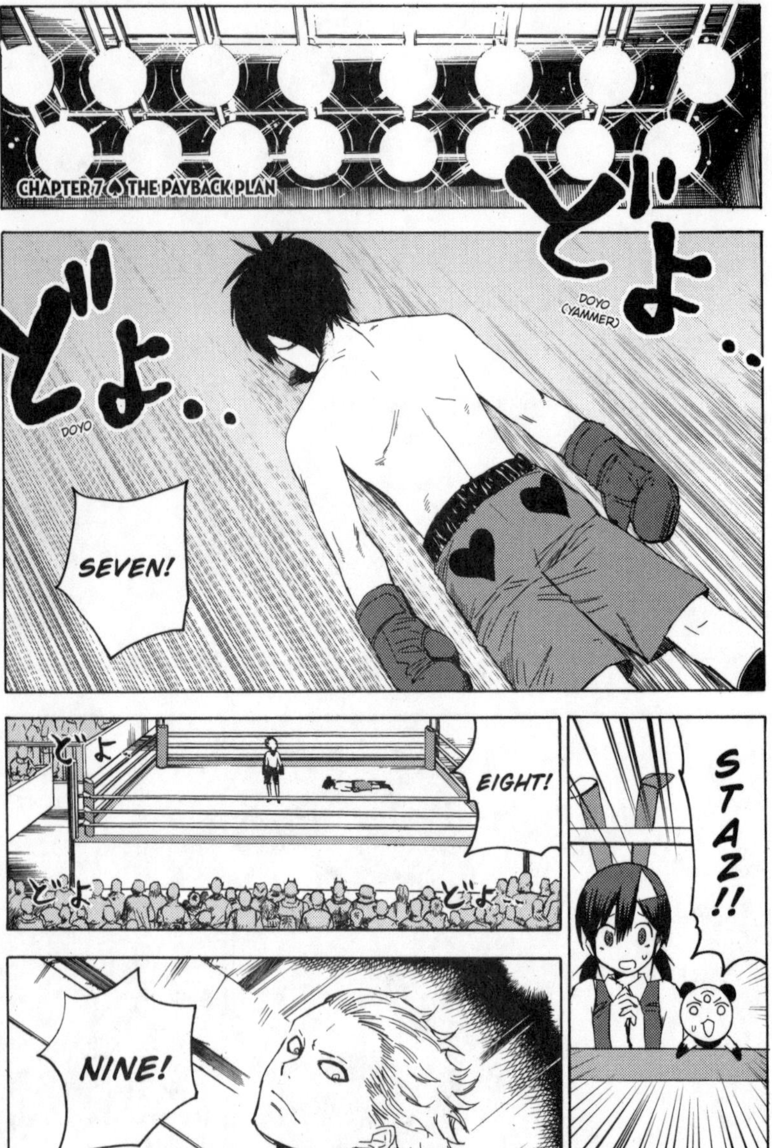
CHAPTER 7 ♠ THE PAYBACK PLAN
どよ..
DOYO (YAMMER)
どよ..
DOYO
SEVEN!
STAZ!!
EIGHT!
どよ
どよ
どよ～
NINE!

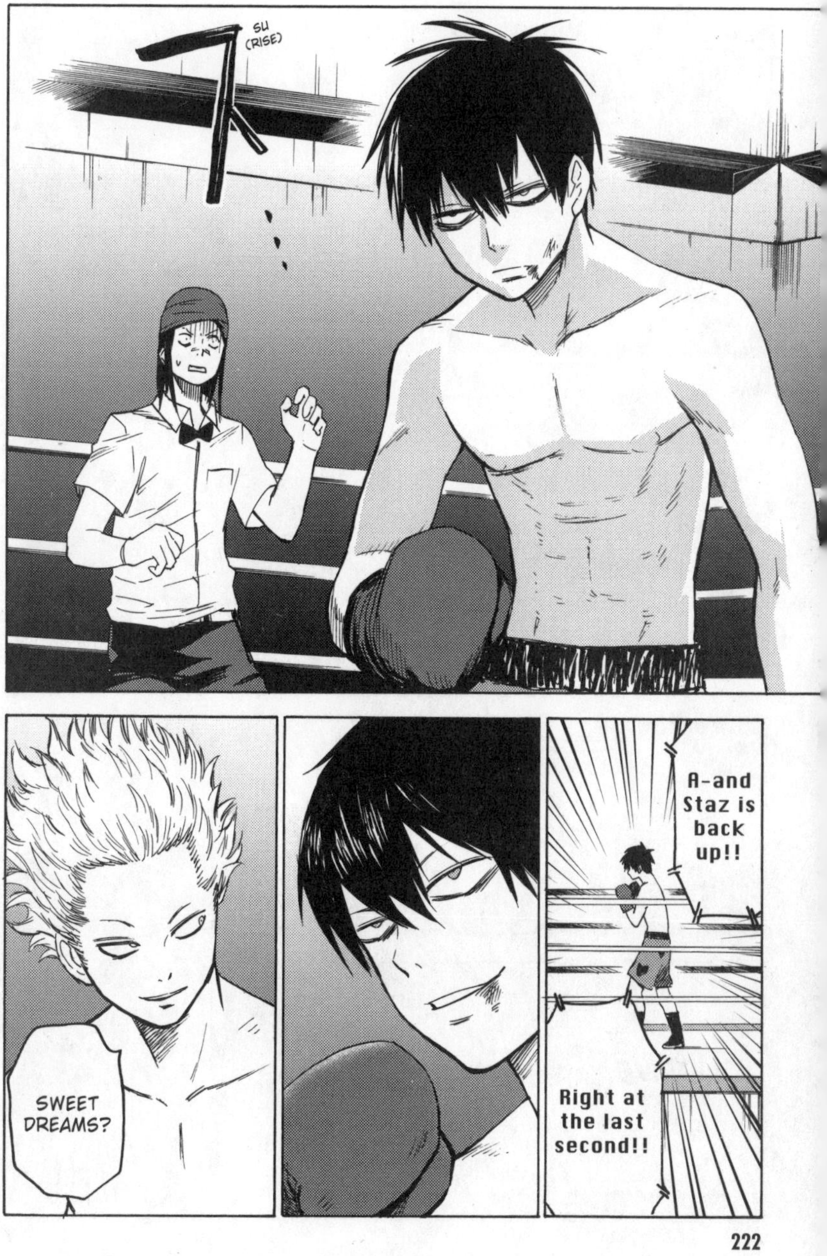
SU (RISE)
A-and Staz is back up!!
Right at the last second!!
SWEET DREAMS?

## CHAPTER 7 ♠ THE PAYBACK PLAN

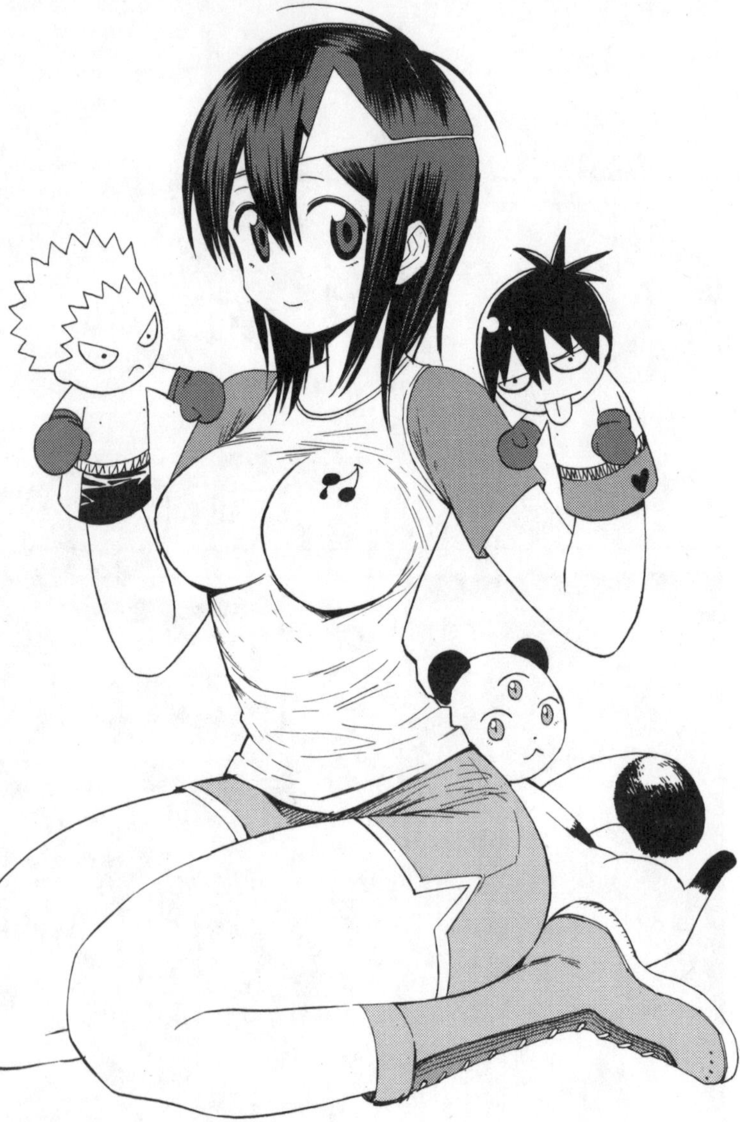

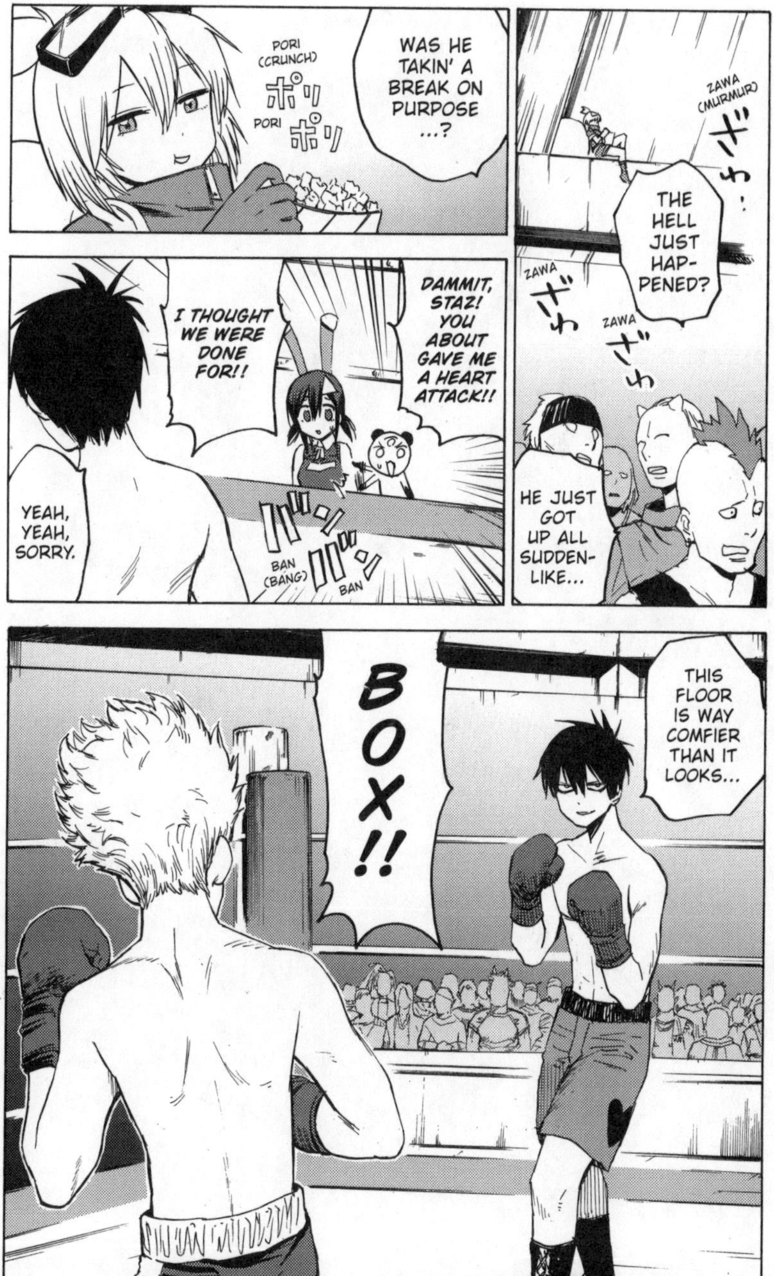
ZAWA (MURMUR)
ざわ
THE HELL JUST HAP-PENED?
ZAWA
ざわ
ZAWA
ざわ
HE JUST GOT UP ALL SUDDEN-LIKE...
WAS HE TAKIN' A BREAK ON PURPOSE ...?
PORI (CRUNCH)
ポリ
PORI
ポリ
DAMMIT, STAZ! YOU ABOUT GAVE ME A HEART ATTACK!!
I THOUGHT WE WERE DONE FOR!!
バン
BAN (BANG)
バン
BAN
YEAH, YEAH, SORRY.
THIS FLOOR IS WAY COMFIER THAN IT LOOKS...
BOX!!

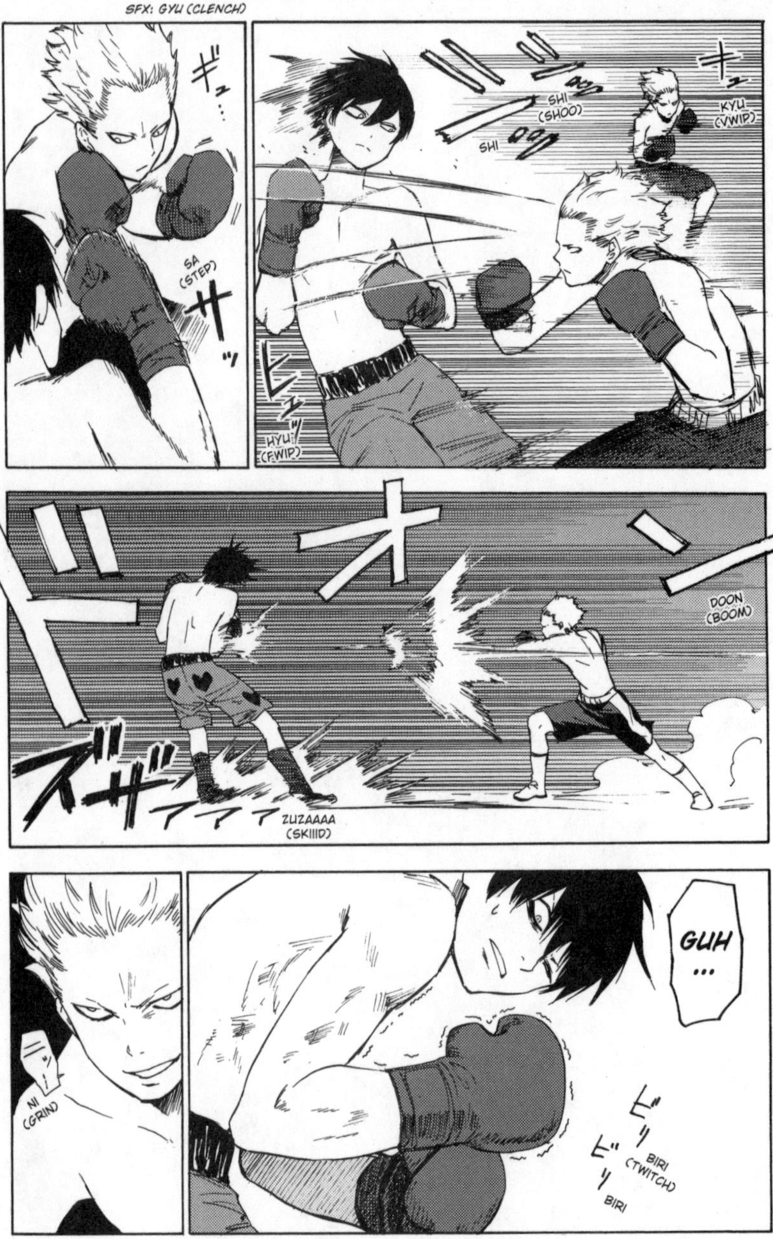
SFX: GYU (CLENCH)
KYU (VWIP)
SHI (SHOO)
SHI
HYU! (FWIP)
SA (STEP)
DOON (BOOM)
ZUZAAAA (SKIIID)
GUH ...
BIRI (TWITCH)
BIRI
NI (GRIN)

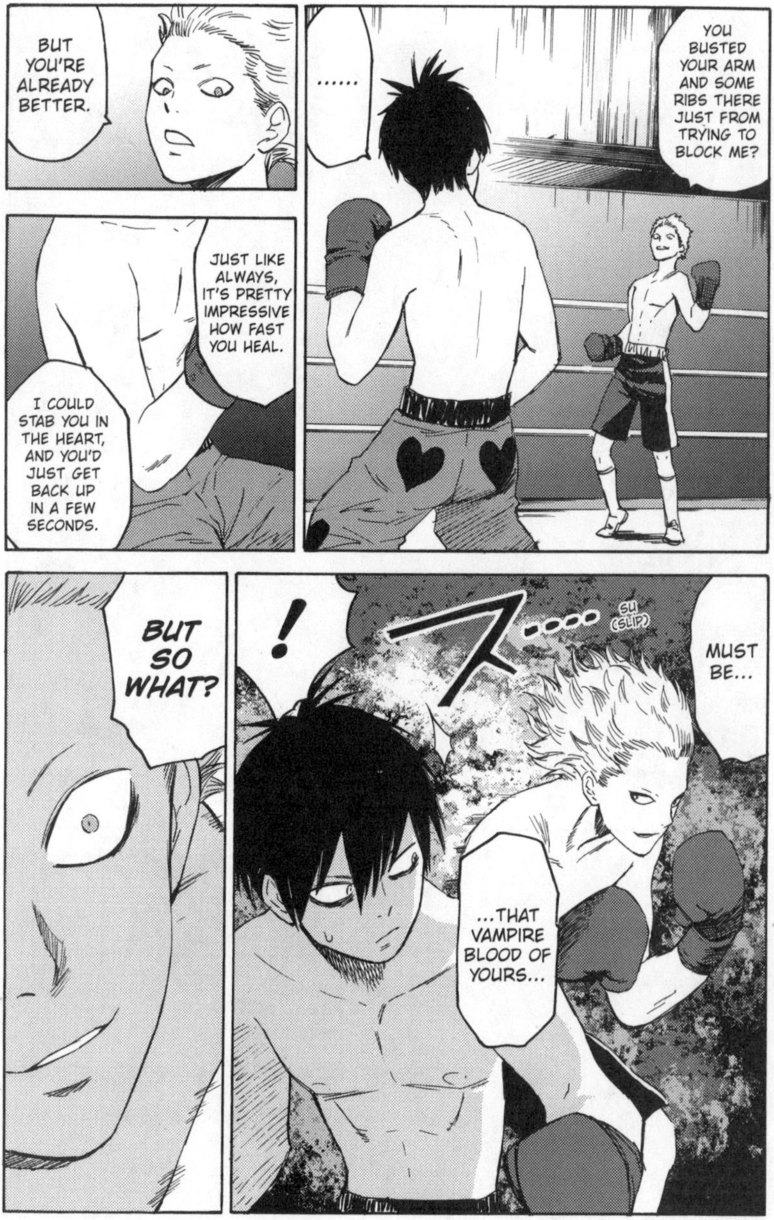

YOU BUSTED YOUR ARM AND SOME RIBS THERE JUST FROM TRYING TO BLOCK ME?
......
BUT YOU'RE ALREADY BETTER.
JUST LIKE ALWAYS, IT'S PRETTY IMPRESSIVE HOW FAST YOU HEAL.
I COULD STAB YOU IN THE HEART, AND YOU'D JUST GET BACK UP IN A FEW SECONDS.
MUST BE...
SU (SLIP)
!
...THAT VAMPIRE BLOOD OF YOURS...
BUT SO WHAT?

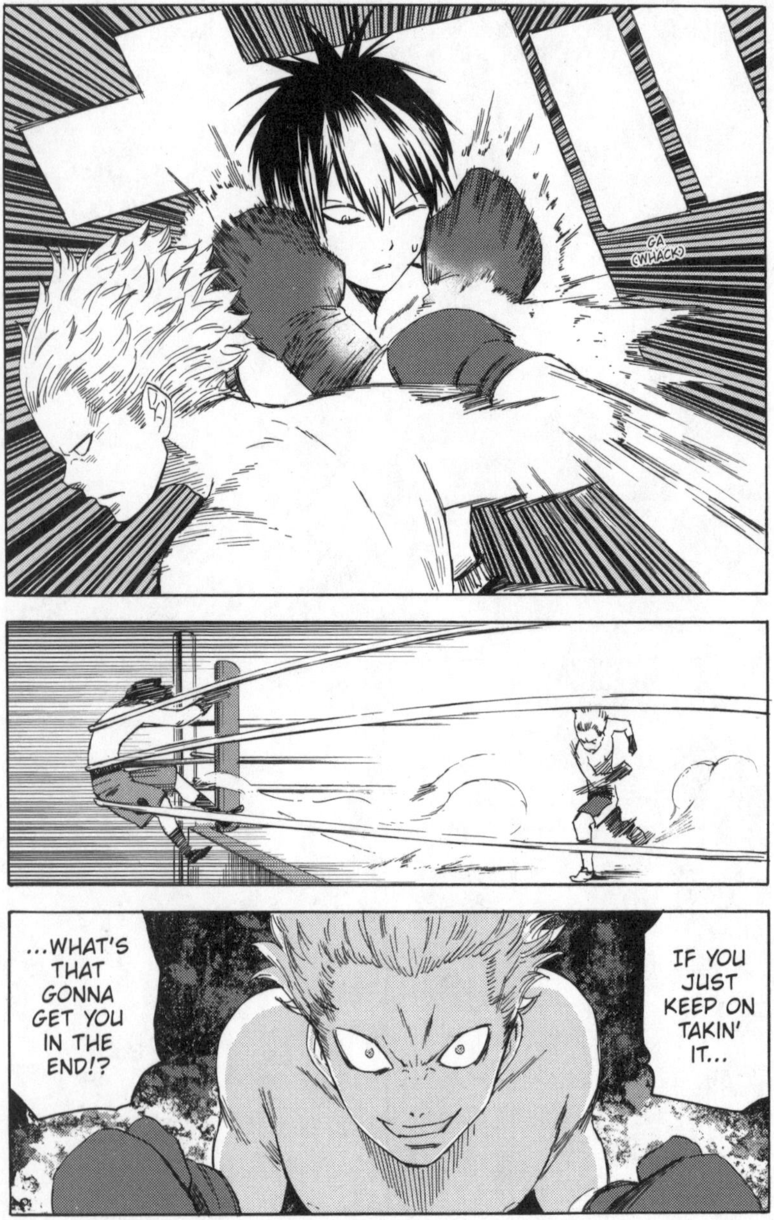
GA (WHACK)
IF YOU JUST KEEP ON TAKIN' IT...
...WHAT'S THAT GONNA GET YOU IN THE END!?

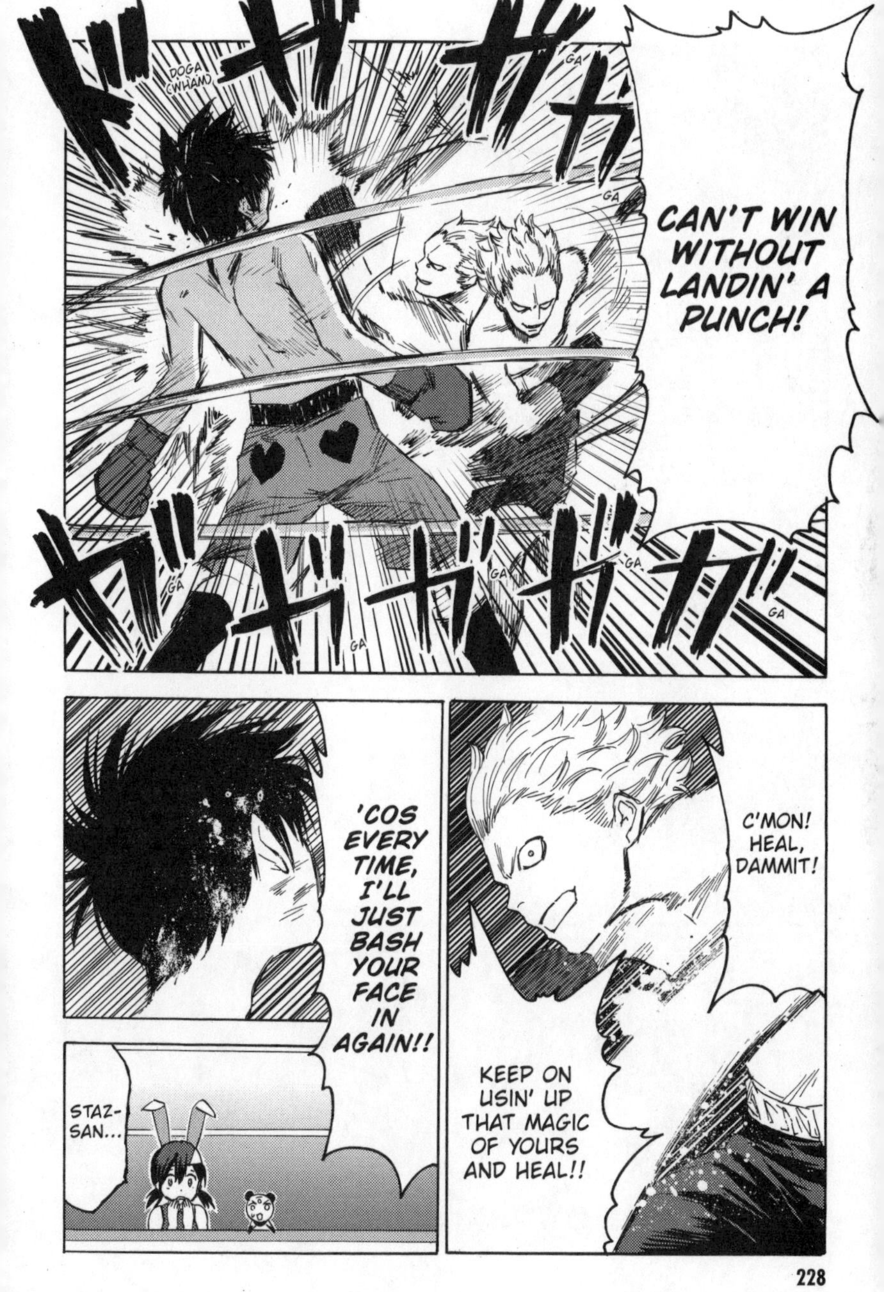
CAN'T WIN WITHOUT LANDIN' A PUNCH!
GA
DOGA (WHAM)
GA
GA
GA
GA
GA
GA
C'MON! HEAL, DAMMIT!
KEEP ON USIN' UP THAT MAGIC OF YOURS AND HEAL!!
'COS EVERY TIME, I'LL JUST BASH YOUR FACE IN AGAIN!!
STAZ-SAN...

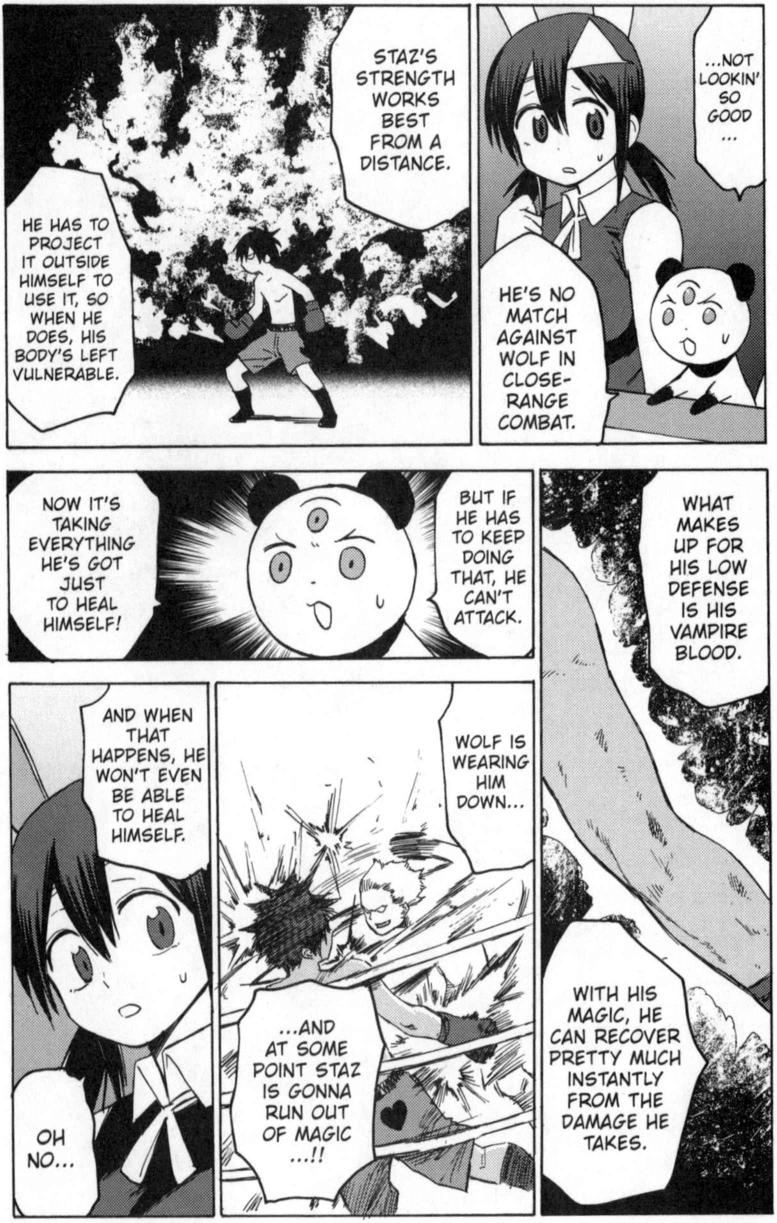
...NOT LOOKIN' SO GOOD...
HE'S NO MATCH AGAINST WOLF IN CLOSE-RANGE COMBAT.
STAZ'S STRENGTH WORKS BEST FROM A DISTANCE.
HE HAS TO PROJECT IT OUTSIDE HIMSELF TO USE IT, SO WHEN HE DOES, HIS BODY'S LEFT VULNERABLE.
WHAT MAKES UP FOR HIS LOW DEFENSE IS HIS VAMPIRE BLOOD.
WITH HIS MAGIC, HE CAN RECOVER PRETTY MUCH INSTANTLY FROM THE DAMAGE HE TAKES.
BUT IF HE HAS TO KEEP DOING THAT, HE CAN'T ATTACK.
NOW IT'S TAKING EVERYTHING HE'S GOT JUST TO HEAL HIMSELF!
WOLF IS WEARING HIM DOWN...
...AND AT SOME POINT STAZ IS GONNA RUN OUT OF MAGIC ...!!
AND WHEN THAT HAPPENS, HE WON'T EVEN BE ABLE TO HEAL HIMSELF.
OH NO...

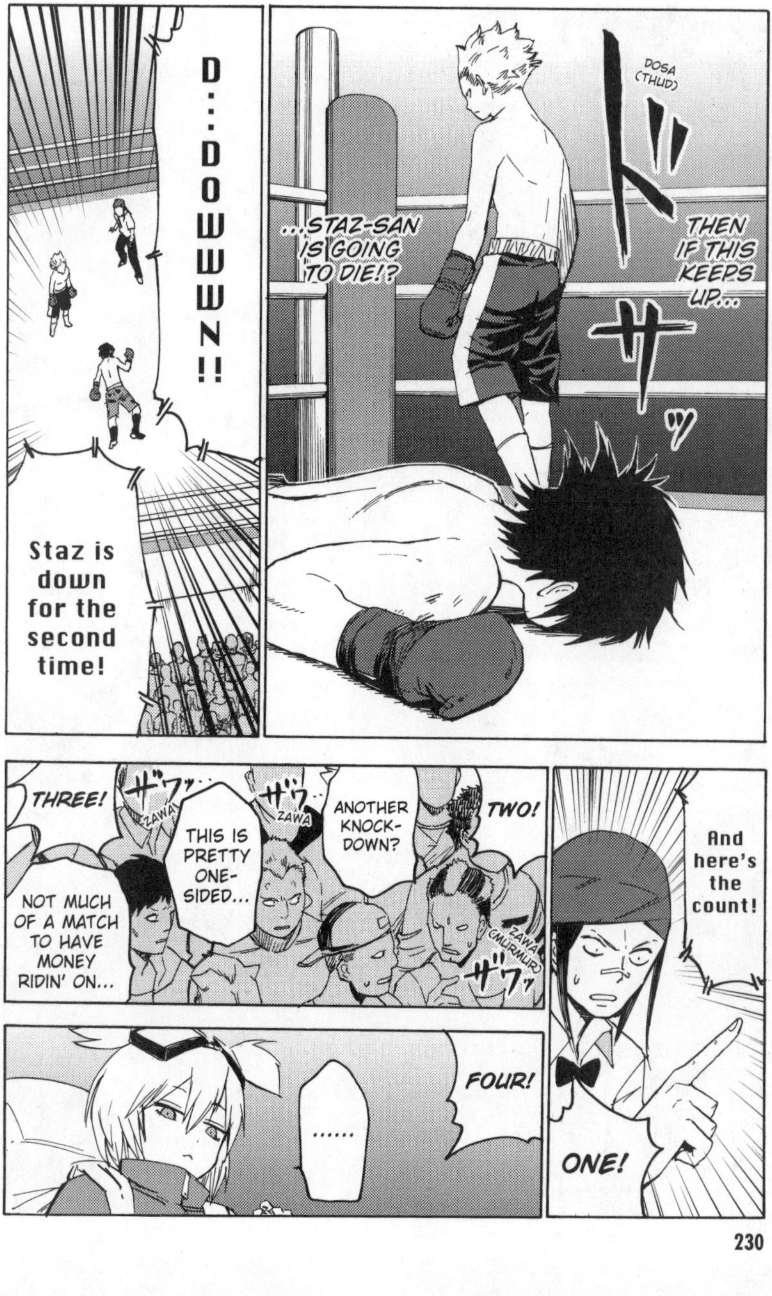
DOSA (THUD)
THEN IF THIS KEEPS UP...
...STAZ-SAN IS GOING TO DIE!?
D...DOWWWWN!!
Staz is down for the second time!
And here's the count!
ONE!
TWO!
ZAWA (MURMUR)
ANOTHER KNOCK-DOWN?
ZAWA
THIS IS PRETTY ONE-SIDED...
ZAWA
THREE!
NOT MUCH OF A MATCH TO HAVE MONEY RIDIN' ON...
FOUR!
......

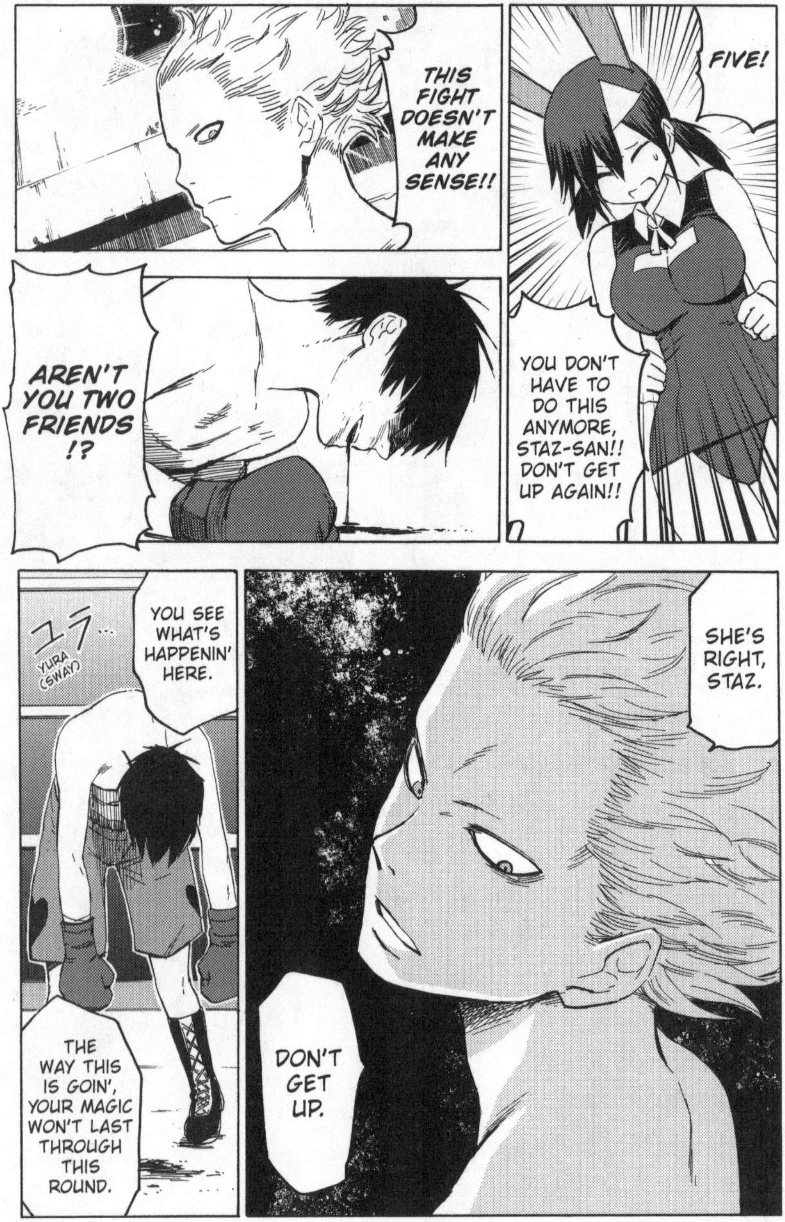
FIVE!
YOU DON'T HAVE TO DO THIS ANYMORE, STAZ-SAN!! DON'T GET UP AGAIN!!
THIS FIGHT DOESN'T MAKE ANY SENSE!!
AREN'T YOU TWO FRIENDS!?
SHE'S RIGHT, STAZ.
DON'T GET UP.
ユラ…
YURA (SWAY)
YOU SEE WHAT'S HAPPENIN' HERE.
THE WAY THIS IS GOIN', YOUR MAGIC WON'T LAST THROUGH THIS ROUND.

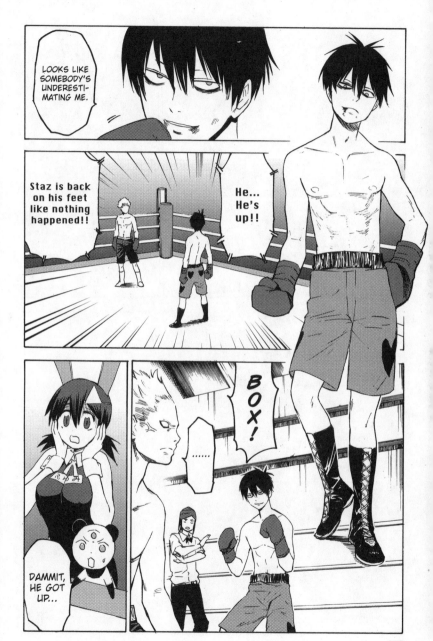

LOOKS LIKE SOMEBODY'S UNDERESTIMATING ME.

Staz is back on his feet like nothing happened!!

He... He's up!!

BOX!

......

DAMMIT, HE GOT UP...

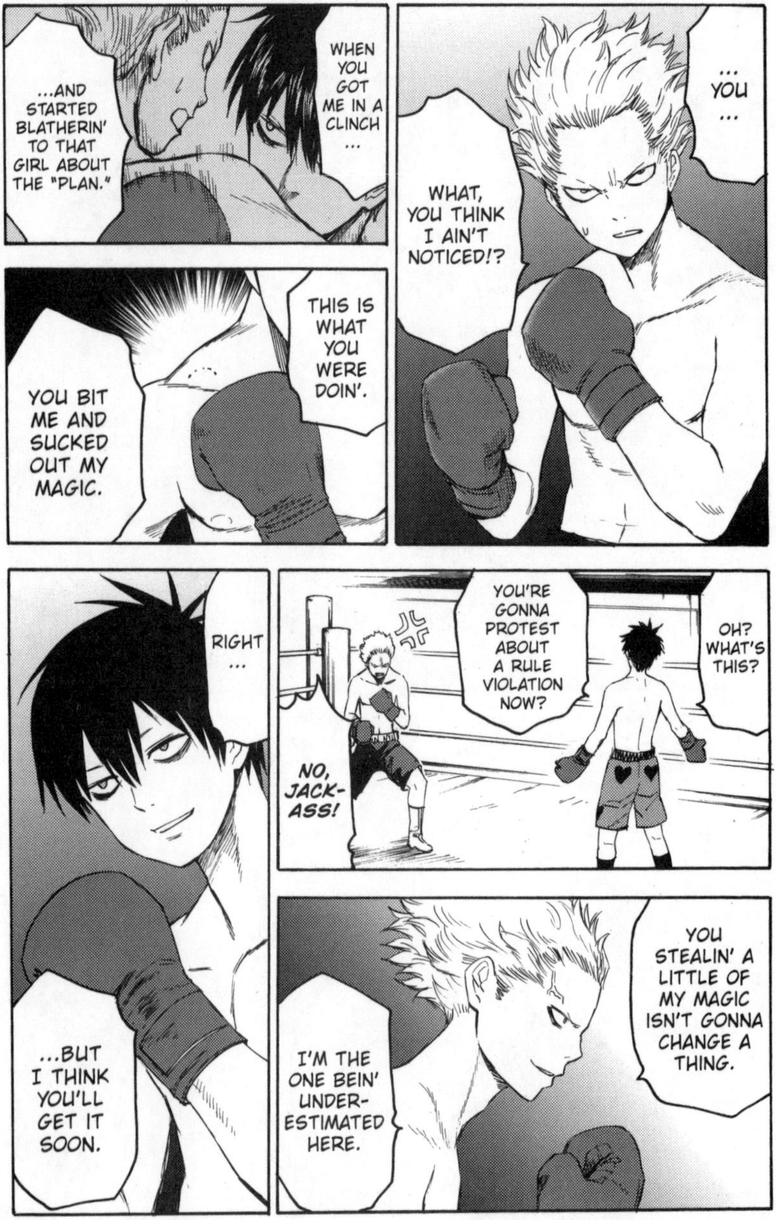
... YOU ...
WHAT, YOU THINK I AIN'T NOTICED!?
WHEN YOU GOT ME IN A CLINCH ...
...AND STARTED BLATHERIN' TO THAT GIRL ABOUT THE "PLAN."
THIS IS WHAT YOU WERE DOIN'.
YOU BIT ME AND SUCKED OUT MY MAGIC.
OH? WHAT'S THIS?
YOU'RE GONNA PROTEST ABOUT A RULE VIOLATION NOW?
NO, JACK-ASS!
YOU STEALIN' A LITTLE OF MY MAGIC ISN'T GONNA CHANGE A THING.
I'M THE ONE BEIN' UNDER-ESTIMATED HERE.
RIGHT ...
...BUT I THINK YOU'LL GET IT SOON.

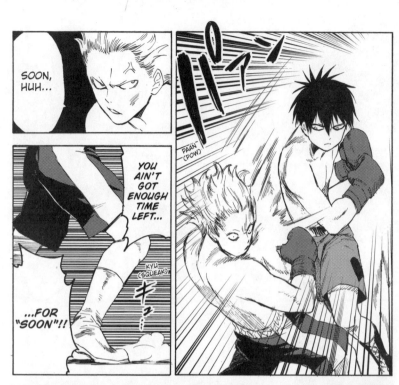

SOON,
HUH...

YOU
AIN'T
GOT
ENOUGH
TIME
LEFT...

KYU
(SQUEAK)

...FOR
"SOON"!!

PAAN
(POW)

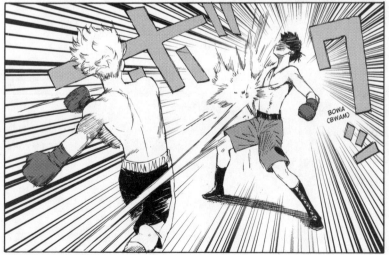

BOWA
(BWAM)

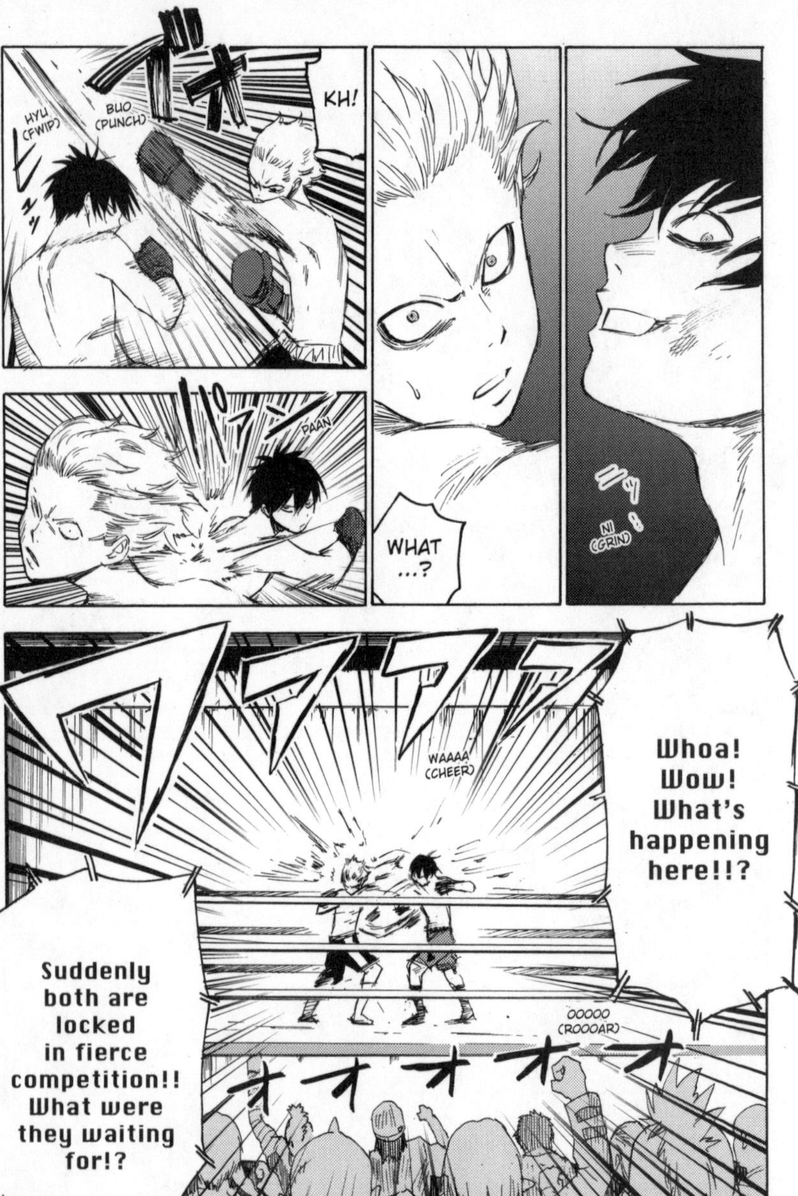
NI (GRIN)
WHAT ...?
KH!
BUO (PUNCH)
HYU (FWIP)
PAAN
Whoa! Wow! What's happening here!!?
WAAAA (CHEER)
OOOOO (ROOOAR)
Suddenly both are locked in fierce competition!! What were they waiting for!?

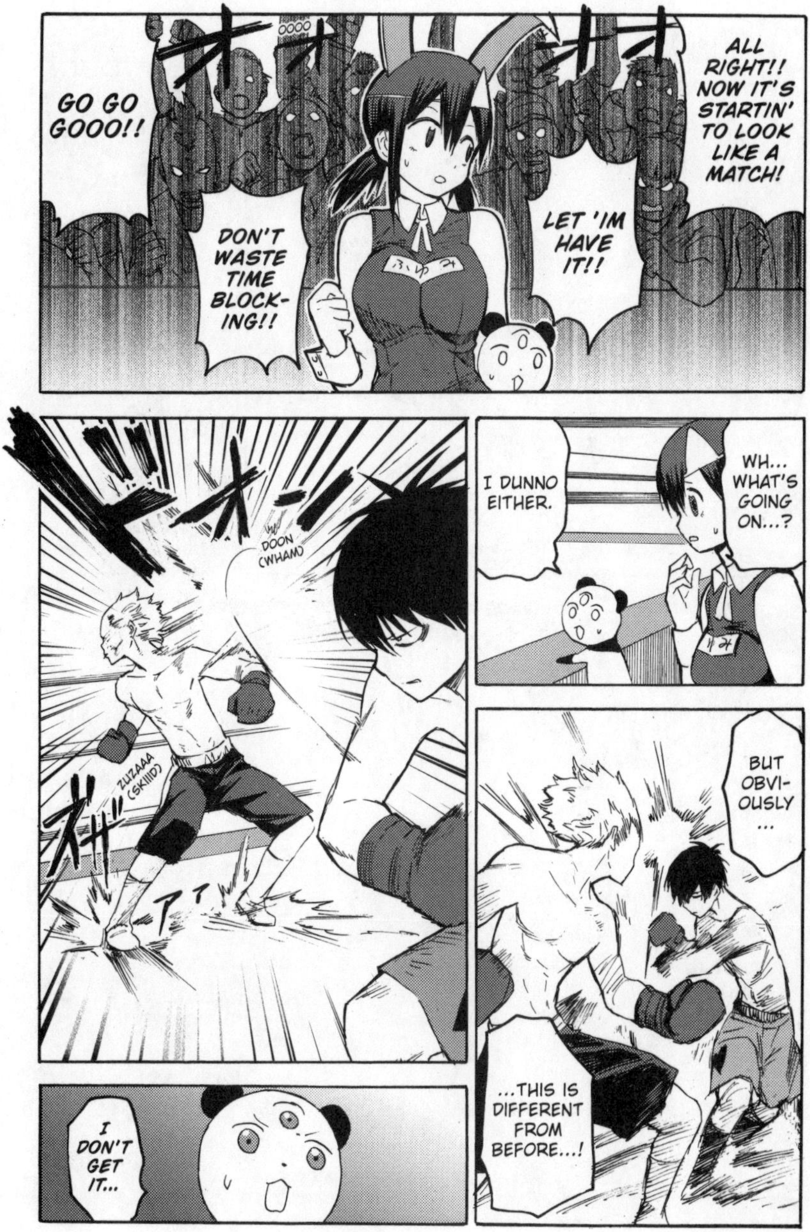
OOOO
ALL RIGHT!! NOW IT'S STARTIN' TO LOOK LIKE A MATCH!
LET 'IM HAVE IT!!
DON'T WASTE TIME BLOCKING!!
GO GO GOOO!!
WH... WHAT'S GOING ON...?
I DUNNO EITHER.
BUT OBVIOUSLY...
...THIS IS DIFFERENT FROM BEFORE...!
DOON (WHAM)
ZUZAAA (SKIIID)
I DON'T GET IT...

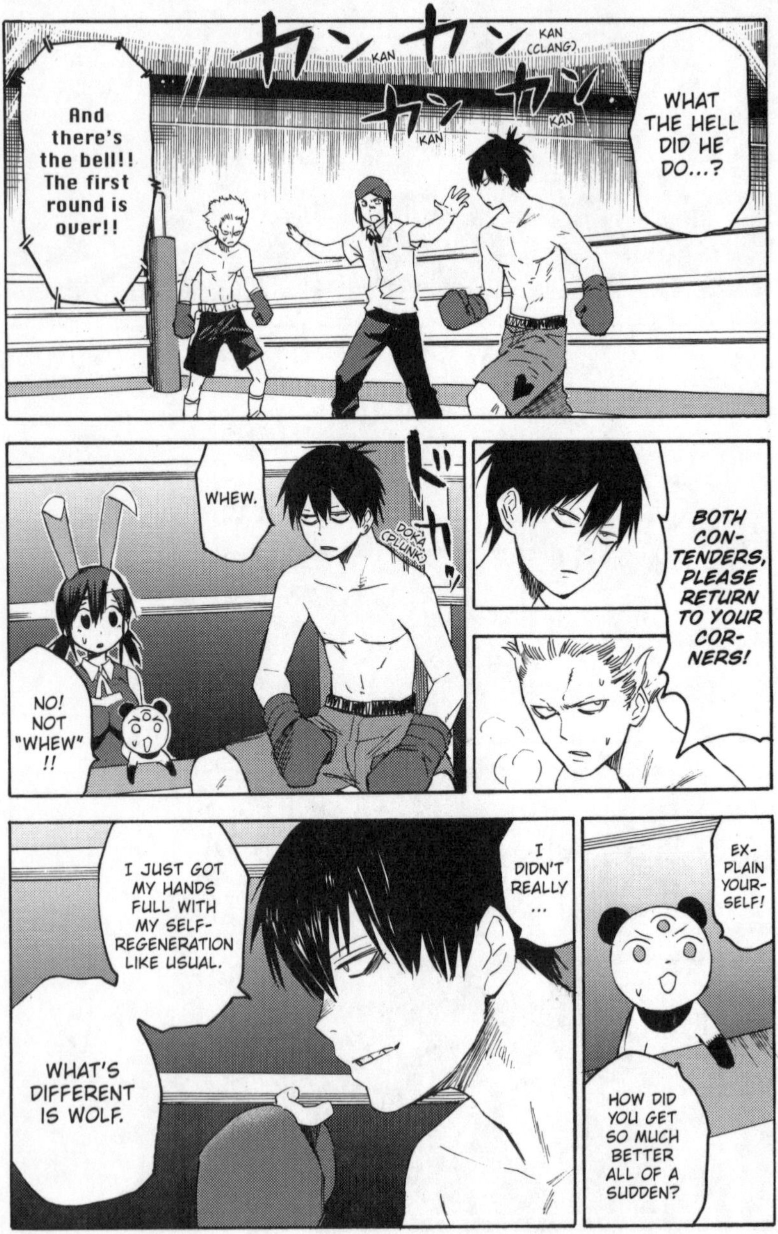
KAN (CLANG)
WHAT THE HELL DID HE DO...?
KAN
KAN
KAN
And there's the bell!! The first round is over!!
BOTH CONTENDERS, PLEASE RETURN TO YOUR CORNERS!
DOKA (PLUNK)
WHEW.
NO! NOT "WHEW" !!
EXPLAIN YOURSELF!
HOW DID YOU GET SO MUCH BETTER ALL OF A SUDDEN?
I DIDN'T REALLY ...
I JUST GOT MY HANDS FULL WITH MY SELF-REGENERATION LIKE USUAL.
WHAT'S DIFFERENT IS WOLF.

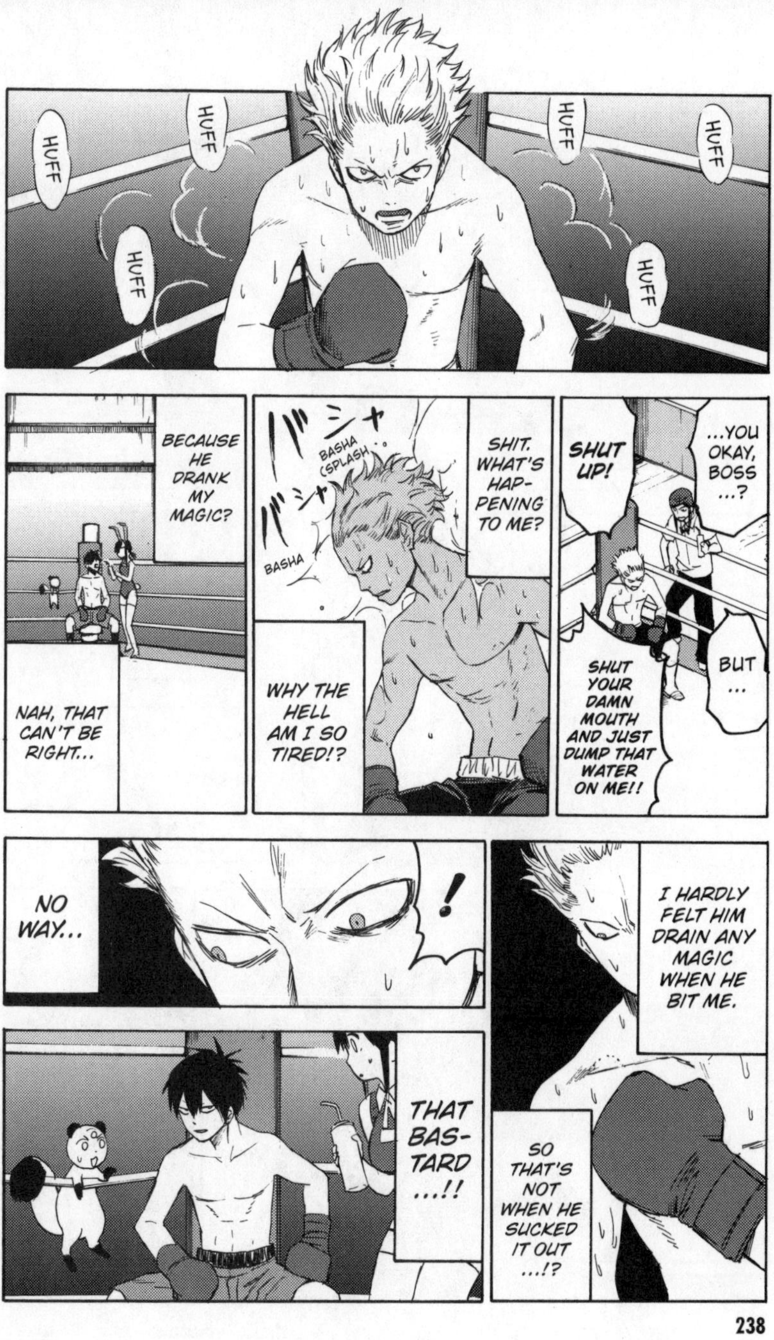
HUFF
HUFF
HUFF
HUFF
HUFF
...YOU OKAY, BOSS...?
SHUT UP!
BUT...
SHUT YOUR DAMN MOUTH AND JUST DUMP THAT WATER ON ME!!
バシャ
BASHA (SPLASH)
SHIT. WHAT'S HAP-PENING TO ME?
バシャ
BASHA
WHY THE HELL AM I SO TIRED!?
BECAUSE HE DRANK MY MAGIC?
NAH, THAT CAN'T BE RIGHT...
I HARDLY FELT HIM DRAIN ANY MAGIC WHEN HE BIT ME.
SO THAT'S NOT WHEN HE SUCKED IT OUT...!?
!
NO WAY...
THAT BAS-TARD...!!

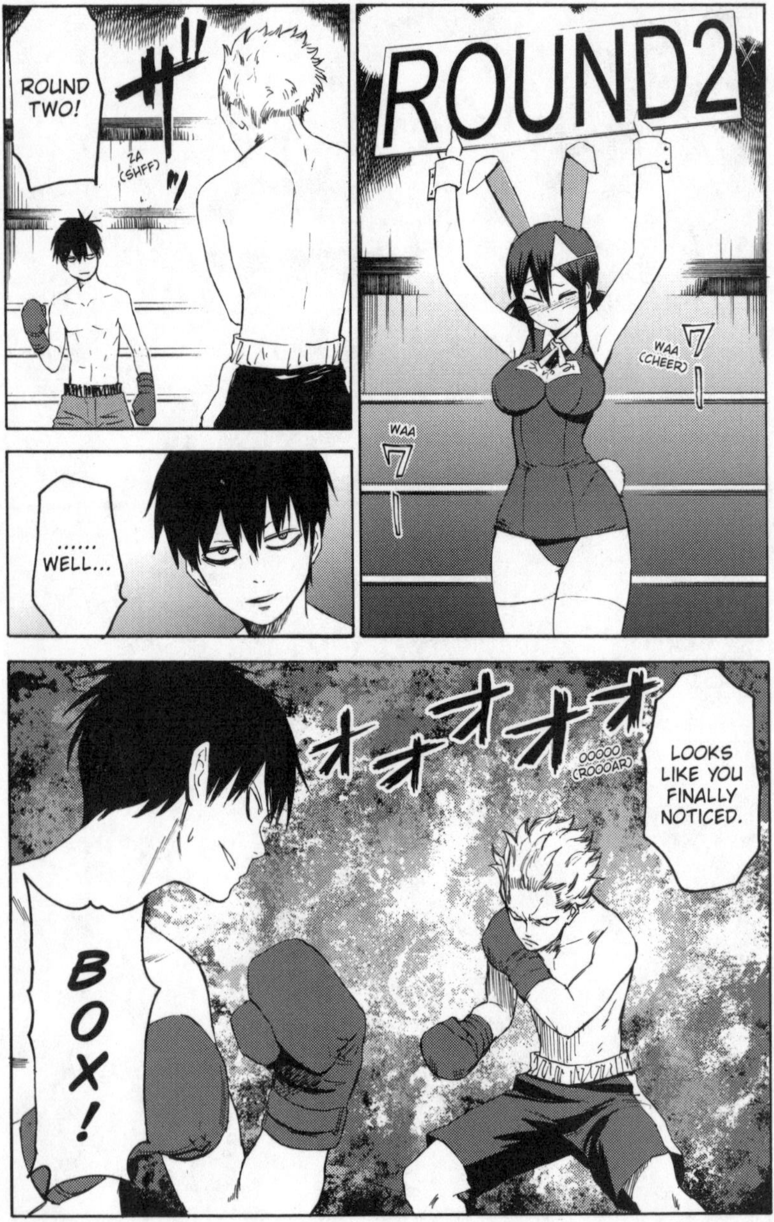
ROUND2
ワー
WAA (CHEER)
ワー
WAA
ROUND TWO!
ザッ
ZA (SHFF)
......WELL...
オォオオオ
OOOOO (ROOOAR)
LOOKS LIKE YOU FINALLY NOTICED.
BOX!

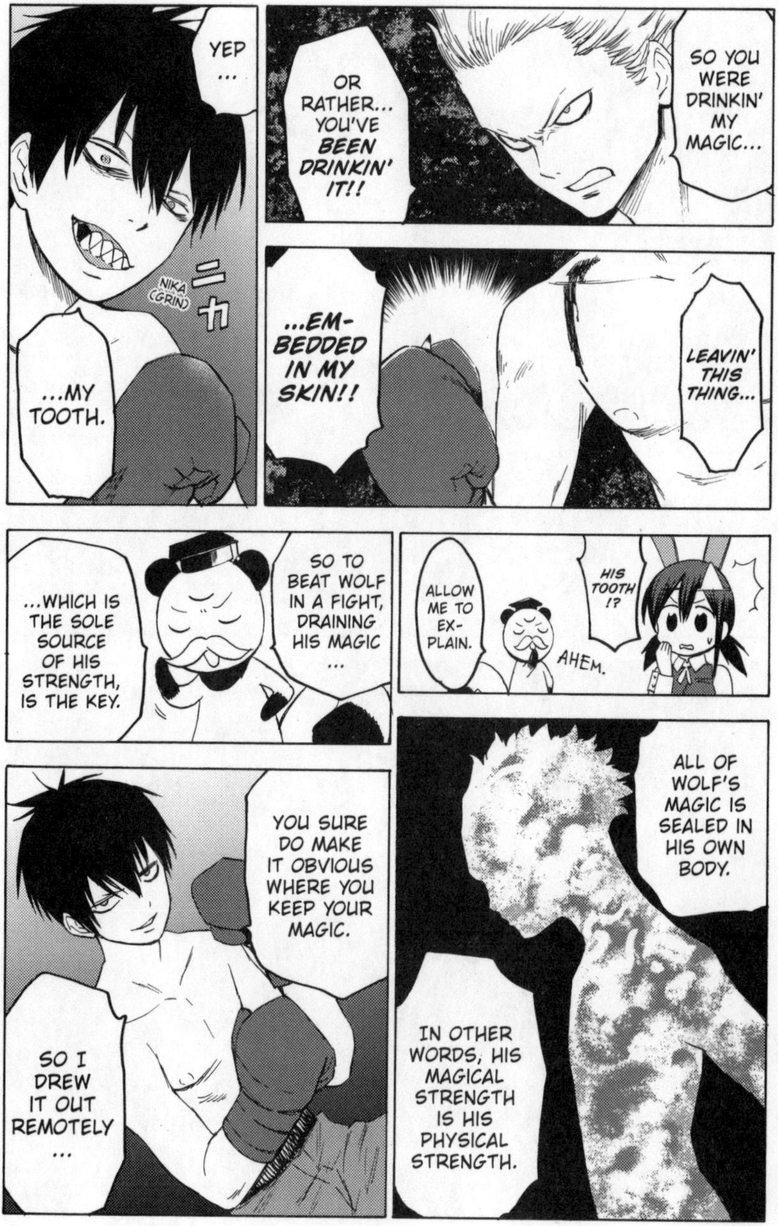
SO YOU WERE DRINKIN' MY MAGIC...
OR RATHER... YOU'VE BEEN DRINKIN' IT!!
LEAVIN' THIS THING...
...EM-BEDDED IN MY SKIN!!
YEP...
NIKA (GRIN)
...MY TOOTH.
HIS TOOTH!?
ALLOW ME TO EX-PLAIN.
AHEM.
SO TO BEAT WOLF IN A FIGHT, DRAINING HIS MAGIC...
...WHICH IS THE SOLE SOURCE OF HIS STRENGTH, IS THE KEY.
ALL OF WOLF'S MAGIC IS SEALED IN HIS OWN BODY.
IN OTHER WORDS, HIS MAGICAL STRENGTH IS HIS PHYSICAL STRENGTH.
YOU SURE DO MAKE IT OBVIOUS WHERE YOU KEEP YOUR MAGIC.
SO I DREW IT OUT REMOTELY...

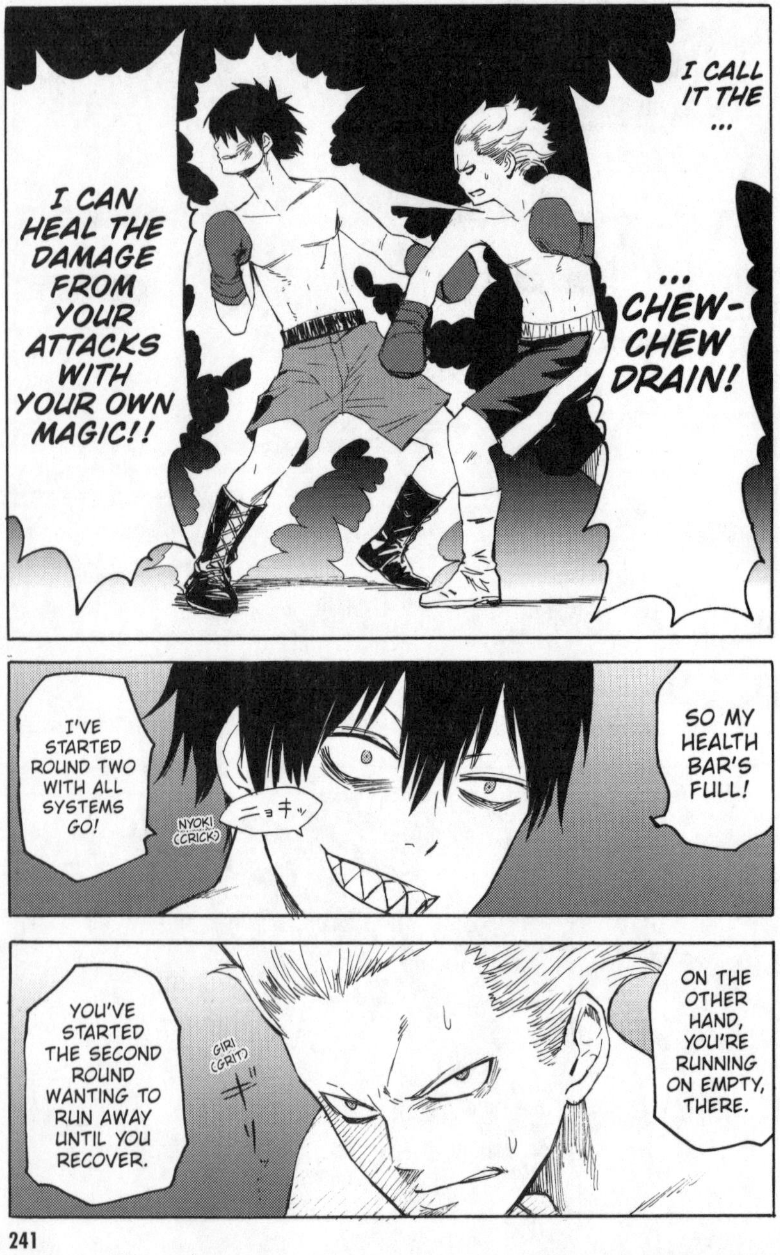
I CALL IT THE ...
... CHËW-CHEW DRAIN!
I CAN HEAL THE DAMAGE FROM YOUR ATTACKS WITH YOUR OWN MAGIC!!
SO MY HEALTH BAR'S FULL!
ニョキッ
NYOKI (CRICK)
I'VE STARTED ROUND TWO WITH ALL SYSTEMS GO!
ON THE OTHER HAND, YOU'RE RUNNING ON EMPTY, THERE.
ギリッ
GIRI (GRIT)
YOU'VE STARTED THE SECOND ROUND WANTING TO RUN AWAY UNTIL YOU RECOVER.

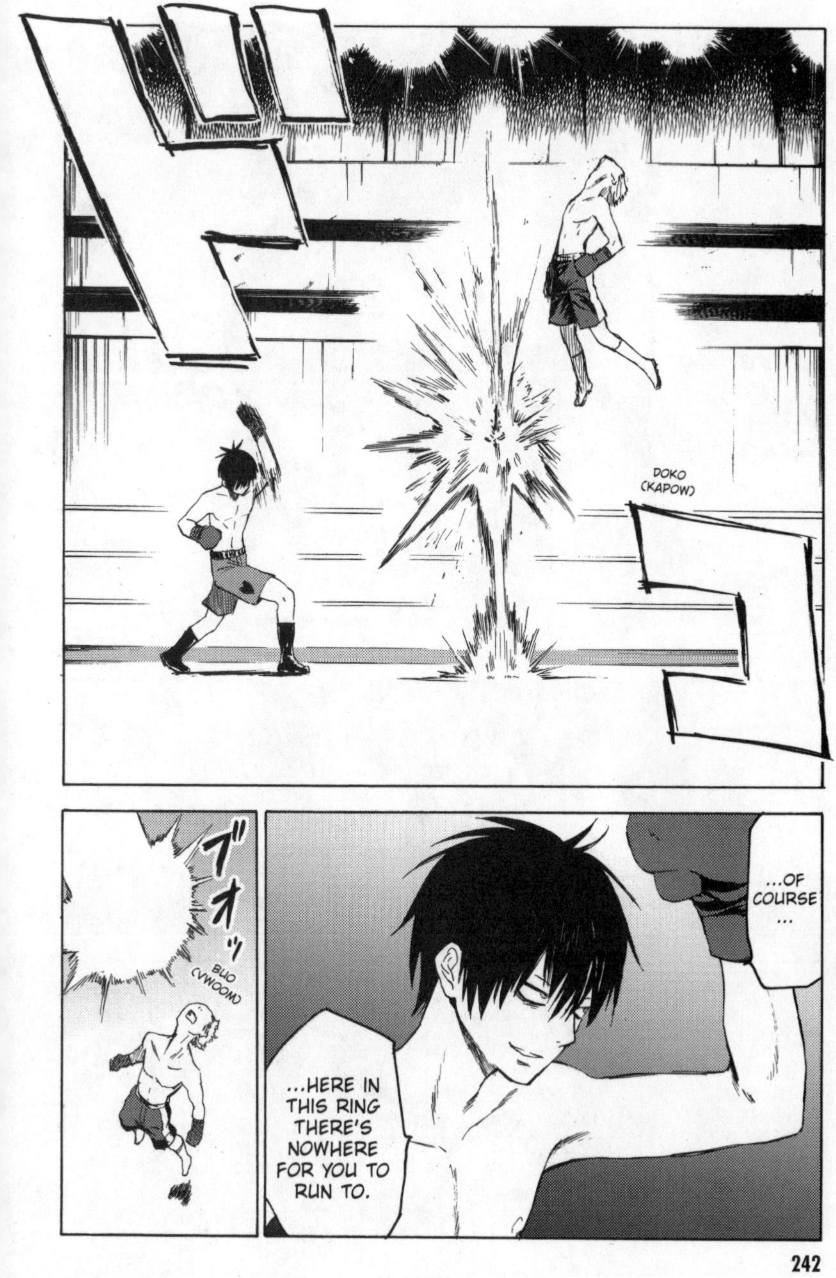
DOKO
(KAPOW)
...OF COURSE ...
...HERE IN THIS RING THERE'S NOWHERE FOR YOU TO RUN TO.
ブオッ
BUO
(VWOOM)

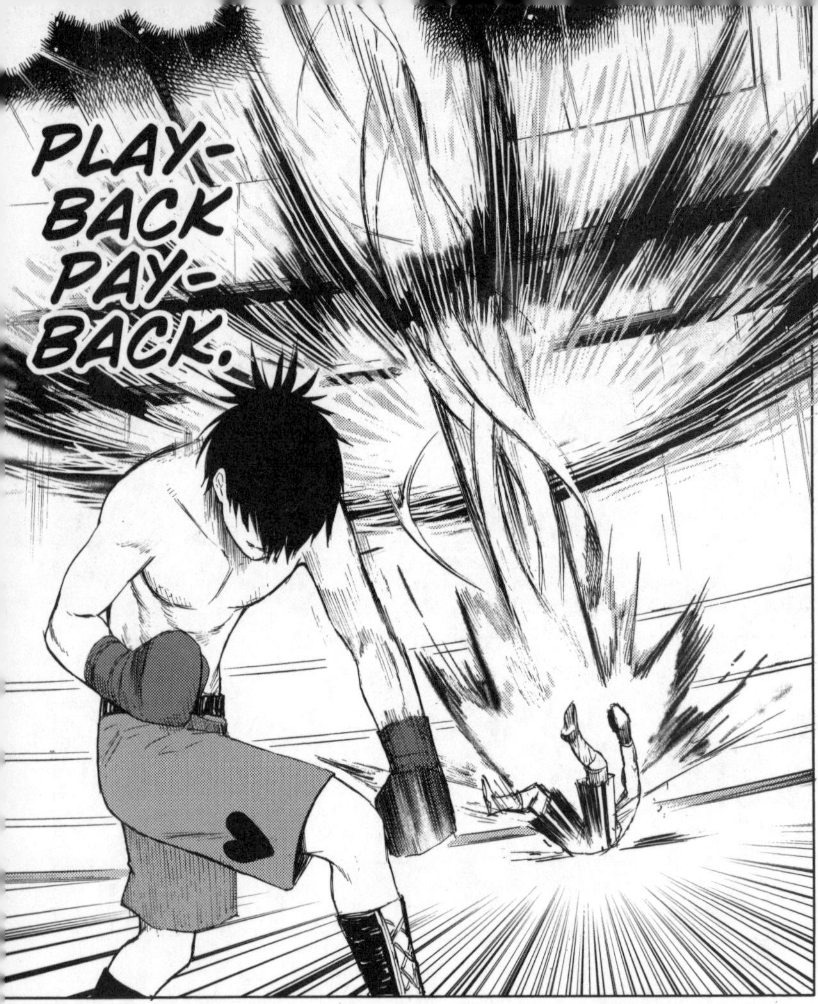
PLAY-BACK PAY-BACK.
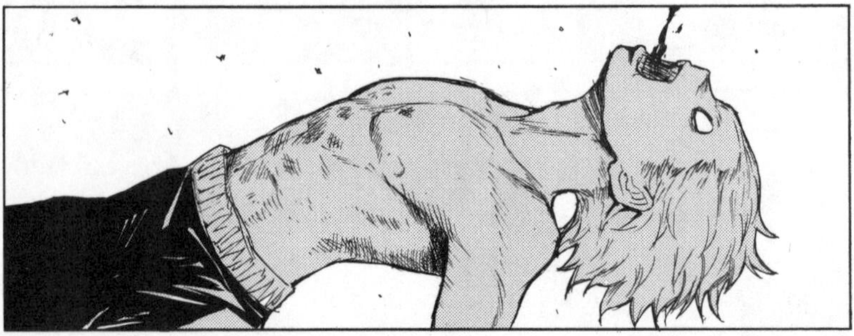

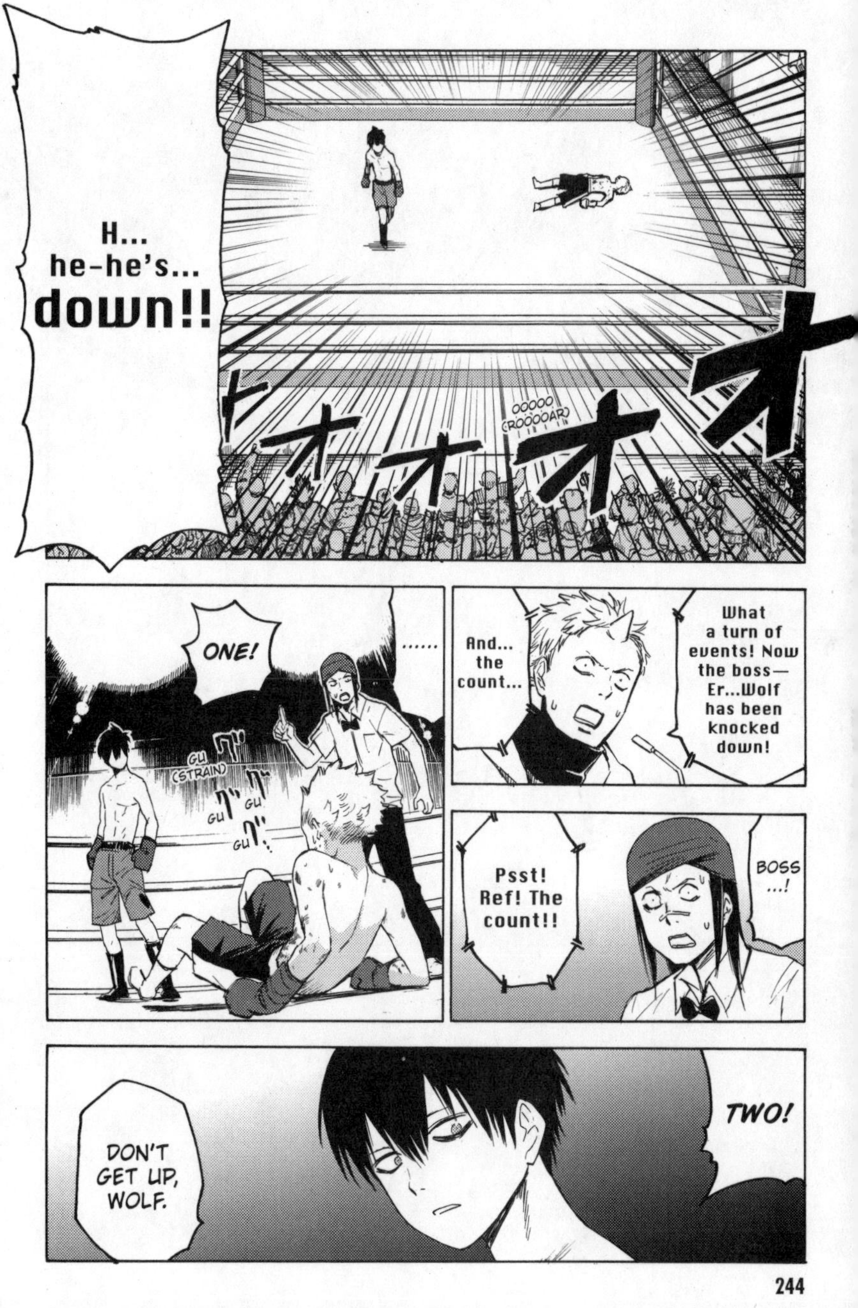
H... he-he's... down!!
OOOOO (ROOOOAR)
What a turn of events! Now the boss— Er...Wolf has been knocked down!
And... the count...
BOSS ...!
Psst! Ref! The count!!
......
ONE!
GU (STRAIN)
GU
GU
GU
TWO!
DON'T GET UP, WOLF.

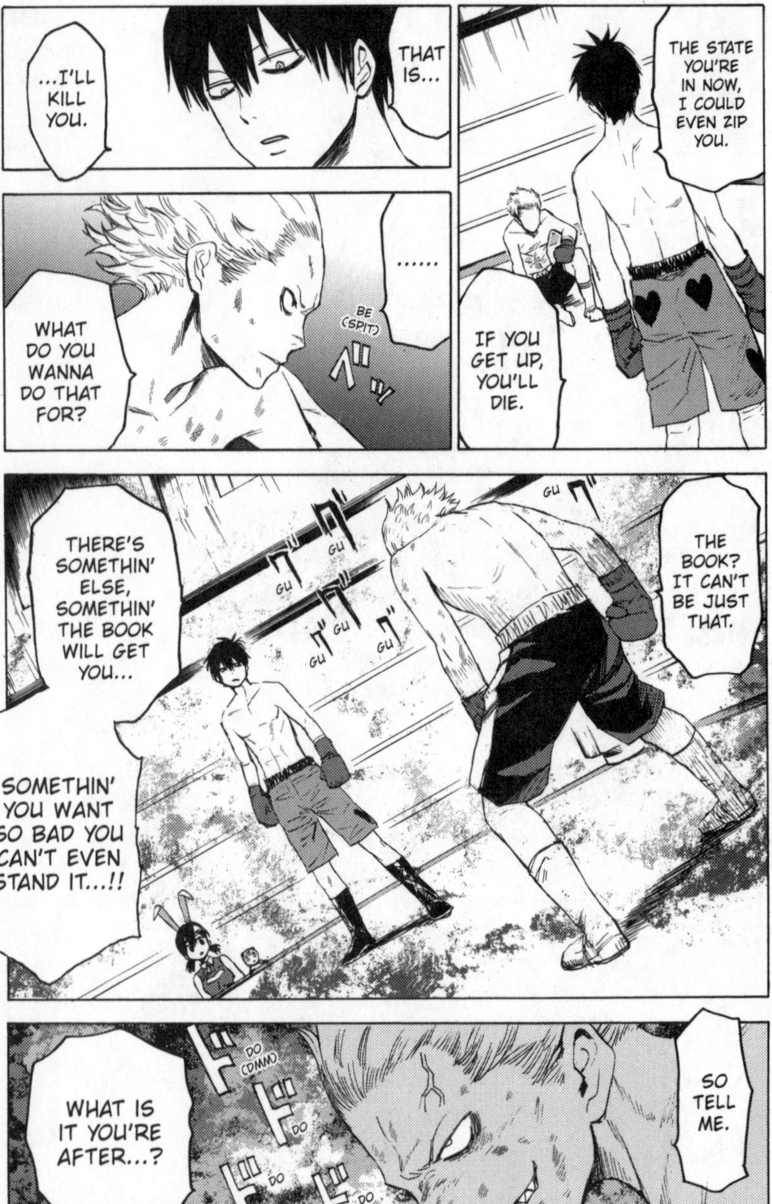
THE STATE YOU'RE IN NOW, I COULD EVEN ZIP YOU.
IF YOU GET UP, YOU'LL DIE.
THAT IS...
...I'LL KILL YOU.
......
BE (SPIT)
WHAT DO YOU WANNA DO THAT FOR?
GU
THE BOOK? IT CAN'T BE JUST THAT.
GU GU GU GU GU
THERE'S SOMETHIN' ELSE, SOMETHIN' THE BOOK WILL GET YOU...
SOMETHIN' YOU WANT SO BAD YOU CAN'T EVEN STAND IT...!!
SO TELL ME.
DO (DMM) DO DO DO
WHAT IS IT YOU'RE AFTER...?

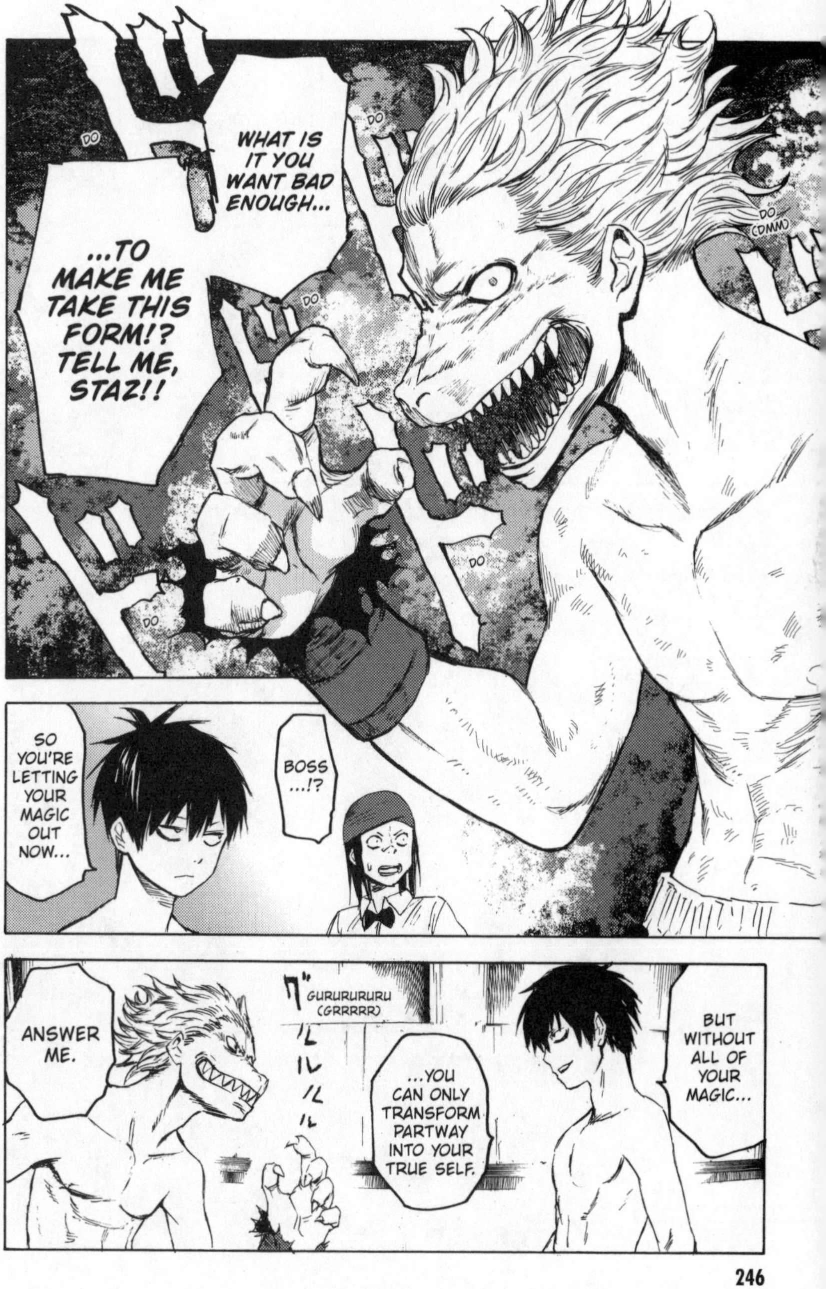
DO
(DMM)
WHAT IS IT YOU WANT BAD ENOUGH...
...TO MAKE ME TAKE THIS FORM!? TELL ME, STAZ!!
DO
DO
DO
DO
DO
BOSS ...!?
SO YOU'RE LETTING YOUR MAGIC OUT NOW...
BUT WITHOUT ALL OF YOUR MAGIC...
...YOU CAN ONLY TRANSFORM PARTWAY INTO YOUR TRUE SELF.
GURURURURU
(GRRRRR)
ANSWER ME.

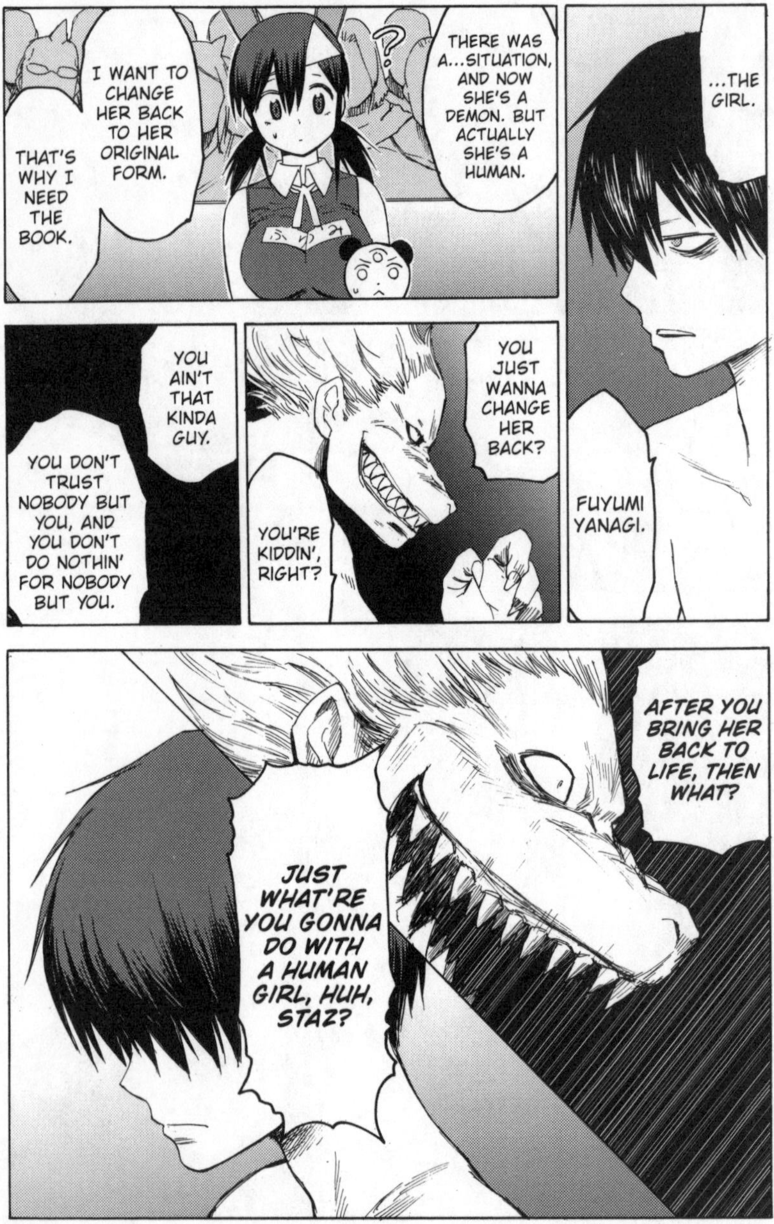
...THE GIRL.
FUYUMI YANAGI.
THERE WAS A...SITUATION, AND NOW SHE'S A DEMON. BUT ACTUALLY SHE'S A HUMAN.
I WANT TO CHANGE HER BACK TO HER ORIGINAL FORM.
THAT'S WHY I NEED THE BOOK.
YOU JUST WANNA CHANGE HER BACK?
YOU'RE KIDDIN', RIGHT?
YOU AIN'T THAT KINDA GUY.
YOU DON'T TRUST NOBODY BUT YOU, AND YOU DON'T DO NOTHIN' FOR NOBODY BUT YOU.
AFTER YOU BRING HER BACK TO LIFE, THEN WHAT?
JUST WHAT'RE YOU GONNA DO WITH A HUMAN GIRL, HUH, STAZ?

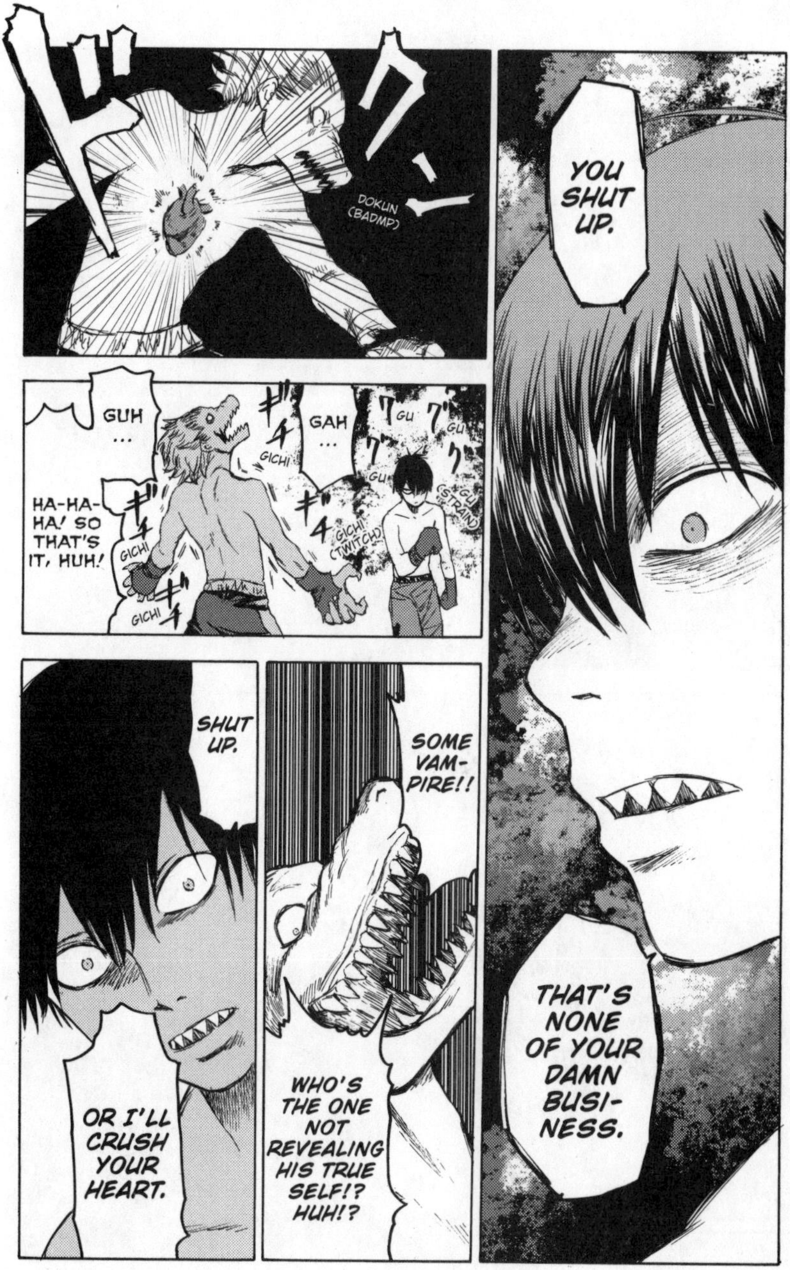

YOU SHUT UP.
THAT'S NONE OF YOUR DAMN BUSINESS.
DOKUN (BADMP)
GAH ...
GU GU GU GU (STRAIN)
GICHI GICHI (TWITCH)
GUH ...
HA-HA-HA! SO THAT'S IT, HUH!
GICHI GICHI
SOME VAMPIRE!!
WHO'S THE ONE NOT REVEALING HIS TRUE SELF!? HUH!?
SHUT UP.
OR I'LL CRUSH YOUR HEART.

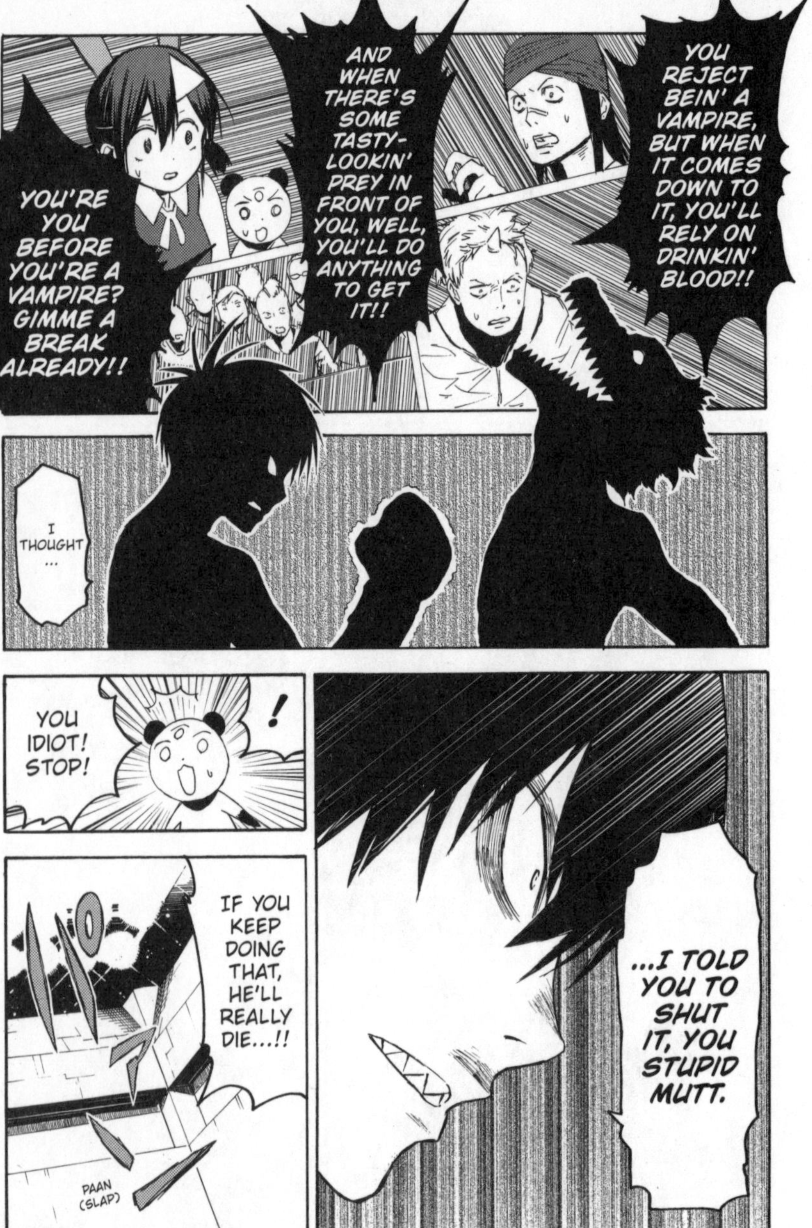
YOU REJECT BEIN' A VAMPIRE, BUT WHEN IT COMES DOWN TO IT, YOU'LL RELY ON DRINKIN' BLOOD!!
AND WHEN THERE'S SOME TASTY-LOOKIN' PREY IN FRONT OF YOU, WELL, YOU'LL DO ANYTHING TO GET IT!!
YOU'RE YOU BEFORE YOU'RE A VAMPIRE? GIMME A BREAK ALREADY!!
I THOUGHT ...
...I TOLD YOU TO SHUT IT, YOU STUPID MUTT.
!
YOU IDIOT! STOP!
IF YOU KEEP DOING THAT, HE'LL REALLY DIE...!!
PAAN (SLAP)

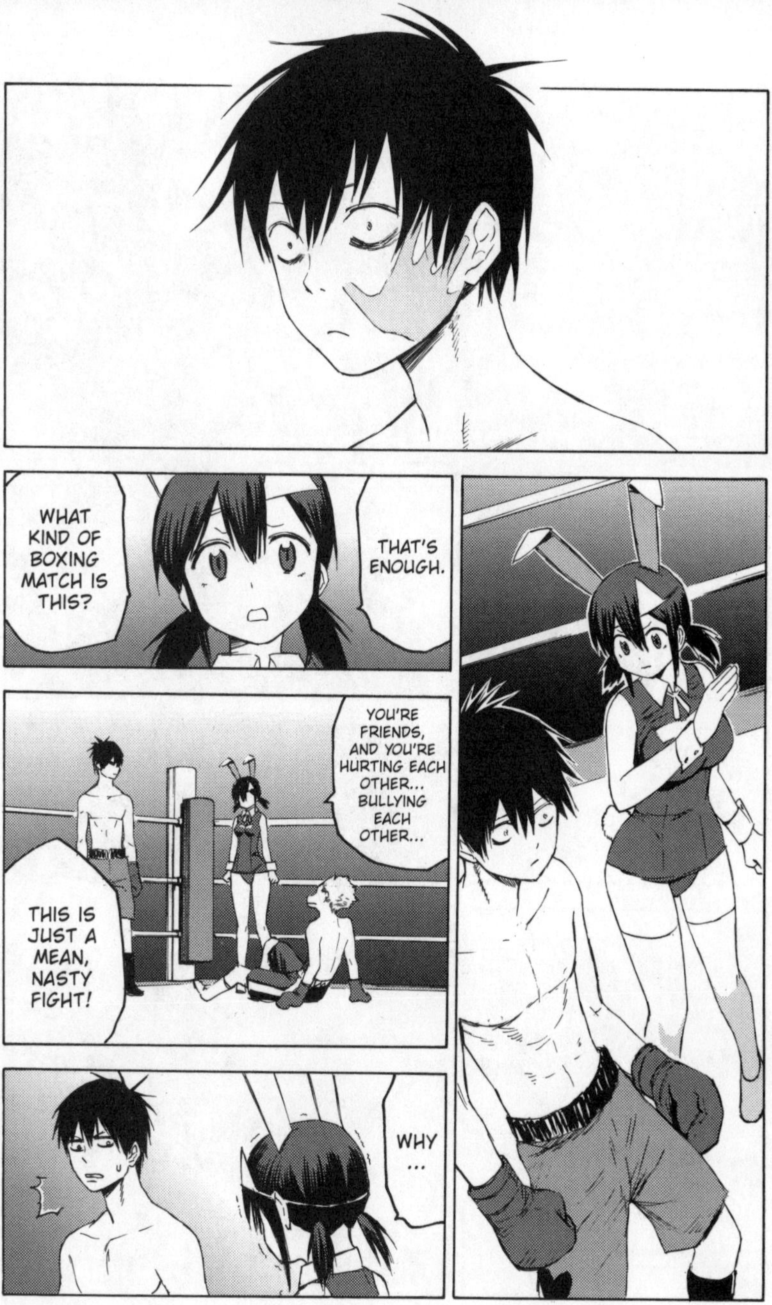
THAT'S ENOUGH.
WHAT KIND OF BOXING MATCH IS THIS?
YOU'RE FRIENDS, AND YOU'RE HURTING EACH OTHER... BULLYING EACH OTHER...
THIS IS JUST A MEAN, NASTY FIGHT!
WHY ...

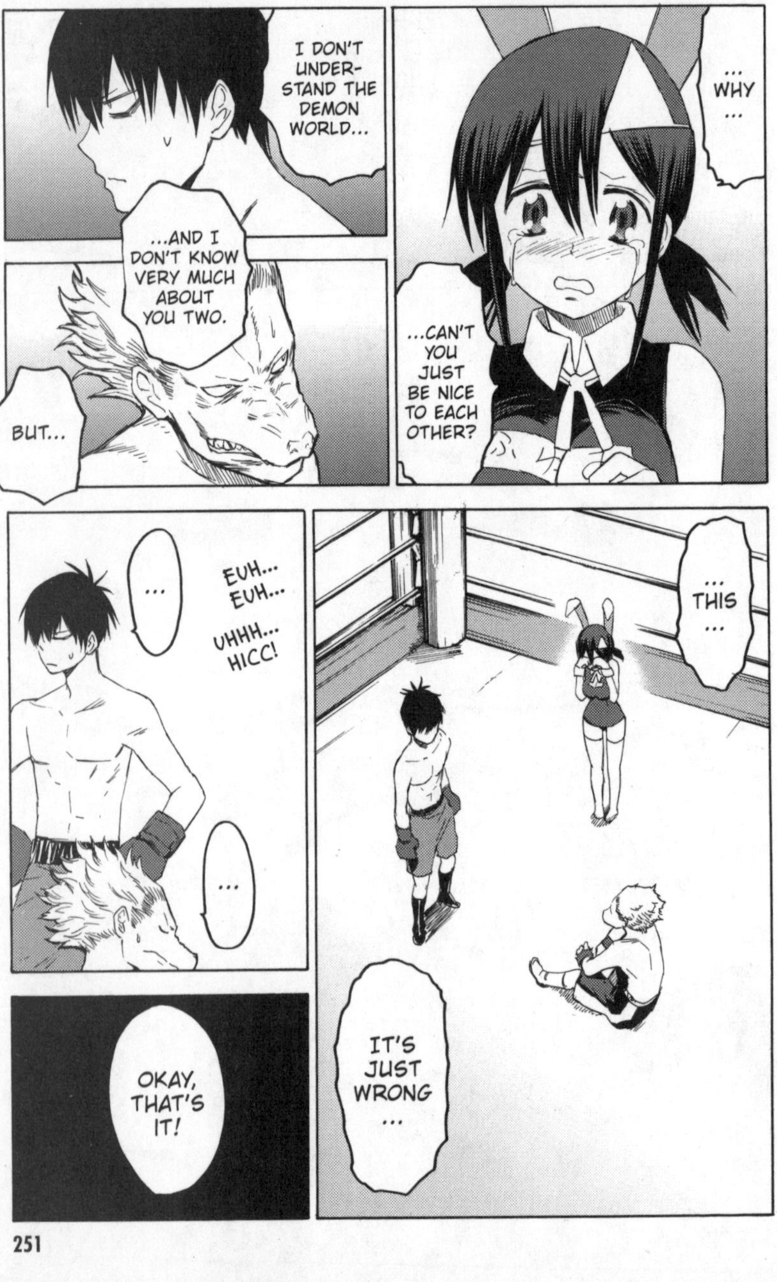
...WHY...
...CAN'T YOU JUST BE NICE TO EACH OTHER?
I DON'T UNDER-STAND THE DEMON WORLD...
...AND I DON'T KNOW VERY MUCH ABOUT YOU TWO.
BUT...
...THIS...
IT'S JUST WRONG...
...
EUH... EUH...
UHHH... HICC!
...
OKAY, THAT'S IT!

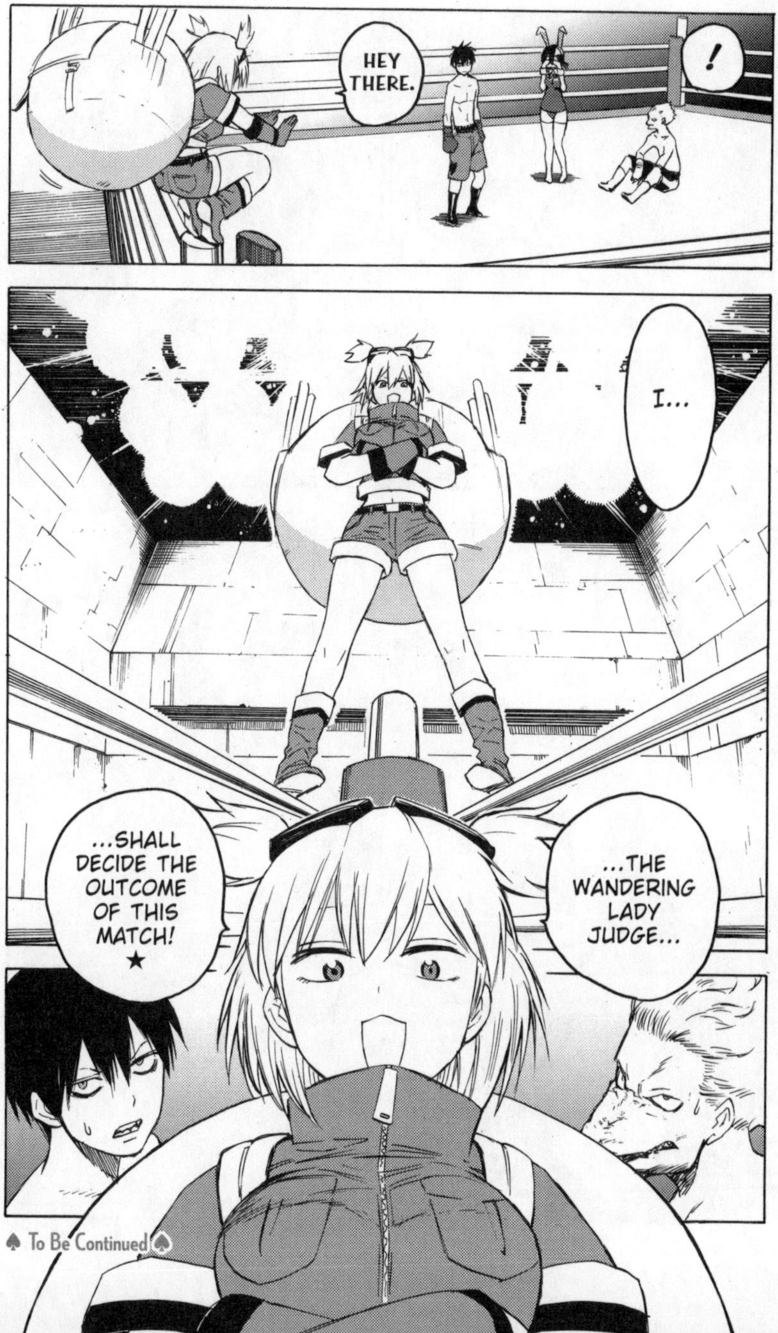
!
HEY THERE.
I...
...THE WANDERING LADY JUDGE...
...SHALL DECIDE THE OUTCOME OF THIS MATCH! ★
To Be Continued

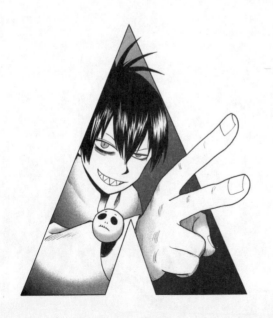

BLOOD LAD

# CHAPTER 8 ♠ THE ACROPOLIS

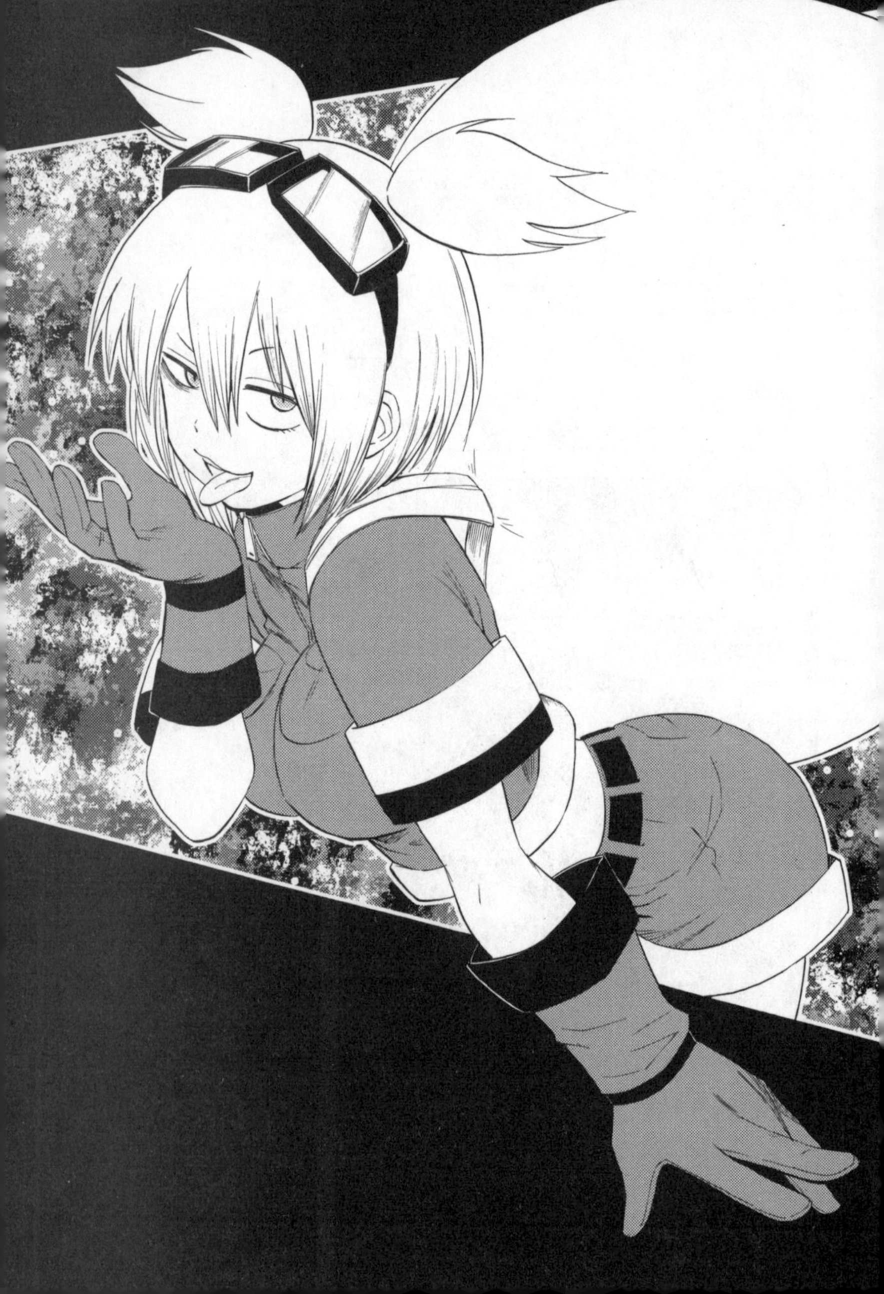

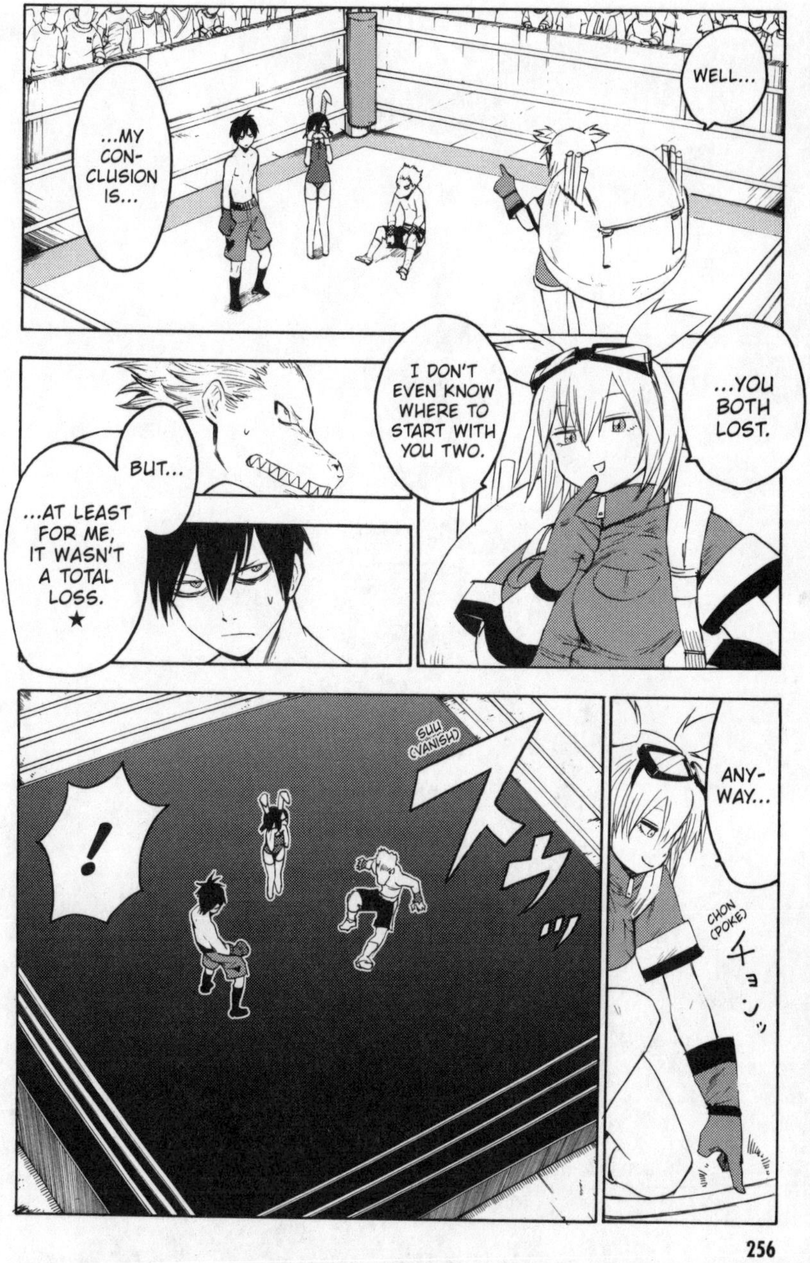
WELL...
...MY CON-CLUSION IS...
...YOU BOTH LOST.
I DON'T EVEN KNOW WHERE TO START WITH YOU TWO.
BUT...
...AT LEAST FOR ME, IT WASN'T A TOTAL LOSS. ★
ANY-WAY...
CHON (POKE)
チョンッ
SUU (VANISH)
スゥッ
!

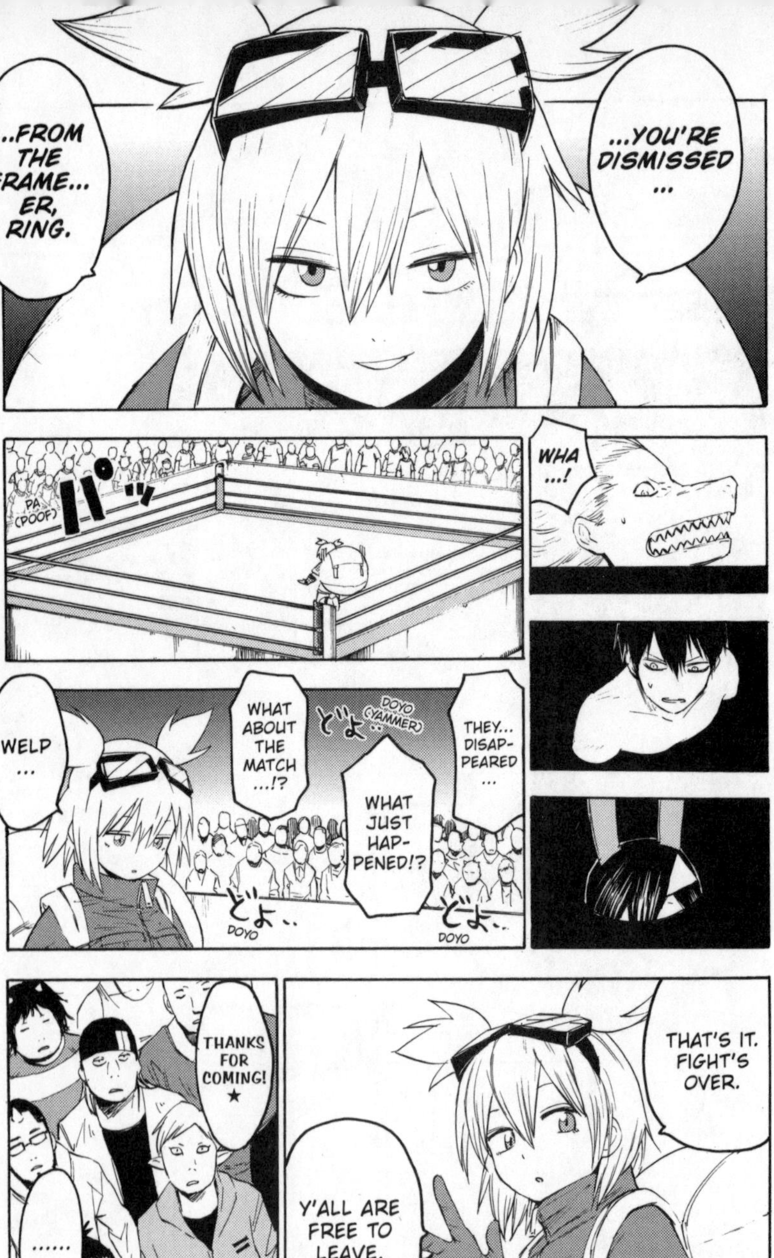
...YOU'RE DISMISSED ...
...FROM THE FRAME... ER, RING.
WHA ...!
パッ
PA (POOF)
THEY... DISAP-PEARED ...
WHAT JUST HAP-PENED!?
どよ
DOYO (YAMMER)
WHAT ABOUT THE MATCH ...!?
WELP ...
どよ
DOYO
どよ
DOYO
THAT'S IT. FIGHT'S OVER.
Y'ALL ARE FREE TO LEAVE.
THANKS FOR COMING! ★
......

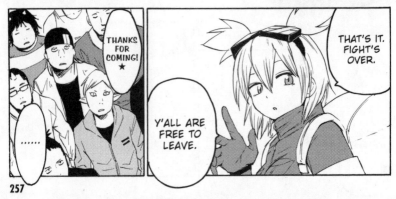

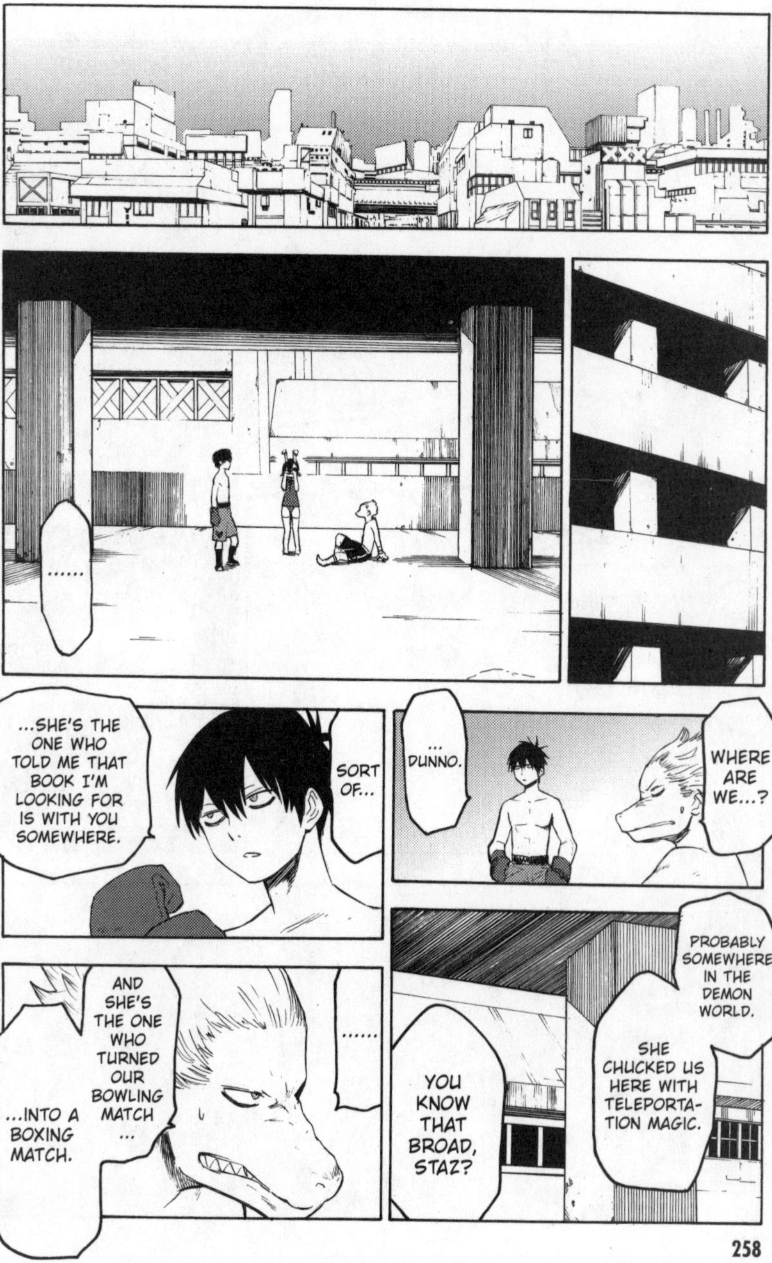
......
WHERE ARE WE...?
... DUNNO.
PROBABLY SOMEWHERE IN THE DEMON WORLD.
SHE CHUCKED US HERE WITH TELEPORTATION MAGIC.
YOU KNOW THAT BROAD, STAZ?
SORT OF...
...SHE'S THE ONE WHO TOLD ME THAT BOOK I'M LOOKING FOR IS WITH YOU SOMEWHERE.
......
AND SHE'S THE ONE WHO TURNED OUR BOWLING MATCH ...
...INTO A BOXING MATCH.

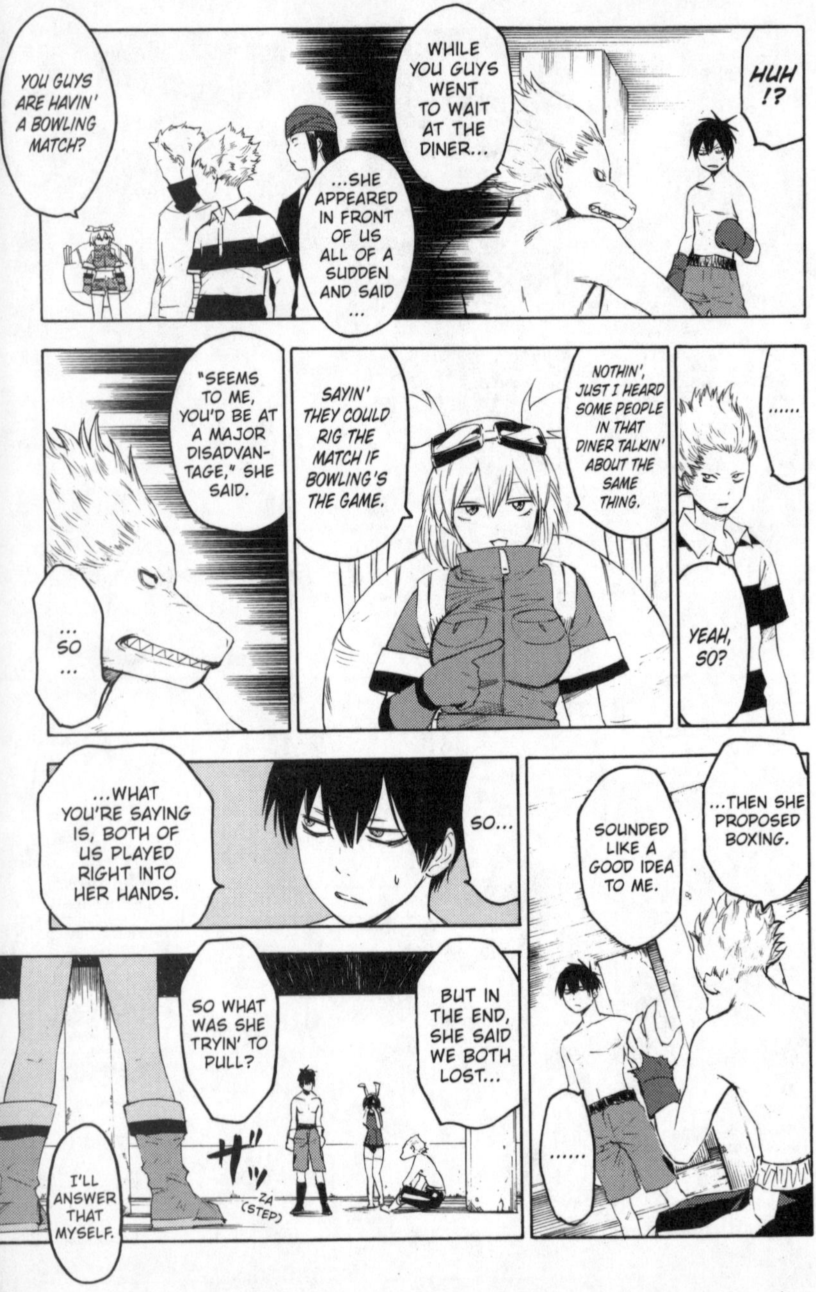
HUH !?
WHILE YOU GUYS WENT TO WAIT AT THE DINER...
...SHE APPEARED IN FRONT OF US ALL OF A SUDDEN AND SAID ...
YOU GUYS ARE HAVIN' A BOWLING MATCH?
......
YEAH, SO?
NOTHIN', JUST I HEARD SOME PEOPLE IN THAT DINER TALKIN' ABOUT THE SAME THING.
SAYIN' THEY COULD RIG THE MATCH IF BOWLING'S THE GAME.
"SEEMS TO ME, YOU'D BE AT A MAJOR DISADVANTAGE," SHE SAID.
... SO ...
...THEN SHE PROPOSED BOXING.
SOUNDED LIKE A GOOD IDEA TO ME.
......
SO...
...WHAT YOU'RE SAYING IS, BOTH OF US PLAYED RIGHT INTO HER HANDS.
BUT IN THE END, SHE SAID WE BOTH LOST...
SO WHAT WAS SHE TRYIN' TO PULL?
ザッ
ZA (STEP)
I'LL ANSWER THAT MYSELF.

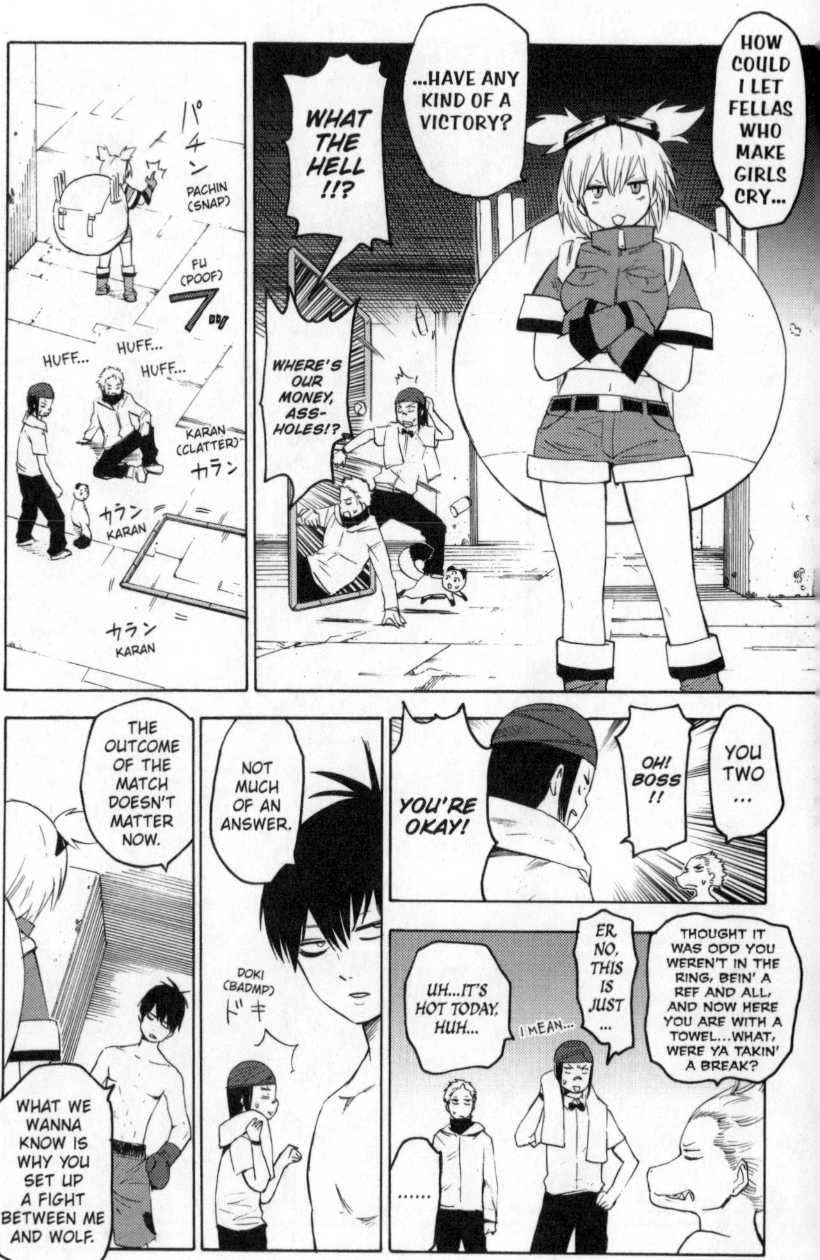
HOW COULD I LET FELLAS WHO MAKE GIRLS CRY...
...HAVE ANY KIND OF A VICTORY?
WHAT THE HELL!!?
WHERE'S OUR MONEY, ASS-HOLES!?
パチン
PACHIN (SNAP)
FU (POOF)
フッ
HUFF...
HUFF...
HUFF...
KARAN (CLATTER)
カラン
カラン
KARAN
カラン
KARAN
YOU TWO...
OH! BOSS!!
YOU'RE OKAY!
THOUGHT IT WAS ODD YOU WEREN'T IN THE RING, BEIN' A REF AND ALL, AND NOW HERE YOU ARE WITH A TOWEL...WHAT, WERE YA TAKIN' A BREAK?
ER, NO, THIS IS JUST...
I MEAN...
UH...IT'S HOT TODAY, HUH...
......
NOT MUCH OF AN ANSWER.
DOKI (BADMP)
ドキ
THE OUTCOME OF THE MATCH DOESN'T MATTER NOW.
WHAT WE WANNA KNOW IS WHY YOU SET UP A FIGHT BETWEEN ME AND WOLF.

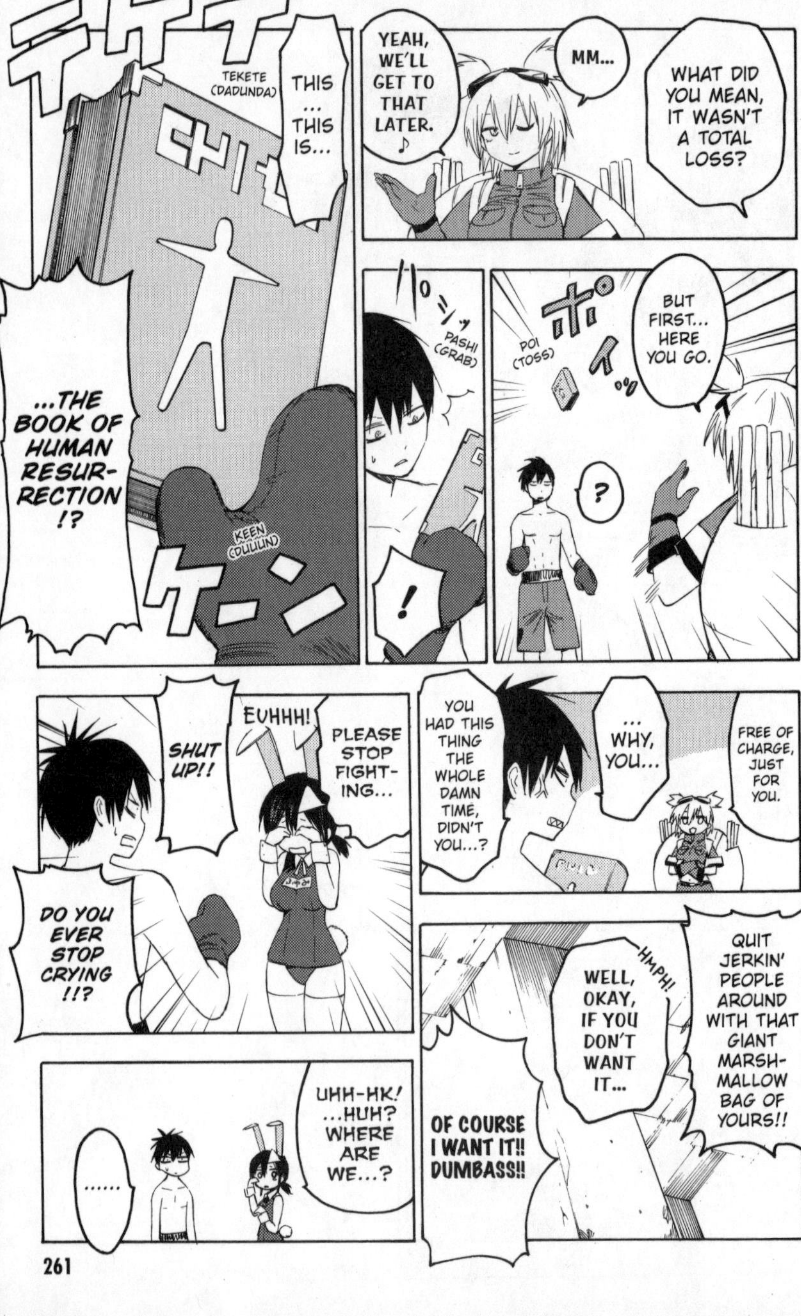
WHAT DID YOU MEAN, IT WASN'T A TOTAL LOSS?
MM...
YEAH, WE'LL GET TO THAT LATER. ♪
BUT FIRST... HERE YOU GO.
POI (TOSS)
?
PASHI (GRAB)
!
THIS ... THIS IS...
TEKETE (DADUNDA)
...THE BOOK OF HUMAN RESUR-RECTION !?
KEEN (DUUUN)
FREE OF CHARGE, JUST FOR YOU.
... WHY, YOU...
YOU HAD THIS THING THE WHOLE DAMN TIME, DIDN'T YOU...?
PLEASE STOP FIGHT-ING...
EVHHH!
SHUT UP!!
DO YOU EVER STOP CRYING !!?
QUIT JERKIN' PEOPLE AROUND WITH THAT GIANT MARSH-MALLOW BAG OF YOURS!!
HMPH!
WELL, OKAY, IF YOU DON'T WANT IT...
OF COURSE I WANT IT!! DUMBASS!!
UHH-HK! ...HUH? WHERE ARE WE...?
......

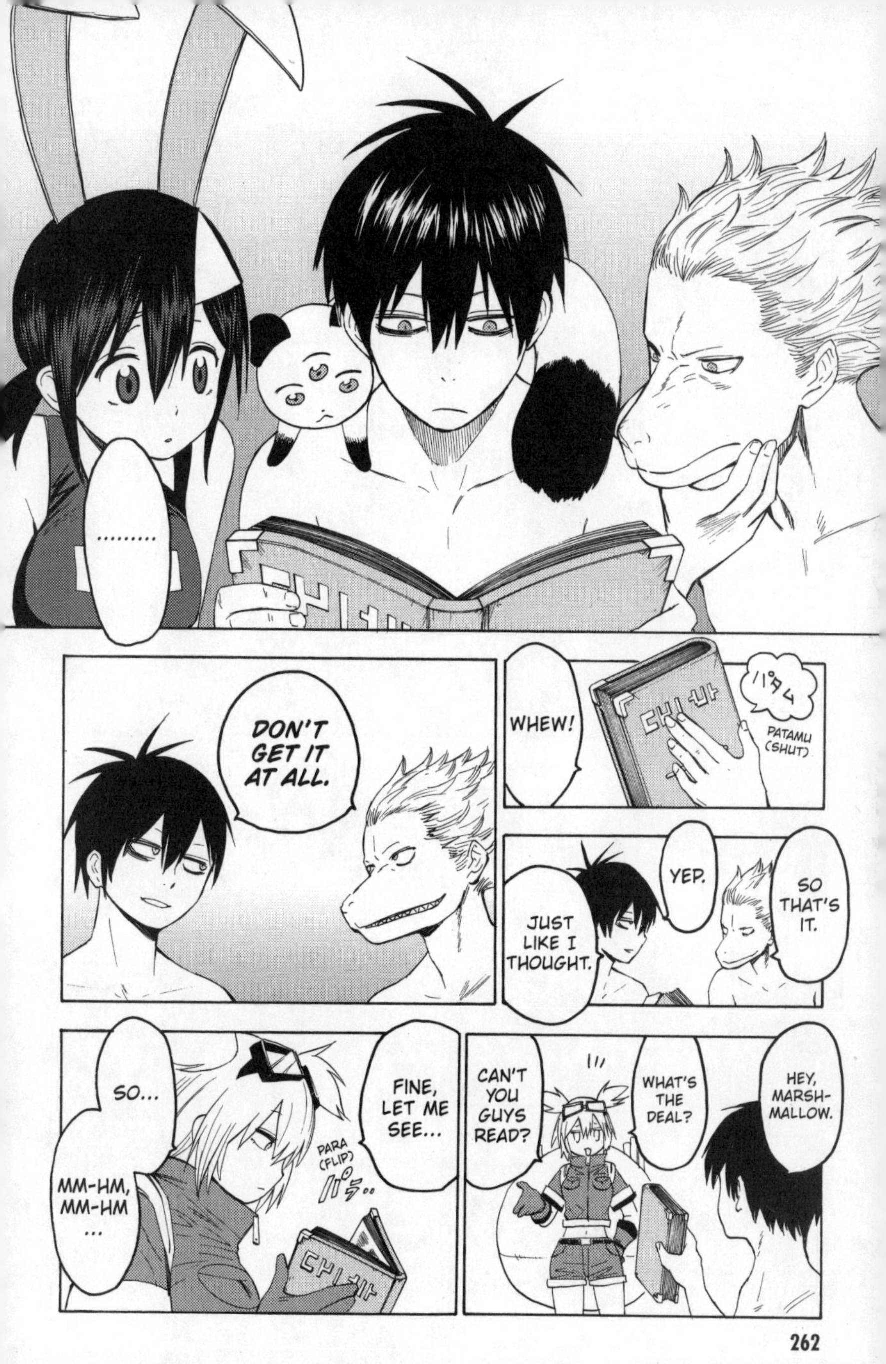
.........
パタム
PATAMU (SHUT)
WHEW!
SO THAT'S IT.
YEP.
JUST LIKE I THOUGHT.
DON'T GET IT AT ALL.
HEY, MARSHMALLOW.
WHAT'S THE DEAL?
CAN'T YOU GUYS READ?
FINE, LET ME SEE...
PARA (FLIP)
パラ..
SO...
MM-HM, MM-HM ...

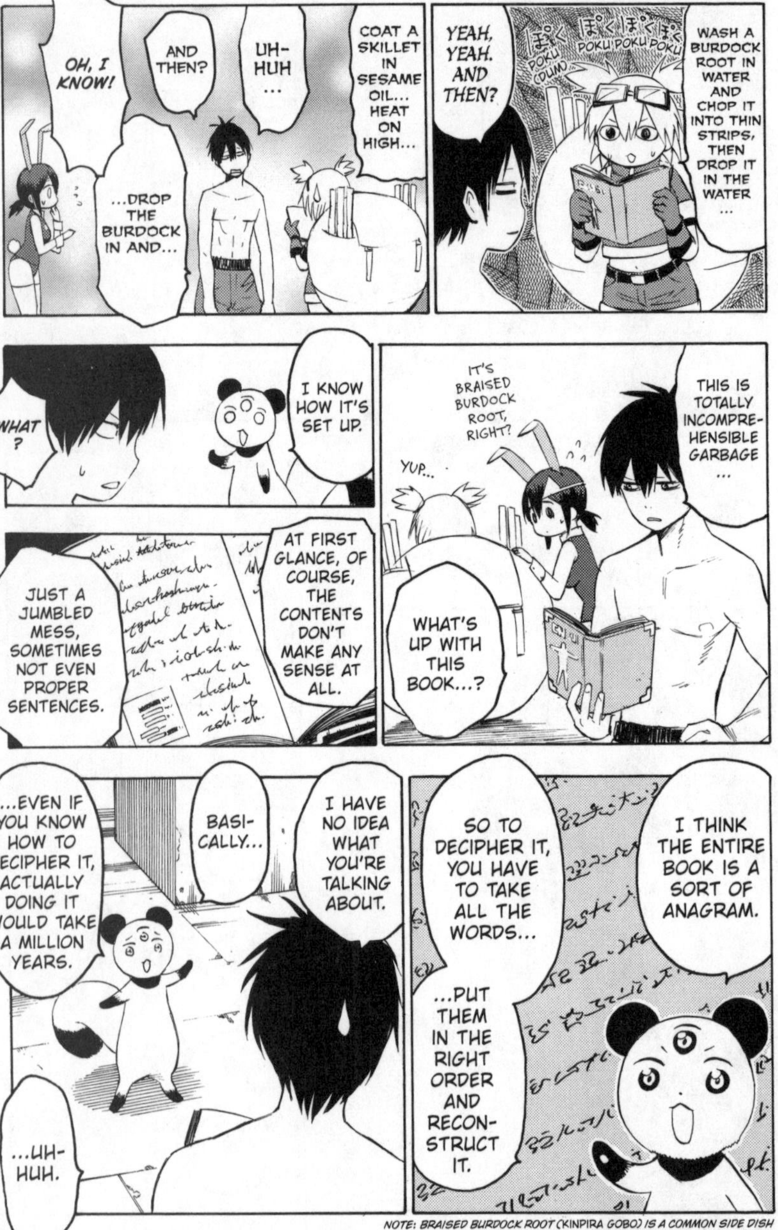
WASH A BURDOCK ROOT IN WATER AND CHOP IT INTO THIN STRIPS, THEN DROP IT IN THE WATER...
ぽく ぽくぽくぽく
POKU POKU POKU POKU (DUM)
YEAH, YEAH. AND THEN?
COAT A SKILLET IN SESAME OIL... HEAT ON HIGH...
UH-HUH...
AND THEN?
OH, I KNOW!
...DROP THE BURDOCK IN AND...
THIS IS TOTALLY INCOMPREHENSIBLE GARBAGE...
IT'S BRAISED BURDOCK ROOT, RIGHT?
YUP...
WHAT'S UP WITH THIS BOOK...?
I KNOW HOW IT'S SET UP.
WHAT?
AT FIRST GLANCE, OF COURSE, THE CONTENTS DON'T MAKE ANY SENSE AT ALL.
JUST A JUMBLED MESS, SOMETIMES NOT EVEN PROPER SENTENCES.
I THINK THE ENTIRE BOOK IS A SORT OF ANAGRAM.
SO TO DECIPHER IT, YOU HAVE TO TAKE ALL THE WORDS...
...PUT THEM IN THE RIGHT ORDER AND RECONSTRUCT IT.
I HAVE NO IDEA WHAT YOU'RE TALKING ABOUT.
BASICALLY...
...EVEN IF YOU KNOW HOW TO DECIPHER IT, ACTUALLY DOING IT WOULD TAKE A MILLION YEARS.
...UH-HUH.

NOTE: BRAISED BURDOCK ROOT (KINPIRA GOBO) IS A COMMON SIDE DISH MADE OF JULIENNED CARROTS AND BURDOCK ROOT THAT YOU MIGHT GET AS A STARTER IN A RESTAURANT OR AS A SIDE IN YOUR BENTO BOX.

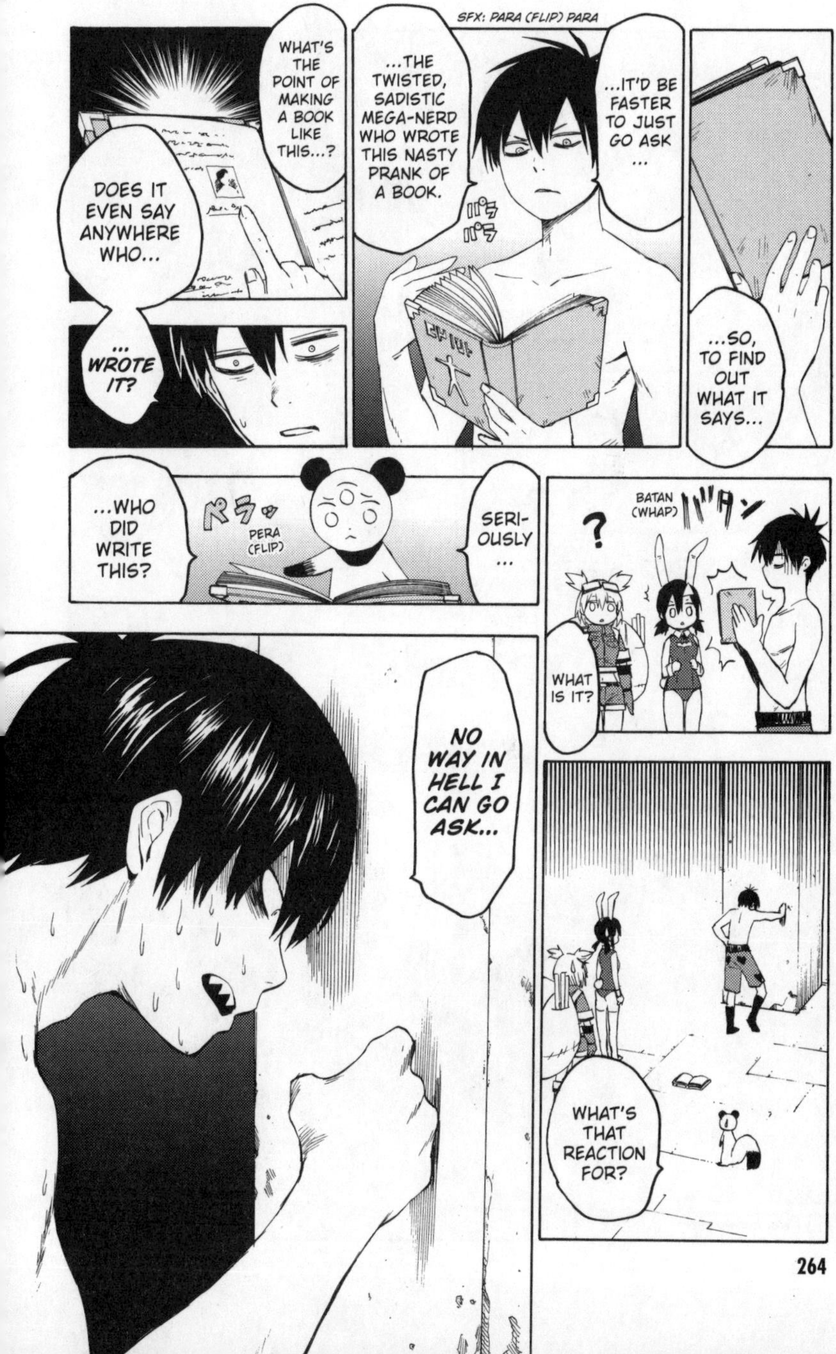
...SO, TO FIND OUT WHAT IT SAYS...
SFX: PARA (FLIP) PARA
...IT'D BE FASTER TO JUST GO ASK ...
...THE TWISTED, SADISTIC MEGA-NERD WHO WROTE THIS NASTY PRANK OF A BOOK.
WHAT'S THE POINT OF MAKING A BOOK LIKE THIS...?
DOES IT EVEN SAY ANYWHERE WHO...
... WROTE IT?
SERI-OUSLY ...
PERA (FLIP)
...WHO DID WRITE THIS?
BATAN (WHAP)
?
WHAT IS IT?
NO WAY IN HELL I CAN GO ASK...
WHAT'S THAT REACTION FOR?

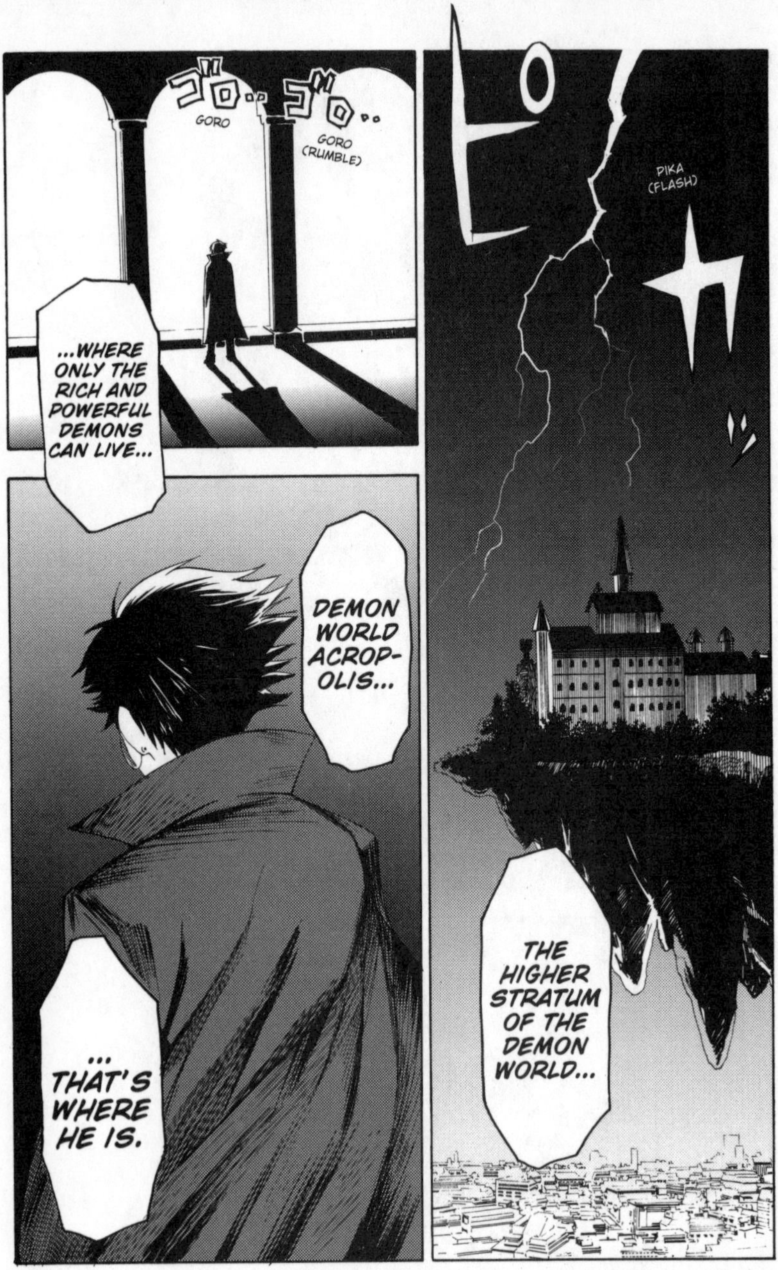
PIKA (FLASH)
THE HIGHER STRATUM OF THE DEMON WORLD...
GORO
GORO (RUMBLE)
...WHERE ONLY THE RICH AND POWERFUL DEMONS CAN LIVE...
DEMON WORLD ACROPOLIS...
...THAT'S WHERE HE IS.

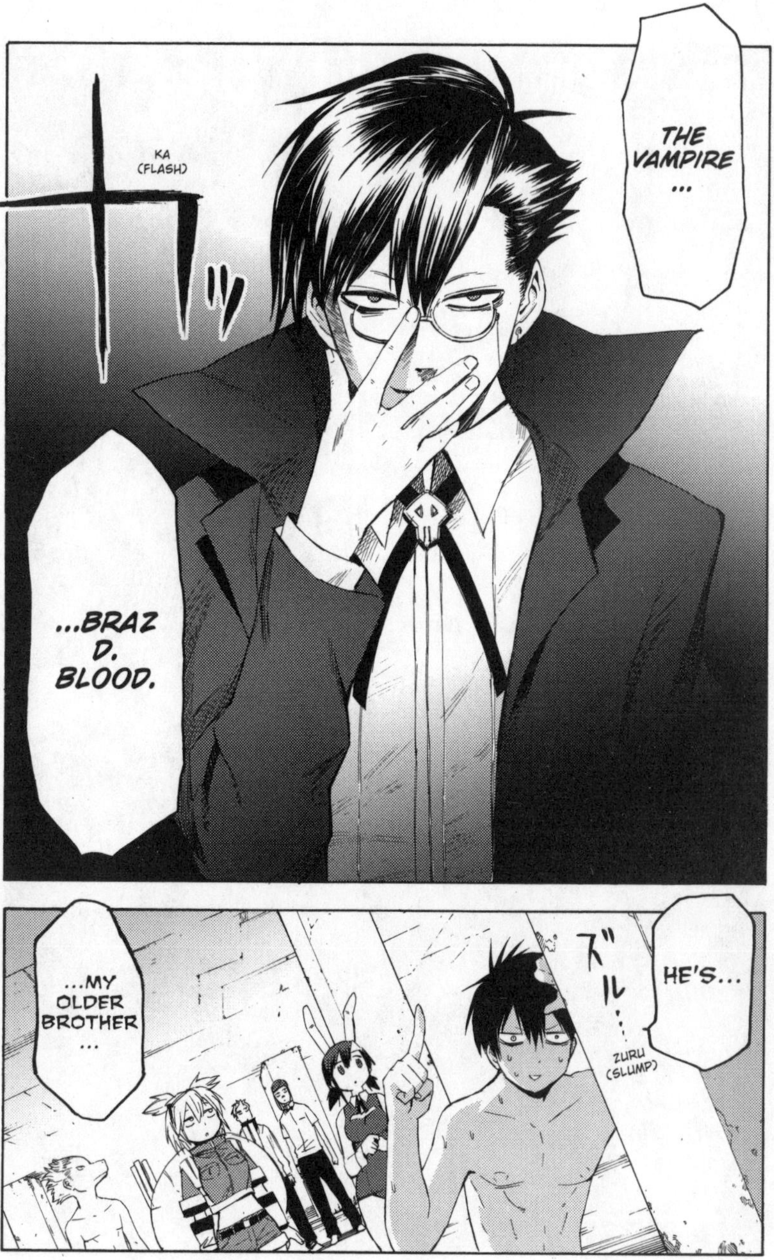
THE VAMPIRE ...
カッ
KA (FLASH)
...BRAZ D. BLOOD.
HE'S...
ズル…
ZURU (SLUMP)
...MY OLDER BROTHER ...

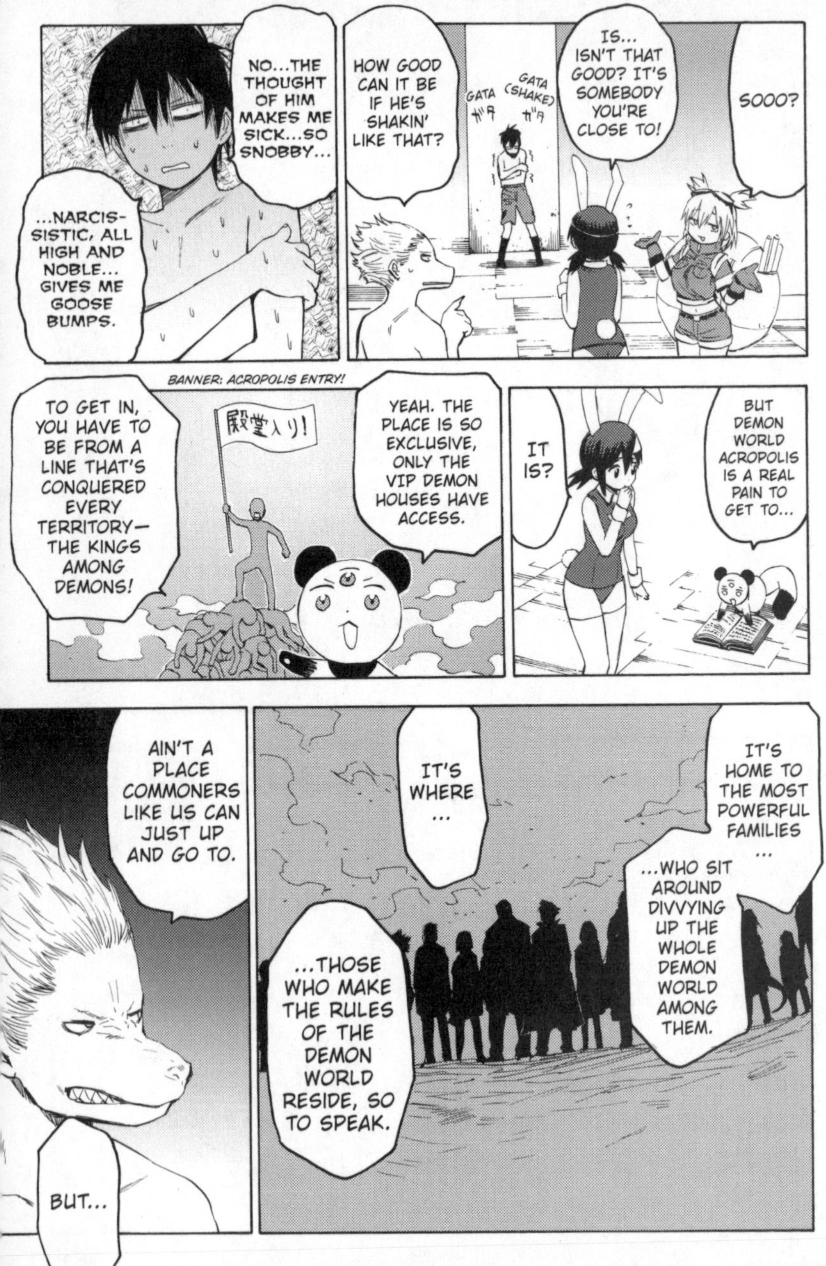
SOOO?
IS... ISN'T THAT GOOD? IT'S SOMEBODY YOU'RE CLOSE TO!
GATA (SHAKE) ガタ
GATA ガタ
HOW GOOD CAN IT BE IF HE'S SHAKIN' LIKE THAT?
NO...THE THOUGHT OF HIM MAKES ME SICK...SO SNOBBY...
...NARCIS-SISTIC, ALL HIGH AND NOBLE... GIVES ME GOOSE BUMPS.
BUT DEMON WORLD ACROPOLIS IS A REAL PAIN TO GET TO...
IT IS?
YEAH. THE PLACE IS SO EXCLUSIVE, ONLY THE VIP DEMON HOUSES HAVE ACCESS.
殿堂入り!
BANNER: ACROPOLIS ENTRY!
TO GET IN, YOU HAVE TO BE FROM A LINE THAT'S CONQUERED EVERY TERRITORY—THE KINGS AMONG DEMONS!
IT'S HOME TO THE MOST POWERFUL FAMILIES...
IT'S WHERE...
...WHO SIT AROUND DIVVYING UP THE WHOLE DEMON WORLD AMONG THEM.
...THOSE WHO MAKE THE RULES OF THE DEMON WORLD RESIDE, SO TO SPEAK.
AIN'T A PLACE COMMONERS LIKE US CAN JUST UP AND GO TO.
BUT...

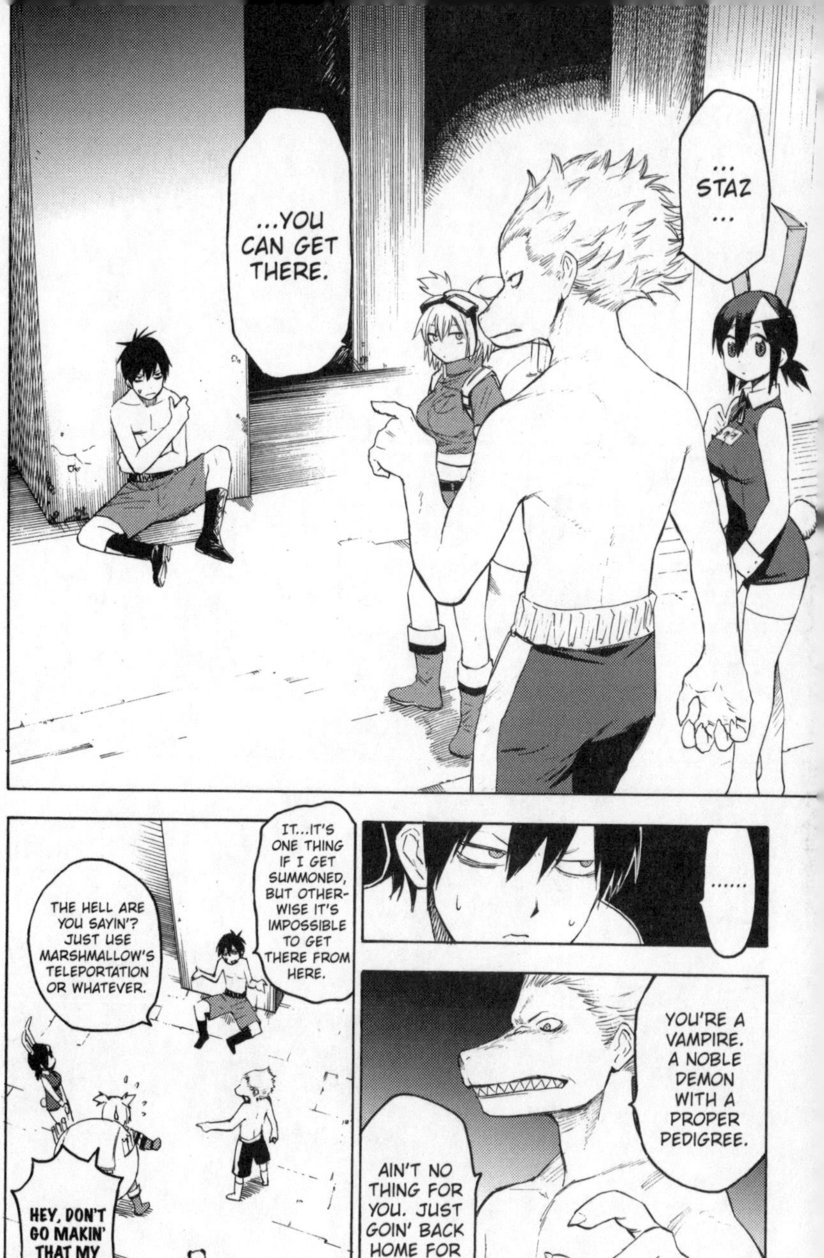
...STAZ...
...YOU CAN GET THERE.
......
YOU'RE A VAMPIRE. A NOBLE DEMON WITH A PROPER PEDIGREE.
AIN'T NO THING FOR YOU. JUST GOIN' BACK HOME FOR A VISIT.
IT...IT'S ONE THING IF I GET SUMMONED, BUT OTHER-WISE IT'S IMPOSSIBLE TO GET THERE FROM HERE.
THE HELL ARE YOU SAYIN'? JUST USE MARSHMALLOW'S TELEPORTATION OR WHATEVER.
HEY, DON'T GO MAKIN' THAT MY NICKNAME!

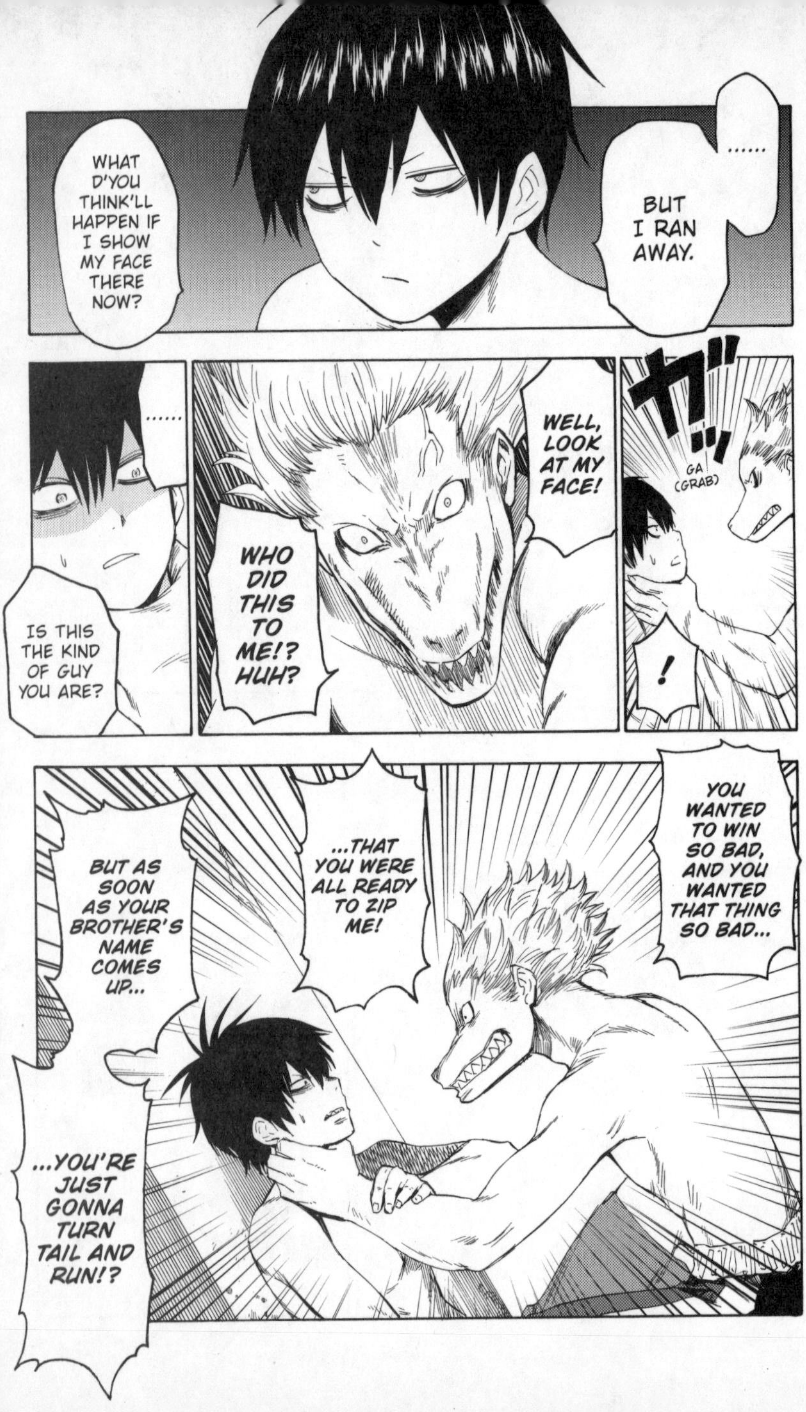
......
BUT I RAN AWAY.
WHAT D'YOU THINK'LL HAPPEN IF I SHOW MY FACE THERE NOW?
ガッ
GA (GRAB)
!
WELL, LOOK AT MY FACE!
WHO DID THIS TO ME!? HUH?
......
IS THIS THE KIND OF GUY YOU ARE?
YOU WANTED TO WIN SO BAD, AND YOU WANTED THAT THING SO BAD...
...THAT YOU WERE ALL READY TO ZIP ME!
BUT AS SOON AS YOUR BROTHER'S NAME COMES UP...
...YOU'RE JUST GONNA TURN TAIL AND RUN!?

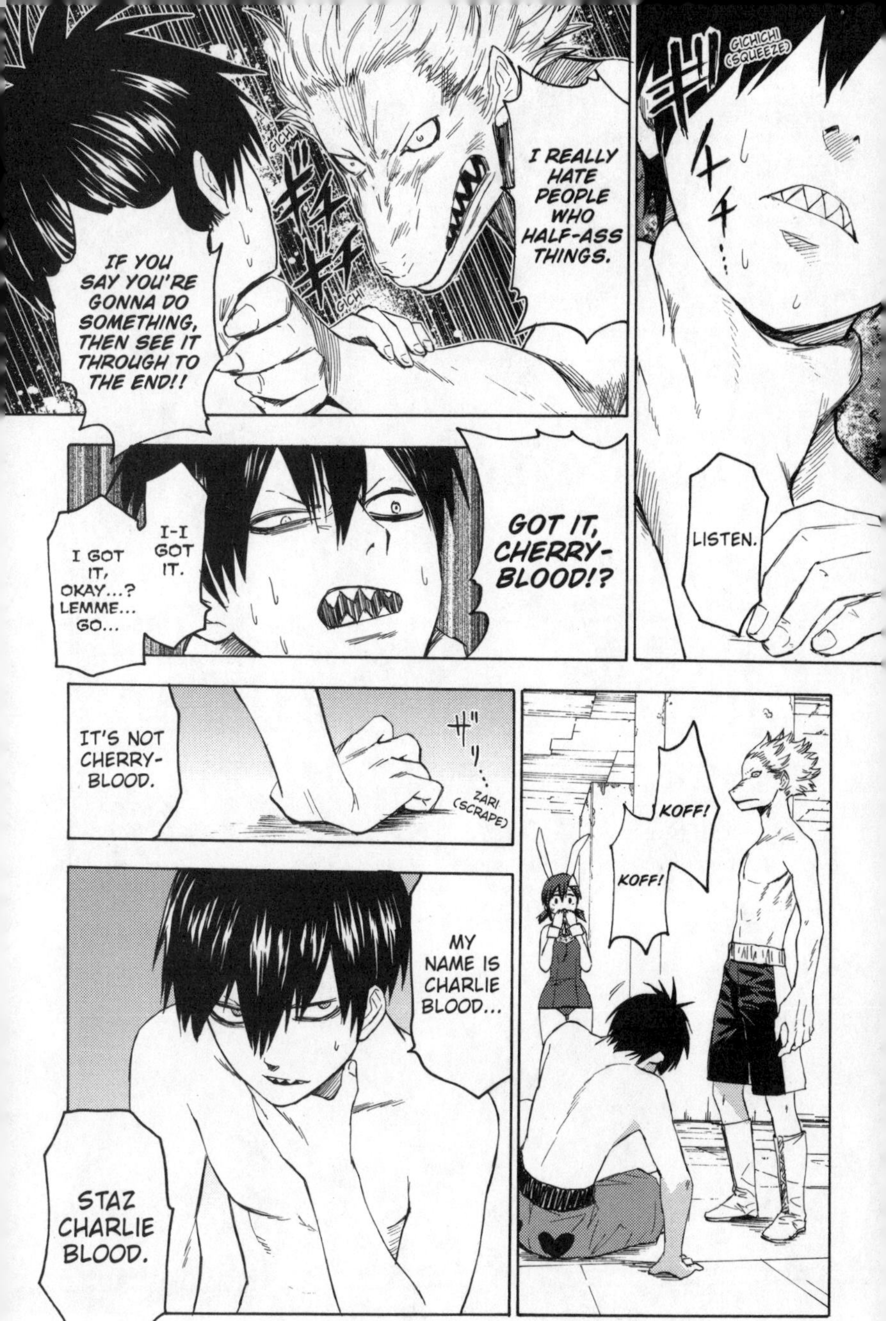

GICHICHI (SQUEEZE)
LISTEN.
I REALLY HATE PEOPLE WHO HALF-ASS THINGS.
GICHI
GICHI
IF YOU SAY YOU'RE GONNA DO SOMETHING, THEN SEE IT THROUGH TO THE END!!
GOT IT, CHERRY-BLOOD!?
I-I GOT IT.
I GOT IT, OKAY...? LEMME... GO...
KOFF!
KOFF!
IT'S NOT CHERRY-BLOOD.
ZARI (SCRAPE)
MY NAME IS CHARLIE BLOOD...
STAZ CHARLIE BLOOD.

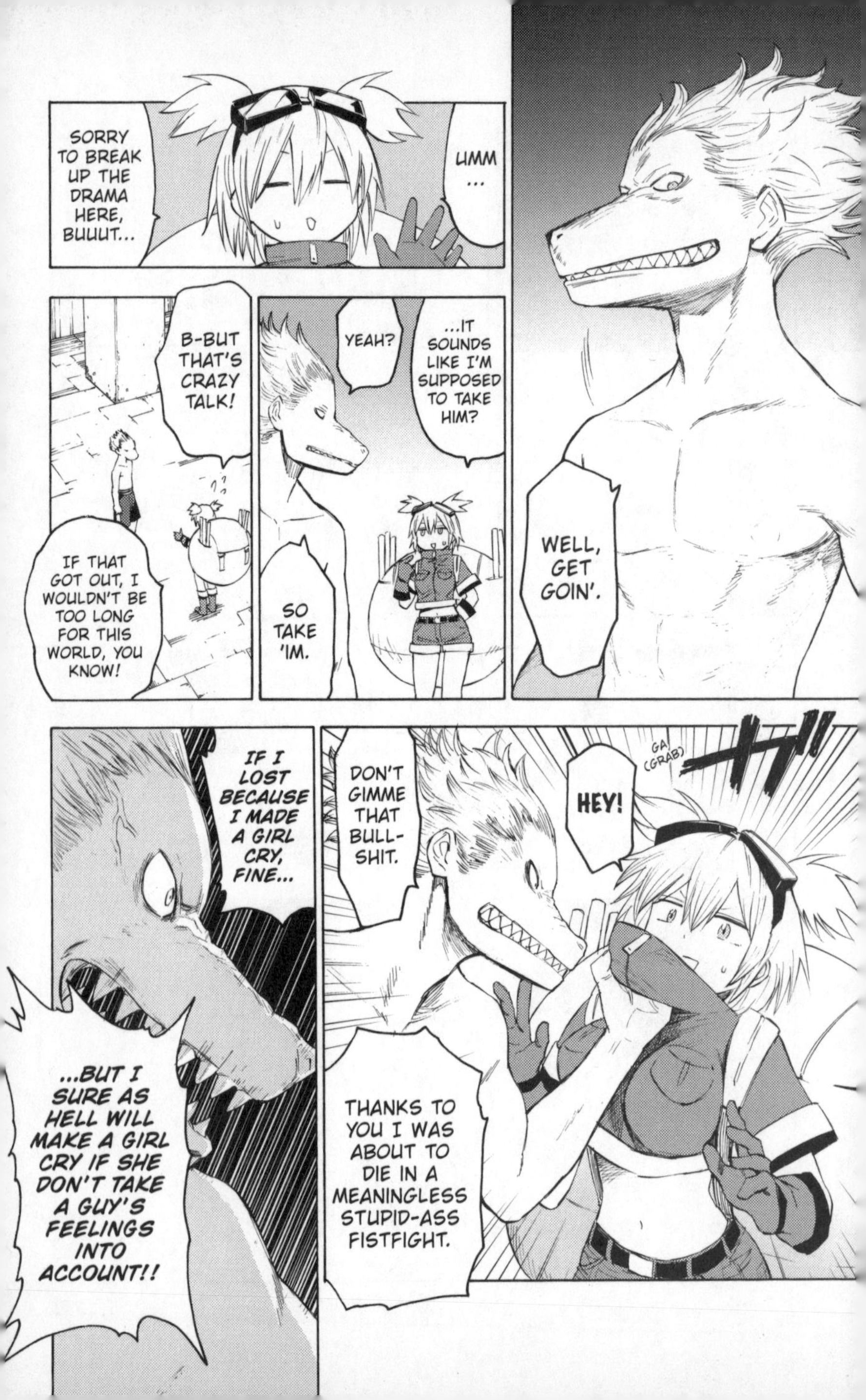
WELL, GET GOIN'.
UMM ...
SORRY TO BREAK UP THE DRAMA HERE, BUUUT...
...IT SOUNDS LIKE I'M SUPPOSED TO TAKE HIM?
YEAH?
SO TAKE 'IM.
B-BUT THAT'S CRAZY TALK!
IF THAT GOT OUT, I WOULDN'T BE TOO LONG FOR THIS WORLD, YOU KNOW!
GA (GRAB)
HEY!
DON'T GIMME THAT BULL-SHIT.
THANKS TO YOU I WAS ABOUT TO DIE IN A MEANINGLESS STUPID-ASS FISTFIGHT.
IF I LOST BECAUSE I MADE A GIRL CRY, FINE...
...BUT I SURE AS HELL WILL MAKE A GIRL CRY IF SHE DON'T TAKE A GUY'S FEELINGS INTO ACCOUNT!!

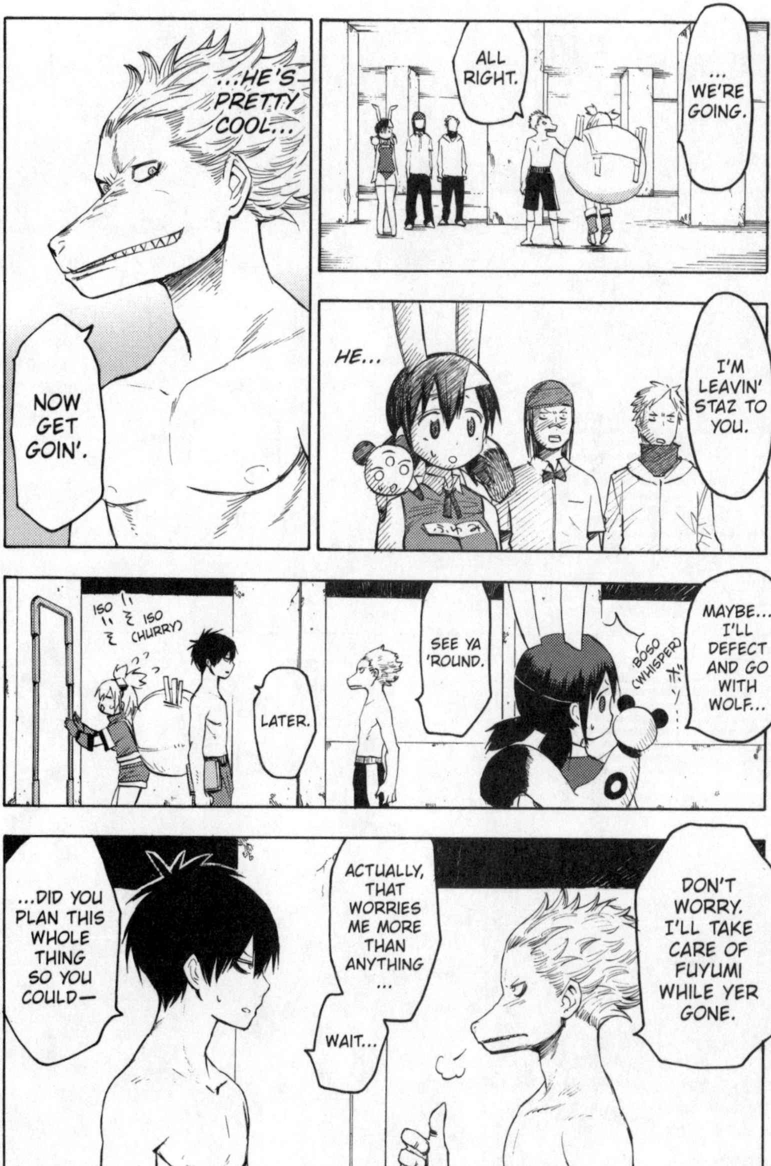
... WE'RE GOING.
ALL RIGHT.
I'M LEAVIN' STAZ TO YOU.
HE...
...HE'S PRETTY COOL...
NOW GET GOIN'.
MAYBE... I'LL DEFECT AND GO WITH WOLF...
BOSO (WHISPER)
SEE YA 'ROUND.
LATER.
ISO ISO (HURRY)
DON'T WORRY. I'LL TAKE CARE OF FUYUMI WHILE YER GONE.
ACTUALLY, THAT WORRIES ME MORE THAN ANYTHING ...
WAIT...
...DID YOU PLAN THIS WHOLE THING SO YOU COULD—

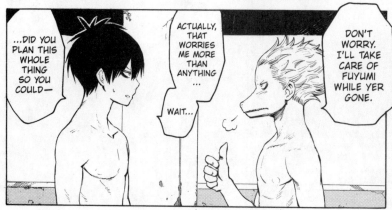

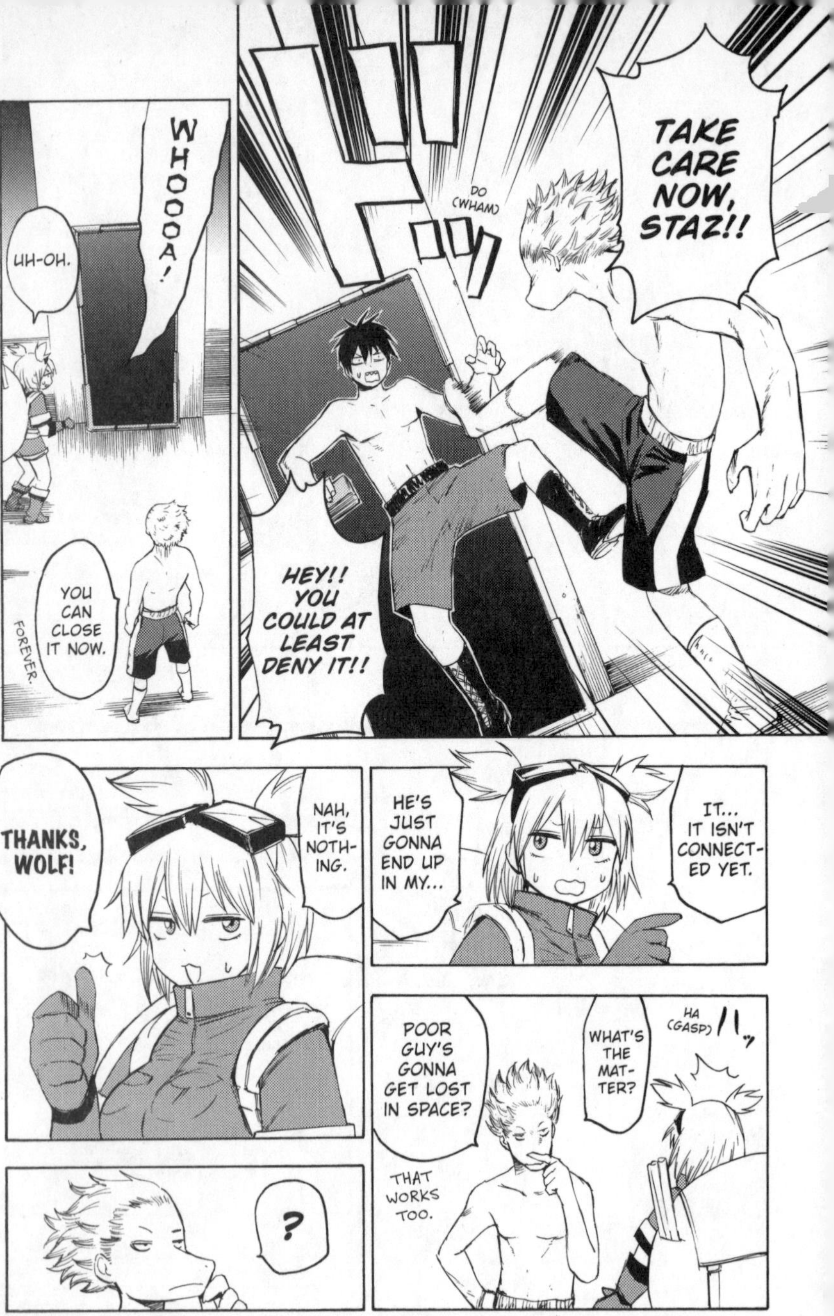

TAKE CARE NOW, STAZ!!
DO (WHAM)
HEY!! YOU COULD AT LEAST DENY IT!!
WHOOOOA!
UH-OH.
YOU CAN CLOSE IT NOW.
FOREVER.
IT... IT ISN'T CONNECTED YET.
HE'S JUST GONNA END UP IN MY...
NAH, IT'S NOTHING.
THANKS, WOLF!
HA (GASP)
WHAT'S THE MATTER?
POOR GUY'S GONNA GET LOST IN SPACE?
THAT WORKS TOO.
?

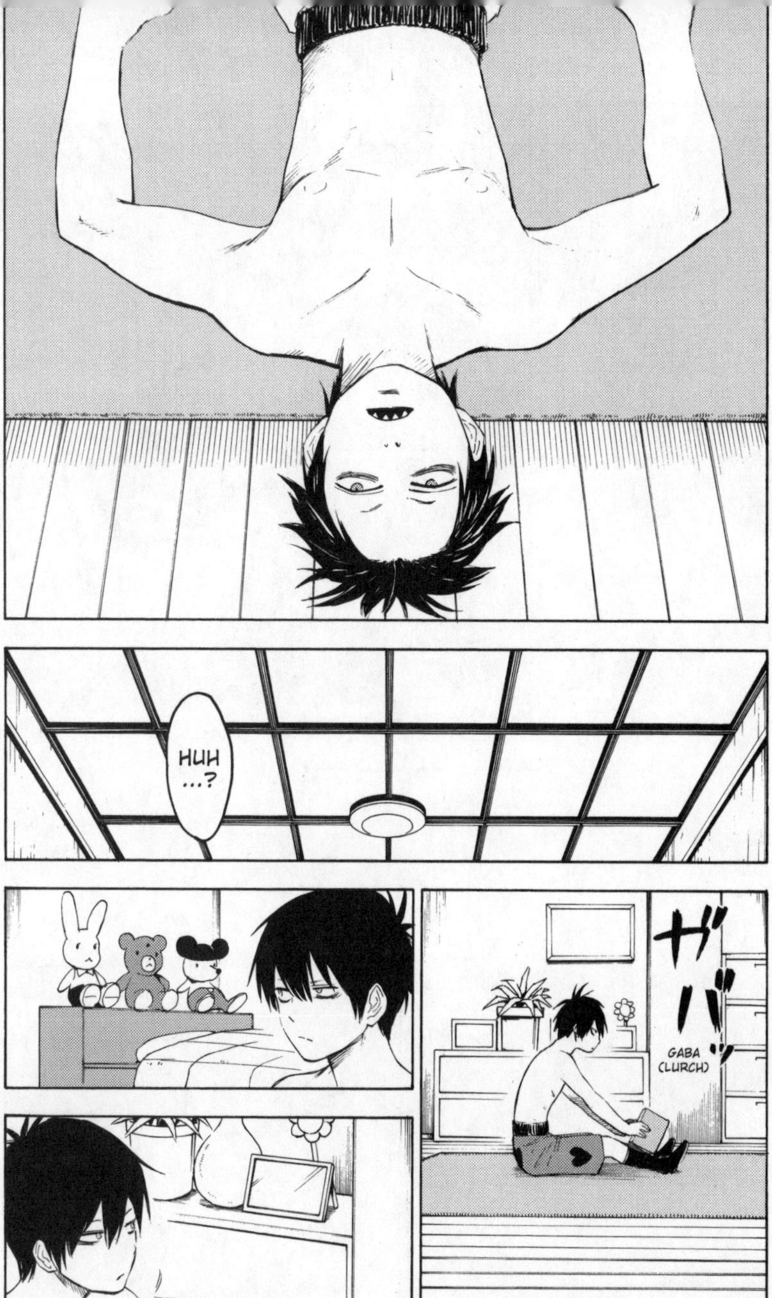
HUH ...?
ザバッ
GABA (LURCH)

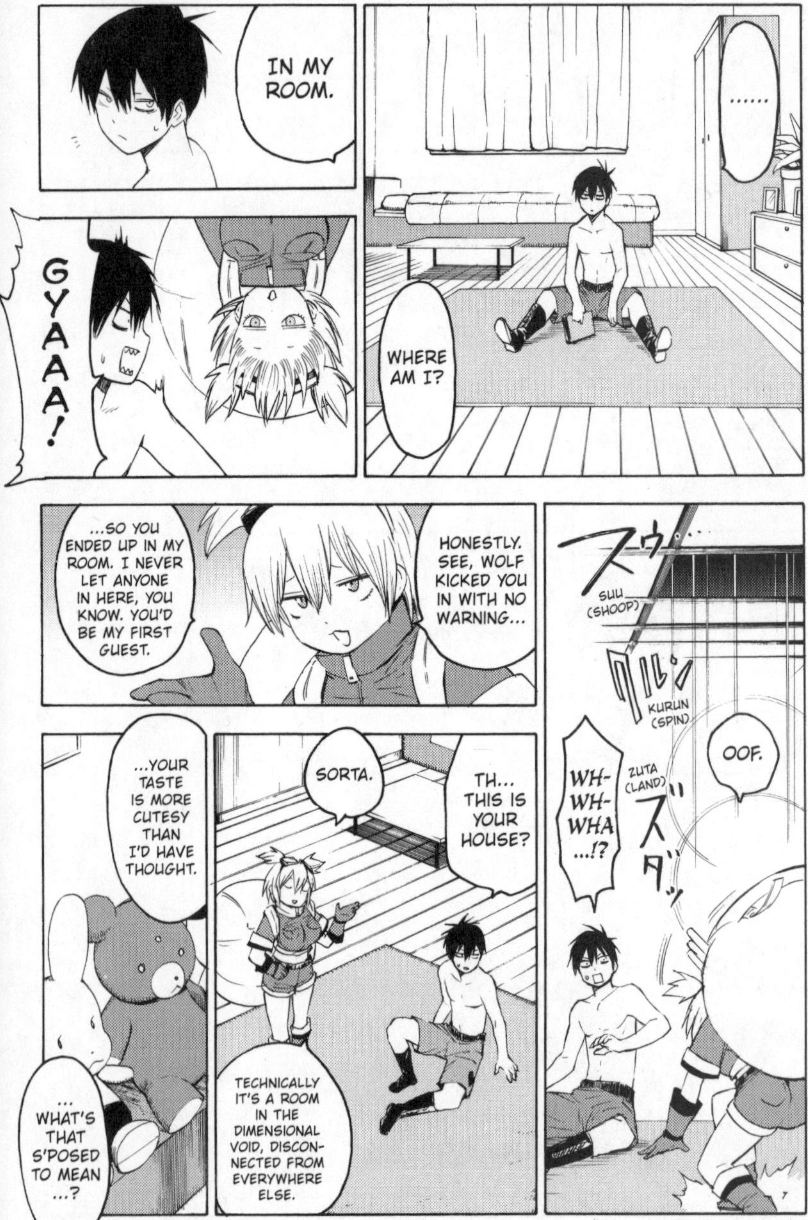
......
WHERE AM I?
IN MY ROOM.
GYAAA!
スゥ…
SUU (SHOOP)
クルン
KURUN (SPIN)
OOF.
ZUTA (LAND)
スタッ
WH-WH-WHA...!?
HONESTLY. SEE, WOLF KICKED YOU IN WITH NO WARNING...
...SO YOU ENDED UP IN MY ROOM. I NEVER LET ANYONE IN HERE, YOU KNOW. YOU'D BE MY FIRST GUEST.
TH... THIS IS YOUR HOUSE?
SORTA.
TECHNICALLY IT'S A ROOM IN THE DIMENSIONAL VOID, DISCONNECTED FROM EVERYWHERE ELSE.
...YOUR TASTE IS MORE CUTESY THAN I'D HAVE THOUGHT.
...WHAT'S THAT S'POSED TO MEAN...?

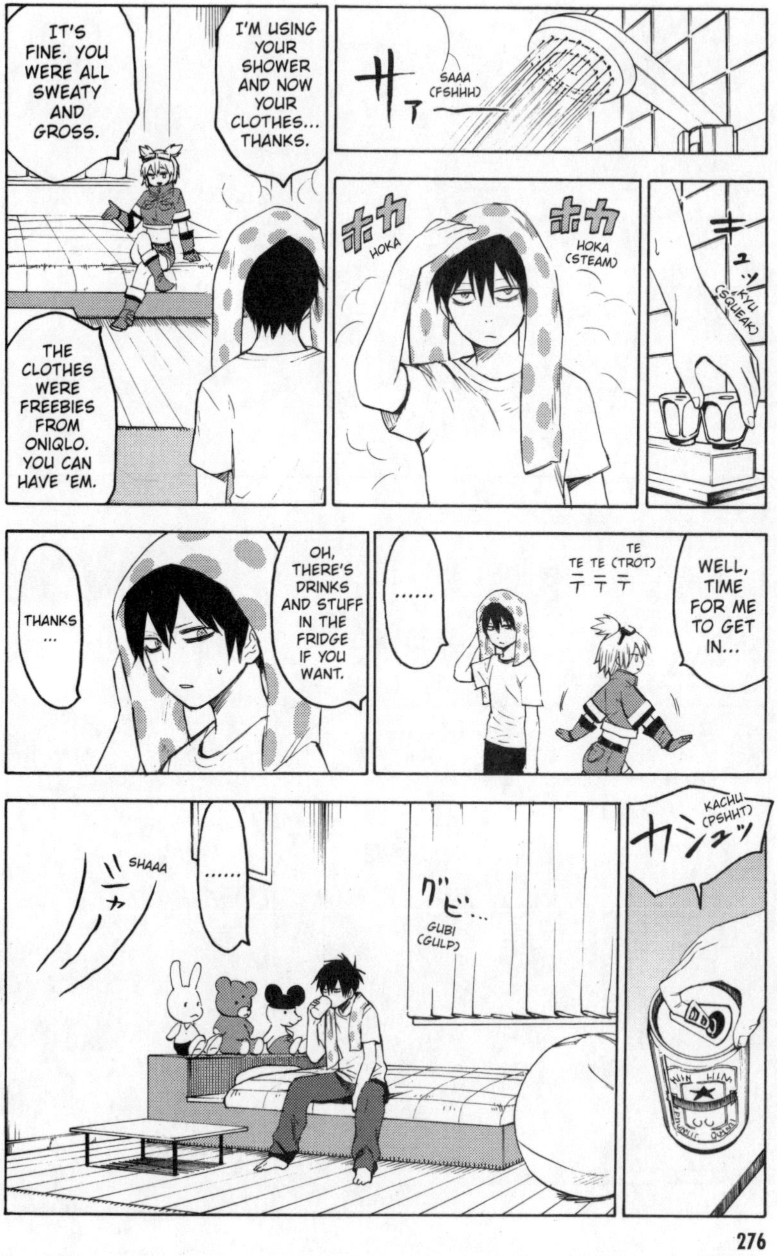
サァ
SAAA (FSHHH)
キュッ
KYU (SQUEAK)
ホカ
HOKA
ホカ
HOKA (STEAM)
I'M USING YOUR SHOWER AND NOW YOUR CLOTHES... THANKS.
IT'S FINE. YOU WERE ALL SWEATY AND GROSS.
THE CLOTHES WERE FREEBIES FROM ONIQLO. YOU CAN HAVE 'EM.
WELL, TIME FOR ME TO GET IN...
テテテ
TE TE TE (TROT)
......
OH, THERE'S DRINKS AND STUFF IN THE FRIDGE IF YOU WANT.
THANKS ...
カシュッ
KACHU (PSHHT)
グビ…
GUBI (GULP)
......
シャ
SHAAA

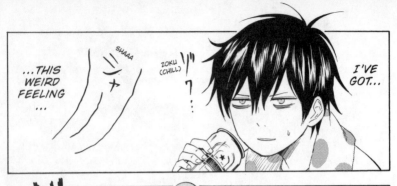

...THIS
WEIRD
FEELING
...

SHAAA

ZOKU
(CHILL)

I'VE
GOT...

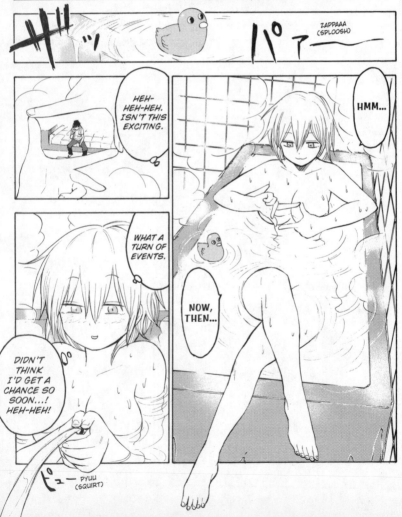

ZAPPAAA
(SPLOOSH)

HEH-
HEH-HEH.
ISN'T THIS
EXCITING.

HMM...

WHAT A
TURN OF
EVENTS.

NOW,
THEN...

DIDN'T
THINK
I'D GET A
CHANCE SO
SOON...!
HEH-HEH!

PYUU
(SQUIRT)

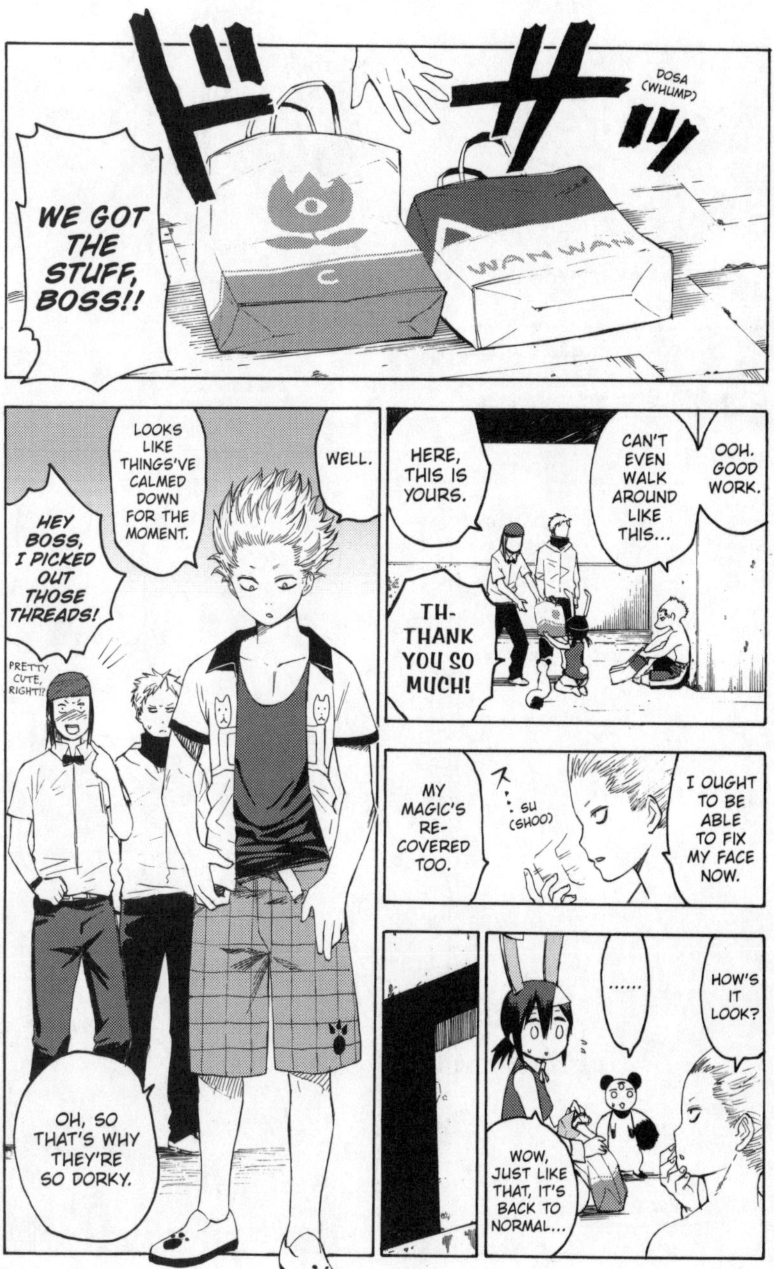
ドサッ
DOSA (WHUMP)
WE GOT THE STUFF, BOSS!!
OOH. GOOD WORK.
CAN'T EVEN WALK AROUND LIKE THIS...
HERE, THIS IS YOURS.
TH-THANK YOU SO MUCH!
I OUGHT TO BE ABLE TO FIX MY FACE NOW.
ス...
SU (SHOO)
MY MAGIC'S RE-COVERED TOO.
HOW'S IT LOOK?
......
WOW, JUST LIKE THAT, IT'S BACK TO NORMAL...
WELL.
LOOKS LIKE THINGS'VE CALMED DOWN FOR THE MOMENT.
HEY BOSS, I PICKED OUT THOSE THREADS!
PRETTY CUTE, RIGHT!?
OH, SO THAT'S WHY THEY'RE SO DORKY.

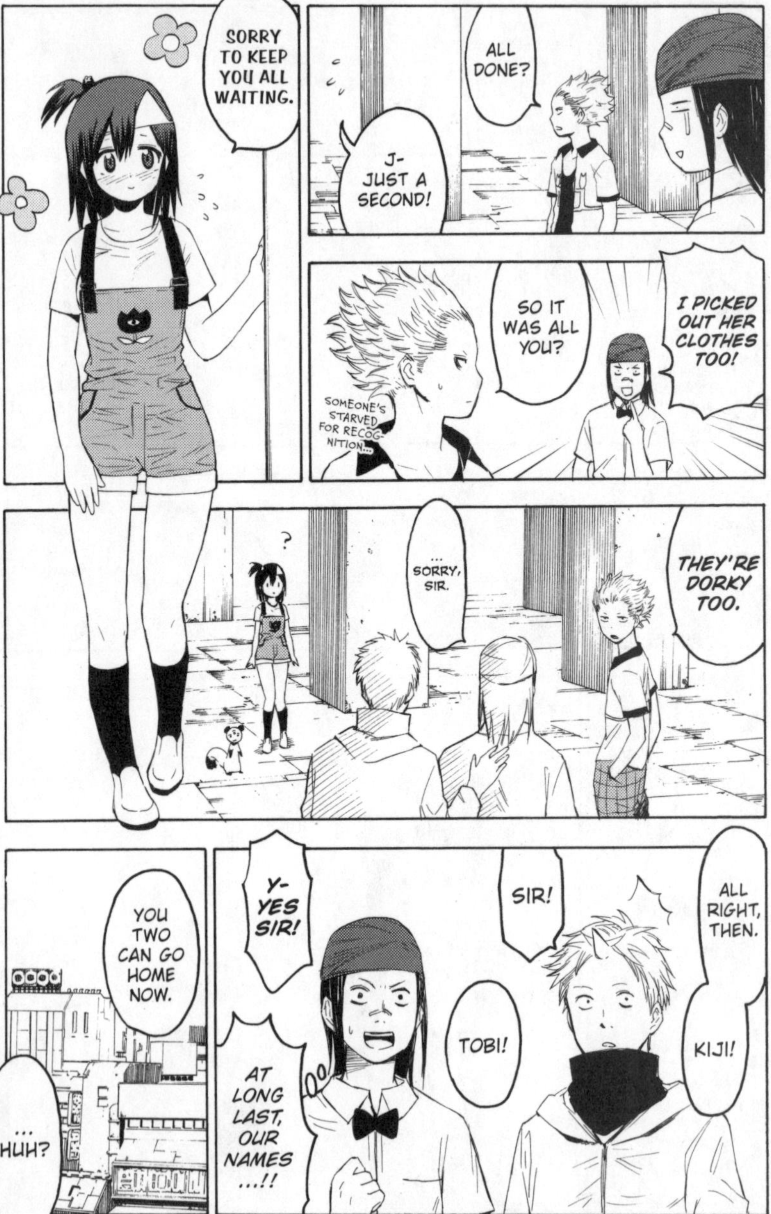
ALL DONE?
J- JUST A SECOND!
I PICKED OUT HER CLOTHES TOO!
SO IT WAS ALL YOU?
SOMEONE'S STARVED FOR RECOG-NITION...
SORRY TO KEEP YOU ALL WAITING.
THEY'RE DORKY TOO.
... SORRY, SIR.
ALL RIGHT, THEN.
SIR!
Y- YES SIR!
KIJI!
TOBI!
AT LONG LAST, OUR NAMES ...!!
YOU TWO CAN GO HOME NOW.
... HUH?

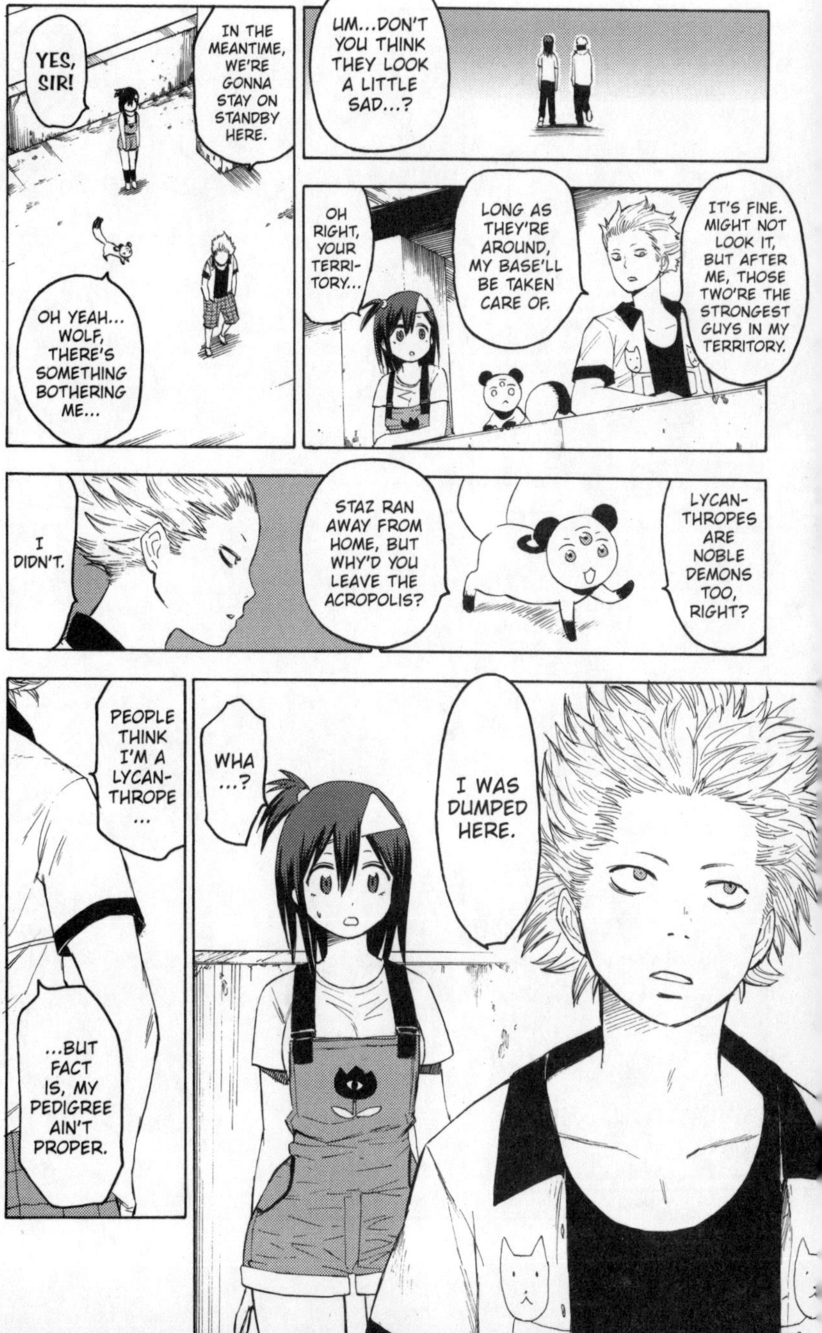
UM...DON'T YOU THINK THEY LOOK A LITTLE SAD...?
IT'S FINE. MIGHT NOT LOOK IT, BUT AFTER ME, THOSE TWO'RE THE STRONGEST GUYS IN MY TERRITORY.
LONG AS THEY'RE AROUND, MY BASE'LL BE TAKEN CARE OF.
OH RIGHT, YOUR TERRI-TORY...
IN THE MEANTIME, WE'RE GONNA STAY ON STANDBY HERE.
YES, SIR!
OH YEAH... WOLF, THERE'S SOMETHING BOTHERING ME...
LYCAN-THROPES ARE NOBLE DEMONS TOO, RIGHT?
STAZ RAN AWAY FROM HOME, BUT WHY'D YOU LEAVE THE ACROPOLIS?
I DIDN'T.
I WAS DUMPED HERE.
WHA ...?
PEOPLE THINK I'M A LYCAN-THROPE ...
...BUT FACT IS, MY PEDIGREE AIN'T PROPER.

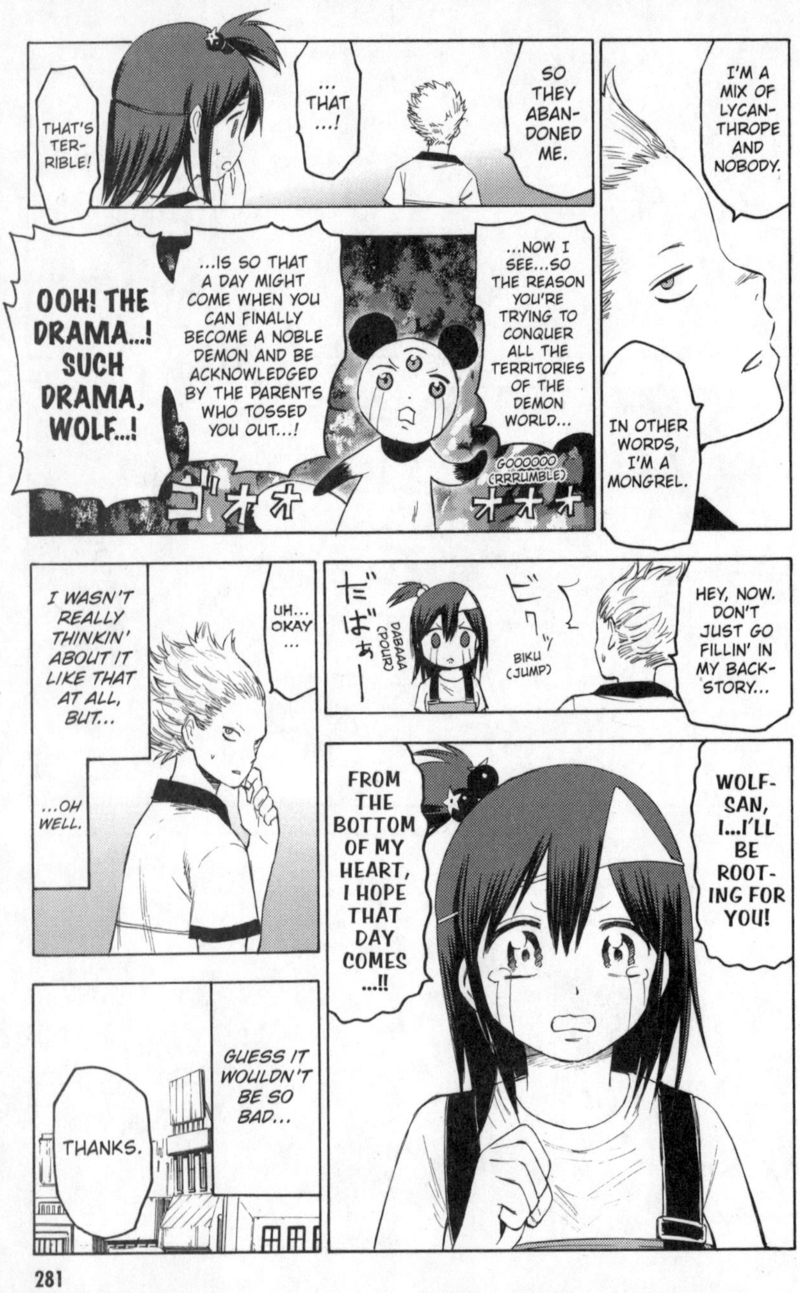
I'M A MIX OF LYCANTHROPE AND NOBODY.
IN OTHER WORDS, I'M A MONGREL.
SO THEY ABANDONED ME.
... THAT ...!
THAT'S TERRIBLE!
...NOW I SEE...SO THE REASON YOU'RE TRYING TO CONQUER ALL THE TERRITORIES OF THE DEMON WORLD...
GOOOOOO (RRRUMBLE)
...IS SO THAT A DAY MIGHT COME WHEN YOU CAN FINALLY BECOME A NOBLE DEMON AND BE ACKNOWLEDGED BY THE PARENTS WHO TOSSED YOU OUT...!
OOH! THE DRAMA...! SUCH DRAMA, WOLF...!
HEY, NOW. DON'T JUST GO FILLIN' IN MY BACK-STORY...
BIKU (JUMP)
DABAAA (POUR)
WOLF-SAN, I...I'LL BE ROOTING FOR YOU!
FROM THE BOTTOM OF MY HEART, I HOPE THAT DAY COMES ...!!
UH... OKAY ...
I WASN'T REALLY THINKIN' ABOUT IT LIKE THAT AT ALL, BUT...
...OH WELL.
GUESS IT WOULDN'T BE SO BAD...
THANKS.

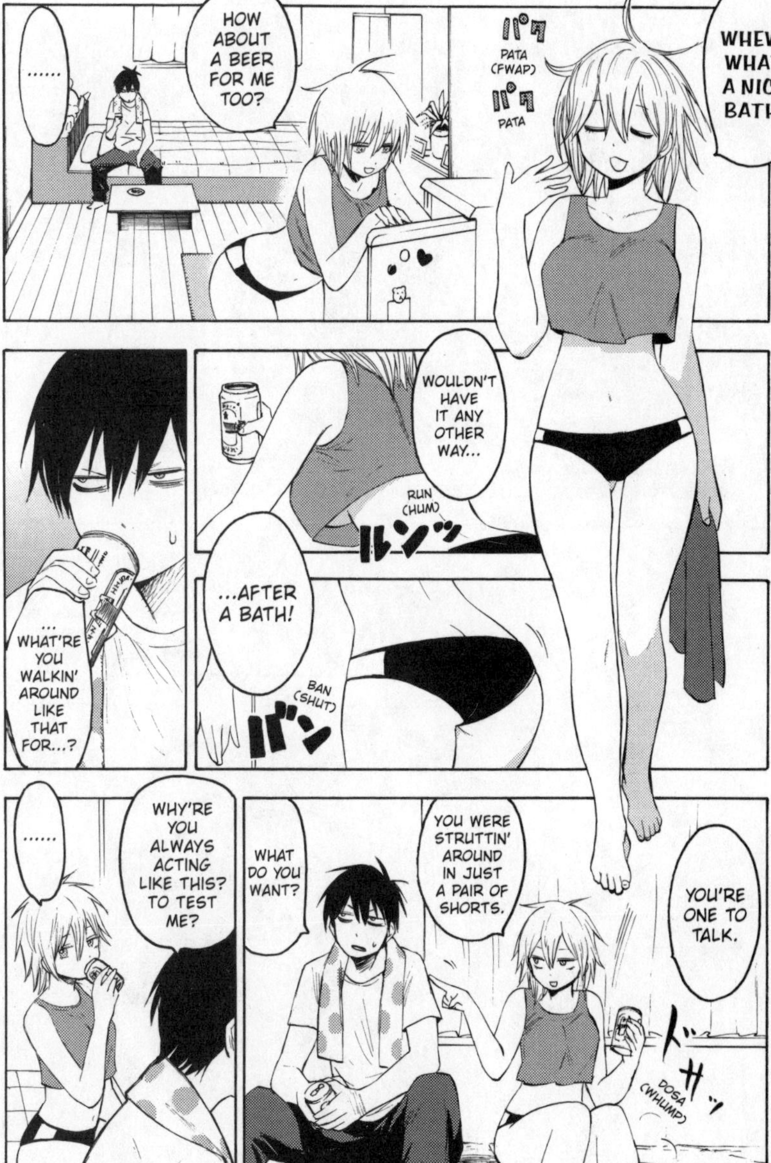
WHEW! WHAT A NICE BATH.
パタ
PATA (FWAP)
パタ
PATA
HOW ABOUT A BEER FOR ME TOO?
......
WOULDN'T HAVE IT ANY OTHER WAY...
ルンッ
RUN (HUM)
...AFTER A BATH!
バン
BAN (SHUT)
...WHAT'RE YOU WALKIN' AROUND LIKE THAT FOR...?
YOU'RE ONE TO TALK.
ドサッ
DOSA (WHUMP)
YOU WERE STRUTTIN' AROUND IN JUST A PAIR OF SHORTS.
WHAT DO YOU WANT?
WHY'RE YOU ALWAYS ACTING LIKE THIS? TO TEST ME?
......

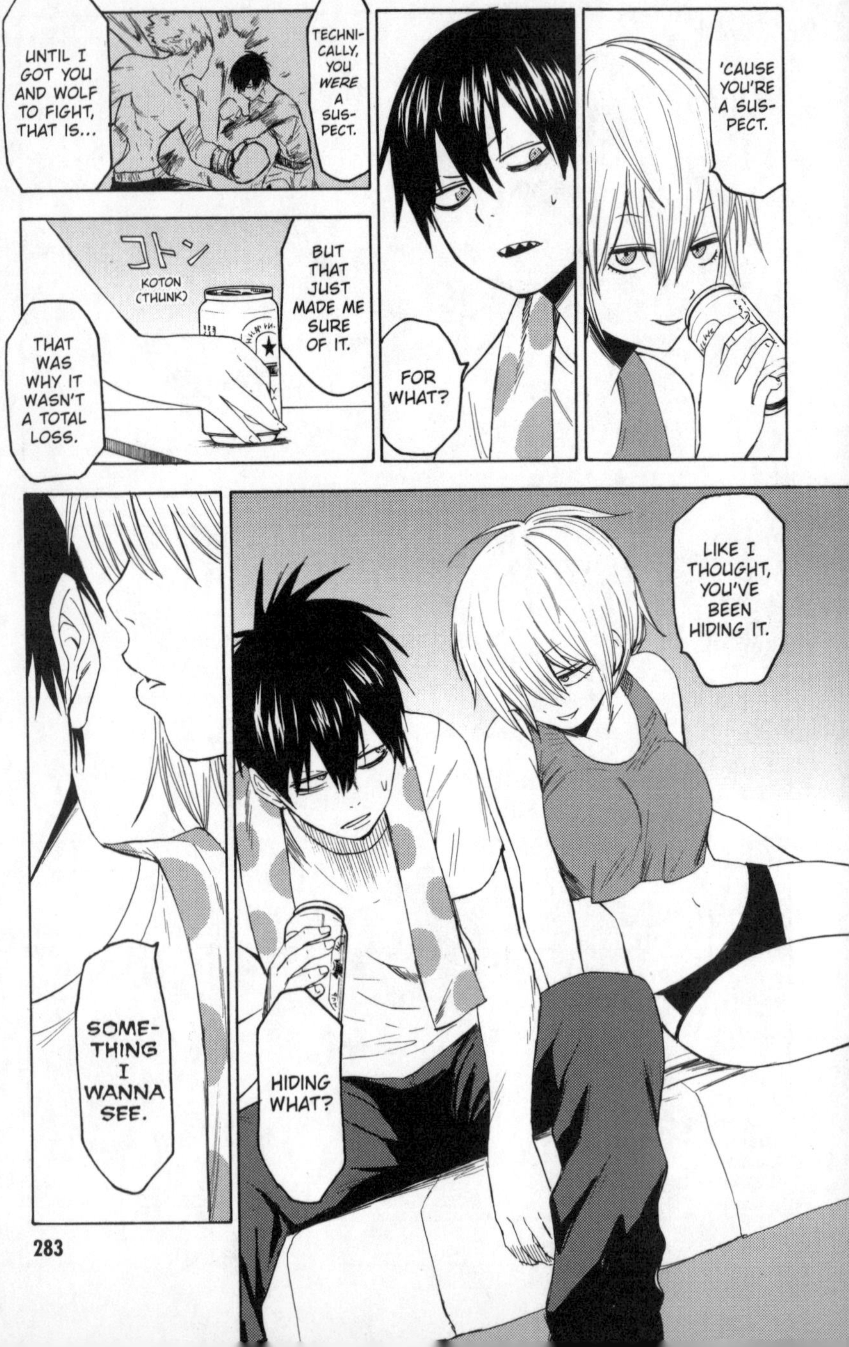
'CAUSE YOU'RE A SUS- PECT.
FOR WHAT?
TECHNI- CALLY, YOU *WERE* A SUS- PECT.
UNTIL I GOT YOU AND WOLF TO FIGHT, THAT IS...
BUT THAT JUST MADE ME SURE OF IT.
コトン
KOTON (THUNK)
THAT WAS WHY IT WASN'T A TOTAL LOSS.
LIKE I THOUGHT, YOU'VE BEEN HIDING IT.
HIDING WHAT?
SOME- THING I WANNA SEE.

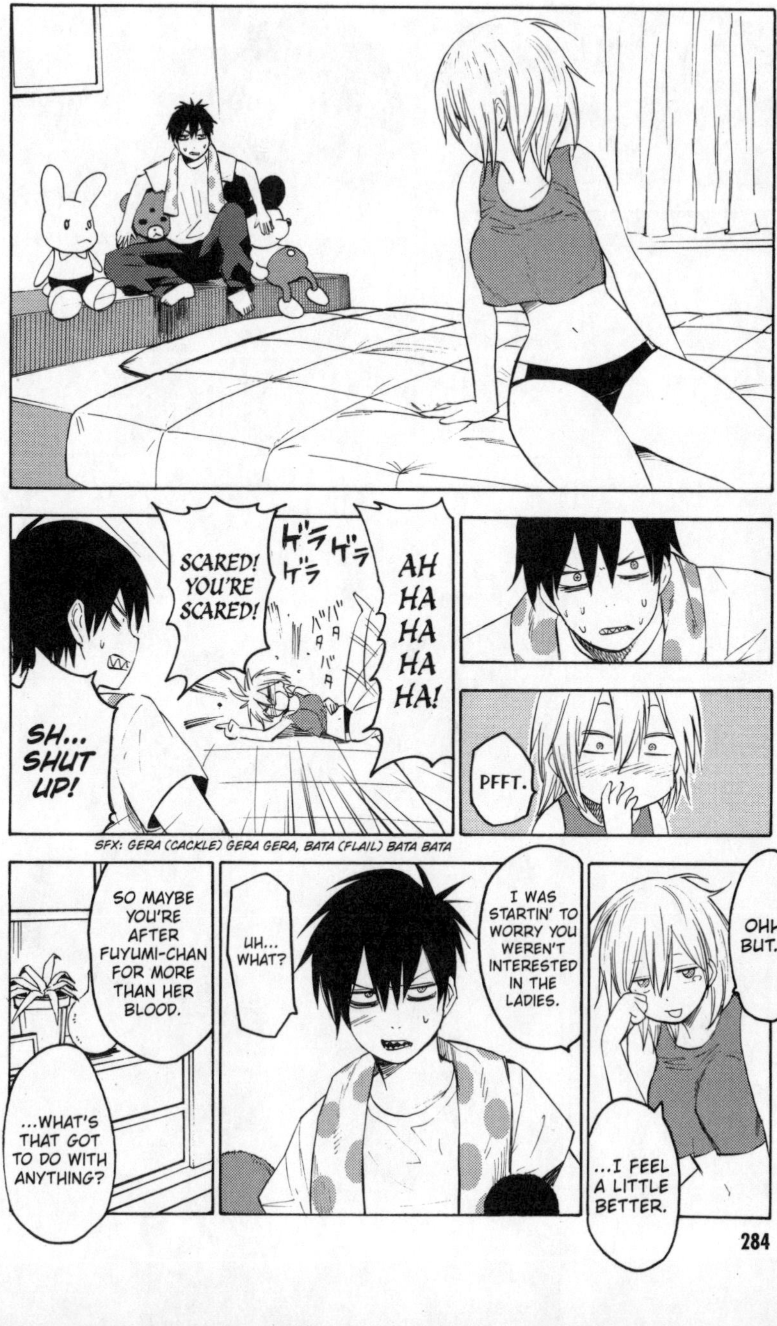
PFFT.
AH HA HA HA HA HA!
ゲラゲラゲラ
SCARED! YOU'RE SCARED!
バタバタバタ
SH... SHUT UP!
SFX: GERA (CACKLE) GERA GERA, BATA (FLAIL) BATA BATA
OHH, BUT...
...I FEEL A LITTLE BETTER.
I WAS STARTIN' TO WORRY YOU WEREN'T INTERESTED IN THE LADIES.
UH... WHAT?
SO MAYBE YOU'RE AFTER FUYUMI-CHAN FOR MORE THAN HER BLOOD.
...WHAT'S THAT GOT TO DO WITH ANYTHING?

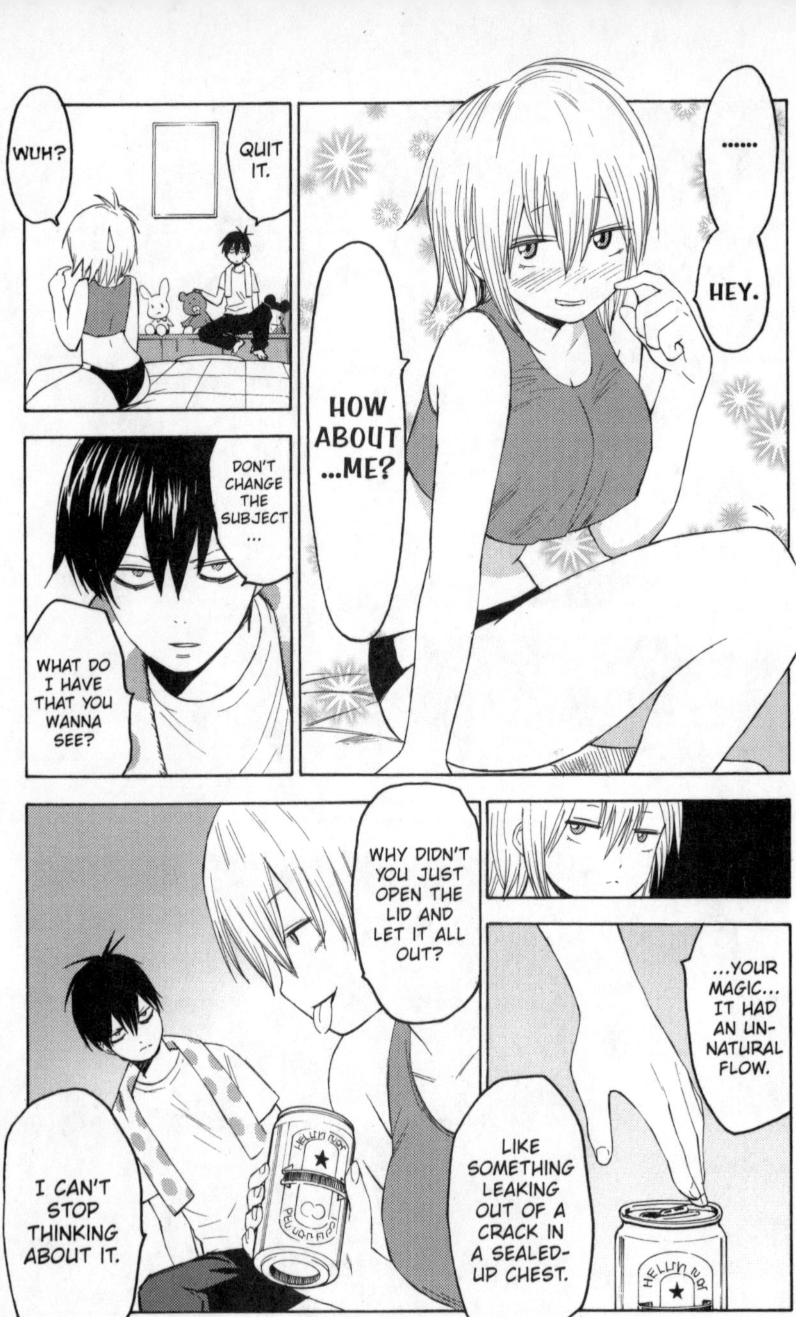
......
HEY.
HOW ABOUT ...ME?
QUIT IT.
WUH?
DON'T CHANGE THE SUBJECT ...
WHAT DO I HAVE THAT YOU WANNA SEE?
...YOUR MAGIC... IT HAD AN UN-NATURAL FLOW.
LIKE SOMETHING LEAKING OUT OF A CRACK IN A SEALED-UP CHEST.
WHY DIDN'T YOU JUST OPEN THE LID AND LET IT ALL OUT?
I CAN'T STOP THINKING ABOUT IT.

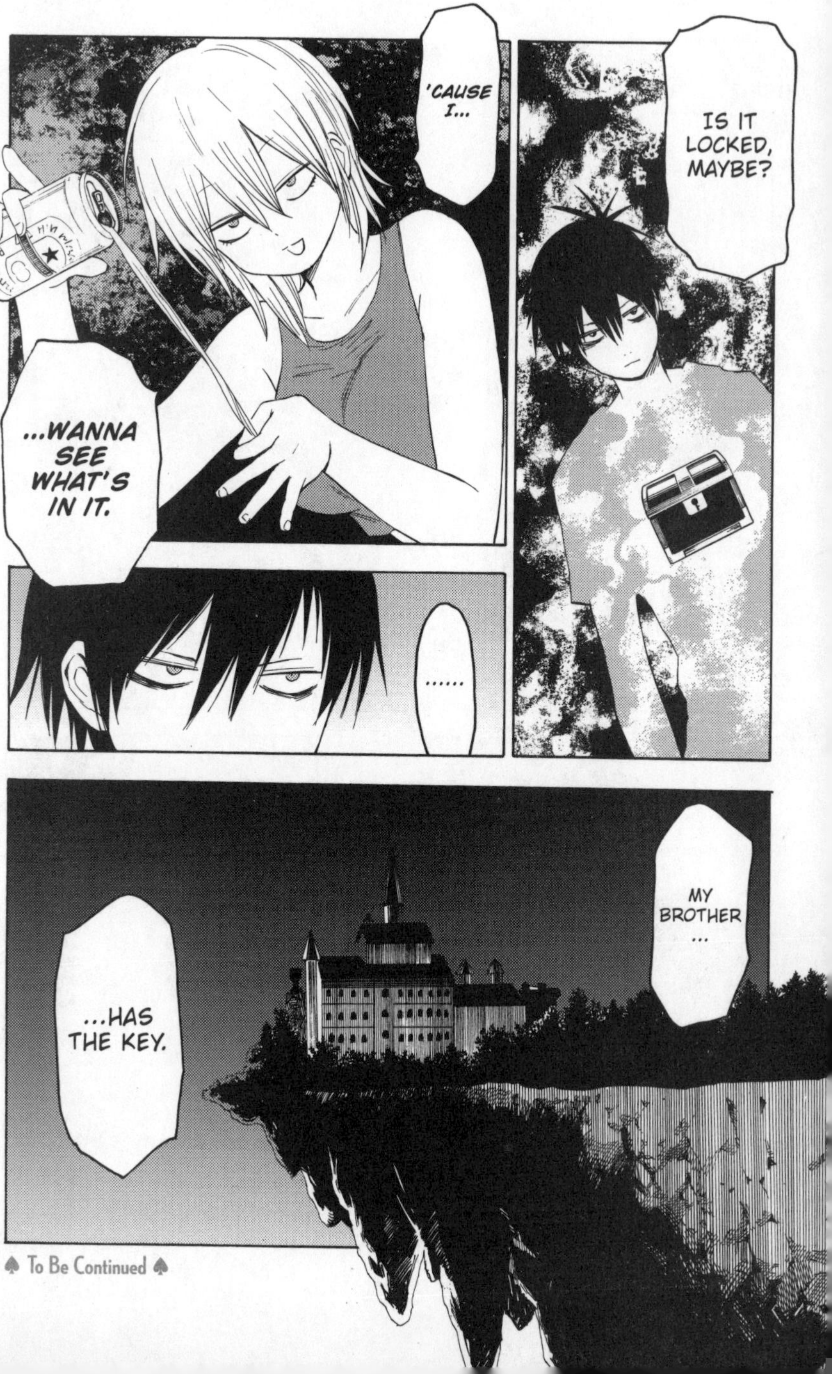
IS IT LOCKED, MAYBE?
'CAUSE I...
...WANNA SEE WHAT'S IN IT.
......
MY BROTHER ...
...HAS THE KEY.

♠ To Be Continued ♠

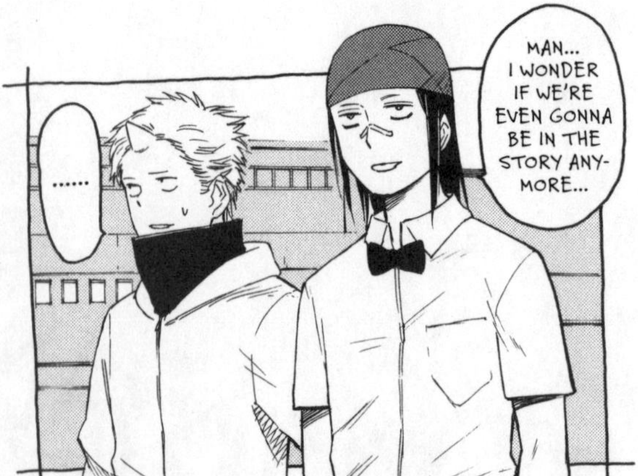
MAN... I WONDER IF WE'RE EVEN GONNA BE IN THE STORY ANY-MORE...
......

BLOOD LAD

# CHAPTER 9 ♠ THE THREE BLOODS

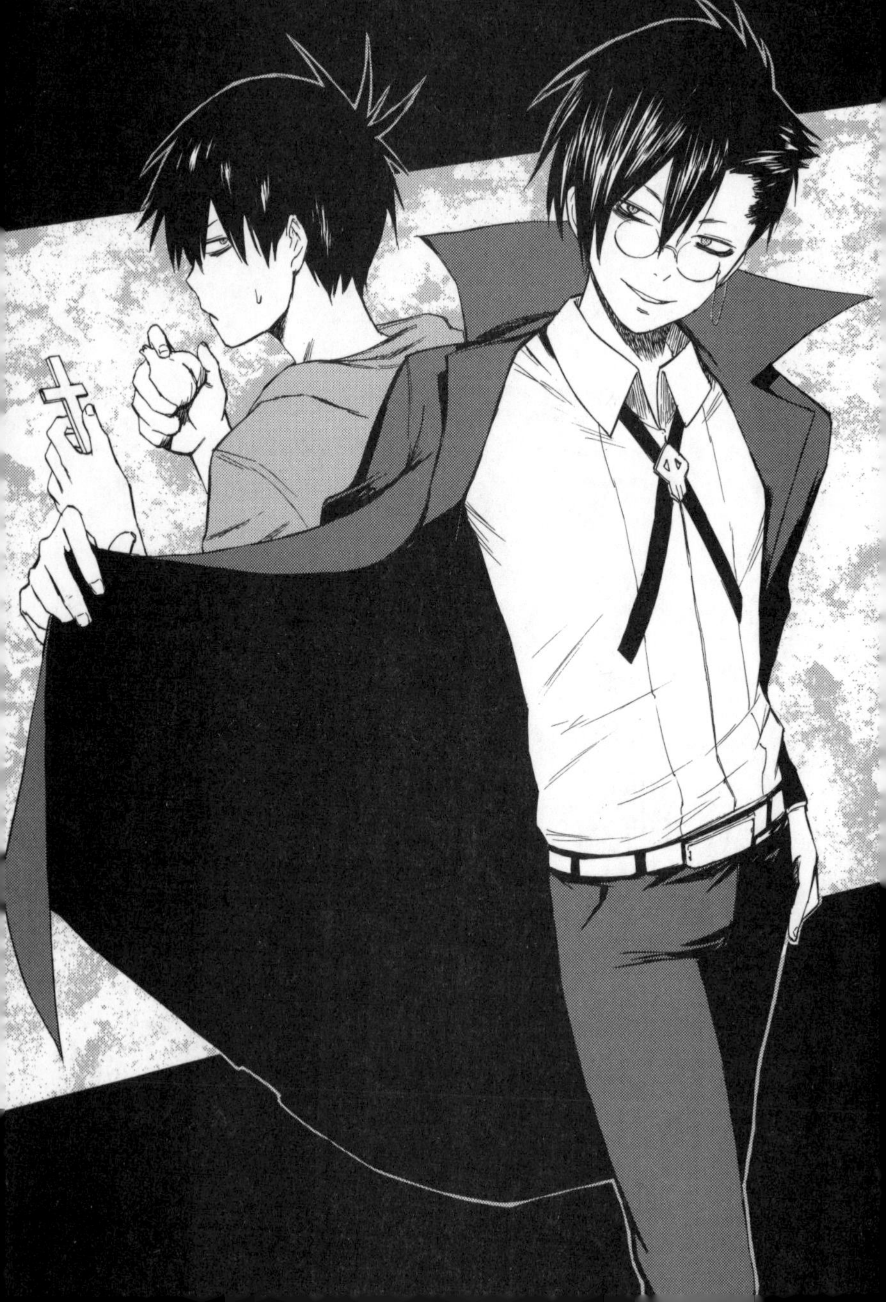

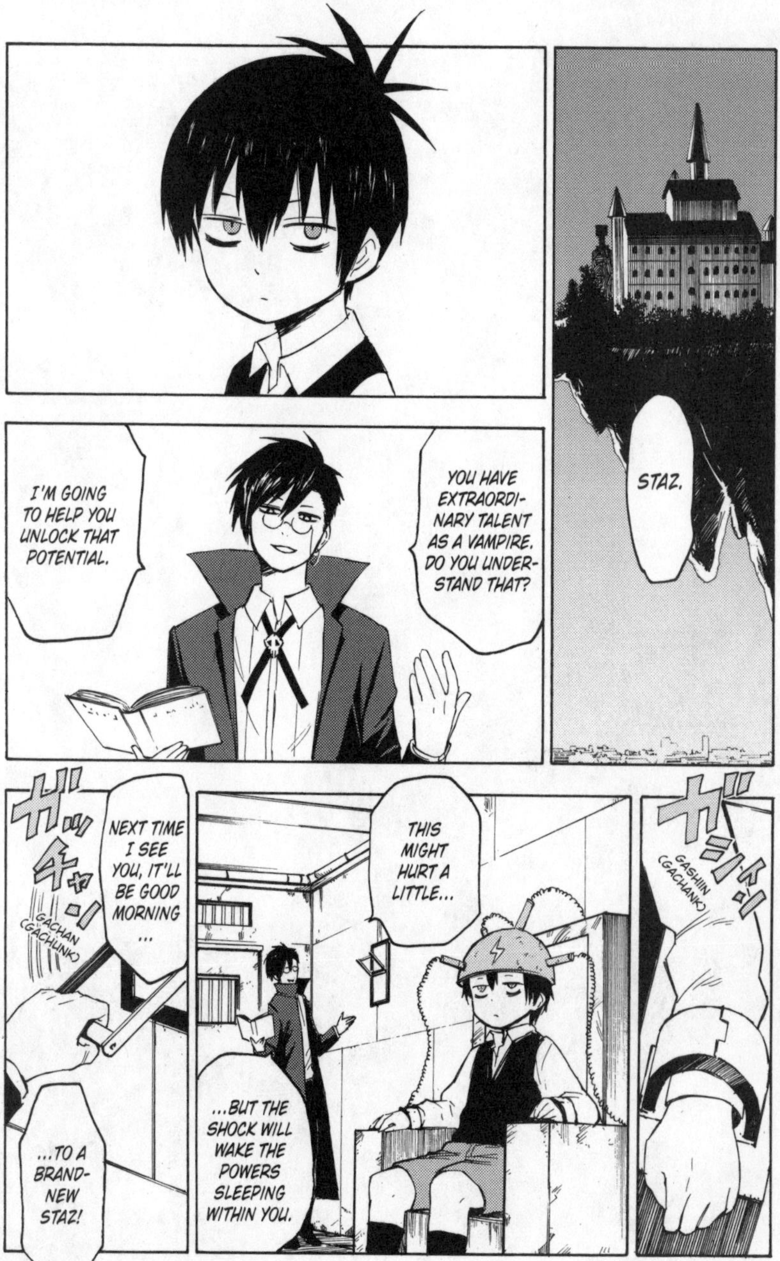
STAZ.
YOU HAVE EXTRAORDINARY TALENT AS A VAMPIRE. DO YOU UNDERSTAND THAT?
I'M GOING TO HELP YOU UNLOCK THAT POTENTIAL.
GASHIIN (GACHANK)
THIS MIGHT HURT A LITTLE...
...BUT THE SHOCK WILL WAKE THE POWERS SLEEPING WITHIN YOU.
NEXT TIME I SEE YOU, IT'LL BE GOOD MORNING ...
GACHAN (GACHLINK)
...TO A BRAND-NEW STAZ!

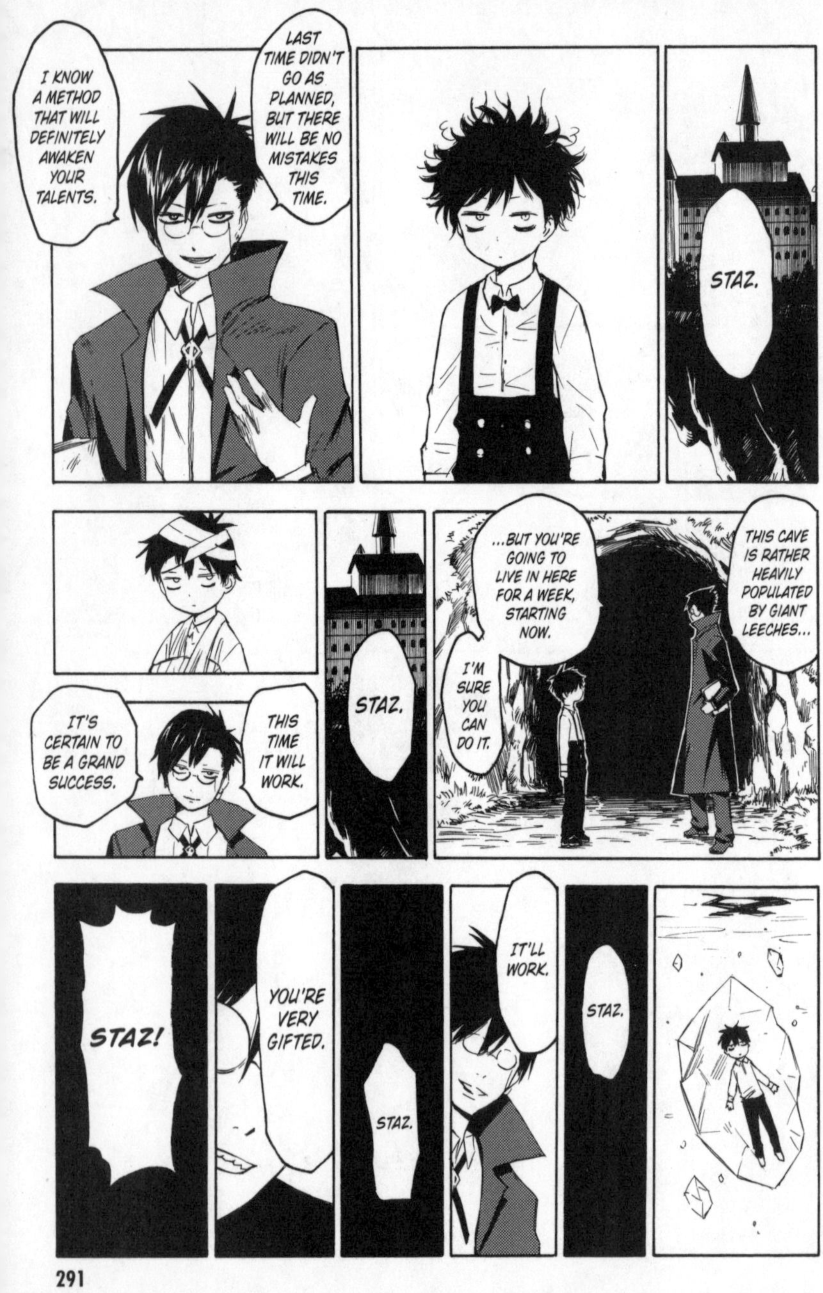

STAZ.
LAST TIME DIDN'T GO AS PLANNED, BUT THERE WILL BE NO MISTAKES THIS TIME.
I KNOW A METHOD THAT WILL DEFINITELY AWAKEN YOUR TALENTS.
THIS CAVE IS RATHER HEAVILY POPULATED BY GIANT LEECHES...
...BUT YOU'RE GOING TO LIVE IN HERE FOR A WEEK, STARTING NOW.
I'M SURE YOU CAN DO IT.
STAZ.
THIS TIME IT WILL WORK.
IT'S CERTAIN TO BE A GRAND SUCCESS.
STAZ.
IT'LL WORK.
STAZ.
YOU'RE VERY GIFTED.
STAZ!

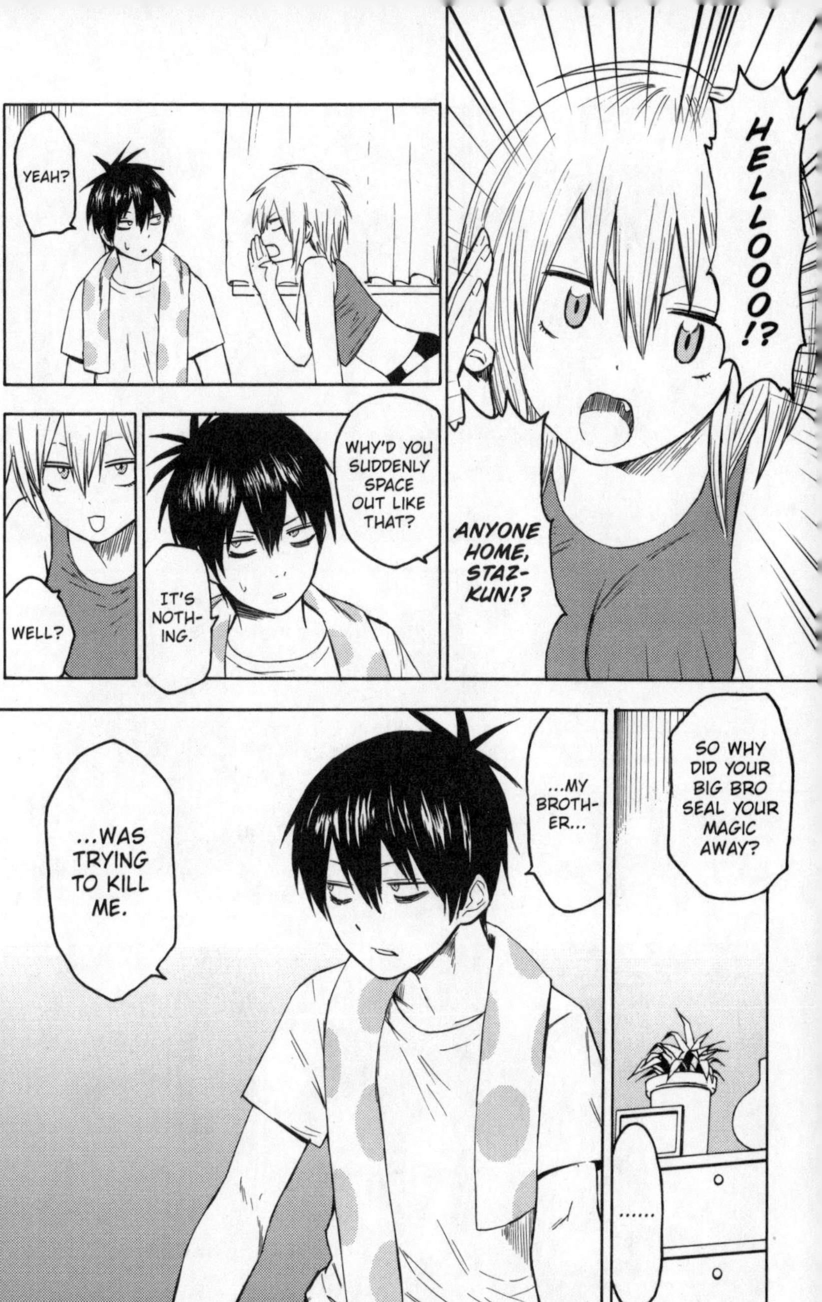
HELLOOOO!?
ANYONE HOME, STAZ-KUN!?
YEAH?
WHY'D YOU SUDDENLY SPACE OUT LIKE THAT?
IT'S NOTH-ING.
WELL?
SO WHY DID YOUR BIG BRO SEAL YOUR MAGIC AWAY?
......
...MY BROTH-ER...
...WAS TRYING TO KILL ME.

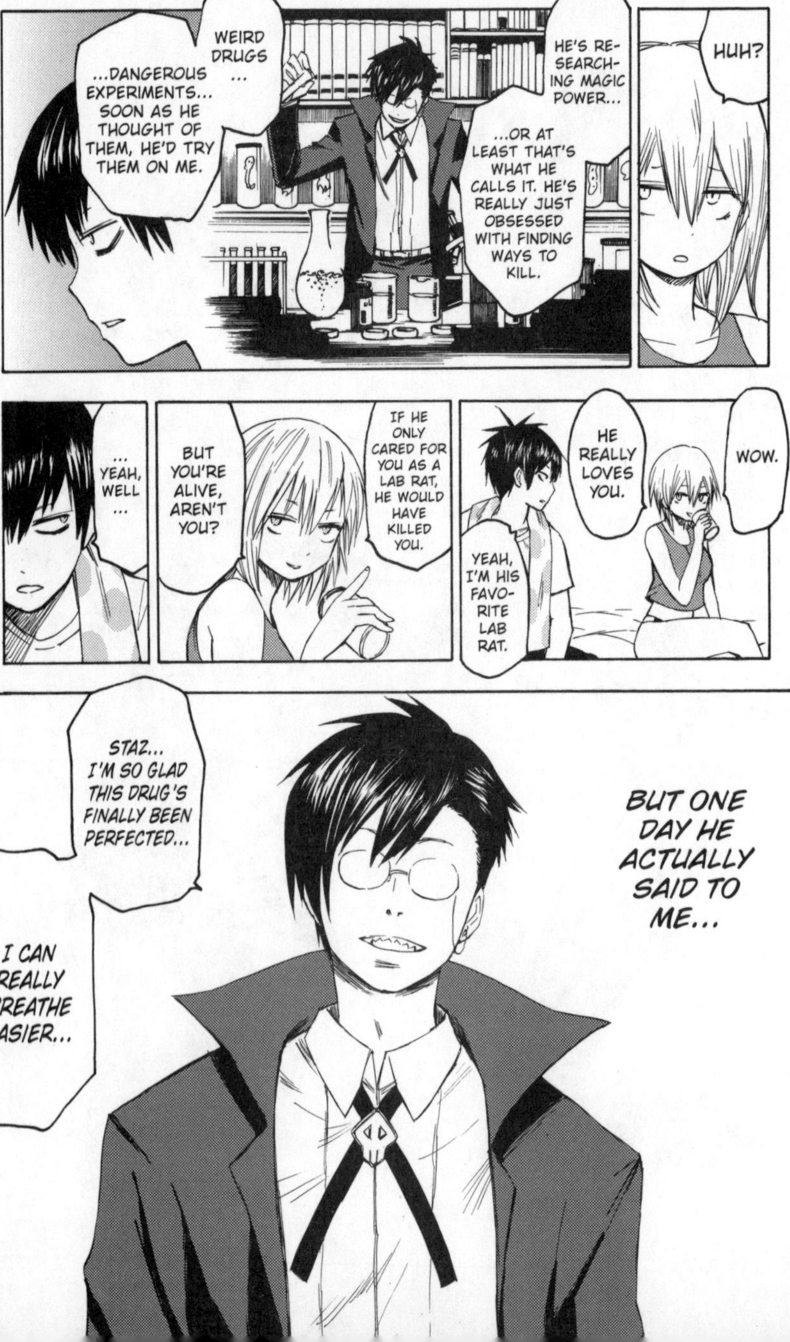
HUH?
HE'S RE-SEARCHING MAGIC POWER...
...OR AT LEAST THAT'S WHAT HE CALLS IT. HE'S REALLY JUST OBSESSED WITH FINDING WAYS TO KILL.
WEIRD DRUGS ...
...DANGEROUS EXPERIMENTS... SOON AS HE THOUGHT OF THEM, HE'D TRY THEM ON ME.
WOW.
HE REALLY LOVES YOU.
YEAH, I'M HIS FAVORITE LAB RAT.
IF HE ONLY CARED FOR YOU AS A LAB RAT, HE WOULD HAVE KILLED YOU.
BUT YOU'RE ALIVE, AREN'T YOU?
... YEAH, WELL ...
BUT ONE DAY HE ACTUALLY SAID TO ME...
STAZ... I'M SO GLAD THIS DRUG'S FINALLY BEEN PERFECTED...
I CAN REALLY BREATHE EASIER...

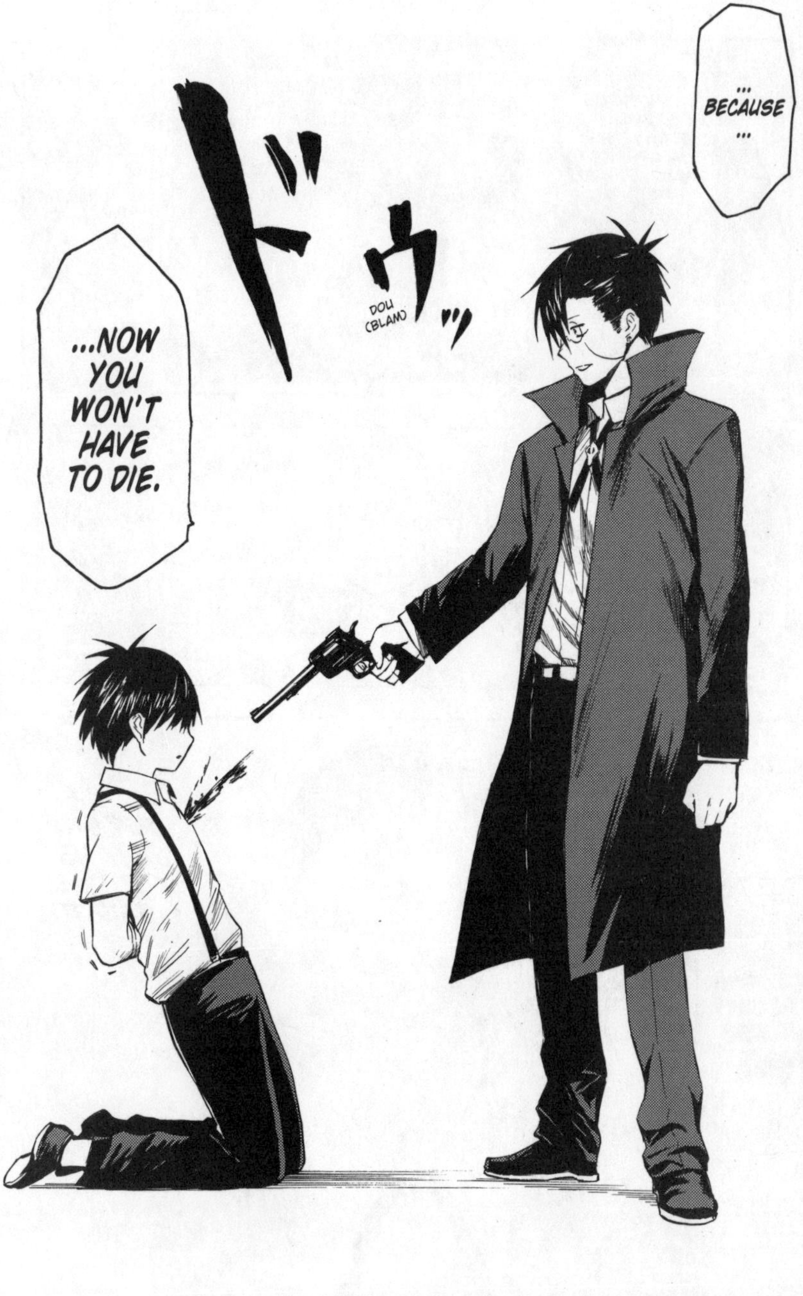
...BECAUSE ...
ドゥッ
DOU (BLAM)
...NOW YOU WON'T HAVE TO DIE.

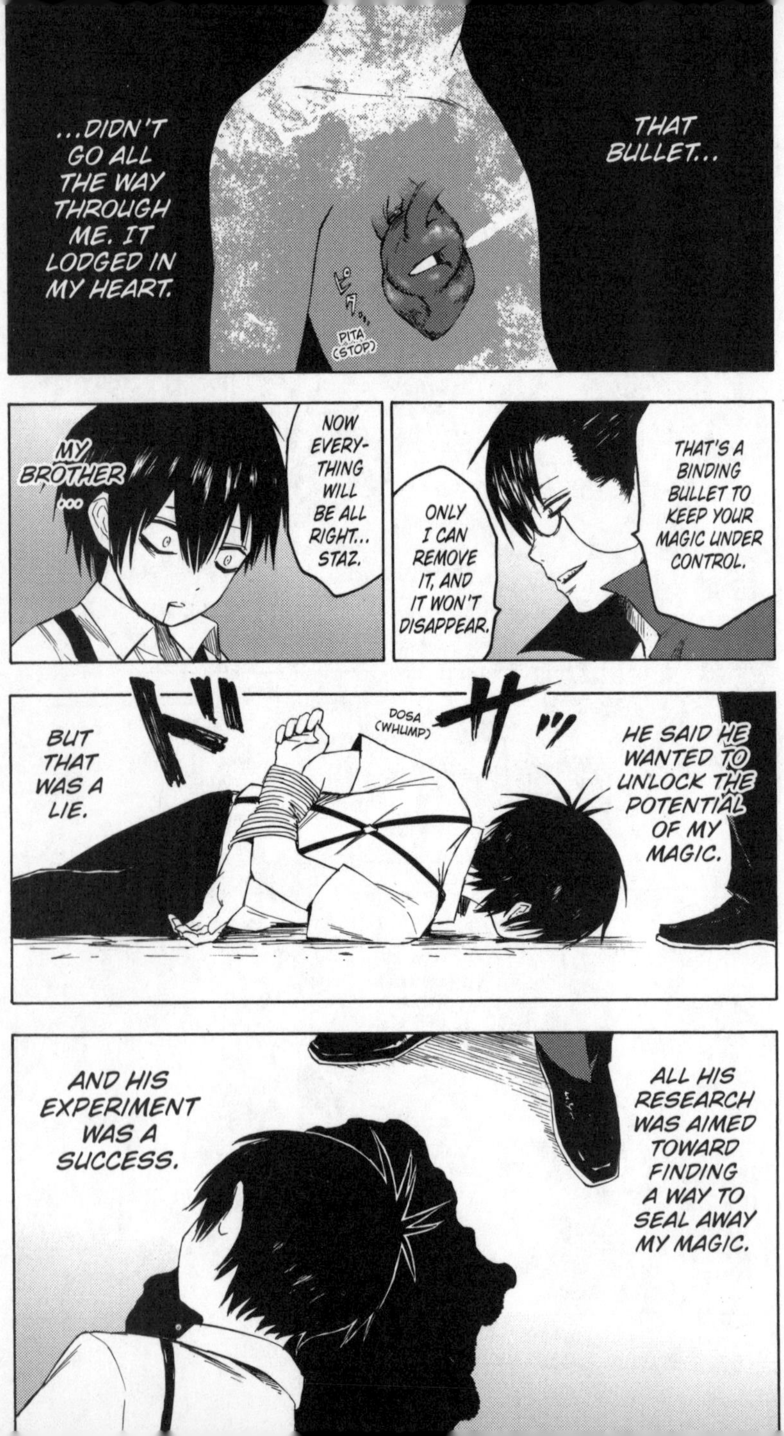
THAT BULLET...
...DIDN'T GO ALL THE WAY THROUGH ME. IT LODGED IN MY HEART.
PITA (STOP)
THAT'S A BINDING BULLET TO KEEP YOUR MAGIC UNDER CONTROL.
ONLY I CAN REMOVE IT, AND IT WON'T DISAPPEAR.
NOW EVERYTHING WILL BE ALL RIGHT... STAZ.
MY BROTHER...
HE SAID HE WANTED TO UNLOCK THE POTENTIAL OF MY MAGIC.
DOSA (WHUMP)
BUT THAT WAS A LIE.
ALL HIS RESEARCH WAS AIMED TOWARD FINDING A WAY TO SEAL AWAY MY MAGIC.
AND HIS EXPERIMENT WAS A SUCCESS.

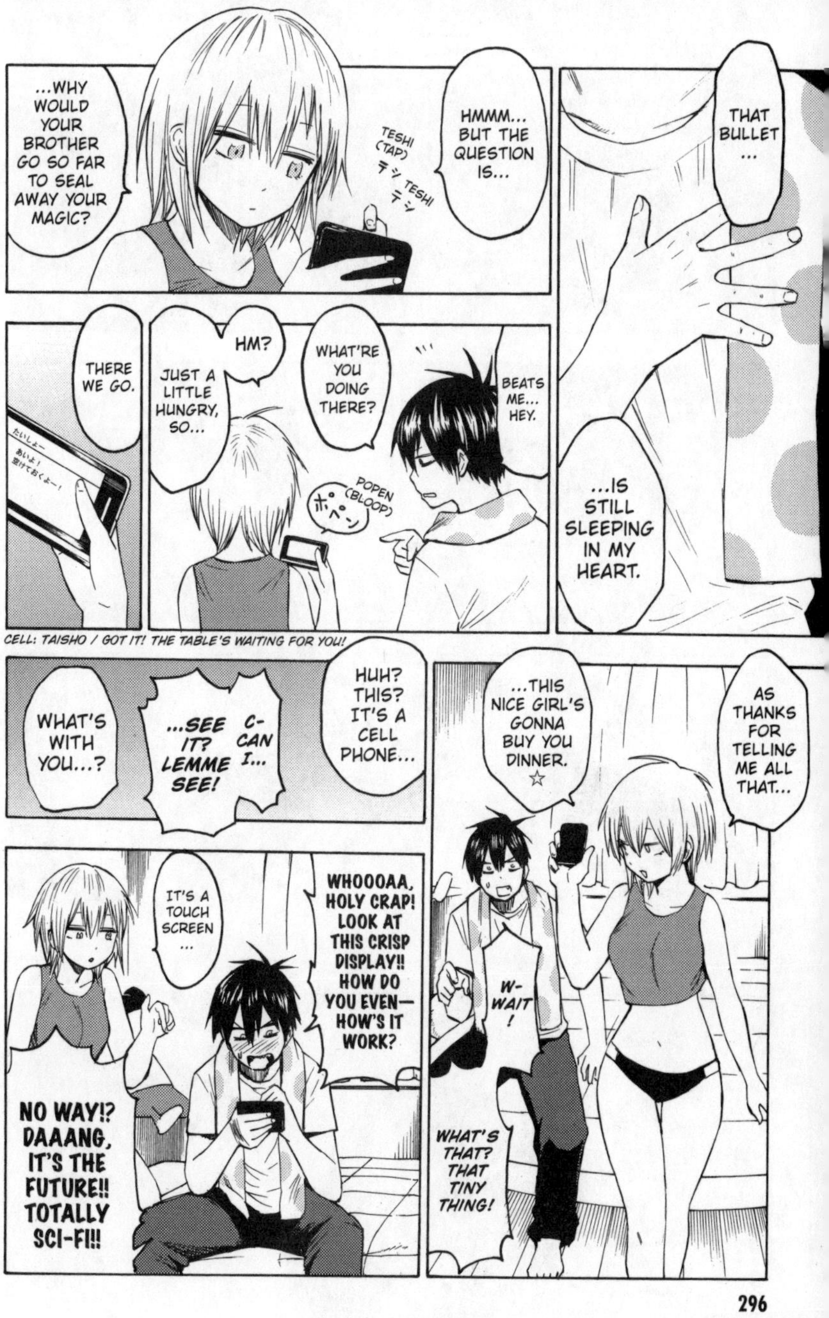
THAT BULLET...
...IS STILL SLEEPING IN MY HEART.
HMMM... BUT THE QUESTION IS...
TESHI (TAP) テシ TESHI テシ
...WHY WOULD YOUR BROTHER GO SO FAR TO SEAL AWAY YOUR MAGIC?
BEATS ME... HEY.
WHAT'RE YOU DOING THERE?
HM?
JUST A LITTLE HUNGRY, SO...
POPEN (BLOOP) ポペン
THERE WE GO.
たいしょー
あいよ！空けておくよー！
CELL: TAISHO / GOT IT! THE TABLE'S WAITING FOR YOU!
AS THANKS FOR TELLING ME ALL THAT...
...THIS NICE GIRL'S GONNA BUY YOU DINNER. ☆
W-WAIT!
WHAT'S THAT? THAT TINY THING!
HUH? THIS? IT'S A CELL PHONE...
C-CAN I...
...SEE IT? LEMME SEE!
WHAT'S WITH YOU...?
WHOOOAA, HOLY CRAP! LOOK AT THIS CRISP DISPLAY!! HOW DO YOU EVEN— HOW'S IT WORK?
IT'S A TOUCH SCREEN...
NO WAY!? DAAANG, IT'S THE FUTURE!! TOTALLY SCI-FI!!

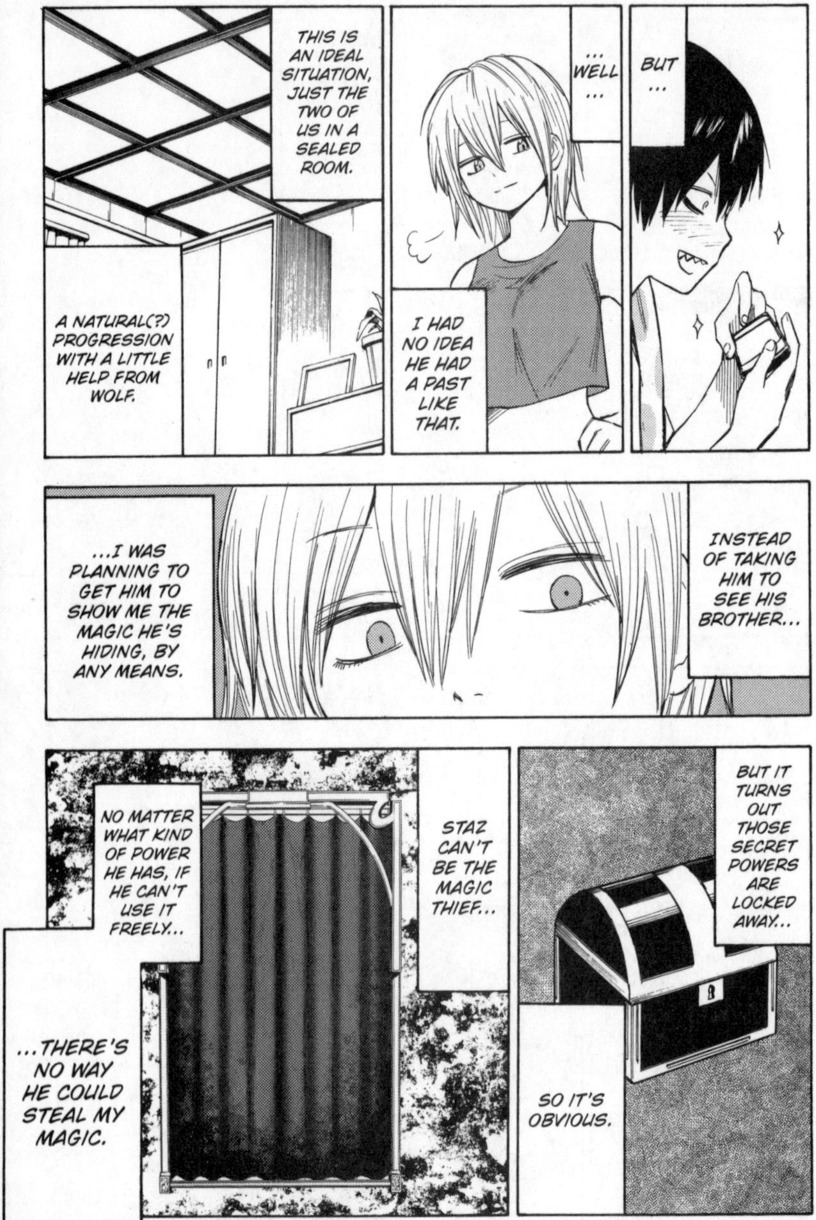
BUT ...
... WELL ...
I HAD NO IDEA HE HAD A PAST LIKE THAT.
THIS IS AN IDEAL SITUATION, JUST THE TWO OF US IN A SEALED ROOM.
A NATURAL(?) PROGRESSION WITH A LITTLE HELP FROM WOLF.
INSTEAD OF TAKING HIM TO SEE HIS BROTHER...
...I WAS PLANNING TO GET HIM TO SHOW ME THE MAGIC HE'S HIDING, BY ANY MEANS.
BUT IT TURNS OUT THOSE SECRET POWERS ARE LOCKED AWAY...
SO IT'S OBVIOUS.
STAZ CAN'T BE THE MAGIC THIEF...
NO MATTER WHAT KIND OF POWER HE HAS, IF HE CAN'T USE IT FREELY...
...THERE'S NO WAY HE COULD STEAL MY MAGIC.

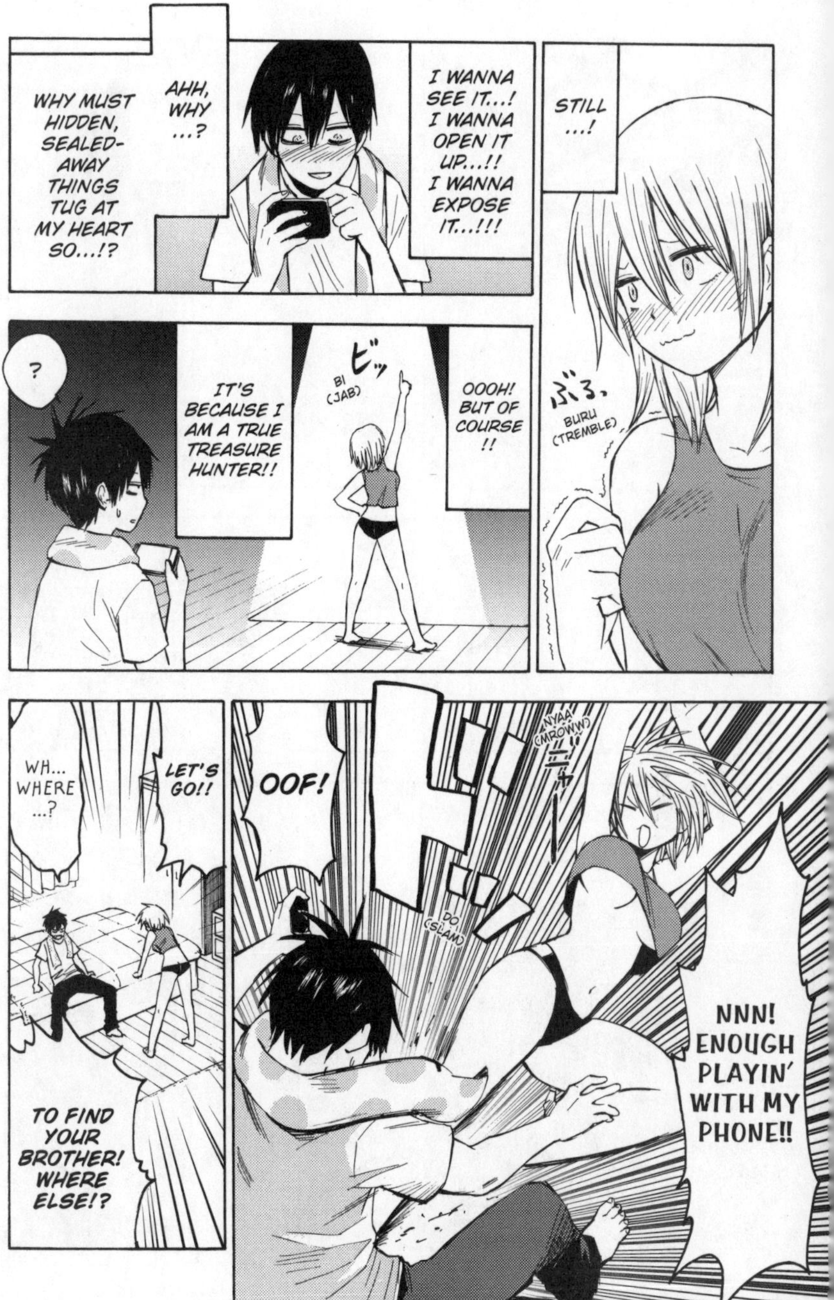
STILL ...!
ぶるっ
BURU (TREMBLE)
I WANNA SEE IT...! I WANNA OPEN IT UP...!! I WANNA EXPOSE IT...!!!
AHH, WHY ...?
WHY MUST HIDDEN, SEALED-AWAY THINGS TUG AT MY HEART SO...!?
OOOH! BUT OF COURSE !!
ビッ
BI (JAB)
IT'S BECAUSE I AM A TRUE TREASURE HUNTER!!
?
NYAA (MROWW)
ニャー
OOF!
DO (SLAM)
NNN! ENOUGH PLAYIN' WITH MY PHONE!!
LET'S GO!!
WH... WHERE ...?
TO FIND YOUR BROTHER! WHERE ELSE!?

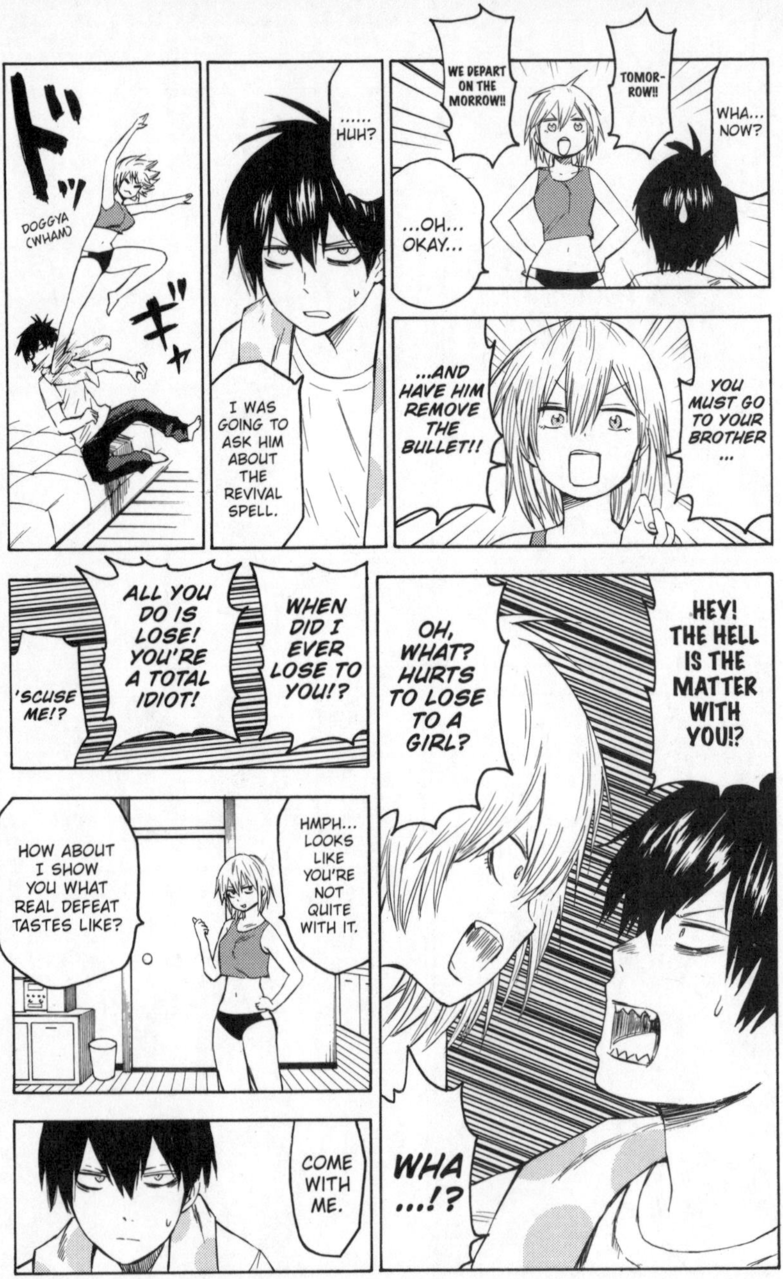
WE DEPART ON THE MORROW!!
TOMOR-ROW!!
WHA... NOW?
...OH... OKAY...
YOU MUST GO TO YOUR BROTHER ...
...AND HAVE HIM REMOVE THE BULLET!!
...... HUH?
I WAS GOING TO ASK HIM ABOUT THE REVIVAL SPELL.
ドッ
DOGGYA (WHAM)
ギャ
HEY! THE HELL IS THE MATTER WITH YOU!?
OH, WHAT? HURTS TO LOSE TO A GIRL?
WHA ...!?
WHEN DID I EVER LOSE TO YOU!?
ALL YOU DO IS LOSE! YOU'RE A TOTAL IDIOT!
'SCUSE ME!?
HMPH... LOOKS LIKE YOU'RE NOT QUITE WITH IT.
HOW ABOUT I SHOW YOU WHAT REAL DEFEAT TASTES LIKE?
COME WITH ME.

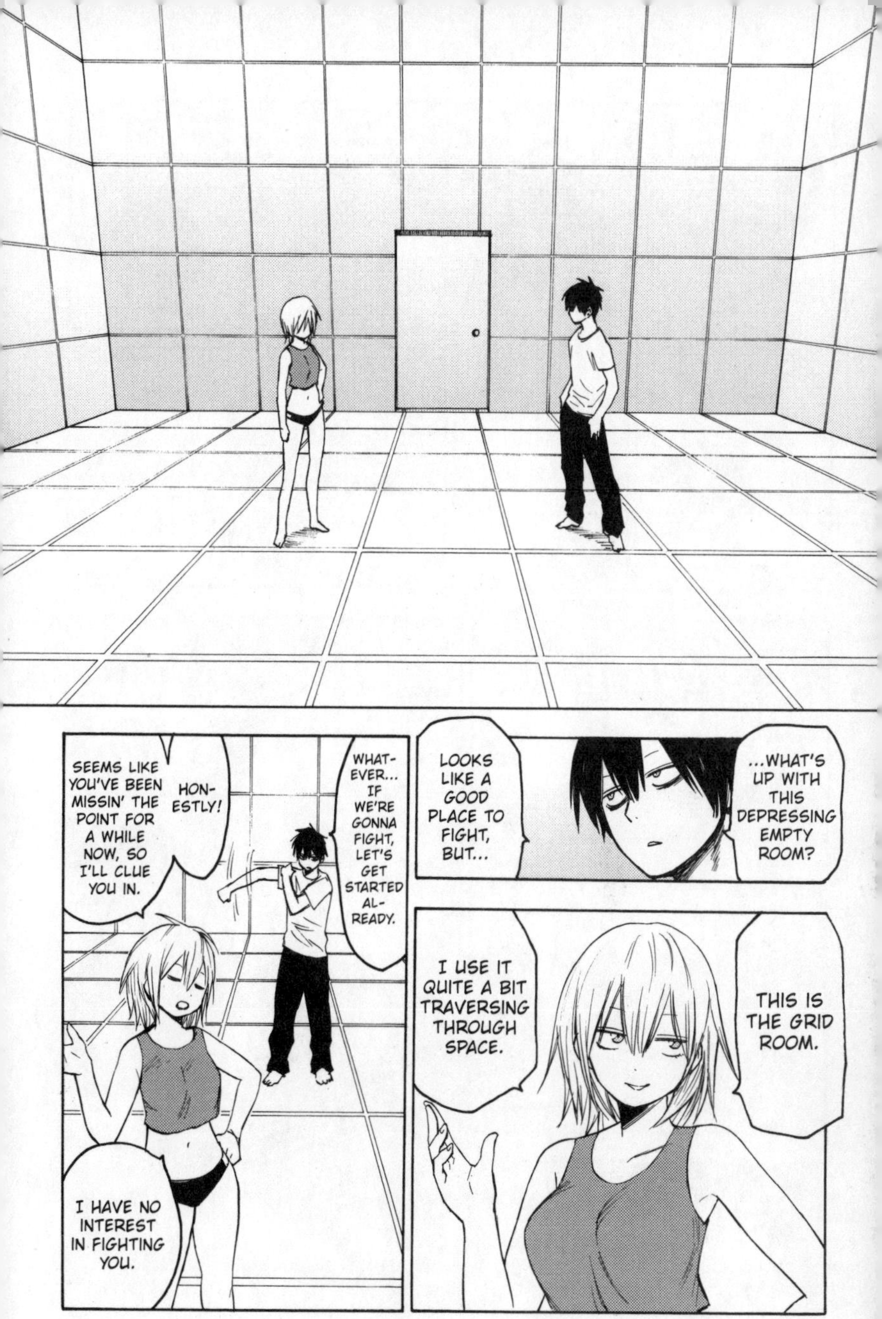
...WHAT'S UP WITH THIS DEPRESSING EMPTY ROOM?
LOOKS LIKE A GOOD PLACE TO FIGHT, BUT...
THIS IS THE GRID ROOM.
I USE IT QUITE A BIT TRAVERSING THROUGH SPACE.
WHAT-EVER... IF WE'RE GONNA FIGHT, LET'S GET STARTED AL-READY.
HON-ESTLY!
SEEMS LIKE YOU'VE BEEN MISSIN' THE POINT FOR A WHILE NOW, SO I'LL CLUE YOU IN.
I HAVE NO INTEREST IN FIGHTING YOU.

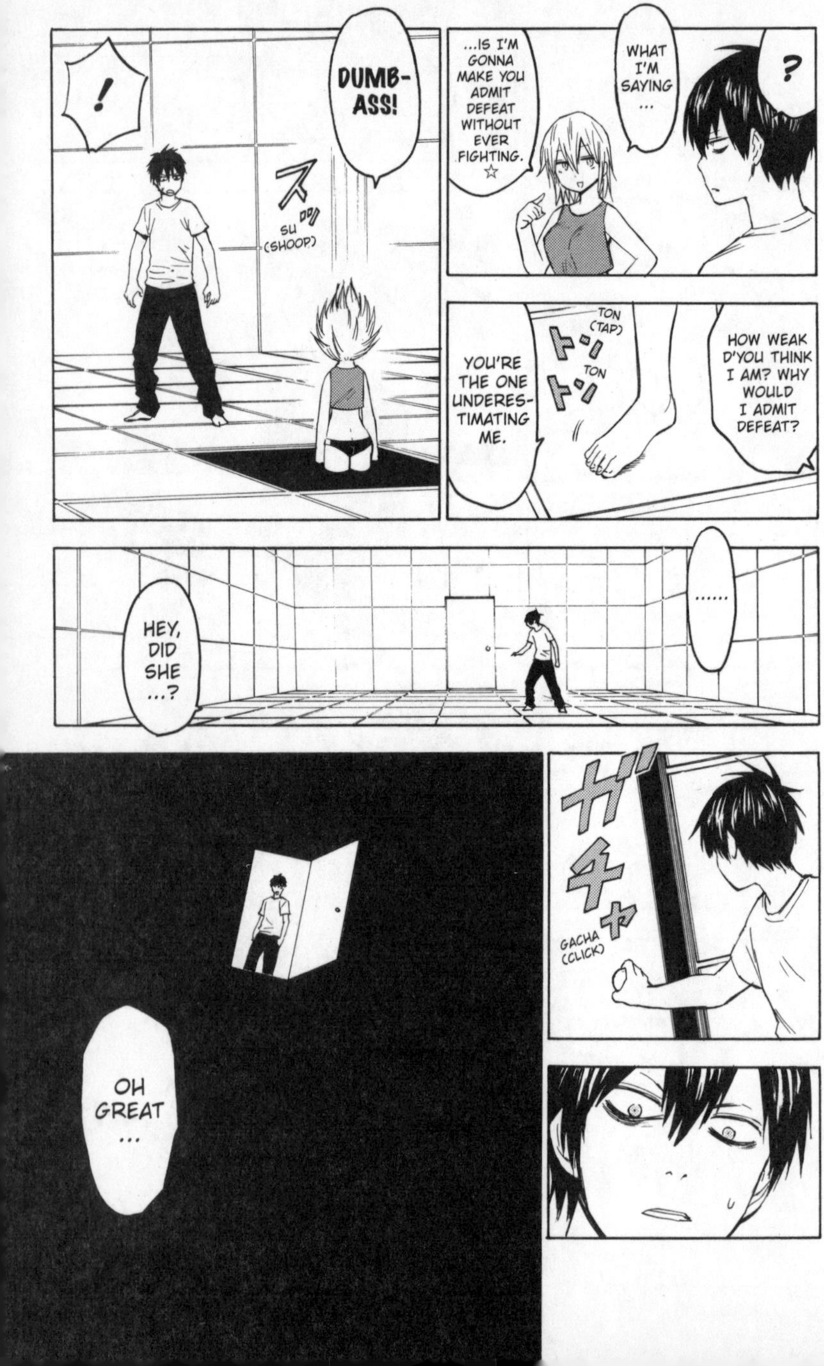
?
WHAT I'M SAYING ...
...IS I'M GONNA MAKE YOU ADMIT DEFEAT WITHOUT EVER FIGHTING. ☆
HOW WEAK D'YOU THINK I AM? WHY WOULD I ADMIT DEFEAT?
TON (TAP)
TON
YOU'RE THE ONE UNDERES-TIMATING ME.
DUMB-ASS!
SU (SHOOP)
!
......
HEY, DID SHE ...?
GACHA (CLICK)
OH GREAT ...

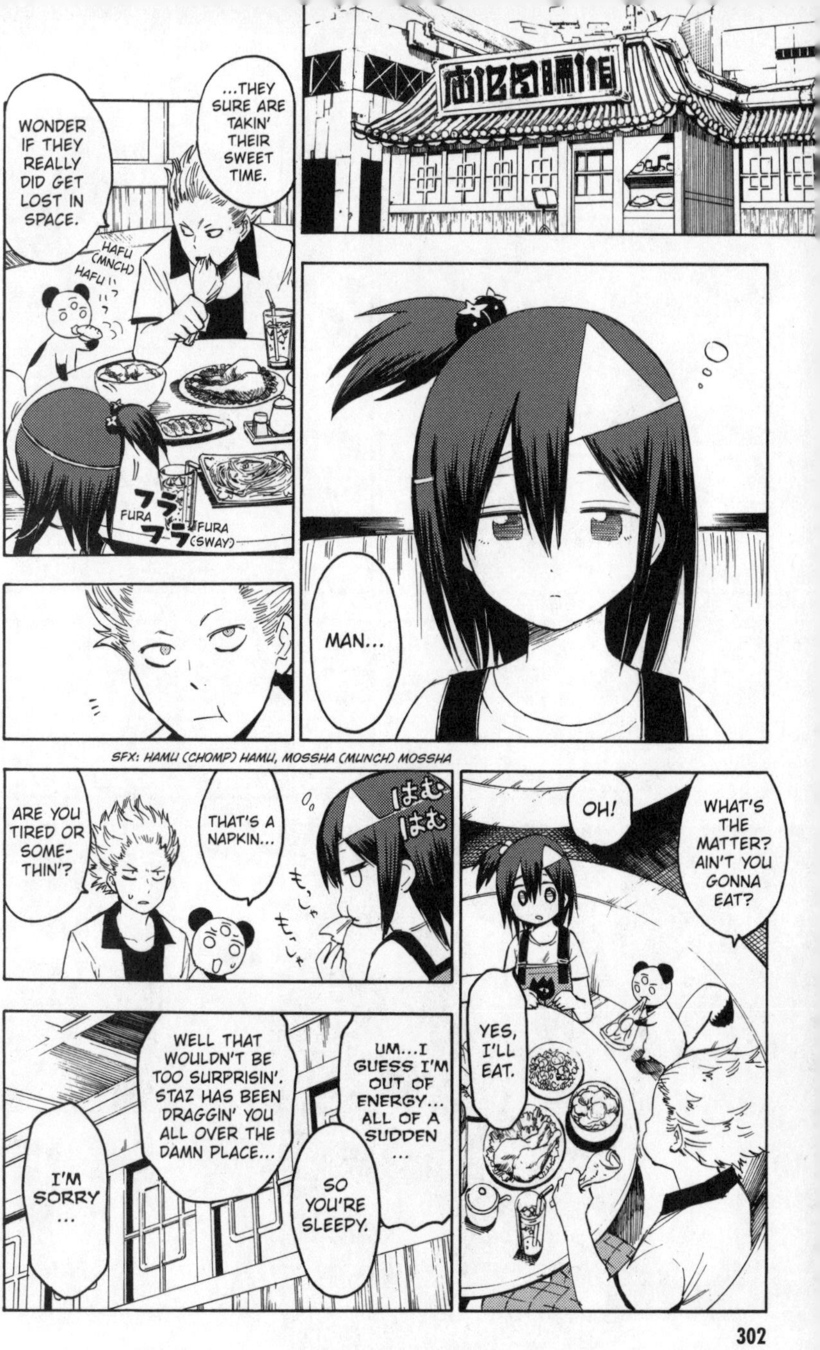
...THEY SURE ARE TAKIN' THEIR SWEET TIME.
WONDER IF THEY REALLY DID GET LOST IN SPACE.
HAFU (MNCH) HAFU
FURA FURA (SWAY)
MAN...
SFX: HAMU (CHOMP) HAMU, MOSSHA (MUNCH) MOSSHA
WHAT'S THE MATTER? AIN'T YOU GONNA EAT?
OH!
YES, I'LL EAT.
はむはむ
THAT'S A NAPKIN...
ARE YOU TIRED OR SOME-THIN'?
UM...I GUESS I'M OUT OF ENERGY... ALL OF A SUDDEN...
SO YOU'RE SLEEPY.
WELL THAT WOULDN'T BE TOO SURPRISIN'. STAZ HAS BEEN DRAGGIN' YOU ALL OVER THE DAMN PLACE...
I'M SORRY...

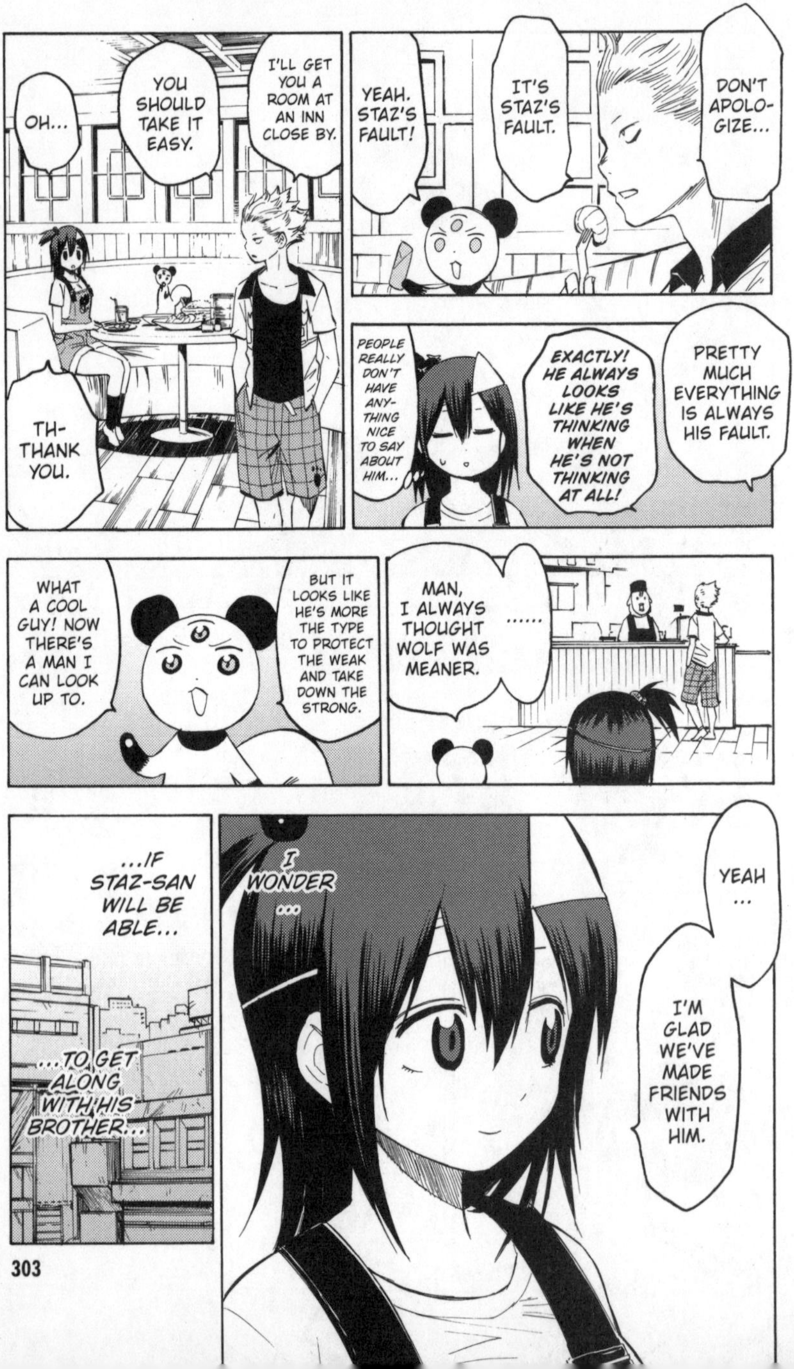
DON'T APOLOGIZE...
IT'S STAZ'S FAULT.
YEAH. STAZ'S FAULT!
PRETTY MUCH EVERYTHING IS ALWAYS HIS FAULT.
EXACTLY! HE ALWAYS LOOKS LIKE HE'S THINKING WHEN HE'S NOT THINKING AT ALL!
PEOPLE REALLY DON'T HAVE ANYTHING NICE TO SAY ABOUT HIM...
I'LL GET YOU A ROOM AT AN INN CLOSE BY.
YOU SHOULD TAKE IT EASY.
OH...
TH-THANK YOU.
......
MAN, I ALWAYS THOUGHT WOLF WAS MEANER.
BUT IT LOOKS LIKE HE'S MORE THE TYPE TO PROTECT THE WEAK AND TAKE DOWN THE STRONG.
WHAT A COOL GUY! NOW THERE'S A MAN I CAN LOOK UP TO.
YEAH...
I'M GLAD WE'VE MADE FRIENDS WITH HIM.
I WONDER...
...IF STAZ-SAN WILL BE ABLE...
...TO GET ALONG WITH HIS BROTHER...

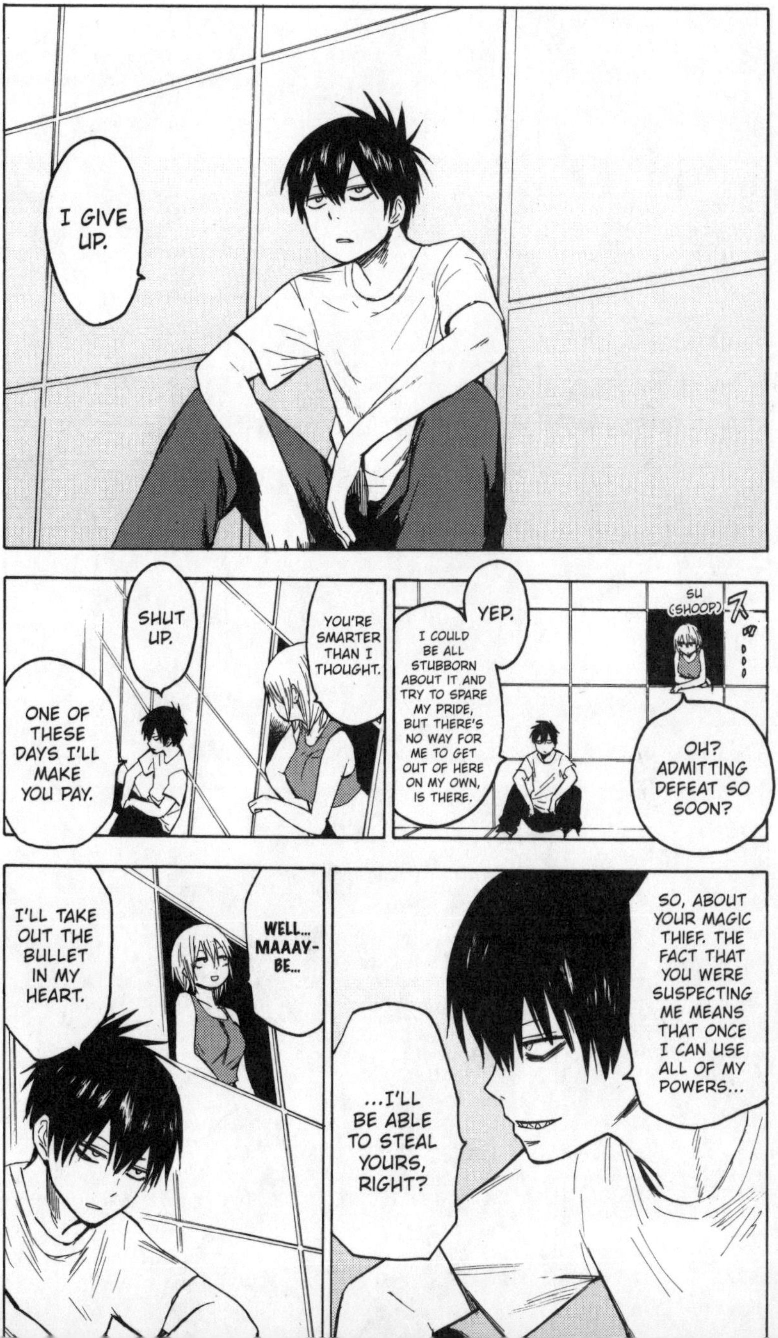
I GIVE UP.
SU (SHOOP)
ス
OH? ADMITTING DEFEAT SO SOON?
YEP.
I COULD BE ALL STUBBORN ABOUT IT AND TRY TO SPARE MY PRIDE, BUT THERE'S NO WAY FOR ME TO GET OUT OF HERE ON MY OWN, IS THERE.
YOU'RE SMARTER THAN I THOUGHT.
SHUT UP.
ONE OF THESE DAYS I'LL MAKE YOU PAY.
SO, ABOUT YOUR MAGIC THIEF. THE FACT THAT YOU WERE SUSPECTING ME MEANS THAT ONCE I CAN USE ALL OF MY POWERS...
...I'LL BE ABLE TO STEAL YOURS, RIGHT?
WELL... MAAAY-BE...
I'LL TAKE OUT THE BULLET IN MY HEART.

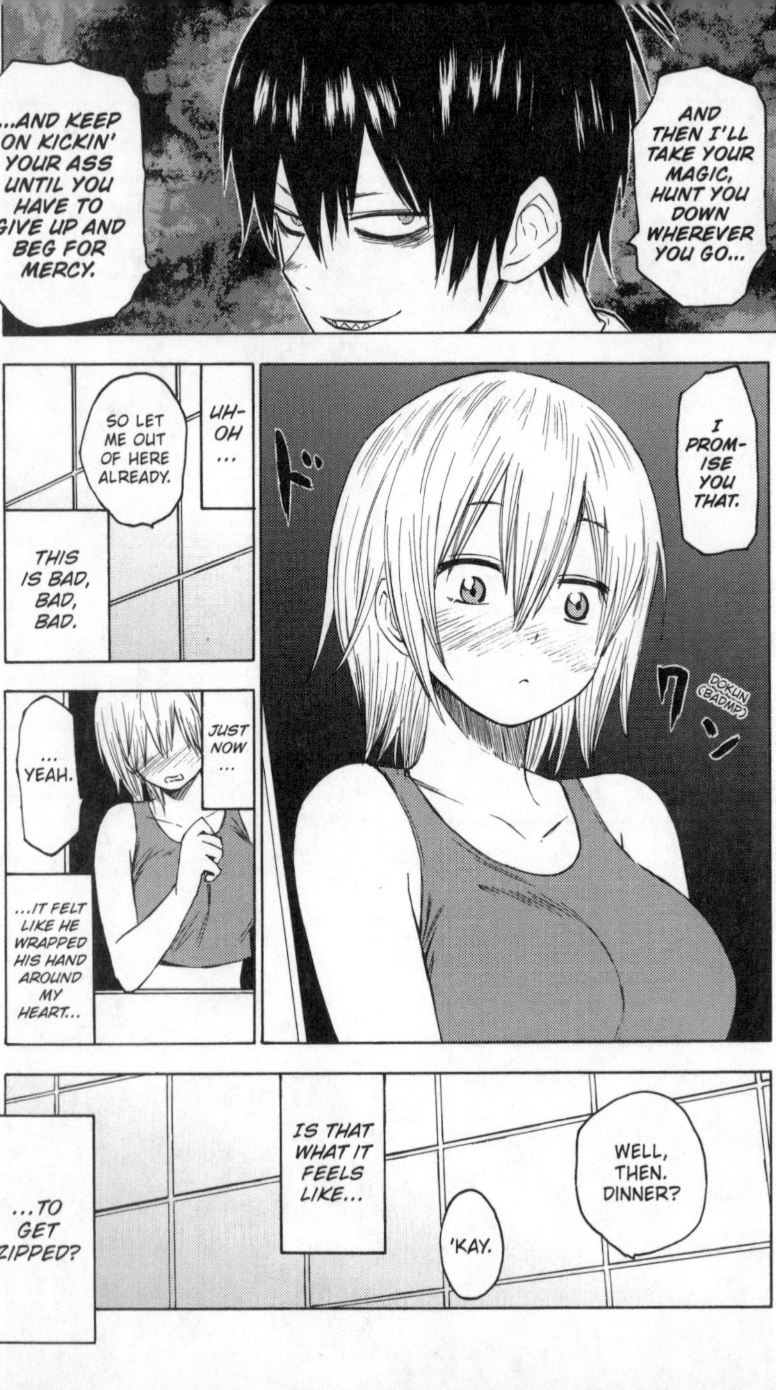
AND THEN I'LL TAKE YOUR MAGIC, HUNT YOU DOWN WHEREVER YOU GO...
...AND KEEP ON KICKIN' YOUR ASS UNTIL YOU HAVE TO GIVE UP AND BEG FOR MERCY.
I PROMISE YOU THAT.
DOKUN (BADMP)
UH-OH...
SO LET ME OUT OF HERE ALREADY.
THIS IS BAD, BAD, BAD.
JUST NOW...
...YEAH.
...IT FELT LIKE HE WRAPPED HIS HAND AROUND MY HEART...
WELL, THEN. DINNER?
'KAY.
IS THAT WHAT IT FEELS LIKE...
...TO GET ZIPPED?

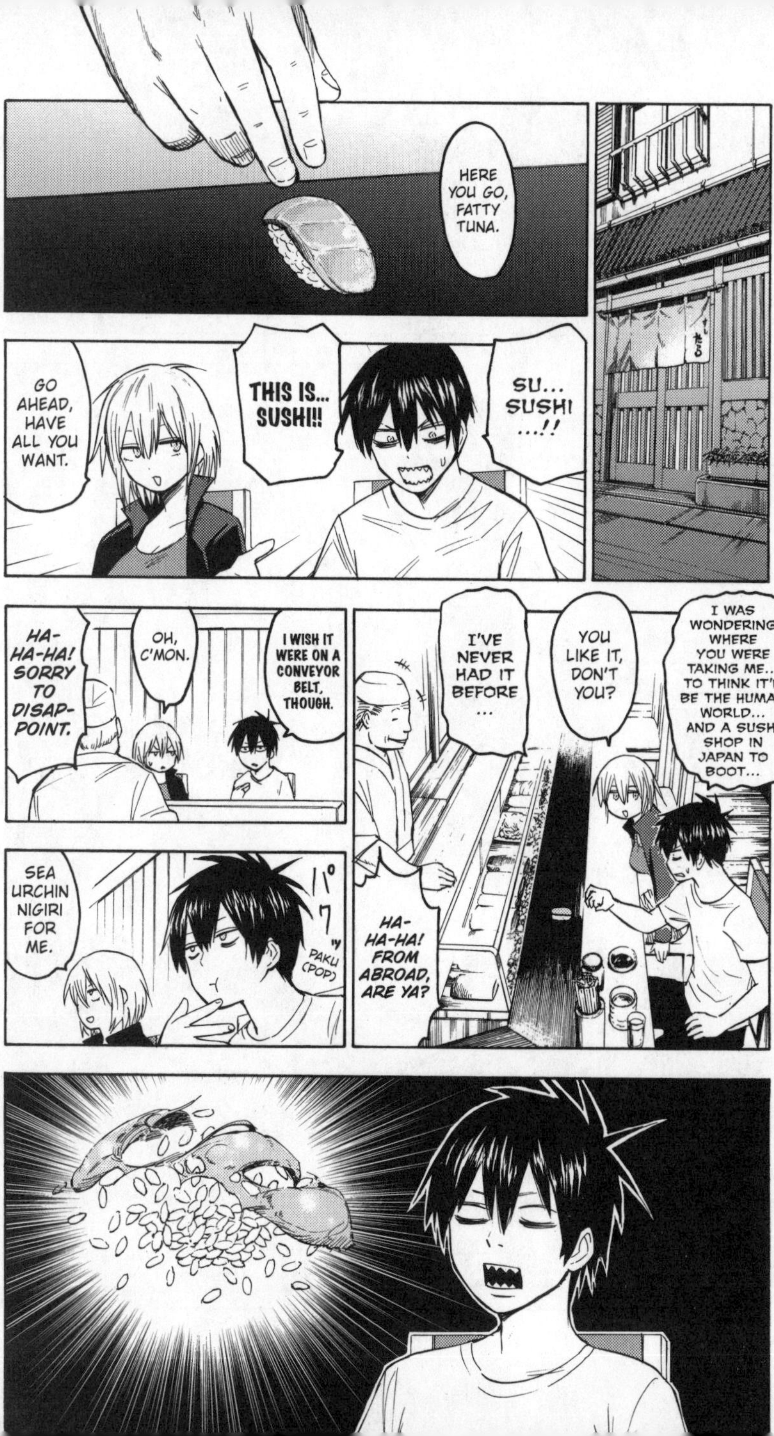
HERE YOU GO, FATTY TUNA.
SU... SUSHI ...!!
THIS IS... SUSHI!!
GO AHEAD, HAVE ALL YOU WANT.
I WAS WONDERING WHERE YOU WERE TAKING ME... TO THINK IT'D BE THE HUMAN WORLD... AND A SUSHI SHOP IN JAPAN TO BOOT...
YOU LIKE IT, DON'T YOU?
I'VE NEVER HAD IT BEFORE ...
HA-HA-HA! FROM ABROAD, ARE YA?
I WISH IT WERE ON A CONVEYOR BELT, THOUGH.
OH, C'MON.
HA-HA-HA! SORRY TO DISAPPOINT.
パク
PAKU (POP)
SEA URCHIN NIGIRI FOR ME.

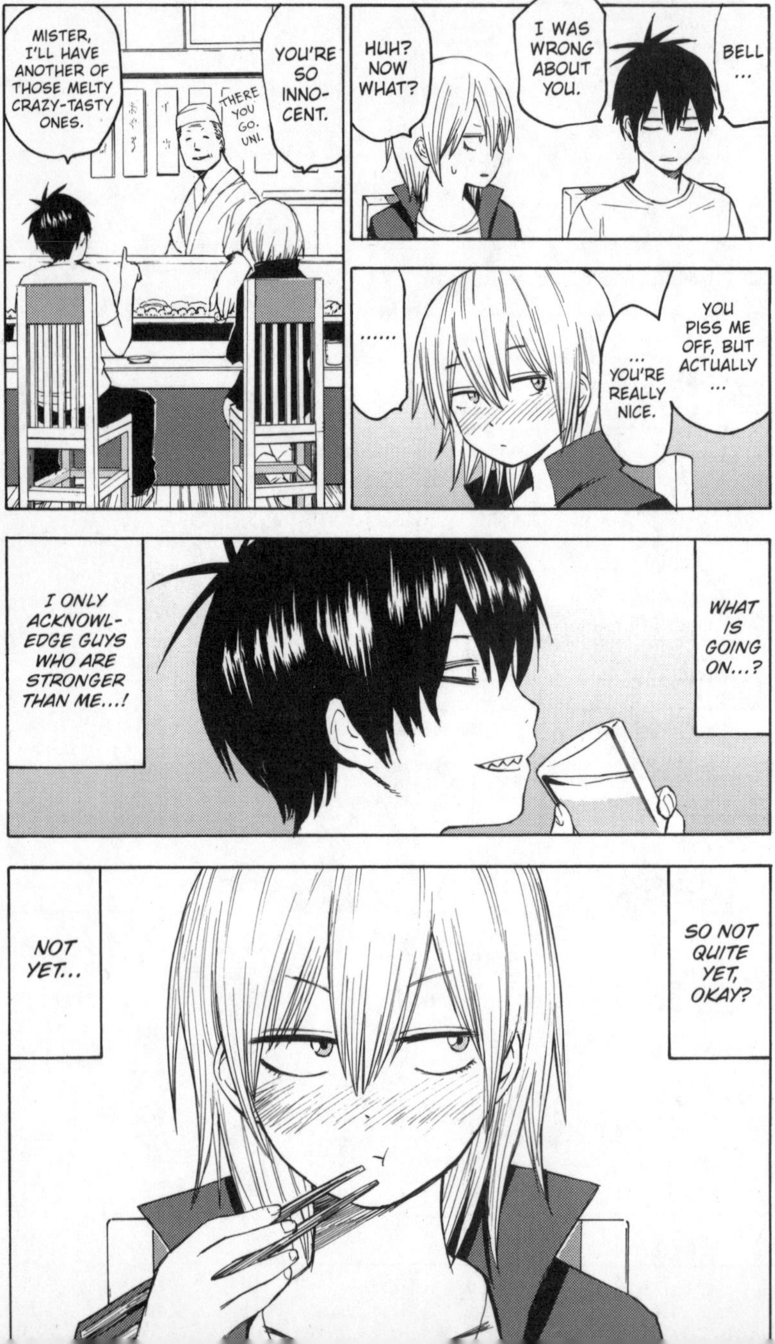
BELL ...
I WAS WRONG ABOUT YOU.
HUH? NOW WHAT?
YOU PISS ME OFF, BUT ACTUALLY ...
... YOU'RE REALLY NICE.
......
YOU'RE SO INNOCENT.
THERE YOU GO. UNI.
MISTER, I'LL HAVE ANOTHER OF THOSE MELTY CRAZY-TASTY ONES.
WHAT IS GOING ON...?
I ONLY ACKNOWL-EDGE GUYS WHO ARE STRONGER THAN ME...!
SO NOT QUITE YET, OKAY?
NOT YET...

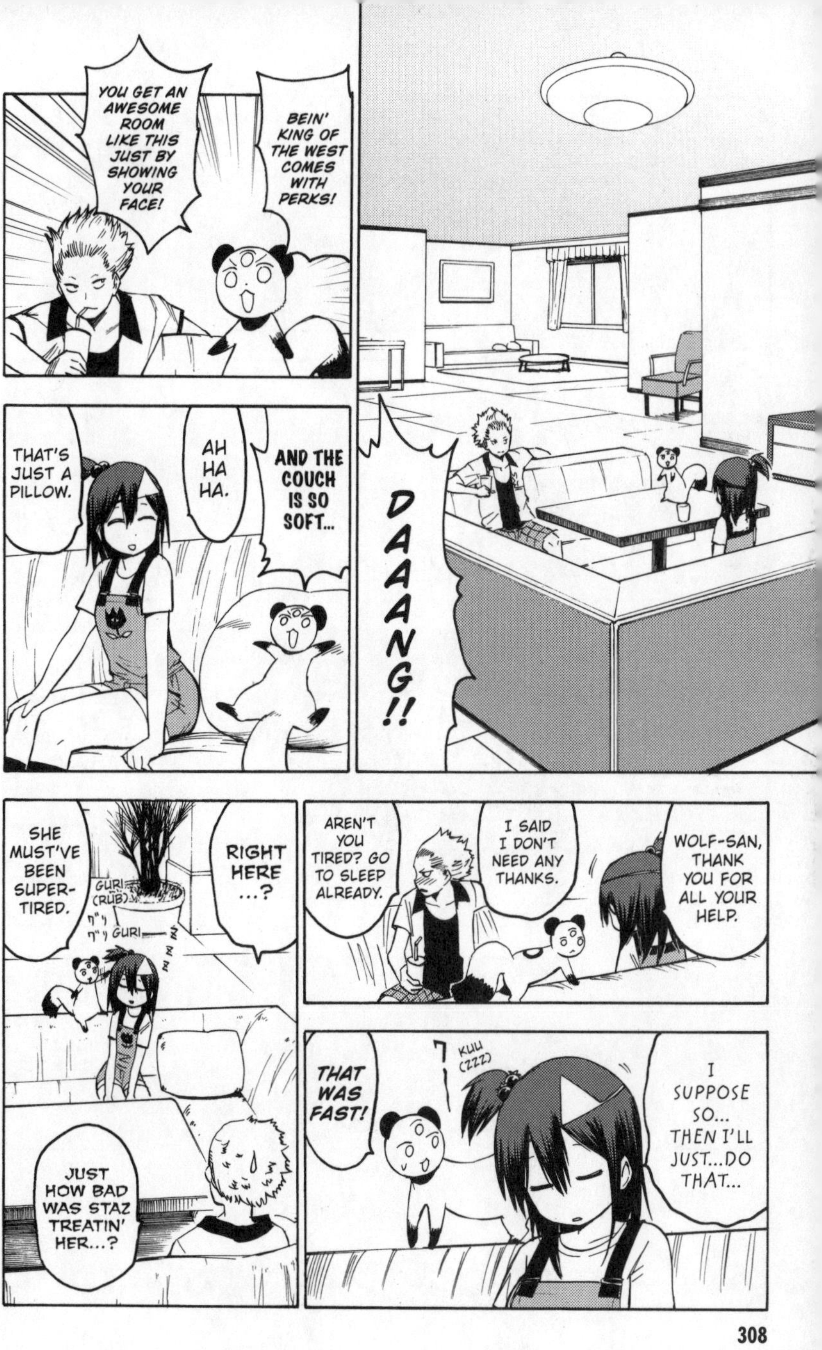
DAAAANG!!
BEIN' KING OF THE WEST COMES WITH PERKS!
YOU GET AN AWESOME ROOM LIKE THIS JUST BY SHOWING YOUR FACE!
AND THE COUCH IS SO SOFT...
AH HA HA.
THAT'S JUST A PILLOW.
WOLF-SAN, THANK YOU FOR ALL YOUR HELP.
I SAID I DON'T NEED ANY THANKS.
AREN'T YOU TIRED? GO TO SLEEP ALREADY.
I SUPPOSE SO... THEN I'LL JUST...DO THAT...
KUU (ZZZ)
THAT WAS FAST!
RIGHT HERE ...?
GURI (RUB)
グリ グリ GURI—
SHE MUST'VE BEEN SUPER-TIRED.
JUST HOW BAD WAS STAZ TREATIN' HER...?

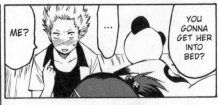

YOU GONNA GET HER INTO BED?
...
ME?
I CAN'T PICK HER UP, CAN I?
W-WELL, I GUESS NOT...
OOF.
SOMETHIN'... SURE DOES...
...FEEL NICE AGAINST MY BACK, THERE.
...BUT SHE'S LIGHTER THAN SHE LOOKS...
HUH?
WHAT?
WH... WHAT'S HAP-PENING...
...FUYUMI'S FEET ARE...

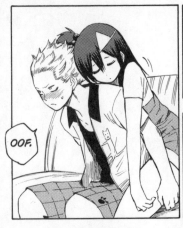

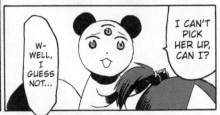

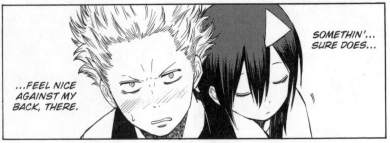

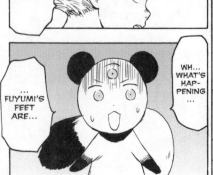

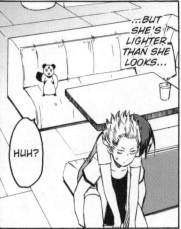

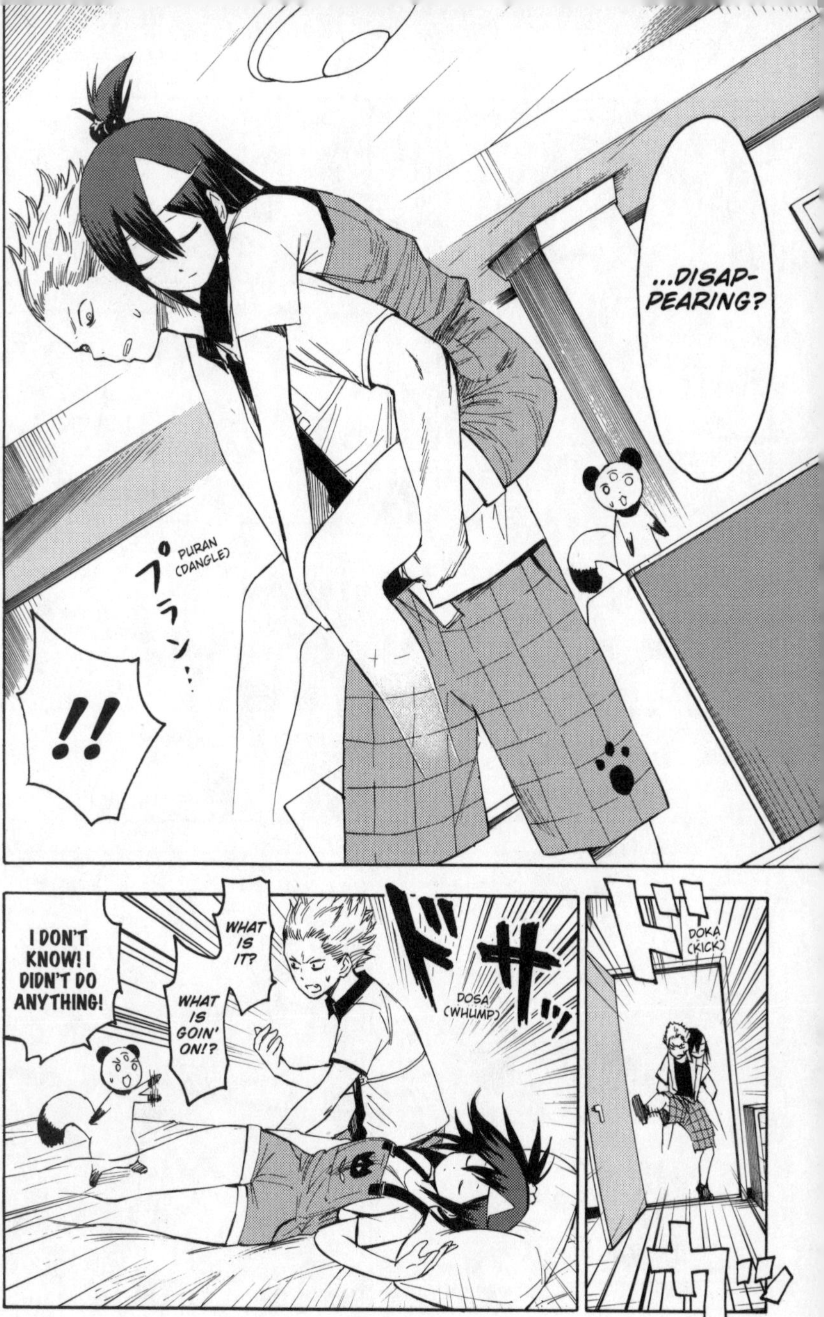

...DISAP-PEARING?
PURAN (DANGLE)
プラン..
!!
DOKA (KICK)
DOSA (WHUMP)
WHAT IS IT?
WHAT IS GOIN' ON!?
I DON'T KNOW! I DIDN'T DO ANYTHING!

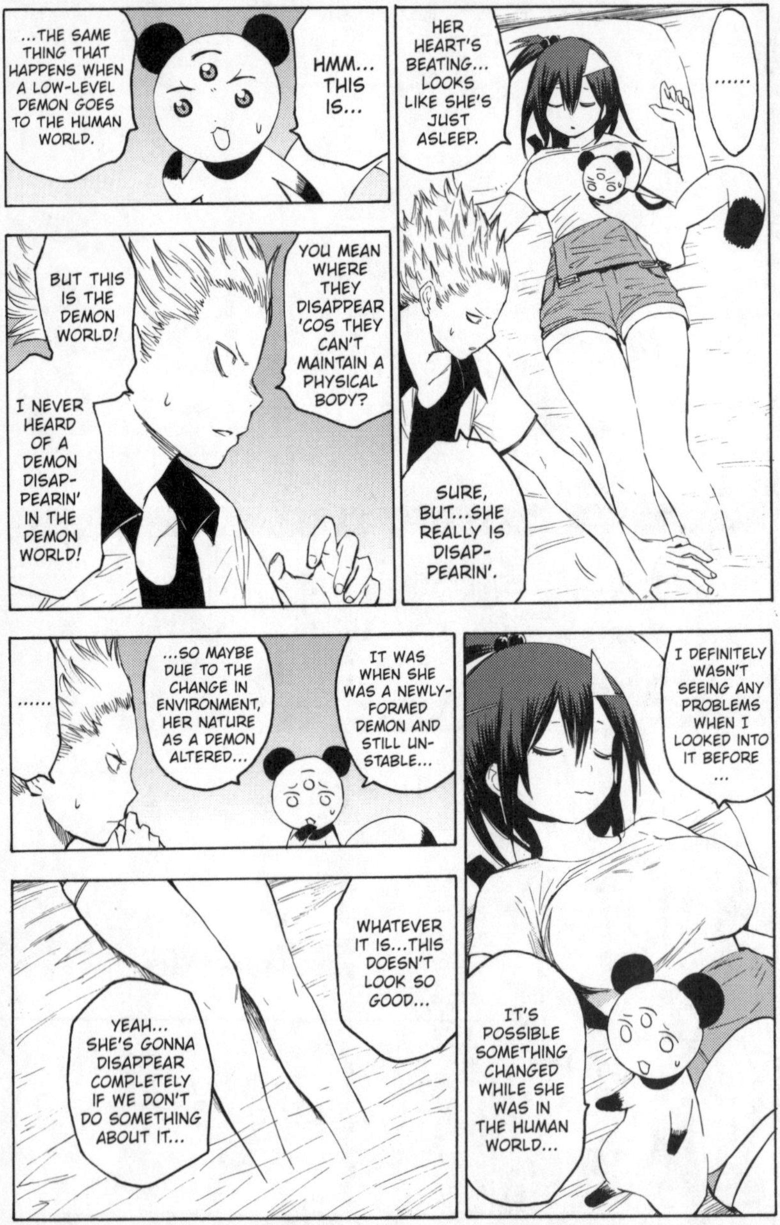
......
HER HEART'S BEATING... LOOKS LIKE SHE'S JUST ASLEEP.
SURE, BUT...SHE REALLY IS DISAP-PEARIN'.
HMM... THIS IS...
...THE SAME THING THAT HAPPENS WHEN A LOW-LEVEL DEMON GOES TO THE HUMAN WORLD.
YOU MEAN WHERE THEY DISAPPEAR 'COS THEY CAN'T MAINTAIN A PHYSICAL BODY?
BUT THIS IS THE DEMON WORLD!
I NEVER HEARD OF A DEMON DISAP-PEARIN' IN THE DEMON WORLD!
I DEFINITELY WASN'T SEEING ANY PROBLEMS WHEN I LOOKED INTO IT BEFORE ...
IT'S POSSIBLE SOMETHING CHANGED WHILE SHE WAS IN THE HUMAN WORLD...
IT WAS WHEN SHE WAS A NEWLY-FORMED DEMON AND STILL UN-STABLE...
...SO MAYBE DUE TO THE CHANGE IN ENVIRONMENT, HER NATURE AS A DEMON ALTERED...
......
WHATEVER IT IS...THIS DOESN'T LOOK SO GOOD...
YEAH... SHE'S GONNA DISAPPEAR COMPLETELY IF WE DON'T DO SOMETHING ABOUT IT...

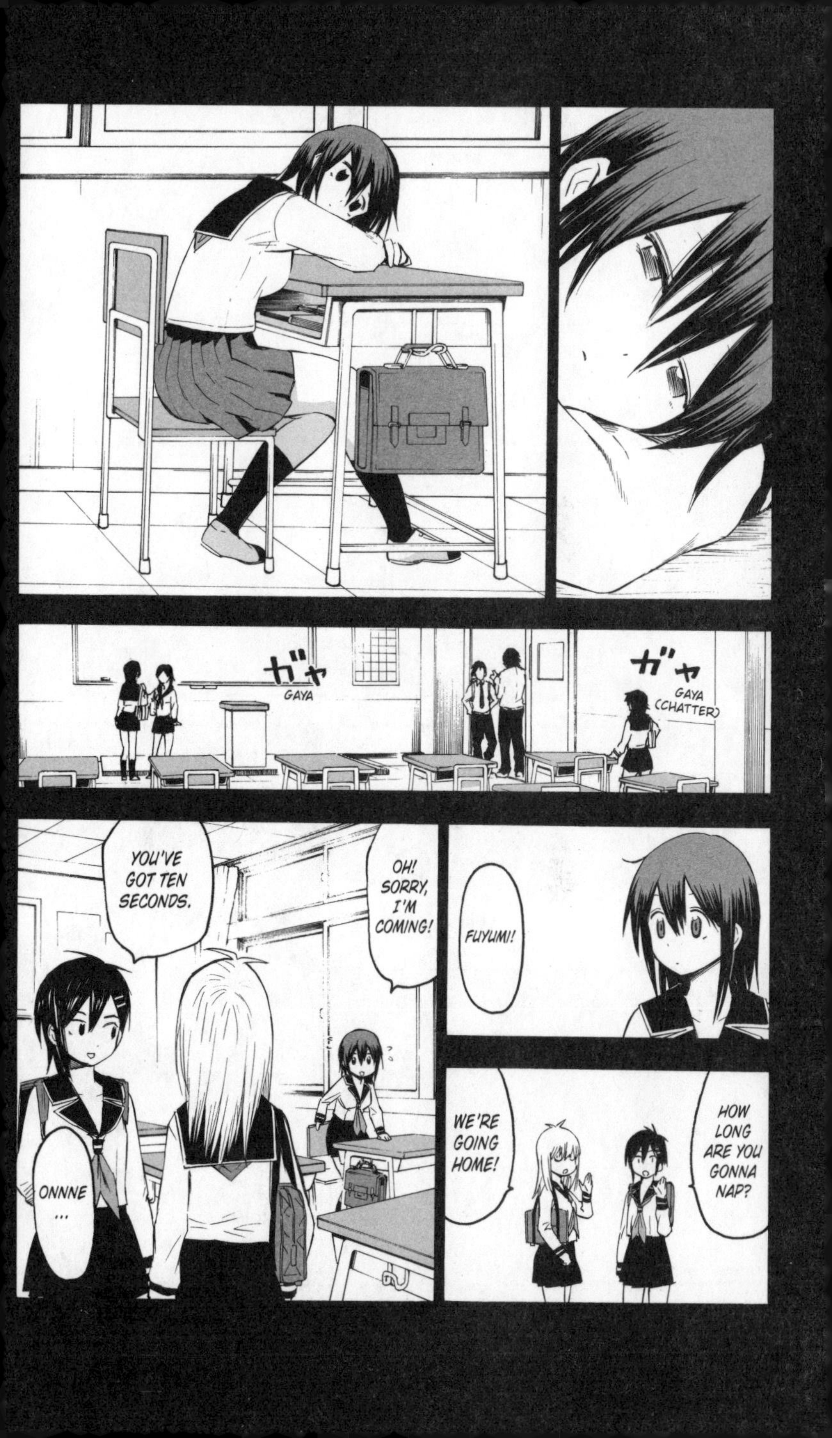
ガヤ
GAYA (CHATTER)
ガヤ
GAYA
FUYUMI!
HOW LONG ARE YOU GONNA NAP?
WE'RE GOING HOME!
OH! SORRY, I'M COMING!
YOU'VE GOT TEN SECONDS.
ONNNE ...

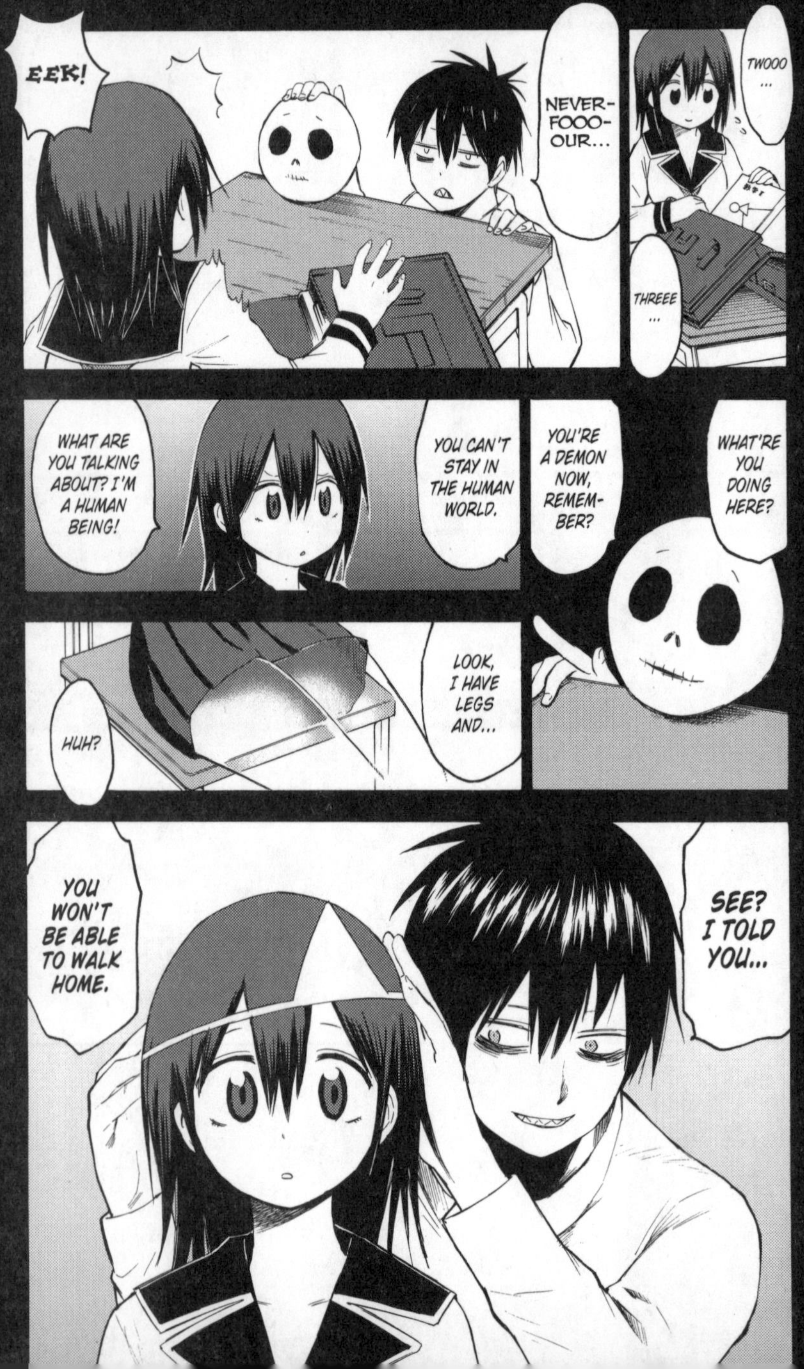
TWOOO ...
THREEE ...
NEVER-FOOO-OUR...
EEK!
WHAT'RE YOU DOING HERE?
YOU'RE A DEMON NOW, REMEMBER?
YOU CAN'T STAY IN THE HUMAN WORLD.
WHAT ARE YOU TALKING ABOUT? I'M A HUMAN BEING!
LOOK, I HAVE LEGS AND...
HUH?
SEE? I TOLD YOU...
YOU WON'T BE ABLE TO WALK HOME.

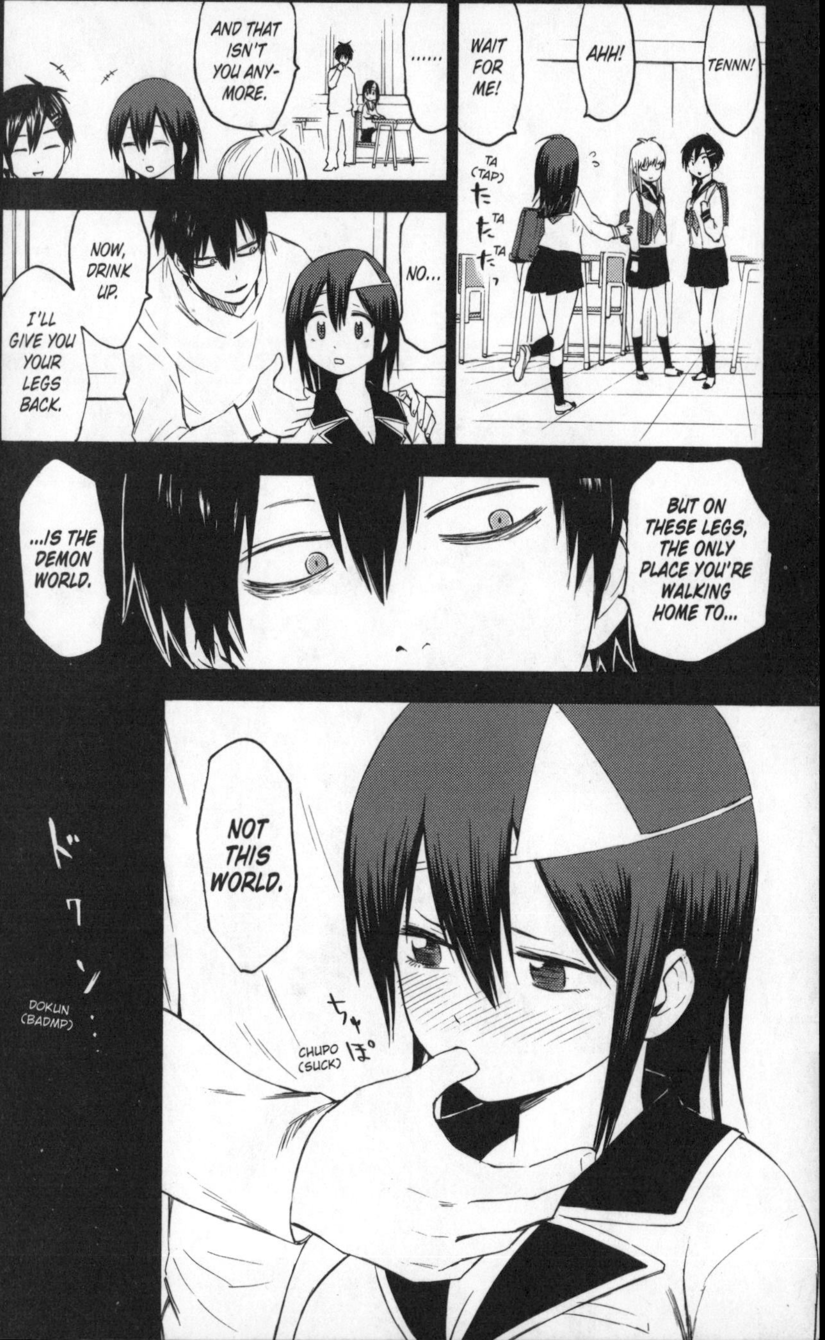
TENNN!
AHH!
WAIT FOR ME!
TA (TAP) た TA た TA た っ
......
AND THAT ISN'T YOU ANY-MORE.
NO...
NOW, DRINK UP.
I'LL GIVE YOU YOUR LEGS BACK.
BUT ON THESE LEGS, THE ONLY PLACE YOU'RE WALKING HOME TO...
...IS THE DEMON WORLD.
ちゅぽ
CHUPO (SUCK)
NOT THIS WORLD.
ドクン
DOKUN (BADMP)

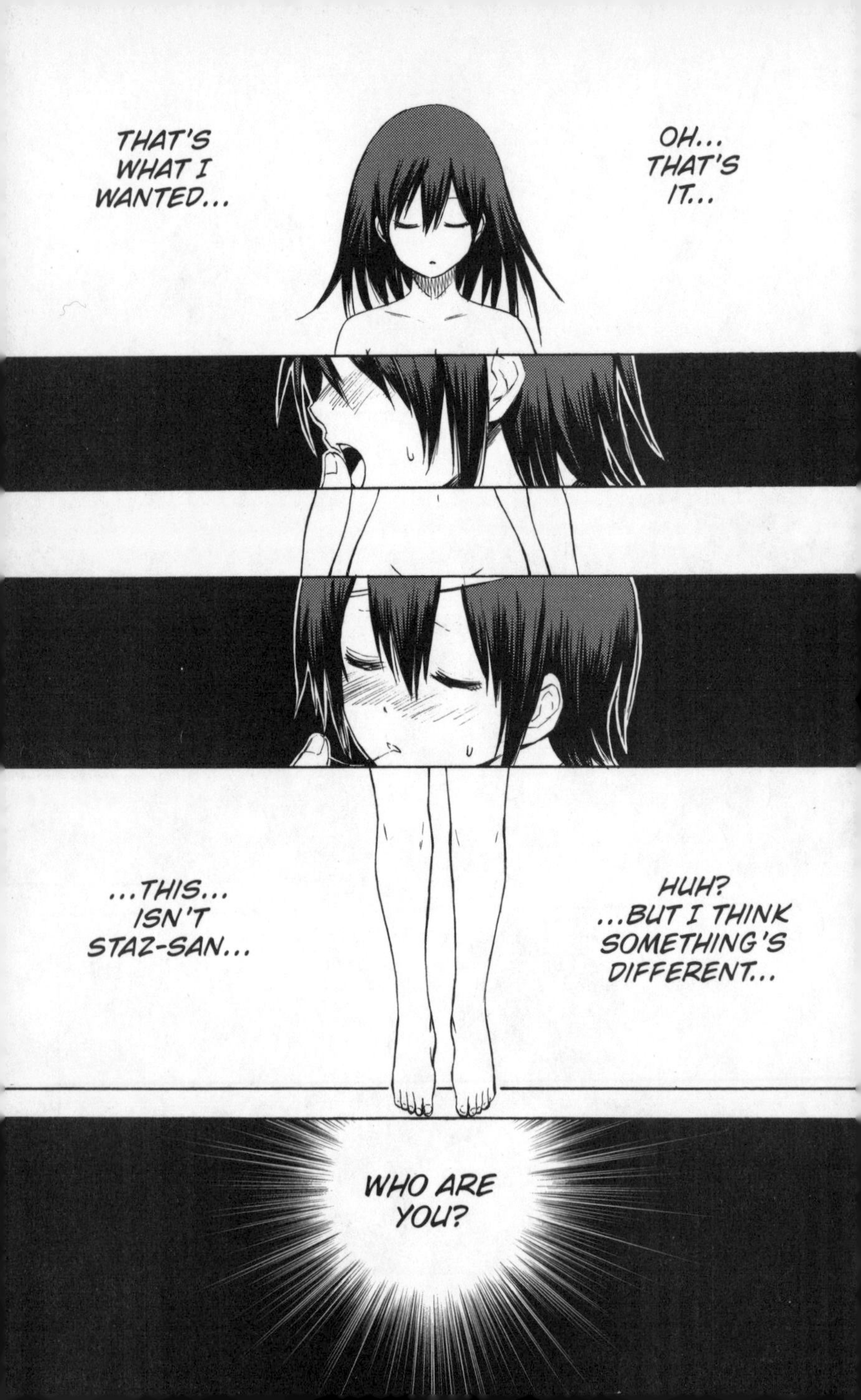
OH... THAT'S IT...
THAT'S WHAT I WANTED...
HUH? ...BUT I THINK SOMETHING'S DIFFERENT...
...THIS... ISN'T STAZ-SAN...
WHO ARE YOU?

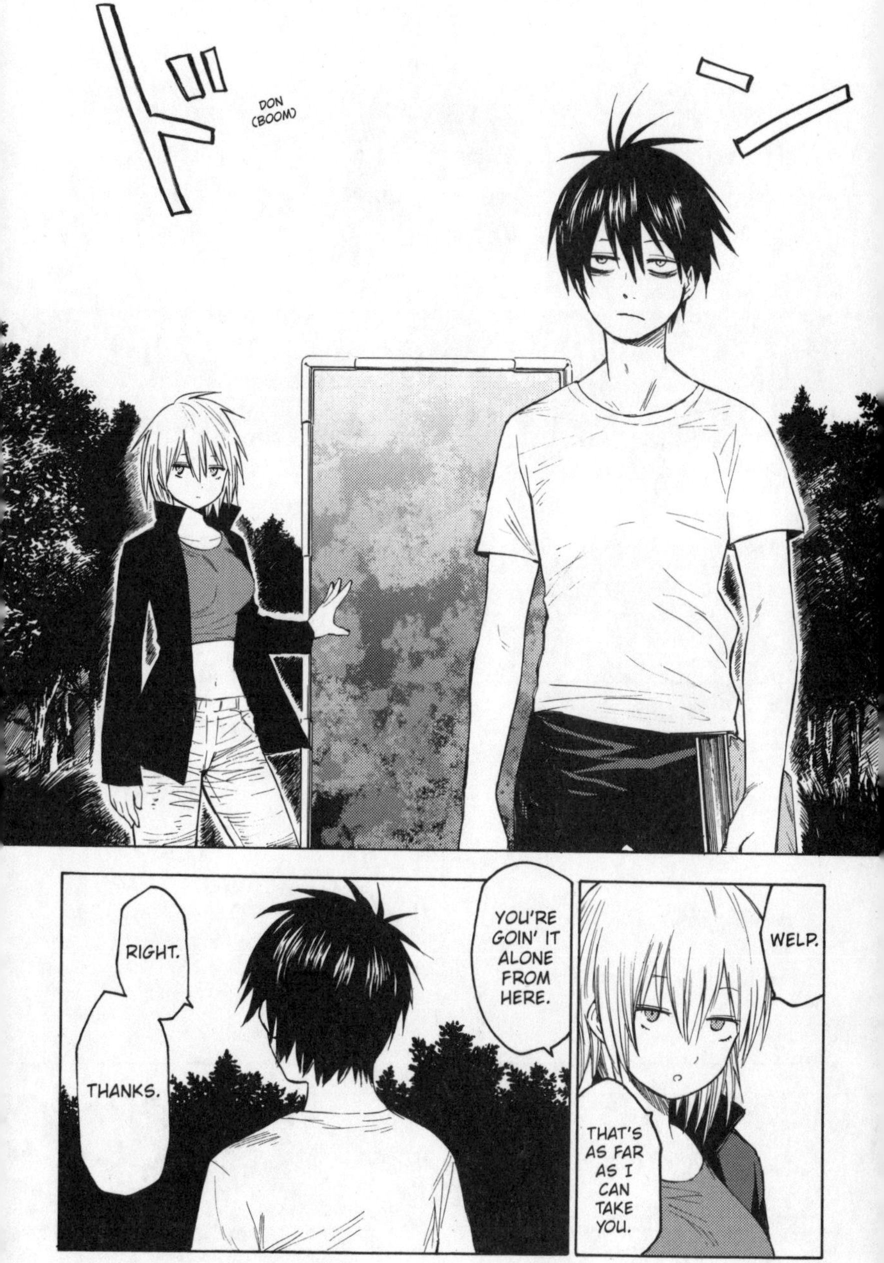
DON (BOOM)
WELP.
THAT'S AS FAR AS I CAN TAKE YOU.
YOU'RE GOIN' IT ALONE FROM HERE.
RIGHT.
THANKS.

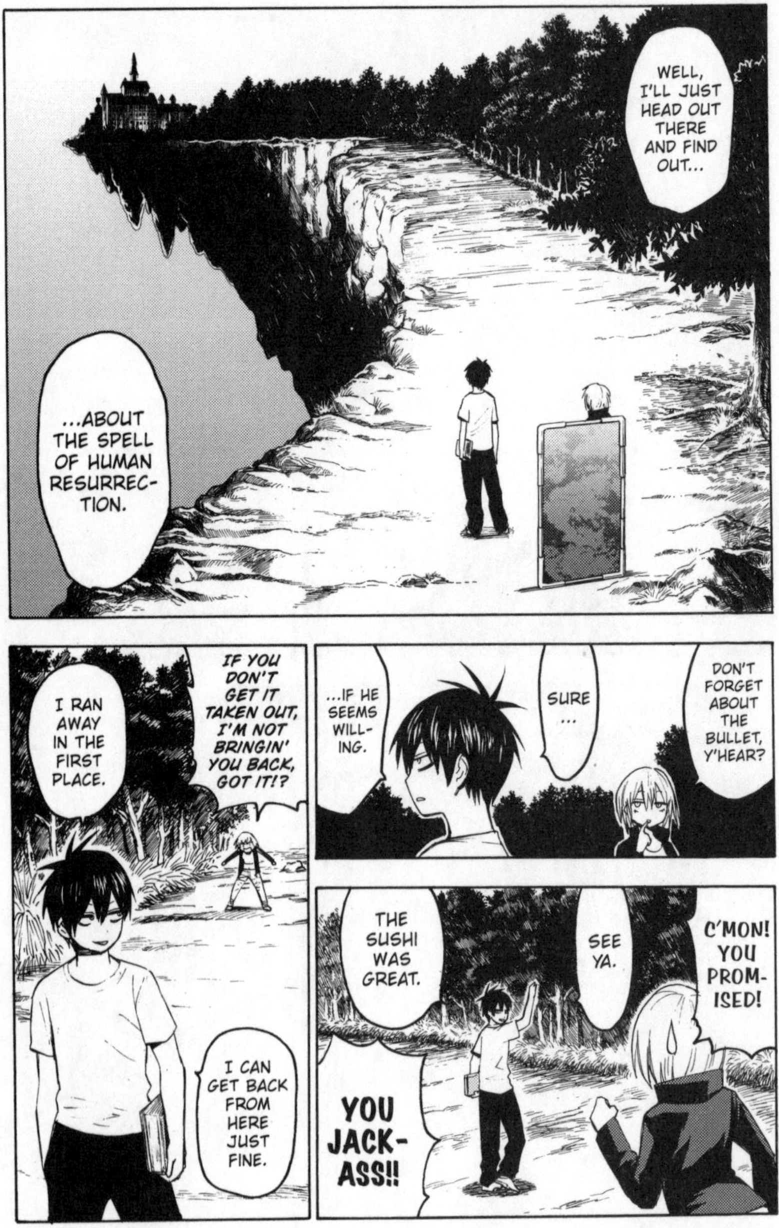
WELL, I'LL JUST HEAD OUT THERE AND FIND OUT...
...ABOUT THE SPELL OF HUMAN RESURREC-TION.
DON'T FORGET ABOUT THE BULLET, Y'HEAR?
SURE...
...IF HE SEEMS WILL-ING.
C'MON! YOU PROM-ISED!
SEE YA.
THE SUSHI WAS GREAT.
YOU JACK-ASS!!
IF YOU DON'T GET IT TAKEN OUT, I'M NOT BRINGIN' YOU BACK, GOT IT!?
I RAN AWAY IN THE FIRST PLACE.
I CAN GET BACK FROM HERE JUST FINE.

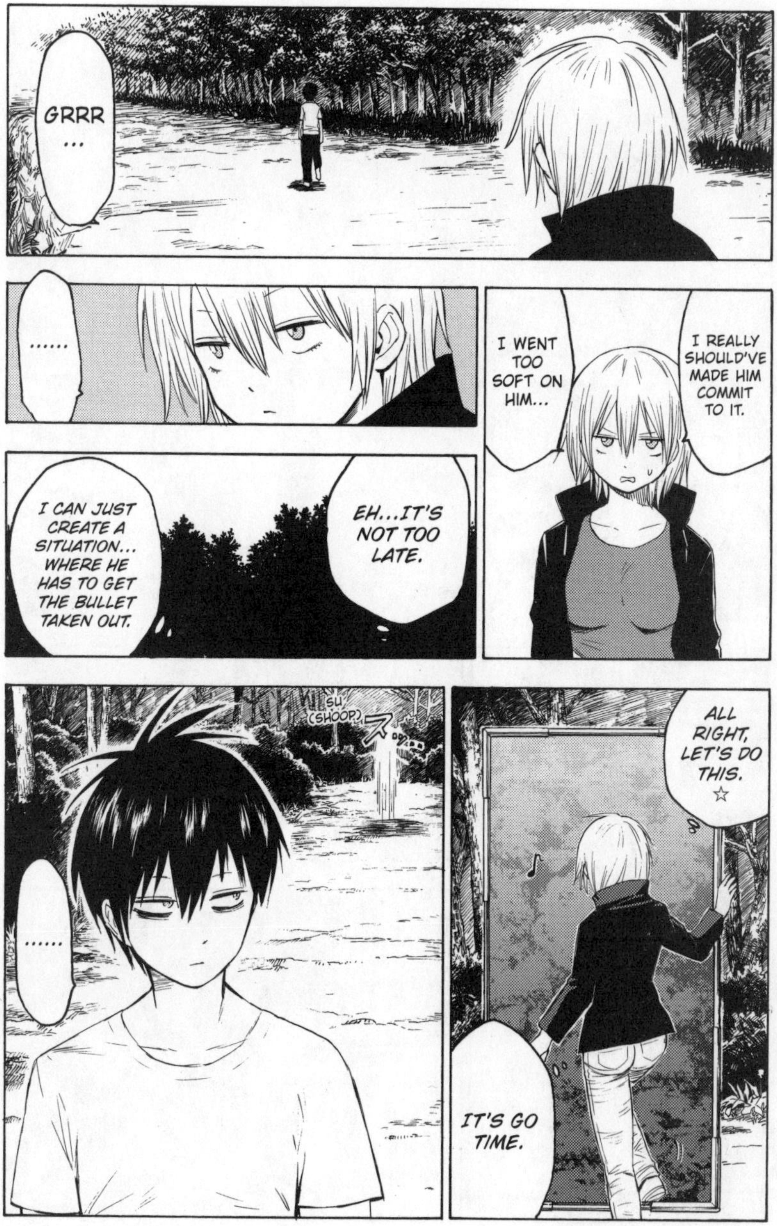
GRRR ...
I REALLY SHOULD'VE MADE HIM COMMIT TO IT.
I WENT TOO SOFT ON HIM...
......
EH...IT'S NOT TOO LATE.
I CAN JUST CREATE A SITUATION... WHERE HE HAS TO GET THE BULLET TAKEN OUT.
ALL RIGHT, LET'S DO THIS. ☆
IT'S GO TIME.
SU (SHOOP)
......

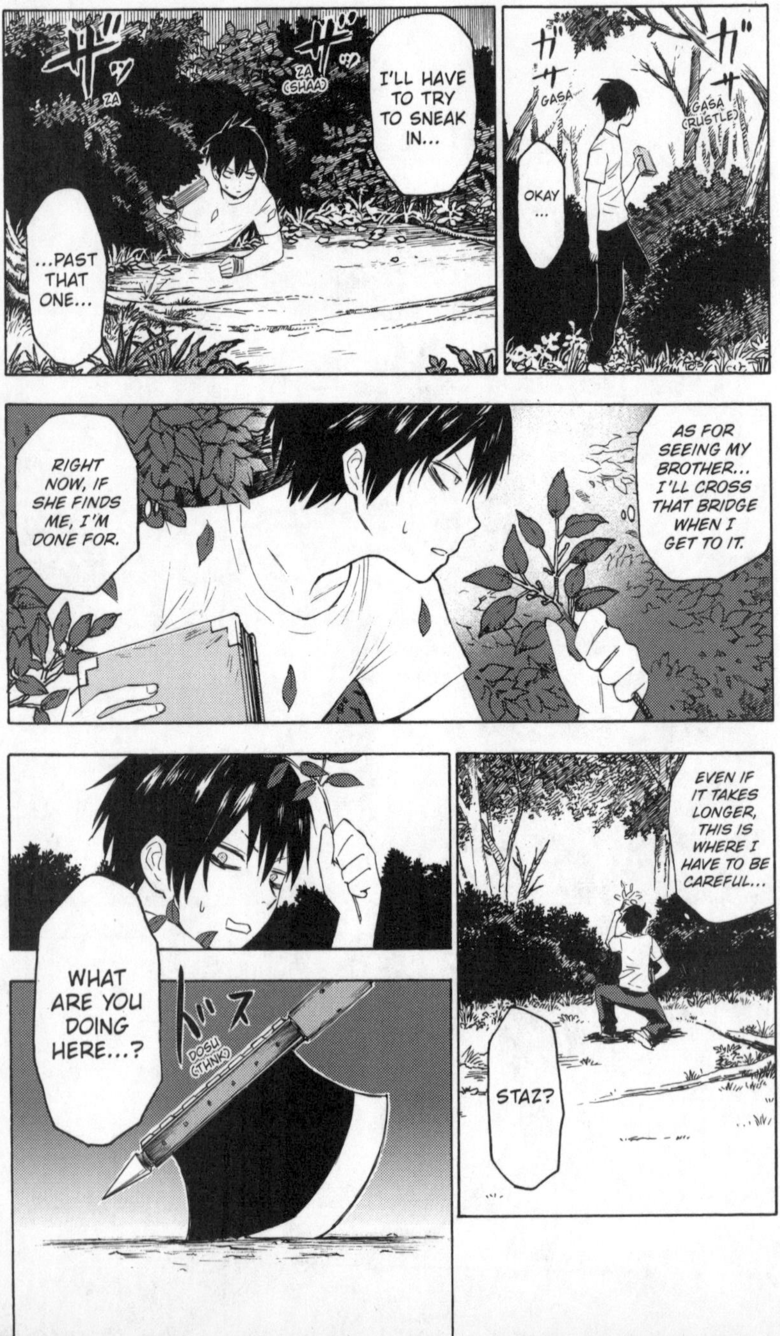
GASA
GASA (RUSTLE)
OKAY...
I'LL HAVE TO TRY TO SNEAK IN...
ZA (SHAA)
ZA
...PAST THAT ONE...
AS FOR SEEING MY BROTHER... I'LL CROSS THAT BRIDGE WHEN I GET TO IT.
RIGHT NOW, IF SHE FINDS ME, I'M DONE FOR.
EVEN IF IT TAKES LONGER, THIS IS WHERE I HAVE TO BE CAREFUL...
STAZ?
WHAT ARE YOU DOING HERE...?
DOSU (THNK)

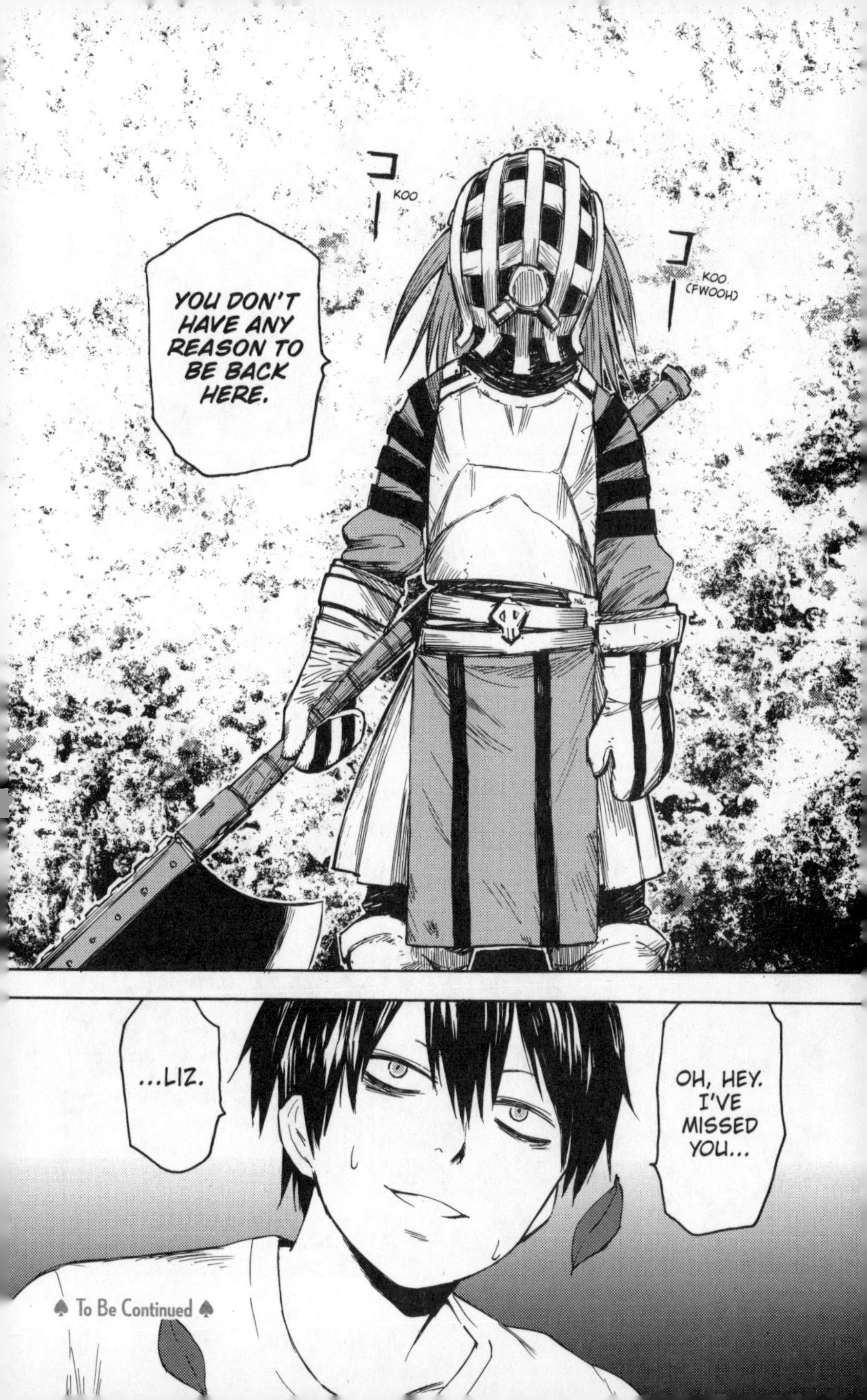
KOO
KOO (FWOOH)
YOU DON'T HAVE ANY REASON TO BE BACK HERE.
OH, HEY. I'VE MISSED YOU...
...LIZ.
To Be Continued

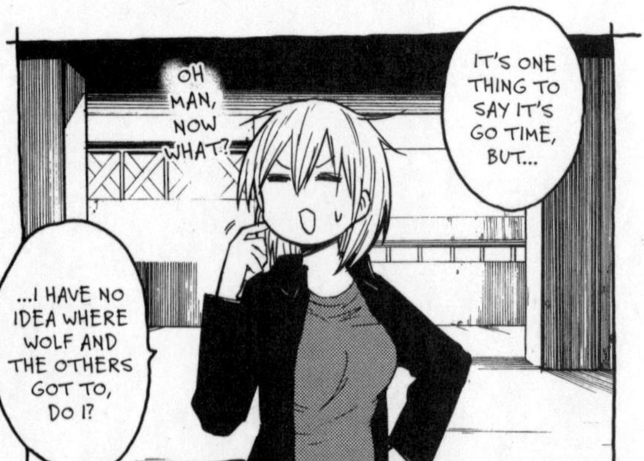
IT'S ONE THING TO SAY IT'S GO TIME, BUT...
OH MAN, NOW WHAT?
...I HAVE NO IDEA WHERE WOLF AND THE OTHERS GOT TO, DO I?

BLOOD LAD

# CHAPTER 10 ♠ FUYUMI INSIDE

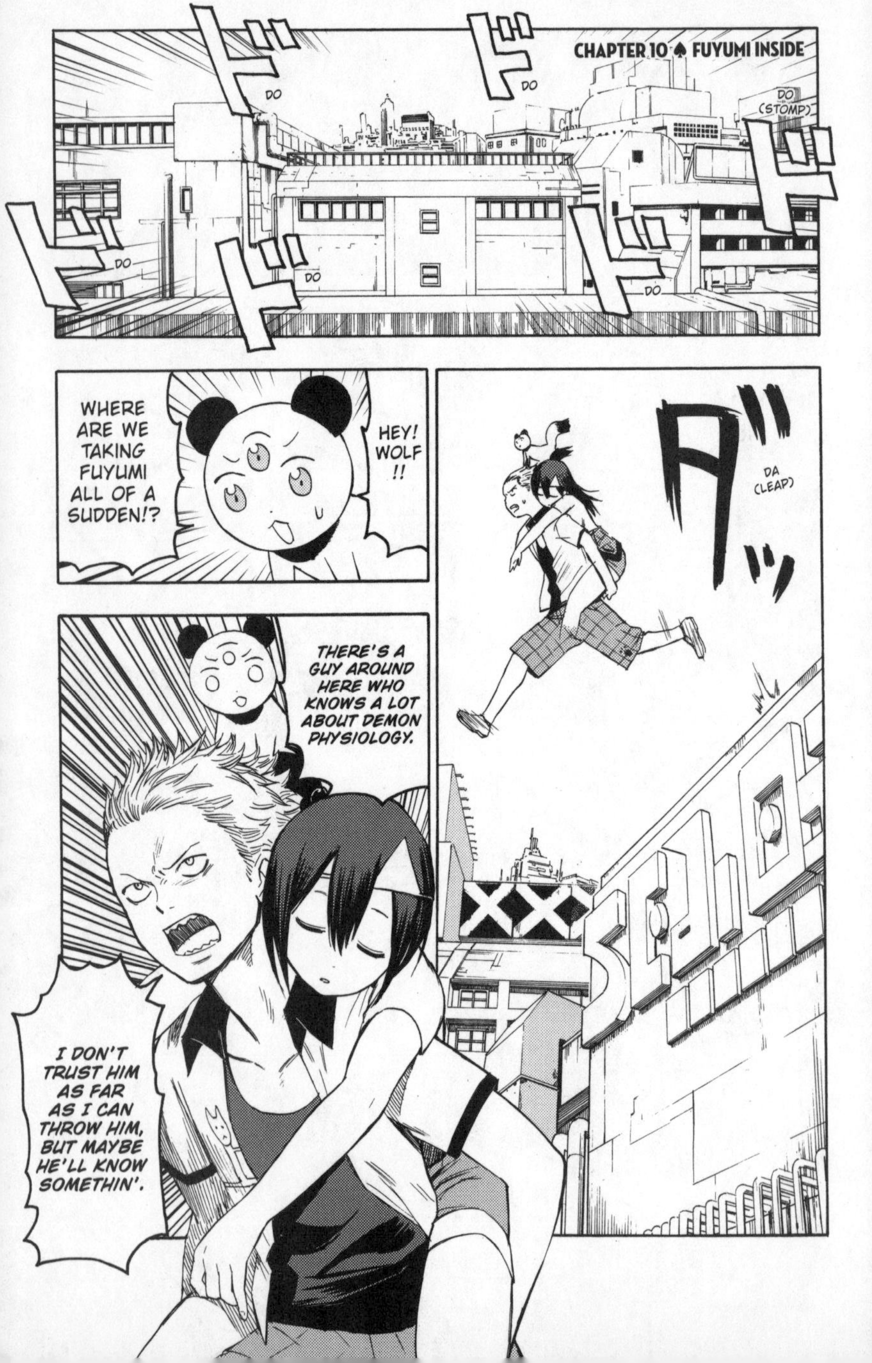

DO (STOMP)
DO
DO
DO
DO
DO
DA (LEAP)
HEY! WOLF !!
WHERE ARE WE TAKING FUYUMI ALL OF A SUDDEN!?
THERE'S A GUY AROUND HERE WHO KNOWS A LOT ABOUT DEMON PHYSIOLOGY.
I DON'T TRUST HIM AS FAR AS I CAN THROW HIM, BUT MAYBE HE'LL KNOW SOMETHIN'.

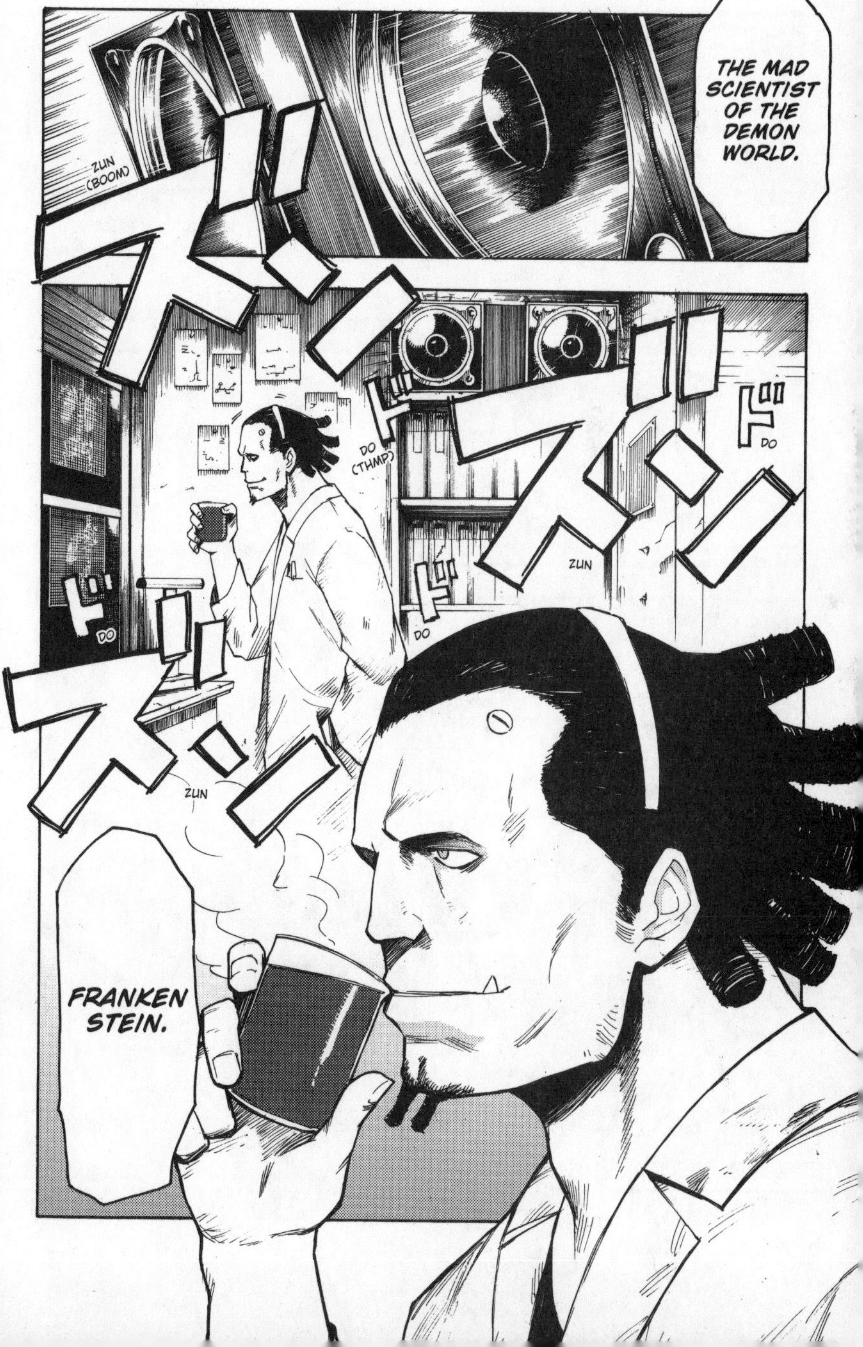
THE MAD SCIENTIST OF THE DEMON WORLD.
ZUN (BOOM)
DO
ZUN
DO (THMP)
DO
DO
ZUN
FRANKEN STEIN.

# CHAPTER 10 ♠ FUYUMI INSIDE

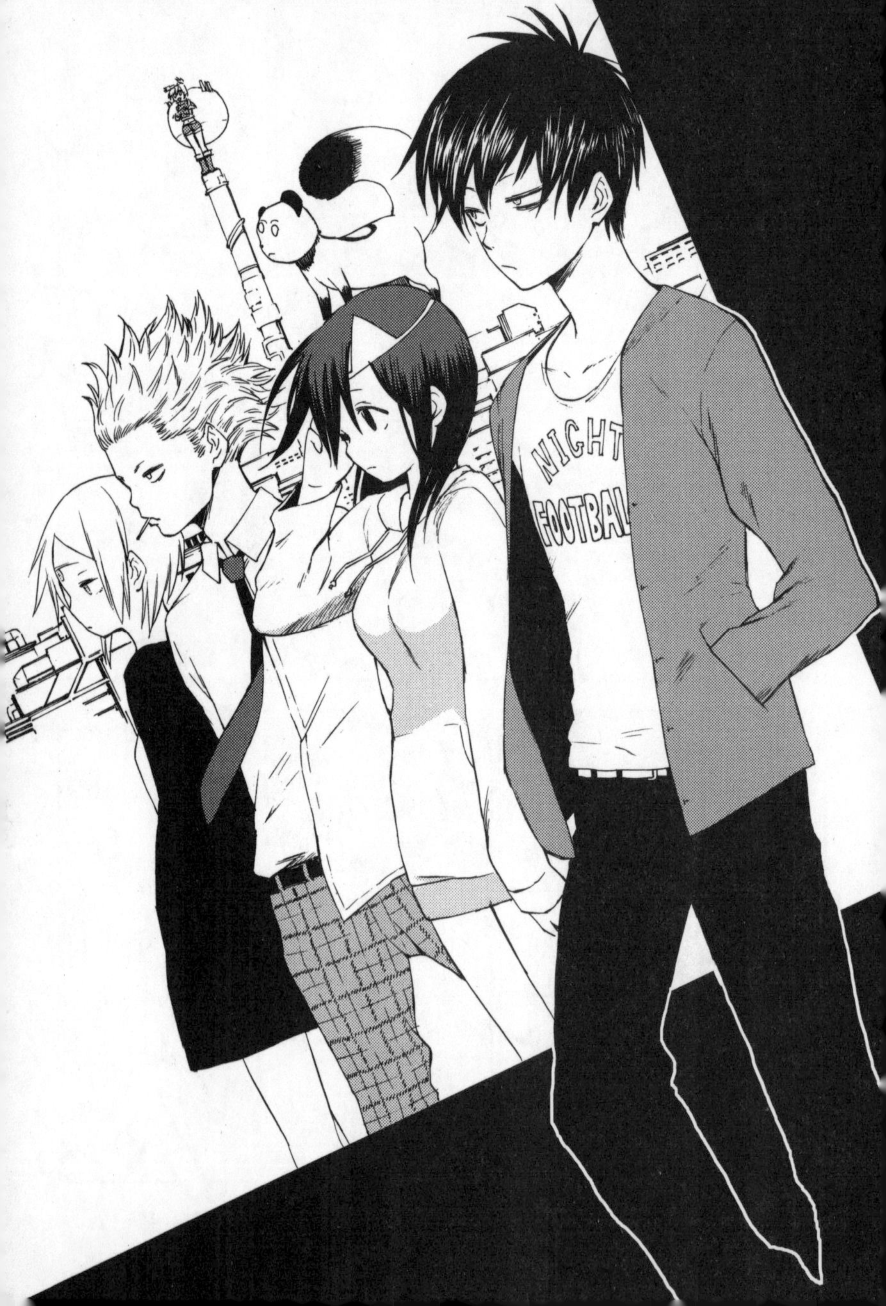
NIGHT
FOOTBAL

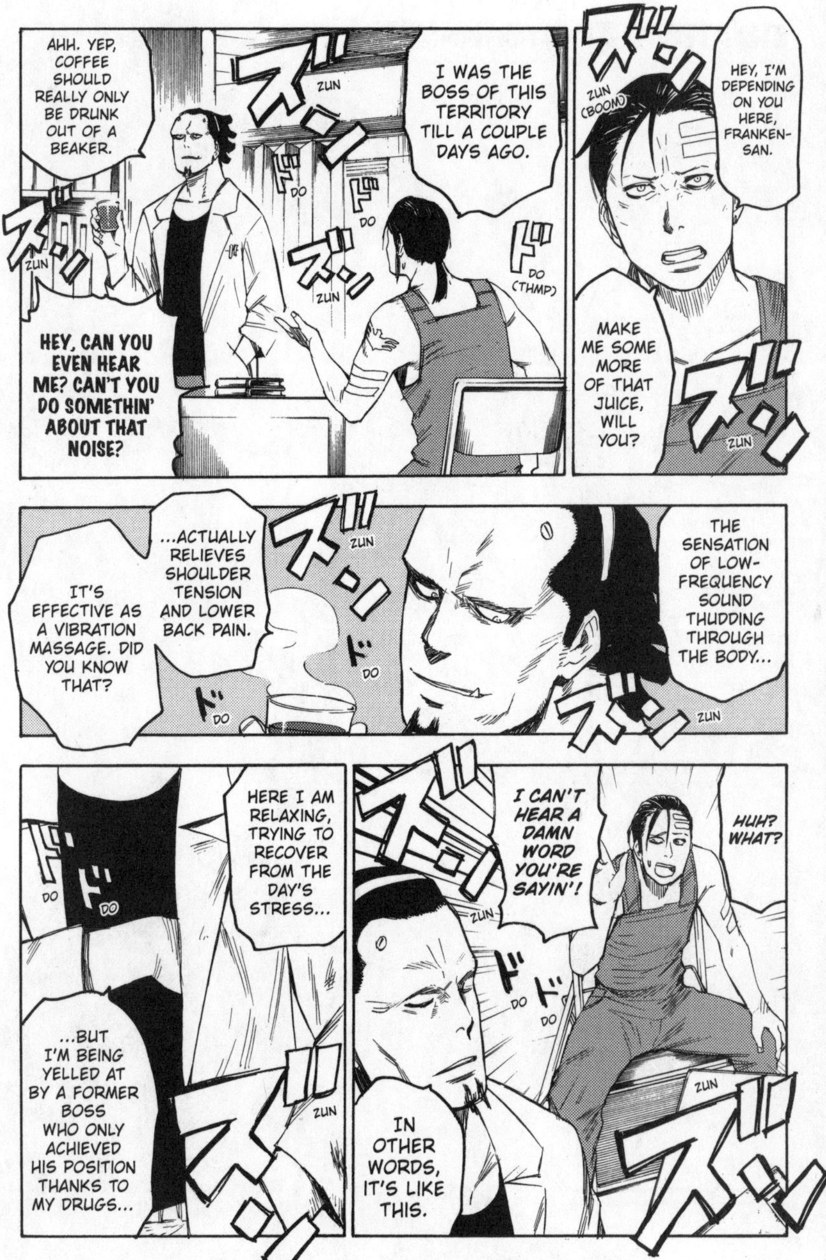
ZUN (BOOM)
HEY, I'M DEPENDING ON YOU HERE, FRANKEN-SAN.
MAKE ME SOME MORE OF THAT JUICE, WILL YOU?
ZUN
I WAS THE BOSS OF THIS TERRITORY TILL A COUPLE DAYS AGO.
ZUN
DO (THMP)
DO
DO
AHH. YEP, COFFEE SHOULD REALLY ONLY BE DRUNK OUT OF A BEAKER.
ZUN
ZUN
HEY, CAN YOU EVEN HEAR ME? CAN'T YOU DO SOMETHIN' ABOUT THAT NOISE?
THE SENSATION OF LOW-FREQUENCY SOUND THUDDING THROUGH THE BODY...
ZUN
ZUN
DO
IT'S EFFECTIVE AS A VIBRATION MASSAGE. DID YOU KNOW THAT?
...ACTUALLY RELIEVES SHOULDER TENSION AND LOWER BACK PAIN.
DO
HUH? WHAT?
I CAN'T HEAR A DAMN WORD YOU'RE SAYIN'!
ZUN
DO
DO
ZUN
IN OTHER WORDS, IT'S LIKE THIS.
HERE I AM RELAXING, TRYING TO RECOVER FROM THE DAY'S STRESS...
DO
DO
ZUN
...BUT I'M BEING YELLED AT BY A FORMER BOSS WHO ONLY ACHIEVED HIS POSITION THANKS TO MY DRUGS...

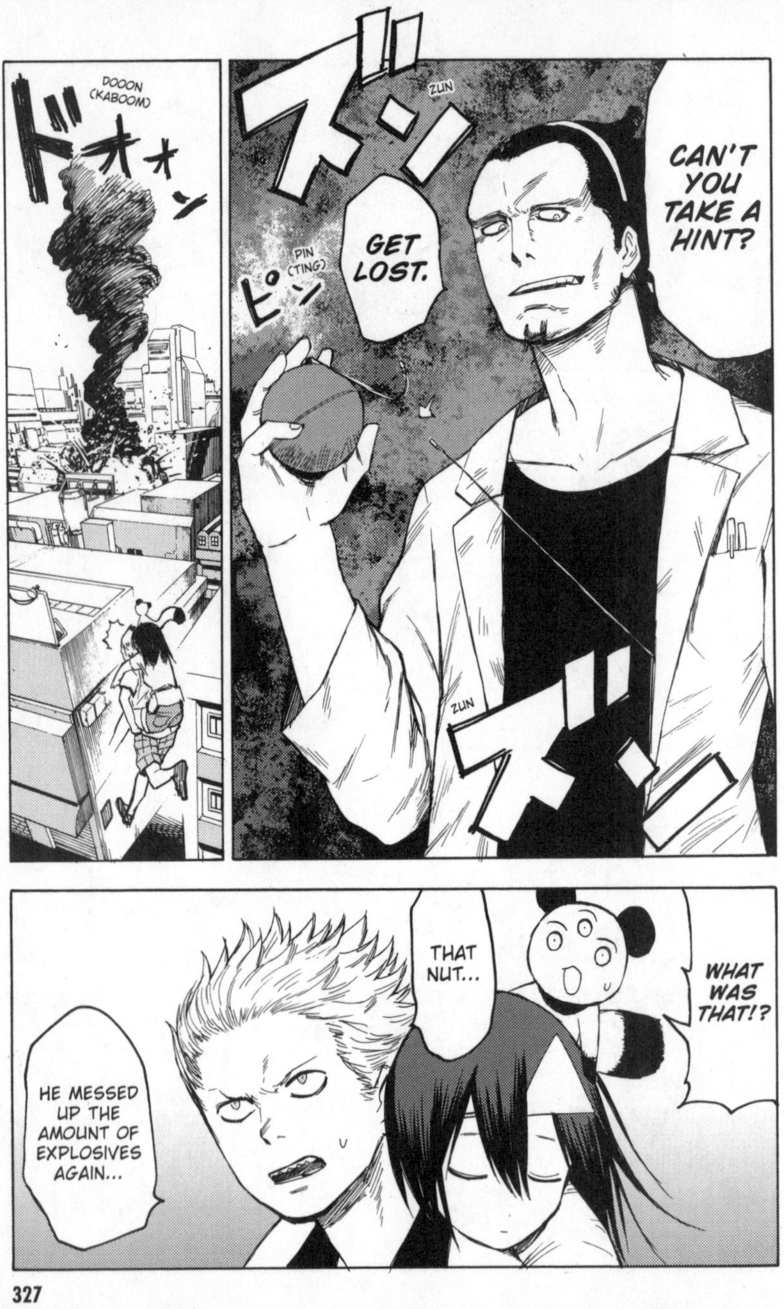

CAN'T YOU TAKE A HINT?
ZUN
GET LOST.
PIN (TING)
ZUN
DOOON (KABOOM)
WHAT WAS THAT!?
THAT NUT...
HE MESSED UP THE AMOUNT OF EXPLOSIVES AGAIN...

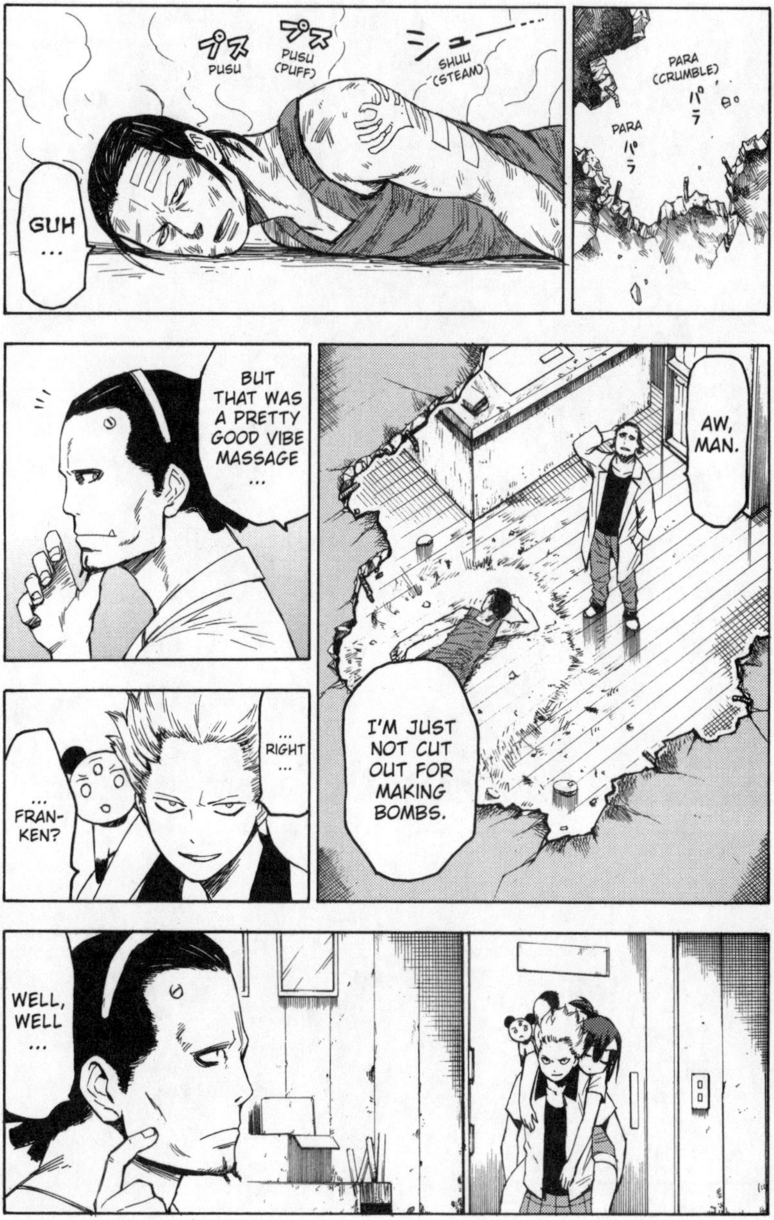
パラ
PARA (CRUMBLE)
パラ
PARA
シュー
SHUU (STEAM)
プス
PUSU (PUFF)
プス
PUSU
GUH …
AW, MAN.
I'M JUST NOT CUT OUT FOR MAKING BOMBS.
BUT THAT WAS A PRETTY GOOD VIBE MASSAGE …
… RIGHT …
… FRAN-KEN?
WELL, WELL …

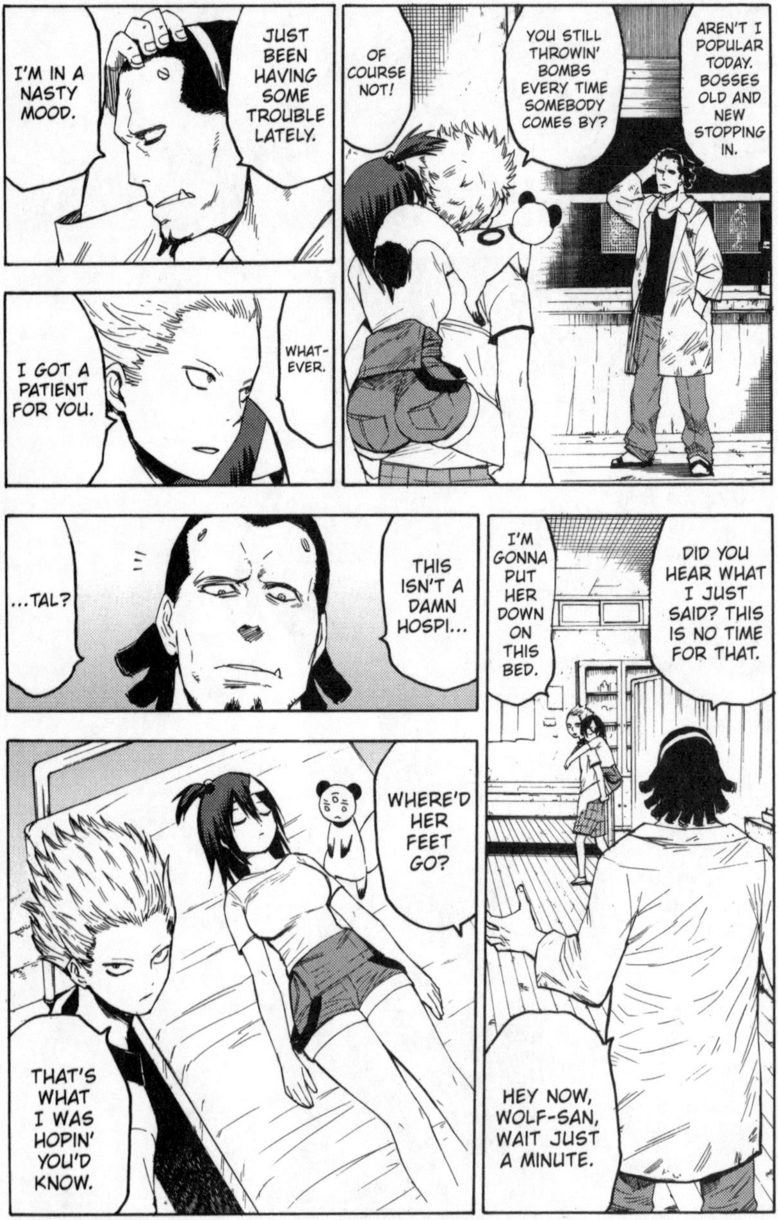
AREN'T I POPULAR TODAY. BOSSES OLD AND NEW STOPPING IN.
YOU STILL THROWIN' BOMBS EVERY TIME SOMEBODY COMES BY?
OF COURSE NOT!
JUST BEEN HAVING SOME TROUBLE LATELY.
I'M IN A NASTY MOOD.
WHAT-EVER.
I GOT A PATIENT FOR YOU.
DID YOU HEAR WHAT I JUST SAID? THIS IS NO TIME FOR THAT.
I'M GONNA PUT HER DOWN ON THIS BED.
HEY NOW, WOLF-SAN, WAIT JUST A MINUTE.
THIS ISN'T A DAMN HOSPI...
...TAL?
WHERE'D HER FEET GO?
THAT'S WHAT I WAS HOPIN' YOU'D KNOW.

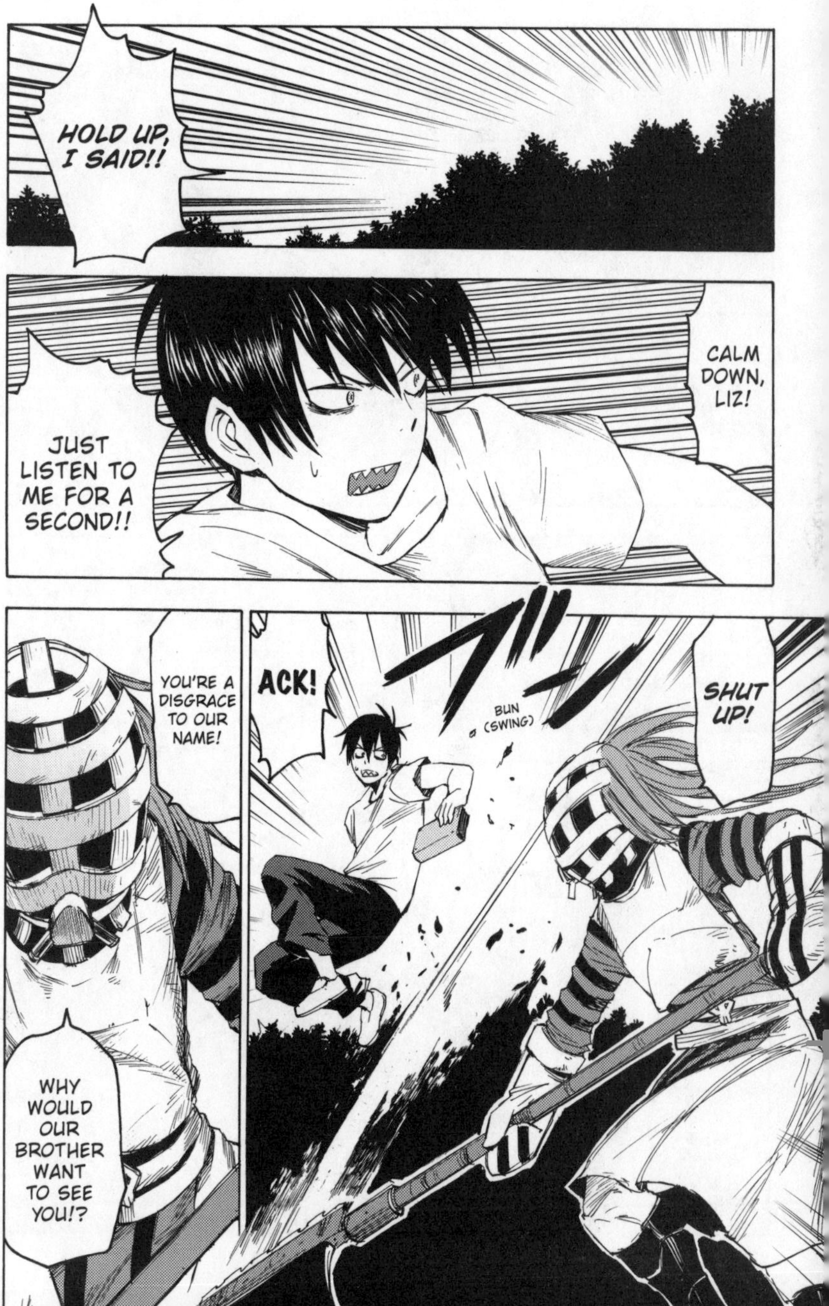
HOLD UP, I SAID!!
CALM DOWN, LIZ!
JUST LISTEN TO ME FOR A SECOND!!
SHUT UP!
ブン
BUN (SWING)
ACK!
YOU'RE A DISGRACE TO OUR NAME!
WHY WOULD OUR BROTHER WANT TO SEE YOU!?

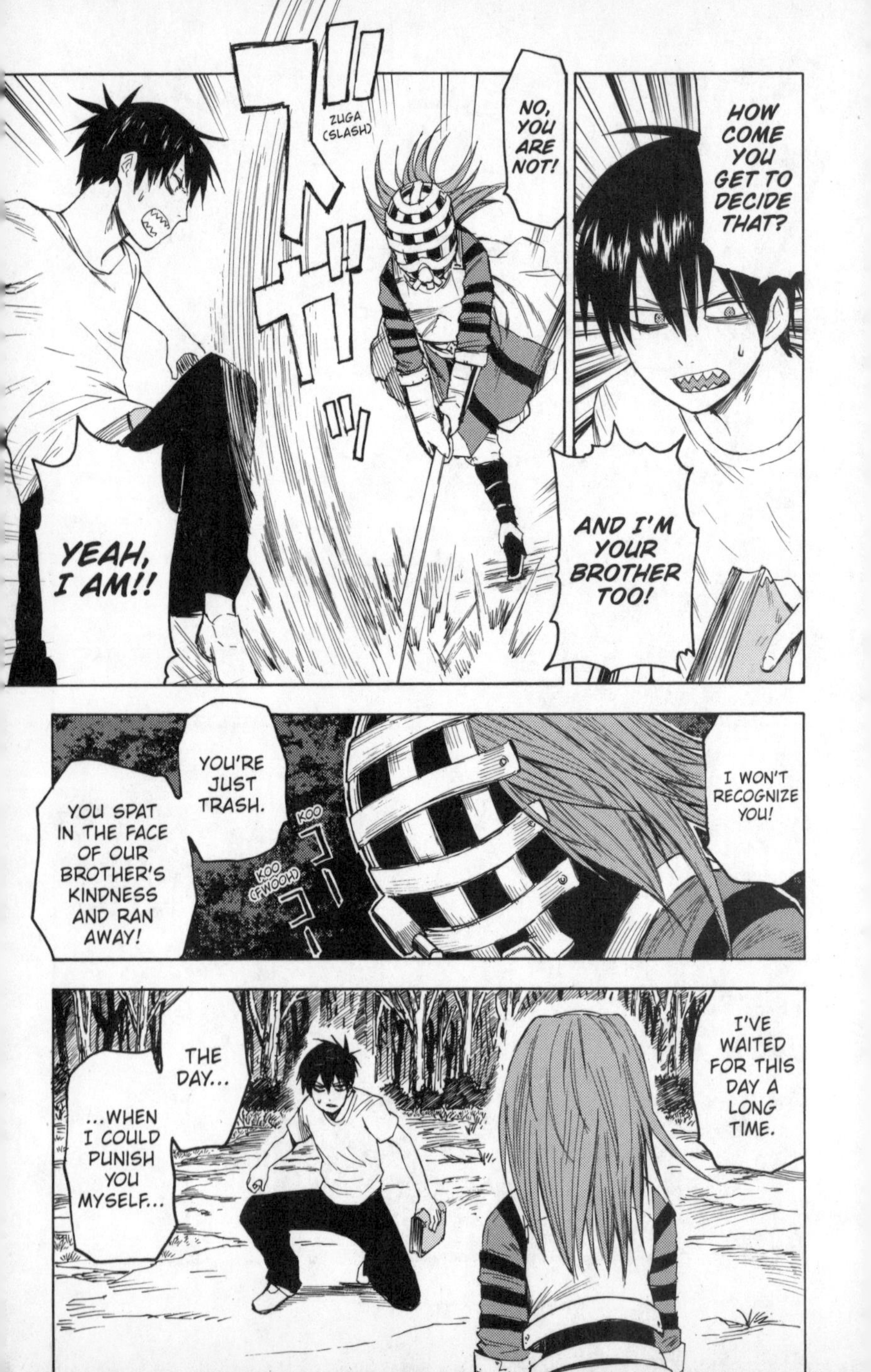
HOW COME YOU GET TO DECIDE THAT?
AND I'M YOUR BROTHER TOO!
NO, YOU ARE NOT!
ZUGA (SLASH)
YEAH, I AM!!
I WON'T RECOGNIZE YOU!
YOU'RE JUST TRASH.
KOO
KOO (FWOOH)
YOU SPAT IN THE FACE OF OUR BROTHER'S KINDNESS AND RAN AWAY!
I'VE WAITED FOR THIS DAY A LONG TIME.
THE DAY...
...WHEN I COULD PUNISH YOU MYSELF...

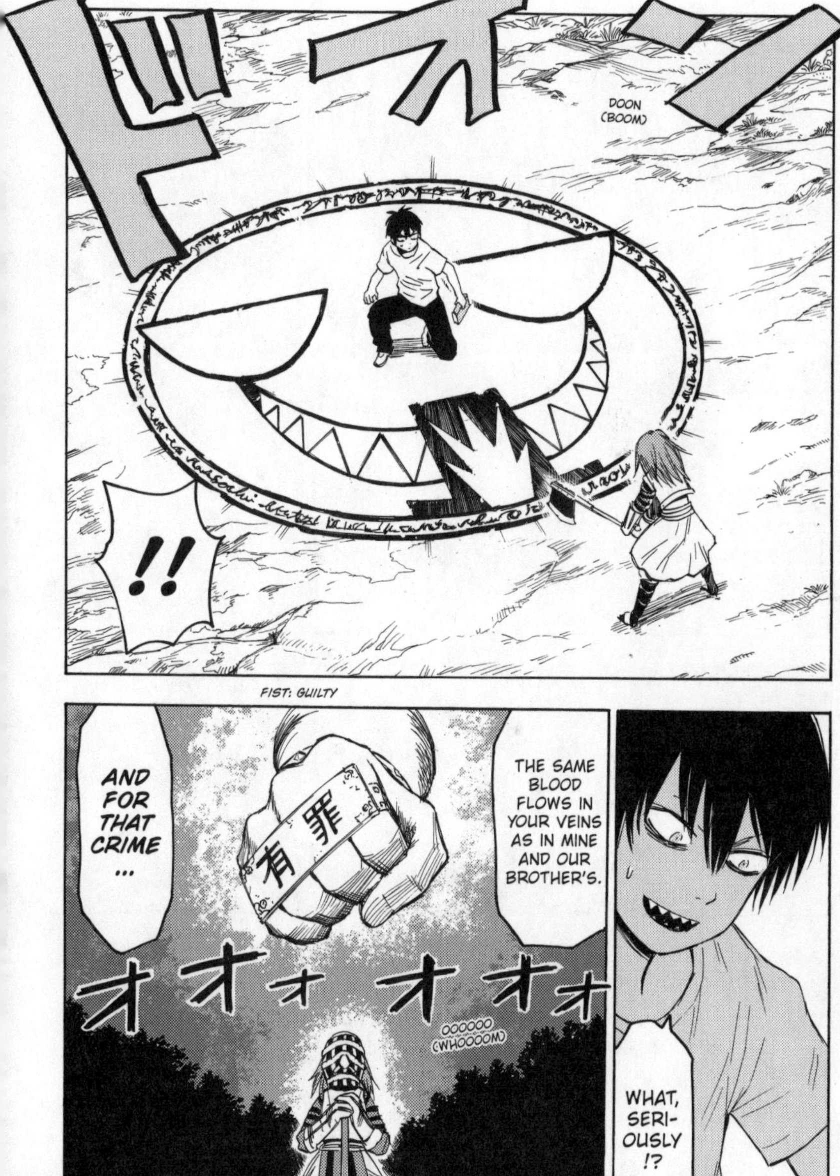
ドオーン
DOON
(BOOM)
!!
FIST: GUILTY
WHAT, SERI-OUSLY!?
THE SAME BLOOD FLOWS IN YOUR VEINS AS IN MINE AND OUR BROTHER'S.
AND FOR THAT CRIME...
有罪
オオォオオォ
OOOOOO
(WHOOOOM)

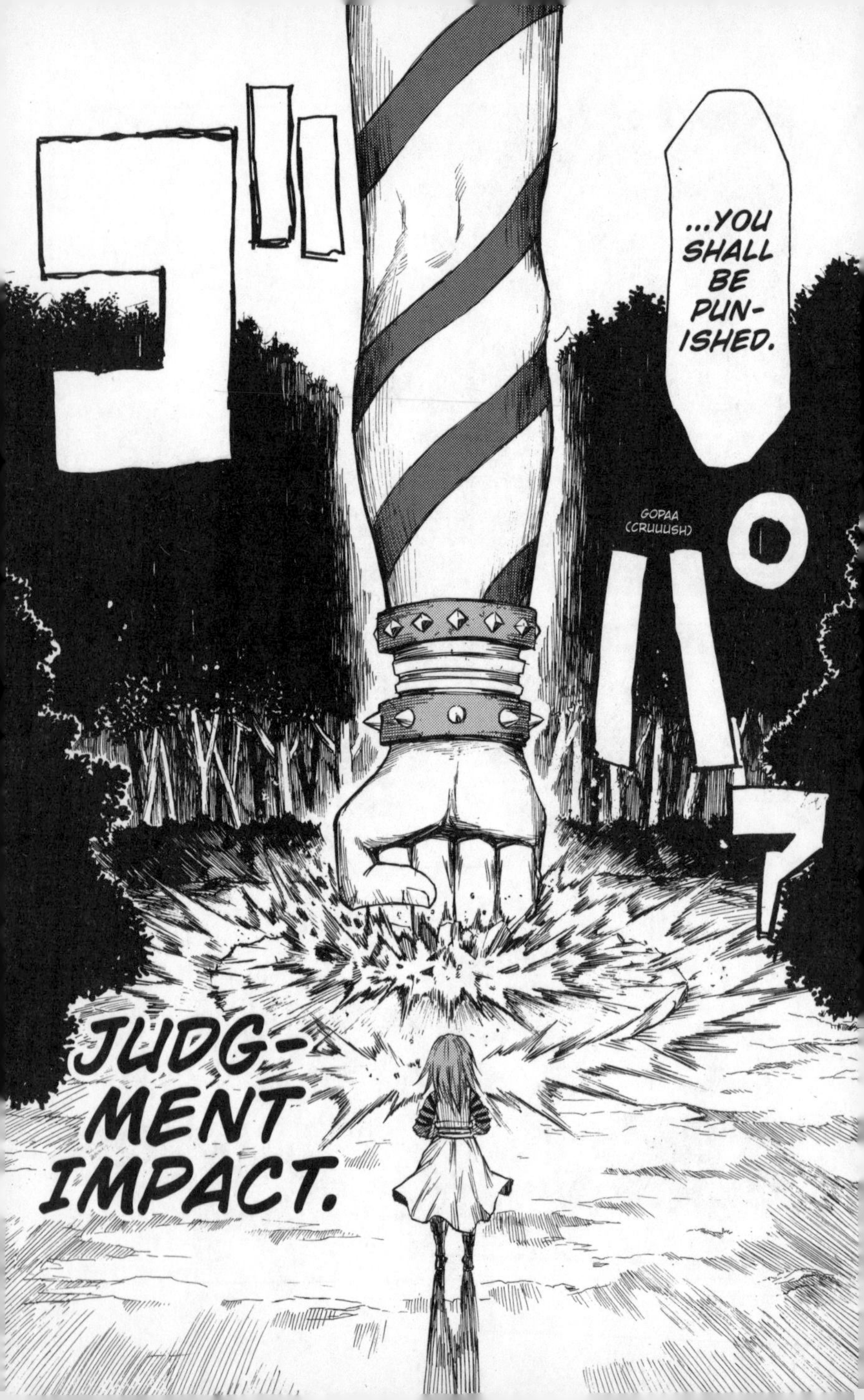
...YOU SHALL BE PUN-ISHED.
GOPAA (CRUUUSH)
JUDG-MENT IMPACT.

FIST: GUILTY

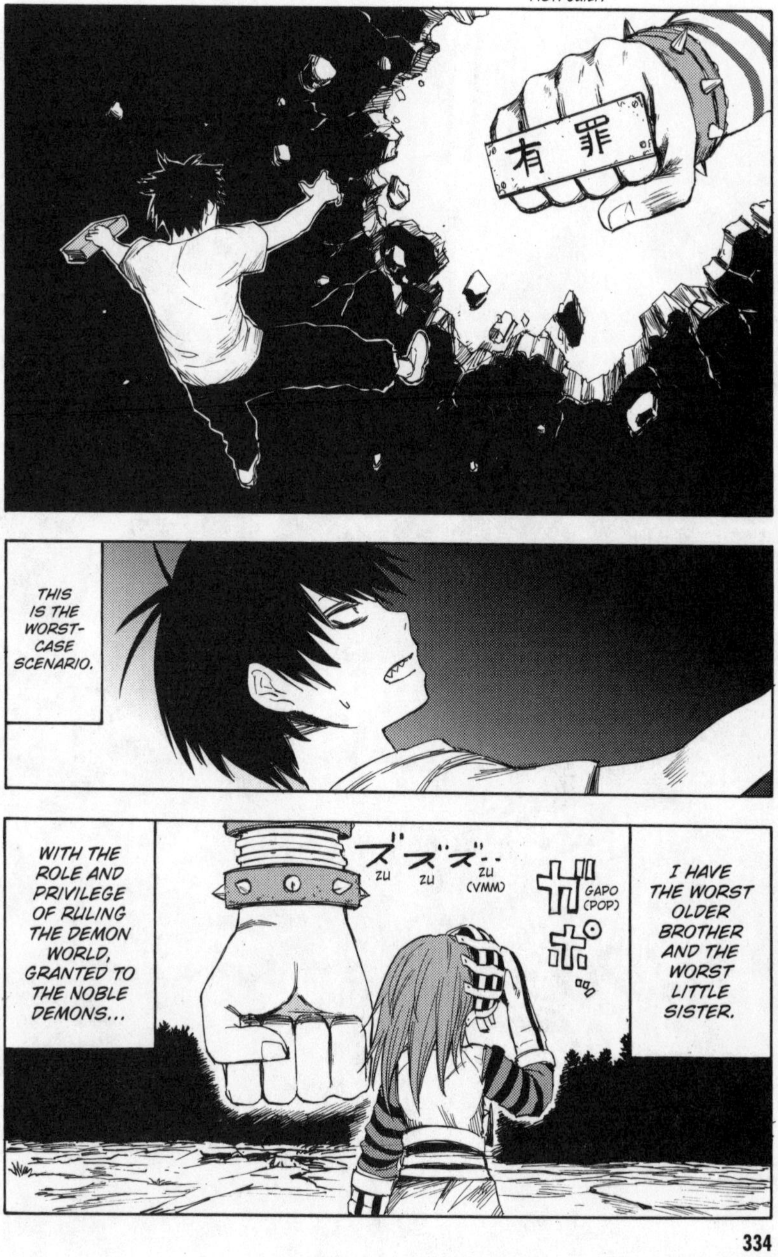
有罪
THIS IS THE WORST-CASE SCENARIO.
I HAVE THE WORST OLDER BROTHER AND THE WORST LITTLE SISTER.
ガポ GAPO (POP)
ズズズ ZU ZU ZU (VMM)
WITH THE ROLE AND PRIVILEGE OF RULING THE DEMON WORLD, GRANTED TO THE NOBLE DEMONS...

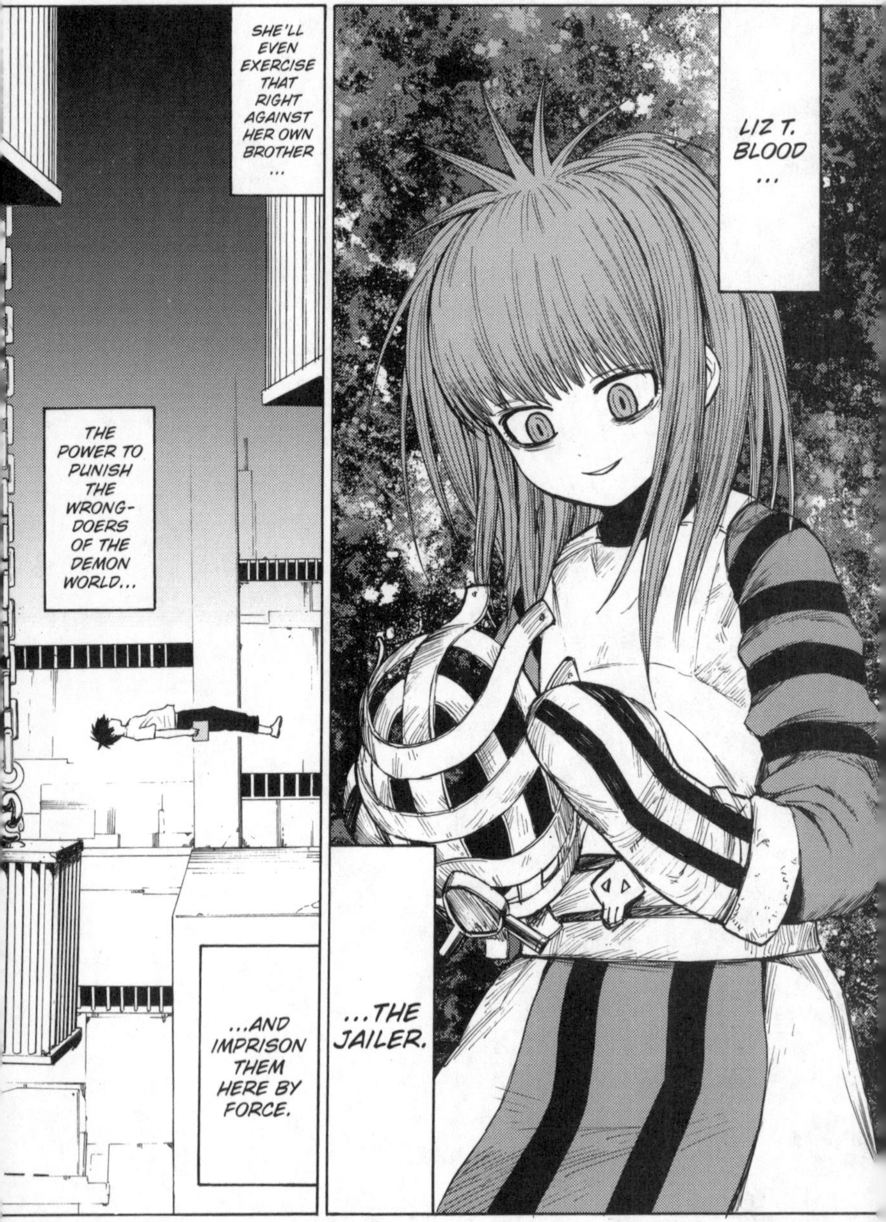
LIZ T. BLOOD ...
...THE JAILER.
SHE'LL EVEN EXERCISE THAT RIGHT AGAINST HER OWN BROTHER ...
THE POWER TO PUNISH THE WRONG-DOERS OF THE DEMON WORLD...
...AND IMPRISON THEM HERE BY FORCE.

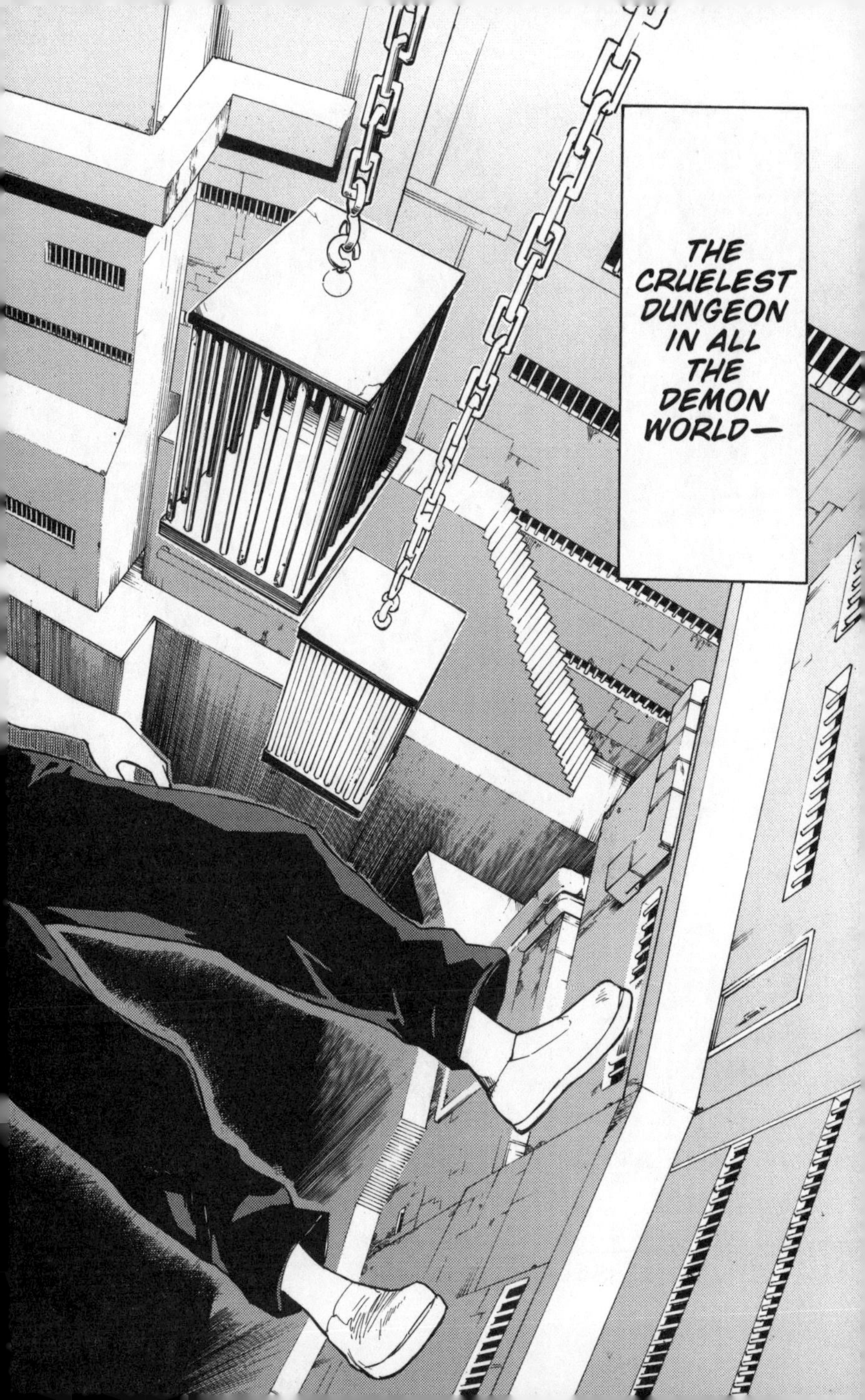
THE CRUELEST DUNGEON IN ALL THE DEMON WORLD—

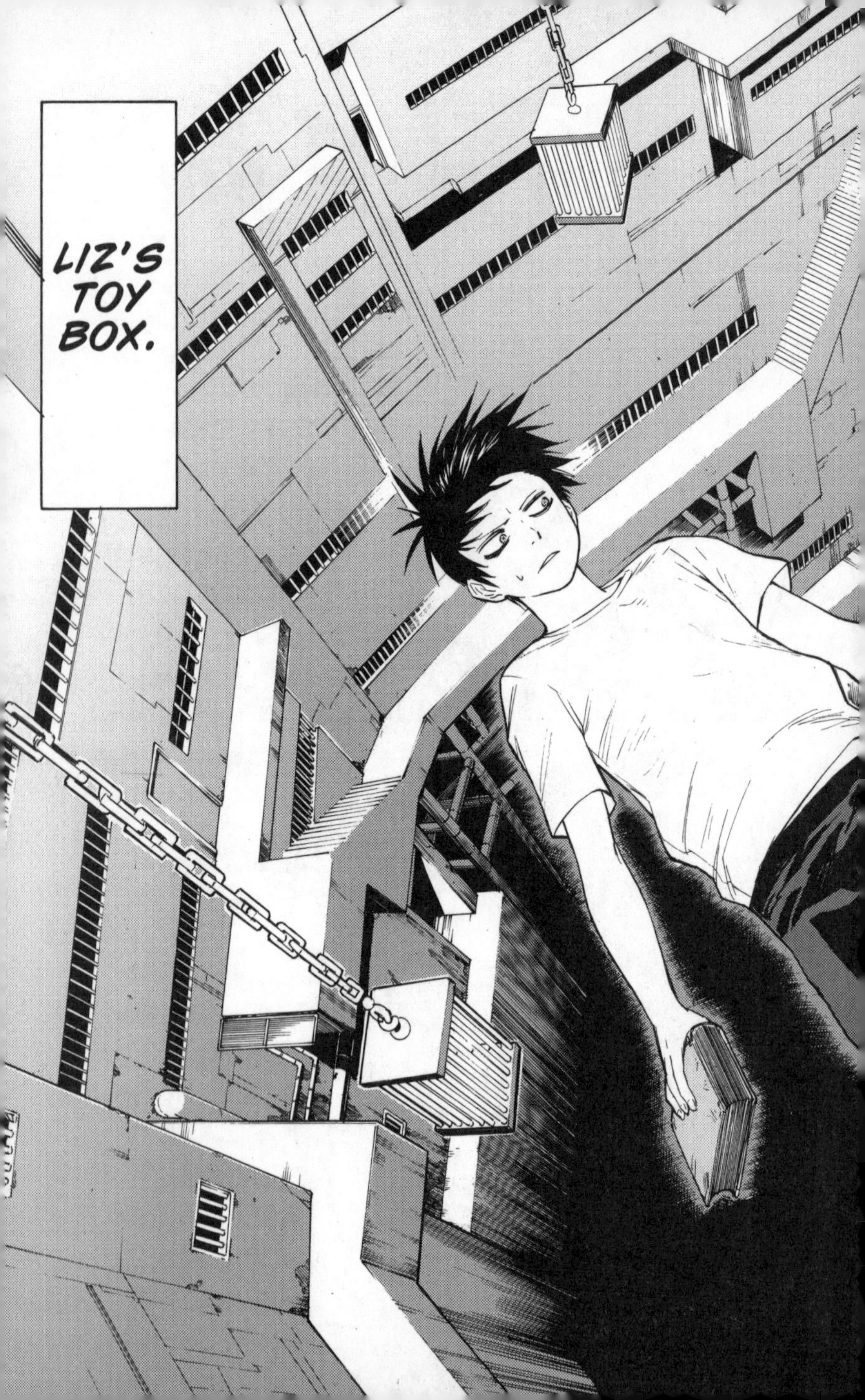
LIZ'S TOY BOX.

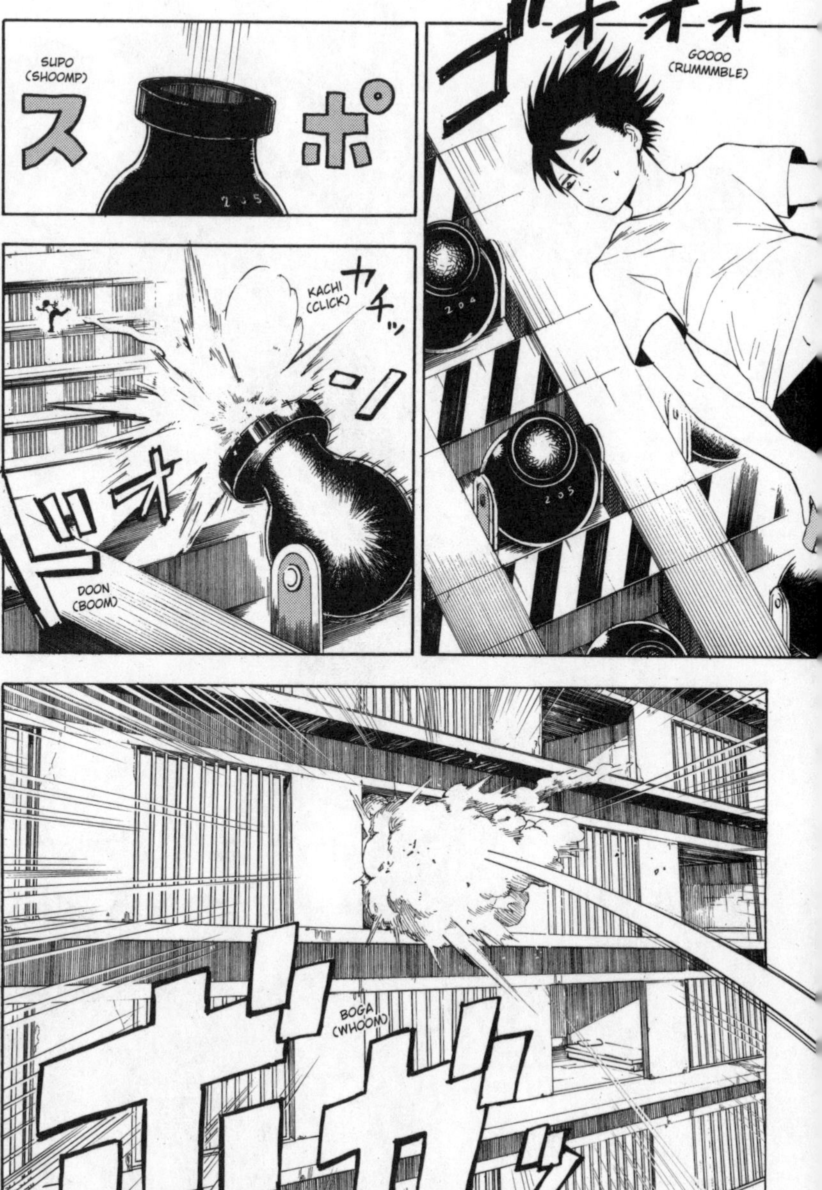
GOOOO (RUMMMBLE)
SUPO (SHOOMP)
KACHI (CLICK)
DOON (BOOM)
BOGA (WHOOM)

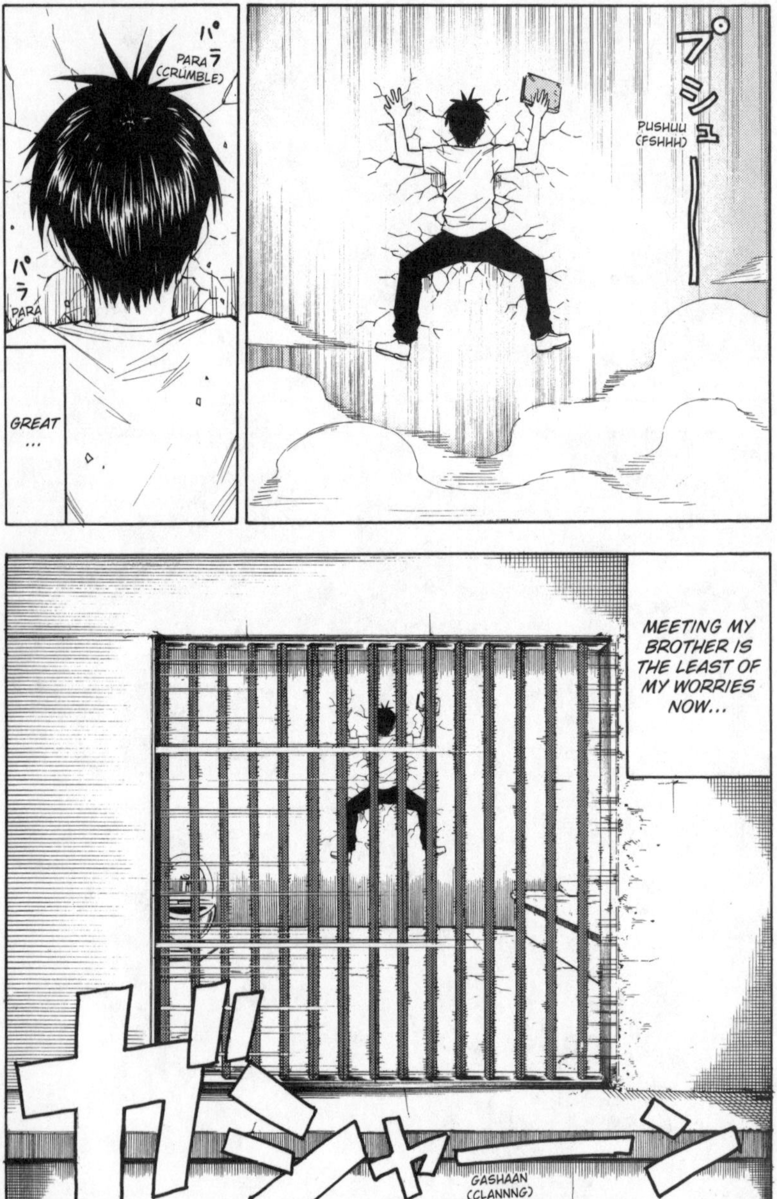
プシュー
PUSHUU (FSHHH)
パラ
PARA (CRUMBLE)
パラ
PARA
GREAT ...
MEETING MY BROTHER IS THE LEAST OF MY WORRIES NOW...
ガシャーン
GASHAAN (CLANNNG)

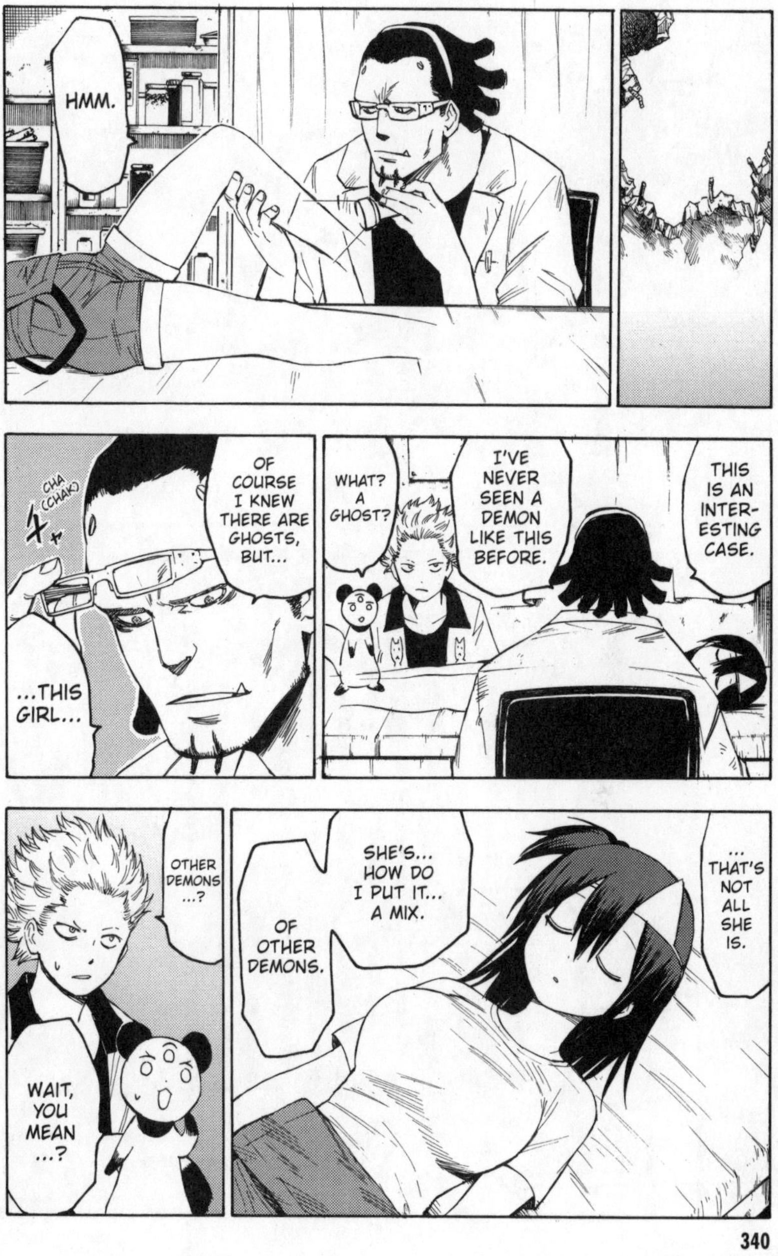
HMM.
THIS IS AN INTERESTING CASE.
I'VE NEVER SEEN A DEMON LIKE THIS BEFORE.
WHAT? A GHOST?
OF COURSE I KNEW THERE ARE GHOSTS, BUT...
CHA (CHAK)
...THIS GIRL...
...THAT'S NOT ALL SHE IS.
SHE'S... HOW DO I PUT IT... A MIX.
OF OTHER DEMONS.
OTHER DEMONS ...?
WAIT, YOU MEAN ...?

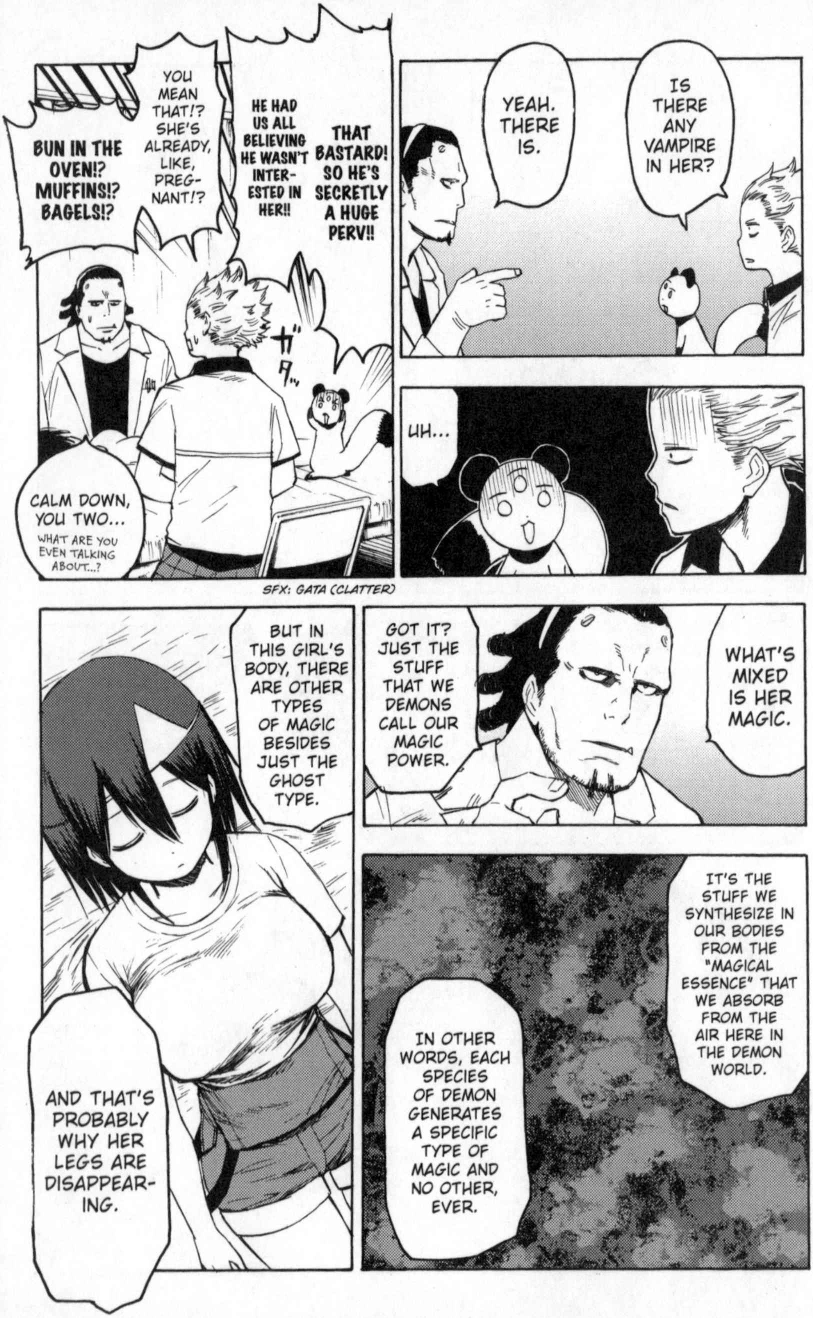
IS THERE ANY VAMPIRE IN HER?
YEAH. THERE IS.
UH...
THAT BASTARD! SO HE'S SECRETLY A HUGE PERV!!
HE HAD US ALL BELIEVING HE WASN'T INTERESTED IN HER!!
YOU MEAN THAT!? SHE'S ALREADY, LIKE, PREGNANT!?
BUN IN THE OVEN!? MUFFINS!? BAGELS!?
CALM DOWN, YOU TWO... WHAT ARE YOU EVEN TALKING ABOUT...?
SFX: GATA (CLATTER)
WHAT'S MIXED IS HER MAGIC.
GOT IT? JUST THE STUFF THAT WE DEMONS CALL OUR MAGIC POWER.
IT'S THE STUFF WE SYNTHESIZE IN OUR BODIES FROM THE "MAGICAL ESSENCE" THAT WE ABSORB FROM THE AIR HERE IN THE DEMON WORLD.
IN OTHER WORDS, EACH SPECIES OF DEMON GENERATES A SPECIFIC TYPE OF MAGIC AND NO OTHER, EVER.
BUT IN THIS GIRL'S BODY, THERE ARE OTHER TYPES OF MAGIC BESIDES JUST THE GHOST TYPE.
AND THAT'S PROBABLY WHY HER LEGS ARE DISAPPEARING.

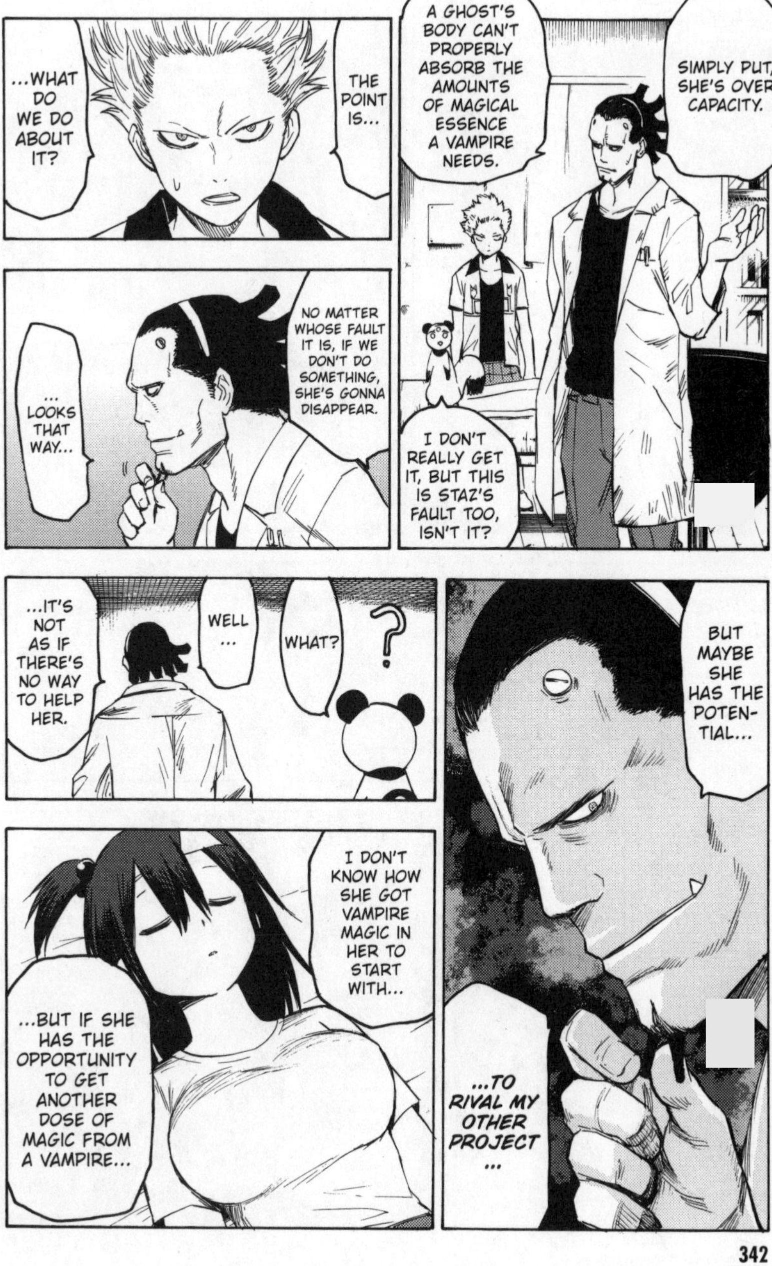
SIMPLY PUT, SHE'S OVER CAPACITY.
A GHOST'S BODY CAN'T PROPERLY ABSORB THE AMOUNTS OF MAGICAL ESSENCE A VAMPIRE NEEDS.
I DON'T REALLY GET IT, BUT THIS IS STAZ'S FAULT TOO, ISN'T IT?
THE POINT IS...
...WHAT DO WE DO ABOUT IT?
NO MATTER WHOSE FAULT IT IS, IF WE DON'T DO SOMETHING, SHE'S GONNA DISAPPEAR.
...LOOKS THAT WAY...
BUT MAYBE SHE HAS THE POTEN-TIAL...
...TO RIVAL MY OTHER PROJECT...
WHAT?
WELL...
...IT'S NOT AS IF THERE'S NO WAY TO HELP HER.
I DON'T KNOW HOW SHE GOT VAMPIRE MAGIC IN HER TO START WITH...
...BUT IF SHE HAS THE OPPORTUNITY TO GET ANOTHER DOSE OF MAGIC FROM A VAMPIRE...

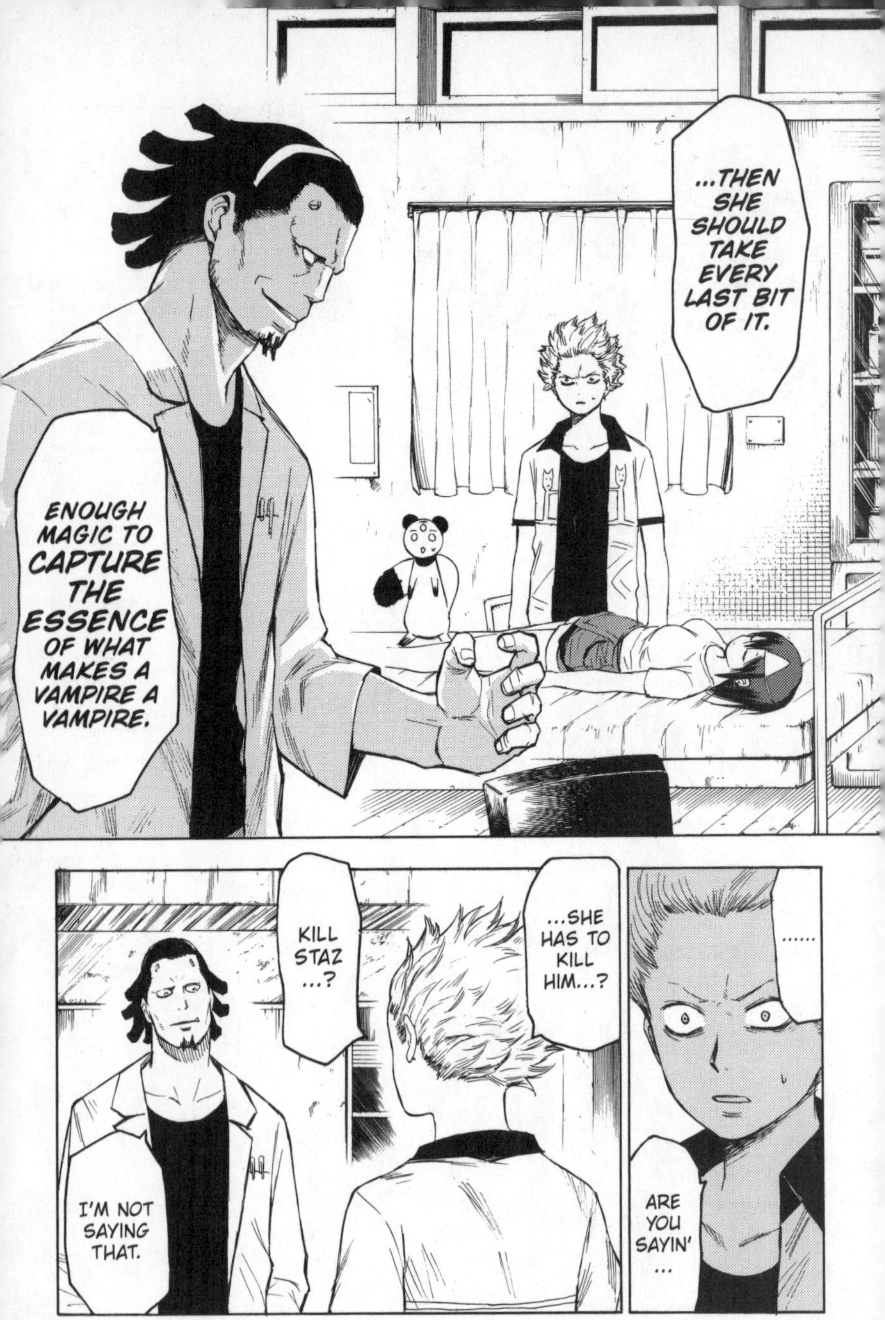
...THEN SHE SHOULD TAKE EVERY LAST BIT OF IT.
ENOUGH MAGIC TO CAPTURE THE ESSENCE OF WHAT MAKES A VAMPIRE A VAMPIRE.
......
ARE YOU SAYIN' ...
...SHE HAS TO KILL HIM...?
KILL STAZ ...?
I'M NOT SAYING THAT.

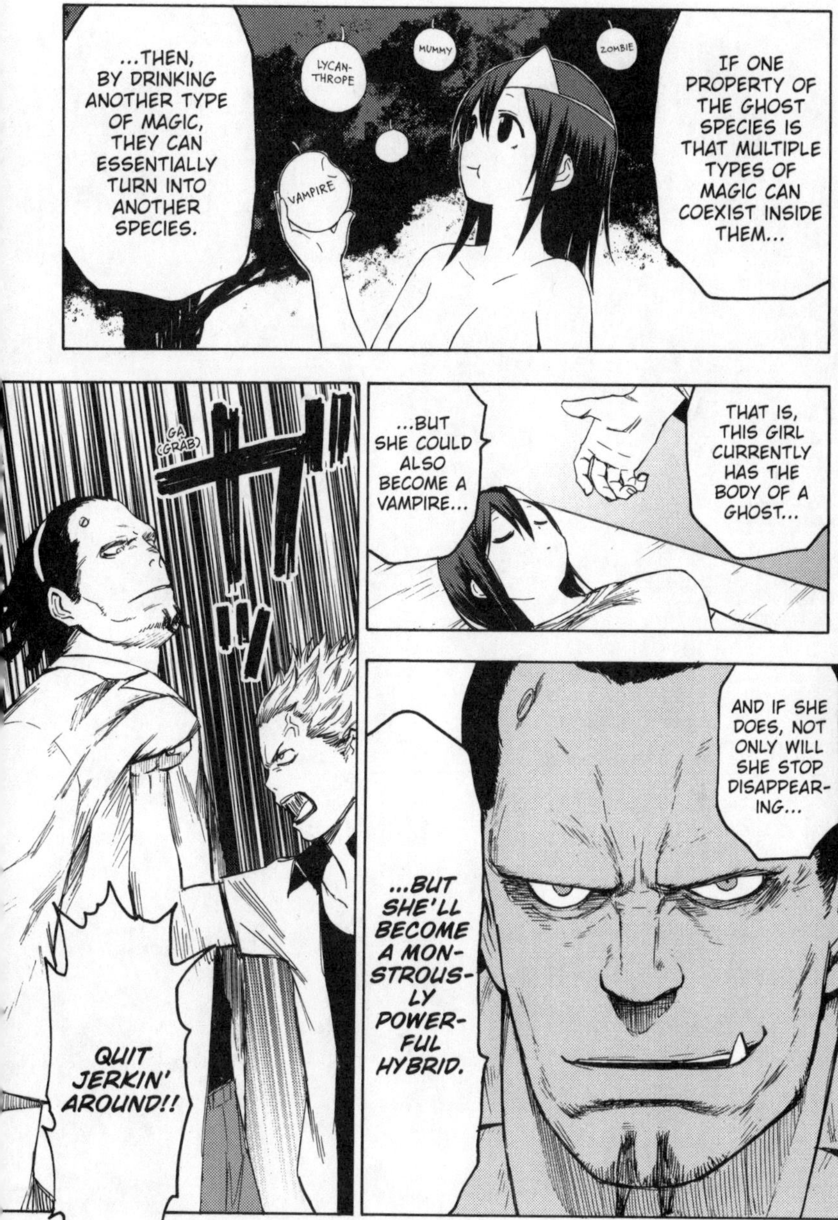
IF ONE PROPERTY OF THE GHOST SPECIES IS THAT MULTIPLE TYPES OF MAGIC CAN COEXIST INSIDE THEM...
ZOMBIE
MUMMY
LYCANTHROPE
VAMPIRE
...THEN, BY DRINKING ANOTHER TYPE OF MAGIC, THEY CAN ESSENTIALLY TURN INTO ANOTHER SPECIES.
THAT IS, THIS GIRL CURRENTLY HAS THE BODY OF A GHOST...
...BUT SHE COULD ALSO BECOME A VAMPIRE...
AND IF SHE DOES, NOT ONLY WILL SHE STOP DISAPPEARING...
...BUT SHE'LL BECOME A MONSTROUSLY POWERFUL HYBRID.
GA (GRAB)
QUIT JERKIN' AROUND!!

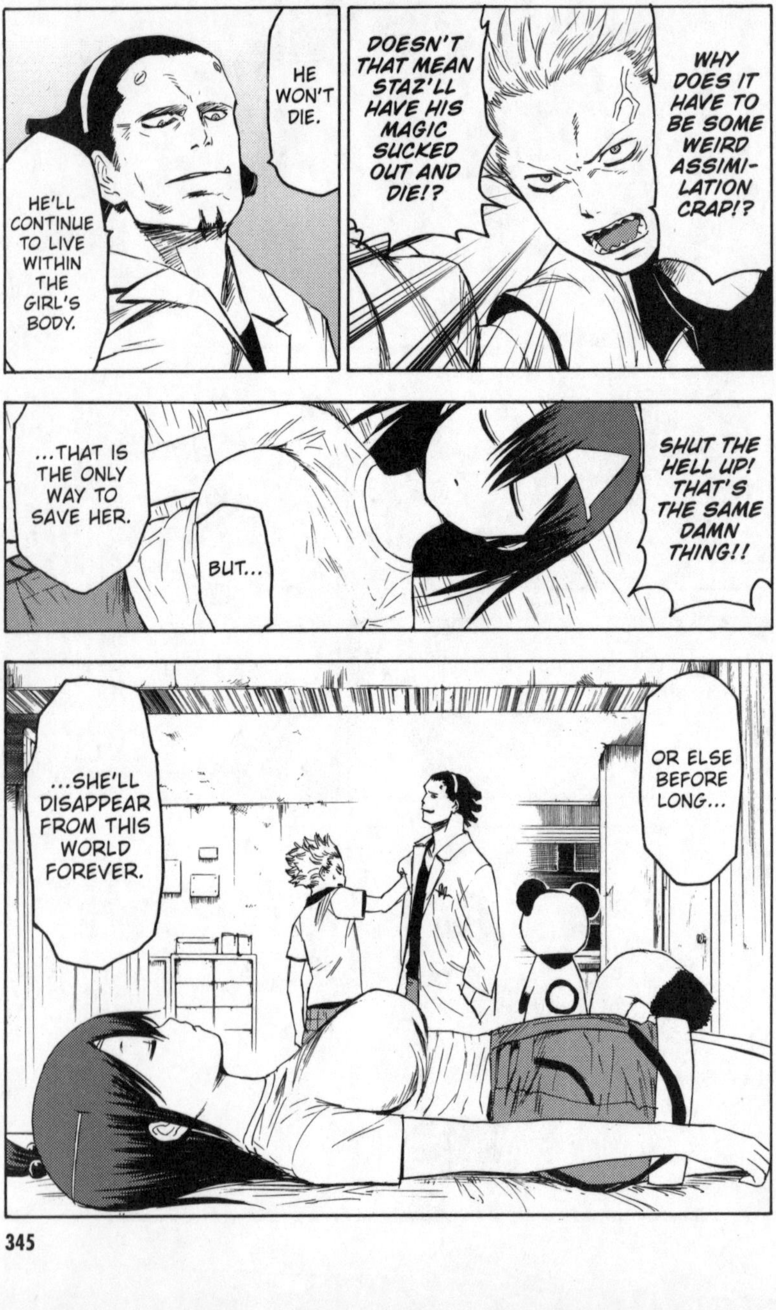
WHY DOES IT HAVE TO BE SOME WEIRD ASSIMILATION CRAP!?
DOESN'T THAT MEAN STAZ'LL HAVE HIS MAGIC SUCKED OUT AND DIE!?
HE WON'T DIE.
HE'LL CONTINUE TO LIVE WITHIN THE GIRL'S BODY.
SHUT THE HELL UP! THAT'S THE SAME DAMN THING!!
BUT...
...THAT IS THE ONLY WAY TO SAVE HER.
OR ELSE BEFORE LONG...
...SHE'LL DISAPPEAR FROM THIS WORLD FOREVER.

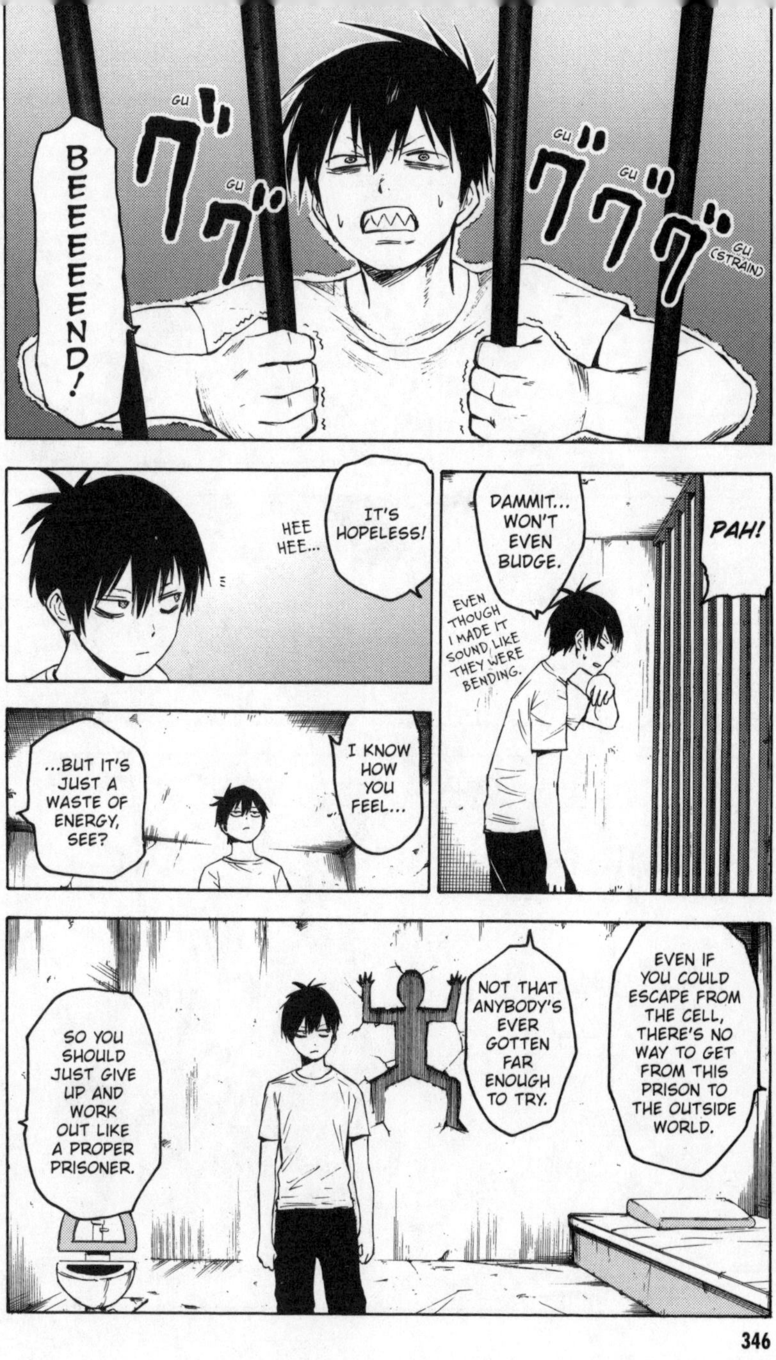
GU
GU
GU (STRAIN)
GU
GU
BEEEEEEND!
PAH!
DAMMIT... WON'T EVEN BUDGE.
EVEN THOUGH I MADE IT SOUND LIKE THEY WERE BENDING.
IT'S HOPELESS!
HEE HEE...
I KNOW HOW YOU FEEL...
...BUT IT'S JUST A WASTE OF ENERGY, SEE?
EVEN IF YOU COULD ESCAPE FROM THE CELL, THERE'S NO WAY TO GET FROM THIS PRISON TO THE OUTSIDE WORLD.
NOT THAT ANYBODY'S EVER GOTTEN FAR ENOUGH TO TRY.
SO YOU SHOULD JUST GIVE UP AND WORK OUT LIKE A PROPER PRISONER.

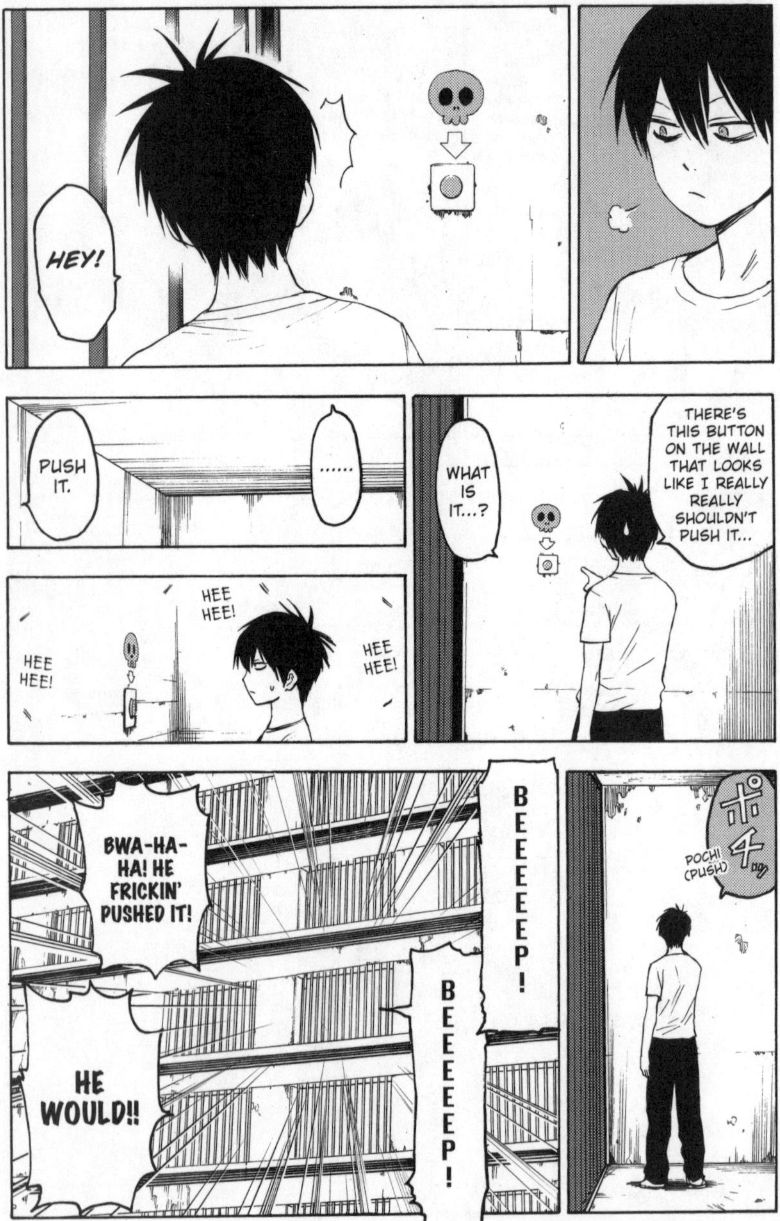
HEY!
THERE'S THIS BUTTON ON THE WALL THAT LOOKS LIKE I REALLY REALLY SHOULDN'T PUSH IT...
WHAT IS IT...?
......
PUSH IT.
HEE HEE!
HEE HEE!
HEE HEE!
ポチ
POCHI (PUSH)
BEEEEEP!
BEEEEEP!
BWA-HA-HA! HE FRICKIN' PUSHED IT!
HE WOULD!!

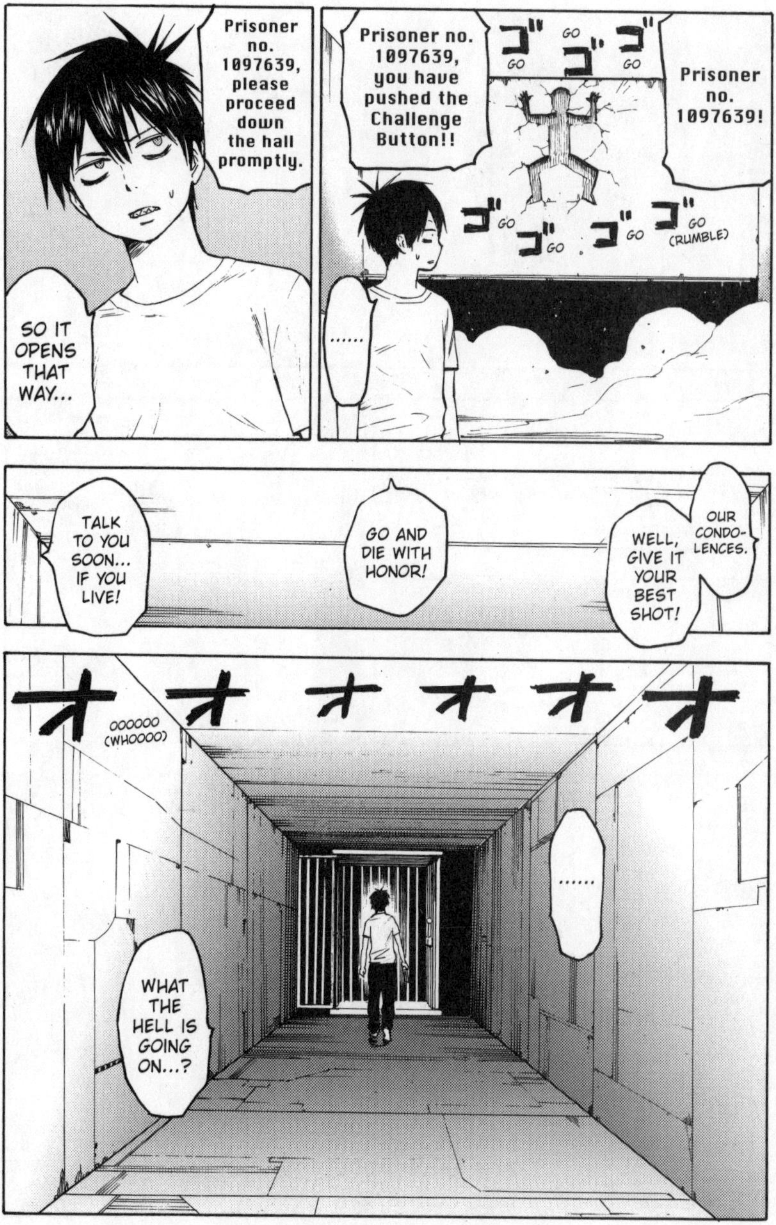
Prisoner no. 1097639!
ゴゴゴ
GO GO GO
Prisoner no. 1097639, you have pushed the Challenge Button!!
ゴゴゴゴ
GO GO GO GO (RUMBLE)
......
Prisoner no. 1097639, please proceed down the hall promptly.
SO IT OPENS THAT WAY...
OUR CONDOLENCES.
WELL, GIVE IT YOUR BEST SHOT!
GO AND DIE WITH HONOR!
TALK TO YOU SOON... IF YOU LIVE!
オオオオオオ
OOOOOO (WHOOOO)
......
WHAT THE HELL IS GOING ON...?

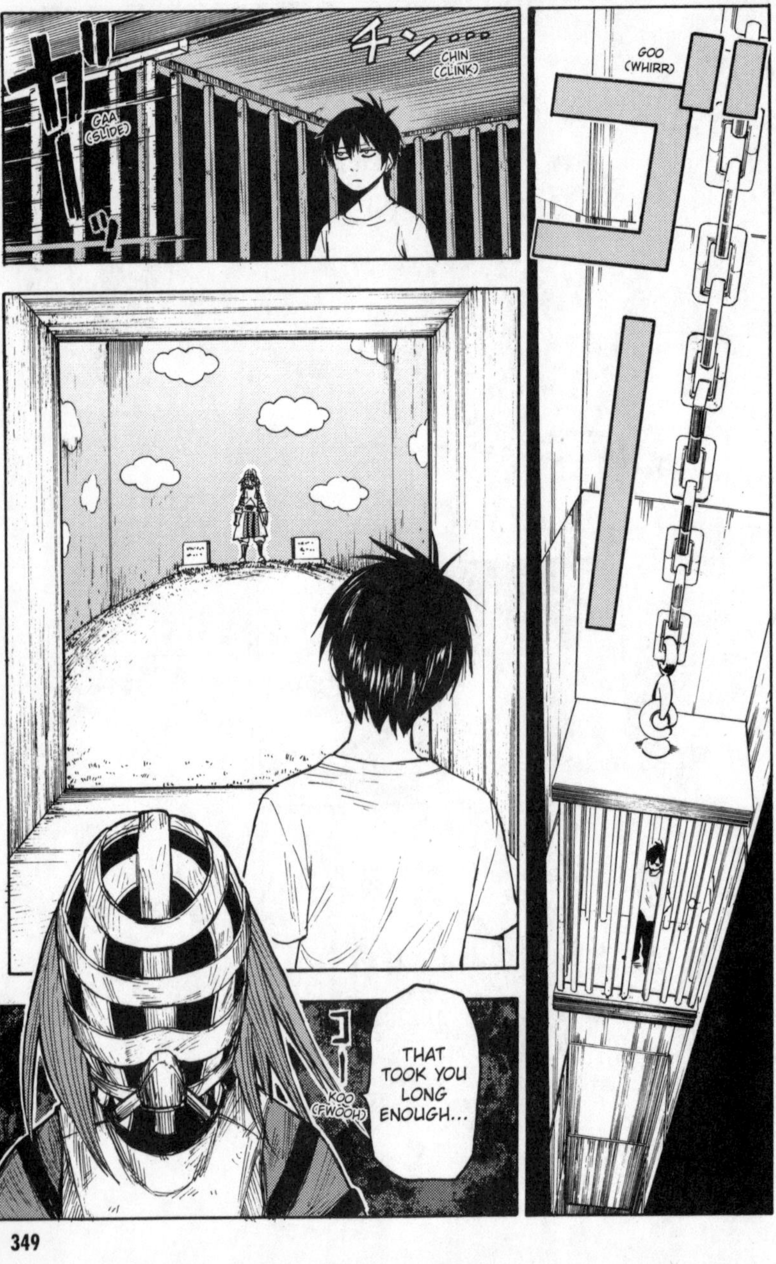
GOO (WHIRR)
CHIN (CLINK)
GAA (SLIDE)
KOO (FWOOH)
THAT TOOK YOU LONG ENOUGH...

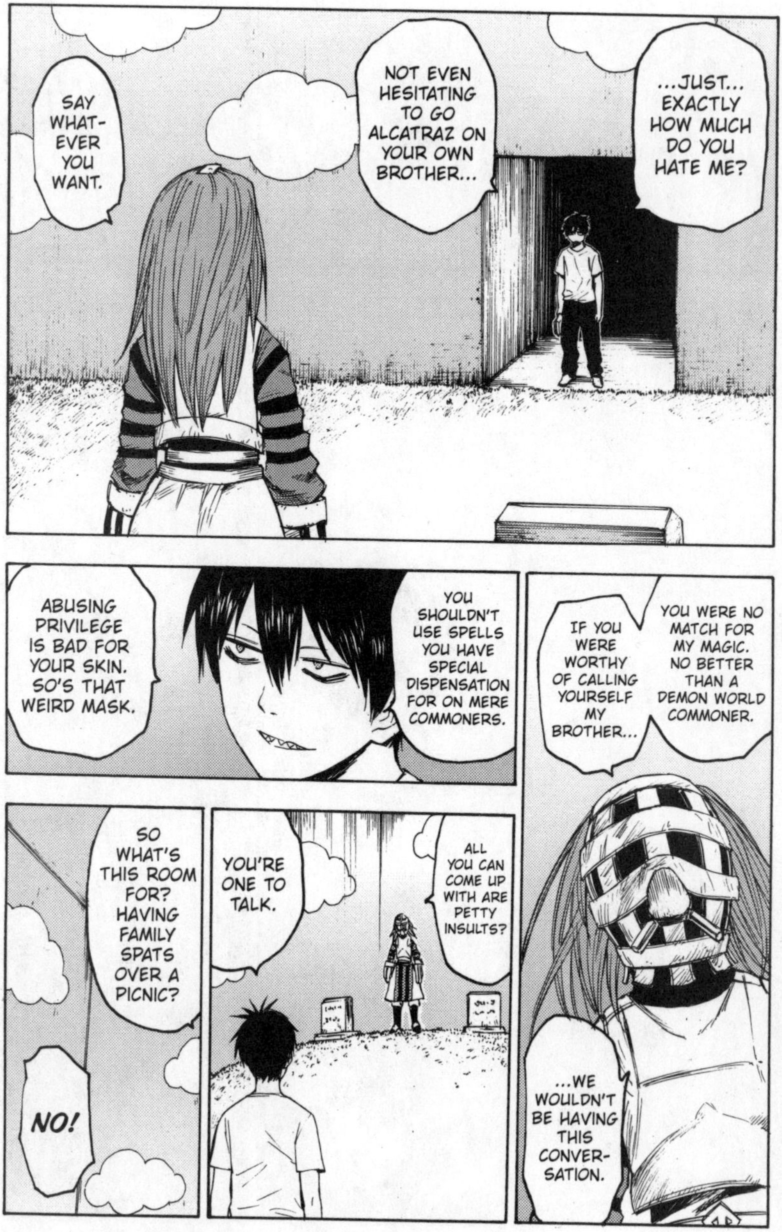
...JUST... EXACTLY HOW MUCH DO YOU HATE ME?
NOT EVEN HESITATING TO GO ALCATRAZ ON YOUR OWN BROTHER...
SAY WHAT-EVER YOU WANT.
YOU WERE NO MATCH FOR MY MAGIC. NO BETTER THAN A DEMON WORLD COMMONER.
IF YOU WERE WORTHY OF CALLING YOURSELF MY BROTHER...
...WE WOULDN'T BE HAVING THIS CONVER-SATION.
YOU SHOULDN'T USE SPELLS YOU HAVE SPECIAL DISPENSATION FOR ON MERE COMMONERS.
ABUSING PRIVILEGE IS BAD FOR YOUR SKIN. SO'S THAT WEIRD MASK.
ALL YOU CAN COME UP WITH ARE PETTY INSULTS?
YOU'RE ONE TO TALK.
SO WHAT'S THIS ROOM FOR? HAVING FAMILY SPATS OVER A PICNIC?
NO!

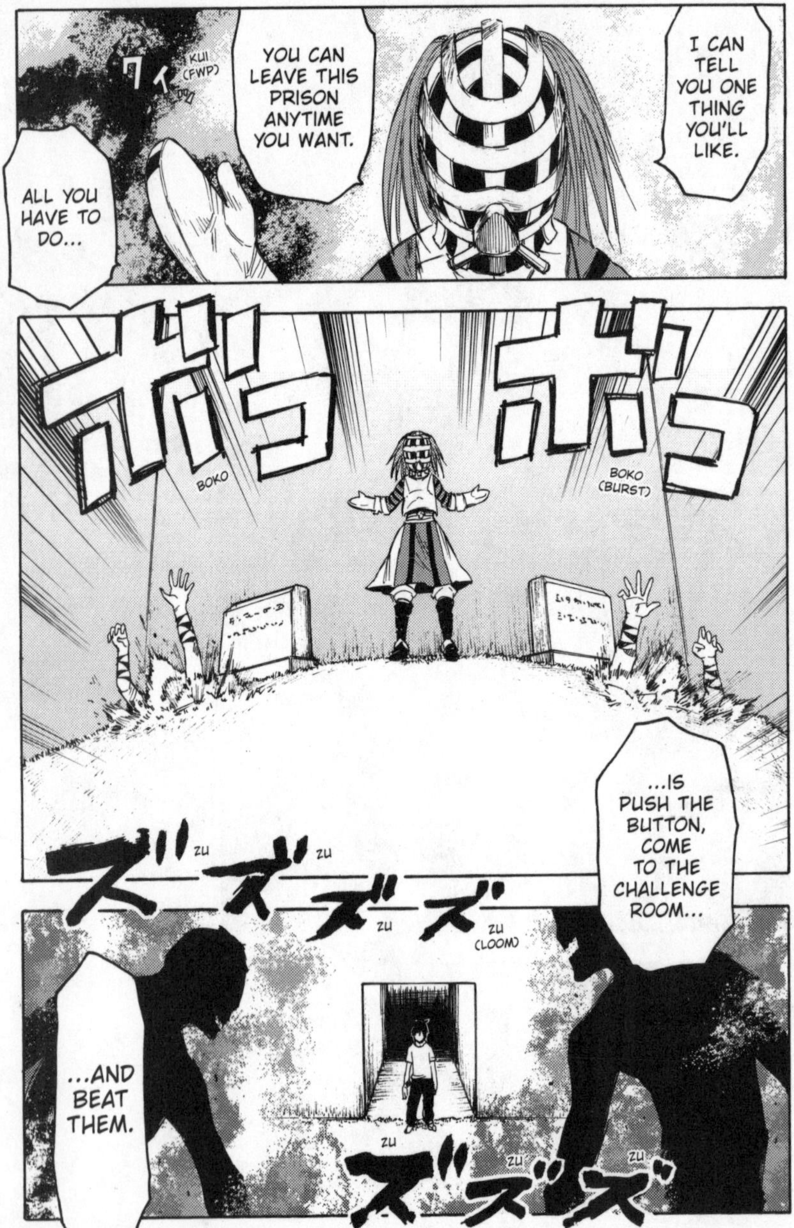
I CAN TELL YOU ONE THING YOU'LL LIKE.
YOU CAN LEAVE THIS PRISON ANYTIME YOU WANT.
KUI (FWP)
ALL YOU HAVE TO DO...
BOKO (BURST)
BOKO
...IS PUSH THE BUTTON, COME TO THE CHALLENGE ROOM...
ZU ZU ZU ZU (LOOM)
...AND BEAT THEM.
ZU ZU ZU

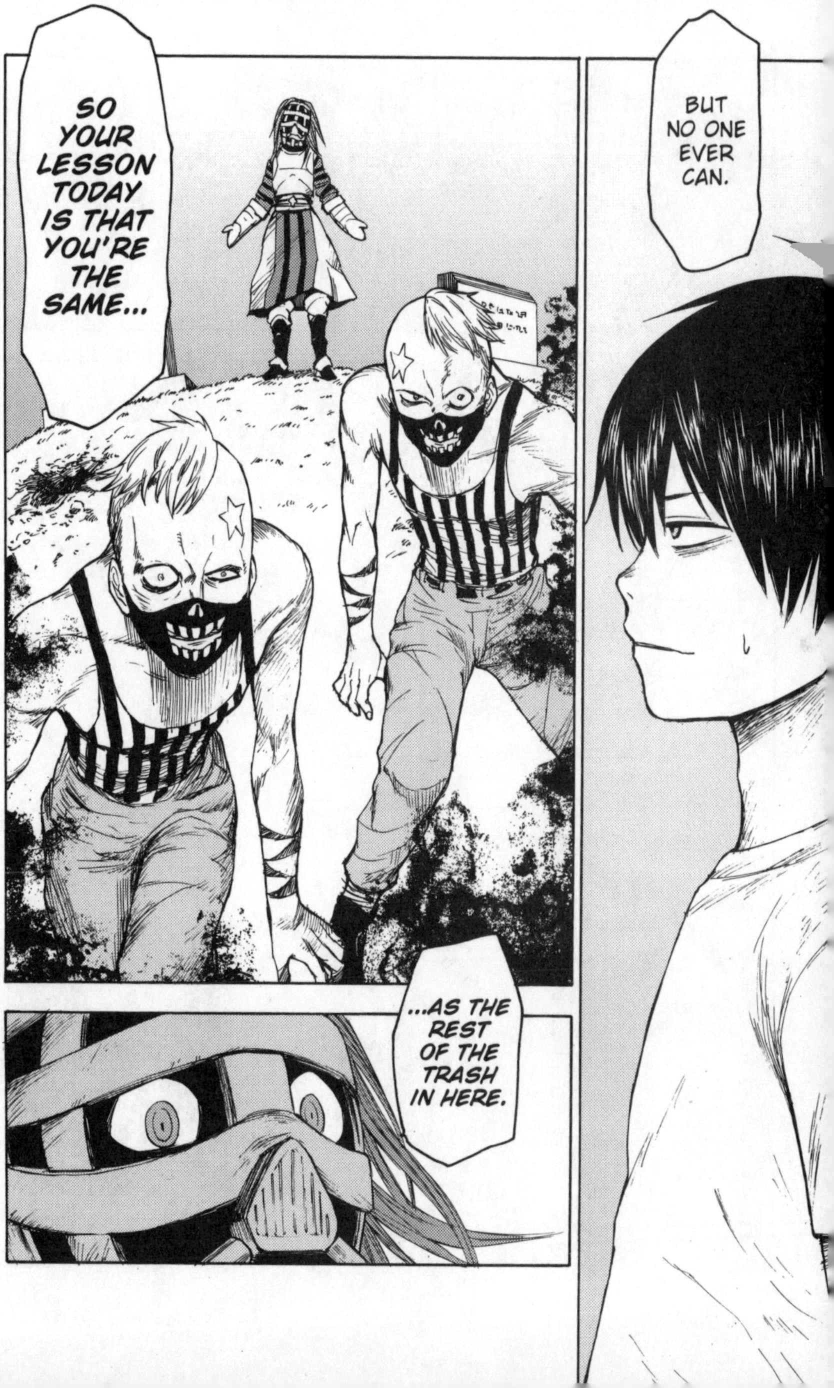
BUT NO ONE EVER CAN.
SO YOUR LESSON TODAY IS THAT YOU'RE THE SAME...
...AS THE REST OF THE TRASH IN HERE.

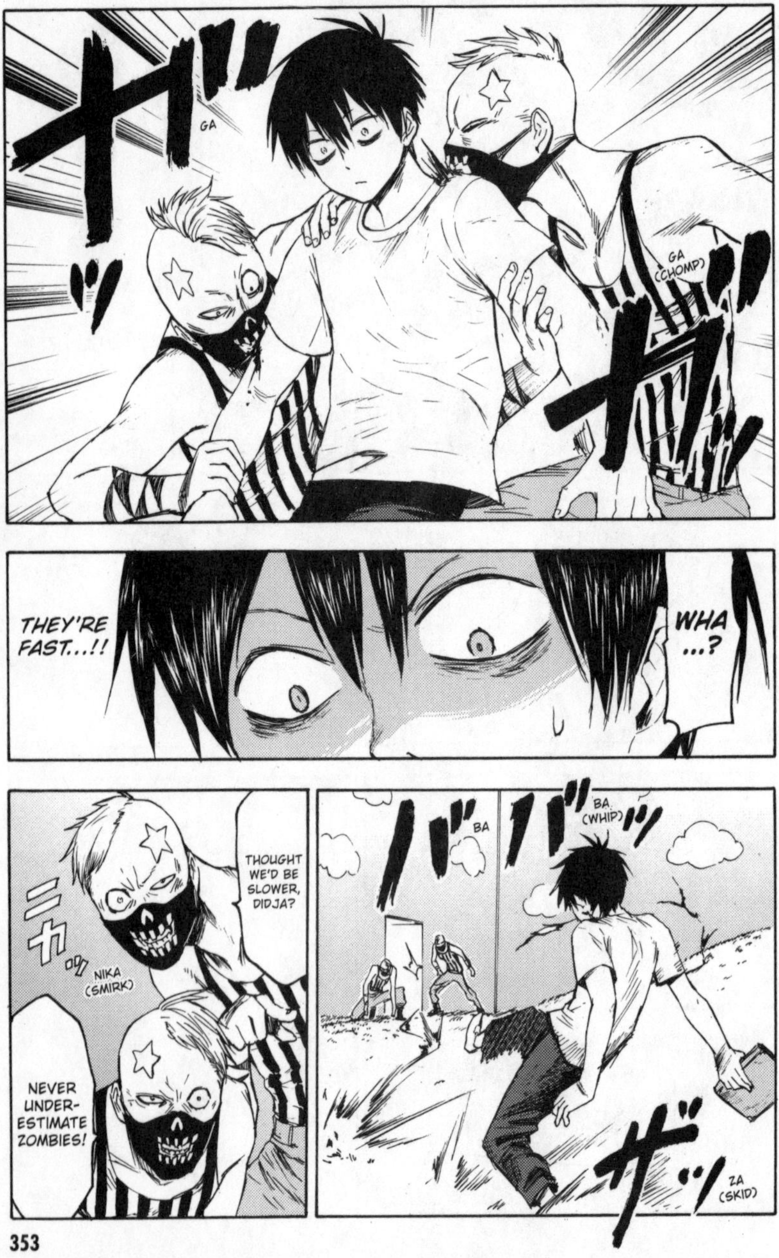
GA
GA (CHOMP)
WHA ...?
THEY'RE FAST...!!
BA (WHIP)
BA
ZA (SKID)
THOUGHT WE'D BE SLOWER, DIDJA?
NIKA (SMIRK)
NEVER UNDER-ESTIMATE ZOMBIES!

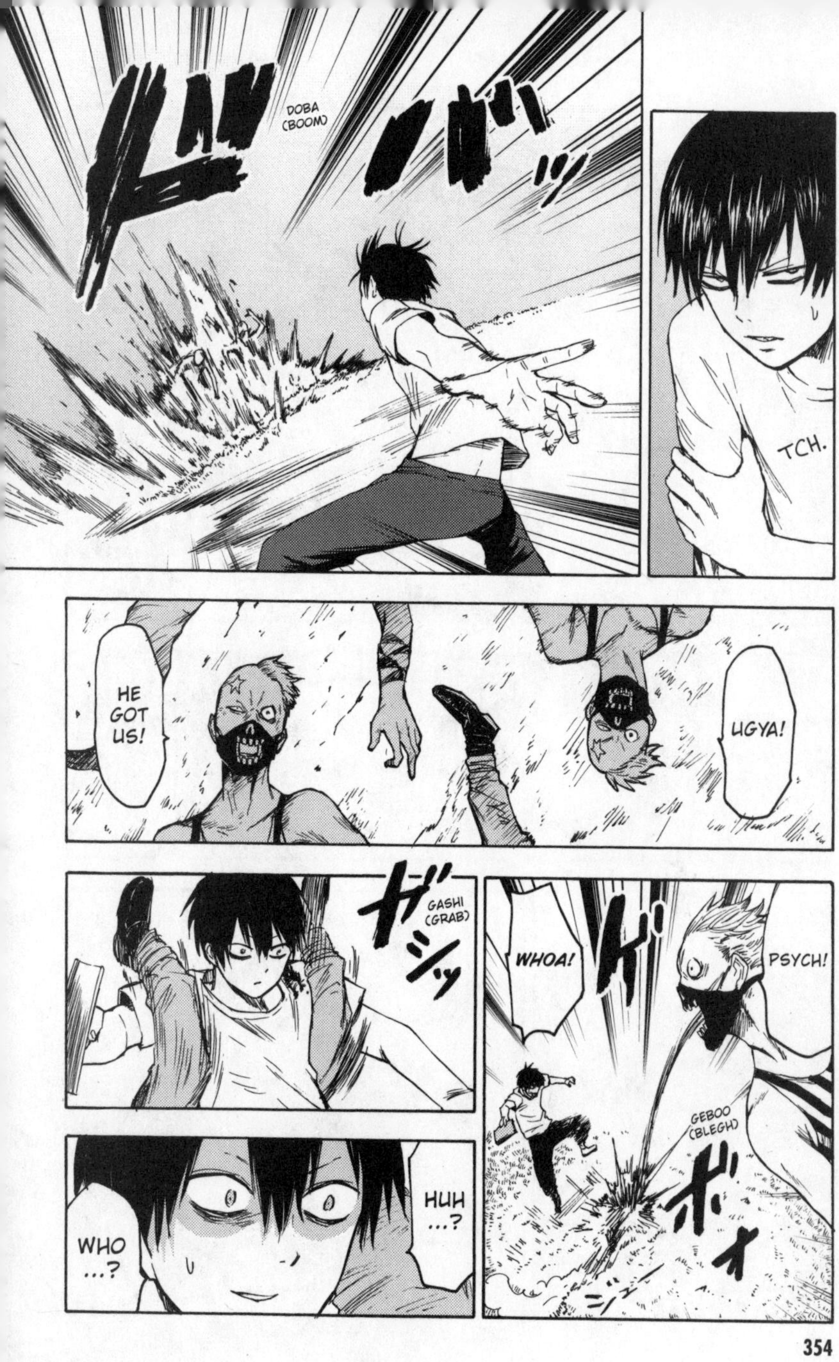
TCH.
DOBA (BOOM)
UGYA!
HE GOT US!
PSYCH!
WHOA!
GEBOO (BLEGH)
GASHI (GRAB)
HUH ...?
WHO ...?

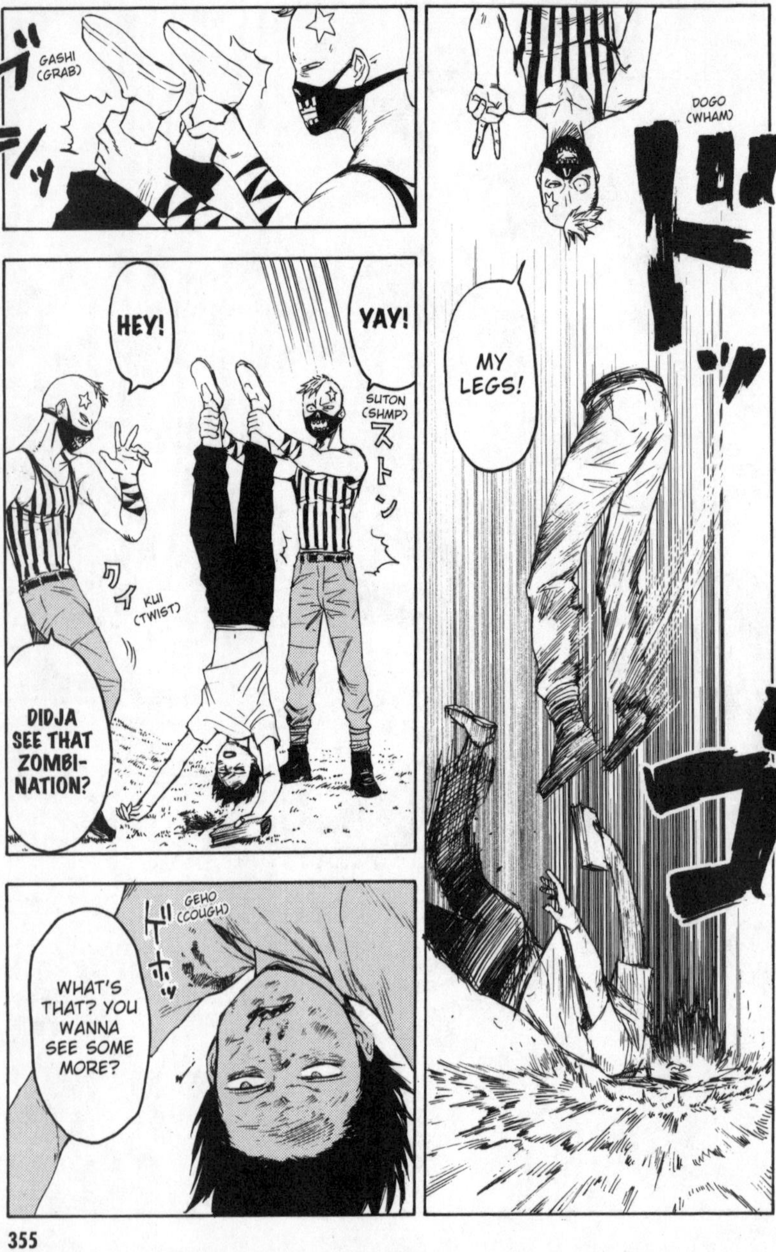
DOGO (WHAM)
ドゴッ
MY LEGS!
ゴッ
GASHI (GRAB)
ガシッ
YAY!
SUTON (SHMP)
ストン
HEY!
クイ
KUI (TWIST)
DIDJA SEE THAT ZOMBI-NATION?
GEHO (COUGH)
ゲホッ
WHAT'S THAT? YOU WANNA SEE SOME MORE?

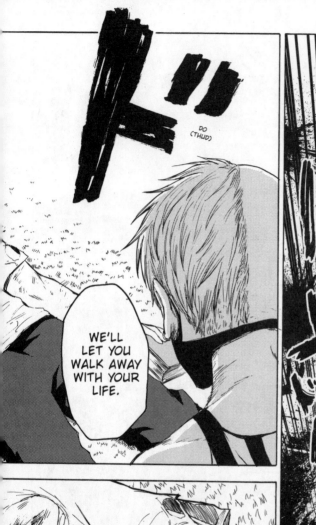

DO
(THUD)

WE'LL LET YOU WALK AWAY WITH YOUR LIFE.

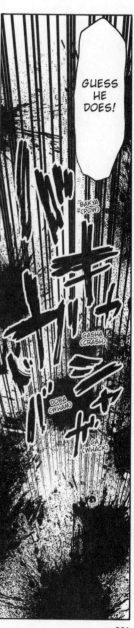

GUESS HE DOES!

BAKYA (CROWD)

GASHA (CRASH)

DOBA (WHAM)

GA (WHACK)

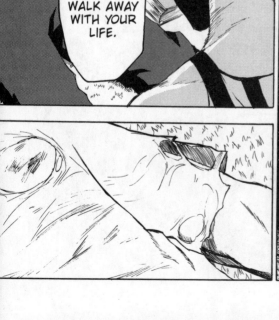

356

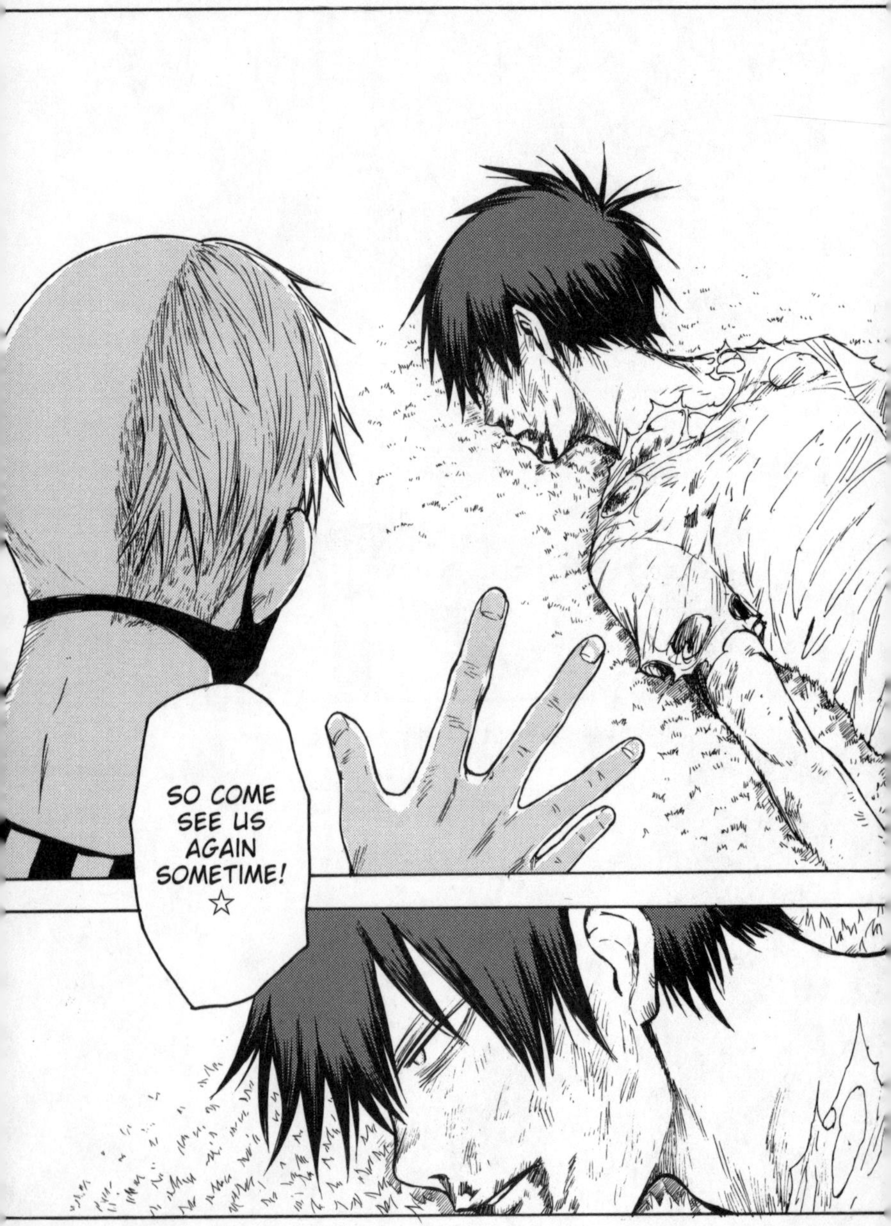
SO COME SEE US AGAIN SOMETIME! ☆

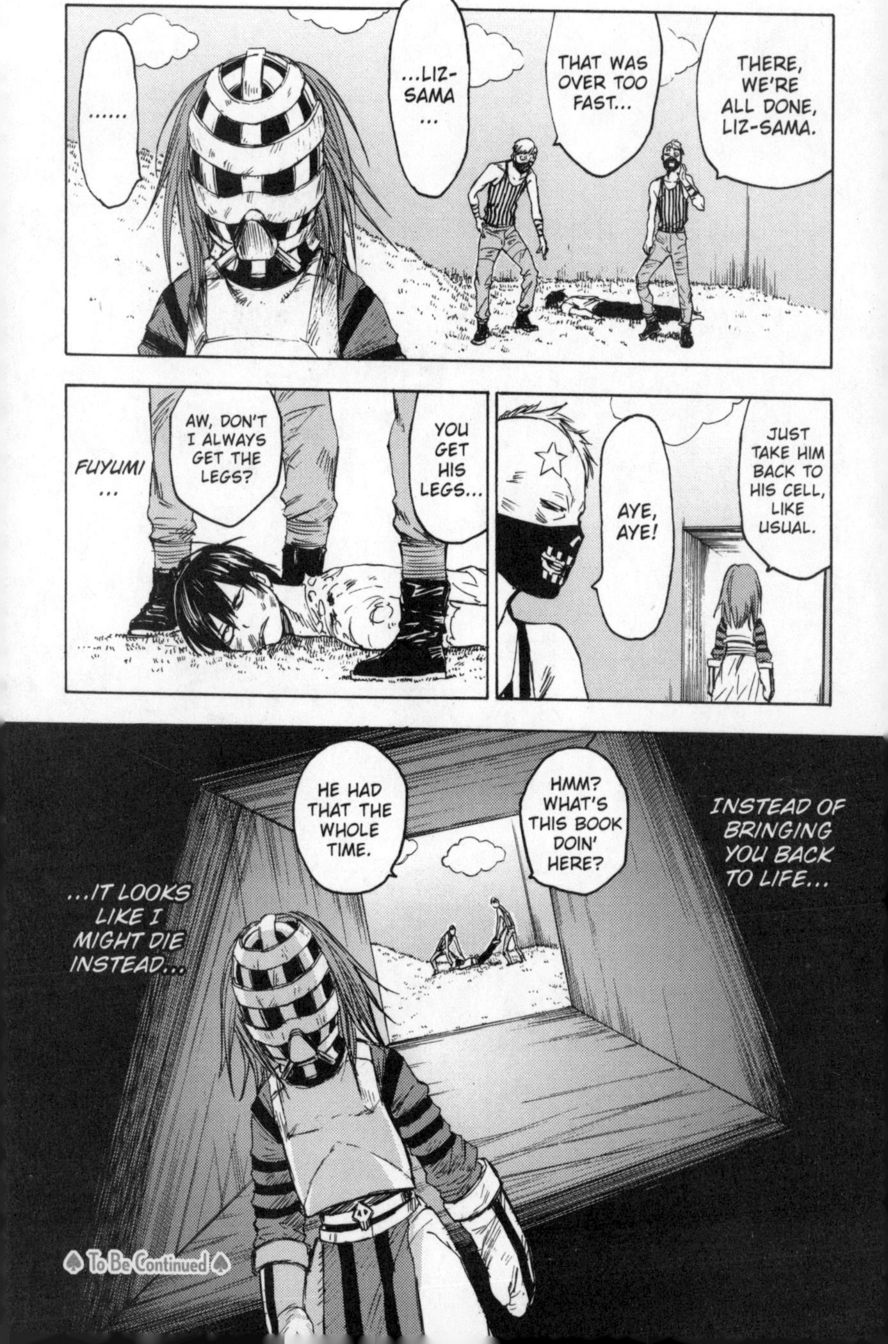
THERE, WE'RE ALL DONE, LIZ-SAMA.
THAT WAS OVER TOO FAST...
...LIZ-SAMA...
......
JUST TAKE HIM BACK TO HIS CELL, LIKE USUAL.
AYE, AYE!
YOU GET HIS LEGS...
AW, DON'T I ALWAYS GET THE LEGS?
FUYUMI...
INSTEAD OF BRINGING YOU BACK TO LIFE...
HMM? WHAT'S THIS BOOK DOIN' HERE?
HE HAD THAT THE WHOLE TIME.
...IT LOOKS LIKE I MIGHT DIE INSTEAD...
To Be Continued

# LIVING IN THE DEMON WORLD

## SATY'S EVERYDAY LIFE

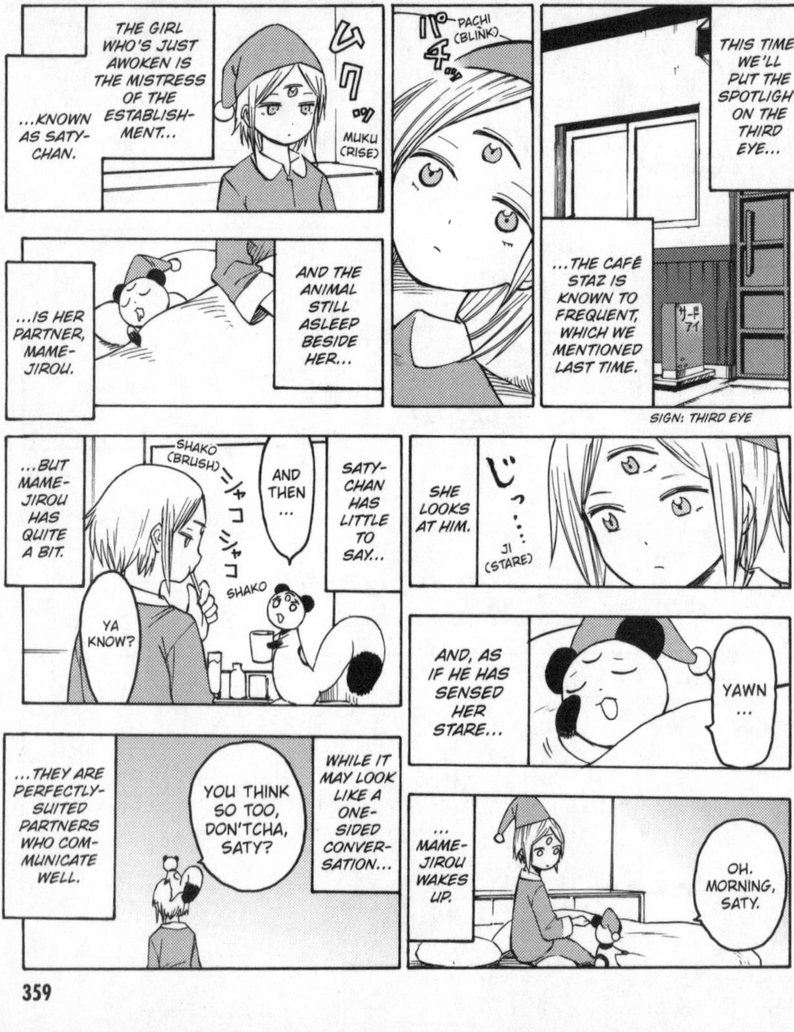

THIS TIME, WE'LL PUT THE SPOTLIGHT ON THE THIRD EYE...
...THE CAFÉ STAZ IS KNOWN TO FREQUENT, WHICH WE MENTIONED LAST TIME.
SIGN: THIRD EYE
PACHI (BLINK)
THE GIRL WHO'S JUST AWOKEN IS THE MISTRESS OF THE ESTABLISHMENT...
...KNOWN AS SATY-CHAN.
MUKU (RISE)
AND THE ANIMAL STILL ASLEEP BESIDE HER...
...IS HER PARTNER, MAMEJIROU.
SHE LOOKS AT HIM.
JI (STARE)
AND, AS IF HE HAS SENSED HER STARE...
YAWN...
...MAMEJIROU WAKES UP.
OH. MORNING, SATY.
SATY-CHAN HAS LITTLE TO SAY...
AND THEN...
SHAKO (BRUSH)
...BUT MAMEJIROU HAS QUITE A BIT.
YA KNOW?
SHAKO
WHILE IT MAY LOOK LIKE A ONE-SIDED CONVERSATION...
YOU THINK SO TOO, DON'TCHA, SATY?
...THEY ARE PERFECTLY-SUITED PARTNERS WHO COMMUNICATE WELL.

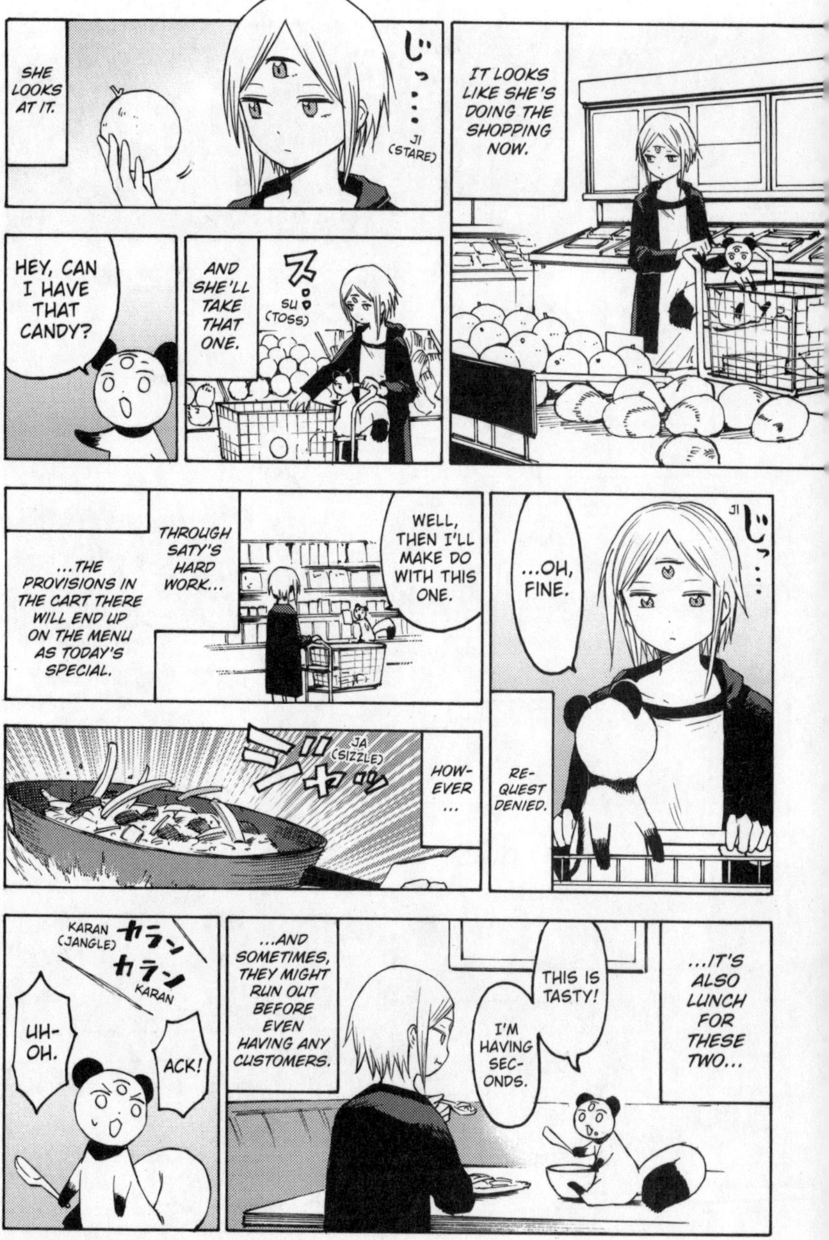
IT LOOKS LIKE SHE'S DOING THE SHOPPING NOW.
SHE LOOKS AT IT.
じっ・・・
JI (STARE)
AND SHE'LL TAKE THAT ONE.
ス
SU (TOSS)
HEY, CAN I HAVE THAT CANDY?
JI
じっ・・・
...OH, FINE.
RE-QUEST DENIED.
WELL, THEN I'LL MAKE DO WITH THIS ONE.
THROUGH SATY'S HARD WORK...
...THE PROVISIONS IN THE CART THERE WILL END UP ON THE MENU AS TODAY'S SPECIAL.
HOW-EVER ...
JA (SIZZLE)
...IT'S ALSO LUNCH FOR THESE TWO...
THIS IS TASTY!
I'M HAVING SEC-ONDS.
...AND SOMETIMES, THEY MIGHT RUN OUT BEFORE EVEN HAVING ANY CUSTOMERS.
KARAN (JANGLE)
カラン
カラン
KARAN
ACK!
UH-OH.

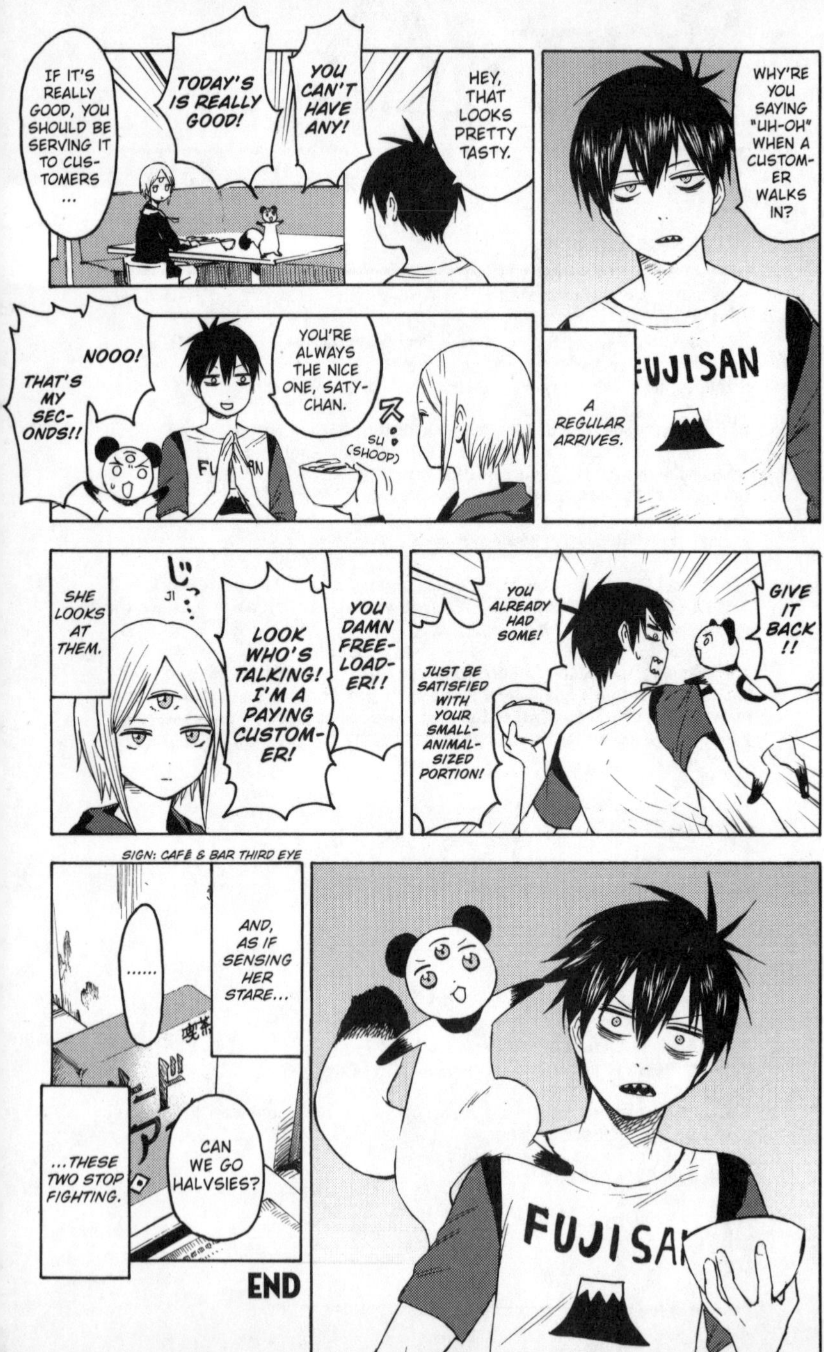
WHY'RE YOU SAYING "UH-OH" WHEN A CUSTOMER WALKS IN?
A REGULAR ARRIVES.
FUJISAN
HEY, THAT LOOKS PRETTY TASTY.
YOU CAN'T HAVE ANY!
TODAY'S IS REALLY GOOD!
IF IT'S REALLY GOOD, YOU SHOULD BE SERVING IT TO CUSTOMERS ...
YOU'RE ALWAYS THE NICE ONE, SATY-CHAN.
ス SU (SHOOP)
NOOO! THAT'S MY SECONDS!!
GIVE IT BACK!!
YOU ALREADY HAD SOME!
JUST BE SATISFIED WITH YOUR SMALL-ANIMAL-SIZED PORTION!
YOU DAMN FREELOADER!!
LOOK WHO'S TALKING! I'M A PAYING CUSTOMER!
じっ JI
SHE LOOKS AT THEM.
SIGN: CAFÉ & BAR THIRD EYE
FUJISAN
AND, AS IF SENSING HER STARE...
......
CAN WE GO HALVSIES?
...THESE TWO STOP FIGHTING.
END

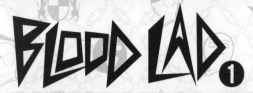

# BLOOD LAD ①

### YUUKI KODAMA

Translation: Melissa Tanaka

Lettering: Alexis Eckerman

BLOOD LAD Volumes 1 and 2 © Yuuki KODAMA 2010. First published in Japan in 2010 by KADOKAWA CORPORATION, Tokyo. English translation rights arranged with KADOKAWA CORPORATION, Tokyo, through TUTTLE-MORI AGENCY, INC., Tokyo.

English translation © 2012 by Yen Press, LLC

Yen Press
1290 Avenue of the Americas
New York, NY 10104

Visit us at yenpress.com
facebook.com/yenpress
twitter.com/yenpress
yenpress.tumblr.com
instagram.com/yenpress

First Yen Press Edition: December 2012

Yen Press is an imprint of Yen Press, LLC.
The Yen Press name and logo are trademarks of Yen Press, LLC.

The publisher is not responsible for websites (or their content) that are not owned by the publisher.

ISBN: 978-0-316-22895-4

20 19 18 17 16 15

WOR

Printed in the United States of America